The American Political Landscape Series

Encyclopedia of Religion in American Politics

Other Titles in the American Political Landscape Series

Encyclopedia of Women in American Politics
Encyclopedia of Minorities in American Politics
Encyclopedia of Media in American Politics
Encyclopedia of Corruption in American Politics

The American Political Landscape Series

Encyclopedia of Religion in American Politics

Edited by
Jeffrey D. Schultz,
John G. West, Jr.,
and
Iain Maclean

Foreword by
Helen Thomas

Oryx Press
1999

The rare Arabian Oryx is believed to have inspired the myth of the unicorn. This desert antelope became virtually extinct in the early 1960s. At that time, several groups of international conservationists arranged to have nine animals sent to the Phoenix Zoo to be the nucleus of a captive breeding herd. Today, the Oryx population is over 1,000, and over 500 have been returned to the Middle East.

Published by The Oryx Press
4041 North Central at Indian School Road
Phoenix, Arizona 85012-3397

Published simultaneously in Canada
Printed and bound in the United States of America

♾ The paper used in this publication meets the minimum requirements of American National Standard for Information Science—Permanence of Paper for Printed Library Materials, ANSI Z39.48, 1984.

Library of Congress Cataloging-in-Publication Data

Schultz, Jeffrey D.
Encyclopedia of religion in American politics / edited by Jeffrey D. Schultz, John G. West, Jr., Iain Maclean.
p. cm.—(The American political landscape series)
Includes bibliographical references and index.
ISBN 1-57356-130-4 (alk. paper)
1. Religion and politics—United States—Encyclopedias. 2. United States—Religion—Encyclopedias.
I. West, John G. II. Maclean, Iain S., 1956- . III. Title. IV. Series.
BL2525.S337 1999
322'.1'097303—dc21 98-47223
CIP

Contents

Contributors

Academic Advisory Board

Daniel L. Dreisbach
The American University

Mark David Hall
East Central University

Martin E. Marty
University of Chicago

Richard John Neuhaus
Institute on Religion & Public Life

Clyde Wilcox
Georgetown University

Christopher Wolfe
Marquette University

Editors

John G. West, Jr.
Seattle Pacific University; Discovery Institute

Iain S. Maclean
James Madison University

Contributors

(AOT) Alvin O. Turner
East Central University

(ARB) Albert R. Beck
Baylor University

(AS) Alan Snyder
Regent University

(BDG) Bryan D. Garsten
Harvard University

(CB) Claire Berlinski

(CH) Crystal Hamilton
Seattle Pacfic University

(DD) Debra Daniels

(DH) David Hudson

(DLD) Daniel L. Dreisbach
American University

(DW) David Weeks
Azuza Pacific University

(EES) Elizabeth Edwards Spalding
George Mason University

(FG) Frank Guliuzza III
Weber State University

(FHJ) Frank H. Julian
Murray State University

(FJB) Francis J. Beckwith
Trinity International University

(GSB Gregory S. Butler
New Mexico State University

(GSS) Gregory S. Strong

(GT) Gary Trogdon

(HLC) H. Lee Cheek
Brewton-Parker College

(HWH) H. Wayne House
Calvin College

(ISM) Iain S. Maclean
James Madison University

(JCW) Jessamyn Charity West

(JDH) J. David Holcomb
Baylor University

(JGW) John G. West, Jr.
Seattle Pacific University; Discovery Institute

(JHM) Jeffry H. Morrison
Georgetown University

(JM) Jack Miller

(JMK) Joseph M. Knippenberg
Oglethorpe University

(JML) J.M. Long
Baylor University

(JP) Jeff Polet
Malone College

(JRV) Jack R. Van Der Slik
University of Illinois—Springfield

(JSF) Joel S. Fetzer
University of Southern California

(JVS) James V. Schall, S.J.
Georgetown University

(KES) Kathryn E. Shea
Harvard University

(KMY) Karen Marie Yust
University of Massachusetts

(KRD) Kevin R. den Dulk
University of Wisconsin—Madison

(MDH) Mark David Hall
East Central University

(MEN) Michael E. Nielson
George Southern University

(MJH) Mary Jane Haemig
Pacific Lutheran University

(MR) Marsha Richards
Seattle Pacific University

(MS) Matthew Spalding
The Heritage Foundation

(MWP) Mike W. Perry
National Writers Group

(PCH) Peter C. Holloran

(PV) Peter Vogt

(PWS) Peter W. Schramm
Ashland University

(RA) Robert Alt
Heritage Foundation

(RAH) Richard Allen Hyde

(RW) Richard Weikart
California State University—Stanislaus

(SEW) Sonja E. West

(SJL) Steven J. Lenzner
Harvard University

(SM) Stephen Monsma
Pepperdine University

(SMN) Steven M. Nolt
University of Notre Dame

(SW) Scott Waalkes
Malone College

(TGJ) Ted G. Jelen
University of Nevada—Las Vegas

(WB) William Binning
Youngstown State University

(WVM) William V. Moore
College of Charleston

(WW) William Woodward
Seattle Pacific University

Foreword

by Helen Thomas

I have always felt greatly privileged to have a ringside seat to instant history at the White House. But I realized after a preview of the Oryx Press encyclopedias on women, religion, and minorities that there are big gaps in my education regarding the role these humanistic trends have played in American politics.

I believe the essays in these volumes are informative, objective, and in-depth, with a wealth of material for scholars, students, and researchers of all kinds. Of course, I was first drawn to the *Encyclopedia of Women in American Politics* for both personal and professional reasons. I am still outraged that women did not get the vote until 1920. Often when I am walking into the White House I look at the big black fence on Pennsylvania Avenue and I think of the suffragettes who chained themselves to it to gain the right to vote.

The strides women have made in the last half of this century are awesome, but not enough. World War II was the defining moment, but it has been a long struggle and women have miles to go to achieve true equality in the workplace.

I have often heard quoted the letter from that remarkable woman, Abigail Adams, who wrote to her husband, John Adams, on March 31, 1776, while he was attending the Continental Congress.

> I desire you would remember the ladies and be more generous and favorable to them than your ancestors. Do not put such unlimited power in the hands of the husbands.

I was covering the White House in 1961 when John F. Kennedy created the President's Commission on the Status of Women by executive order. It was considered a great leap forward in those days and the panel included the most prominent women leaders of the times, those who had reached the top in their fields. Eleanor Roosevelt, who had worked for so many years on behalf of women, was chosen as the chair.

Two years later, the Commission wrote a report that documented "pervasive discrimination against women in state and national laws in work and at schools." State commissions later pursued the goals of equal opportunity for women and followed up on complaints of sex-based employment discrimination.

Women then began to focus their efforts on ratification of the Equal Rights Amendment, but they failed to achieve the necessary two-thirds of the states. I thought it was a very sad day for the Republic. Women began to venture forth afterward more strongly into the path of political acceptance, and, by the 1970s, the women's movement to empower females had gained great momentum. But the movement hit a plateau when President Ronald Reagan moved into the White House in 1981 and the country became more conservative.

So women have had their hills and valleys, which are vividly illustrated in the biographies and the other entries in the *Encyclopedia of Women in American Politics*.

Every student of American history has some insight into the role that religion has played in the founding of the United States and into the profound impact of religious groups on the politics of different eras, dating back to colonial times. School children learn of the flight of the Pilgrims from religious persecution in England. The *Encyclopedia of Religion in American Politics* is a gold mine of information. As its introductory essay explains,

> The story of religion in American politics is largely an account of the quest to harness the moral idealism of religion for political purposes while attempting to restrain the potential of religion for bigotry. The overwhelming success of that quest for a civic-minded religion can be seen in the thriving diversity of religious groups in the United States today.

Fortunately, the *Encyclopedia* shows that religions fostered in the United States have not been all-consuming, domineering, or fanatical, so as to nurture the kind of age-old religious-cultural hatreds that have torn apart Northern Ireland, Bosnia, and the Middle East. Everyday, the United States is involved in seeking to bring peace to these lands, where religion is a tinder box.

Ministers in the colonial era used their tracts and sermons to lay the groundwork for the American Revolution. The founding fathers were mostly religious, but they also devoutly believed in religious freedom.

Almost from its beginning, the United States has had a multiplicity of religions and therefore an admirable tolerance. The First Amendment stipulated that "Congress shall make no law respecting an establishment of religion or prohibiting the free exercise thereof." The founding fathers, while trying to reconcile the influences of reason and revelation on moral law, believed strongly in the separation of church and state.

Politics in the new Republic depended on a shared morality rather than on a shared theology. The ministers of the post-colonial era fought the removal of the Cherokees from Georgia to the West, an infamous episode in American history known as the "Trail of Tears." The churches in the North were also leaders in the movement to abolish slavery, while religious institutions in the South played an equally important role on the other side of the controversy.

In this century, the best known minister in the struggle for civil rights was Martin Luther King, Jr., who first came to national attention when he spearheaded the boycott of segregated buses in Montgomery, Alabama, in 1955–56. Later, many religions banded together in support of the civil rights movement and it took a southern president, Lyndon B. Johnson, to push through Congress the Civil Rights Act of 1964 and the Voting Rights Act of 1965.

But the influence of religion in American politics during the twentieth century has swung from left to right. During the late 1970s and 1980s, the Moral Majority gained a foothold and, after its demise, was replaced by the Christian Coalition. The domestic agenda of the political conservatives includes restoring prayer in public schools and promoting family and pro-life values. Despite the strict wall that the Supreme Court has interposed between church and state in the past, recent years have seen a chipping away at that barrier with rulings permitting religious groups to gather and use schoolrooms and public facilities for their meetings.

Equally fascinating is the documentation in the *Encyclopedia of Minorities in American Politics* of the struggle for political rights of minorities, who have been historically under-represented in the American political system and who have had to fight to attain their rightful place as citizens. The discrimination against racial and ethnic groups is vividly chronicled in the *Encyclopedia's* biographies and historical references to past eras that were dominated by white males. Included among those discriminated against were blacks, Latinos, Asian Americans, and Native Americans. I can remember how often President John F. Kennedy was appalled to see signs at Boston job sites that read, "No Irish allowed." A sea change is occurring in the nation, and once deprived groups are becoming increasingly involved in shaping the political dialogue in this country and in winning public office. Witness the number of big city black mayors currently holding office in the United States. Furthermore, no politician would dare to ignore the Cubans in Florida or the Hispanics in the Southwest and expect to get elected.

All this is to the good. It makes real the unity and validity of the melting pot and there is no question that these groups will have an even bigger voice in the future. My only hope and prayer is that they do not divide along ethnic and racial lines and forget that we are one people.

The three volumes in Oryx's American Political Landscape Series are a treasure trove for scholars and students, and provide the key to the significant historic trends that have made the United States great.

Helen Thomas is White House Bureau Chief for United Press International.

Preface

In the last two decades, political scientists and journalists have noted an increased political activity on the part of religious Americans. This period has seen the rise of the Moral Majority, the creation of the Christian Coalition, and the presidential campaigns of Jesse Jackson and Pat Robertson. But to believe that American politics has only recently been influenced by religion is to believe incorrectly. As school children, we learned of the brave Pilgrims who settled here for religious freedom. We, at times, seem to forget those religious roots in an age that is largely secular. However, even the secular nature of modern American society is the result of conflict—at times political—between those who see the U.S. as a "City on the Hill" and those who see it as the embodiment of the separation of church and state. The complex history that has shaped current relations between religion and politics is one that *The Encyclopedia of Religion in American Politics* traces by covering individuals, events, ideas, and issues. Religion and politics in the U.S. are inextricable from one another. To attempt to separate them is to ignore our very roots and aspirations.

In selecting entries for the volume, the emphasis was placed upon being as comprehensive as limitations would allow. The work consists of nearly 700 alphabetically arranged entries written by more than 50 scholars. The entries cover religious leaders who were politically active and political leaders who were actively religious. It also covers significant historical events, court cases, concepts, and specific denominations and sects. Longer entries address some of the key issues that face religion in politics in the U.S. These issue entries, like abortion, free exercise, and separation of church and state (to name just a few), were written to give context to current politics and to current efforts to resolve those issues.

Being a reference work, the *Encyclopedia* gives accurate information in manageable doses. And because a good reference work must be able to lead the reader to more information, *every entry* in the *Encyclopedia* has a bibliography that can serve as the next step for further research by the user of the volume. In addition to bibliographies, entries are cross-referenced in two ways to aid the reader in successfully using the resources of the work. First, the work is internally cross-referenced through the use of **bold-faced** type. Bold-faced word(s) indicate to the reader that there is a separate entry on that person, event, concept, or issue. Second, many articles have *See also* listings at the end of the entry to offer other areas the reader may want to investigate. These two features in addition to the index will facilitate the user's ability to navigate the volume.

The volume has three appendices. The first appendix reprints a selection of important documents and speeches, including the First Amendment, Washington's Farewell Address, Lincoln's Second Inaugural, and the Humanist Manifesto. The second appendix is a directory of organizations that are directly or indirectly involved in religion and politics. The directory contains brief descriptions of each organization as well as contact information, including web sites (where possible). The third appendix is a four-column timeline of religion in American politics. Starting with the adoption of the Constitution and running to the present day, the timeline draws attention to American religious history in a comparative context.

The Encyclopedia of Religion in American Politics is the most comprehensive single source of its kind. Its pages contain entries on the people and events that have shaped the past and present, while looking forward to a political sphere that continues to be influenced by religion.

Acknowledgments

Every encyclopedia is the work of many people who share in the volume's success, and *The Encyclopedia of Religion in American Politics* is no different. John G. West, Jr. and Iain Maclean, my coeditors, have contributed to the volume in numerous ways, including editing entries, writing last minute additions or no-shows, shaping the table of contents, suggesting documents, and simply lending an ear to a swamped series editor. John has been a good friend and intellectual fellow traveler for many years and I have had the honor of working with him on other projects, including the recently released *C.S. Lewis Readers' Encyclopedia*. Iain is one of those rare individuals who sheds light on every encounter. They both have made this volume better than originally envisioned. The Board of Advisors, especially Daniel L. Dreisbach and Mark Hall, were instrumental in reviewing the table of contents and giving other helpful advice. The volume's contributors also share in any praise that the volume may find. All of them should take heart to know that they have helped to write a worthwhile and timely reference work.

Two of my former teachers deserve special mention because I learned a lot about religion and politics from them both: Fr. James V. Schall, SJ, of Georgetown University and Professor Emeritus Leonard W. Levy of The Claremont Graduate School. In different ways, both taught me about the importance of understanding the impact that religion has on politics and vice versa. Though, I would guess that both think I was too dense to get the point.

Everyone at The Oryx Press has been wonderful in making the *Encyclopedia* a better volume. However, Phyllis B. Steckler, the president of The Oryx Press, deserves special mention as the second volume of the series goes into print. Her vision for The Oryx Press and for The American Political Landscape Series has been steadfast. Her commitment to me as an editor has meant much in putting this series together. I look forward to many years of working together to produce meaningful reference works.

Every work I do deserves a special note to George and Annie Kurian who have been unwavering supporters of me. George has helped make this particular volume better in lots of ways. However, his biggest contribution is always as a friend, confidant, and moral advisor. He continues to teach me much about faith and living it.

And finally, to my wife Elena and our son Sasha, who are always there for me.

Introduction

Religion in American Politics

by John G. West, Jr.

Religion, Frances Wright declared to American audiences in the 1800s, is "a system of error, which from the earliest date of human tradition, has filled the earth with crime, and deluged its bosom with blood, and which, at this hour, fills your country with discord, and impedes its progress in virtue." Born in Scotland, the fiery Wright toured American cities in the late 1820s, lecturing to packed auditoriums on such subjects as education, science, and God. Condemning traditional religion as the source of bigotry, tyranny, and ignorance, Wright promised her listeners a heaven on earth if only they would abandon the superstitions of faith and embrace the truths taught by modern science about the material universe.

Wright's critics derided her proposals as a half-baked prescription for an earthly hell rather than a secular heaven. Labelling Wright the "female apostle of atheistic liberty," the Rev. Lyman Beecher said that anyone who believed a republic could exist without religion was deluded. For a nation to remain politically free, Beecher argued, its citizens must be morally bound, and religious institutions—Christian ones, in particular—were the only efficacious method of moral restraint. In Beecher's view, the Christian religion was the best method of inculcating the habits needed for republicanism to flourish. Far from undermining liberty (as Wright claimed), "Christianity . . . rocked the cradle of our liberties, defended our youth, and brought us up to manhood."

Wright and Beecher encapsulate the two views of religion in politics that have been at loggerheads since at least the start of the Enlightenment in the eighteenth century. One view sees religion as the source of nearly all earthly evils. The other view sees religion as the source of virtually every earthly good. Both views have a point. Religion has been used to justify a whole parade of iniquities throughout history, including the caste system in India, the Inquisition in Spain, anti-Semitism in Germany, and slavery in the American South. At the same time, religious believers can be credited with working to abolish slavery, sheltering Jews during World War II, promoting democratic governments that guarantee human rights, and creating programs that care for the poor. Herein lies the paradox of religion in politics throughout human history: Religious zeal may be a breeding ground for intolerance, but religious idealism may be the seedbed of justice and human rights. Moreover, in democratic governments that depend on the character of their citizens to survive, religion may inculcate the moral habits that make democratic government possible.

The story of religion in American politics is largely an account of the quest to harness the moral idealism of religion for political purposes while attempting to restrain the potential of religion for bigotry. The overwhelming success of that quest for civic-minded religion can be seen in the thriving diversity of religious groups in the United States today. Despite the continued piety of Americans (more than 40 percent attend a religious service each week), and despite the vigorous political activities of many religious groups, contemporary Americans have little experience with the religious-cultural hatreds presently tearing apart such places as Northern Ireland, Bosnia, and the Middle East. This relative harmony among competing sects in the United States represents an amazing achievement in world history, and the history of religion in American politics helps explain how the current situation came about.

Religion and Politics in Colonial America

The role of religion in American politics reaches back to the earliest European settlements on the continent, when religious adherents facing persecution in the Old World fled to North America to practice their respective faiths in freedom. Puritans migrated to Massachusetts and Connecticut. Quakers settled in New Jersey and Pennsylvania, the latter colony being founded by Quaker William Penn. Roman Catholics came to Maryland, the proprietary colony of the Roman Catholic Lord Baltimore. Rhode Island served as a refuge for people of all faiths, including Jews. Given the number of immigrants who came to America for avowedly religious reasons, it is no surprise that the politics of the time were inextricably intertwined with the religious views of the inhabitants.

The connection between religion and politics was especially close in the Puritan-led communities of New England. To understand why this was the case, one needs to know something about the Puritans' history. Beginning as reformers within the Anglican Church in England during the reign of Queen

Elizabeth in the late sixteenth century, the Puritans wished to purge their church of the last vestiges of Roman Catholicism, secure adherence to the doctrines of reformed theology (as expounded by John Calvin and others), and promote renewed personal piety among both clergy and laypeople. The Puritans immersed themselves in the Bible and believed that the worship of God should be simple and direct, not burdened with elaborate rituals and liturgies. Eventually, the Puritan movement splintered into numerous factions, largely over the issue of church government. Some Puritans accepted the existing Anglican system of government by bishops and the monarch. Others sought a more decentralized presbyterian form of church government. A third group believed that local congregations ought to rule themselves by means of a voluntary compact among their members. This faction was itself split over how far to go in promoting congregationalism. Most congregationalists accepted the existing Church of England, though they wanted to reform it according to their principles; a smaller, more radical group (known as "separatists") viewed the Anglican Church as thoroughly apostate and formed their own congregations outside the authority of the Church. These Puritan separatists faced the harshest persecution in England, and the Pilgrims who arrived at Plymouth on the *Mayflower* in 1620 were among their numbers. By contrast, the Puritans who began settling in Massachusetts Bay Colony about 1630 were congregationalists but not separatists. As a practical matter, these distinctions among Puritan congregationalists blurred once they arrived in America, and the Puritan churches in Massachusetts soon operated as independently of the Anglican Church in England as the churches of their Plymouth brethren.

Modern culture likes to caricature the Puritans in America as a rather sour and intolerant lot. Indeed, to be a "Puritan" in modern parlance is to be prudish, repressive, and tyrannical. But as is often the case, the modern stereotype and historical reality are two different things. Admittedly, New England Puritans espoused their religion with great earnestness. In the words of historian Perry Miller, a gathering of Puritan servants and yeoman could produce "long and unbelievably technical discussions of predestination, infant damnation, and the distinctions between faith and works." Nevertheless, the Puritans' cultural legacy is far richer than the modern stereotype suggests.

Although the Puritans shunned secular entertainments like the theater, they did not spurn either learning or art. Anyone who reads the sermons of Puritan clergymen will be struck by both the volume and the variety of allusions to Greek and Roman literature. Similarly, anyone who reads American Puritan poets, such as Anne Bradstreet and Edward Taylor (not to mention Puritan literary giants in England such as John Milton and Edmund Spenser), will realize that Puritanism cannot be equated with philistinism. The Puritans also believed in witches, a belief that opened the door to the horrendous Salem witch trials of 1692. But belief in witchcraft was not peculiar to the Puritans of that era, and for their time, the Puritans were not particularly superstitious. They certainly did not oppose modern science. In England, nearly two-thirds of the scientists belonging to the Royal Society in the early 1660s were Puritans; in America, Puritans Samuel Danforth and Thomas Brattle pursued astronomy, and in the 1720s the Revs. Increase and Cotton Mather supported experiments with smallpox vaccines against considerable public opposition.

In politics, the Puritans were not the proponents of authoritarianism that some make them out to be today. The Puritans and their religious beliefs were key in laying the foundations of democracy in America. It is no coincidence that New England is known as the cradle of "town hall" democracy. The democratic institutions in New England grew out of the fertile soil of Puritan theology. Perhaps the Puritans' most important contribution to American democratic theory was the idea of compact (or covenant) as the foundation of legitimate government. The Puritans who came to America believed that a church was created whenever Christians voluntarily compacted with each other and with God. This idea of compact as the source of communal authority in the church easily transferred to political institutions. When the *Mayflower* landed off Plymouth, the Puritan separatists on board decided that they needed a compact to provide the proper basis for civil government, so 41 of the passengers signed what became known as the Mayflower Compact, declaring "solemnly and mutualy in the presence of God, and one of another, [that we] covenant and combine our selves togeather into a civill body politick, for our better ordering and preservation and furtherance of the ends aforesaid."

Later compacts supplied the basis for governments at settlements in New Hampshire, Providence, Hartford, and along the Connecticut River. Perhaps the most significant of these documents was the Fundamental Orders of Connecticut, which, according to Alfred Kelly and Winfred Harbison, was "for all practical purposes the first of modern written constitutions." Like modern constitutions, the Fundamental Orders was "a written compact of the people by which a fundamental frame of government was erected." Citizens of the Massachusetts Bay Colony did not explicitly form a compact for civil government (a compact of sorts already having been formed at the founding of the Massachusetts Bay Company). Nevertheless, the same ideas about government by compact permeated Massachusetts. Boston minister John Cotton declared that "all civill Relations are founded in Covenant . . . . For. . . there is no other way whereby a people . . . free from naturall and compulsory engagements, can be united or combined together into one visible body to stand by mutuall Relations, fellow-members of the same body but only by mutual Covenant; as appeareth between husband and wife in the family, Magistrates and subjects in the Commonwealth, fellow-citizens in the same cities."

A second Puritan contribution to American democratic philosophy was less concrete but just as significant: an emphasis on sin. The Puritans had no illusions about the perfectibility of human beings by human effort, and their unswerving realism about the darker side of human nature sowed the seeds of skepticism in America about unchecked government power. In the words of Rev. John Cotton, it is a necessity "that all power . . . on earth be limited, Church-power or other . . . . It is counted a matter of danger to the State to limit Prerogatives; but it is a further danger, not to have them limited. . . ." The Puritans' realism about human nature cast a long shadow, and historian Sydney Ahlstrom did not exaggerate when he suggested that "*The Federalist Papers* . . . as well as John Adams's defenses of the American constitutions, can be read as Puritan contributions to Enlightenment political theory."

The main point on which the Puritans sharply diverged from modern notions of democracy was religious liberty. Although the Puritans themselves had fled persecution in England, they relentlessly persecuted those in their settlements who did not adhere to Puritan orthodoxy. The Massachusetts Bay Colony was especially vigilant when it came to rooting out heretics, real or imagined. When clergyman Roger Williams proclaimed his unorthodox views on both church and state—including a stubborn insistence that the civil magistrates could not punish people for their religious beliefs—the colony expelled him in 1635. Anne Hutchinson met the same fate two years later for spreading various heterodox doctrines, including a claim that she was receiving direct revelations from God. The modern mind can easily condemn the Puritans as hypocrites on the subject of religious liberty. But in their own minds, Puritans were not being hypocritical. To more easily grasp Puritan reasoning on this point, it helps to think of the Puritan settlements in America as something more akin to private communes than modern political communities. The Puritans fled to America to form a community where God could be honored. In their view, when non-Puritans sought to live within their holy commonwealth, they ought to abide by Puritan ways; if not, they should live somewhere else. This insular mindset could not hope to last. As new emigrants with differing beliefs arrived in the colonies, and as the children of the first generation of Puritans grew up and adopted their own views, the link between church membership and civil liberties and citizenship was severed. But it took time, and it was a struggle.

Yet even the Puritans' religious intolerance was not without its beneficial effects, as Puritan descendant Nathaniel Hawthorne observed much later. Often remembered for his skewering of Puritan pride and prejudice in *The Scarlet Letter*, Hawthorne actually held a remarkably nuanced view of his forebears. He admired their realism and devotion to principle just as much as he deplored their bigotry. The former traits he lucidly depicted in his short story "The Gray Champion" (1835), where a first-generation Puritan mysteriously returns to Boston in 1689 to thwart the subjugation of the colonies by King James II. Like a fiery Old Testament prophet, the old Puritan—the "Gray Champion" of the title—denounces the usurpations of royal Governor Sir Edmund Andros and urges the people to resist. Hawthorne understood how the same rigid idealism that spawned the Puritans' religious bigotry also produced a powerful commitment to moral principle that made Puritans resist political tyranny. Hawthorne saw this hard-nosed Puritan temperament as one of the wellsprings of the American Revolution. Hence, the paradox of religion in politics broached earlier: Religion's intolerance may subvert republican government, but its rigorous attachment to moral principle may be necessary to defend it. Crusading religious ideals may provide people with the backbone they need to fight oppression.

If the Puritans were not the architects of religious liberty in the American colonies, other religious groups were. Roman Catholic George Calvert, Lord Baltimore, planned his colony of Maryland as a safe haven for fellow Catholics. When his son Cecilius was able to bring the colony to reality, he charged his governors with protecting the rights of all who "believe in Jesus Christ," Protestants as well as Catholics. Maryland's legislature followed this pronouncement in 1649 with a Toleration Act for all confessing Christians.

Like Lord Baltimore, Quaker William Penn saw his colony of Pennsylvania as a place where fellow believers could find refuge from the persecution they suffered in England. The colony subsequently guaranteed complete freedom of worship for all who believed in "one Almighty God." Government offices were restricted to those who believed in Jesus Christ, but even here the generic wording encompassed Catholics as well as Protestants.

By far the most comprehensive theoretician of religious freedom in colonial America was Roger Williams. Starting out as a Puritan, Williams became a Baptist, and ended up a "Seeker." He was indefatigable in his support for the rights of conscience, and he explicitly founded Providence, Rhode Island, as "a shelter for persons distressed for conscience." Williams's literary legacy includes *The Bloudy Tenet of Persecution* (1644), in which he pressed a vigorous case for religious toleration more than four decades before John Locke's more celebrated *Letter on Toleration*. Williams condemned religious persecution squarely on Christian grounds, arguing that persecution contradicted the meek example of Jesus and promoted fraudulent conversions. In Williams's view, the separation of church and state was good for the church because it helped safeguard its purity. Williams ultimately called for a civil society where the state acted in the area of morality but not theology. His view on the proper role of government vis-à-vis religion is expressed most succinctly and beautifully in a letter he wrote to the town of Providence in January 1655, wherein he compares civil society to life on a ship at sea.

> It hath fallen out sometimes, that both papists and protestants, Jews and Turks, may be embarked in one ship; upon which supposal I affirm, that all the liberty of conscience, that ever I pleaded for, turns upon these two hinges—that none of the papists, protestants, Jews, or Turks, be forced to come to the ship's prayers or worship, nor compelled from their own particular prayers or worship, if they practice any. . .

> notwithstanding this liberty, the commander of this ship ought to command the ship's course, yea, and also command that justice, peace and sobriety, be kept and practiced, both among the seamen and all the passengers. . . . [I]f any refuse to obey the common laws and orders of the ship, concerning their common peace or preservation; if any shall mutiny and rise up against their commanders and officers. . . in such cases. . . the commander or commanders may judge, resist, compel and punish such transgressors, according to their deserts and merits.

In this letter, Williams articulated a theory of church and state that would eventually be accepted as the common sense of the subject by nearly all Americans: Let the civil authorities focus on civil wrongs like murder and theft and leave theological wrongs to be decided by persuasion alone.

Despite glimmers in such places as Rhode Island, religious liberty in the American colonies as a whole was still an idea struggling to be born during the seventeenth and eighteenth centuries. This was true in both the North and the South. Southern colonies were perhaps the worst offenders when it came to restricting religious freedom. The Anglican Church was the established religion and taxpayers were compelled to pay for its support. Non-Anglican Protestants, such as Baptists, often found life difficult in the southern colonies. As late as 1774, James Madison could complain about the "diabolical Hell conceived principle of persecution" after learning that some non-Anglican clergymen had been jailed in an adjacent Virginia county for (in his words) "publishing their religious Sentiments which in the main are very orthodox."

Times were changing nonetheless. On the eve of the Revolutionary War, four American colonies had never had an official state church (New Jersey, Pennsylvania, Rhode Island, and Delaware) and four colonies (New York, New Hampshire, Massachusetts, and Connecticut) allowed local taxpayers to support more than one Protestant denomination. In the latter colonies, members of churches that received no state money (such as Quakers and Baptists) were often exempted from church taxes. What was developing in America was a situation where people were taxed to support the churches of their choice; and political pressures from many non-established Christian groups were building for broader religious freedoms for all. Those pressures would ultimately produce, during the Revolutionary and Founding periods, a system of religious liberty unparalleled in human history.

Religion and Politics during the Revolution and Founding of the United States

Nathaniel Hawthorne ended his short story, "The Gray Champion," by drawing a connection between the fierce spirit of the Puritans and the American Revolution. For Hawthorne, the "Gray Champion" symbolized the Puritan spirit, and he wrote that this mysterious hero reappeared "whenever the descendants of the Puritans are to show the spirit of their sires." The old man came again "at Lexington, where now the obelisk of granite, with a slab of slate inlaid, commemorates the first fallen of the Revolution. And when our fathers were toiling at the breastwork on Bunker's Hill, all through that night the old warrior walked his rounds." While it would be simplistic to describe the American Revolution as a consequence of Puritanism, Hawthorne was perceptive. The spirit of fierceness inculcated by the Puritans helped develop a culture of resistence in New England that culminated in the Revolutionary generation's opposition to what they saw as English tyranny.

But the connections between religion and politics in the American Revolution were also more explicit. In the decades preceding the Revolution, colonial clergy—especially the Congregationalists and Presbyterians who were heirs to the Puritan tradition—laid the groundwork for rebellion in countless sermons and tracts. An election sermon by Massachusetts minister Gad Hitchock in 1774 was typical. Hitchcock declared that government "is from the people, who have not only a right, but are bound in duty . . . to lodge it in such hands as they judge best qualified to answer its intention; so when it is misapplied to other purposes . . . they have the same original right . . . to transfer it to others." Hitchcock was, if anything, fearless. The audience for his sermon included the newly appointed military governor of Massachusetts, General Thomas Gage. Gage listened politely to the entire sermon, but many audience members walked out, causing Hitchcock to observe dryly that his sermon had apparently been a moving one. When the Revolution commenced in earnest, clergymen like Hitchcock continued to fan the flames of resistence. These ministers have sometimes been criticized for taking their political ideas more from British political writers such as John Locke than the Bible; but one should never forget that the Puritans' compact theory of government predated Locke. American Christians likely cited Locke because they found his ideas compatible with what they already knew to be true on other grounds.

All Christians in America did not agree on the Revolutionary War, of course. Recent scholarship has underscored the fact that most Christian denominations had members on both sides of the conflict. "Nevertheless," writes Mark Noll, "it is true that vast numbers of American Christians offered wholehearted support to the movement leading to separation from Great Britain. Certainly the overwhelming majority of clergymen who wrote about the conflict lent Christian support to the Patriot cause. In particular, the direct descendants of Anglo-American Puritanism, Congregationalists and Presbyterians distinguished themselves in defense of colonial prerogatives. To some observers, in fact, colonial Patriots took on the appearance of religious crusaders."

Those clergymen who did not support the patriot cause were split among pacifists and loyalists. Pacifist denominations, such as the Quakers and Mennonites, had deep objections to the sinfulness of war and sat out the conflict, often provoking persecution from supporters of the Revolution. Loyalists who supported Great Britain, meanwhile, were scattered throughout the denominations, though the largest group likely resided in the Anglican Church. Given the anticlericalism rampant in both the later French and Russian revolutions, the American Revolution is unusual for the number of prominent church leaders who not only preached revolution, but who actively helped found the new order. One of the most prominent of these was the Rev. John Witherspoon, president of the Presbyterian College of New Jersey (later Princeton).

Elected in 1776 to the Continental Congress, Witherspoon signed the Declaration of Independence and served with distinction on more than 100 committees. He left Congress only after victory had been assured and the Articles of Confederation had been ratified, returning to Princeton in 1782 to rebuild his war-ravaged college. From 1783 to 1789, he served in the New Jersey legislature, and in 1787 he was selected as a delegate to the New Jersey convention called to ratify the Constitution. Witherspoon remained a respected and influential national figure until his death in 1794. Witherspoon's most profound impact on the new republic probably came in his role as teacher. As president of his college, he taught the required course in moral philosophy to each senior class, and his students included 20 future senators, 25 future congressmen, 3 future justices of the United States Supreme Court, 13 future governors, and one future president—James Madison, who remained at Princeton after graduation to pursue further studies under Witherspoon.

Witherspoon defended the right of clergymen to hold public office, and he viewed churches and ministers as exercising an independent moral voice for the good of society. In Witherspoon's view, churches created the moral conditions necessary for popular government to survive. Republics were based on the rule of the people, and the people must be moral to rule well. But the existence of social morality depended on the vitality of the churches. Witherspoon went so far as to claim that churches in modern republics served the same function as the *censor morum,* the public official in Rome who safeguarded public manners and morals. According to Witherspoon, "the only thing which we have now to supply the place of this is the religious discipline of the several sects with respect to their own members; so that the denomination or profession which shall take the most effectual care of the instruction of its members and maintain its discipline in the fullest vigor, will do the most essential service to the whole body." The churches fulfilled a vital political function by inculcating in their members the virtues and habits that produced good citizens.

Witherspoon further thought that religion could be helpful in dampening the extremism spawned by political passions. On the eve of the Revolutionary War, he drafted a pastoral letter for the churches in his synod that urged parishoners to exhibit "a spirit of humanity and mercy" in the coming conflict. Noting that "civil wars are carried on with a rancor and spirit of revenge much greater than those between independent states," Witherspoon argued that it was all the more incumbent on Christians in the conflict to curb their natural passions: "That man will fight most bravely, who never fights till it is necessary, and who ceases to fight as soon as the necessity is over."

Because of religion's vital public role, Witherspoon believed that the government ought to be favorably disposed toward religion, but he did not think that it should try to enforce theological orthodoxy. To the contrary, he defended religious liberty as vigorously as he did the public role of religion. According to Witherspoon, the government "ought to defend the rights of conscience, and tolerate all in their religious sentiments that are not injurious to their neighbors." Indeed, in Witherspoon's view, the government should probably forgo interference with religion even in cases where a religious group's opinions are deemed subversive. Chiding those political theorists (like John Locke) who maintained that religious toleration should not extend to Roman Catholics, Witherspoon noted that

> It is commonly said . . . that in case any sect holds tenets subversive of society and inconsistent with the rights of others, that they ought not to be tolerated. On this footing Popery is not tolerated in Great Britain; because they profess entire subjection to a foreign power, the See of Rome . . . . But however just this may be in a way of reasoning, we ought in general to guard against persecution on a religious account as much as possible; because such as hold absurd tenets are seldom dangerous. Perhaps they are never dangerous, but when they are oppressed. Papists are tolerated in Holland without danger to liberty. And though not properly tolerated, they are now connived at in Britain.

Witherspoon's view of the importance of religious liberty was widely shared by the time of the Revolution, and the movement to expand the freedom of religion continued to grow both during and after the war. In New England, the system of allowing people to pay their religious tax to the church of their choice (or exempting religious dissenters from the taxes) generally prevailed. New York went further, ending all government support for churches. But the most significant reforms came in the South, where the Anglican Church had maintained a monopoly on tax support and other privileges prior to the Revolution. All the Southern states abolished the Anglican monopoly as a consequence of the Revolution, but they did so in different ways. Some states replaced the exclusive establishment of the Anglican Church with a general tax that required citizens to support the church of their choice (as in New England). Other Southern states abandoned tax support of churches altogether.

A difference of opinion over the definition of religious liberty manifested itself during the Founding period. Proponents of requiring taxpayers to support the church of their choice did not think that the scheme violated the rights of conscience. After all, taxpayers did not have to support a church with which they disagreed. Opponents of all tax support for churches disagreed. They argued that using the government to fund clergy salaries corrupted both the church and state, and they pointed out that some of the exemption schemes for adherents of minority sects were cumbersome and discriminatory.

The latter position was favored by James Madison and Thomas Jefferson in Virginia, where they sought not only to end the Anglican establishment but to stop proposals to provide tax support for all the churches in the state. It is sometimes argued that Madison and Jefferson's opposition to any state subsidy for churches proved their Enlightenment secularism. The actual situation is more complicated. While Jefferson and Madison's opposition to state subsidies may have been animated by their secularism, neither of them were typical of the majority of citizens who opposed such schemes. Most opponents of tax-supported churches were anything but Englightenment secularists. They were evangelical Baptists, Presbyterians, and the like. Accordingly, historians have noted that James Madison's arguments against general tax support for churches largely synthesized arguments made in petitions drafted by evangelical Christians. Baptists, in particular, saw any state support for churches as likely to contaminate the purity of the church, and they argued that churches that were forced to raise their own support would be more likely to keep themselves to the true faith.

Two things were critical in the development of religious liberty in the new United States during the post-Revolutionary period. The first was the sheer mutiplicity of sects. The U.S. after the Revolution was awash in differing religious traditions, albeit most of them were within the larger Christian tradition: Quakers, Mennonites, Baptists, Methodists, Congregationalists, Lutherans, Presbyterians, Covenanters, Unitarians, Catholics, and many more. Given the variety of religious sects even within many states, it became increasingly difficult for any single sect to expect that it could use the government to dominate its competitors. As a result, religious believers in general were encouraged to lower their expectations as to what they could achieve through government. Rather than expect the government to promote their own particular church to the exclusion of others, religious adherents settled for the guarantee of equal rights. The government would be an honest broker that treated members of different religious sects fairly. That way members of each sect would not be oppressed if their religious opponents gained control of the government.

James Madison had already recognized the connection between sectarianism and religious freedom during the battle for disestablishment in Virginia in the 1780s. Writing to Thomas Jefferson in 1785, he expressed his happiness with the animosity among competing sects because he believed that it secured liberty by preventing an unjust coalition that could endanger fundamental rights. Three years later at Virginia's convention to ratify the Constitution, Madison gave a more extended defense of this line of thinking.

> Happily for the states, they enjoy the utmost freedom of religion. This freedom arises from that multiplicity of sects, which pervades America, and which is the best and only security for religious liberty in any society .... The United States abound in such a variety of sects, that it is a strong security against religious persecution, and it is sufficient to authorize a conclusion, that no one sect will ever be able to outnumber or depress the rest.

By itself, however, a multiplicity of sects would not have produced religious liberty in the U.S. Conceivably, the variety of sects could have generated even sharper strife as competing sects jockeyed for the reins of government power. Something beyond sheer variety was needed to lay the groundwork for religious liberty, and that was found within the Christian tradition that so dominated early colonial thought. Christianity (especially in its Protestant manifestations) emphasized the necessity of voluntary conversion of the heart. Laws that compelled citizens to become Christians were ultimately futile; they could produce hypocrites, but not real penitents. In addition, the example of Jesus—the one who meekly suffered—was difficult to square with a policy of compulsory conversions. Thus, the seeds of religious liberty existed within the Christian tradition from the very start. Though it was some time before most Christians accepted the full doctrine of religious liberty, it is no surprise that the loudest proponents of the concept were Baptists, Quakers, and others who made the case largely on Christian grounds.

The battle over state support for churches was the main issue involving religion in politics after the Revolutionary War, and it was fought out at the state and local level for the most part. Yet the political status of religion also found its way into the national arena with the Constitution of 1787 and the subsequent Bill of Rights. The Constitution forbade religious tests for federal offices (Article VI, Section 3), a departure from the practice of many states, which still required public officials to make various kinds of professions of religion to hold office. The Constitution also allowed government officials to pledge their loyalty to the Constitution by either "Oath or Affirmation" (Article II, Section 1), an accommodation to the scruples against swearing harbored by religious groups such as the Quakers.

The First Amendment to the Constitution broached the subject of religion more broadly, stipulating that "Congress shall make no law respecting an establishment of religion, or prohibiting the free exercise thereof." While there has been considerable debate about the precise meaning of this language, the best scholarship (by Leonard Levy among others) suggests that it was designed to prevent any sort of direct funding of churches by the federal government. However, the First Amendment does not appear to have prohibited many less direct ways to favor religion. Presidents could issue thanksgiving proclamations that emphasized the nation's dependence on God as did the nation's first two presidents, George Washington and John Adams (the next president, Thomas Jefferson, declined to do so because he thought the practice exceeded federal power). Presidents could also make appeals to God in their public utterances, as did all the early presidents, including Jefferson. In addition, the government could aid religious groups incidentally to pursue otherwise secular policy objectives. From the earliest days of the republic, tax dollars subsidized missionary efforts among the Indians in the hope of gaining secure borders and tempering the inevitable problems created by western expansion. These subsidies were sanctioned even by James Madison and Thomas Jefferson, otherwise strong supporters of a strict separation between church and state. In at least one area, the federal government could actually hire clergy for explicitly religious purposes, as it did in the case of chaplains for Congress and the armed services. Although James Madison privately believed that this practice violated the rights of conscience, his view was exceptional. Generally speaking, the founding generation seemed to believe that there were many ways that the government could treat religion favorably even while securing religious liberty for all.

Despite clear evidence that religion served an important public role during the Founding period, debate has persisted over the years concerning the views of major founding statesmen on religion, society, and politics. What were the personal religious beliefs of such founders as George Washington, Alexander Hamilton, James Madison, and Thomas Jefferson? Did they ultimately regard religion as a threat or as a help to republican government? What political role did they envision for religion, if any? The answers to such questions have been vigorously disputed, and it is impossible to deal with them comprehensively in this essay. But it might be useful to describe some of the major schools of thought.

Some scholars, notably Walter Berns and Thomas Pangle, claim that the major founders were primarily Enlightenment rationalists who rejected Christianity and sought to replace it with a vague political religion that could be used as a tool for social control by elected officials. According to this view, the founders wanted to subordinate religion to the government. While a generic belief in God and the afterlife might be useful as a tool to promote social morality, the existence of religious believers who thought that they had the one true way to God was dangerous to republicanism and had to be undermined. In this understanding, the founders' prescription for religion in politics becomes almost indistinguishable from the vision offered by Rousseau in *The Social Contract* or by Machiavelli in *The Prince* and *The Discourses*.

At the other end of the spectrum from Berns and Pangle are proponents of what might be termed the "Christian America" thesis. According to their view, the founders did not subordinate religion to the government; they subordinated the government to religion—or, more precisely, to Christianity. In its most radical form, the Christian America thesis is a legacy of New England Puritanism, positing America as a new Israel, chosen and directed by Providence. Less strenuous adherents to this position contend that Christianity, if not officially established during the founding, certainly provided the foundation upon which everything else was built; moreover, it was a necessary ingredient for the republic's continued existence. The most important political consequence of this view is that the laws must never contradict—and perhaps should sometimes positively encourage—the teachings of Christianity.

The Christian America thesis was vigorously advocated by many evangelical Protestants in the early nineteenth century, and it continued to reappear as the century progressed. More recently, the Christian America idea has been revived by elements of the Christian Right. Constitutional lawyer John Whitehead has argued that the Constitution's framers sought to create a government based on the higher law of the Bible, because they "knew very well that the higher law with its reference point in the Bible provided advantages beyond what was called natural justice."

In between the polarities represented by Berns and Pangle on the one hand, and the "Christian America" advocates on the other, are those who think the founders' goal was to protect the integrity of both the spiritual and political realms. In the view of Harry Jaffa, the founders confined politics to areas where human reason and divine revelation could agree, leaving religious groups free to compete for support outside politics. In this view, the spiritual and political spheres were placed on an equal footing. Neither was subordinate to the other. Church and state were both supreme within their respective spheres.

Which of these views better fits with historical reality? The founders' personal religious beliefs offer some insight, but not much. The charge that the major founding fathers were invariably the champions of the Enlightenment and opposed traditional religion is manifestly false, but so too is the claim that most of them were either devout Christians or believed that all morality is derived from the Bible. The major statesmen of the founding era were a curious mixture of the devout, the semi-devout, and the secularist, as several examples will illustrate.

- **John Jay**, chief justice of the Supreme Court and negotiator of the final peace treaty with Great Britain, was perhaps the most prominent evangelical Christian in national politics in the 1780s and 1790s. His private letters are replete with discussions of religious issues, including Bible prophecy, and he spent the latter part of his life as the president of the American Bible Society.
- **Alexander Hamilton**, the nation's first Treasury secretary, who functioned as virtual prime minister in the Washington administration, likewise began his life as a devout Christian. But he apparently fell away from his faith during his climb to power, only to return to it near the end of his life after one of his sons was killed in a duel.
- **George Washington**, the first president, is harder to pin down. He was an active Episcopalian, and his personal correspondence is filled with references to a personal God who intervenes in human affairs;

but whether he actually believed that Christ was God and savior is somewhat unclear. He apparently declined to take the sacrament of Holy Communion during at least parts of his adult life, which at least raises doubts about his view of Christ.

- **Benjamin Franklin**, **Thomas Jefferson**, and **John Adams** were Unitarians of various stripes. Adams and Jefferson were hostile to the teachings of orthodox Christianity, lampooning the Trinitarian conception of God in their personal letters to each other. However, they were careful not to broach such subjects in their public utterances, with Adams choosing to follow the maxim, "honor the gods established by law."
- **James Madison** is perhaps the greatest religious enigma among the major founders. During his college years, his private papers show evangelical fervor, and he spent an extra year at college to study theology under John Witherspoon. But his silence on theological topics later in life is deafening.

In some respects, the diversity of personal religious beliefs among the founders obscures more than it explains. Despite their widely differing theological persuasions, the leading statesmen of the Founding era agreed substantially on the proper relationship between church and state. James Madison outlined the common sense of the subject as follows in his "Memorial and Remonstrance" in 1785:

> Before any man can be considered as a member of Civil Society, he must be considered as a subject of the Governor of the Universe: And if a member of Civil Society, who enters into any subordinate Association, must always do it with a reservation of his duty to the general authority; much more must every man who becomes a member of any particular Civil Society, do it with a saving of his allegiance to the Universal Sovereign. We maintain therefore that in matters of Religion, no man's right is abridged by the institution of Civil Society, and that Religion is wholly exempt from its cognizance.

Reminiscent of the two kingdoms approach championed by Roger Williams in the seventeenth century in Rhode Island, the founders' political philosophy argued for an institutional separation between church and state not to subvert religion but to safeguard it. It was precisely because the duty to God comes first that religion must be exempt from civil authority. Of course, this two-sphere approach advocated by the founders required a major corollary to work in practice: a belief that citizens of different religious faiths would agree on the moral basis of political action. Religion encompasses the realm of action as well as belief. Hence, what happens if a church inculcates duties contrary to civil policy, and its adherents act accordingly? Will not the government have to intervene against those religious adherents to preserve social order? And will not this very intervention subjugate religion to the state, thus reintroducing conflict between religion and politics? Only if church and state can agree on the moral standard for political action can this result be avoided. In other words, reason (the operating principle of civil government) and revelation (the ultimate standard for religion) must concur on the moral law for the founders' system to work.

The founders agreed with this proposition. Evangelical Christians like Witherspoon and Jay, no less than champions of the Enlightenment like Jefferson and Franklin, concurred that the morality of revelation was largely coincident with the morality of reason and conscience. This conceit that reason and revelation agreed on the moral law so permeated the founding era that the modern reader may miss it because authors of the period more often assume it rather than demonstrate it. When citing authority for fundamental propositions, writers of the founding era appealed to both reason and revelation as a matter of course.

This pervasive belief during the Founding era that reason and revelation agreed on morality undercuts much of Walter Berns's analysis. According to Berns, the founders thought that sectarian religion must "be reformed and rendered harmless" by the spread of Unitarianism if their scheme of republican government was to succeed. But one strives in vain to see how this could be the case. Politics in the new republic depended on a shared morality rather than a shared theology. Thus, there was little reason for the government to be concerned about continued theological differences. As long as competing religious sects promoted the same reasonable morality, they helped, rather than hindered, republican government. Since even rationalists like Jefferson and Franklin acknowledged that sectarian religion promoted the requisite civic virtues, it becomes difficult to take Berns's position seriously. Whatever theoretical grounds certain founders might have had for opposing sectarian theology, they saw no pressing political reason to supplant sectarianism with Unitarianism. If anything, founders such as James Madison wanted sectarian religion to flourish because they knew that continued differences in theology would make a tyrannical combination of religious sects more difficult.

But if the founders' belief in a morality shared by both reason and revelation undercuts the analysis offered by Berns, it also undermines the claims of those who advocate the "Christian America" thesis. The existence of a common moral order shared by Christians and non-Christians makes a peculiarly "Christian" republic largely unnecessary, particularly when the government of the republic has no say over theology. Civil society can be founded upon God's general revelation to all humans through the law of nature, rather than on tenets peculiar to the Bible. Hence, it is understandable that evangelicals among the founders, such as Witherspoon and Jay, mostly eschewed rhetoric connecting the American regime to Christian revelation.

Still, one must not claim too much for the rapprochement between religion and politics that was devised during this period. The founders never claimed that human reason and divine revelation could agree on everything, even in the realm of morality. The founders well knew that religion and unassisted reason might sometimes disagree on the course of civic action, and that this meant that the independence between theology and politics might be difficult to maintain. But knowing this, they still insisted that the area of agreement between reason and revelation was sufficiently broad that both church and state might benefit by being institutionally separate.

If the founders' system separating church and state was theoretically coherent, their political science also contained the seeds of further strife between religion and politics. This situation becomes apparent when one recognizes the nearly universal opinion during the period that civic morality was necessary for republican government and churches were either necessary or helpful to defend that morality. In the words of George Washington's famous "Farewell Address,"

> Of all the dispositions and habits which lead to political prosperity, religion and morality are indispensable supports . . . . And let us with caution indulge the supposition that morality can be maintained without religion . . . reason and experience both forbid us to expect that national morality can prevail in exclusion of religious principle.

If religion is necessary for morality, and morality is necessary for republican government, then it constitutes no great leap to conclude that religious groups should become involved in politics—at least insofar as politics intersects with morality. Admittedly, this conclusion was not something most of the founders thought a great deal about, although some of them certainly foresaw it.

The result was that even as the founders defused the conflict between church and state, they created the conditions for the conflict to rise again in another form. Whether intended or not, the political system that the founders created issued a de facto invitation to the nation's churches to enter politics as the defenders of civic morality. What this would mean for the nation—and for its churches—became sharply evident in the early decades of the nineteenth century.

Religion and Politics to the Civil War

"[T]he American clergy stands aloof from public business. That is the most striking, but not the only, example of their self-restraint. Religion in America is a world apart in which the clergyman is supreme, but one which he is careful never to leave . . . ." So observed the famed French political observer Alexis de Tocqueville after his visit to the United States in 1831. Tocqueville claimed that religion may have been the primary American political institution, but its influence was indirect at best; it helped fashion the morals of society, but did not actively participate in matters for legislation. Indeed, American clergy were "at pains to keep out of affairs and not mix in the combinations of parties."

Tocqueville's analysis of religion and American politics in the early 1800s is so frequently cited today that it has almost become a truism, but it is a truism that is largely untrue. Far from eschewing political strife, American clergy in the early decades of the new nation embarked upon a great era of political and social reform. Clergymen and their congregations were active in party strife from the inception of American party politics. During the bitter battles between the Federalists and the Jeffersonian Republicans in the 1790s, religion became a key campaign issue—so much so that clergy aligned with the Federalists tried to turn the presidential election of 1800 into a referendum on candidate Thomas Jefferson's religious beliefs.

Although Jefferson for the most part hid his theological opinions, rumors swirled about that he was actually a "howling athiest." Federalists subsequently presented the upcoming election as a stark choice between "God and a Religious President" and "Jefferson and No God." Evangelicals aligned with the party did their best to fan the flames of fear. In a pamphlet titled *The Voice of Warning to Christians*, the Rev. John Mason of New York (a friend of Alexander Hamilton) bore down upon Jefferson with all the eloquence he could muster. Delivering an exacting exegesis of Jefferson's one published book, *Notes on the State of Virginia*, Mason rebuked Jefferson for undercutting the Biblical account of the universal deluge, for implicitly denying that the Jews are God's chosen people, and for asserting that atheism has no ill political consequences. Mason further castigated Jefferson for his ambivalent speculations about blacks, accusing him of hinting that blacks were actually subhuman. At best, Jefferson merely acknowledged that blacks "perhaps" were on the same level of being as whites. Such waffling was, according to Mason, in flagrant contradiction to divine revelation's teaching that all human beings were made "of one blood."

Mason's jeremiad against Jefferson constituted the last gasp of a long campaign by evangelicals to counter the onslaught of the Jeffersonians. Not all evangelicals were Federalists, but many of the evangelical leaders most openly involved in politics were; these tended to be Congregationalist and Presbyterian clergymen. In the years leading up to the election of 1800, their sermons had repeatedly warned about the scheming proponents of infidelity who wished to re-enact the bloody French Revolution on American soil. In 1798, the Rev. Jedidiah Morse identified these national traitors as members of a vast subversive organization known as the Illuminati. Yale President Timothy Dwight succinctly summarized the objectives of this secret group as "the overthrow of religion, government, and human society civil and domestic." Federalist evangelicals left few doubts about which political party wished to enact the Illuminati's program; nor were they reluctant to prescribe partisan solutions to the problem.

The aftermath of the election of 1800 was a great anticlimax as far as Federalist evangelicals were concerned. Contrary to the apocalyptic predictions of one Boston newspaper, Jefferson's election did not place "the seal of death . . . on our holy religion" or result in the installation of "some infamous prostitute, under the title of the Goddess of Reason . . . [to] preside in the sanctuaries now devoted to the Most

High." Once in office, the "howling atheist" from Virginia hid his religious views more furtively than before. He signed laws funding both military chaplains and missionaries among the Indians, and he was ever careful to make pious appeals to Providence in his public speeches.

Yet there had been a price exacted for the injection of religion into the politics of the time. Many people had soured on the experience, viewing the active partisanship of the clergy as unseemly at best. After the Federalist Party disintegrated, even some clergymen who had been actively involved in the political strife expressed second thoughts. They began to wonder whether they had allowed themselves to be used as pawns in political battles that they should not have been fighting in the first place.

The Rev. Timothy Dwight, president of Yale and a fierce Federalist, was one of the ones who looked back with dismay on the role of Christians in the party battles of the early nation. In his charge to graduating students in 1816, Dwight declared that

> [O]ur countrymen have spent a sufficient time in hostilities against each other. We have entertained as many unkind thoughts, uttered as many bitter speeches, called each other by as many hard names, and indulged as much unkindness and malignity; as might satisfy our worst enemies, and as certainly ought to satisfy us. From all these efforts of ill-will we have not derived the least advantage . . . Friends and brothers have ceased to be friends and brothers; and professing Christians have dishonoured the religion which they professed.

Religious leaders such as Dwight did not completely foreswear politics, but they did begin to see a different way of exerting influence. Rather than latching onto existing parties, they discovered that they could exercise an independent moral voice outside the parties. The first example of what this might mean at the national level occurred during the summer of 1804, when Vice President Aaron Burr shot and killed Alexander Hamilton in a duel. The killing set off a wave of revulsion and sparked a movement among the religious community to end the barbaric practice of duelling. The anti-duelling crusade was the first national political movement separate from party politics to involve religion. Neither party wanted to tackle the issue because among the ruling elite duelling was an accepted way of handling affronts. Accordingly, many clergymen initially declined to take a stand on the issue, fearing they would offend upper-class gentlemen in their congregations who supported the practice. But in the months following the death of Hamilton, the hands-off attitude started to change. Ministers around the nation began delivering sermons demanding an end to duelling, citizens formed anti-duelling associations, and church bodies enacted resolutions condemning the practice.

The duelling controversy catapaulted an obscure young preacher from Long Island, New York, into the national limelight. After reading about the Burr-Hamilton duel, Lyman Beecher was both horrified and outraged and wrote a pamphlet urging that citizens withhold their votes from candidates who fought duels. The pamphlet was a tour de force of both reasoned argument and passionate moralism. It attacked duelling as contradicting reason, the Bible, and civil liberty. Remembered today chiefly as the father of author Harriet Beecher Stowe and abolitionist preacher Henry Ward Beecher, the elder Beecher was a towering preacher and reformer in his own right in the early decades of the nineteenth century. As one of his colleagues commented after his death in 1863, "in massive talent Lyman Beecher stood among his brethren like Daniel Webster in the Senate—alone."

Beecher moved to Connecticut in 1810 and soon became one of the most perceptive champions of what some historians have called the country's "voluntary establishment of religion." Like most ministers of his era, Beecher believed that republican government could not survive without a virtuous citizenry, and that a virtuous citizenry depended on religion. He was therefore disturbed that public officials were increasingly reticent about enforcing either morality or piety by law and that there was growing political support for abolishing all tax subsidies for churches, which had long been the bulwark of Protestantism in New England. Beecher viewed these developments with alarm and feared the worst. But instead of despairing, he came up with a brilliant response. If the government could no longer be relied on to support religion and morality, he announced, religious adherents themselves had to do what the government could not. Government once promoted civic virtue by compelling people to "support the gospel and attend the public worship of God," Beecher told the Connecticut legislature in 1826. "But these means of moral influence the law can no longer apply; and there is no substitute but the voluntary energies of the nation itself, in associations for charitable contributions and efforts, patronized by all denominations of Christians, and by all classes of the community who love their country."

Beecher advocated replacing government as a supporter of religion and morality with a network of voluntary societies that would spread the gospel, inculcate moral habits in the young, and reclaim the dissolute. In those cases where government action might still be necessary, the associations would seek to create a public consensus through educational efforts, because, as Beecher realized, in a free society persuasion had to precede coercion.

Following the lead of Beecher and others, evangelicals organized scores of voluntary associations for evangelism, missions, and social and political reform. They formed groups to help end poverty, to teach reading and writing to the poor, and to prevent the abuse of alcohol. Beecher himself took part in many of these efforts, such as the American Temperance Society and a group that promoted the voluntary observance of the sabbath. This multitude of private associations transformed American society in a way that few government programs ever could. By the 1830s, a well-developed system of voluntary activity and benevolence existed in the United States. "They say ministers have lost their influence," Beecher wrote years later. "The fact is, they have gained. By voluntary efforts, societies, missions, and revivals, they exert a deeper influence than ever they could" have done by state support. He had learned through experience that the free enterprise system in religion, far from being hostile to faith, created the conditions for true piety and civic virtue to flourish.

But even as Beecher championed Christianity's civic role, he had a keen appreciation for the limits of religious activism. Unlike many later reformers, he had a firm belief in human sinfulness, and he harbored no illusions that human beings could create an earthly paradise. Beecher further recognized the dangers that political activism posed for Christianity. Political ambitions could easily overwhelm the gospel and provoke public censure. He subsequently advised Christians to restrict their political efforts to the "great questions of national morality" instead of trying to formulate an explicitly Christian position on every conceivable political issue.

> When great questions of national morality are about to be decided, such as the declaration of war; or, as in England, the abolition of the slave trade . . . it becomes Christians to lift up their voice, and exert their united influence. But, with the annual detail of secular policy, it does not become Christians to intermeddle, beyond the unobtrusive influence of their silent suffrage.

As a result of the ideas of Beecher and others, significant numbers of evangelical Christians entered the public arena on a variety of issues prior to the Civil War. In the domestic sphere, evangelicals waged crusades against poverty, alcoholism, lotteries, and prostitution. They boycotted businesses that opened on Sundays, and they sought to improve what can only be called the hellish conditions then prevalent in American prisons. In foreign affairs, evangelicals and Unitarians joined to establish societies for the promotion of pacifism during the War of 1812. The peace movement continued in later years under the auspices of the American Peace Society, which was formed in 1827. One of the goals of the peace movement was the establishment of a world court for the arbitration of international disputes.

Perhaps the most consistent involvement of religious believers in foreign affairs was caused by concerns for the human rights of fellow Christians and missionaries in other parts of the world. For example, when the Ottoman Empire tried to quell the Greek uprising in the 1820s, American pulpits resounded with appeals to help Greek Christians overthrow their Moslem rulers. In 1826, when American naval officer "Mad Jack" Percival fomented riots against missionaries in Hawaii (largely because they had convinced Hawaiian chiefs to end the prostitution on the island that serviced foreign sailors), missionary activists demanded a court-martial for Percival. Although Percival was ultimately cleared by a court of inquiry, the next naval vessel to arrive in Hawaii carried a letter from President John Quincy Adams that all but apologized for the incident. More generally, supporters of Christian missionaries abroad prodded the federal government to be more solicitous of the interests of American missionaries. After many years of lobbying by missionary groups, Secretary of State Daniel Webster in 1842 finally instructed the American minister in Constantinople that American missionaries should receive the same help and protection from American consular officers as American businessmen.

Of all the issues to involve religious adherents in the public arena before the Civil War, three stand out as the high-water marks of religious activism in politics: Sunday mails, Cherokee removal, and slavery. All three issues showed how people of faith could articulate an independent moral voice in politics within the limits outlined by the founders. The Sunday mails controversy erupted in 1810 after Congress required many post offices to open on Sundays. Congress was soon flooded with hundreds of petitions demanding both the closure of post offices on Sunday and the curtailment of Sunday mail routes. The first wave of petitions came between 1811 and 1816. The petitions failed to bring about the desired relief, so a second and larger petition campaign commenced in the late 1820s. Critics of Sunday mails largely attacked the practice as a two-fold violation of religious liberty. First, and most obviously, it forced postal workers who believed that Sunday was God's ordained day of rest to choose between their faith and their job. More subtly, Sunday mails placed the government in the role of undercutting the religious beliefs of a large number of citizens. By requiring mail service on Sundays, the government was declaring as official policy that the sabbath need not be respected.

Defenders of Sunday mails rejected the religious liberty claims of postal workers, arguing that postmasters and their clerks were not really being coerced because they could always resign. These defenders further maintained that to stop the mails on Sunday would contravene the First Amendment and establish a religion by officially sanctioning Sunday as God's sabbath. Finally, they denounced their opponents as scheming to unify church and state and implied that they did not even have the right to petition Congress on the subject. This last attack was decried by the Sunday mail protestors, who pointed out that religious adherents had the same constitutional rights to become involved in politics as other citizens.

The second petition campaign against Sunday mails also ended without petitioners obtaining their desired relief, although in later decades the scope of Sunday postal service was reduced substantially. This reduction was achieved for economic as well as religious reasons. By 1863, one evangelical reformer could boast that the Sunday mails crusade had "caused a reduction of Sunday-mail service to an amount scarcely one fourth of what it was when the question was first mooted."

Almost simultaneous with the second Sunday mails petition campaign was the battle over Cherokee removal from Georgia. Federal treaties had guaranteed the Cherokees their lands upon the condition that they become both peaceful and civilized. The Cherokees kept their part of the bargain. They embraced agriculture, became educated, adopted Christianity, and pursued republican self-government. The Georgians, however, had no intention of respecting Cherokee treaty rights, and in 1828 and 1829 the Georgia legislature tried to legislate the Cherokee Nation out of existence, extending its laws over Cherokee lands and demanding that the federal government remove the recalcitrant Indians.

The evangelical missionaries who had been working among the Indians rose to the Cherokees' defense, led by the corresponding secretary of the American Board of Commissioners for Foreign Missions, Jeremiah Evarts. Evarts, a lawyer, helped turn the removal issue into a major national controversy. Under the nom de plume "William Penn," he wrote 26 essays for the *National Intelligencer* defending the Cherokees. The essays were a tour de force of logic, morality, and law. Evarts and other evangelicals based their arguments against removal not simply on biblical morality, but on the natural right of property, the inviolability of contracts, and the God-given equality of all men proclaimed in the Declaration of Independence, which they argued applied to Indians as well as whites.

Both Congress and President Andrew Jackson rebuffed the evangelicals' efforts on behalf of the Cherokees, and the government eventually relocated the Indians further West in a scandalous episode of American history known as the "Trail of Tears." The controversy nevertheless demonstrated that religious adherents could fulfill the role that the founders had carved out for them: They could put their idealism to constructive use by intervening in politics on the basis of principles of natural justice rather than doctrines of sectarian theology.

The greatest moral issue to involve religion in politics during the first half of the nineteenth century was slavery. Although the religious connections to the slavery controversy are clear, they are also multifaceted, and there is considerable truth to Abraham Lincoln's observation in his Second Inaugural Address that both sides of the controversy "read the same Bible, and pray[ed] to the same God; and each invoke[d] His aid against the other." The animating impulses of northern abolitionism were overwhelmingly Christian. From the Revolutionary War onward, an increasing number of clergymen and religious groups called for an end to slavery. The Quakers were the earliest denomination to make the abolition of slavery a defining issue, with Quakers in Pennsylvania producing the first published condemnation of the practice in America in 1688. In New England, Puritans Samuel Sewall and Cotton Mather produced early antislavery tracts. By the time of the Revolution, the Quakers in Pennsylvania had decided to expel members who did not free their slaves; and by the early 1800s, clergymen from a variety of denominations were calling for an end to the evil on the grounds that the Bible taught the doctrine of human equality. Presbyterian minister Samuel Stanhope Smith, for example, defended the natural equality of blacks and whites in his *Essay on the Causes of the Variety of Complexion and Figure in the Human Species*. President of Princeton, Smith went so far as to advocate racial intermarriage between blacks and whites as a way of breaking down the social barriers between them.

The abolitionist cause did not become a major movement with significant popular support until the 1830s. That decade saw the founding of the American Anti-Slavery Society, which soon became the focal point for much of the antislavery crusade. Backers of the Society included the brothers Lewis and Arthur Tappan, evangelical businessmen who supported a variety of reform efforts in the antebellum era.

On a practical level, antislavery forces often differed among themselves on what their political agenda should be. Given the Constitution's implicit protection of slavery in the South, it was unclear how much could be done to actually end the practice. At a bare minimum, opponents of slavery agreed that the South's "peculiar institution" should be contained. Thus, when Congress abrogated the Missouri Compromise and allowed slavery to spread north with the adoption of the Kansas-Nebraska Act in 1854, many in the religious community were outraged. During the debate over the bill, Congress received petitions from ministers around the nation attacking the proposal, including one memorial signed by more than 3,000 clergymen from New England, including Lyman Beecher. After passage of the Kansas-Nebraska Act, many churches supported an organized movement to bring antislavery settlers to the Kansas Territory to ensure that it would enter the union as a free state.

Some religious activists went beyond the policy of containment, supporting such activities as the underground railroad to smuggle slaves to freedom. Others tried passive resistance. In 1851, two Quakers were charged with treason for refusing to participate in a posse to capture fugitive slaves as required by the Fugitive Slave Act. They were tried, but acquitted.

Religion also played an important role in the battle for public opinion over slavery. The novel *Uncle Tom's Cabin*, perhaps the era's ultimate indictment of the evils of slavery, was a deeply religious manifesto. Written by Lyman Beecher's daughter Harriet Beecher Stowe, and published in 1852, the novel was undeniably melodramatic; but it was also a masterful piece of political fiction and Christian social thought. Ironically, the title figure of the novel was far from an "Uncle Tom" as that term is presently understood. Instead, he was a magnanimous hero who sacrificed himself to protect his family and fellow slaves. He was, in fact, a Christ figure. Nor was the book merely northern propaganda, for Stowe was just as critical of northern hypocrisy toward free blacks as she was toward southern slaveowners. Some 300,000 copies of *Uncle Tom's Cabin* were sold in its first year of publication, and it galvanized popular support behind the antislavery cause. When Stowe met Lincoln at the White House during the Civil War, he described her as "the little woman who wrote the book that made this great war." The comment was hyperbolic, but it was also insightful.

If religion in the North played a pivotal role in undermining support for slavery, religious institutions in the South played an equally important role on the other side of the controversy. While northern Christians increasingly condemned slavery as against God's law, southern Christians plunged into full-scale denial. As early as 1822, South Carolina Baptists accepted Richard Furman's scriptural justification of slavery, and many more embraced such arguments as time went on. Admirably, a few Christians in slave states took a different view. Antislavery clergyman John Dixon Long labored in Maryland until 1856, when he finally removed to Philadelphia for the sake of his family. Others accepted slavery, but refused to parrot the claims of southern spokesmen that blacks were subhuman. On the whole, however, southern Christians acquiesced—and then supported—the social system in which they found themselves. The controversy over slavery demonstrated how one's religious convictions could be overpowered by self-interest.

As the nation entered the 1840s, the chasm between southern and northern Christians on the subject of slavery became too cavernous to bridge, and national religious bodies began to disintegrate. Methodists and Baptists split into separate Northern and Southern denominations in 1844 and 1845, respectively. Presbyterians eventually divided as well. The controversy over slavery polarized the nation and helped propel it toward war. Yet it also demonstrated the vital moral currency of faith in politics. Like the crusade against duelling, the movement against slavery germinated in the churches rather than the structures of political power. Indeed, for years the political parties evaded the issue because it was so divisive. Only after antislavery agitation by religious reformers had grown into a significant force were new political groups created (like the Republican Party), which explicitly opposed the practice.

The vigorous political activity by churches before the Civil War was not without controversy. Critics charged that evangelical Christians and their reform associations constituted a threat to freedom just as grave as established churches had been. In their view, this "Christian party in politics" sought to unify church and state and impose its religious beliefs by law. The coalition opposing religion in politics was a mixture of secular and religious elements. On the secular side stood freethinkers like Frances Wright, quoted at the beginning of this essay. Lecturing around the country, Wright excoriated traditional religion as superstition and offered up science in its place. Wright attacked the clergy of the time as strident and intolerant, but her own views were not exactly mild. To mold the next generation to fit her views, she proposed taking children away from their parents at age two and sending them off to boarding schools that would supply an education "national, rational, and republican." Wright's friend, socialist Robert Owen, proposed a similar educational scheme. In addition, as part of his "Declaration of Mental Independence" in 1826, Owen denounced private property, traditional religion, and even the institution of marriage as "a trinity of the most monstrous evils that could be combined to inflict mental and physical evil upon his whole race."

Wright and Owen were radical secularists, but the opponents of religion in politics also included devout Christians who thought that Christianity should not taint itself by becoming so involved in earthly affairs. Among these were the followers of Alexander Campbell, who believed that reform associations were not sanctioned by scripture and emphasized personal piety over social reform.

Still other critics of Christian political activists were simply looking for a slogan with which to browbeat their political opponents. The charges of "priestcraft" and "union of church and state" provided powerful rhetorical weapons. Thus, during the Cherokee removal controversy in the 1830s, U.S. Senator Wilson Lumpkin openly attacked Christians who defended the Cherokee as "canting fanatics" and suggested they were a menace to the republic because they became involved in politics. Ironically, Lumpkin praised clergy who advocated removal. Apparently their efforts did not involve a dangerous mingling of church and state. Similar charges against clergy in politics were levelled during the debate on the Kansas-Nebraska bill, with Senator Stephen A. Douglas accusing clergy opposed to the bill of "having prostituted the sacred desk to the miserable and corrupting influences of party politics."

The charge that political activism by religious believers was illegitimate was a convenient way to attack religious reformers in politics without answering their arguments. In reality, the vast majority of religious efforts in politics during the antebellum period did not seek to impose a particular set of religious dogmas or entangle church with state. By the Civil War, nearly all denominations accepted disestablishment, and when religious believers advocated political or social reforms they generally articulated them in terms that could be accepted by citizens regardless of religious affiliation.

Nevertheless, there were some problem areas. Minority religious groups, especially Catholics and Mormons, faced open hostility. In 1844, anti-Catholic riots broke out in Philadelphia largely because the school board refused to compel Catholic children to read the Protestant version of the Bible in public schools. Anti-Catholic violence continued throughout the 1840s and 1850s. Ironically, much anti-Catholic agitation was conducted under the banner of protecting religious freedom. Critics claimed that American Catholics threatened the rights of conscience and wished to unify church and state. The charge was unfounded because American Catholicism had embraced religious liberty from the start. Even so, the position of American Catholics was not helped by papal encyclicals of the time, such as *Mirari Vos* (1832), which attacked as "absurd and erroneous" the "proposition which claims that liberty of conscience must be maintained for everyone." Anti-Catholic agitation spanned the theological spectrum, encompassing Protestants, freethinkers, and Jews.

Mormons faced even harsher persecution, aroused largely by practices such as polygamy and their penchant for establishing theocratic governments wherever they settled. They ultimately removed to Utah in search of greater freedom, much like the Puritans had fled to New England centuries before.

But conflict followed them west. When Utah became a territory of the United States, church leader Brigham Young was appointed governor. He was subsequently replaced in an effort to establish a genuinely secular government. When resistance followed, President James Buchanan sent in federal troops.

Despite the intolerance displayed toward religious minorities during this period, religion on the whole was a constructive force in American politics prior to the Civil War. People of faith defended human rights for disenfranchised groups such as the Cherokee and African-American slaves, worked to heal social ills like poverty and alcoholism, and called the nation to account when it acted unjustly. The religious activism during this era also had a liberating effect on the role of women in society. Women became heavily involved in various religious reform associations, carving out a public role for themselves that could not easily be taken back. Perhaps the first national political controversy where women sought to exercise their influence was Cherokee removal, when groups of religious women sent petitions to Congress seeking to defend Cherokee rights.

Prior to the Civil War, the churches largely fulfilled the role of the nation's political conscience, which had been created for them by the founders. This vigorous entry of religion into politics established a pattern for religious activism that would continue and expand in the latter part of the nineteenth century.

Religion and Politics from the Civil War through World War I

For the most part, churches in the North and South supported the war efforts of their respective governments during the Civil War. After peace had been secured, northern churches that had opposed slavery worked to establish educational institutions in the South for newly freed blacks to prepare them for their new life as citizens.

Unfortunately, civil rights for freedmen never became the post-war issue that slavery had been before the conflict, and it was soon dwarfed by other concerns. A brief review of the economic conditions of the time reveals why. The latter part of the nineteenth century brought the U.S. both phenomenal growth and unprecedented instability. On the one hand, the country's total wealth surged (reaching nearly $90 billion by 1900), modern manufacturing supplied the common man with a vast array of new products, and inventors like Thomas Edison and Alexander Graham Bell ushered in the age of technological marvels. On the other hand, there was a great deal of misery among ordinary people, especially those living in cities. Part of the misery was due to an unstable business cycle. As Charles and Mary Beard put it, the latter half of the nineteenth century "was . . . characterized by panics and depressions, nationwide in scope, unprecedented in extent" and accompanied by "unemployment, poverty, violence, and the destruction of property." American cities soon spawned vast slums dominated by decadance, disease, and disorder. Those fortunate enough to have jobs were often subjected to intolerable working conditions for meager wages. The arrival of hundreds of thousands of new immigrants exacerbated the situation, sparking a revival of virulent nativism by such groups as the American Protective Association and the Ku Klux Klan (which was anti-Catholic and anti-Jewish as well as anti-black). Protestant religious intolerance played a part in the creation of these nativist organizations, but economic fears of being displaced by foreign workers were probably more central.

The extremes of social distress during this period led churches to pay more attention to social problems, especially those tied to urbanization. This awakening to the social challenges of wealth and poverty spread beyond the churches, producing secular political movements such as populism and progressivism. These secular movements often drew heavily on the religious community for new recruits; nevertheless, the churches also maintained their own agenda.

The churches began to give greater attention to the problems of the urban poor soon after the Civil War. Evangelists like Dwight L. Moody brought revival meetings to major urban centers in the 1870s and 1880s. Missionaries set up urban rescue missions, settlement houses, and a variety of private social service agencies to dispense both material and spiritual aid. Religious leaders lobbied the government to attack the social conditions that bred poverty.

The idealistic zeal animating these religious reformers was clearly displayed in the novel *In His Steps*. Written by Congregationalist minister Charles Sheldon and published in 1896, the novel describes the social revolution that occurs in one city when a pastor persuades several people to guide their actions by the question, "What would Jesus do?" Much as *Uncle Tom's Cabin* galvanized the abolitionist movement, Sheldon's book proved to be a manifesto for this new crusade for social reform. By the mid-1920s, it had sold more than eight million copies. Translated into over 20 different languages, it remains in print even today.

The religious community's campaign on behalf of the poor was not monolithic; it encompassed different groups that did not always agree on either methods or goals. Perhaps the best known group of religious social reformers was made up of liberal Protestants who championed what became known as the "social gospel." Proponents of the social gospel generally rejected the infallibility of the Bible, redefined traditional Christian doctrines to downplay the supernatural, and hoped to create the kingdom of heaven on earth through political and social reform. Key figures in this movement included Congregationalists Josiah Strong and Washington Gladden, and Baptist theologian Walter Rauschenbusch. The number of clergy in the "social gospel" camp was limited, but the group exerted a powerful influence on public policy.

However, liberal Protestants were not the only religious adherents to focus on the problems of the poor. Catholics did as well, and recent scholarship has shown that theologically conservative Protestants promoted an ambitious social welfare agenda of their own. As Norris Magnuson points out in his book *Salvation in the Slums*, evangelists who preached a traditional message of salvation among the urban poor "attracted hundreds of thousands of recruits and converts within a few decades. Their continuing experience in the slums soon led them into varied and extensive social welfare programs. Thus combining evangelism and welfare they formed one of the largest and most influential contingents of field workers in American cities during those decades." The Salvation Army was the best-known organization promoting the theologically conservative approach to social reform. Some items on the political agendas of these social reformers were unfinished business from previous reform movements. Efforts to promote the observance of Sunday, discourage the distribution of alcohol, and curb such vices as gambling and prostitution all predated the Civil War. Other agenda items were new, especially those dealing with workers' rights.

The last part of the nineteenth century was a time of incredible tension between business and labor, and the religious community struggled to come up with a coherent response to the emerging conflict. Some clergymen embraced socialism as the solution, and a Christian Socialist Party was founded in the United States in 1889. Others, like the Rev. Henry Ward Beecher (son of Lyman Beecher), championed the benefits of capitalism in moving people out of poverty. Still other religious leaders supported free enterprise in general, but urged greater government regulation to curb its excesses. As labor organized and strikes became frequent, clergy often intervened as peacemakers. As Anson Phelps Stokes noted, "cases where individual clergymen took part in industrial conflicts—generally on the side of labor but opposing violence—became frequent toward the close of the nineteenth century. Roman Catholic priests were then often active in trying to protect the rights of miners and factory workers. Protestant ministers also played their part." Increasingly, church leaders were asked to serve on government boards that arbitrated labor disputes.

By the early 1900s, major religious bodies such as the Federal Council of Churches, the Central Conference of American Rabbis, and the National Catholic War Council all weighed in on the labor question, issuing statements that defended the rights of workers to decent paying jobs at reasonable hours. They also called for the right of arbitration in labor disputes and for a ban on child labor. A demonstration of how effective the religious community could be in securing justice for workers came during the bitter steel strike of 1919. A commission of the Inter-Church World Movement investigated the working conditions in the steel industry and then issued a blistering report that exposed how workers were expected to work 12-hour days seven days a week. The report mobilized public opinion on behalf of the strikers, and the United States Steel Corporation quickly announced the abolition of the seven-day work week and declared its intention to eventually eliminate the 12-hour day (which finally occurred in 1923).

In some cities, religious leaders became frustrated by the way local political machines stifled potential reforms, and so they openly worked to overthrow existing elected officials. Perhaps the most notable case was the campaign waged against Tammany Hall in New York City by Presbyertian minister Charles Parkhurst. Parkhurst declared war on the city administration after determining that illegal saloons, gambling, and prostitution flourished in New York because of police protection. When city officials attacked Parkhurst for making unfounded charges, he secured 284 affidavits backing up his claims. A grand jury subsequently issued a presentment against the police department, and the Tammany Hall machine was on its way out.

Although domestic social problems dominated the public agenda of the religious community during this era, a few foreign policy issues also gained attention. The safety of American missionaries abroad remained an issue of concern, and most presidents during this time mentioned their diplomatic efforts to protect American missionaries abroad in their annual messages to Congress. In 1898, the successful conclusion of the Spanish-American War sparked a debate about whether the United States should become a colonial power by acquiring the Philippines.

President William McKinley told a group of ministers that after praying about the matter, he had decided that it was God's will for the United States to keep the Philippines to "Christianize" the inhabitants ("Protestantize" would have been more accurate, since the Filipinos were already largely Catholic Christians). Most of the American religious community accepted McKinley's policy, but a few religious reformers joined secular critics to raise serious objections. Perhaps the best-known Protestant critic of the Philippines policy was former U.S. Congressman William Jennings Bryan. Nominated three times as the Democratic Party's candidate for president, Bryan made a critique of imperialism central to the election campaign of 1900. A devout evangelical Christian, Bryan ridiculed the idea that American control of the Philippines was required to spread the gospel there. In his acceptance speech at the Democratic National Convention, Bryan declared

> If true Christianity consists in carrying out in our daily lives the teachings of Christ, who will say that we are commanded to civilize with dynamite and proselyte with the sword? . . . . Imperialism finds no warrant in the Bible. The command, "Go ye into all the world and preach the gospel to every creature," has no Gatling gun attachment. . . . Love, not force, was the weapon of the Nazarene; sacrifice for others, not the exploitation of them, was His method of reaching the human heart.

Bryan's impassioned plea against colonialism fell on deaf ears, and he lost the election. The U.S. was a rising world power, and most Americans of the time—including church members—weren't interested in hearing criticism of American expansionism. Many ministers on both the right and left defended the imperialist impulse as part of God's providential plan. Social gospel champion Josiah Strong claimed that God was preparing the "Anglo-Saxon race" for the time when it would "spread itself over the earth. . . destined to dispossess many weaker [races], assimilate others, and mould the remainder, until, in a very true and important sense, it has Anglo-Saxonized mankind."

For William Jennings Bryan, the country's embrace of imperialism was disheartening, but not disabling. There were other causes to champion and other battles to fight. Although Bryan also lost the presidential election of 1908, he kept pushing an aggressive agenda of domestic reforms, including a national income tax, the direct election of United States senators, woman suffrage, and—the longtime hope of religious activists—a national prohibition on the production and distribution of alcohol. Bryan lived to see all four reforms enacted into law, not exactly a bad track record (especially given that all four proposals required the passage of constitutional amendments).

Nevertheless, by the dawn of the 1920s, Bryan's faith in progress was finally shaken. Appointed secretary of state in the administration of Woodrow Wilson, Bryan resigned his office in despair when he proved unable to keep the United States out of World War I. The incredible carnage of that conflict (more than 12 million civilians and soldiers dead) sobered many Americans who had thought that the history of modern civilization was one of inevitable progress.

Bryan eventually came to believe that the war resulted from a sinister new philosophy tied to modern science. He was led to this view in part by the book *Headquarters Nights* (1917) by Stanford University zoologist Vernon Kellogg. Kellogg's book described how German military leaders embraced a Darwinian philosophy of survival of the fittest and viewed it as a justification for war. Appalled at the social implications of Darwinism, Bryan was convinced that he had identified the nation's next great threat, and in the following decade he sought to wake his fellow citizens to the new menace.

Religion and Politics from the 1920s to the 1970s

"It may be said with truth that we are all materialists now," wrote Hugh Elliot in *Modern Science and Materialism* (1919). Elliot overstated the case, but the sentence effectively encapsulates the intellectual revolution that had occurred by the early decades of the twentieth century. Even while American religious reformers were trying to remake the world at the end of the nineteenth century, the highest levels of American culture were being shaped by a new philosophy that was anything but religious. That philosophy could be given several names, but the one that will be employed here is "scientific materialism"—the idea that human beings and the universe can be completely explained by material products and conditions. Put another way, scientific materialism is the claim that we are simply the sum of our chemical, biological, and environmental building blocks.

The basic idea has many variations. In England, Charles Darwin argued that everything in the natural world—including man and his moral beliefs—could be understood as the product of an impersonal and unplanned process of "survival of the fittest." In Germany, Karl Marx contended that one's ideas are the product of economic conditions. In the U.S., behavioral psychologists like John Watson argued that the soul was a myth and reason was merely the physical processes of the brain. The effect of these views on ideas about free will and personal responsibility was devastating. By the 1930s, American criminologist Nathaniel Cantor could write that "Man is no more 'responsible' for becoming willful and committing a crime than the flower for becoming red and fragrant."

The progress of scientific materialism in the United States was slow at first, partly because Americans were eager to find ways of reconciling new scientific theories with their religious and social views. But by the early 1900s, the situation changed. As historian Edward Larson points out in his book *Summer for the Gods*, new advances in genetics made the Darwinian account of survival of the fittest more compelling, and the scientific and cultural elites began to adopt the view in earnest. The acceptance of Darwinism had immediate practical implications, for it gave scientific backing to advocates of sterilization laws designed to check the spread of the "unfit."

Perhaps no event of the 1920s seemed to better symbolize the emerging conflict between traditional religion and scientific materialism than the Scopes trial in Dayton, Tennessee. Tennessee was one of several states that had passed laws forbidding the teaching of evolution to public school students. Opponents of the law enlisted John Scopes, a high school biology teacher, to bring a test case against the statute in 1925. The dramatic highlight of the trial was the gruelling cross-examination of William Jennings Bryan by famed lawyer Clarence Darrow. Darrow subjected Bryan's religious beliefs to withering scorn and attempted to expose what he thought was the irrationality of those who accepted the Bible as infallible.

The Scopes trial is seen today largely through the eyes of the play (later a film) *Inherit the Wind*. Unfortunately, that heavily fictionalized account of the trial supplies little insight into the real nature of the conflict. In the contemporary view, the battle over Darwinism arose primarily because of fears about evolution's consequences for religion. In fact, the conflict was fueled just as much by concern over Darwinism's consequences for society. William Jennings Bryan made this point with vigor. He explained how the doctrine of "survival of the fittest" had been employed by Social Darwinists to frustate reforms to help the poor and disadvantaged. He also described how evolutionary biology was being used to deny the personal accountability of criminals. Bryan relished pointing out that Clarence Darrow, his Scopes-trial nemesis, had defended a murderer just a year earlier on the grounds that he was the victim of bad heredity.

Bryan further warned that Darwinism could be used to support a program of "scientific breeding . . . under which a few supposedly superior intellects, self-appointed, would direct the mating and the movements of the mass of mankind." Those who think that Bryan's concerns on this point were chimerical might want to peruse George Hunter's *Civic Biology*, the textbook used by John Scopes. It includes the following chilling discussion of what to do with the mentally handicapped, criminals, and others deemed unfit by society: "If such people were lower animals, we would probably kill them off to prevent them from spreading. Humanity will not allow this, but we do have the remedy of separating the sexes in asylums or other places and in various ways preventing intermarriage and the possibility of perpetuating such a low and degenerate race."

Edward Larson frames the Scopes trial as a battle between majoritarianism and individual rights, but it is better understood as a conflict over the question of whose individual rights take precedence. Proponents of Darwinism defended the academic freedom of teachers to teach what they wanted free from government interference. But in Bryan's view, the individual rights of parents came first. While teachers had the right to promote evolution (or any other doctrine) as private citizens, they had no right to do so in the public school classroom. According to Bryan, teachers who undercut the religious beliefs of students by teaching evolution violated the religious liberties of both students and their parents.

Today the Scopes trial is often regarded as a turning point in the history of religion in American politics, with some historians implying that it caused religious traditionalists to retreat from public life. As Edward Larson points out, that assessment is inaccurate. At the time, neither religious fundamentalists nor their opponents thought that the trial was especially consequential. Both continued as they had before. Nevertheless, the fact remains that after the 1920s, religious traditionalists (especially evangelical Protestants) did largely retreat from the public arena. Rather than engage the world as Lyman Beecher or William Jennings Bryan had done, they sought safety among themselves, forming their own colleges, starting their own publishing houses, and creating their own social institutions. While the Scopes trial itself had little to do with this retreat, the philosophy of scientific materialism that provided the subtext for the Scopes controversy was pivotal. By equating traditional religious beliefs with irrationality and prejudice, the proponents of scientific materialism made the public square increasingly hostile for traditional religious believers, so they abandoned the public square.

Scientific materialism also impacted the heirs to the social gospel, although here the effects were more subtle. Scientific materialism did not cause them to abandon politics, but their social agenda became increasingly indistinguishable from that of more secular forms of liberalism—to the point that one must seriously question whether some of them remained "religious" reformers in the genuine sense of the term. While American religious traditions have unquestionably disagreed on a variety of points, most have maintained as core propositions that (1) human beings are spiritual beings who are morally accountable for their actions, and (2) human beings are bound by a transcendent moral code ordained by God. Under the assault of scientific materialism, however, some strands of religious liberalism gradually gave up on these propositions.

Consider the issue of moral accountability. Scientific materialism undermined the case for accountability by reducing human behavior to the product of heredity and environment. In the materialist understanding, poverty, crime, and other social problems were produced more by heredity and environment than personal choice. This theory made sense to a point. Yet early proponents of the social gospel refused to adopt the theory wholesale, arguing that human beings could still be held accountable because as spiritual beings they had the power to overcome their material conditions. Thus, Washington Gladden urged people not to blame their faults on either heredity or environment: "Heredity is no excuse . . . . Your heredity is from God. He is your Father. Deeper than all other strains of ancestral tendency is this fact that your nature comes from God . . . . Environment is no excuse for you. . . God is the great first fact in all our environment, no matter where you may be. There is no place of temptation in which he is not nearer to you than any human influence can be." But gradually Gladden's point was lost. As Marvin Olasky points out in *The Tragedy of American Compassion*, by the 1930s and 1940s, many religious liberals viewed social problems as almost wholly the function of material causes.

Despite the corrosive effects of scientific materialism, there were still areas where churches raised an authentic voice in politics during this period. In conservative churches, the great issue became the spread of communism and the persecution of religious believers under communist regimes. Among liberal churches, the great issue was civil rights. Like the abolitionist movement in the nineteenth century, the civil rights struggle of the mid-twentieth century largely sprang from churches—in this case, the black churches of the South, supported by the heirs to the social gospel tradition in the North. The best-known leader of the movement, Martin Luther King, Jr., was a Baptist minister born in Georgia. King was thrust into the limelight by spearheading the boycott of segregated city buses in Montgomery, Alabama, in 1955-56. Several years later, King's "Letter from a Birmingham Jail" presented an eloquent defense of the Christian grounds for nonviolent civil disobedience. Written while King was jailed for his participation in civil rights protests, the essay responded to an open letter by liberal white ministers in Alabama who urged King to discontinue civil disobedience and entrust the civil rights struggle to the courts.

The civil rights movement eventually drew support from a variety of religious groups, and when Congress deliberated on the Civil Rights Act of 1964, national Jewish, Catholic, and Protestant organizations all lobbied on behalf of the legislation. In many ways, the civil rights struggle reinvigorated the social gospel tradition in the United States; and during the latter part of the 1960s, it fed the vigorous political efforts on the part of liberal churches in opposition to the Vietnam War.

Ironically, even as religious liberals reasserted their voice in American politics, the acceptable sphere of religion in public life was shrinking due to a series of decisions by the U.S. Supreme Court. In 1948, the Court banned public schools from offering voluntary religion classes on school grounds, although it later allowed schools to release students early to attend religious classes elsewhere. In the 1960s, the Court issued a series of decisions that prohibited devotional Bible readings and teacher-led prayers in public schools. While many prominent Protestant and Catholic leaders criticized the rulings, liberal Protestant groups such as the National Council of Churches applauded them for defending the rights of students who did not want to participate in religious exercises. Supporters of the rulings often pointed out that the Court did not actually ban prayer in schools, only officially sponsored prayers. Students were still free to pray on their own.

This was true of the initial Supreme Court decisions. Yet the logic driving those rulings was susceptible of a much broader interpretation, as subsequent cases began to demonstrate. By the late 1970s, lower federal courts began to interpret the Constitution so as to prohibit even student-initiated religious activities on school grounds. Secularization, not religious freedom, seemed to be the goal. In *Brandon v. Guilderland* (1980), for example, a group of high school students sought permission to meet before school in an empty classroom to pray and read the Bible. A federal appellate judge ultimately ruled that the school district had to stop the students from meeting, otherwise the school would impermissibly advance religion. According to the judge, "to an impressionable student even the mere appearance of secular involvement in religious activities might indicate that the state has placed its imprimatur on a particular creed. This symbolic inference is too dangerous to permit."

Under this logic, even voluntary religious activities in public spaces constituted a threat to the separation of church and state. Adopting similar reasoning, local governments began to prevent religious groups from using parks, libraries, and other public facilities on the same basis as secular groups. In some schools, students were disciplined for revealing their religious beliefs to other students. In one particularly egregious case, a mentally handicapped girl was ordered to refrain from reading her Bible on the bus on the way to school. What began in the 1960s as a defense of religious liberty became during the 1970s and 1980s a movement toward wholesale secularization.

At the same time that voluntary expressions of religion in public were being restricted, a social revolution was underway that called into question traditional restraints on sexuality that reflected the religious consensus of earlier decades. States enacted no-fault divorce laws, social taboos against pre-marital sex eroded, and homosexuals argued for public acceptance. The Supreme Court furthered the process by making the prosecution of pornography more difficult and declaring laws against abortion unconstitutional in *Roe v. Wade* (1973). Religious believers who continued to adhere to traditional moral norms became increasingly frustrated because of their political impotence.

The legitimate public role of religion, meanwhile, continued to constrict. When religious traditionalists (especially Catholics) tried to restrict taxpayer-funded abortions, the ACLU came up with the creative argument that such a restriction would constitute an "establishment of religion" in violation of the Constitution. The ACLU's primary target was the law authored by Congressman Henry Hyde that limited federal funding for abortions. Because Hyde is a Catholic, the ACLU believed that he was unconstitutionally attempting to enact the dogmas of the Catholic Church into law. To prove its theory, the ACLU even sent someone to observe Representative Hyde participating in Mass.

The ACLU's implication seemed to be that a political agenda inspired by religious beliefs was illegitimate. This was a curious view considering most of American history. Few would contend that the abolitionist and social gospel movements were illegitimate because of the religious motives of their supporters. The ACLU was unsuccessful in getting this rationale adopted by the courts in the case of taxpayer-funded abortions, but in *Stone v. Graham* (1980), the Supreme Court invoked a similar argument to prevent Kentucky public schools from posting copies of the Ten Commandments in classrooms. Kentucky claimed that the purpose of the policy was to inform students of the influence of the Ten Commandments on secular history; the Commandments were to be accompanied by a message pointing out their influence on the development of Western law. While the Court didn't dispute the historical influence of the Ten Commandments on Western culture, it decided that the real motivation behind the law must be religious, therefore the law was unconstitutional. Religious conservatives attacked the ruling as yet another attempt by the Supreme Court to limit the public role of religion.

The issues raised by *Stone v. Graham* were not about to disappear. By the time the decision was handed down in the fall of 1980, the U.S. was embroiled in a national debate about the legitimacy of religious believers in politics, a debate that would turn out to be one of the defining controversies of the coming decade.

Religion and Politics in the 1980s and the 1990s

Conservative evangelical Christians who had been in political hibernation for much of the post-World War II era returned to politics in a big way in 1980, helping elect Ronald Reagan to the presidency and helping defeat such notable liberals in Congress as Frank Church and George McGovern. Critics of what soon became known as the "new Christian right" lost little time in sounding the alarms. An article in *Penthouse* magazine predicted that "the homegrown Ayatollahs of the New Right . . . plan to turn America into a religious dictatorship" by 1984. Even liberal religious activists who had mixed religion and politics for years accused Christian conservatives of exhibiting "the kind of attitude which in previous eras led to holy wars." The rhetoric was reminiscent of the reaction faced by evangelical reformers like Lyman Beecher in the 1820s and 1830s.

The domestic agenda of religious conservatives included re-establishing school prayer, restricting abortion, defending the traditional two-parent family, and carving out a greater role for religious expression in public life. In foreign policy, religious conservatives supported efforts to stop communism and curtail religious persecution abroad. On the surface, the new Christian right was not especially successful in the 1980s. *Roe v. Wade* was not overturned, and school prayer was not re-established. In 1988, when religious broadcaster Pat Robertson ran for president, his campaign was a flop. The Moral Majority, which had been the flagship organization of the movement, disbanded. By the end of the decade, disenchantment with politics was spreading among grassroots supporters of the Christian right. Nowhere was this more apparent than the anti-abortion movement.

When it became clear that enacting new abortion restrictions was futile because the Supreme Court would simply invalidate them, a large segment of the anti-abortion movement gave up on politics and turned to mass civil disobedience in the mid-1980s. Thousands became involved in a loose-knit organization known as Operation Rescue, which staged nonviolent sit-ins to shut down abortion clinics. The protests were self-consciously modelled after the efforts of the civil rights movement of the 1960s.

When tried for criminal trespass, members of Operation Rescue commonly invoked the necessity defense, arguing that they were compelled by a higher law to engage in civil disobedience to save human life. The magnitude of the protests is indicated by the number of protestors arrested, estimated at between 28,000 and 35,000 during one 18-month period. As the protests grew in size and number, some fairly drastic measures were taken to stop the organization, including lawsuits based on the Racketeer Influenced and Corrupt Organizations Act (RICO). Protestors also encountered widespread police brutality. In Buffalo, male protestors were handcuffed, beaten with clubs, and dragged face-down down a flight of stairs. In Dobbs Ferry, New York, women protestors were strip-searched and photographed nude by prison guards. In Los Angeles, police broke a nonresisting man's arm twice, pounded the faces of other peaceful protestors into the asphalt, and repeatedly inflicted pain on protestors who were trying to comply with police requests. Reports of police brutality became so widespread that in late 1989 the United States Commission on Civil Rights voted to launch an investigation. Most public officials and members of the media, however, paid scant attention to the protestors' plight. Much more attention was paid to a handful of extremists who tried to burn down abortion clinics, even though they were clearly disavowed by the rest of the anti-abortion movement.

The inability of the religious right to enact its major agenda items led many observers to conclude by the early 1990s that the resurgence of religious conservatism in politics had peaked. That assessment seemed confirmed by the election of Democrat Bill Clinton to the presidency in 1992. While Clinton campaigned as an economic moderate, his social views on such issues as abortion and gay rights were a clear repudiation of the religious right. On closer inspection, however, the view that the religious right had achieved little during the 1980s and had become ineffectual by the 1990s was flawed. American democracy, embodying as it does an interlocking system of checks and balances, is notoriously slow, and political movements rarely achieve all they want as quickly as they want. So it is no great surprise that the religious right did not fulfill its initial objectives.

The fact remains that the religious right made a significant impact on the American political landscape in several ways. First, it effectively countered the claim that religious motivations somehow disqualify one from speaking out on public issues. With some justice, religious conservatives pointed out that the First Amendment guaranteed freedom of speech for everyone and secularists who denounced religious conservatives as illegitimate because they were religious were being inconsistent. By the early 1990s, thoughtful observers outside the religious right were making the same point, such as Stephen Carter in his influential book, *The Culture of Disbelief* (1993).

Second, religious conservatives focused attention on the way religion was being discriminated against in the public square. They showed how many public school textbooks ignored the contributions of religious believers in American history, a criticism subsequently echoed by religious liberals. They also highlighted the way religious groups were routinely denied the same free speech rights as other groups, especially in public schools. High school students who wanted to pray or read the Bible during lunch or before school were frequently denied access to school facilities, even though nonreligious student groups were allowed to meet at the same times. Students were sometimes prevented from distributing religious tracts to classmates, even when the distribution of political leaflets was allowed. Religious groups were also prohibited from renting school facilities after hours, even in school districts that allowed a wide variety of nonreligious community groups to rent school facilities.

Religious conservatives challenged such policies as violations of free speech, and they pursued an aggressive legal strategy to secure "equal access." The idea behind equal access was that religious individuals and groups should be accorded the same access to public facilities as nonreligious individuals and groups. For example, if a city allowed a community group to stage a rock concert at a public park, it should not be able to forbid a religious group from holding a worship service there because this would be discriminating against certain groups on the basis of the content of their speech. Congress guaranteed religious student groups equal access to public high schools in the Equal Access Act of 1984, a law which the Supreme Court upheld in *Board of Education v. Mergens* (1990). The Supreme Court subsequently guaranteed religious groups equal access to the rental of school facilities in *Lamb's Chapel v. Center Moriches Union Free School District* (1993) and to university activity fees in *Rosenberger v. The Rector and Visitors of the University of Virginia* (1995). The Rutherford Institute, a public interest law group, was one of the early pioneers of the equal access concept.

Finally, the religious right showed that it had staying power by institutionalizing itself and building coalitions. Although the Moral Majority went defunct, many other lobbying groups and policy organizations took its place, including the Christian Coalition, the Family Research Council, Focus on the Family, and Concerned Women for America. Moreover, though the religious right began primarily with evangelical Christians, it eventually expanded into a larger coalition of religious conservatives representing a variety of religious traditions. By the 1990s, an extensive network was developing between culturally conservative Catholics, Jews, and Protestants, given voice by such publications as *First Things*, a journal edited by Catholic priest Richard John Neuhaus.

The major failing of the religious right in the 1980s and early 1990s was its inability to articluate its agenda in a manner that was persuasive on secular grounds. While religion has traditionally served as the nation's public conscience, the logic of the system set up by the founders demands that public policy be based squarely on public principles. Therefore, religious believers must offer public arguments for their policy positions if they hope to persevere. Religious conservatives, evangelical Christians especially, had a difficult time coming up with a coherent public philosophy, often basing their appeals ultimately on the moral authority of the Bible.

In some ways, the appeals to divine revelation were to be expected because the United States no longer had much of a common moral vocabulary by the end of the twentieth century. Scientific materialism had largely undermined it, claiming that human reason disproved traditional morality and showed moral norms to be a function of culture or biology. Whether or not this claim was persuasive (or even coherent), it had a devastating effect on many evangelical Protestants in the twentieth century. Told that their moral beliefs were inherently unreasonable, they chose to reject their reason rather than their morality. Whereas American evangelicals of a previous era (like John Witherspoon) had insisted that Biblical morality could be shown true by reason, it became fashionable among modern evangelicals to argue that morality should be based on the Bible alone. In fact, reason was to be avoided, because it would mislead you. Given this mentality, the difficulty among the religious right of articulating a coherent public philosophy was understandable.

By the 1990s, many in the religious right recognized the need to think more systematically about political rhetoric in a pluralistic society, and there was renewed interest in such topics as natural law as a way of bridging the gap between religious adherents and secularists in the public arena. There also was a willingness among some members of the religious right to seek incremental policy advances to attract more political support. A good example of this was the effort to secure a ban on partial-birth abortions, which drew widespread backing from both legislators and the public.

While the return of religious conservatives to the political arena was the main story of the 1980s and 1990s, the heirs to the social gospel did not retreat from the public arena. These Protestants and Catholics were especially active in foreign affairs during the 1980s, playing an important part in the nuclear freeze movement and in opposition to Reagan administration policies in Central America. Many liberal churches in the 1980s participated in what became known as the "sanctuary movement," which sheltered illegal aliens from Central America who feared political retribution if forced to return to their countries. In the domestic realm, liberal churches criticized the resurgence of the death penalty and fought against proposed cuts in welfare spending in the 1990s. Despite their impressive number of lobbyists, and their ability to generate demonstrations, the ability of liberal churches to mobilize electoral support paled in comparison to the religious right.

Religion and Politics in the Twenty-First Century

Religious conservatives dominated religion in politics during the final decades of the twentieth century, and if the past is any indication, they will likely continue to dominate the arena at least through the early decades of the twenty-first century. Past waves of religious activism have lasted for several decades at a stretch, and there is little reason to believe that the religious right will dissipate more quickly.

In looking at the broad picture of religion in politics across American history, one is struck by how religious activism has stayed for the most part within the confines layed out by the founders of the United States. Except for a handful of fringe groups on both the right and the left, religion in the U.S. is not associated with political violence. Nor does any major religious group seriously advocate that taxpayers fund ministers or enact religious tests for public office. Moreover, to be successful in American politics, religious groups have had to find a way to frame their arguments in secular terms. The result of all this is that the U.S. has been able to temper (for the most part) the bitter religious strife in politics that has dominated so much of human history.

If religion in American politics has largely avoided the costs of religion in politics, it has reaped its benefits. Throughout American history, religious groups have exercised a dynamic, positive influence on social and political change.

From slavery and Cherokee removal to labor conditions and civil rights, religious adherents have sought to hold the existing moral order accountable to the timeless dictates of justice and mercy. American political history would have been substantially poorer if religious adherents had stayed outside the political arena.

Whether or not religion will continue to be a constructive voice in politics in the decades ahead is an open question. Scientific materialism has made it more difficult for religious believers to effectively join the public debate; and the dramatic secularization of public life in recent years has added new barriers to mixing faith and politics. Even so, the United States remains one of the most religious nations of the industrialized world, and it would be foolish to discount the inherent power of religious idealism for animating social and political reform.

BIBLIOGRAPHY

Ahlstrom, Sydney E. *A Religious History of the American People*. New Haven, CT: Yale University Press, 1972.

Andrew, John A., III. *From Revivals to Removal: Jeremiah Evarts, The Cherokee Nation, and the Search for the Soul of America*. Athens: University of Georgia Press, 1992.

Banner, Lois W. "Religious Benevolence as Social Control: A Critique of an Interpretation." In John M. Mulder and John F. Wilson, eds. *Religion in American History: Interpretive Essays*. Englewood Cliffs, NJ: Prentice-Hall, Inc., 1978.

Beecher, Lyman. *Autobiography of Lyman Beecher*. Barbara M. Cross, ed. Cambridge, MA: Belknap Press, 1961.

——. *Works of Lyman Beecher*. Boston: Jewett, 1852.

Berns, Walter. *The First Amendment and the Future of American Democracy*. New York: Basic Books, 1976.

Boles, John, ed. *Masters and Slaves in the House of the Lord: Race and Religion in the American South, 1740-1870*. Lexington: University Press of Kentucky, 1988.

Borden, Morton. *Jews, Turks, and Infidels*. Chapel Hill: University of North Carolina Press, 1984.

Carter, Stephen. *The Culture of Disbelief: How American Law and Politics Trivialize Religious Devotion*. New York: Anchor Books, 1994.

Carwardine, Richard. *Evangelicals and Politics in Antebellum America*. New Haven, CT: Yale University Press, 1993.

Curry, Thomas J. *The First Freedoms: Church and State in America to the Passage of the First Amendment*. New York: Oxford University Press, 1986.

Dreisbach, Daniel. *Real Threat and Mere Shadow: Religious Liberty and the First Amendment*. Westchester, IL: Crossway Books, 1987.

Evarts, Jeremiah. *Cherokee Removal: The "William Penn Essays" and Other Writings by Jeremiah Evarts*. Francis Paul Prucha, ed. Knoxville: University of Tennessee Press, 1981.

Goodman, Paul. *Towards a Christian Republic: Antimasonry and the Great Transition in New England, 1826-1836*. New York: Oxford University Press, 1988.

Hudson, Winthrop. *The Great Tradition of the American Churches*. New York: Harper and Row, 1953.

Jaffa, Harry V. *The American Founding as the Best Regime: The Bonding of Civil and Religious Liberty*. Claremont, CA: Claremont Institute for the Study of Political Philosophy and Statesmanship, 1990.

John, Richard. "Taking Sabbatarianism Seriously: The Postal System, the Sabbath, and the Transformation of the American Political Culture." *Journal of the Early Republic* 10 (Winter 1990): 517-67.

Larson, Edward. *Summer for the Gods: The Scopes Trial and America's Continuing Debate over Science and Religion*. New York: Basic Books, 1997.

Levy, Leonard W. *The Establishment Clause: Religion and the First Amendment*. New York: Macmillan, 1986.

Long, John Dixon. *Pictures of Slavery in Church and State*. 1857; repr. New York: Negro Universities Press, 1969.

Magnuson, Norris. *Salvation in the Slums: Evangelical Social Work, 1865-1920*. Grand Rapids, MI: Baker Book House, 1990.

McLoughlin, William G. *Revivals, Awakenings, and Reform*. Chicago: University of Chicago Press, 1978.

Niebuhr, H. Richard. *The Kingdom of God in America*. New York: Harper Torchbooks, 1959.

Noll, Mark A. *One Nation Under God? Christian Faith and Political Action in America*. San Francisco: Harper and Row, 1988.

Olasky, Marvin. *The Tragedy of American Compassion*. Washington, DC: Regnery, 1992.

Pangle, Thomas. *The Spirit of Modern Republicanism: The Moral Vision of the American Founders and the Philosophy of Locke*. Chicago: University of Chicago Press, 1988.

Pfeffer, Leo. *Church, State and Freedom*. rev. ed. Boston: Beacon Press, 1967.

Sandoz, Ellis, ed. *Political Sermons of the American Founding Era, 1730-1805*. Indianapolis: Liberty Press, 1991.

Schaeffer, Francis A. *Complete Works of Francis A. Schaeffer: A Christian Worldview*. Westchester, IL: Crossway Books, 1982.

Smith, Elwyn A. "The Voluntary Establishment of Religion." In Elwyn A. Smith, ed. *The Religion of the Republic*. Philadelphia: Fortress Press, 1971.

Smith, Samuel Stanhope. *An Essay on the Causes of the Variety of Complexion and Figure in the Human Species*. 2nd ed. New Brunswick, NJ: J. Simpson and Co., 1810.

Smith, Timothy L. *Revivalism and Social Reform in Mid-Nineteenth-Century America*. New York: Abingdon Press, 1957.

Smith-Rosenberg, Carroll. "Women and Religious Revivals: Anti-Ritualism, Liminality, and the Emergence of the American Bourgeoisie." In *The Evangelical Tradition in America*. Macon, GA: Mercer University Press, 1984.

Stokes, Anson Phelps. *Church and State in the United States*. 3 vols. New York: Harper and Brothers, 1950.

Tocqueville, Alexis de. *Democracy in America*. George Lawrence, trans. J.P. Mayer, ed. Garden City, NY: Anchor Books, 1969.

West, John G., Jr. "The Changing Battle over Religion in the Public Schools." *Wake Forest Law Review* 26, no. 2 (1991): 2.

———. *The Politics of Revelation and Reason: Religion and Civic Life in the New Nation*. Lawrence: University Press of Kansas, 1996.

Whitehead, John W. *The Second American Revolution*. Elgin, IL: David C. Cook Publishing Co., 1982.

Witherspoon, John. *Annotated Edition of Lectures on Moral Philosophy*. Jack Scott, ed. Newark: University of Delaware Press, 1982.

Encyclopedia of Religion in American Politics

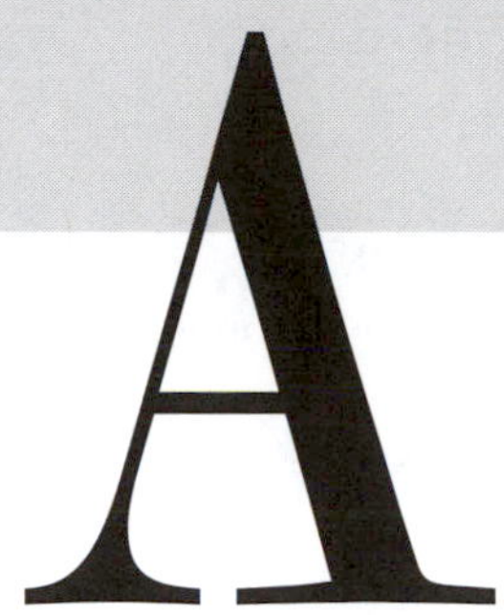

Lyman Abbott (1835–1922)

Lyman Abbott was a leading spokesman for the **Social Gospel**. Initially a lawyer, he became an editor for *Harper's Magazine*, *Illustrated Christian Weekly,* and *Christian Union.* He used his editorial positions to support the North in the Civil War. In 1888, he returned to the pastorate, taking over **Henry Ward Beecher**'s pulpit at the Plymouth Congregation Church. He remained in the political mainstream throughout his life and supported progressive ideas and candidates, including **Theodore Roosevelt** in his 1912 third-party run for president. (MWP)

Abolitionist and social reformer Lyman Abbott, shown in this photo from December 1919, supported Theodore Roosevelt's third party run for the presidency in 1912. Underwood and Underwood. Library of Congress.

Bibliography

Abbott, Lyman. *Christianity and Social Problems.* New York: Johnson Reprint Co., 1970.

———. *The Evolution of Christianity.* New York: Johnson Reprint Co., 1969.

———. The Spirit of Democracy. Boston: Houghton Mifflin, 1910.

Brown, Ira V. *Lyman Abbott: Christian Evolutionist.* Cambridge, MA: Harvard University Press, 1953.

Ralph David Abernathy (1926–1990)

Ralph Abernathy was a cofounder of the **Southern Christian Leadership Conference, (SCLC),** a **Baptist** minister and close friend of **Martin Luther King, Jr.** Born in Linden, Alabama, on March 11, 1926, and educated at Alabama State College and Atlanta University, he became pastor of First Baptist Church, Montgomery, Alabama, in 1951. Instrumental in electing King as president of the Montgomery Improvement Association, he coordinated support for the Montgomery bus boycott, cofounded the Southern Christian Leadership Conference, and in 1961 became the SCLC's full-time vice president. He organized the 1960–62 sit-ins and Freedom Rides, designed to desegregate public facilities, and led with King the 1963 Good Friday march in Birmingham. He was with King at the time of King's assassination in Memphis in 1968 and subsequently delivered the eulogy at King's funeral. He succeeded King as president of the Southern Christian Leadership Conference and served until 1977, when he ran unsuccessfully for the House of Representatives. He estranged many **civil rights** leaders by his 1980 endorsement of **Ronald Reagan.** He died on April 17, 1990. (ISM)

Bibliography

Abernathy, Ralph D. *And The Walls Came Tumbling Down: An Autobiography.* New York: Harper & Row, 1989.

Abington Township v. Schempp (1963)

Abington Township v. Schempp, 374 U.S. 203 (1972), was one of many cases decided by the U.S. Supreme Court following the precedent of ***Everson v. Board of Education*** 330 U.S. 1 (1947) and the direction of ***Engel v. Vitale*** 370 U.S. 421 (1962). A Pennsylvania law required Bible reading in public school every day. Upon written request, a child could be excused from the exercise. Readings were done by students under teacher supervision. Following the reading, students recited the Lord's Prayer. The Court declared these requirements invalid according to the **Establishment Clause** of the **First Amendment**, because the state was not supposed to conduct religious services. The Court said, "there must be a secular legislative purpose and a primary effect that neither advances nor inhibits religion." The elements of purpose and primary effect became a twin standard for states to meet for constitutional approval. For a later addition, see ***Lemon v. Kurtzman*** 403 U.S. 602 (1971). The Court's opinion held that, although children could be excused, this was not a **Free Exercise Clause** issue. Such government support for religion violated the Establishment Clause whether there was coercion or not. (JRV)

Bibliography

Pfeffer, Leo. "The New York Regents' Prayer Case *(Engel v. Vitale):* Its Background, Meaning and Implications." *CLSA Reports.* New York: Commission on Law and Social Action of the American Jewish Congress, 1962.

Smith, Rodney K. *Public Prayer and the Constitution: A Case Study in Constitutional Interpretation.* Wilmington, DE: Scholarly Resources, 1987.

Abolition

Abolition, the nineteenth-century movement to abolish **slavery** in the United States, drew heavily on the theology and biblical interpretations of religious people for its justification. Both apocalyptic and judgmental in tone, the movement capitalized on the American public's millennial belief in Christ's Second Coming and a concomitant Last Judgment. The language of vindication for the righteous and damnation for the opponent encouraged both abolitionists and slaveholders to pursue war as a means of illustrating God's favor. The force of these catastrophic images of judgment is particularly apparent in **Julia Ward Howe**'s *Battle Hymn of the Republic,* the war anthem of the North.

As early as 1818, the **Presbyterians** issued a condemnation of slavery. Yet they cautioned against hasty emancipation, fearing the social effects of black freedom, and prohibited their clergy from making anti-slavery statements from the pulpit. The movement began in earnest following the passage of the British Slavery Abolition Act of 1831. In that year, the **American Anti-Slavery Society** was formed, and **William Lloyd Garrison** and **Arthur Tappan** began publishing abolition tracts and speaking against the institution of slavery. However, the abolition message was fiercely opposed by the public—both in the North and South—until 1840.

This illustration depicts the April 19, 1866, celebration in Washington of the abolition of slavery in the District of Columbia. Much of the language and impetus for the abolition movement came from religiously motivated people. Library of Congress.

Several events contributed to the movement's eventual success in formally emancipating the slaves. **Henry Ward Beecher** used his pulpit to raise money for rifles, dubbed "Beecher's Bibles," to defend Kansas and the surrounding territory against the legalization of slavery. **Theodore Dwight Weld**, one of **Charles Grandison Finney's** revival converts, helped found Oberlin College with an abolitionist agenda in mind. His wife, **Angelina Grimke**, published a pamphlet in 1836 entitled "Appeal to the Christian Women of the South." In it, she laid forth the liberal perspective on scripture and the American **Declaration of Independence** that formed the heart of the abolition message. The publication of **Harriet Beecher Stowe**'s novel ***Uncle Tom's Cabin*** in 1852 drew significant popular attention to the moral critique of slavery. The use of fiction to convey the message succeeded where philosophical and religious tracts had only begun to sway opinion.

Abolitionists particularly sought to bring the force of church sanctions to their side of the debate. Holding that slavery was inherently sinful, they urged local congregations to bar slaveholders from church fellowship and the sacrament of communion. Such action had social as well as spiritual consequences for those so barred, since being a member in good standing of a church affected one's business opportunities and social status in nineteenth-century culture. However, even prominent abolitionists like Garrison met resistance in their own churches to such demands, and few southern churches heeded the call for disfellowship.

By the late 1840s, most northern churches had become outspoken in their disapproval of slavery, although few were willing to condemn slavery as inherently sinful or to endorse immediate emancipation. Congregationalists and **Unitarians** emerged as powerful anti-slavery voices. Both denominations were concentrated in the North, and thus did not have to contend with dissenting voices from churches in the slaveholding states. Several denominations experienced North-South splits before the Civil War or shortly thereafter. The Roman Catholic Church declined to support abolition, even though it agreed with the theological condemnation of slavery.

It was not until the outbreak of the Civil War that the churches fully assented to the abolitionist agenda. Many denominations that had simply articulated their disapproval of slavery issued stronger statements prohibiting slaveholding and blatant racial discrimination. Congregations engaged in fund-raising and propaganda campaigns with abolitionist groups. The hesitation of the churches to engage intimately in the politics of race remained, but the urgency of the issue once the southern states seceded forced them to choose a side, and most chose abolition.

The abolition movement ultimately served as a prelude to the **Social Gospel** movement. Its attention to biblical interpretation and application to social issues, as well as its practice of tying together several nineteenth-century social movements—women's rights, **temperance**, **education**—served as a model for **Solomon Washington Gladden** and **Walter Rauschenbusch** in the early twentieth century. (KMY) **See also** Congregationalism; Roman Catholicism.

BIBLIOGRAPHY

Ceplair, Larry, ed. *The Public Years of Sarah and Angelina Grimke: Selected Writings, 1835–1839.* New York: Columbia University Press, 1989.

Chesebrough, David B., ed. *"God Ordained This War": Sermons on the Sectional Crisis, 1830–1865.* Columbia: University of South Carolina Press, 1991.

Loewenberg, Bert James, and Bogin, Ruth. *Black Women in Nineteenth-Century American Life.* University Park: The Pennsylvania State University Press, 1976.

McKivigan, John R. *The War against Proslavery Religion: Abolitionism and the Northern Churches, 1830–1865.* Ithaca, NY: Cornell University Press, 1984.

Abortion and Birth Control

Two of the most controversial legal, social, and religious issues in American politics in the late twentieth century have been birth control and abortion. Since they touch on fundamental questions surrounding gender, personhood, and community, one's view of birth control and abortion, especially the latter, is inexorably linked to one's religious and philosophical commitments. They also both relate to public policy concerns regarding governmental intrusiveness into the reproductive rights of women and men.

The use of contraceptives is ancient. In Egypt, for example, five different papyri, dating from 1900 B.C. to 1100 B.C., give recipes for contraceptives that are used in a woman's vulva. Some other papyri speak of blocking or killing semen. One also finds similar formulas in Europe starting in the medieval period (A.D. 450–1450) and continuing to the premodern period (A.D. 1450–1750).

Historically, Jewish and Christian traditions have viewed contraceptives, especially artificial ones, with disdain, or have discouraged their use. Rabbinic scholars read the mandate of Genesis 1:28 to "be fruitful and multiply" as precluding attempts to prevent the conceiving of children (Talmud, Nid. 13a).

Contraception was discouraged or forbidden during much of Christian history, and marriage was viewed as being primarily for the bearing of children. Some Church fathers even viewed intercourse apart from the intent to conceive a child as sinful. Part of the reason for limiting sex to procreation, and consequently for discouraging birth control, related to the influence of Stoicism, which exalted self-control, on intellectual writers within Christian circles.

The Church's early views on birth control continued through the Middle Ages and until recently remained the dominant view where Christian influence prevailed. Today, **Roman Catholicism**, unlike the majority of Protestant sects, continues its general prohibition of most birth control techniques, as evidenced by the papal encyclical *Humanae Vitae* (1965).

The modern American birth control movement is synonymous with the name Margaret Sanger. Sanger (1879–1966) is largely responsible for the rise of birth control in the United States, and indirectly, for legalized abortion. She began an influential magazine, the *Birth Control Review*, in which she and various activists argued for birth control and **eugenics**. Sanger became the first president of Planned Parenthood, the most powerful organization advocating birth control and abortion.

In spite of Sanger's successes, numerous scandals clouded her career and caused her to leave the United States. Many of her ideas against birth control, as well as her promotion of **pornography** and greater sexual license in general, were related to her disdain of Christianity and **capitalism**. In the early 1940s, she supported the Nazi program of eugenics. As editor of *The Birth Control Review*, she allowed Hitler's director of genetic sterilization and founder of the Nazi Society for Racial Hygiene, Ernst Rudin, to publish his views in her magazine. She also published the works of various Malthusian eugenicists who advocated Aryan/white supremacy. In 1932, Sanger advocated coercive sterilization and rehabilative concentration camps for all dysgenic stocks. Only after the atrocities of Hitler's **Holocaust** came to light did she retreat from such public espousals. She saw birth control as the best way to eliminate undesirable groups of people in American society, people whom she called "feebleminded." She estimated that such people constituted almost 50 percent of the U.S. population.

In the United States, various laws attempted to regulate or outlaw birth control. The first case to address the matter of reproductive freedom was *Griswold v. Connecticut,* 381 U.S. 479, 484 (1965), in which the Supreme Court determined that though the Bill of Rights did not specifically protect the intimate private rights of a married couple, the Bill of Rights contained penumbras which did intend that such rights be protected. Though the law, which banned the sale of contraceptives, had never been enforced by Connecticut against any couple, and was apparently on the law books simply to set forth certain values of the state regarding the family, it was ideal for challenging the constitutionality of laws that regulatedcontraception. The subsequent case of *Eisenstadt v. Baird,* 405 U.S. 438 (1972), extended this protection beyond married couples and applied the *Griswold* privacy rights to all citizens. These two cases served as the basis of the landmark abortion decision, ***Roe v. Wade*** (410 U.S. 113 [1973]).

Generally, birth control is divided into three categories: natural, social, and artificial. Natural disasters are the first catagory. Throughout history major natural catastrophes have been followed by periods of famine and disease, which lower birthrates.

The second catagory of birth control consists of such social factors as selective parenting or planned parenthood. This selectivity has been influenced greatly by the science of eugenics, which holds that births should be controlled so as to produce superior offspring. Famous figures who have contributed to this thinking are Sir Francis Galton (1822–1911), who invented the term eugenics; Charles Darwin (1809–1882), whose evolutionary view argued for the survival of superior species and racial groups; and Gregor Mendel (1822–1884), who discovered modern genetics. Though this selectivity is regularly practiced in animal breeding with little discussion, many social and religious factors make human eugenics suspect in the eyes of most. Besides eugenics, other social factors have affected the birthrate. The rising status and independence of women, for example, have caused many women not to marry, or at least to marry later, and this reality has lowered birthrates

The third catagory, artificial birth control, attempts to prevent the fertilization of the ovum of the woman. One of the oldest forms of birth control is periodic marital continence, often called the rhythmic cycle, which even has the approval of the Roman Catholic Church, a staunch opponent of most birth control. Other forms include hormone additives (the pill), condoms, sponges, spermicides, surgical operations (vasectomy for males and salpingectomy for females), castration, abortion, and such practices as coitus interruptus or coitus reservatus.

Contraception is usually practiced for one or more of three reasons. First, there is the desire to better society, which includes the raising of health standards and the more equitable distribution of food allowed by smaller families. Second, much of the push for birth control is attached to the belief in eugenics (attempts to weed out individuals viewed to represent inadequate or undesirable genetic or racial traits) and the desire for higher quality of life for infants. Last, the rise of egalitarianism in Western society has allowed greater independence for women, part of which required control over their reproductive rights.

A major argument that underlies all the arguments for the ready availability of contraceptives is the increasingly overpopulated world. Thomas Malthus (*Essay on the Principle of Population* [1789]) is credited with the first emphasis on birth control. The three postulates that Malthus made regarding overpopulation are (1) food is necessary for human existence, (2) the passion for sex is necessary and will continue to be so, and (3) the power of the population is infinitely greater than the capacity of the planet to produce food adequate to the needs of the population. Malthus and others postulated that the population increases geometrically (e.g., 1, 2, 4, 8, 16), while subsistence increases only arithmetically (e.g., 1, 2, 3, 4, 5). Based on these factors, Malthus and his followers believed that only a planned strategy of late marriage and abstinence could control the birthrate and thus save the planet.

The predictions and underlying assumptions of Malthus have proved to be wrong. The food supply of the world is outstripping the population. Three factors must always be taken into account when discussing the issue of overpopulation, namely, land, natural resources, and food. Based on the amount of space an individual person reasonably occupies, the earth has room for many times the approximately six billion people living here. With each person receiving 1,700 square feet, a comfortable, but small, home, the entire population of earth could fit inside the state of Texas. Current evidence indicates that the population of the earth is levelling out. The real problem involves the distribution of food and natural resources, oppression by dictators, and the crowding of people into dense areas. Because of these problems, lowering birthrates through contraception and other means is still viewed favorably by many people.

Although the issue of birth control has been controversial at times in the United States, it has paled in comparison to the controversy surrounding abortion. The two most important U.S. Supreme Court decisions on abortion are ***Roe v. Wade*** (1973) and *Casey v. Planned Parenthood* (1992). Dividing pregnancy into trimesters, Justice **Harry Blackmun** argued in *Roe* that the right to abortion is as constitutionally fundamental as the freedom of religion or expression. Except for guidelines to ensure the pregnant woman's protection, a state has no right to restrict abortion in the first two trimesters. In the last trimester (after the fetus is viable), a state can, though it need not, restrict abortions to only those cases in which the mother's life or health is in danger. But, this health exception is so broad that it makes *Roe* more permissive than is often thought. In *Doe v. Bolton* (1973), a companion to *Roe*, the Court ruled that "health" must be taken in its broadest possible context, in light of all factors physical, emotional, psychological, familial, and the woman's age relevant to the well-being of the patient. All these factors relate to health.

In *Casey*, although the Court upheld *Roe* as precedent, it rejected *Roe*'s trimester breakdown (which it had done in *Webster v. Reproductive Health Services* [1989]) as well as its conclusion that abortion is a fundamental right. In this case, the Court was asked to consider the constitutionality of five provisions of a Pennsylvania statute related to abortion. It upheld four of the five provisions as constitutional, rejecting only the one that requires a married woman seeking an abortion to sign a statement indicating that she has notified her husband, unless certain exceptions apply. The Court allowed Pennsylvania's restrictions, including parental notification and a waiting period based on what it calls the "undue burden" standard.

This standard is different from what is found in *Roe*, which affirms abortion as a fundamental constitutional right and thus makes any possible restrictions subject to strict scrutiny. To be valid, possible restrictions must be essential to meeting a compelling public need. For example, laws that prohibit shouting "fire" in a crowded theater pass strict scrutiny when subject to the fundamental right of freedom of expression. But, according to *Casey*, states may restrict abortion by passing laws that may not withstand strict scrutiny but nevertheless do not result in an undue burden for the pregnant woman.

Ethicists have argued for and against abortion rights in primarily two ways: (1) from the moral status of the fetus, or (2) from the bodily rights of the pregnant woman. Arguments from the moral status of the fetus maintain that the beginning of individual human life begins at conception and does not end until natural death. At the moment of conception, when sperm and ovum cease to exist as individual entities, a new being with its own genetic code comes into existence. No new genetic information is added from this moment until natural death. All that is needed for its development is food, water, air, and an environment conducive to its survival.

These facts are not denied by those who believe that abortion should be allowed at some point during pregnancy. They argue that the fetus, though a human being from conception, is not a person until some decisive moment after conception. Some argue that personhood does not arrive until brain waves are detected (40 to 43 days). Others define a person as a being with certain functions, such as consciousness and the ability to solve complex problems, which would put the arrival of personhood after birth. Traditional pro-lifers respond to these views by maintaining that there are good reasons to continue to accept and no good reason to deny that human personhood begins at conception. Still others argue that human personhood does not arrive until the fetus is sentient, which occurs possibly as early as the middle weeks, and no later than the end, of the second trimester of pregnancy.

Although agreeing that the moral status of the fetus is important, some argue that when personhood begins is not. The real question for these people is whether a being has a future-like-ours (FLO), for it is typically considered wrong to kill any being that has an FLO. Since the ordinary fetus does have an FLO, then abortion is generally considered wrong.

Arguments from the bodily rights of the pregnant woman disagree that the abortion debate hinges on the moral status of the fetus. They argue that even if the fetus is a human person from conception, abortion is still morally justified. Some argue that the fetus's physical dependence on the pregnant woman's body entails a conflict of rights if the pregnant woman did not consent to the pregnancy. Consequently, the fetus cannot use another's body without her consent. Thus, a pregnant woman's removal of the fetus by abortion, though it will result in its death, is no more immoral than an adult person's refusal to donate her kidney to someone who needs one, though this refusal will probably result in the death of the person who needs the kidney. (HWH; FJB)

BIBLIOGRAPHY

Beckwith, F. J. *Politically Correct Death: Answering the Arguments for Abortion Rights*. Grand Rapids, MI: Baker, 1993.

Brody, B. *Abortion and the Sanctity of Human Life: A Philosophical View.* Boston, MA: M.I.T. Press, 1975.

Douglas, E. (1970) *Margaret Sanger: Pioneer of the Future*. New York: Holt, Rinehart and Winston, 1970.

Glendon, M.A. *Abortion and Divorce in Western Law*. Cambridge, MA: Harvard University Press, 1987.

Lee, P. *Abortion and Unborn Human Life*. Washington, DC: The Catholic University of America, 1996.

Noonan J., Jr., *Contraception*. Cambridge, MA: Harvard University Press, 1966.

Pavlischek, K. "Abortion Logic and Paternal Responsibilties: One More Look at Judith Thomson's 'A Defense of Abortion.'" *Public Affairs Quarterly* 7 (October 1993): 38–52.

Pojman, L. P. and Beckwith, F. J., eds. *The Abortion Controversy 25 Years After Roe v. Wade: A Reader*. Belmont, CA: Wadsworth, 1998.

Schwarz, S.D. *The Moral Question of Abortion*. Chicago: Loyola University Press, 1990.

Sowell, T. *The Economics and Politics of Race*. New York: William Morrow and Company, 1983.

Sumner, L.W. *Abortion and Moral Theory*. Princeton, NJ: Princeton University Press, 1981.

Tooley, M. *Abortion and Infanticide*. New York: Oxford University Press, 1983.

Wennberg, R. *Life in the Balance: Exploring the Abortion Controversy*. Grand Rapids, MI: Eerdmans, 1985.

Abortion Rights Mobilization v. United States Catholic Conference (1990)

After the 1980 national election, Abortion Rights Mobilization and several other abortion rights groups, frustrated by the Roman Catholic Church's political opposition to abortion during the campaign, sued the IRS in an effort to revoke the Church's tax exempt status. The litigants became embroiled in several complex procedural battles and a final decision on the case was not reached until 1990. Ultimately, in *Abortion Rights Mobilization v. United States Catholic Conference,* 495 U.S. 918 (1990), the U.S. Supreme Court refused to hear an appeal by Abortion Rights Mobilization after a lower court decided that a decision on the matter was best left to the political process. (KRD) **See also** Roman Catholicism.

BIBLIOGRAPHY

Carroll, Anne Berrill. "Religion, Politics, and the IRS: Defining the Limits of Tax Law Controls on Political Expression by Churches." *Marquette Law Review* 76, no. 1 (Fall 1992): 217-63.

Accommodationism

The **First Amendment** to the United States Constitution reads, in part, "Congress shall make no law respecting an establishment of religion. . . . ." Accommodationism is a general theory of the **Establishment Clause**, which entails the assumption that government is permitted to approach religion from the standpoint of "benevolent neutrality." Accommodationists generally believe that the Establishment Clause prohibits government from aiding or supporting *particular* religions or denominations. However, the Establishment Clause is not taken to prohibit nondiscriminatory support for religion in general. Thus, accommodationists are likely to support nondenominational affirmations of religious belief, such as nonsectarian prayers in public schools, religious observances at public events, and the like. The opposite of accommodationism is *separationism,* which would impose much more stringent limitations on government support for religion.

Underlying accommodationism are two assumptions about the relationship between religion and public life. First, it is generally assumed that the behavioral consequences of religion are similar across denominations. Although American religions differ substantially in terms of doctrinal beliefs, there is thought to exist a common set of religiously based morals. Such values as chastity, honesty, charity, and frugality ultimately are regarded as having a religious basis, but are common to virtually all religious traditions. Second, accommodationists tend to believe that the moral implications of religious belief are generally beneficial, and, therefore, government is not required to be indifferent between religion and irreligion. By contrast, separationists tend to assume that religion is a dangerous source of social division and factionalism, and that certain behavioral consequences of religious belief (self-righteousness, intolerance, or anti-intellectualism) are undesirable in democratic politics.

At present, the state of Establishment Clause jurisprudence is generally separationist. The operative precedent is ***Lemon v. Kurtzman*** (1971) which has recently been reaffirmed in ***Lee v. Weisman***. (TGJ)

BIBLIOGRAPHY

Jelen, Ted G. and Clyde Wilcox. *Public Attitudes Toward Church and State.* Armonk, NY: M.E. Sharpe, 1995.

Monsma, Stephen V. *Positive Neutrality: Letting Religious Freedom Ring.* Westport, CT: Praeger, 1993.

Neuhaus, Richard John. *The Naked Public Square.* Grand Rapids, MI: Eerdmans, 1984.

Reichley, A. James. *Religion in Private and Public Life.* Washington, DC: The Brookings Institution, 1985.

Wald, Kenneth D. *Religion and Politics in the United States.* 3rd ed. Washington, DC: CQ Press, 1997.

Act of Toleration (Maryland Colony, 1649)

The Act of Toleration, also known as An Act Concerning Religion, was passed in 1649 by the colony of Maryland in the hopes of ending religious conflict between Roman Catholic and Protestant colonists. **Maryland Colony** had been established by **Cecilius Calvert, Lord Baltimore**, as a safe haven for Catholics in the New World, but Protestant settlers did not want to be ruled by Catholics, whom they believed were under allegiance to the pope. The act guaranteed freedom of religion for all who believed in Jesus Christ. Political participation (voting and holding public office) required that one believe in the Trinity. Additionally, the act forbade all disparaging remarks and protected Sundays as the sabbath. The act did little to settle the religious and political conflicts of Maryland. It was repealed in 1654 when Protestant forces took control of the colony and enacted several anti-Catholic statutes. (The Maryland Act of Toleration is reprinted in Appendix 1.) **See also** Colonial America; Roman Catholicism.

Bibliography

Aubrey, C.L. *Colonial Maryland.* Millwood, NY: KTO Press, 1981.

Ellis, John T. *Catholics in Colonial America.* Baltimore: Helicon Press, 1965.

James Luther Adams (1901–1994)

James Adams, a professor of Christian ethics at the Harvard Divinity School from 1956 to 1968 is known for his pioneering work in the sociology of religion, particularly on the role of churches as voluntary associations in creating and sustaining free democratic societies. He edited translations of **Max Weber's** *Sociology of Religion* and of **Ernst Troeltsch's** writings. Deeply influenced by Hugo Grotius, Althusius, Otto von Gierke, Ernst Troeltsch, and **Paul Tillich**, he recognized the social implications that radical Protestantism had for the emergence of modern **democracy**. The lack of independent organizations witnessed by Adams in his years in prewar Germany only confirmed his views on the role of such voluntary organizations (nonprofit and public interest groups) in sustaining democratic societies. Adams studied the political, sociological, and institutional dimensions of such organizations as well as their religious and ethical meanings. (ISM)

Bibliography

Adams, James Luther. *Voluntary Associations.* Ronald Engel, ed. Chicago: Exploration Press, 1986.

Robertson, D.B., ed. *Voluntary Associations. A Study of Groups in Free Societies.* Richmond, VA: John Knox Press, 1966.

Wilcox, John R. *Taking Time Seriously: James Luther Adams.* Washington, DC: University Press of America, 1978.

Jasper Adams (1793–1841)

Jasper Adams was an educator, **Episcopal** clergyman, and moral philosopher. His most influential work was a published sermon entitled "The Relation of Christianity to Civil Government in the United States," preached in 1833 before the South Carolina Diocese of the Protestant Episcopal Church. Adams argued that Christianity was indispensable to social order, good government, and national prosperity. Although he opposed the establishment of a state church, he believed a Christian ethic must inform all civil, legal, and political institutions. His prescient discourse anticipated the emergence of a dominant secular culture and the inevitable conflict with the formerly ascendant religious establishment. Adams's sermon was among the major polemics to come from the embattled religious traditionalists of this era, who were attempting to controvert the vision of a secular polity and church-state separation attributed to **Thomas Jefferson**. (DLD)

Bibliography

Dreisbach, Daniel L., ed. *Religion and Politics in the Early Republic: Jasper Adams and the Church-State Debate.* Lexington: University Press of Kentucky, 1996.

John Adams (1735–1826)

John Adams, the second president and first vice president of the United States, was encouraged by his father to become a clergyman. Although Adams eventually decided to pursue legal studies, his religious faith continued throughout his life to exercise a strong influence on his political thoughts and actions. Over the course of his career, Adams's theological views moved from an early Puritanism to **Unitarianism** in later life. However, Adams continued to affirm the imperfectability of humankind and the perfectability of God as necessary doctrines. He believed the Bible was the primary guide for ordering the moral life, and that it served as the "most republican book in the world" because its limitations on human behavior were necessary for republican government to survive. Throughout his life, Adams affirmed Christianity as the one, true religion; however, in old age, he refused to accept any denominational label, preferring to be a "fellow disciple" of all Christians.

Although professing deep commitment to Christianity, John Adams, the second president of the United States, refused to accept any denominational label. Library of Congress.

(HLC) **See also** American Revolution; John Quincy Adams; Thomas Jefferson; Puritans; George Washington.

BIBLIOGRAPHY

Smith, Page. *John Adams*. Garden City, NY: Doubleday, 1963.

Fielding, Howard Ioan. "John Adams: Puritan, Deist, Humanist." *The Journal of Religion* 12 (January 1940): 33-46.

John Quincy Adams (1767–1848)

John Quincy Adams, sixth president of the United States, is remembered more often for his triumphs in the field of foreign diplomacy and his late-life abolitionism than for his work as chief executive. Son of the revolutionary leader and second American president **John Adams**, he was raised in the Calvinist tradition but later abandoned this for a **Unitarianism** that saw the United States as the realization of God's moral order on earth. Additionally, Adams was a firm believer in **natural law** and the ability of human reason to discuss God's will. Like many of his era, he saw the political and social importance of religion and religious toleration. As secretary of state under President James Monroe, Adams is said to have been the guiding hand behind the Monroe Doctrine, and he played a large role in the negotiations to acquire Florida from Spain. He ran for president against **Andrew Jackson** and Henry Clay in 1824, winning the election in the House of Representatives. Jackson won the next election, and Adams returned to Congress where he spoke out against slavery, most notably in his defense of the Amistad mutineers before the U.S. Supreme Court in 1841. (BDG) **See also** Amistad Case; Calvinism.

A practicing Unitarian, John Quincy Adams, the sixth president of the United States, believed that the United States must conform to the will of God. Library of Congress.

BIBLIOGRAPHY

Richards, Leonard. *The Life and Times of Congressman John Quincy Adams*. New York: Oxford University Press, 1986.

Weeks, William Earl. *John Quincy Adams and American Global Empire*. Lexington: University Press of Kentucky, 1992.

Samuel Adams (1722–1803)

Believing in the role of the covenant in life and politics, Samuel Adams was a radical **Puritan** during America's Revolutionary era. He believed individuals accepted divine will through their own efforts, and government was just when it was created and ruled by consent. Adams, like the Puritan founders of **Massachusetts Bay**, believed that the New World was established to reflect biblical principals of justice and morality. (GT) **See also** John Adams; American Revolution.

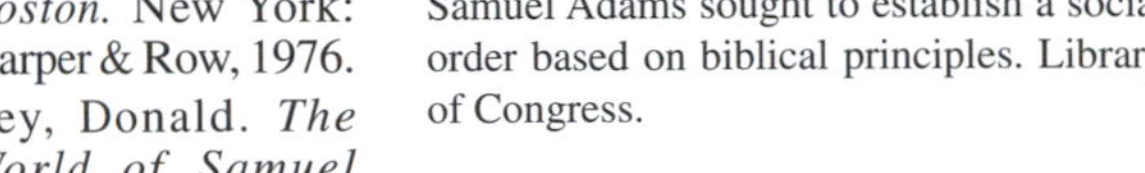

A radical Puritan, American revolutionary Samuel Adams sought to establish a social order based on biblical principles. Library of Congress.

BIBLIOGRAPHY

Canfield, Cass. *Samuel Adam's Revolution, 1765–1776: With the Assistance of George Washington, Thomas Jefferson, Benjamin Franklin, John Adams, George III, and the People of Boston*. New York: Harper & Row, 1976.

Chidsey, Donald. *The World of Samuel Adams*. Nashville: Thomas Nelson Publishers, 1974.

Fowler, William M., Jr. *Samuel Adams: Radical Puritan*. New York: Longman, 1997.

Jane Addams (1860–1935)

One of the most respected social reformers of the late nineteenth and early twentieth centuries, Jane Addams received the 1931 Noble Peace Prize (with Nicholas Butler). Addams graduated from Rockford Seminary in 1881 and was encouraged by the school's president to become a church missionary. In 1887, she experimented with Auguste Comte's system of theology, which placed science over theology. She is best known for Hull House, a settlement house in a working class, immigrant neighborhood of Chicago. Modeled after Toynbee Hall in London, it had social workers live in the same neighborhood as those they were trying to help. Its services included a gymnasium, a boarding school, a day nursery, and vocational training. In 1910, Addams became the first woman president of the National Conference of Social Work. She used her fame to advance many causes, including women's suffrage and international peace. (MWP) **See also** Women in Religion and Politics.

BIBLIOGRAPHY

Addams, Jane. *The Second Twelve Years at Hull House*. New York: Macmillan, 1930.

———. *Twelve Years at Hull House*. New York: Macmillan, 1911.

Davis, Allen F. *American Heroine: The Life and Legend of Jane Addams*. New York: Oxford University Press, 1973.

Adolescent Family Life Act (1981)

Congress passed the Adolescent Family Life Act in 1981 to change the way federal programs dealt with teen sexuality and pregnancy. Sometimes called the "Chastity Act," it funded programs that stressed abstinence and adoption. In 1987, a group of taxpayers challenged a provision of the act that specifically allowed money to go to religious groups. The Washington, D.C., Circuit Court found the statute unconstitutional, but that decision was overturned by the United States Supreme Court in *Bowen v. Kendrick*, 487 U.S. 589 (1988). (MWP)

Bibliography

Sweeny, Coreen K. *"Establishment Clause: Adolescent Family Life Act Upheld." Drake Law Review* 39 (Spring 1990): 783-95.

African-American Churches

African-American churches are the synthesis of African religions brought to the United States by enslaved Africans and the predominantly evangelistic Christianity of the eighteenth and nineteenth centuries. African-American religion was fundamentally marked by **slavery** and the accompanying racism that continued after emancipation. The racial discrimination within the then dominant **Baptist, Episcopal,** Methodist, and **Presbyterian** churches led to the founding of independent African-American churches, both in the antebellum and postbellum periods. The most well-known of these is the **African Methodist Episcopal (AME) Church**, formed by **Richard Allen** and Absalom Jones and incorporated in 1816. Similar withdrawals of African Americans from predominantly white denominations led to the founding in 1821 of the African Methodist Episcopal Zion Church, and, after the **Civil War**, the Christian Methodist Church, and independent Black Baptist congregations.

African-American religion served as a means of survival under slavery, being the single institution controlled by African Americans. **W.E.B. Du Bois** described these churches as serving not just spiritual ends, but also as centers for black social life, lending banks, and mutual-aid societies. Thus, in African-American churches, the spiritual, economic, political, and the social were never sharply demarcated and this has remained a defining characteristic of African-American religion. As early as the 1830s, ministers of existing African-American denominations had organized the National Negro Convention Movement to agitate for social reform and **abolition**.

African-American religion has often been misunderstood as a "haven for the masses," the implication being that it was individualistic, pietistic, and without a social impact. However, modern scholarship, beginning with the work of W.E.B. Du Bois, has challenged this passive view of the African-American church and has devoted much attention to African-American religion (and churches) and its complex dialectic of accommodation and opposition. While African-American churches did serve as otherworldly refuges, they also served both as preservers of black identity and as sources of resistance to slavery and racism. Thus, even prior to the Civil War, African-American ministers and congregations in the North championed abolitionism, and during **Reconstruction**, black ministers filled numerous federal and state positions. The failure of Reconstruction caused an upsurge in religious Ethiopianism (from Psalm 68:31), a movement that claimed a messianic role for Christianized black people. These beliefs fostered black nationalism, the movement for African Americans to establish their own separate black nation, and Pan-Africanism, a movement that sought to unite blacks from around the world to exert political, economic, and social force.

Martin Luther King, Jr., leader of the **civil rights** movement until his assassination in 1968, was himself a Baptist minister and founder of the **Southern Christian Leadership Conference** (SCLC). King, through his synthesis of Christianity, American **civil religion**, and Ghandian nonviolence, led the movement to establish the equality of African Americans. After his death, his more radical successors in the Black Power and **Black Theology** movements sought not so much reform as revolution. This was the central theme of the Black Theology espoused by **Albert B. Cleage** and **James H. Cone**, which understood Jesus as struggling against oppression, thus justifying the black political struggle against racism. While Black Theology never deeply influenced African-American churches, the post-1960s social and political coalitions had great influence.

In the 1970s, coalitions between African-American churches, political leaders, and other racial minorities began to address common social and economic issues. Two clergy prominent in these movements were the Rev. Benjamin Chavis (**United Church of Christ**) and the Rev. **Jesse Jackson** (Baptist). Chavis, a church civil rights organizer, became a controversial director of the NAACP from 1993 to 1994 and then founder of the National African-American Leadership Summit. Jackson, one of King's assistants in the Southern Christian Leadership Conference's Chicago projects, used his Operation Breadbasket organization to initiate Operation PUSH (People United to Save Humanity) and eventually ran as Democratic contender for the presidency in 1984 and 1988, with support from African-American churches.

An African-American church often overlooked is the **Pentecostal** Church of God in Christ (the fastest growing black denomination), which was initiated by an African-American pastor, William Seymour, and led modern Pentecostal Churches. Earlier scholarly treatments of Pentecostalism overlooked Seymour's role and that of African Americans, and the interracial make-up of the early Pentecostal movement. Belatedly entering the social and political arenas, black Pentecostals made news in 1994, when the white Pentecostal Fellowship of North America voted to merge with its African-American counterparts. (ISM) **See also** Methodism; Race Relations.

Bibliography

Baer, Hans A. and Singer, Merrill. *African-American Religion in the Twentieth Century. Varieties of Protest and Accommodation.* Knoxville: University of Tennessee Press, 1992.

Cox, Harvey. *Fire from Heaven: The Rise of Pentecostal Spirituality and the Reshaping of Religion in the Twenty-First Century.* Reading, MA: Addison-Wesley, 1995.

Du Bois, W.E.B. *The Negro Church.* Atlanta: Atlanta University Press, 1903.

Frazier, E. Franklin. *The Negro Church in America.* New York: Schocken, 1974.

Paris, Peter J. *The Social Teaching of the Black Churches.* Philadelphia: Fortress, 1985.

Raboteau, Albert J. *Slave Religion: The "Invisible Institution" in the Antebellum South.* New York: Oxford University Press, 1978.

African Methodist Episcopal (AME) Church

The African Methodist Episcopal Church is the largest African-American Methodist denomination in the United States. Former slave **Richard Allen** founded the AME Church in 1816. Because blacks were denied access to worship at St. George's Methodist Episcopal Church in Philadelphia, Allen and others had initially formed the Free African Society in 1787, which eventually developed into the African Methodist Episcopal Church. Until his death in 1831, Allen served as the first bishop of the AME Church. Under Allen's leadership, the church devoted itself to the spiritual and social teachings of John and Charles Wesley, the originators of the Methodist movement, and to serving the African-American community. These attributes remain the hallmarks of the AME Church, which today claims over 3.5 million members.(HLC)

Women were active as preachers in the early years of the African Methodist Episcopal Church. Library of Congress.

See also African-American Churches; Methodism.

Bibliography

George, Carol V.R. *Segregated Schools: Richard Allen and the Rise of Independent Black Churches, 1760-1840.* New York: Oxford University Press, 1973.

Agostini et al. v. Felton et al. (1997)

In *Agostini v. Felton,* 117 S. Ct. (1997), the Supreme Court by a 5-4 margin overturned ***Aguilar v. Felton*** (1985), which prohibited public school teachers from teaching federally mandated remedial classes on the grounds of parochial schools, and its companion case *Grand Rapids School District v. Ball* (1985), which determined that Shared Time programs also violated the **Establishment Clause**.

In *Aguilar*, the Court ruled that New York City's program sending public school teachers into parochial schools to provide remedial education was unconstitutional. The city's program was designed to meet the requirements of Title I of the Elementary and Secondary Education Act of 1965. Relying on ***Lemon v. Kurtzman*** (1971), Justice **William J. Brennan**, writing for the majority in *Aguilar*, concluded that there was an excessive entanglement between church and state because of the need to have ongoing inspections to ensure that the inculcation of religion did not take place as part of the remedial instruction provided by the state.

The *Agostini* Court rejected the conclusion of the *Aguilar* Court that the programs violated the second prong—the impermissible effect of advancing religion—and the third prong—excessive government entanglement with religion—of the **Lemon Test**. In response to the *Aguilar* Court's second prong claim, the *Agostini* Court, citing ***Zobrest v. Catalina Foothills School District*** (1993)—in which the Court permitted a deaf student to bring his state-employed sign language interpreter with him to his Roman Catholic high school—concluded that the presence of a public employee on the grounds of a parochial school does not constitute a symbolic union between church and state.

Further, the Court rejected the claim that any public employee who works on a religious school's grounds is presumed to inculcate religion. The Court relied on the fact that there was no evidence that any of the public teachers had attempted to inculcate religion in students. Citing ***Witters v. Department of Services for the Blind*** (1986)—a case which held that the Establishment Clause did not bar a state from issuing a vocational tuition grant to a blind person who wished to attend a Christian college and become a pastor, missionary, or youth director—the majority ruled that not all government aid that benefits the educational functions of religious schools is invalid.

In response to the third prong question, Justice Sandra Day O'Connor's opinion noted that the New York City Title I Program does not give aid recipients any incentive to modify religious beliefs or practices to obtain access to the program. In fact, the aid is given in a neutral manner that neither favors nor disfavors religion.

Bibliography

Levy, Leonard. *The Establishment Clause.* Chapel Hill: University of North Carolina Press, 1996.

Aguilar v. Felton (1985)

In 1985, the United States Supreme Court ruled in the *Aguilar* case that it was a violation of the **Establishment Clause** of the United States Constitution for New York City to send public school teachers into parochial schools to provide remedial education to disadvantaged children under the Title I federal program. As a way around this decision, New York City bussed parochial school students who needed remedial help to public schools after school hours and put mobile units on city land near the parochial schools.

In October 1996, the Clinton administration joined with the New York City public schools and a group of Roman Catholic parents to ask the Supreme Court to reverse its 1985 decision. In a rare move, the Court agreed to review the case. In June 1997, in a 5-4 vote, the Court overturned ***Aguilar v. Felton*** and its companion case, *Grand Rapids School District v. Ball*, arguing that the Title I program did not violate the criteria used to evaluate whether government aid had the effect of advancing religion. **See also** William Jefferson Clinton; Roman Catholicism. (WVM)

Bibliography

Levy, Leonard W. *The Establishment Clause: Religion and the First Amendment.* New York: Macmillan, 1986.

Amos Bronson Alcott (1799–1888)

Amos Alcott, an educator of children, philosopher, and renowned lecturer, was a leader of the Transcendentalist movement, which stressed an indwelling God and the significance of intuitive thought. A Deist, Alcott thought Christianity was the "best [religion] yet promulgated." Many of his Transcendentalist beliefs were drawn from Plato and neo-platonic texts. He founded the Fruitlands community as a utopian experiment in Concord, Massachusetts, in 1843. At its height, the community only had 11 members, and by 1845 the community failed. (JCW) **See also** Deism; Trancendentalism; Utopianism.

Bibliography

Dahlstrand, Frederick C. *Amos Bronson Alcott, An Intellectual Biography.* London: Associated University Press, 1982.

Ethan Allen (1738–1789)

Shouting "In the name of the Great Jehovah and the Continental Congress," Ethan Allen captured Fort Ticonderoga from the British. Revolutionary hero and leader of Vermont's Green Mountain Boys, Allen was a descendant of Church of England separatists, but proclaimed himself a Deist. Allen believed that the great danger of religion lay in the manipulation of people by clergy and churches. Allen argued that free will was the measure of morality in that it enabled humans to know God's will. (GT) **See also** American Revolution; Deism.

Bibliography

Allen, Ethan. *A Narrative of Colonel Ethan Allen's Captivity Containing His Voyages and Travels.* New York: The Georgian Press, 1930.

Bellesiles, Michael. *Revolutionary Outlaws: Ethan Allen and the Struggle for Independence on the Early American Frontier.* Charlottesville: University Press of Virginia, 1993.

Richard Allen (1760–1831)

Born in 1760 as the slave of a **Quaker** master, Richard Allen eventually purchased his freedom in 1786. At the age of 17, he experienced a religious conversion and began an itinerant preaching ministry. In 1787, after joining the Methodist Church, Allen established the first church for blacks in the United States in Philadelphia. He became the first black man ordained into the Methodist Church in 1799. Starting with his Philadelphia church, Allen later founded a separate denomination, the **African Methodist Episcopal (AME) Church**.

Richard Allen (center) was the founder of the African Methodist Episcopal (AME) Church. Library of Congress.

Allen served as the first bishop of the AME Church from 1816 until his death in 1831, and led the denomination in all its early religious, social, and political initiatives. (HLC) **See also** African-American Churches; Methodism; Slavery.

Bibliography

Allen, Richard. *Life Experience and Gospel Labors of the Rt. Rev. Richard Allen.* Nashville: Abingdon Press, 1960.

George, Carol V.R. *Segregated Schools: Richard Allen and the Rise of Independent Black Churches, 1760-1840.* New York: Oxford University Press, 1973.

American and Foreign Anti-Slavery Society. See Liberty Party.

American Anti-Slavery Society

Founded in Philadelphia in 1833, the American Anti-Slavery Society became one of the first and most influential abolitionist organizations. Filled with religious zeal and rejecting quietism, the Society sought an immediate end to **slavery**.

A convention of the American Anti-Slavery Society. Photo by B.R. Haydon. National Portrait Gallery.

Declaring their victory assured by God, organizers at the first convention constructed a multifaceted strategy to combat the immorality of slavery.

Society activities included the establishment of similarly organized societies in cities and towns across the country, distribution of tracts and publications, such as *The American Anti-Slavery Almanac,* and direct lobbying of Congress and state legislatures. Public speeches, rallies, and declarations from church pulpits sought to persuade fellow citizens through logical augmentation and impassioned moral rhetoric. Black orators often spoke to demonstrate their intellectual capacities and offer a living testimony to the equality of blacks and whites.

Some members of the Society also sought equality for women and the organization served as a springboard for the early suffrage movement. The issue of equal rights for women was one of the key factors that split the society into two main groups in 1839. The radical faction under **William Lloyd Garrison**, a journalist and editor of the first **temperance** paper, was inspired by **Quaker** teachings of egalitarianism, activism for justice, and nonviolence. While the Society's constitution strictly forbid resorting to physical force, at times the Society's activities incited a violent response. The blunt and fiery charges against slaveholders and the complicity of citizens in the institution of slavery at times incited mob violence and threats and led to jail terms for the more radical abolitionists. These activities and reactions also contributed to the split among the religious members of the Society, who experienced the same righteous passion for the cause but advocated reforms through prayer and revival to awaken the public's consciousness. The two factions saw their mission completed with the passage in 1865 of the Thirteenth Amendment abolishing slavery. (DD) **See also** Abolition; Women in Religion and Politics.

Bibliography

Goodman, Paul. *Of One Blood: Origins of Racial Equality and the Emergence of Abolitionism, 1820–1840.* Berkeley: University of California Press, 1998.

Magdol, Edward. *The Anti-Slavery Rank and File: A Social Profile of the Abolitionists Constituency.* Westport, CT: Greenwood Publishing Group, 1986.

American Board of Commissioners for Foreign Missions

Founded in 1806 by students at Williams College in Massachusetts, the American Board of Commissioners for Foreign Missions was incorporated in 1810 to serve as a mission society for **Congregational** and **Presbyterian** churches and was the first American foreign mission organization. In addition to its primary focus on India, China, the Far East, the Ottoman Empire (Turkey and Armenia), and the Zulus of Southern Africa, the Board's **missionaries** worked among freed slaves, Native American Indians, and Hawaiians. It established social institutions such as schools and hospitals as part of its aim to establish self-supporting and self-propogating churches. In 1961, with the union creating the **United Churches of Christ**, the Board merged with the UCC's Board of World Ministries. (ISM) **See also** Jeremiah Evarts.

One of the major goals of missionary societies was the distribution of the Gospel. Library of Congress.

Bibliography

Andrew, John. *Rebuilding the Christian Commonwealth: New England Congregationalists and Foreign Missions, 1800–1830.* Lexington: University of Kentucky Press, 1976.

Phillips, Clifton Jackson. *Protestant America and the Pagan World: The First Half-Century of the American Board of Commissioners for Foreign Missions, 1810–1860.* Cambridge, MA: Harvard University Press, 1968.

American Civil Liberties Union (ACLU)

The American Civil Liberties Union was founded by Roger Baldwin in 1920 as a public interest law firm dedicated to protecting the basic civil liberties of all Americans. It has grown into a nationwide, non-partisan, non-profit organization of over 275,000 members with 52 state affiliates and hundreds of local chapters. The ACLU's mission is to uphold the Bill of Rights, including **First Amendment** rights, and to guarantee equal protection under the law, due process, the right to privacy and the expansion of those rights to cover previously non-covered groups, such as Native Americans, mental patients, and homosexuals. At the time the ACLU was founded, the U.S. Supreme Court had never upheld a free speech claim under the First Amendment.

The ACLU has been a steadfast supporter of the individual's right to freedom of religion, including the strict separation of church and state. The ACLU's stated position is "The Constitution's framers understood very well that religious liberty can flourish only if the government leaves religion alone. The **Free Exercise Clause** of the First Amendment guarantees the right to practice one's religion free of government interference. The **Establishment Clause** requires the separation of church and state. Combined, they ensure religious liberty." Specific religious issues the ACLU has addressed include opposing prayer in schools, upholding the religious rights of prisoners, and protecting the worship practices of minority religions.

To this end, the ACLU has supported politically diverse groups, ranging from the American Nazi Party, to the Black Panthers, to members of the Communist Party. In 1925, the ACLU defended John Scopes in the highly publicized **Scopes Trial** concerning a teacher's right to free speech in the face of Tennessee's new anti-**evolution** law. Scopes lost the trial but the decision was eventually reversed by the Tennessee Supreme Court. The ACLU later opposed the internment of Japanese Americans on the West Coast in 1943, fought segregation in the notable case, *Brown v. Board of Education,* and was instrumental in the legalization of abortion in the landmark case ***Roe v. Wade***.

The ACLU was a subject in the 1988 presidential elections in which Democratic candidate Michael Dukakis was accused by his opponent, **George Bush**, of being a "card carrying ACLU member," equating such membership with liberal or left-leaning politics. Dukakis, who had a 17-point lead at the time, lost the election. (JCW) **See also** School Prayer.

BIBLIOGRAPHY

Walker, Samuel. *In Defense of American Liberties: A History of the ACLU.* New York: Oxford University Press, 1990.

American Exceptionalism

"American Exceptionalism" represents the belief that the United States is fundamentally exceptional, different, and even unique compared with other nations. The phrase was coined by the Frenchman **Alexis de Tocqueville**, but some variant of the idea behind it had been present in America since **John Winthrop** spoke of **Massachusetts Bay Colony** as a "city upon a hill" in 1630. From the deliberate act of "founding" in the eighteenth century, to the westward expansion in the nineteenth century, which was thought to fulfill the country's "**manifest destiny**," to the anticipation in the twentieth of an "American century," there has been a continuing sense that the U.S. is different from the rest of the world and must therefore be understood differently.

American exceptionalism has been exemplified by persons as diverse as seventeenth-century New England **Puritans** and twentieth-century Marxists. The distinctiveness is thought to lie in many different aspects of American life, in formal institutions such as government and education, in economics, and in mediating institutions like religion. Some have pointed to the unusual aspects of American government: the extraordinarily limited government with its so-called "checks and balances" between the branches, the lack of viable socialist and labor parties in American history, and the strength and durability of the two national political parties. Others have pointed to the formal separation of the state from religion. Americans have always been, and continue to be, an exceptionally religious people — measured by church attendance and profession of belief in God — especially in comparison with Western Europe. In spite of this great religiosity, Americans have seen fit to separate in some degree, by banning religious test oaths and the establishment of a national religion, and by separating the state from the church. (JHM)

BIBLIOGRAPHY

Shafer, Byron E., ed. *Is America Different?: A Look at American Exceptionalism.* New York: Oxford University Press, 1991.

American Indian Religious Freedom Act (1978)

The American Indian Religious Freedom Act (AIRFA) was first introduced into Congress by Senator James Abourezk of South Dakota who sought to clarify federal policy in respect to Native American religions. The act states that it was the policy of the federal government "to protect and preserve for American Indians their inherent right of freedom to believe, express and practice traditional religions." While the language seemed to settled the conflict, it had little practical impact on changing federal policies or protecting Native American religions.

In 1988, the U.S. Supreme Court ruled in ***Lyng v. Northwest Indian Cemetery Protective Association*** that the government's leasing of land—believed to be sacred by Native Americans—for a logging road was not an infringement of AIRFA. Additionally, in 1990, the Court ruled in ***Employment Division of Oregon v. Smith*** that a practitioner of the Native American religious practice of consuming peyote could be denied unemployment benefits.

Congress once again tried to rectify the situation by passing the **Religious Freedom Restoration Act (RFRA)**, specifically designed to overturn the ruling of the Supreme Court in *Smith*. However, RFRA was ruled unconstitutional in the 1997 decision ***City of Boerne v. Flores***. **See also** Cherokee Removal; Native American Religions.

BIBLIOGRAPHY

Vecsey, Christopher. *Handbook of American Indian Religious Freedom.* New York: Crossroad, 1991.

American Missionary Fellowship. See American Sunday School Union.

American Revolution

The American Revolution (1775-1783) is inextricably tied to religion in two key ways. First, religious influence on American political structures helped provide the theoretical underpinning of the Revolution. Second, the Revolution itself was critical in defining American **civil religion**, that is, in placing religion in the service of the American Republic.

The Revolution's two key theoretical sources were Puritanism and the **Enlightenment**. Puritanism contributed the idea that America was a "city on a hill," a shining beacon to the rest of the world. This notion was reinforced by the **First Great Awakening** that swept the English colonies in America in the 1730s and 1740s. Also derived from Puritan tradition was the idea that the people being governed should decide who governs them. Much of the language of the American

Revolution was derived from biblical sources, while Enlightenment political thinking (especially the writings of **John Locke**) reinforced the notion that "just government was derived from the consent of the governed."

Specific sects, however, were divided on the issue of American political separation from Great Britain. Generally, Congregationalists and Presbyterians favored the American cause while Anglicans (although not Southern ones), Methodists, and **Baptists** were loyalists. Being pacificists, **Quakers**, Morovians, and **Mennonites** were generally neutral.

Through the principles enunciated in the **Declaration of Independence**, the American Revolution was also responsible for establishing American civil religion. Specifically acknowledging God several times, the Declaration sets forth a philosophy (largely borrowed from John Locke) that identifies the fundamental ideals of the country and casts them in religious terms as articles of faith to be held by all Americans. These ideals and the belief that the United States enjoyed a special divine favor were reinforced by the American victory in the war.

Throughout American history, political leaders have drawn upon these foundations of civil religion. For example, **Abraham Lincoln** cited the Declaration of Independence's assertion that "all men are created equal" as the central truth of the American experience, and **Ronald Reagan** identified the United States as a beacon to the rest of the world. **See also** Congregationalism; Methodism; Presbyterian Church; Puritans.

BIBLIOGRAPHY

Albanese, Catherine L. *Sons of the Fathers: Civil Religion of the American Revolution*. Philadelphia: Temple University Press, 1976.

Noll, Mark. *Christians in the American Revolution*. Grand Rapids, MI: Eerdmans, 1977.

Pierard, Richard V. and Robert D. Linder. *Civil Religion and the Presidency*. Grand Rapids, MI: Zondervan, 1988.

American Sunday School Union

Begun in 1817 in Philadelphia as the Sunday and Adult School Union, the organization's name was changed to the American Sunday School Union in 1824. Founded by **evangelical** Protestants, it taught reading, morality, and religion in communities without public schools. In 1828, these schools had 127,000 students. In 1830, the Union developed a plan to place a school in every community west of the Alleghenies. By 1835, there were 1 million students enrolled in 16,000 schools taught by 140,000 unpaid, volunteer teachers. In 1974, the name was changed to the American Missionary Fellowship. (MWP) **See also** Missionaries.

BIBLIOGRAPHY

Boglan, Anne M. *Sunday School: The Formation of an American Institution, 1790–1880.* New Haven, CT: Yale University Press, 1988.

Americanism

The term Americanism described attempts by nineteenth-century Roman Catholics to define their patriotism. The term was carefully and critically defined by Pope Leo XIII in his apostolic letter, *Testem Benevolentiae Nostrae* (1899), which condemned some ideas of Americanism, such as the notion that the Church should accommodate itself to modernity and especially to the principles of individual liberty and the democratic political process. This papal letter came down on the conservative side of an ongoing controversy among American Catholics on the extent of Roman Catholic accommodation to American culture. (*Testem Benevolentiae Nostrae* is reprinted in Appendix 1.) (ISM) **See also** Roman Catholicism.

BIBLIOGRAPHY

Fogarty, G. P. *The Vatican and the American Hierarchy from 1870 to 1965.* Stuttgart, Germany: Hiersemann, 1985.

Reher, M. M. "Pope Leo XIII and 'Americanism.'" *Theological Studies* 34 (1973): 679-89.Americans United for the Separation of Church and State

Americans United for the Separation of Church and State

In 1947, a group of Protestant religious, political, and educational leaders formed Americans United for the Separation of Church and State. Americans United has focused on the principle of church-state separation in public education, although the group has been involved in other important **First Amendment** cases. Tactically, Americans United has relied heavily on litigation; it has participated as counsel or amicus curiae in dozens of legal disputes, including the landmark case of ***Lemon v. Kurtzman*** (1971). Today, Americans United claims more than 50,000 members of all faiths and representation in nearly 4,000 churches and other places of worship. (KRD)

BIBLIOGRAPHY

Sorauf, Frank J. *The Wall of Separation: The Constitutional Politics of Church and State.* Princeton, NJ: Princeton University Press, 1976.

Amish

The Amish trace their roots to the Swiss bishop Jacob Amann, who broke from the **Mennonite** Church in 1693. The group fled to America in the early part of the eighteenth century to avoid religious persecution, with the earliest settlements locating in Lancaster County Pennsylvania. There are no Amish settlements left in Europe, though they are located all over the United States and Canada, with the largest concentration living in Lancaster County and Holmes County, Ohio. Amish life has traditionally been marked by pietist devotion, a strong emphasis on family and community, and a primarily agrarian lifestyle.

Despite many common misperceptions, the Amish are not stuck in time, nor are they anti-technology. Rather, they evaluate any new technology or change carefully before incorporating it into the life of the community. All decisions about incorporating new technologies are rationally debated by the communal council until they reach a consensus. The Amish are primarily concerned about the potential of any technology to disrupt the life of the family and the possibility of increasing their dependency on forces outside the community. Thus, for example, the Amish do not disapprove of telephones but they do not allow them inside the house where they will disrupt family activities. Likewise, they do not oppose the use of pesticides or many other modern farming technologies, but will not employ any pesticides that are not "land-friendly" or tools that they cannot easily repair themselves. Traditional Amish adherence to agrarianism, however, has been threatened recently by land shortage, forcing more Amish to work in factories.

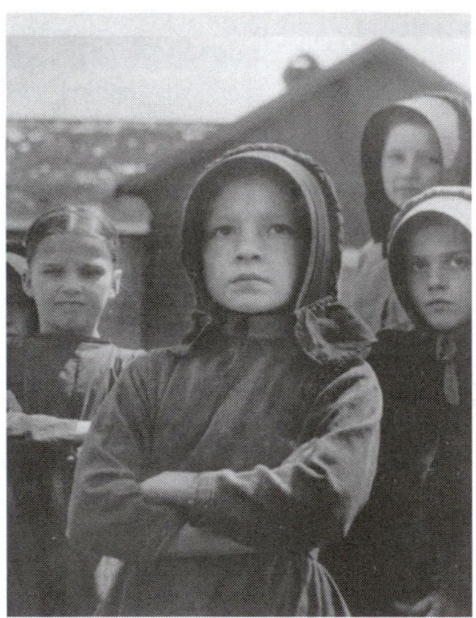

The U.S. government has accommodated the Amish with a number of legal exemptions. This Amish girl was photographed in the early 1950s. Photo by A. Aubrey Bodine, *Baltimore Sun*. Library of Congress.

The Amish have been embroiled in a number of legal battles. In ***Wisconsin v. Yoder,*** the U.S. Supreme Court ruled the Amish were not required to send their children to school past the eighth grade since such a requirement would violate their religious freedom and be superfluous in terms of the children's future. The Amish pay taxes but refuse all government aid; for this reason, they refuse to pay Social Security, which they believe to be an immoral intrusion upon the children's responsibility to care for their parents. (JP) **See also** Pietism.

BIBLIOGRAPHY

Bowen, Keith. *Among the Amish.* Philadelphia: Running Press, 1996.

Friesen, Bruce. *Perceptions of the Amish Way.* Dubuque, IA: Kendall-Hunt, 1966.

Hostetler, John. *The Amish.* Scottdale, PA: Herald Press, 1995.

Amistad Case (1841)

The Amistad Case was one of the few cases ever tried before the U.S. Supreme Court. In 1839, a group of Africans who had been sold into **slavery** were transported from Africa to Cuba. They were then put on a ship, the *Amistad*, to be sent elsewhere. However, the defendants in the case took control of the ship and were attempting to return to Africa when the ship was seized by a U.S. warship. The Africans were held as pirates. President Martin Van Buren wanted to return the men to Cuba, but the U.S. Supreme Court ruled that the men were free because of international agreements banning the slave trade. The cause of the Africans was championed by **Lewis Tappan** and by former President **John Quincy Adams** who acted as their attorney. Abolitionist groups helped support the safe return of the men to Africa, where they established a Christian mission. **See also** Abolition.

BIBLIOGRAPHY

Jones, Howard. *Mutiny on the Amistad.* New York : Oxford University Press, 1987.

Martin, B. Edmon. *All We Want Is Make Us Free.* Lanham, MD : University Press of America, 1986.

Joan Andrews (1948–)

A leading activist in the abortion clinic sit-ins (or rescues) of the 1980s, Joan Andrews began her involvement in the late 1970s by joining St. Louis University students in clinic sit-ins. By 1986, she was so well-known that a judge in Pensacola, Florida, sentenced her to five years in prison for refusing to promise not to go into an abortion clinic. After serving half of her sentence, she was pardoned by the governor. (MWP) **See also** Abortion and Birth Control.

BIBLIOGRAPHY

Andrews, Joan and John Cavanaugh-O'Keefe. *I Will Never Forget You.* New York: Ignatius Press, 1989.

Cowden, Guido. *You Reject Them, You Reject Me.* New York: Trinity, 1988.

Susan Brownell Anthony (1820–1906)

An early advocate of **temperance** and **abolition**, Susan B. Anthony is best known for her support of women's rights. Her energy and organizational abilities made her a driving force behind most of the significant women's rights organizations in the nineteenth century.

Anthony was the daughter of **Quaker** abolitionists and a product of Quaker schools. The moralism and independence emphasized by the Quakers had an enormous impact on her life's work. Initially, her beliefs led her to join temperance and abolitionist organizations, but, upon meeting discrimination in male-dominated reform organizations, she became more concerned with the rights of women.

In 1851, Anthony formed a partnership with **Elizabeth Cady Stanton** that lasted until the latter's death in 1902. With Stanton doing most of the speaking and writing and Anthony doing most of the organizing, the two lobbied unceasingly for women's rights. Most significantly, in 1869, they founded the National Woman Suffrage Association and in 1890 the National American Woman Suffrage Association. Anthony and Stanton also published a suffrage newspaper, *The Revolution* (1868–1870), and Anthony was a major contributor to the first four volumes of *The History of Woman Suffrage (1881–1922).* (MDH)

BIBLIOGRAPHY

Anthony, Katharine. *Susan B. Anthony: Her Personal History and Her Era.* New York: Russell and Russell, 1975.

Barry, Kathleen. *Susan B. Anthony: A Biography of a Singular Feminist.* New York: New York University Press, 1988.

Anti-Catholicism

Anti-Catholicism has been a feature of American society from the beginning, despite Roman Catholic contributions and demographic impact by the eighteenth century. With over 58 million members today, the Catholic church is the largest religious denomination in the United States. However, at the time of the **American Revolution**, Catholics were a distrusted minority, mostly French and Spanish colonists and a few German or Irish Catholics in the Middle Colonies and **Maryland**.

American culture was initially pluralistic, although Massachusetts supported the Congregational church with state funds until 1833. In contrast, Roman Catholics insisted as a matter of faith that theirs was the one true faith. In addition, the **Puritan** origins of American society imbued the United States with individualistic, anti-authoritarian, anti-clerical, anti-hierarchical values in contrast to papal and episcopal authority. Catholic priests and bishops exercised much greater control than Protestant clergymen. Anti-Catholic riots in Boston in 1834 and Philadelphia in 1844 and the sudden growth of the nativist **Know-Nothing Party** in the 1850s demonstrated powerful anti-Catholic bias.

Until the 1950s, the Catholic Church in the U.S. was an immigrant church due to repeated waves of German and Irish Catholics in the 1840s and 1850s, followed by post-Civil War immigrants from Quebec, Italy, and Poland—and from Latin America from the 1830s to present. This immigration expanded both the Catholic Church and religious prejudice. Although **Civil War** service by loyal Catholics in both the Union and Confederate armies diminished some anti-Catholicism, new immigrants in the late nineteenth century, clinging to their Old World religion and customs, aroused fears that Catholics would never assimilate into American society.

European Catholic leaders, who expressed doubts about modern culture, supported American Catholic efforts to protect immigrants with new parochial schools, parish organizations, social services, and hospitals. This separation seemed inimical to the American values of the expanding public school system, and the authority and influence of parish priests seemed sinister to many non-Catholics. In the Progressive Era, most Catholic bishops were social conservatives opposed to reform and union movements, causing further distrust. In the 1880s, anti-Catholic bias was evident in the nativist American Protective Association and in the revived **Ku Klux Klan** in the 1920s. The defeat of **Alfred E. Smith** as the Democratic candidate for president in 1928 was due in part to anti-Catholicism, which was overcome somewhat by the election of **John F. Kennedy** in 1960. Despite the enormous success of millions of Catholic Americans who today are a quarter of the U.S. population, anti-Catholicism still lingers in American society. (PCH) **See also** Colonial America; Congregationalism; Roman Catholicism.

Bibliography

Greeley, Andrew M. *An Ugly Little Secret: Anti-Catholicism in North America.* Kansas City: Sheed Andrews and McMeel, 1977.

Schwartz, Michael. *The Persistent Prejudice: Anti-Catholicism in America.* Huntington, IN: Our Sunday Visitor, 1984.

Anti-Defamation League of B'nai B'rith

The Anti-Defamation League of B'nai B'rith (ADL) champions the rights of Jews in the United States and around the world. It was founded in 1913 "to stop, by appeals to reason and conscience, and if necessary by appeals to law, the defamation of the Jewish people."

Since its inception in 1843, B'nai B'rith, parent organization to the ADL, has advanced the rights of Jews. When General Ulysses S. Grant issued his General Order No. 11 on December 17, 1862, expelling all Jews from Tennessee, Missouri, and other southern states, rabbis affiliated with B'nai B'rith protested to President **Abraham Lincoln**, who quickly overturned the command. When 45 Jews were killed and hundreds more injured in a Russian pogrom in 1903, B'nai B'rith organized a petition to be presented to the czar with the signatures of more than 13,000 leading American businessmen, clergy, and other civic leaders. Most who signed were not Jews.

From the 1920s through the 1940s, the ADL countered a rising tide of **anti-Semitism** led by a resurgent **Ku Klux Klan** and by American fascist organizations like the German-American Bund. When B'nai B'rith endorsed **Zionism** in 1947, the ADL worked and lobbied on behalf of the new Jewish nation.

The ADL expanded its defense of civil rights after **World War II**. Believing that all minority rights are intertwined, it participated in the **civil rights** struggle of the 1960s. The ADL also championed the strict separation of church and state, strongly condemning the proposed "religious freedom amendments" as attempts to impose religious majoritarianism upon minority faiths.

The ADL continues to focus on its three-fold mission of education, legislation, and "vigilance work." It produces curriculum guides on prejudice, anti-Semitism, and the **Holocaust**. Amicus briefs are filed by the ADL in numerous civil liberty cases and the group continues to lobby Congress on behalf of Jews worldwide. Anti-Semitic bigotry is carefully monitored and the work of extreme elements in society, like the militia movement and the **Nation of Islam,** is exposed. The ADL publishes numerous books and reports, as well as the *ADL Bulletin*, a monthly report of ongoing ADL efforts and concerns. (ARB) **See also** Judaism.

Bibliography

Grusd, Edward E. *B'nai B'rith: The Story of a Covenant.* New York: Appleton-Century, 1966.

_______. *Not the Work of a Day: The Story of the Anti-Defamation League of B'nai B'rith.* New York: B'nai B'rith, 1965.

Anti-Masonic Movement

The Anti-Masonic Party, one of the first single-issue parties in American politics, was founded in 1828 as a reaction to the Freemasons' perceived preferential treatment in the political arena. After the 1826 disappearance of William Morgan, a New York Mason allegedly on the verge of revealing secrets of the order, rumors circulated that the Masons had abducted and murdered him and anti-Masonic sentiment became widespread. The Masons involved in the kidnapping received light jail terms and lodges did nothing to punish those responsible. Anti-Masons believed that Masons sought to subvert American political and religious institutions for their own benefit and thought themselves to be above the law.

In 1827, fifteen anti-Masonic candidates were elected to the New York State Assembly. Anti-Masonic Party candidates were elected governors of Vermont and Pennsylvania, controlled some state legislatures, and won seats in the U.S. Congress. Following this, there was a rapid spread of anti-Masonic newspapers, especially in the Eastern states, with over 100 different papers being published in 1832. The number of Masons was estimated to have dropped from 100,000 to 40,000, and an estimated 85 percent of Masonic lodges closed in the state of New York.

By 1831, the Anti-Masonic Party had announced a platform and held a nominating convention. They chose **William Wirt** of Maryland to be their standard bearer and Amos Ellmaker of Pennsylvania for the vice presidency. However, the Anti-Masonic candidates served mostly to draw votes away from Henry Clay, assuring victory for Democrat and Mason **Andrew Jackson**. After the elections of 1836, the Anti-Masonic Party went into decline. (JCW) **See also** Freemasonry.

BIBLIOGRAPHY

Vaughn, William Preston. *The Anti-Masonic Party in the United States, 1826–1843.* Lexington: University Press of Kentucky, 1983.

Antinomian Controversy

Antinomianism is a belief that Christians, having been freed from obedience to any rules or laws as a means of salvation, are also freed from the requirement to obey moral laws. In America, the doctrine was first encountered in the **Massachusetts Bay Colony** in 1636. **Anne Hutchinson** rejected the claim that personal behavior was a guide to grace and salvation. Her position challenged the authority of the **Puritan** leadership and led to Hutchinson's excommunication and banishment in 1637. (MWP)

BIBLIOGRAPHY

Bathis, Emery John. *Saints and Sectaries.* Chapel Hill: University of North Carolina Press, 1962.

Hall, David D. *The Antinomian Controversy, 1636–1638: A Documenting History.* Durham, NC: Duke University Press, 1990.

Anti-Saloon League

Founded in 1895, the Anti-Saloon League was one of the most important **temperance** organizations in the country. The League adopted the motto "the saloon must go," believing that saloons created enormous social problems, particularly among working-class men and their families. An interdenominational group, it used local churches to carry its message to the people and to solicit the funds.

In addition to its networking of local churches, the League worked within the two-party system by backing individual candidates who supported its cause. Initially, the group had adopted a town-by-town, county-by-county approach to prohibition. The political influence of the League grew, as did the temperance movement, in the early decades of the twentieth century. In 1905, the growing power of the League was illustrated when the Ohio League led a successful campaign to unseat the wet Republican Governor Myron P. Herrick and replace him with dry Democratic Governor John M. Pattison.

In 1913, the League shifted its goals of local victories to national prohibition. Its first attempt, the Hobson-Sheppard bill, failed to achieve the necessary two-thirds vote of both houses, but its failure only reinforced the League's activities. When national prohibition was finally enacted in 1919, the League continued its educational pamphleteering. The end of prohibition in 1933 largely saw an end to the League's activities. Though it continued its educational activities, its influence was isolated. In 1950, the remnants of the League were merged with two other temperance organizations to form the National Temperance League. (MWP) **See also** Eighteenth Amendment.

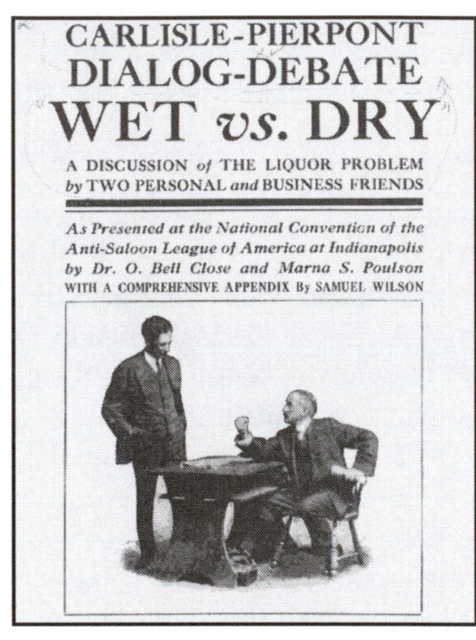

This poster advertises the Carlisle-Pierpont debate on prohibition, which was sponsored by the Anti-Saloon League. National Archives.

BIBLIOGRAPHY

Dohn, Norman Harding. *The History of the Anti-Saloon League.* Ann Arbor, MI: University Microfilms, 1976.

Lien, Jerry. *The Speechmaking of the Anti-Saloon League.* Los Angeles: University of Southern California, 1968.

Odegard, Peter H. *Pressure Politics: The Story of the Anti-Saloon League.* New York: Columbia University Press, 1928.

Anti-Semitism

The term "anti-Semitism" was first used by Wilhelm Marr, a German political activist, to denote anti-Jewish movements in Europe during the eighteenth century. Over time, anti-Semitism has become synonymous with racism in politics directed towards Jews. Anti-Semitism has played a large and tragic role in Jewish history, especially in the last two centuries.

While it existed in many forms in **colonial America**, where the colonies of **Maryland** and **Rhode Island** refused Jews the right to vote, anti-Semitism was of little significance in American politics until the end of the **Civil War**. Between 1880 and 1924, about one million Jewish immigrants came to the United States, many of them fleeing the pogroms of Russia and Poland. Although Jewish immigrants saw the United States as a safe haven from European oppression, many newly arrived Jews found that the "golden land" was not as hospitable as they had thought. Rural Americans resented the rapid growth of American cities caused by swelling numbers of Jewish and other immigrants. Other immigrant groups resented the competition for jobs represented by Jewish workers. And the widespread association of Jews with international financial affairs promoted anti-Semitic sentiments throughout the United States, as it did in much of Europe.

The rebirth of the **Ku Klux Klan** in the early twentieth century and statements by prominent Americans like Henry Ford that Jews were trying to dominate the world only enflamed American anti-Semitism. Several American anti-Jewish publications appeared in the first half of the twentieth century, including *The American Vindicator*, *The Cross and the Flag* (both published by Rev. Gerald L.K. Smith), the *Jeffersonian*, *Watson's Magazine* (published by Thomas E. Watson), and *Social Justice*, an anti-**New Deal** and anti-Semitic newspaper published by Father **Charles E. Coughlin**. These magazines and newspapers promoted anti-Jewish bigotry throughout the country.

Since the 1980s, racial tensions between Jews and African Americans has grown. Although Jews and blacks worked together for **civil rights** in the 1960s, black leaders in the 1990s have specifically attacked **Judaism**. Civil rights leader **Jesse Jackson** called New York City "Hymie Town" and **Nation of Islam** leader **Louis Farrakhan** called Judaism a "gutter religion." This new wave of American anti-Semitism seems to stem largely from a growing disagreement between Jews and blacks over the issue of affirmative action. **See also** Holocaust; Zionism.

BIBLIOGRAPHY

Dinnerstein, Leonard. *Anti-Semitism in America*. New York: Oxford University Press, 1994.

Gerber, David A., ed. *Anti-Semitism in American History*. Urbana: University of Illinois Press, 1986.

Poliakov, Leon. *The History of Anti-Semitism*. New York: Schocken Books, 1965.

Anti-Sunday Law Convention (1848)

The Anti-Sunday Law Convention (1848) was organized by **William Lloyd Garrison** in response to the efforts of the National Sabbath Convention of 1844 and the American and Foreign Sabbath Union. The Convention's supporters believed in the importance of observing the Sabbath, but felt that using government force to enact mandatory Sunday-observance laws violated the principles of church-state separation and religious freedom. They believed that observance of the Sabbath was a personal matter and individuals had an inalienable right to follow their own religious convictions without state interference. (MR) **See also** Sabbatarianism.

BIBLIOGRAPHY

Stokes, Anson Phelps. *Church and State in the United States*. Volume 3. New York: Harper & Brothers Publishers, 1950.

Arver v. United States (1918)

The Draft Act of May 18, 1917, was challenged on the grounds that it violated the Thirteenth Amendment's prohibition of involuntary servitude and the religion clauses of the **First Amendment**. In *Arver v. United States*, 245 U.S. 366 (1918), a ruling that dealt extensively with military history and little with questions of religion, the U.S. Supreme Court upheld the draft and its imposition on all citizens, regardless of religious beliefs. The Court was "unable to conceive upon what theory [the draft] can be said to be the imposition of involuntary servitude" because the draft was duly voted on by the elected representatives of the people and therefore embodied a chosen form of servitude. (JM)

BIBLIOGRAPHY

Beck, Carl, ed. Law and Justice. Durham, NC: Duke University Press, 1970.

Francis Asbury (1745–1816)

Francis Asbury was a founder of the Methodist Episcopal Church in the the United States. Asbury came to America in 1771 to work as a Methodist missionary. He was recalled to Great Britain on the outbreak of the **American Revolution** in 1775, but refused to return and became a citizen of Delaware in 1778. Asbury repudiated John Wesley's authority over the American Methodist churches, and in 1785 became bishop of the new American Methodist Episcopal Church, a position that he held until his death in 1816. During his leadership, the Church experienced a period of remarkable growth, which Asbury assisted by establishing the itinerant system of circuit-riding ministers, who helped evangelize the country.

Asbury was a religious and political pragmatist. All his activities were grounded in a deliberate effort to present the gospel of Jesus Christ and to advance the Methodist movement. While possessing an affinity for the historic forms of worship and Christian life, Asbury realized that he had to rearticulate this understanding for Americans. Asbury's stress on personal and societal holiness encouraged **Methodism**'s complex political involvement during the nineteenth century. (HLC) **See also** African Methodist Episcopal (AME) Church; Richard Allen.

BIBLIOGRAPHY

Asbury, Francis. *The Journal and Letters of Francis Asbury*. Nashville: Abingdon Press, 1958.

Rudolph, L.C. *Francis Asbury*. Nashville: Abingdon Press, 1966.

Assemblies of God

The Assemblies of God is the largest **Pentecostal** denomination and among the fastest growing Protestant denominations. The foundations for the denomination were established in 1914 when Pentecostal Christians broke away from their churches as tensions developed over the manifestations of the "gifts of the Holy Spirit." Designed as an extra-church organization, the national office, the General Council of the Assemblies of

God, still considers its primary function to be a cooperative fellowship with local churches operating with a high degree of autonomy.

Associated churches are required to accept the "Statement of Fundamental Truths" that includes the recognition of the Bible as the inspired and infallible Word of God, water baptism by immersion, divine healing, and baptism in the Holy Spirit. Drafted in 1915, the statement reflects **fundamentalist** theology and an affirmation of **Reformation** beliefs. While united in a common evangelical faith, local churches differ over such issues as qualifications for ministry, the structure of worship services, the role of women in the ministry, and divorce and remarriage. The focus on local governance and local responsibility for funding has generated a variety of ministries and movements that have at times generated controversy.

Jim Bakker and the financial dealings of the PTL Club and Jimmy Swaggart and his sexual scandals during the 1980s raised concerns about the weak structure of the church, since both men were Assemblies of God ministers. However, these loose links also minimized public damage to the denomination and continue to allow the Assemblies of God to benefit from the growth of other charismatic ministries.

Pat Robertson, televangelist, presidential candidate, and **Baptist** minister, has created both a significant public ministry and a new political force. His 1988 presidential campaign, while unsuccessful, moved many charismatic Christians into the **Republican Party** and provided an organizational base for the **Christian Coalition.** (DD)

Bibliography

Blumhofer, Edith. *Restoring the Faith: The Assemblies of God, Pentecostalism, and American Culture.* Urbana: University of Illinois Press, 1993.

Poloma, Margaret M. *The Assemblies of God at the Crossroads: Charisma and Institutional Dilemmas.* Knoxville: University of Tennessee Press, 1989.

Atheism

Atheism is the lack of belief in God. Throughout American history, atheism has always been a minority viewpoint. However, the philosophical influence of the **Enlightenment** and its stress on religious toleration and rationality enabled atheism to take on some politically acceptable forms. For instance, he U.S. Constitution forbids **religious tests and oaths** as a condition to hold office, and the **First Amendment's Establishment Clause** specifically prevents the national government from recognizing any denomination as the official religion of the United States. However, despite the prohibition against religious tests to hold public office, every president of the United States, with the possible exception of Ulysses S. Grant, has acknowledged the role of religion in politics in one form or another. This homage (whether false or not) is recognition that religion, or more specifically believing, is an important element in American politics.

Although today most politicians (and most Americans) believe in some sort of deity, the Constitution and the increasingly secular nature of American society mean that atheists are relatively free from persecution. However, this has not always been the case. In the mid-nineteenth century, the secret society of the Masons, an organization many considered atheistic and anti-American, generated much religious and political furor. A short-lived third party movement, the Anti-Masonic Party, formed in New York State with the specific goal of limiting the political influence of Masons. Other nineteenth-century groups, like the transcendentalists and the communitarians, were also suspect to many orthodox Christians.

After the **Civil War**, the rise of Darwinian social science resulted in the growing acceptance of atheism in the form of **secular humanism**. Influential thinkers like **John Dewey** were at liberty to issue documents like the **Humanist Manifesto**, which minimized God's role in human affairs. However, in the early twentieth century, the 1925 **Scopes Trial** in Tennessee and the growing debate over **evolution** signalled an increasing struggle between rationalist science and the traditional Judeo-Christian values of the United States.

In the last half of the twentieth century, tension between believers and non-believers has largely focused around Supreme Court rulings in the areas of church-state relations, **abortion**, and other questions of morality. Atheists, who were strong supporters of the high wall of separation of church and state, have suffered some defeats as the Court has again chosen to recognize that the United States is fundamentally a religious nation. **See also** Anti-Masonic Movement; Communitarianism; Freemasonry; Transcendentalism.

Bibliography

Truner, James. *Without God, Without Creed.* Baltimore: Johns Hopkins University Press, 1985.

B

Isaac Backus (1724–1806)

Isaac Backus was an American clergyman who helped define the policies of separation of church and state in the new nation. Under the influence of the **First Great Awakening,** Backus abandoned **Congregationalism** to become a **Baptist** and served as pastor of the First Baptist Church of Middleborough, Massachusetts, from 1756 until his death in 1806. He believed that the United States should be both Christian and Protestant and his defense of liberty of conscience before the **Continental Congress** and in subsequent writings helped shape the definitions of religious freedom in the Massachusetts state constitution and the U.S. Constitution. (AOT)

Bibliography

Grenz, Stanley. *Isaac Backus—Puritan & Baptist: His Place in History, His Thoughts, & the Implications for Modern Baptist Theology*. Macon, GA: Mercer University Press, 1983.

McLoughlin, William G. *Soul Liberty: The Baptist Struggle in New England, 1630-1833*. Hanover, NH: Brown University Press, 1991.

Leonard Bacon (1802–1881)

A Congregational preacher and church historian, Leonard Bacon was active in many social reform causes. He supported the gradual emancipation and recolonization of African Americans to Liberia. He also spoke out against abolitionists and their tactics. After the **Civil War** he became a leader in the **temperance** movement. (MWP) **See also** Abolition; Congregationalism; Slavery.

Bibliography

Bacon, Leonard. *Leonard Bacon: A Statesman in the Church.* New Haven, CT: Yale University Press, 1931.

Bacon, Leonard. *A Plea for Africa.* 1825.

Robert Baird (1798–1863)

A Presbyterian clergyman and religious historian, Robert Baird is best known for his epic work *Religion in America*, which exhaustively chronicles the development of religious groups in the United States. As general agent of the **American Sunday School Union**, he established thousands of such schools. Traveling in Europe, he promoted **temperance** and Protestant unity. (MWP)

Bibliography

Baird, Henry M. *Life of the Rev. Robert Baird*. New York: A. D. F. Randolph, 1866.

Baird, Robert. *Religion in America*. New York: Harper and Brothers, 1856.

Hosea Ballou (1771–1852)

A leader in New England's Universialist Church, Hosea Ballou believed that everyone would go to heaven, denied the Trinity and Original Sin, and claimed that Christ died merely to demonstrate God's love. Emphasizing reason in understanding faith, he was a leading advocate of religious liberalism. (MWP)

Bibliography

Cassara, Ernest. *Universalism in America.* Boston: Beacon Press, 1971.

Douglas Leighton Bandow (1957–)

Douglas Bandow writes on politics and social policy from the perspective of a Christian libertarian. In his *The Politics of Envy*, he criticized attempts to substitute an enlarged government for God. He served in the Reagan administration as a special assistant for policy development and is currently with the Cato Institute. (MWP) **See also** Ronald Reagan.

Bibliography

Bandow, Douglas L. *The Politics of Envy.* New Brunswick, NJ: Transaction, 1994.

Baptists

Baptists are established worldwide, particularly in Russia, Nigeria, Kenya, Liberia, Brazil, and English-speaking nations. The Baptist Church successfully promoted religious freedom in England as well as in the United States and is the largest Protestant body in the U.S. Best understood by reference to shared ideas rather than organizations, Baptists have maintained their individualism while adhering to key principles since the early **Reformation**. Their best-known doctrines reserve baptism for believers and define immersion as its only acceptable form. Both baptism and the Lord's Supper are considered symbols. Adherents claim that relying on God's promise rather than one's own merits assures salvation. Belief in soul liberty and the priesthood of all believers, explains their avoidance of creeds and opposition to any authority other than scripture for religious matters. Church governance is local; congregations may unite for common goals in associations or conventions but such organizations remain voluntary.

Accounts of Baptist origins include claims to continuity with an unbroken succession of churches from the first century, roots among sixteenth-century Anabaptists, or beginnings within **Puritan** separatism. English persecution of religious dissenters led to the first identifiable Baptist churches in the Netherlands (1608) and two years later in London. Baptists grew rapidly during the next 50 years despite dividing over **Calvinism**. Both branches supported Oliver Cromwell's revolution and consequently faced severe persecution after the Stuart restoration until the Glorious Revolution of 1688.

Baptist growth in the American colonies mirrored English developments, but colonial isolation from authority also fostered indigenous movements. From beginnings in **Rhode Island** in 1638, credited to either **Roger Williams** or **John Clarke**, Baptists were soon to be found in every colony, and the **First Great Awakening** made them a leading denomination and political force. They were especially successful in the South and on frontiers where their democratic practices and flexibility were uniquely suited for scattered populations. Severe harassment in Virginia and Massachusetts produced leaders such as **John Leland** and **Isaac Backus,** who helped shape state and national constitutional provisions calling for separation of church and state during and after the **American Revolution**.

A call for American Baptist support of missions to India led to the formation of the General Missionary Convention of the Baptist Denomination in the United States for Foreign Missions in 1814. This early expression of unity was strengthened by societies promoting publications, home missions (including significant steps to Christianize Native Americans), and Bible distribution. The **slavery** question and other issues produced a division and the formation of the **Southern Baptist Convention** in 1845. Northern churches continued under society structures until 1907 and the establishment of the organization presently known as the American Baptist Churches, USA. **African-American churches** began forming after the **Civil War**, establishing the National Baptist Convention of America in 1880. The convention divided in 1907; the smaller segment retained the original name while the larger incorporated as the National Baptist Convention, USA. Both Southern and American Baptists also continued to divide through the last 100 years, spawning new Baptist groups to add to those that were defined locally or by ethnic identities. Today, Baptist groups include the Regular, Swedish, Free Will, Landmark, Seventh Day, and Two Seed-in-the-Spirit Predestinarian Baptists, with numerous other groups and thousands of unaffiliated congregations.

Most of the groups organized since 1900 were due to **fundamentalist** opposition to perceived modernist tendencies in larger conventions. In contrast, Baptists such as **Walter Rauschenbusch** led liberal church movements in the early twentieth century. While Baptists were typically isolated from national movements—other than fundamentalism—this never meant an abandonment of social goals or localized political efforts. While promoting the spread of colleges and orphanages, they also focused on moral issues—most notably, **temperance and prohibition** and anti-**evolution** campaigns—in state and local politics. A Baptist minister, **Martin Luther King, Jr.**, provided moral and political leadership for the civil rights movement. Currently, Baptists are in the forefront of campaigns opposing **abortion**, advocating **school prayer**, and promoting other social changes. Since 1939, numerous Baptist bodies have joined to support the Baptist Joint Committee on Public Affairs, which lobbies for separation of church and state and similar concerns in Washington, D.C. (AOT)

Bibliography

Barnes, Irwin. *Truth Is Immortal: The Story of Baptists in Europe.* New York: Attic Press, 1950.

Brackney, William H. *The Baptists.* Westport CT: Greenwood, 1994.

Clarke, John & McLoughlin, William G. *Colonial Baptists: Massachusetts & Rhode Island.* Stratford, NH: Ayer, 1980.

Dawson, Joseph M. *Baptists & the American Republic.* Stratford, NH: Ayer, 1980.

George, Timothy & George, Denise, eds. *Baptist Confessions, Covenants, & Catechisms.* Nashville: Broadman, 1996.

Goodwin, Everrett C., ed. *Baptists in the Balance: The Tension Between Freedom & Responsibility.* New York: Judson, 1997.

McBeth, Leon. *Baptist Heritage.* Nashville: Broadman, 1987.

McLoughlin, William G. *New England Dissent, 1630–1833: The Baptists & the Separation of Church & State.* 2 vols. Cambridge, MA: Harvard University Press, 1971.

Torbet, Robert G. *A History of the Baptists.* New York: Judson, 1973.

Robert Barclay (1648–1690)

Robert Barclay was a leading **Quaker** theologian and advocate of religious liberty. He joined the Society of Friends in 1667 and was frequently imprisoned for his beliefs and practices. Befriended by the Duke of York, who would later become King James II, Barclay, along with other Quakers, including **William Penn**, was given title to land in East Jersey (present-day New Jersey). Barclay's *Apology for the True Christian Divinity* (1676) contains a classic expression of the Christian grounds against religious persecution. (MWP)

Bibliography

Freiday, Dean, ed. *Barclay's Apology in Modern English.* Newberg, OR: The Barclay Press, 1967.

Trueblood, Elton. *Robert Barclay.* New York, Harper & Row, 1967.

Samuel June Barrows (1845–1909)

A reporter, then a Unitarian clergyman, Samuel Barrows' most lasting impact concerned prison reform. Beginning in 1905, he served as International Prison Commissioner for the United States, bringing many European ideas about prison construction to this country. He also played a major role in enacting a federal parole system. (MWP) **See also** Prisoners, Religious Rights of; Unitarianism.

Bibliography

Barrows, Isabel C. *A Sunny Life, The Biography of Samuel June Barrows.* Boston: Little, Brown, and Co., 1913.

Clarissa Harlowe Barton (1821–1912)

During both the U.S. **Civil War** and the Crimean War, Clara Barton worked to improve the hospital conditions and medical treatment of wounded soldiers. A woman of great charity and mercy, she convinced U.S. officials to join the Swiss-based Red Cross, an international relief organization founded in 1863. In 1881, she became the American Red Cross's first president. (MWP)

BIBLIOGRAPHY

Barton, Clara. *The Red Cross: A History.* 1898.

———. *The Story of the Red Cross.* 1904.

Ross, Ishbel. *Angel of the Battlefield.* New York: Harper, 1956.

Gary Bauer (1946–)

Gary Bauer is the president of the Family Research Council, a group that promotes conservative family values. Born in Covington, Kentucky, he earned his B.A. degree from Georgetown College and a law degree from Georgetown University. In the 1970s, he was director of research for the Republican National Committee, and in the 1980s he served in a number of positions in the Reagan administration before eventually becoming chairman of the White House Working Group on the Family from 1987 to 1988. Bauer became president of the Family Research Council in 1988, and frequently appears in the national media as a spokesperson for conservative family values. **See also** Conservatism; Ronald Reagan; Religious Right; Republican Party.

BIBLIOGRAPHY

Bauer, Gary. *Our Hopes—Our Dreams: A Vision for America.* Colorado Springs, CO: Focus on the Family, 1996.

Dobson, James and Gary Bauer. *Children at Risk.* Nashville: Word, 1992.

Becker Amendment

The Becker amendment was proposed by New York Congressman Frank Becker after the U.S. Supreme Court issued its decisions banning prayer (1962) and Bible reading (1963) in public schools. The amendment would have permitted voluntary prayer and Bible reading in all schools. While the amendment had strong support initially, this support waned after religious leaders disagreed over whether including or excluding religion was coercive. (MWP) **See also** School Prayer.

BIBLIOGRAPHY

Green, Steven K. "Evangelicals and the Becker Amendment." *Journal of Church and State* 33 (Summer 1991): 541-67.

Catherine Beecher (1800–1878)

One of Congregational (later **Presbyterian**) minister **Lyman Beecher**'s 13 children, Catherine Beecher was raised a strict Calvinist. Although she abandoned some of **Calvinism**'s harsher doctrines, she never rejected the core of her father's evangelical beliefs. Her religious convictions led her to embrace a concept of domesticity wherein women were to submit to their husbands, focus on their families, and attempt to reform society through education.

A prolific and influential author, Beecher spread her view of domesticity through her significant and popular work, *A Treatise on Domestic Economy* (1841), which went through 14 editions and later became the basis for the influential *The American Woman's Home* (1869), co-authored with **Harriet Beecher Stowe**.

Beecher also believed that women should help reform society by serving as schoolteachers. Toward this end she founded the Hartford Female Seminary in 1823 and the Western Female Institute in Cincinnati, Ohio, in 1832. Unlike many female academies of the time, Beecher's schools provided young women with solid academic educations.

Convinced of the need to train and send teachers to the American frontier, Beecher founded the Central Committee for Promoting National Education in 1843 and the American Woman's Educational Association in 1852. Both organizations contributed significantly to the professionalization of teaching and to the substantial increase in the number of female teachers in the nineteenth century. (MDH) **See also** Edward Beecher; Henry Ward Beecher; Congregationalism.

BIBLIOGRAPHY

Sklar, Katheryn Kish. *Catherine Beecher: A Study in American Domesticity.* New York: W. W. Norton, 1976.

Edward Beecher (1803–1895)

The son of **Lyman Beecher** and a member of the illustrious Beecher family, Edward Beecher was a vocal and influential abolitionist. He used his post as editor of *The Congregationalist* (1849–1853) to reject the recolonization of African Americans in favor of evangelical **abolition**. He also warned against the dangers of **Roman Catholicism** to the United States. (MWP) **See also** Catherine Beecher; Henry Ward Beecher; Evangelicals; Harriot Beecher Stowe.

BIBLIOGRAPHY

Beecher, Edward. *Narrative of Riots at Alton.* 1838.

Beecher, Edward. *The Papal Conspiracy Exposed.* 1855.

Merideth, Robert. *The Politics of the Universe: Edward Beecher, Abolition and Orthodoxy.* Nashville: Nelson, 1963.

Henry Ward Beecher (1813–1887)

A widely acclaimed nineteenth-century preacher, Henry Ward Beecher articulated the vision and the values of the emerging urban middle class. His sermons coupled the issues of **slavery**, immigration, women's rights, and political reform with a romantic Christianity that emphasized God's love and human self-control. He trumpeted the American themes of individualism, **democracy**, self-help, and progress as reasons for optimism in the face of increased urban violence. He opposed the theater and other urban entertainments, and emphasized the importance of the family, school, and church as organizations charged with teaching good habits and enforcing social standards.

Although opposed to socialist politics and liberal theology, he shared many of the concerns of the **Social Gospel** movement, and condemned the corrupt tax practices of city politicians that exacerbated the hardships of the working poor. He also worked tirelessly to eradicate slavery. Following the passage of the Kansas-Nebraska Act of 1854, he raised money from the pulpit to purchase rifles—dubbed "Beecher's Bibles"—for abolitionists on the Great Plains. He believed that the South's leaders would be condemned by God on the final judgment day, and was an avid supporter of President Andrew Johnson's Union Restoration plan following the **Civil War**. (KMY) **See also** Abolition; Catherine Beecher; Edward Beecher; Lyman Beecher; Reconstruction; Harriot Beecher Stowe.

Bibliography

Clark, Clifford E. *Henry Ward Beecher: Spokesman for a Middle-Class America.* Chicago: University of Illinois Press, 1978.

Lyman Beecher (1775–1863)

Lyman Beecher was an influential Congregational and **Presbyterian** minister who championed many political and religious causes and actively opposed the growing **Unitarianism** of his day. After the death of **Alexander Hamilton** in a duel with Aaron Burr, Beecher led an anti-dueling campaign. He also opposed the **disestablishment** of the Congregational Church in Connecticut in 1818, but later came to think of disestablishment as advantageous to religion. In 1832, he became president of Lane Theological Seminary in Cincinnati, Ohio. In 1835, Beecher published *A Plea for the West,* in which he bemoaned the increase in Catholic settlements. He was tried for heresy the same year because of his moderate Calvinism, but was acquitted. Many of his 13 children would also be influential in religion and politics, especially his daughter **Harriet Beecher Stowe**, author of ***Uncle Tom's Cabin***. **See also** Catherine Beecher; Edward Beecher; Henry Ward Beecher; Congregationalism; Roman Catholicism.

Lyman Beecher, an influential and controversial minister, championed many religious and political causes. Engraving by L. E. Wagstaff and J. Andrews. Library of Congress.

Bibliography

Caskey, Marie. *Chariot of Fire.* New Haven CT: Yale University Press, 1978.

Cross, Barbara, ed. *The Autobiography of Lyman Beecher.* Cambridge, MA: Belknap Press, 1961.

Bernard Iddings Bell (1886–1958)

Born in Dayton, Ohio, Bernard I. Bell was educated at the University of Chicago (B.A., 1907), Western Theological Seminary (S.T.B., 1912), and The University of the South (S.T.D., 1923). Bell also later received numerous honorary degrees. In college, Bell temporarily rejected his **Episcopal Church** upbringing. Under the influence of a local Catholic priest and his reading of G. K. Chesterton's *Orthodoxy*, Bell returned to a belief in the classic, consensual tradition of Christianity, and spent the remainder of his life defending such a faith. Ordained a priest in the Episcopal Church in 1910, he served as vicar and dean of a midwestern Episcopal church and cathedral until his appointment in 1919 as warden (president) of St. Stephen's College (now Bard College) in New York State, a position he held until 1933. As a college president, Bell demonstrated an unusual propensity for spiritual and administrative leadership. During the last three years of his tenure at St. Stephen's, Bell also taught at Columbia University in New York City.

The remainder of Bell's life was devoted to the religious training of adults. He served as a canon (i.e., a member of the regular clerical staff) of St. John's Cathedral in Providence, Rhode Island, from 1933 to 1946, and as a canon of the Cathedral of Saints Peter and Paul and St. James Cathedral Church in Chicago. He also served as a consultant on education to the Episcopal bishop of Chicago, and as a highly popular and influential preacher and lecturer throughout the country.

The author of over 20 books, Bell believed the future of the West depended upon reclaiming the virtues of the Christian life. As a gifted man of letters, Bell attempted to relate the Christian faith to his contemporaries in a "postmodernist" United States, a term that Bell used to describe a renewal of doubt about the accepted ideological formulations of American social, religious, and political life. **See also** Roman Catholicism. (HLC)

Bibliography

Bell, Bernard Iddings. *Beyond Agnosticism.* New York: Harper and Brothers, 1929.

Robert Bellah (1927–)

Robert Bellah, a professor of sociology at the University of California (Berkeley), is known for his works on **civil religion**. His works warn prophetically about unrestrained individualism destroying American society. Rejecting "value-free" approaches to sociology, he has argued for a greater valuation of culture, in particular religion, as an integrating social force. His scholarly interest in civil religion blossomed during the **Vietnam War** era as he noted the similarities between popular cultural expressions such as the celebration of the "American Way of Life" (the blessings of freedom, individualism, Christianity, **democracy**, and **capitalism**) and religious ritual. Bellah continued his critique in his bestselling *Habits of the Heart* (1985). (ISM)

BIBLIOGRAPHY

Bellah, Robert. *Broken Covenant: American Civil Religion in Time of Trial.* New York: Seabury Press, 1975.

———. "Public Philosophy and Public Theology in America Today." Leroy S. Rourner, ed. *Civil Religion and Political Theology.* Notre Dame, IN: University of Notre Dame, 1986, 79-97.

Bellah, Robert, Steve Tipton et al. *Habits of the Heart: Individualism in American Life.* Berkeley: University of California Press, 1985.

Edward Bellamy (1850–1898)

Edward Bellamy was a successful author and leading spokesman for the **Social Gospel** movement who turned his attention to **social justice** in his 1887 utopian novel, *Looking Backward, 2000–1887*. In this novel, Bellamy describes the U.S. in the year 2000, when everyone lives in "God's kingdom of fraternal equality." The success of the book led Bellamy to pursue projects in an effort to aid the realization of his Christian socialist view. The book widely influenced the Populist Party platform in 1892. (MWP) **See also** Socialism and Communism; Utopianism.

BIBLIOGRAPHY

McClay, Wilfred M. "Edward Bellamy and the Politics of Meaning." *Current* 375 (September 1995): 31-37.

Samuels, Warren J. "A Literary Reconsideration of Bellamy's *Looking Backward*." *The American Journal of Economics and Sociology* 43 (April 1984): 130-48.

Ezra T. Benson (1899–1994)

President of the **Church of Jesus Christ of Latter-day Saints** from 1985 through 1994, Ezra Benson was active in conservative politics throughout his life, and served as U.S. secretary of agriculture in the Eisenhower administration. His *Crossfire: The Eight Years with Eisenhower* (1962) is characteristic of his conservative views. (MEN) **See also** Dwight D. Eisenhower.

BIBLIOGRAPHY

Dew, Sheri L. *Ezra Taft Benson: A Biography.* Salt Lake City: Desert Book Co., 1987.

Joseph Bernardin (1928–1996)

Cardinal Joseph Bernardin was Archbishop of Cincinnati, and then of Chicago and was known as a conciliatory figure in the American Catholic Church. As a Church leader, he sought common ground among various factions within Catholicism, and between the Church and the secular world.

Bernardin was an active participant in the **National Conference of Catholic Bishops (NCCB)**, and was its president from 1974 to 1977. He headed the NCCB committee that produced the pastoral letter, ***The Challenge of Peace: God's Promise and Our Response*** (1989). In this document, the NCCB sought to lay out the moral imperatives relevant to the conduct of modern warfare, and was sharply critical of the nuclear arms race.

Bernardin was perhaps best known for his championing of the concept of "A Consistent Ethic of Life," which held that Church teachings on war, **abortion**, contraception, **capital punishment**, and economics were all part of a single gestalt, and constituted a "seamless garment." Thus, Catholics were called upon to be "pro-life" in all areas of social and political life, and were encouraged to apply the same affirmation and celebration of life to all areas of human endeavor. This idea constituted an attempt to bridge the gap between liberals and conservatives and encourage practical responses to wide-ranging political and social issues. (TGJ) **See also** Conservatism; Liberalism; Nuclear Disarmament; Roman Catholicism.

BIBLIOGRAPHY

Kennedy, Eugene. *Bernardin: Life to the Full.* New York: Bonus, 1997.

Daniel Berrigan (1921–)

Born Irish Catholic, Daniel Berrigan entered the Jesuit order in 1939 and received his ordination in 1952. His commitment to aggressive **pacifism** came during the **Vietnam War,** when under the influence of his brother, **Philip Berrigan**, he became a member of Clergy Concerned about Vietnam. (MWP) **See also** Roman Catholicism.

BIBLIOGRAPHY

Berrigan, Daniel. *To Dwell in Peace: An Autobiography.* San Francisco: Harper & Row, 1987.

Philip Berrigan (1923–)

Born into a large Irish-American family, Philip Berrigan fought in **World War II** but became an aggressive pacifist during the late 1950s under the influence of the Fellowship of Reconciliation. Like his older brother **Daniel Berrigan**, he is best known for his protests against the **Vietnam War**. (MWP) **See also** Pacificism; Roman Catholicism.

BIBLIOGRAPHY

Berrigan. Philip. *Fighting the Lamb's War.* Monroe, ME: Common Courage Press, 1996.

Mary McLeod Bethune (1875–1955)

Mary McLeod Bethune, an African-American and Christian educator and **civil rights** advocate, was president and founder of a school for girls in Daytona Beach, Florida, which became Bethune-Cookman College. She also founded a human rights organization, the National Council of Negro Women and was appointed as special advisor on minority affairs to Franklin D. Roosevelt. (WVM)

BIBLIOGRAPHY

Wolfe, Rinna E. *Mary McLeod Bethune.* Franklin Watts, 1992.

Bible Belt

The term Bible Belt was a derogatory label coined by **H.L. Mencken** in the 1920s. Mencken applied the term to areas of the country that were dominated by people who believed the Bible was literally true. While Mencken did not assign a specific geographic area to the term, he did use it for the rural areas of the Midwest and the South. He once designated Jackson, Mississippi, as "the heart of the Bible and Lynching Belt."

The origins of the Bible Belt can be traced to the evangelical nature of the early settlers of the backcountry of Virginia, North Carolina, and South Carolina. Mostly Methodists, Presbyterians, and **Baptists**, and combining antebellum evangelism with the cultural Puritanism of New England, these settlers moved west to escape the Anglican domination of the coastal communities.

In modern application, the term refers to a path that runs across the country from the Atlantic seaboard through Texas and eastern New Mexico. Its borders are formed on the north by the state lines of Virginia, Kentucky, Missouri, and Oklahoma. Within this belt, conservative churches dominate religious, social, and political life. Therefore, public policy makers and politicians who want to appeal to these areas must be well versed in the Bible and generally must take conservative views, akin to those held by the dominant Southern Baptists, on social and political issues.

Although the economic relocation of millions of Americans has brought a growing religious diversity to the South, a deep-seated southern subculture still regards the Bible as the best (if not only) guide to life and politics. However, the influence of the Bible Belt is clearly not as strong as it was 25 years ago. The continuing movement of populations and the growth of southern cities will likely continue to weaken this American subculture. **See also** Conservatism; Evangelicals; Methodism; Presbyterian Church; Puritans; Southern Baptist Convention.

Bibliography

Cornfield, Michael. "What the Beltway Could Learn from the Bible Belt." *Washington Monthly* 22, no.11 (December 1990): 50-53.

Heyrman, Christine L. *Southern Cross: The Beginnings of the Bible Belt*. New York: Knopf, 1998.

Lord, Lewis J. "New Strains on Dixie's Bible Belt." *US News and World Report* 99 (December 9, 1985): 59.

Mencken, H.L. *Prejudices: Sixth Series*. New York: Octagon, 1977.

Reed, John Shelton. *The Enduring South*. Chapel Hill: University of North Carolina Press, 1986.

Biotechnology

Powerful new biotechnological techniques developed in recent decades have provoked significant theological concern in the United States. Yet the traditional wisdom of organized religion, oriented to technologically simpler times, is often silent or oblique about the anxieties to which these new technologies give rise—the Talmud prescribes codes and laws for many things, to be sure, but recombinant DNA is not among them. Among religious activists there has been hesitation in advancing a broad political agenda in response to rapid gains in biotechnological acumen. Certain religious groups have strong opinions about particular biotechnologies, but there is no consensus among religious bodies about the disposition government should demonstrate toward research and development in this field, and thus there has been comparatively little organized and effective political action in the pursuit of policy goals.

The term "biotechnology" is itself a broad umbrella, used loosely to mean the manipulation of living things, from the leavening of bread to the cloning of the baker. In debate, however, the term generally signifies the dramatic new recombinant DNA technologies developed in the mid-1970s and 1980s, tools that ushered in an era of intense moral debate and speculation.

Genetic engineering moved beyond the realm of imagination when geneticists developed techniques to cut a copy of a segment of DNA containing a gene and paste it into another segment of DNA. The DNA segment can be taken from any organism and transferred into any other, where it remains, in principle, active and inheritable. It is thus now possible to place a basset hound's genes into a bacterium, and vice-versa. The watershed year was 1977, when a man-made gene was used to manufacture a human protein in a bacteria. Breakthrough upon breakthrough followed. In 1978, Genentech, Inc. and The City of Hope National Medical Center announced the laboratory production of human insulin using recombinant DNA technology. In 1978, Stanford University scientists successfully transplanted a mammalian gene, and in 1979, the gene for human growth hormone was cloned. In 1981, researchers at Ohio University produced the first transgenic animals by transferring genes from other animals into mice. Sophisticated selection and breeding tools were concomitantly developed, as were techniques such as chromosome analysis, which is used, for example, to diagnose Down's Syndrome. Technological competence grew exponentially. Tissue culture techniques used in plant propagation and in the production of drugs such as penicillin and monoclonal antibodies were perfected, as were techniques for DNA analysis used in DNA fingerprinting and in massive DNA sequencing efforts such as the Human Genome Project.

What, precisely, does all this entail? No one concerned with human well-being could fail to be optimistic about some of the prospects these techniques suggest. New genes and genetically altered plant and animal species provide hope for the treatment of fatal or crippling human diseases. Biotechnology also offers less spectacular but significant possibilities, such as the production of crops resistant to pests and inclement weather. Milk production has, for example, been augmented by the administration of genetically engineered hormones to cows.

Obviously, however, there are profoundly rebarbative ethical and theological ramifications to biotechnological techniques such as cloning, inserting human genes into other species, xenografting organs, releasing altered microbes into the environment, or using fetal brain cells to treat adult diseases. The implications of this new technology raise immediate concerns: Will the new enterprises of genetic modification undermine our conception of ourselves and other species? Will tampering with nature's genetic disposition give rise to the manipulation of animals for commodification and the genetic manipulation of humans? The specter of genetic monsters let loose, interfering with the fundamental processes and rhythms of nature, gives pause to ponder.

Policy makers in the United States have been something less than cohesive and vigorous in response to these questions. In 1974, in the wake of an outpouring of public concern about biotechnological research on human subjects, Congress established the National Commission for the Protection of Human Subjects of Biomedical and Behavioral Research, and in 1977, 16 bills were introduced in Congress to regulate recombinant DNA research. None passed. A Presidential Ethical Advisory Board, established in 1978, was charged with considering the question of federal funding for research on in vitro fertilization. The Board's recommendation that such research be funded met strong opposition from the Right-to-Life movement; as a result, proposals to provide research funding for the biotechnology associated with assisted reproduction, particularly in vitro fertilization, failed. When a fetal transplantation panel was formed in the 1990s, the ethical debate was starkly polarized, and although the panel voted 19 to 2 for government support for research into treating patients with Parkinson's disease and diabetes, the minority prevailed until the next presidential election. A subsequent Human Embryo Research Panel formed to advise the National Institute of Health met a similar fate; the majority panel report, in favor of funding such research, was rejected. In Congress, an Ethics Advisory Board on biotechnology, with equal representation from the House and Senate and the two parties, foundered over balancing members of appropriate religions and viewpoints on the status of fetal life. The committee languished, ultimately disbanding over its irreconcilable differences.

In the political realm, ethics must be considered in tandem with economics. By the year 2000, the biotechnology industry is projected to have sales reaching $50 billion in the United States, with obvious significance for the economy and the employment rate. Biotechnology-related industry in the United States is characterized by close linkage to its research base; over the past three decades, with research support from the federal government, the United States has become the international leader in biotechnology research, development, and commercialization.

This matter-of-fact commercialization has been a source of particular concern to religious activists. The United States Supreme Court ruled in *Diamond v. Chakrabarty*, 447 U.S. 303 (1980), that genetically altered life forms could be patented, opening enormous possibilities for the commercial exploitation of genetic engineering. A concert of religious groups began lobbying the United States Patent Office to cease issuing patents protecting new gene developments, and issued a manifesto demanding a change in patent policy. Educational campaigns in synagogues and churches were coordinated to raise political awareness of the issue. Should gene patenting become a priority on the political agendas of various conservative religious groups, Republican politicians, who have generally been the beneficiaries of their support, will certainly take notice. This would be a significant development; the absence of patent protection would make it impossible for private firms to raise capital, and reduce the necessary research investments required to pursue promising biotechnological solutions.

Theologically speaking, cloning is the biotechnological technique now receiving the highest profile, with concerns often voiced about the putative violation of the dignity and uniqueness of the individual and the instrumental attitude towards human beings such experimentation necessarily implies. The threat of abuses of new cloning techniques has figured conspicuously in religious tracts and pronouncements, particularly those of the Catholic Church.

On February 23, 1997, Dolly the sheep, the world's first mammal cloned from an adult cell, was presented to the world, bleating peaceably before a chaos of snapping camera shutters. The unprecedented media excitement surrounding the event did not always result in balanced or nuanced coverage and debate. Claims about rapid progress towards human cloning should be treated with skepticism; Dolly's patrimony is far from clear. Nonetheless, in 1998, a little-known American physicist announced his intention to create cloned human beings for U.S. infertility clinics. Instant national queasiness ensued, with the executive branch moving swiftly to introduce countervailing legislation.

While organized religion has yet to make a pronounced impact on the politics of biotechnology, this is almost sure to change if certain techniques, now merely hypothetical, become commonplace. Religious authorities are unlikely to remain on the sidelines where matters of such profound human significance as cloning and the genetic manipulation of humans are concerned. As biotechnology develops, political and religious groups will almost certainly raise these issues to the tops of their agenda. If religious activism in issues such as **abortion** and **euthanasia** is anything to go by, this will result in a significant pressure on United States policy, although what form this pressure will take is not yet clear. (CB)

Bibliography

Kimbrell, Andrew. *The Human Body Shop: The Engineering and Marketing of Life.* San Francisco: HarperSanFrancisco, 1993.

Rifkin, Jeremy. *The Biotech Century.* New York: Putnam, 1998.

Smith, George Patrick. *The New Biology: Law, Ethics and Biotechnology.* New York: Plenum Press, 1989.

Spallone, Patricia. *Generation Games: Genetic Engineering and the Future for Our Lives.* Philadelphia: Temple University Press, 1992.

Thobaben, Robert G. *Issues in American Political Life: Money, Violence, and Biology.* Englewood Cliffs, NJ: Prentice Hall, 1991.

Webber, David J. *Biotechnology: Assessing Social Impacts and Policy Implications.* New York: Greenwood Press, 1990.

Black Theology

Black Theology, as a specifically African-American development in response to white racism, is to be distinguished from two other forms of theology, African Theology and **Liberation Theology**. The former developed from indigenous African conceptions as a response to European colonialism and served in part to express Christianity in African terms. The latter emerged from in Latin America from Gustavo Gutierrez's *Theology of Liberation* (1971), which emphasized human dignity and the socio-political forces that oppress the poor. Black Theology seeks to deal with the ethical and theological implications of the black experience. It uses elements from both of these contemporary theologies in describing the black situation in the United States.

Black Theology emerged as the **civil rights** movement, after the assassination of Dr. **Martin Luther King, Jr.**, faced both the challenge of more radical black leaders (**Malcolm X** and Black Power leaders) and the realization that racist attitudes could be more easily changed than the economic and social forces that dominated society. The first expressions of Black Theology are found in the 1966 Statement by the National Committee of the Negro Churches and in **Albert Cleague**'s *Black Messiah* (1969) and **James Cone**'s *Black Theology and Black Power* (1969).

These works argued that blackness describes a condition of social, economic, and political powerlessness and that theology's task is to analyze such conditions, locate the source of these conditions in the white world, and prepare blacks for revolutionary action in overcoming their situation. Such a definition of theology and blackness explains why Jesus can be described as black, for he is one who also experienced suffering, powerlessness, and death. Black Theology was a sharp indictment of traditional Christianity, but in its attempts to describe and valorize the black experience, it runs the danger of becoming the mirror-image of white nationalism and racism. Unfortunately, Black Theology in the United States, though connected to and with African theologies and Latin American liberation theologies, has largely remained in academic enclaves and has not reached the majority of black churchgoers, though its radical political implications disturbed many white churchgoers and its proponents when viewed as threats to national security. (ISM) **See also** African-American Churches.

Bibliography

Baker-Fletcher, Garth. *Somebodyness: Martin Luther King Jr., and the Theory of Dignity.* Minneapolis, MN: Fortress Press, 1993.

Cone, James H. *A Black Theology of Liberation.* New York: Orbis, 1970.

Wilmore, Gayraud S. and James H. Cone, eds. *Black Theology: A Documentary History: 1966-1979.* New York: Orbis, 1979.

Young, Joseph U. *Black and African Theologies: Siblings or Distant Cousins?* New York: Orbis, 1986.

Hugo L. Black (1886–1971)

Hugo Black was a U.S. Supreme Court justice from 1937 to 1971. An exponent of the freedoms in the Bill of Rights, he convinced the court that through the Due Process Clause of the **Fourteenth Amendment**, those freedoms limited states as well as the federal government. Black's opinion for the Court in ***Everson v. Board of Education of the Township of Ewing***, 330 U.S. 1 (1947), broadly interpreted prohibitions under the **Establishment Clause** of the **First Amendment,** which erected "a wall of separation between church and state." In ***Engel v. Vitale***, 370 U.S. 370 (1962), Black's opinion barred a state-composed prayer in public schools. (JRV) **See also** School Prayer.

Bibliography

Mauney, Connie Pat. "Justice Black and First Amendment Freedoms: Thirty-Four Influential Years." *The Emporia State Research Studies* 35, no. 2 (1986).

Harry Andrew Blackmun (1908–)

Appointed to the U.S. Supreme Court by **Richard Nixon** in 1970, Harry Blackmun was a "strict constructionist." By the time he retired in 1994, he had changed considerably, opposing **capital punishment** as well as taking liberal positions on many other issues. Blackmun grew up in Minnesota, a boyhood friend of Chief Justice **Warren Burger**, and was educated at Harvard. Blackman practiced and taught law in Minnesota before being appointed to the Court of Appeals in 1959. His most notable decision for the Court was ***Roe v. Wade*** (1983), creating a constitutional right to **abortion**. (JRV)

Harry A. Blackmun, associate justice of the U.S. Supreme Court, wrote the Court's opinion in the landmark *Roe v. Wade* (1973) abortion case. Library of Congress.

Bibliography

A Documentary History of the Legal Aspects of Abortion in the United States: Roe v. Wade. Littleton, CO: F. B. Rothman, 1993.

Blaine Amendment

On August 14, 1875, Representative **James G. Blaine** of Maine submitted a proposed constitutional amendment to Congress that, among other things, declared: "No public property, and no public revenue of . . . the United States, or any State, Territory, District or municipal corporation, shall be appropriated to, or made or used for, the support of any school, educational or other institution, under the control of any religious or anti-religious sect, organization, or denomination." The amendment was approved in the House by a vote of 180 to 7, with 98 not voting, but failed to receive the necessary two-thirds majority in the Senate to send it to the states. Senate votes were cast along party lines: 28 Republicans for, 16 Democrats against, and 27 absent or abstaining.

The Blaine Amendment reflected a growing consensus among Protestants that public education must be free from sectarian control. In large measure, the impetus for such an amendment came from nativist tendencies hostile to the growing Roman Catholic population. As early as 1855, the American or **Know-Nothing Party** had declared that to resist the "corrupting tendencies of the Roman Catholic Church," schools should be "provided by the State, which schools shall be common to all, without distinction of creed or party, and free from any influence or direction of a denominational or partisan character." President Ulysses S. Grant echoed these sentiments in a famous address to the Army of the Tennessee on September 29, 1875.

The spirit of the amendment was taken up by the states. By 1913, 33 states had incorporated into their constitutions provisions forbidding state funding of religious education. A condition of admission to statehood for the western territories was their agreement to provide for the establishment of public schools, "open to all children and free from sectarian control." The non-sectarian reading of the Bible was often exempted from this provision.

The Blaine Amendment briefly re-emerged as an important state issue in the 1960s when New York rewrote its constitution and some suggested the provision prohibiting state funding of religiously directed education be left out of the new document. (ARB) **See also** Nativism; Roman Catholicism.

BIBLIOGRAPHY

Larson, Edward J. "The Blaine Amendment in State Constitutions." In James W. Skillen, ed. *The School-Choice Controversy: What is Constitutional?* Washington, DC: Center for Public Justice, 1993.

Stokes, Anson P. *Church and State in the United States.* Vol. II. New York: Harper & Brothers, 1950.

James G. Blaine (1830–1893)

A leading Republican during the last four decades of the nineteenth century, James Blaine served in the U.S. House of Representatives from 1863 to 1876 and in the U.S. Senate from 1877 until 1881. He barely lost his 1884 bid for the presidency to Democratic candidate **Grover Cleveland**. Blaine's campaign was marred by the anti-Catholic comments of a prominent supporter who characterized the Democratic Party as the party of "rum, Romanism, and rebellion." Benjamin Harrison appointed Blaine as secretary of state in 1888, a post from which he retired in 1892. Particularly interested in improving relations between the countries of the Western hemisphere, Blaine served as the first chairman of the Pan-American Conference in 1889. Blaine is also remembered for his introduction and support for a constitutional amendment—the **Blaine Amendment**—that would have barred any public funds for religious activities. (MWP) **See also** Anti-Catholicism; Roman Catholicism.

James G. Blaine (above), the Republican presidential candidate in 1884, sponsored a constitutional amendment that would have banned any public money for religious activities. Photo by Cosack and Company. Library of Congress.

BIBLIOGRAPHY

Muzzey, David S. *James G. Blaine: A Political Idol of Other Days.* New York: Dodd Mead, 1934

Paul Blanshard (1892–1980)

A liberal journalist who specialized in exposes, Paul Blanshard wrote several widely selling books exposing the alleged threat **Roman Catholicism** posed to American **democracy**. In addition to his anti-Catholic writings, he also wrote in support of **eugenics** and forced sterilization, which at the time were respectable, progressive ideas. (MWP) **See also** Anti-Catholicism.

BIBLIOGRAPHY

Blanshard, Paul. *Personal and Controversial: An Autobiography.* Boston: Beacon, 1973.

Blue Laws

The history of Sunday closing laws, also known as Blue laws, goes back to **colonial America**. Commonly, such laws required the observance of the Christian Sabbath as a day of rest, and the closing of most businesses. Although these laws were originally efforts at promoting church attendance, and more specifically, Christian church attendance, more non-religious arguments for Sunday closing were put forward over time. When the U.S. Supreme Court heard a **First Amendment** challenge to these laws, in *McGowan v. Maryland, 266 U.S. 420* (1961), many states were justifying these laws as necessary not for religious rest but to provide the state with a uniform day of rest. The Court accepted these arguments and ruled that most existing Sunday closing laws were secular rather than religious in character, tending to provide a uniform day of rest for all citizens. The Court found that such laws did not contravene the **Establishment Clause** of the First Amendment. Even though Sunday was a day of significance to Christians, that fact did not prevent the state from using Sunday to achieve its goals in establishing a day of rest. Though sanctioned by the Supreme Court, many states have repealed their Blue laws or scaled them back to encompass only certain activities, such as the sale of liquor. (JM) **See also** Sabbatarianism.

BIBLIOGRAPHY

Solberg, Winton N. *Redeem the Time.* Cambridge, MA: Harvard University Press, 1977.

Stone, Geoffrey R., et al. *Constitutional Law.* Boston: Little, Brown and Company, 1991.

Board of Airport Commissioners of Los Angeles v. Jews for Jesus (1987)

The Board of Airport Commissioners of Los Angeles attempted to ban all soliciting in the central terminal of Los Angeles International Airport, except airport-related communication. The board claimed the airport was not a public forum for free speech purposes and soliciting by groups such as the plaintiffs added to the confusion and disruption of the traveling public. In *Board of Airport Commissioners of Los Angeles v. Jews for Jesus,* 482 U.S. 569 (1987), the U.S. Supreme Court held that an absolute ban on **First Amendment** free speech by a government agency could not conceivably advance a legitimate governmental interest, even if the airport were a non-public forum. (FHJ)

BIBLIOGRAPHY

Reuben, Richard C. "Unanimous Justices Void Rule Banning 'Free Speech Activities' at LAX." *The Los Angeles Daily Journal* 100 (June 16, 1987): 8.

Board of Education of Kiryas Joel Village School District v. Grumet (1994)

The U.S. Supreme Court decided in this case that the creation of a public school district for a particular religious community violated the **Establishment Clause** of the **First Amendment.** The court forbade the state to delegate authority to a group selected on the basis of its religion.

Kiryas Joel is a New York village occupied entirely by practitioners of a strict form of **Judaism**. The New York legislature enacted a separate public school district for special education students following village lines. A taxpayer's suit charged that the act violated the Establishment Clause of the First Amendment.

In *Board of Education of Kiryas Joel Village School District v. Grumet,* 512 U.S. 687 (1994), the Court noted that the legislature knowingly used village lines to favor a religious group. Thus, civil authority followed religious belief, not neutral principles. The court used "the test of neutrality," a departure from most previous cases interpreting the Establishment Clause, which used the ***Lemon* Test.** This case may foreshadow future changes to the *Lemon* Test, but for now it has not been overruled. (JRV)

BIBLIOGRAPHY

Souter, David H. "*Board of Education of Kiryas Joel Village School District v. Louis Grumet et al* [Text of U.S. Supreme Court Decision; JE 27, 1994]." *Journal of Church and State* 36 (Summer 1994): 656-92.

Board of Education of the Westside Community Schools v. Mergens (1990)

The federal **Equal Access Act** makes it unlawful for any public secondary school that receives federal financial assistance, and which allows one or more non-curriculum-related student groups to meet on school premises during non-instructional time, to deny equal access to any students who wish to conduct meetings on similar terms because of religious, political, philosophical, or other content of their speech. In *Board of Education of the Westside Community Schools v. Mergens*, 110 St.Ct. 2356 (1990), the U.S. Supreme Court upheld an **Establishment Clause** challenge to the act, ruling that a prohibition against discrimination on the basis of political as well as religious speech was a permissible secular purpose, and that equal access would not have the effect of conveying a message of government endorsement of religion. The Court stated, "We think that secondary school students are mature enough and are likely to understand that a school does not endorse or support student speech that it merely permits on a nondiscriminatory basis." (JM)

BIBLIOGRAPHY

West, John G., Jr. "The Changing Battle over Religion in the Public Schools." *Wake Forest Law Review* 26 (1991): 2.

Bob Jones University v. United States (1983)

Prior to 1970, the Internal Revenue Service (IRS) granted tax-exempt status to private schools, independent of racial admissions policies, but in that year, the IRS concluded that it could no longer justify allowing tax-exempt status to private schools that practiced racial discrimination. Bob Jones University, which allowed the enrollment of unmarried blacks but denied admission to applicants engaged in an interracial marriage or known to advocate interracial marriage or dating, had its tax-exempt status revoked following this change. The university brought suit against the IRS for exceeding its powers and violating the **Free Exercise Clause** of the **First Amendment**. *In Bob Jones University v. United States*, 461 U.S. 574 (1983), the U.S. Supreme Court ruled that the university did not qualify as a tax-exempt organization, stating that "tax exemption depends on meeting certain common-law standards of charity—namely, that an institution seeking tax-exempt status must serve a public purpose and not be contrary to established public policy." To warrant exemption, "an institution . . . must demonstrably serve and be in harmony with the public interest, and the institution's purpose must not be so at odds with the common community conscience as to undermine any public benefit that might otherwise be conferred." (JM)

BIBLIOGRAPHY

Miller, R. Charles. "Rendering Unto Caesar." *University of Pennsylvania Law Review* 134, no. 2 (January 1986); 433-56.

Pepper, Stephen. "A Brief for the Free Exercise Clause." *The Journal of Law and Religion* 7, no. 2 (Summer 1989): 323-62.

Born-Again Christians

Born-again Christians report a conversion experience whereby they accept Jesus Christ as their Lord and Savior. The term "born again" refers to Jesus's response to Nicodemus in John 3:3: "I tell you the truth, no one can see the kingdom of God unless he is born again." While born-again Christians are a diverse group and represent roughly one-third of the population, the term is generally associated with **Evangelical** Protestants who reject the idea that a person is naturally born into a religion but instead must make a conscious choice to accept Christ's lordship. Being born again is regarded as a life changing experience whereby one enters into a personal relationship with Christ and seeks to follow his commands.

Public and political focus on born-again Christians increased in 1976, in what *Time* magazine declared the year of the born-again Christian. Presidential candidate **Jimmy Carter** announced he was a **Baptist** and born-again Christian. **Ronald Reagan**, from a **fundamentalist** background, and President **Gerald Ford** made similar pronouncements. (DD)

BIBLIOGRAPHY

Jorstad, Erling. *Evangelicals in the White House: The Cultural Maturation of Born Again Christians, 1960–1981.* New York: Edwin Mellon Press, 1982.

M(elvin) E(ustace) Bradford (1934–1993)

A Southern Baptist and a professor of English, M.E. Bradford attempted to explain the motivations and intentions of the framers of the U.S. Constitution, as well as to understand the distinctiveness of the American South as a social, political, and religious entity. Advocating decentralization in religious and political life, Bradford contributed significantly to the fields of American history and literature, and to political philosophy. His scholarship on the Constitution suggested the importance of Christianity as an influence upon the framers. (HLC) **See also** Baptists.

BIBLIOGRAPHY

Bradford, M.E. *Founding Fathers: Brief Lives of the Framers of the United States Constitution, Second Revised Edition.* Lawrence: University of Kansas Press, 1994.

———. *Original Intentions: On the Making and Ratification of the United States Constitution.* Athens: University of Georgia Press, 1993.

William Bradford (c. 1589–1657)

A **Pilgrim** Father, William Bradford came to the New World aboard the *Mayflower* in 1620 to help found the Plymouth colony. He was an author and signatory of the famous **Mayflower Compact** (1620), considered by many to be one of the first American political documents. Bradford was Calvinist in his theology and Congregationalist with respect to church polity. He was a perennial governor of the colony from his first election in 1621 until 1656, excepting only five years, although he unsuccessfully urged rotation of that office. As governor, Bradford combined Christian charity, forgiveness, and humility with liberality and political shrewdness. (JHM) **See also** Calvinism; Congregationalism; Puritanism.

BIBLIOGRAPHY

Bradford, William. *Of Plymouth Plantation.* Edited by Francis Murphy. New York: Modern Library, 1981.

Branch Davidians

The Branch Davidians were a small **Seventh-Day Adventist** splinter group that came under the influence of Vernon Howell (i.e., David Koresh) in 1987. Howell often preached on the coming apocalypse and urged his followers to prepare for the eschatological conflict. In May 1992, the Bureau of Alcohol, Tobacco and Firearms (BATF) received reports that the Davidian compound near Waco, Texas, was receiving unusual arms shipments. On February 29, 1993, BATF agents raided the Davidian compound in an attempt to arrest Howell. A shootout followed in which four BATF agents and six Davidians were killed. A protracted standoff ensued, lasting 51 days. The FBI, which had taken over the federal operation, began tear-gassing the Davidians early on April 19. When fires broke out six hours later, the compound was quickly engulfed in flames. Seventy-four Davidians died in the inferno, including at least 21 children.

The Davidian standoff remains clouded in controversy. Many thoughtful commentators have noted the disturbing implications of the Waco debacle concerning the role society assigns to alternative religious movements (or "**cults**"), and the threat by heavily armed groups on the fringes of society. The bombing of the Oklahoma City Federal Building in 1995 was apparently an antigovernment response to the Davidian incident. (ARB)

BIBLIOGRAPHY

Lewis, James R., ed. *From the Ashes: Making Sense of Waco.* Lanham, MD: Rowman & Littlefield Publishers, 1994.

Wright, Stuart A., ed. *Armageddon in Waco: Critical Perspectives on the Branch Davidian Conflict.* Chicago: University of Chicago Press, 1995.

Louis Dembitz Brandeis (1856–1941)

One of the most influential justices in the history of the U.S. Supreme Court, Louis Brandeis pioneered new legal approaches to labor regulation and individual liberties, as well as leading the American wing of the Zionist movement. He introduced both the practice of including sociological data in legal briefs and the idea that the Constitution protected a "right of privacy." Outside of his legal practice, Brandeis persuaded many Americans, including President **Woodrow Wilson**, to support a Jewish homeland in Palestine. Nominated to the Court in 1916, he was confirmed after facing **anti-Semitic** opposition. Usually dissenting from the majority, he advocated judicial restraint and supported most **New Deal** reforms. (BDG) **See also** Zionism.

Bibliography
Strum, Philippa. *Louis D. Brandeis: Justice for the People.* Cambridge, MA: Harvard University Press, 1984.
Urofsky, Melvin I. *Louis D. Brandeis and the Progressive Tradition.* Boston: Little, Brown & Co., 1981.

William J. Brennan, Jr. (1906–1997)

Appointed to the U.S. Supreme Court by President **Dwight D. Eisenhower** in 1956, William J. Brennan—a lifelong Democrat—was the first Roman Catholic to serve on the Court. His selection was based in part on his religion and in part on the president's desire to be bipartisan in his administration. One of the Court's leading liberal members, he would occasionally get conservative support for his decisions by writing the decision on narrow grounds. During his 34 years on the Court, Brennan wrote several important religion clause cases, including the majority opinion in ***Aguilar v. Felton*** (1985), a concurring opinion in ***Abington Township v. Schempp*** (1963), the unanimous decision in ***Sherbert v. Verner*** (1963), and a dissent in ***Goldman v. Weinberger*** (1986). Brennan supported the use of the ***Lemon* Test** to decide free exercise cases and supported the concept of a "high wall of separation" between religion and government. He retired from the Court in 1990. **See also** Free Excercise Clause; Roman Catholicism.

Bibliography
Eisler, Kim Isaac. *A Justice for All.* New York: Simon & Schuster, 1993.
Marion, David E. *The Jurisprudence of Justice William J. Brennan, Jr.* Lantham, MD: Rowman & Littlefield, 1997.

David J. Brewer (1837–1910)

David Josiah Brewer, associate justice of the U.S. Supreme Court, was born in Asia Minor, the son of American **missionaries**. Educated at Wesleyan College and Yale College, he followed his famous uncles, Justice Stephen J. Field and David Dudley Field, into the legal profession. He authored the opinion of a unanimous Supreme Court in ***Church of the Holy Trinity v. United States*** (1892), in which he surveyed the history of the nation, concluding that the United States is "a Christian nation." Brewer elaborated on this dictum in a slender volume entitled *The United States a Christian Nation* (1905). (DLD)

Bibliography
Brewer, David J. *The United States: A Christian Nation.* Philadelphia: John C. Winston, 1905; reprint, Atlanta, GA: American Vision, 1996.
Brodhead, Michael J. *David J. Brewer: The Life of a Supreme Court Justice, 1837–1910.* Carbondale: Southern Illinois University Press, 1994.

John Brown (1800–1859)

John Brown, also known as Old Brown of Osawatomie, was a radical abolitionist whose activities in the Kansas Territory and his raid on Harpers Ferry,Virginia, gave the country both a martyr and a villain. In 1855, Brown and his five sons moved to the Kansas Territory, which was in the process of deciding if it would enter the United States as a slave or free state. Avenging an attack by pro-slavery forces at Lawrence, Brown and his sons killed five pro-slavery settlers at Pottawatomie Creek on May 24, 1856. His continued militant attacks on pro-slavery settlers at Osawatomie in Missouri, brought Brown national fame. This national reputation was useful in raising funds for his activities.

This idealized depiction of John Brown (center) shows him as a protector of the helpless. Library of Congress.

However, Brown became too radical even for many of his backers when he began to hatch a plan to create an army of freed slaves. On October 16, 1859, Brown and 18 other men captured the federal arsenal at Harpers Ferry, Virginia (now West Virginia). Rather than fight his way out immediately against a smaller local militia, Brown's raid failed when the militia was reinforced by Marines under the command of Colonel Robert E. Lee.

At his trial, Brown defended his actions as just in the eyes of God. Hanged on December 2 in Charleston, he became a powerful symbol for both sides in the slave debate. He became the subject of a famous song "John Brown's body lies a-mould'ring in the grave" which is sung to the same tune as **Julia Ward Howe's** anthem, "The Battle Hymn of the Republic." **See also** Abolition; Civil War; Slavery.

Bibliography
Boyer, Richard O. *The Legend of John Brown: A Biography and a History.* New York: Knopf, 1973.
Oates, Stephen B. *To Purge This Land with Blood: A Biography of John Brown.* New York: Harper, 1970.

Judie Brown (1944–)

A devout Catholic, Judie Brown has been active in the pro-life movement since 1969. A decade later she founded, with her husband Paul, the American Life League, the nation's largest grass-roots pro-life educational organization, with over 300,000 American families as members. Brown has served as the organization's president since its founding. She is a dynamic speaker and is committed to the sacredness of human life without compromise, exception, or apology. In addition to championing the pro-life cause, she has been an outspoken opponent of the use of fetal tissue in research and has been an advocate of the rights of handicapped newborns. She was also instrumental in the development of the "Baby Doe" regulations, a 1984 federal law that prohibits the withholding of medically indicated treatment from any disabled newborn. (MWP) **See also** Abortion and Birth Control Regulation; *Roe v. Wade*.

BIBLIOGRAPHY

Brown, Judie. *It is I Who Have Chosen You.* Stafford, VA: American Life League, 1992.

Orestes Augustus Brownson (1803–1876)

Orestes A. Brownson was perhaps the most important American Catholic thinker of the nineteenth century. During his dynamic career, he embraced a variety of intellectual and spiritual traditions, ranging from Presbyterianism and Universalism to a socialist-inspired "religion of humanity." While he is often remembered for his socialist tract "An Essay on the Laboring Classes" (1841), the piece is not characteristic of his mature thought, for soon after its publication he questioned whether the philosophical assumptions of socialist ideology were capable of sustaining a commitment to the rights and dignity of the human person. He concluded that all morality is undermined by the removal of the transcendent God from the socialist consciousness, and with this conclusion he began to investigate the claims of Catholicism. He found them convincing, and embraced the Catholic faith in 1844. One of the consistent themes throughout Brownson's post-conversion writings is that Catholicism is the only reliable corrective to the modern errors of libertinism and **socialism**. It was on this account that he became passionately devoted not only to the Church but to the American liberal order, and actively engaged the Catholic leadership of his day in controversies over church-state relations, immigration, the **Civil War**, and **education**. (GSB) **See also** Presbyterian Church; Roman Catholicsim.

BIBLIOGRAPHY

Butler, Gregory S. *In Search of the American Spirit: The Political Thought of Orestes Brownson.* Carbondale: Southern Illinois University Press, 1992.

Ryan, Thomas R. *Orestes A. Brownson: A Definitive Biography.* Huntington, IN: Our Sunday Visitor, 1976.

William Jennings Bryan (1860–1925)

William Jennings Bryan was an American political and religious leader whose ideas shaped major debates affecting American politics from 1896 until his death. Born and educated in Illinois, he entered politics in Nebraska, winning two terms to Congress (1891–1895), the only elective offices he ever held. A three-time presidential nominee of the **Democratic Party** (1896, 1900, and 1908), Bryan gained national influence following his famed "Cross of Gold" speech at the Democratic National Convention of 1896. Though endorsed by Populists and other third party alliances, he lost to **William McKinley**. His advocacy of free silver (a silver monetary standard) and other changes, usually deemed radical at the time, identified many of the major reforms enacted during the subsequent Progressive Era.

At varied times, he advocated direct election of U.S. senators, a graduated income tax, prohibition, and tariff reform. Although he served as a voluntary colonel in the Spanish-American War, he campaigned for anti-**imperialism** in 1900, arguing that colonialism was anti-Christian. As secretary of state, 1913–1915, he negotiated the Bryan-Chamorro Treaty that granted the U.S. an option to build a canal in Nicaragua. He resigned from President **Woodrow Wilson**'s cabinet in protest of policies that he believed could lead to **war** with Germany.

Three-time (1896, 1900, 1908) Democratic presidential nominee William Jennings Bryan (left) was a devout fundamentalist Christian. National Archives.

Though contributing significantly to campaigns for women's suffrage and the passage of the **Eighteenth Amendment**, he increasingly devoted himself to the anti-**evolution** crusade. An enduring success on the Chautauqua circuit, a series of Bible camps, conference centers, and summer resorts for evangelicals located in Chautauqua, New York, he expanded both his speaking and writing to promote that crusade. An active Presbyterian, he served as vice moderator of the General Assembly of the **Presbyterian Church** the year before his death. Bryan died five days after the conclusion of the **Scopes Trial** in Dayton, Tennessee, in which he played a pivotal role. (AOT)

BIBLIOGRAPHY

Glad, Paul W. *McKinley, Bryan, & the People.* New York: Elephant Paperbacks, 1991.

Levine, Lawrence W. *Defender of the Faith: William Jennings Bryan: The Last Decade 1915–1925.* Cambridge MA: Harvard University Press, 1987.

Patrick Buchanan (1938–)

Patrick Buchanan, an unsuccessful candidate for the Republican presidential nomination in 1992 and 1996, was born in Washington, D.C. and graduated from Georgetown University. After earning a master's degree in journalism from Columbia University, he began his journalistic career as an editorial writer for the *St. Louis Globe Democrat*. In 1962, he became a speechwriter for **Richard M. Nixon**. He was an articulate voice for conservative policies in the **Republican Party** and later served as a communications director for President **Ronald Reagan**.

Patrick Buchanan became popular with conservatives and especially religious conservatives, because of the forceful expression of his strong views on CNN's *Crossfire*. In 1992, challenging **George Bush** for the Republican presidential nomination, Buchanan enjoyed a strong showing in New Hampshire and at the 1992 GOP Convention he spoke on prime time television claiming that the U.S. was in a "**culture war**," due in large part to what he saw as a decline in morality and traditional religious values.

In 1996, Buchanan ran for the GOP presidential nomination a second time. He articulated a strong pro-life position and a protectionist foreign policy. He carried New Hampshire, but then his campaign faded. Fearful of making the same mistake Bush made, the Dole forces would not give Buchanan a major role at the 1996 GOP Convention. (WB) **See also** Conservatism.

BIBLIOGRAPHY

Buchanan, Patrick J. *Conservative Votes, Liberal Victories: Why the Right has Failed.* New York: Quadrangle/NY Times Books, 1975.

Buchanan, Patrick J. *Right from the Beginning.* Boston: Little, Brown, 1988.

Grant, George. *Buchanan: Caught in the Crossfire.* Nashville: Thomas Nelson, 1996.

Frank Buchman (1878–1961)

After serving many years as a Lutheran minister in Philadelphia, Frank Buchman experienced a religious conversion while in Europe. Upon returning to the United States, he founded a religious movement at Princeton in 1922 that became known as the Oxford Group and later as **Moral Re-Armament**. The movement sought to prevent **war** through moral reawakening. Critics complained that his views led to appeasement policies in the late 1930s. (MWP) **See also** Lutheran Church.

BIBLIOGRAPHY

Buchman, Frank. *Remaking the World.* New York, 1949.

Howard, Peter. *The World Rebuilt: The True Story of Frank Buchman.* New York: Doubleday, 1951.

Howard, Peter. *Frank Buchman's Secret.* New York: Doubleday, 1962.

William Frank Buckley, Jr. (1925–)

One of the most influential American conservatives, William Buckley is best known for his long-time editorship of the *National Review*. An early public television commentator on public affairs, he created a stir in 1951 with the publication of his book, *God and Man at Yale*, in which he attacked the influence of liberals in the study of humanities. In later years, he has become a successful novelist. (WB) **See also** Conservatism; Liberalism.

BIBLIOGRAPHY

Buckley, William F. *Nearer, My God: An Autobiography of Faith.* New York: Doubleday, 1997.

Judis, John B. *William F. Buckley, Jr., Patron Saint of the Conservatives.* New York: Simon and Schuster, 1988.

Buddhism

Buddhism is a religion based on the teachings of Siddhartha Gautama — otherwise known as Buddha, meaning "enlightened one" — who lived and taught in northern India in the sixth century BCE. The Four Noble Truths are the core teachings of Buddhism: the truth of suffering, the truth of the origin

Students in a Buddhist monastery in Freewood Acres, NJ. N. Haynes. Library of Congress.

of suffering, the truth of the cessation of suffering, and the truth of the path leading to the cessation of suffering (the Noble Eightfold Path). There are three major sects within Buddhism: Theravada, Mahayana, and Vajrayana. A major foundation of Buddhist practice is meditation, where one learns to focus on the moment and cultivate a clear, stable, and non-judgmental awareness. Zen Buddhism began to spread to the U.S. via Japanese monks in the 1930s, was popularized by the Beats in the 1950s, and came to the forefront of American consciousness during the **Vietnam War** with images of Buddhist monks setting themselves on fire to protest. Today, there are roughly three million Buddhists living in the United States. Politically, Buddhism has had an influence in recent years on such disparate public figures as former California Governor Jerry Brown and film actor Richard Gere. The latter has crusaded to build international support for Tibetan Buddhists facing repression by the communist government of China. (JCW) **See also** *Cruz v. Beto*.

BIBLIOGRAPHY

Rahula, Walpola. *What the Buddha Taught.* New York: Grove Weidenfeld, 1979.

Sangharakshita, Bhikshu. *A Survey of Buddhism: Its Doctrines and Methods Through the Ages.* Glasglow: Windhorse, 1993.

Warren E. Burger (1907–1995)

As chief justice of the U.S. Supreme Court for 17 years, Warren Burger presided over the Court's shift from the liberal activism of the 1960s to a more conservative stance. Born in St. Paul, Minnesota, he was appointed in 1959 to the U.S. Court of Appeals in Washington, D.C. by President **Dwight D. Eisenhower**. From that bench he criticized the procedural laxity of the decisions of the Supreme Court under Chief Justice **Earl Warren**, and was rewarded when newly elected President **Richard Nixon** wanted to dismantle Warren's legacy. Convinced that Burger would practice judicial restraint and defer to the executive, Nixon nominated him to be the fifteenth chief justice of the high court in 1969. Burger did not retire until 1986. During that long term, he did not succeed in undoing the work of the Warren Court, but he did ease the Court away from further activism. Among his most important decisions were the unanimous ***Lemon v. Kurtzman*** (1971), which outlined criteria for judging whether a law endangers the separation of church and state, and ***Lynch v. Donnelly*** (1984) which suggested that those criteria are not always applicable. (BDG)

BIBLIOGRAPHY

Lamb, Charles and Stephen C. Halpern, eds. *The Burger Court: Political and Judicial Profiles.* Chicago: University of Illinois Press, 1971.

Schwartz, Bernard. *The Ascent of Pragmatism: The Burger Court in Action.* Reading, MA: Addison-Wesley Publishing Co., 1990.

John Joseph Burke (1875–1936)

A Roman Catholic clergyman of Irish descent, John Burke was a member of the Paulist Fathers and helped found the Paulist Press. After the United States entered **World War I**, he organized the National Catholic War Council to aid the war effort and directed all Catholic contributions to the war except those by the Knights of Columbus. After the war, the Council became the National Catholic Welfare Council. He served as general secretary of this organization and the one that supplanted it, the **National Catholic Welfare Conference**, until his death. (MWP) **See also** Roman Catholicism.

BIBLIOGRAPHY

Shering, John B. *Never Look Back: The Career and Concerns of John J. Burke.* New York: Paulist Press, 1975.

Joseph Burstyn, Inc. v. Wilson (1952)

In *Joseph Burstyn, Inc. v. Wilson*, 343 U.S. 495 (1952), the U.S. Supreme Court voided a New York law that authorized the denial of a license to show a motion picture based on a censor's conclusion that that particular film was "sacrilegious." The crucial aspect of the case was the Court's ruling that films counted as speech and therefore deserved the protection of the free speech clauses of the **First** and **Fourteenth Amendments**: "It cannot be doubted that motion pictures are a significant medium for the communication of ideas. Their importance as an organ of public opinion is not lessened by the fact that they are designed to entertain as well as to inform." (JM)

BIBLIOGRAPHY

Amsterdam, Anthony B. "The Void-for-Vaguenism Doctrine and the Supreme Court." *University of Pennsylvania Law Review* 109 (1960): 67-116.

Timothy Byrnes (1958–)

A specialist in Roman Catholic politics, Timothy Byrnes has studied the abortion controversy, the political role of the American Catholic hierarchy, and the actions of the Catholic Church in newly democratized Eastern Europe. In his study, *Catholic Bishops in American Politics*, Byrnes showed how American bishops' political strategies reflected the changing political environment. (JSF) **See also** Roman Catholicism

BIBLIOGRAPHY

Byrnes, Timothy A. *Catholic Bishops in American Politics.* Princeton, NJ: Princeton University Press, 1991.

Segers, Mary C. and Timothy A. Byrnes, eds. *Abortion Politics in American States.* Armonk, NY: M.E. Sharpe, 1995.

Richard H. Cain (1825–1887)

Richard Cain was a free African American who at the age of 19 became a Methodist preacher in Missouri. He later left the Methodist church and became a minister of the **African Methodist Episcopal (AME) Church**. During the **Civil War**, he served as a chaplain, eventually settling in South Carolina after the war. In 1868, he was elected as a delegate to the state constitutional convention. From 1868 to 1872, he served as a state senator after being elected as a Republican. In 1872, Cain was elected to the U.S. House of Representatives. He did not stand for re-election in 1874 but was a successful candidate in 1876. He left politics in 1880 after he was appointed bishop of the African Methodist Episcopal Church. **See also** Chaplaincy; Methodism.

BIBLIOGRAPHY

Mann, Kenneth E. "Richard Harvey Cain: Congressman, Minister and Champion of Civil Rights." *Negro History Bulletin* 35 (March 1972): 64–66.

Call to Renewal (1976)

As part of a number of Bicentennial projects, American Catholics conducted a survey of more than 800,000 questionnaires and held a meeting of more than 1,300 lay and clerical delegates at a convention in Detroit from October 21-23, 1976. The delegates adopted a number of resolutions that they thought would update the Catholic Church and make it fit better into American society. These proposals included the ordination of women, married men as priests, and freedom of conscience with respect to artificial birth control. It also recommended an end to the uniquely American policy of automatic excommunication of divorced Catholics who remarry. The **National Conference of Catholic Bishops** met on May 6-7, 1977 in Chicago to review the proposals. Although they voted to end the automatic **excommunication**, the bishops also issued a 4,500-page statement that rejected artificial birth control, ordination of women, and married priests. The bishops did, however, agree to establish a committee to review other, less radical proposals. (MWP) **See also** Abortion and Birth Control Regulation; Roman Catholicism.

BIBLIOGRAPHY

D'Antonio, William V. *Laity, American and Catholic*. Kansas City, MO: Sheed & Ward, 1996.

Glem, Richard J. *Politics and Religious Authority*. Westport, CT: Greenwood, 1994.

Weigel, George. *Freedom and Its Discontents*. Washington, DC: Ethics and Public Policy Center, 1991.

Cecilius Calvert, Lord Baltimore (1606–1675)

Cecilius Calvert, the second Lord Baltimore, fulfilled the plan of his father, **George Calvert**, first Lord Baltimore, for a colony open to English Catholics by founding **Maryland Colony** in 1634. Calvert sent out two ships (the *Ark* and the *Dove*) of colonists, along with his brother Leonard, who served as governor of the colony. Although initially founded for Catholics and open to members of other persecuted religions, Maryland soon fell into religious turmoil, and Calvert lost control of the colony to Protestant forces in the early 1640s. He regained his authority in 1647 and two years later issued the **Act of Toleration** in hopes of ending the religious fighting. However, in 1654 the colony was again taken over by Protestant forces who disenfranchised Catholics and members of various other religious groups. In 1658, Calvert was again able to re-establish his control and the colony remained peaceful until his death in 1675. **See also** Colonial America; Roman Catholicism.

Cecilius Calvert, Lord Baltimore, fulfilled the wishes of his father by founding a colony for Catholics in Maryland. Library of Congress.

Bibliography

Browne, William H. *George Calvert and Cecilius Calvert.* New York: Dodd Mead, 1890.

Ellis, John Tracy. *Catholics in Colonial America.* Baltimore: Helicon, 1965.

George Calvert, Lord Baltimore (1580?–1632)

George Calvert, first Lord Baltimore, was an English nobleman who established a safe haven for Roman Catholics in 1623 when he founded a colony at Ferryland in Newfoundland. However, after he visited the colony in 1628, he sought to settle a new colony to the south where the climate was more mild. King Charles I originally agreed to land south of Virginia, but when that colony complained the new location was changed to north of the Potomac River. Although Calvert died before the **Maryland Colony** was founded in 1634, his vision of a Catholic colony in America was fulfilled by his heir, **Cecilius Calvert**, the second Lord Baltimore. (MWP) **See also** Colonial America; Roman Catholicism.

Bibliography

Browne, William H. *George Calvert and Cecilius Calvert.* New York: Dodd, Mead, 1890.

Ellis, John T. *Catholics in Colonial America.* Baltimore: Helicon, 1965.

John Calvin (1509–1564)

After **Martin Luther**, John Calvin was the best known of the Protestant **Reformation** leaders. His teachings, referred to as **Calvinism**, emphasized God's perfection and sovereignty in contrast to the sinful helplessness of humans. He is remembered for his cogent teaching of predestination, although Augustine, Luther, and Huldrych Zwingli held similar doctrines. His enduring work, the *Institutes of the Christian Religion*, first published in 1536, and later issued in expanded editions, circulated widely throughout Europe.

French by birth, Calvin studied theology and law. Fleeing persecution in France, he lived in Strasbourg and then in Geneva, Switzerland, where his church reforms were accomplished. His doctrine of the church held that it should not be subject to the state, that church leaders should be chosen only with the consent of members, and that church authority should be stratified through representation. Calvinism is displayed in modern Reformed, **Presbyterian**, and Congregational churches. Their practices of representation encouraged representational **democracy** in Western governments. (JRV) **See also** Congregationalism; Reformation.

Bibliography

Bouwsma, W.I. *John Calvin: A Sixteenth Century Portrait.* New York: Oxford University Press, 1988.

Calvinism

Calvinism as a term has two meanings. One is the teaching and practice of Calvinistic or Reformed (**Presbyterian**, Dutch Reformed, and Congregational) churches, which trace their origins to the Protestant reformer, **John Calvin** (1509-1564). The other, much broader meaning refers to a complex of social and ethical ideals that have influenced Western society since Calvin's time.

Calvinistic thought and practice, while acknowledging the supremacy of Scripture, finds its original expression in Calvin's *Institutes of the Christian Religion* (1559) and in subsequent Reformed confessions such as the Belgic (1561), Scot (1580), and Westminster (1647), and in the Thirty-Nine Articles of the Church of England (1563) and the Canons of the Synod of Dort (1619). All these docrinal formulations agree in accepting the sola scriptura principle which emphasizes the primacy of the Bible and belief in God's sovereignty, humanity's sin, and the election of the chosen. The Calvinist world view has, in **H. Richard Niebuhr's** terms, led to a "transformationist" approach to culture, seeking not to separate the "secular" and the "spiritual" but rather to view them as equally areas for divine and human activity. Thus the doctrine of divine sovereignty led to a great emphasis on human responsibility and action in the world.

The term Calvinism then also refers to the sociological and political impact of Calvin's thought and institutions on subsequent Western history, particularly in Switzerland, France, Great Britain, the Netherlands, and the United States. The sociological impact, brought into prominence by the seminal work of **Max Weber** (*The Protestant Ethic and the Spirit of Capitalism*) connects the "this-worldly" ascetic, self-denying Calvinistic ethic, with its emphasis on fulfilling one's calling in all spheres of life, with the rise of rationalized capitalist production. This Weberian thesis has come under sharp critique for not taking into account other variables and for failing to explain its inapplicability in such "Calvinist" regimes as Scotland and Afrikaner South Africa. Calvinism (as understood by Theodore Beza, Duplessis-Mornay, and George Buchanan) had radical political implications with its teaching concerning the right to resist unjust or impious rulers and its teaching on conciliar and representative forms of government, which exists to serve the common good. This social concern is reflected in the work of modern Calvinists, such as **Reinhold Niebuhr**, Emil Brunner, and Karl Barth.

Calvinism was the doctrinal basis of the founders of the New England colonies, and, following the example of Calvin's Genevan Academy, the source of the **Puritan** stress on lay and clerical education, which led in New England to the founding of Harvard College in 1638. Calvinism, primarily in its Congregational variant, set the sociological and political agenda for the early American colonies. Its emphasis on the covenant, God's elect/chosen people, and human depravity led to later political ideas of a "social contract" (Jean-Jacques Rousseau) and to the idea of institutional checks and balances to curb a ruler's power. The representative and local form of church government made Calvinism both highly adaptable and a precursor of democratic political institutions. (ISM) **See also** Capitalism; Colonial America; Congregationalism; Democracy; Massachusetts Bay Colony.

BIBLIOGRAPHY

Hancock, Ralph C. *Calvin and the Foundations of Modern Politics*. Ithaca, NY: Cornell University Press, 1989.

Hopfl, Harro. *The Christian Polity of John Calvin*. New York: Cambridge University Press, 1982.

Johnson, William S. and John Leith, eds. *Reformed Reader: A Sourcebook in Christian Tradition.* Westminister: John Knox Press, 1993.

McNeill, John T. *The History and Character of Calvinism*. New York: Oxford University Press, 1967.

Skinner, Quentin. "Calvinism and the Theory of Revolution." *The Foundations of Modern Political Thought* 2 (1978): 189-358.

Cambridge Platform

In the middle of the seventeenth century, the **Puritans** of England became critical of certain trends in the Puritan colonies of New England. In response, the colonies decided in 1646 to call what became known as the Cambridge Synod to settle "questions of church government and discipline." In 1648, ministers and their representatives met in Cambridge, Massachusetts, where they adopted the Westminster Confession as their statement of faith and drew up the Cambridge Platform to describe their form of church government.

The platform was based on the experiences and practices of New England Congregational churches. Each church was to be independent, tied to other churches only for advice and fellowship. Churches were formed when a group of believers chose to unite themselves in a covenant. In this form of government, power rested in the congregation, and even the minister's authority rested on the congregation's approval of him. This democratic form of church government had a major impact on the development of **democracy** in America. (MWP) **See also** Colonial America; Congregationalism; Massachusetts Bay Colony.

BIBLIOGRAPHY

Walker, Williston. *The Creeds and Platforms of Congregationalism*. Philadelphia: Pilgrim Press, 1960.

Alexander Campbell (1788–1866)

In 1832, Alexander Campbell founded the **Disciples of Christ** by uniting the churches he led in Virginia with those of Barton Stone in Kentucky. He worked for ecclesiastical harmony by emphasizing the common elements of Christianity and its American heritage. In 1840, he started Bethany College in West Virginia and remained its president until his death. (MWP)

BIBLIOGRAPHY

Campbell, Alexander. *Popular Lectures and Addresses*. 1863.

Denton, Ray Lindley. *Apostle of Freedom*. St. Louis: Bethany Press, 1957.

Lunger, Harold C. *The Political Ethics of Alexander Campbell*. St. Louis: Bethany Press, 1954.

Anthony "Tony" Campolo (1935–)

A professor of sociology at Eastern College, St. Davids, Pennsylvania, Tony Campolo is a popular writer and lecturer on the evangelical left. He has served in postions of ministry, including starting Beyond Borders, a community-based ministry in Haiti, and Urban Promise, an urban ministry in Camden, New Jersey. He is also the founder of Evangelicals for the Advancement and Promotion of Education (E.A.P.E) in North Philadelphia. A signer of the "Cry for Renewal," he has been sharply critical of both **capitalism** and the **Religious Right**. (SEW) **See also** Evangelicals.

BIBLIOGRAPHY

Campolo, Anthony. *Is Jesus a Republican or a Democrat?* Dallas: Word Books, 1995.

Nash, Ronald. *Why the Left Is Not Right: The Religious Left—Who They Are and What They Believe*. Grand Rapids: Zondervan, 1996.

James Cannon, Jr. (1864–1944)

As a bishop in the Southern Methodist Church, James Cannon was a leader in the **Anti-Saloon League** and head of the World League Against Alcoholism. During the 1928 presidential campaign, Cannon repeatedly denounced Democratic candidate **Alfred E. Smith** because of his Catholicism and his stance on national **temperance**. Cannon's influence declined after 1928 because of growing personal scandals, including adultery and stock market speculation. (MWP) **See also** Democratic Party; Methodism; Roman Catholicism.

BIBLIOGRAPHY

Dabney, Virginius. *Dry Messiah: The Life of Bishop Cannon*. Westport, CT: Greenwood, 1970.

Watson, Richard L., Jr. *Bishop Cannon's Own Story*. Durham, NC: Duke University Press, 1955.

Canon Law

Most major Christian churches have some form of regulations, but the term "canon law" is most commonly used by the Church of England, the Orthodox Church, and the Roman Catholic Church. "Canon" comes from the Greek and means "rule" or "standard." The process of establishing canons dates from the fourth century, although ecclesiastical orders can be found in earlier documents. Although elements of canon law emerged in antiquity and in the medieval and early modern periods, the first systematic codification of Roman Catholic canon law took place in 1917. Pope John XXIII appointed a Pontifical Commission to revise the code in 1959. In 1983, Pope John Paul II promulgated a new code that contains 1,752 canons, a reduction from the 1917 code's 2,414 canons. The Code of Canon Law serves as the legal structure for the Roman Catholic Church, defining its relationship with civil authority and its role in the modern world. (HLC) **See also** Roman Catholicism.

BIBLIOGRAPHY

Code of Canon Law: Latin-English Edition. Washington, DC: Canon Law Society of America, 1983.

Cantwell v. State of Connecticut (1940)

Newton Cantwell and his two sons, Jesse and Russell, ordained ministers of the **Jehovah's Witnesses**, were convicted of violating a Connecticut statute that required licensing of religious organizations by the public welfare council. The statute made it a crime for unlicensed organizations to solicit money, services, "or any valuable thing" for the cause, except from other members of the organization. The Cantwells appealed their convictions on the grounds that the statute violated the **First Amendment** by denying them freedom of speech and the free exercise of religion, protections made applicable to the states by the **Fourteenth Amendment**.

In *Cantwell v. State of Connecticut*, 310 U.S. 296 (1940), the U.S. Supreme Court struck down the Connecticut statute with a ruling that broke new ground in the jurisprudence of religious freedom and became an important precedent that was to be often quoted in Court decisions in the years that followed. In *Cantwell*, the Court declared that "The [First] Amendment embraces two concepts—freedom to believe and freedom to act. The first is absolute but, in the nature of things, the second cannot be. Conduct remains subject to regulation for the protection of society." The Court elucidated the ways in which regulation of action may be carried out without violating the Constitution, noting that "a state may by general and non-discriminatory legislation regulate the times, the places, and the manner of soliciting upon its streets, and of holding meetings thereon; and may in other respects safeguard the peace, good order and comfort of the community, without unconstitutionally invading the liberties protected by the Fourteenth Amendment. . . . The general regulation, in the public interest, of solicitation, which does not involve any religious test and does not unreasonably obstruct or delay the collection of funds, is not open to any constitutional objection." Although future cases overturned the legitimacy of most forms of regulation upon solicitation, often in cases involving Jehovah's Witnesses, the Court tended to follow the doctrine that regulation of conduct was permissible as long as it made no specific reference to particular groups or religious activities. (JM) **See also** Free Exercise Clause; Free Speech Approach to Religious Liberty.

Bibliography

Eastland, Terry. *Religious Liberty in the Supreme Court*. Washington, DC: Ethics and Public Policy Center, 1993.

Capital Punishment

Capital punishment is the legally sanctioned execution of persons who have committed crimes that society has determined to be so heinous as to warrant such an extreme penalty. The term comes from the Latin *caput*, used by the Romans to mean the head, the life, or the civil rights of an individual. Capital punishment has been practiced in almost all societies from the beginning of recorded human history. Only during this century has there been a concerted effort to abandon this practice, especially in Europe, though the seeds of the abolition of the death penalty were planted at least two centuries ago with abolitionists such as Cesare Bonesana and Jeremy Bentham.

The reasons why various ancient societies practiced the death penalty is not altogether clear but most likely it is related to a religious need to rid society of persons who had brought down the wrath of a deity. Throughout the societies of the Ancient Near East, such as Babylonia and **Israel**, as well as in ancient Rome, execution was the penalty for several offenses, including homicide, treason, and sexual crimes. Israel and Babylonia followed the practice of *lex talionis*, the law of retaliation, in which the penalty was measured according to the severity of the crime, although in Israel the *lex talionis* was more moderate in expression. In Rome and several other societies, offenses against persons, including homicides, were the private concern of individuals or their kinsmen and were settled privately. Crimes against the state were usually limited to treason and certain religious violations. The state had only one punishment—death.

From medieval Europe through the eighteenth century, unbridled use of the death penalty was practiced; even petty offenses could bring death, age of the offender not being a discriminating factor.

The English colonies in America practiced capital punishment, but in much more reserved manner than in England, where in the eighteenth and early nineteenth centuries anywhere from 160 to 260 crimes could be punished by death. In **colonial America**, no one questioned the right of the death penalty. The **Puritan** colony of **Massachusetts Bay** inflicted it for a number of crimes while other colonies reserved it for only severe crimes such as treason or murder. Both England and her American colonies punished witchcraft with the death penalty. This was largely because of the belief that witches had the power to inflict death upon their victims; the penalty was thus consistent with the universal view that homicide brought the just execution of the offender.

In modern times, the death penalty is preserved in most countries of the world except for portions of Western Europe, though in those countries that practice the death penalty, it is used more sparingly than in former ages. The work of Cesare Bonesana, marquis of Beccaria (1738-1794), in his influential *An Essay on Crimes and Punishments* (1764), and the moral recoil against the French Revolution had more to do with the move toward abolition of capital punishment than anything else. Generally today it is exacted only in cases of treason or murder.

The manner of executing criminals has changed much from ancient times. Except in rabbinic tradition, where the desire to preserve the body was paramount, numerous forms of execution have been practiced. The major forms of capital punishment have been stoning, burning, decapitating, and thrusting through with a sword, though more cruel and unusual methods have been practiced in different cultures, such as drawing and quartering, boiling in oil, and flaying. The most common method in human history has been beheading. Modern methods in the United States are electrocution, poison gas, hanging, firing squad, and lethal injection.

The religious traditions of historic **Judaism** and Christianity have strongly supported the exercise of the death penalty. Rabbis and Christian theologians and statesmen have considered it to be just action against malicious crimes such as murder. The Hebrew Scriptures advocate this view in Genesis 9:6-7; the laws of Israel and rabbinic tradition also support this perspective. The New Testament also seems to accept the state as a servant of God in using the sword (Rom. 13:1-3), and Paul considered such punishment acceptable for one truly guilty of a captial offense (Acts 25:11). Recently, many moral theologians in both the Roman Catholic and Protestant communions, as well as Jewish scholars, have favored abolition of the death penalty.

Those advocating capital punishment have employed the following arguments:

1. Retribution is probably the earliest reason for the death penalty and still is the favored justification for capital punishment. Murderers receive their just reward; they are paid back for their crime. This may even be the sense of Genesis 9:6-7. Since punishment is in general the payment of just due for the deeds of a person, in which the individual earns payment for his or her behavior, the punishment fits the crime.
2. Deterrence is regularly given as a major justification for the death penalty, though a distinction must be made between the general and individual intent of deterrence. General deterrence does not concern the future behavior of a particular criminal; it is concerned with the effect of that criminal's punishment on society as a whole. It is intended to make examples of criminals so that other members of society will do no harm. Individual deterrence is aimed specifically at the particular potential criminal and has as its object to teach the criminal not to perform a more severe act that might lead to the imposition of capital punishment. This deterrence might even be seen as a form of rehabilitation, encouraging the criminal offender not to commit a crime worthy of death.
3. Incarceration of the criminal is a primary means to separate the offender from the rest of society to protect members of society from criminal acts. In less severe cases, the criminal might be reformed so as not to perpetrate further acts against society; but for the murderer, capital punishment provides the ultimate protection by removing him or her from society with no possibility of further aggression. This might be viewed as a subset of the deterrence view in that it actually deters the offender from committing another murder.
4. Today, the death penalty usually is exacted only for first degree murder or for treason against the state. However, the theonomic view, advocated by some in more conservative Christian circles, follows the Mosaic legislation of the Hebrew Scriptures in listing a variety of reasons for capital punishment. In the Hebrew culture, 21 different capital crimes could bring the death penalty (Exod. 31:14), some of which were directed against profane service by priests in the temple (Lev. 10:8-11; Num. 4:15).

Arguments against capital punishment include the following:

1. A major tactic is to undermine the idea that the exercise of the death penalty has any significant deterrent value. Often studies have been done showing the limited impact on the crime rate of the death penalty. Those advocating the death penalty point out that the studies are half-truths, in that the death penalty was not being practiced during the time studied, or at least not consistently and speedily practiced, so that the most the study proves is that laws that are not consistently and quickly applied have little impact on crime. Moreover, death penalty advocates point out that deterrence cannot be expected to work with many citizens. There are always some persons who will refrain from crime regardless of the penalty, and some who will commit crime regardless of the severity of the penalty. Deterrence, instead, is intended for the large center group of persons. Genuine fear of being caught and paying for violations of the law does work. Simply observing how cars slow down in the presence of a police car proves the point.
2. Another argument is to call the state's use of the death penalty hypocritical because it does the same thing for which it wants to punish the murderer. Those who argue for capital punishment distinguish between the actions of an individual and societal mandated acts of the government after due process. For example, private citizens are not to pay back a criminal for any crime, be it robbery, rape, murder, or trespass. The punishment is justly left in the hands of the state. Yet it is not acting like a criminal to imprison someone against his or her will for falsely imprisoning or kidnapping someone else.
3. The fact that the death penalty may not be evenly applied across racial and gender groups has been used by some to support the abolition of capital punishment. It has rightly been pointed out that a disproportionate number of minorities, especially blacks, are on death row. Those for the death penalty would aver that any imbalance does not change the fact that those so punished deserved the punishment. Those persons were tried and found guilty by courts of law that required guilt beyond a reasonable doubt and afforded the opportunity for appeal.

4. One of the more persuasive arguments against inflicting the death penalty is that it is impossible to correct a miscarriage of justice when the system convicts the wrong person.
5. The constitutional provision advocated against the death penalty relates to the Eighth Amendment (applied to the states through the **Fourteenth Amendment**) against cruel and unusual punishment. It is argued that the death penalty is cruel and unusual, but historically the phrase referred to punishments which were more severe than the offense, to torture or to prolonging the pain of dying. Since the Constitution and Bill of Rights provide for captial crimes, it is difficult to argue that captial punishment is unconstitutional.

The state of the law on the matter of capital punishment has fluctuated for several decades. From the 1930s through the 1960s, the tendency of the Supreme Court was to remand any sentence of death. The Supreme Court, through expansive jurisprudence, nullified many death sentences in *Furman v. Georgia* (1972), which required considerable statutory guidelines. Public opinion, however, even since *Furman*, has largely favored the death penalty. The Court, in *Gregg v. Georgia* (1976) ended the moratorium on executions but required states to create statutory sentencing guidelines. A major decision for the death penalty was *Butler v. McKellar* (1990), in which the Court removed many of the obstacles to implementing the death sentence and to limiting the endless appeals process. It appears that the current Court will allow states to continue the practice of capital punishment within certain guidelines. (HWH) **See also** Roman Catholicism; Theonomist.

Bibliography

Bedau, Hugo Adam, ed. *The Death Penalty in America*. New York: Oxford University Press, 1997.
Berns, Walter. *For Capital Punishment*. New York: Basic Books, 1979.
House, H. Wayne and John Howard Yoder. *The Death Penalty Debate*. Dallas: Word, 1991.
van den Haag, Ernest and John P. Conrad. *The Death Penalty, a Debate*. New York: Plenum Press, 1983.

Capitalism

Capitalism is a comparatively modern economic system. From antiquity through the Renaissance and **Reformation**, what we call "goods and services" were bartered, sold, and bought. Yet capitalism, in the sense that we know it, did not exist in those various societies. For example, in *Economics Explained*, Robert Heilbroner and Lester Thurow call those societies precapitalist for the following reasons: (1) they lacked economic freedom and an extensive system of private property; (2) they allowed their members to seek wealth through the exercise of power but officially condemned the making of money for its own sake (e.g., the medieval Church considered usury—the practice of lending money at interest, one of the mainstays of modern capital formation—to be sinful); and (3) their technologies and economic systems were almost static in comparison to the technological innovations and business cycles of modern capitalist systems.

Likewise, while religious thinkers have long examined matters of money and business, the rise of capitalist economies has engendered in the modern era extensive thought among religious people. There are many reasons why. Among them is the attempt to grapple with the profound effects of capitalism, such as the parallel urbanization of societies; vast accumulation of new wealth by individuals; disparities in wealth, labor and capitalist tensions; the surge of technology; and environmental issues. Additional motivators for modern religious examination of economics include the critique of capitalism by Karl Marx and Frederick Engels in the mid-1800s, with the subsequent developments of **socialism and communism**, and the arguments in the early 1900s of **Max Weber** and others that Protestant Christianity significantly shaped and spurred the character and growth of capitalism.

What then is capitalism? While we speak of capitalism commonly, it can be difficult to define simply and precisely. This is because the term "capitalism" refers to a complex of elements with variations over time and in different settings. Generally, capitalism denotes economic systems in which the autonomy of private ownership, the incentive of profit for the individual, and market supply and demand — not authority and tradition — are the prevailing determinants of production, costs, prices, and distribution. In capitalist systems, labor, land, and capital (the means of production) are no longer static elements but dynamic commodities. For example, capitalism means a certain freedom for **labor**, at least in principle. Specifically, workers are not bound to land or ruler (as in serfdom), nor are they bound to a traditional trade or type of work (such as being born into cobbling or peasant farming). Workers have more choice and opportunity. At the same time, labor in capitalist systems tends to become merely one of various tools necessary for production and distribution — to be hired ("bought") or dismissed ("sold") by owners according to efficiencies of cost. Hence, workers have fewer guarantees of stability and security in making a livelihood. Other aspects of capitalism include the tendency toward expanding, not static, economies. In this regard, capitalism intrinsically possesses a strong historical dimension, not in being backward oriented, but in being dynamic rather than static. This dynamism is marked by an impetus for change and a hope in the possibilities of the future. Thus, capitalism is often linked with assumptions of the progress of human society.

Capitalism in this modern sense began to develop in eighteenth-century England in connection with industrialization. In England's American colonies, much economic activity remained local, geared to subsistence. But in the early 1800s, modern capitalism and industrialism began to develop in the new United States. The **Civil War**, with its huge requirements for goods and services, and the following half century witnessed a great acceleration in the transformation of the U.S. into a capitalist, industrial society. The massing of the means of production in large factories with numerous laborers increased, which required concentrations of raw materials and energy sources, and extensive, efficient transportation systems.

Technological advances mechanized many aspects of labor and vastly raised productivity. More and more laborers not only did not own their means of production (tools and shops), but they became basically another of the means of production. Division of labor, so that workers repetitively made only a small part of a product, became standard. Social and economic conflicts between workers and owners heightened, especially as workers organized into unions to protect and improve their work. More and cheaper goods were produced. Living standards in general rose, even recognizing the terrible conditions for many workers and their families in the capitalist, industrial U.S. Moreover, a comparatively small segment of the population accumulated vast amounts of wealth. Certain companies and corporations expanded dramatically in size and in their portion of the national economy.

Between the Civil War and the first quarter of the twentieth century, the U.S. rapidly and radically changed into a capitalist, industrial, urban society. Then the Great Depression of the 1930s severely strained the American economy and society. The federal government's **New Deal** response — spurring job creation and guaranteeing social welfare systems — established government intervention in the economy in new ways, though without really challenging the capitalist foundations of the economy. Since the end of **World War II**, the U.S. has moved, with considerable trauma, into a largely post-industrial society, still urbanized and still broadly capitalist.

What is the relationship between capitalism and religion? If capitalism is a complex, religious influences on and responses to capitalism also involve a complex of elements and perspectives, from ardent support to uncritical acceptance to outright opposition. Certain historians and social philosophers have tied the origin and growth of capitalism to the spirit and ethic of the Protestant **Reformation**, particularly the **Puritan** movement in England and America. Max Weber, in his *The Protestant Ethic and the Spirit of Capitalism*, contended that the sense of duty and dynamism embedded in the religious idea of calling is central to the spirit of capitalism. He pointed out that **Martin Luther** and **John Calvin** emphasized the religious significance of calling. From this emphasis Weber saw the development of an "ascetic Protestantism"—a dutiful, self-disciplined effort at worldly affairs that both manifests righteousness and produces results—that laid the foundations for a worldly asceticism, critical to the spirit of capitalism. While the religious significance faded over time, the sense of calling remained as a "moral justification of worldly activity," influencing the character and rise of capitalism. Many have followed Weber in this contention, whereas others have qualified or criticized his arguments (e.g. compare *The Spirit of Democratic Capitalism* by **Michael Novak**).

The dramatic changes in American society and economics from the Civil War to the 1930s profoundly affected many religious people. A few were unabashed supporters of capitalism and the wealth it can engender. For example, William Lawrence, Episcopal bishop of Massachusetts (1893-1927), declared two principles that expressed well a "gospel of wealth"—that the strong person conquers nature, and that only the moral person gains wealth. For others, serious concern about the effects of capitalism, industrialism, and urbanization led to the **Social Gospel** movement, with its moderate critiques of American society and economics and its reform proposals. More radical critiques and proposals, especially in the 1920s and 1930s, came from Christians and Jews persuaded that socialism was more just and more consonant with their religious worldviews than capitalism. However, most people of faith in the U.S., with little critical reflection on issues of religious belief and economic systems, simply accepted capitalism as good, even if mildly questioning some of its excesses.

Some American religious thinkers have argued for a close, even necessary, connection between capitalism, **democracy**, and Christianity. Michael Novak represents a recent example of this position as does **Richard John Neuhaus** in his *Doing Good and Doing Well: The Challenge to the Christian Capitalist*. Certainly, economic, political, and religious freedoms were shaping streams in the founding and formation of the American character and system. Indeed, American Christians have often conceived of them as essentially linked; and that all three, so connected, are foundational to the very essence, purpose, and success of the American nation. In this view, the fortunes of each—and hence, the fortunes of the nation—are bound together, reinforcing each other or together falling.

While serious questions about American capitalist economics continue to be raised—for example, **liberation theologies** influenced by Marxist analyses, the **Sojourners** community, and the Catholic bishops' statement on economics in the early 1980s — there has also been a resurgence of religious examination of and support for capitalism, particularly in light of the demise of communism in Russia and elsewhere. (GSS) **See also** Calvinism; Episcopal Church; Massachusetts Bay Colony; National Conference of Catholic Bishops; Roman Catholicism.

BIBLIOGRAPHY

Ahlstrom, Sydney E. *A Religious History of the American People.* New Haven, CT: Yale University, 1972.

Heilbroner, Robert L. *The Worldly Philosophers: The Lives, Times, and Ideas of the Great Economic Thinkers.* New York: Simon and Schuster, 1953.

Heilbroner, Robert, and Lester Thurow. *Economics Explained: Everything You Need to Know about How the Economy Works and Where It's Going.* New York: Simon & Schuster, 1982.

Nash, Ronald H. *Poverty and Wealth: The Christian Debate over Capitalism.* Westchester, IL: Good News Publishers, 1986.

Neuhaus, Richard John. *Doing Well and Doing Good: The Challenge to the Christian Capitalist.* New York: Doubleday, 1992.

Novak, Michael. *The Spirit of Democratic Capitalism.* New York: Simon & Schuster, 1982.

Tamari, Meir. *Jewish Ethics and Economic Life.* New York: Macmillan, 1987.

Tawney, R. H. *Religion and the Rise of Capitalism: A Historical Study.* New York: Harcourt, Brace, 1926.

Wauzzinski, Robert A. *Between God and Gold: Protestant Evangelicalism and Industrial Revolution, 1820-1914.* Madison, NJ: Fairleigh Dickinson University, 1993.

Weber, Max. *The Protestant Ethic and the Spirit of Capitalism.* Trans. by Talcott Parsons. New York: Charles Scribner's Sons, 1930.

Capitol Square Review Board v. Pinette (1995)

In *Capitol Square Review Board v. Pinette*, 515 U.S. 753 (1995), the Supreme Court ruled 7-2 that it was not unconstitutional for the **Ku Klux Klan** to erect a Christian cross on the plaza surrounding the Ohio state capitol building during the Christmas season. In the opinion by Justice **Antonin Scalia**, the Court stated that the cross represents private religious speech, that the capitol plaza is a public forum as evidenced by periodic displays of a United Way thermometer and a menorah during Chanukah, and that no promotion or favoring of religion would therefore be implied by allowing the cross. (SM) **See also** First Amendment; Judaism.

BIBLIOGRAPHY

Cleary, Edward J. *Beyond the Burning Cross: The First Amendment and the Landmark R.A.V. Case.* New York: Random House, 1994.

Benjamin N. Cardozo (1870–1938)

Widely admired for his gentle character as well as for his legal scholarship, Benjamin Cardozo was one of the most popular Supreme Court justices of his day. Born in New York City to a family of Orthodox Sephardic Jews, Cardozo enjoyed an influential career on the New York Court of Appeals before being nominated by President **Herbert Hoover** in 1932 to replace Justice Oliver Wendell Holmes, Jr., on the U.S. Supreme Court. Endorsing a pragmatic approach to jurisprudence which he outlined in his 1921 book *The Nature of the Judicial Process*, Cardozo helped to introduce the doctrine that freedom of religion and certain other protections in the Bill of Rights could limit state as well as federal laws. (BDG) **See also** First Amendment; Judaism.

BIBLIOGRAPHY

Cardozo, Benjamin. *The Nature of the Judicial Process.* New Haven, CT: Yale University Press, 1957.

Polenberg, Richard. *The World of Benjamin Cardozo: Personal Values and the Judicial Process.* Cambridge, MA: Harvard University Press, 1997.

John Carroll (1735–1815)

John Carroll became the first Roman Catholic bishop in the United States when he was appointed the bishop of Baltimore in 1789. Educated in Europe, Carroll was a member of a wealthy and influential **Maryland** family. In 1769, he entered the Society of Jesus (the Jesuits). During the Revolutionary War, Carroll accompanied his cousin, Charles Carroll, and **Benjamin Franklin** on a diplomatic mission to the French Canadians. Carroll was also active in the founding of several colleges, including Georgetown University in 1789, Mt. St. Mary's College in Annapolis, Maryland, in 1792, and St. Joseph's College in Emmitsburg, Maryland, in 1809. Unlike most colleges in the United States at the time, the colleges established by Carroll admitted all qualified students regardless of their religious affiliations. **See also** Roman Catholicism.

BIBLIOGRAPHY

Melville, Annabelle M. *John Carrol of Baltimore.* New York: Scribners, 1955.

James Earl "Jimmy" Carter (1924–)

President of the United States from 1977 through 1981, James Earl "Jimmy" Carter, Jr., was both an overtly evangelical politician and a southern political moderate. However, his presidency marked a watershed in the declining commitment of both southerners and **evangelicals** to his **Democratic Party**. In one term as Georgia governor, Carter's racial policies and reforms gained national recognition. His presidential campaign garnered support with his promise of openness, separating his candidacy from the recent political turmoil of the Watergate era, while his claim to "**born-again**" status spurred national popularization of that term. Carter's religious beliefs were central to his political identity. He publicly professed his deep commitment to Christian morality and knew that those values were central to his appeal to the American people.

Jimmy Carter's religious beliefs were fundamental to his political identity. Library of Congress.

Carter's presidency was largely defined by failures. Unable to implement his energy policy, welfare reform, or national health insurance, his greatest accomplishments were in foreign policy, notably the 1979 treaty between **Israel** and Egypt. These successes were diminished by growing opposition to his human rights emphasis in foreign policy and to his policy toward Latin America, particularly the Panama Canal Treaty. Double-digit inflation, high unemployment, and the Iranian hostage crisis assured his defeat in 1980 and strengthened a conservative resurgence in national politics. Since his defeat, Carter has written extensively while continuing to work for world peace and other causes, notably with Habitat for Humanity.

Some commentators found hypocrisy in Carter's religious affiliation with the **Southern Baptist Convention** and his interest in modern theology, especially the writings of **Reinhold Niebuhr**, and its emphasis on **social justice**. An orthodox Christian, Carter never quite fit in the **fundamentalist** mold. (AOT) **See also** Moral Majority; Ronald Reagan; Religious Right.

BIBLIOGRAPHY

Ariail, Dan and Cheryl Heckler-Felz. *The Carpenter's Apprentice: The Spiritual Biography of Jimmy Carter*. Grand Rapids, MI: Zondervan, 1996.

Bourne, Peter G. *Jimmy Carter: A Comprehensive Biography from Plains to Post-Presidency.* New York: S & S Trade, 1997.

Carter, Jimmy. *Living Faith*. New York: Random House, 1996.

Thornton, Richard C. *The Carter Years: Toward a New Global Order*. Washington, DC: Washington Institute Press, 1992.

Stephen L. Carter (1954–)

Stephen Carter is a leading constitutional scholar and law professor. In his 1993 book, *The Culture of Disbelief*, Carter presents a strong set of arguments that government should be more accommodating of religious belief, and should defer more frequently to the religious scruples of those whose beliefs make compliance with the law difficult. Carter argues that Supreme Court rulings, in particular, have made the public assertion of religious values problematic, and that religion has been relegated to a private and unimportant sphere of human activity. (TGJ) **See also** First Amendment.

BIBLIOGRAPHY

Carter, Stephen L. *The Culture of Disbelief: How American Law and Politics Trivialize Religious Devotion*. New York: Basic Books, 1993.

Robert P. Casey (1932–)

Born in New York and trained as a lawyer, Robert Casey has held a number of political positions in Pennsylvania, including serving as governor from 1987 to 1995. During his tenure, he signed the **abortion** control law that ultimately led to the U.S. Supreme Court case, ***Planned Parenthood of Southeastern Pennsylvania v. Casey*** (1992). A devout Catholic, Casey has tried unsuccessfully to get the **Democratic Party** to reconsider its support of abortion rights. In 1992, he asked to speak at the Democratic National Convention, but his request was denied because organizers feared he would use the opportunity to speak out against the party's abortion plank. (MWP) **See also** Roman Catholicism.

BIBLIOGRAPHY

Casey, Robert P. *Fighting for Life*. Dallas: Word Publishing, 1996.

Catholic Worker Movement

The Catholic Worker Movement was and continues to be a radical Catholic movement for social witness and action on behalf of the poor, the working class, and pacifism. In one sense, the Catholic Worker Movement began with the first appearance of the monthly *Catholic Worker* in the midst of the Great Depression of the 1930s. The inaugural issue was sold by hand, at a penny a copy, at the May Day rally in New York City on May 1, 1933. From this beginning grew a movement. The founders of the paper and the movement were **Dorothy Day** (1897-1980) and **Peter Maurin** (1877-1949). Day's roots had been in the radical community of socialists, communists, and anarchists in New York City. After her conversion to Catholicism, she sought to show that being a Christian intrinsically involved identification with the very people the atheistic socialists and communists championed. Peter Maurin, a French-born immigrant to the United States, longed for a society where work and living conditions recognized and fostered the God-given dignity of each person. He lived in self-chosen poverty until his death. These two people of different backgrounds came together to struggle against poverty, joblessness, and homelessness. Their chief means were the paper, the informal education of people attracted to the movement through participation in protests and strikes, a simplicity of lifestyle, Houses of Hospitality, and farming communes. The Houses of Hospitality and family communes were an attempt to live in a society free of the profit motive, wherein the holiness of the individual could be expressed.

The Catholic Worker Movement, a minority in the Catholic Church, nevertheless significantly influenced many Catholics toward a radical, activist Catholicism. These include Thomas Merton, the well-known Trappist monk and writer on spiritual and socio-political topics, and the **Berrigan** brothers, **Daniel** and **Philip**, both priests and activists for social change in the 1960s. Even the influential socialist commentator Michael Harrington had roots in this movement; he was an editor for *The Catholic Worker* in the early 1950s. More than 130 Catholic Worker Hospitality Houses and farm communes exist today in the United States and abroad, and *The Catholic Worker* continues to be published. (GSS) **See also** Atheism; Roman Catholicism; Socialism and Communism.

BIBLIOGRAPHY

Diehl, Mel. *Breaking Bread: The Catholic Worker and the Origin of Catholic Radicalism in America.* Philadelphia: Temple University, 1982.

Ellis, Marc H. *Peter Maurin: Prophet in the Twentieth Century*. New York: Paulist Press, 1981.

Miller, William D. *Dorothy Day: A Biography*. San Francisco: Harper & Row, 1982.

Roberts, Nancy L. *Dorothy Day and the Catholic Worker*. Albany: State University of New York, 1984.

Censorship

Censorship is the practice of removing access to material because it is found objectionable. This can be done on a personal, social, or institutional level. The **First Amendment** states that "Congress shall make no law respecting an establishment of religion, or prohibiting the free exercise thereof; or abridging the freedom of speech, or of the press." While laws that contradict the First Amendment can be considered censorship at a governmental level, organizations or individuals can also attempt to censor material.

One of the earliest censorship campaigns in the United States was led by Anthony Comstock. He was a crusader for the removal of all material considered to be contrary to public morals. He founded the New York Society for the Suppression of Vice and was designated an unpaid U.S. postal inspector for the purpose of inspecting the mail for obscenity or contraceptive information. His urging prompted Congress to pass the federal anti-obscenity law of 1873, known as the Comstock Act, which banned the sale of items "for the purpose of contraception" or "obscene, lewd and lascivious" publications.

The current criteria for banning material at a governmental level is the Miller Standard, which legislated that obscene material can be legally banned. Obscene material is defined as being material that appeals to a "prurient" interest in sex, is patently offensive under contemporary community standards, and lacks significant scientific, literary, artistic, or political value. Many people attempting to ban materials argue that their communities, whether they are geographical or ideological, find material to be offensive that is otherwise not bound by the Miller standard. They often object to public money in the form of taxes being used to purchase for libraries and schools material that is counter to their personal beliefs.

Groups that try to censor books have many different justifications for their requests: e.g., material that portrays women or minorities in unfavorable lights, that contains strong language or imagery some people find personally offensive, that makes adult subject matter available to children, or that promotes lifestyles and attitudes that some people find objectionable. An example includes the book *Daddy's Roommate,* which deals with a family with two gay male parents and is not considered legally obscene. Groups like Family Friendly Libraries have been attempting to get this book banned from public schools and public libraries because of its "pro-gay-agenda." The American Library Association's Office of Intellectual Freedom offers assistance to libraries that are facing challenges to books in their collections.

Popular music has also been the subject of intense censorship debates. In the 1950s, as the popularity of rock n' roll increased, Billie Holiday's song, "Love For Sale," was banned from ABC radio because of its prostitution theme. In the mid-1980s, a group called the Parents Music Resource Center was founded by Tipper Gore to get record companies to monitor and rate their artists' releases with a system similar to the MPAA system for movies. The group convinced the Recording Industry Association of America to develop a labeling system to indicate whether a recording contained explicit lyrics regarding drugs, sex, violence, or other "potentially objectionable material." Many large retailers refused to sell products with the warning labels, causing musicians to record two versions of controversial material, one as originally intended and one with questionable material removed.

As an inexpensive, efficient, and rapidly expanding means of information transfer, the Internet has also come under censorious scrutiny. In 1994, Democratic Senator Jim Exon of Nebraska sponsored a bill known as the Communications Decency Act that sought to make transmission of "indecent" speech via the Internet a felony. The bill was signed into law in 1996, but was immediately challenged for being too vague and for criminalizing speech that is protected by the First Amendment and relevant case law. The act was overturned in June 1997 in the *ACLU v. Reno* decision.

Censorship can take many forms and be in opposition to many different types of subject matter. While the First Amendment protects many individuals and organizations from governmental censorship, it does not always ensure free access to information at every level. **See also** Abortion and Birth Control Regulation; Free Exercise Clause; Free Speech Approach to Religious Liberty.

BIBLIOGRAPHY

Busha, Charles H. *An Intellectual Freedom Primer*. Littleton, CO: Libraries Unlimited, 1977.

Daily, Jay. *The Anatomy of Censorship*. New York: Marcel Dekker, 1973.

DeGrazia, Edward. *Girls Lean Back Everywhere: The Law of Obscenity and the Assault on Genius.* New York: Random House, 1992.

Demac, Donna. *Liberty Denied, The Current Rise of Censorship in America*. New Brunswick, NJ: Rutgers University Press, 1990.

The Challenge of Peace

In 1983, the **National Conference of Catholic Bishops (NCCB)** issued a pastoral letter on war and peace, entitled *The Challenge of Peace: God's Promise and Our Response*. In this teaching document, the NCCB examined the moral and ethical issues of modern warfare, with an emphasis on the use and purposes of nuclear weapons. *The Challenge of Peace* represented, if not a reversal, at least a radical shift in emphasis from the American Catholic Church's traditional anti-communist and just **war** stance. The pastoral letter constituted an attempt to extend the church's "pro-life" stance beyond the **abortion** issue, and into the area of defense and foreign policy. The letter applied a particularly stringent version of Augustine's concept of the "just war" to the contemporary deployment of nuclear weapons, and found that the prospect of nuclear war (including the concept of deterrence) violated two provisions of the just war tradition: proportionality and noncombatant immunity. The requirement of proportionality means that, since warfare is inherently evil, engaging in warfare can only be justified if the good to be gained outweighs the evil to be endured by warfare. Under such a criterion, the indiscriminate and widespread destruction that would result from the deployment of nuclear weapons would clearly (in the eyes of the bishops) be entirely disproportionate to any possible gain. Similarly, the just war tradition proscribes the intentional killing of civilians and noncombatants. Again, nuclear weapons would make no distinctions between combatants and noncombatants. Indeed, civilians would be among the most likely casualties in any "countervalue" strategy (in which population centers would be targeted), which represented the stated policies of both the United States and the Soviet Union. For these reasons, the use or threat of nuclear weapons could, according to the peace pastoral letter, never be morally justified.

The timing of *The Challenge of Peace* appears to have been dictated by the pattern of electoral politics in the United States. Work on the document began shortly after the election of **Ronald Reagan** to the U.S. presidency in 1980. As a presidential candidate, Reagan voiced strong support for the importance of American nuclear superiority, and occasionally cited analysts who suggested that nuclear war was potentially winnable, or that a limited nuclear war could be confined to Europe. The bishops' letter can be seen as a reaction to this change in the political climate of the United States.

In the letter, the bishops address Roman Catholics with arguments specifically supported by Catholic doctrine, but they also explicitly enter the wider debate about military and foreign policy with policy recommendation directed to "people of goodwill." (TGJ) **See also** Just War Theory; Nuclear Disarmament; Peace Movement; Roman Catholicism; Socialism and Communism.

BIBLIOGRAPHY

Byrnes, Timothy A. *Catholic Bishops in American Politics*. Princeton, NJ: Princeton University Press, 1991.

National Council of Catholic Bishops. *The Challenge of Peace: God's Promise and Our Response*. Washington, DC: United States Catholic Conference, 1983.

William Ellery Channing (1780–1842)

William Ellery Channing was a religious liberal and social progressive who launched a new Christian denomination and assisted in the development of the American **peace movement**. His abhorrence of the doctrine of original sin and his belief in the perfectibility of humanity led him to advocate the reformation of society according to the liberal moral principle of self-determination. His liberal theological views led him to reject the doctrine of the Trinity, which explained the divinity of Jesus and was a centerpiece of traditional Christian faith, and to espouse a unitarian Christianity that became the foundation for contemporary Unitarian Universalist churches.

He was strongly influenced by Scottish common sense philosophy, and used its principle of acting in accordance with clearly held beliefs to justify his **pacifism**. In 1815, he helped organized the Massachusetts Peace Society, which spawned the American Peace Society in 1828. He condemned the War of 1812 as unnecessary, and was a strong supporter of the antislavery movement. Both stances were unpopular with the wealthy patrons of his Boston congregation, yet he served the Federal Street Church for 40 years because the members of his congregation admired his rhetorical style and rational argumentation. (KMY) **See also** Abolition; Liberalism; Unitarianism; War.

Delbanco, Andrew. *William Ellery Channing: An Essay on the Liberal Spirit in America*. Cambridge, MA: Harvard University Press, 1981.

Wright, Conrad. *3 Prophets of Religious Liberalism: Channing—Emerson—Parker*. Boston: Unitarian Universalist Association, 1986.

Chaplaincy

Chaplaincy, although designating a variety of religious functions throughout history, most often describes an institutional but non-parish ministry, with service in the military, hospitals, educational programs, prisons, industry, and government. In a more specialized sense, the term may also indicate the spiritual advisor to a religious house or the private secretary to a bishop. The prototype for the chaplaincy extends to ancient Egypt where the priests of Amon-Re accompanied the army, as did Aaronic priests with the Israelite army. "Chaplain" derives from Latin *cappella*, "little cloak," and described the cape of St. Martin of Tours (d. 397), which was kept as a relic by Frankish kings. "Chapel" designated the place of its keeping, and "chaplain," the one charged with its custody. The term later came to mean a minister to the king who said Mass and could do clerical work. The office grew in importance to a post of royal advisor on both secular and ecclesiastical affairs.

In the United States, chaplaincy took on its more familiar contours during the Revolutionary War when the **Continental Congress** appointed chaplains to serve with the army. The legislative chaplaincy also dates to the same time. Congress arranged for a minister to open its first session with prayer in 1774, formalizing the office two years later. During the **Civil War**, Congress dropped the stipulation that military chaplains must be Christian, specifying only the individual be a "regularly ordained minister" with ecclesiastical endorsement. The pattern is followed today: most chaplains complete a course of specialized study, are ordained or otherwise recognized by the sponsoring organization, and are then endorsed to a particular service. **Establishment Clause** issues are raised when a chaplain receives public funds, as in the case of prison, military, and legislative chaplains. *Katkoff v. Marsh* turned back a challenge to the military chaplaincy, reasoning that it promotes good order and discipline and supports free exercise rights of military personnel, a rationale courts continue to accept. In ***Marsh v. Chambers***, 463 U.S. 783 (1983), the Supreme Court supported the legislative chaplaincy, arguing its legitimacy from historical precedent. (JML) **See also** First Amendment; Israel; Military Service; Prisoners, Religious Rights of.

BIBLIOGRAPHY

Hutcheson, Richard G. *The Churches and the Chaplaincy*. Atlanta: John Knox Press, 1975.

Stokes, Anson, and Leo Pfeffer. *Church and State in the United States*. New York: Harper and Row, 1964.

Thompson, Parker C. *From Its European Antecedents to 1791*. Volume I of *The United States Army Chaplaincy*. Washington, DC: Office of the Chief of Chaplains (Department of the Army), 1978.

Zahn, Gordon. *The Military Chaplaincy*. Toronto: University of Toronto Press, 1969.

Chaplinsky v. State of New Hampshire (1942)

Chaplinsky, a **Jehovah's Witness**, was taken to jail for creating a public disturbance with his denouncements of religion. He was later arrested for violating a New Hampshire statute that prohibited the use of derisive or offensive words. On appeal, Chaplinsky's lawyers argued that the statute restricted the **First Amendment**'s religious and speech rights. In *Chaplinsky v. State of New Hampshire*, 315 U.S. 568 (1942), the U.S. Supreme Court ruled in favor of New Hampshire, stating that certain words or phrases are not necessary to the exposition of ideas and that the state has a legitimate interest in order and morality. (JP)

BIBLIOGRAPHY

"The Demise of the Chaplinsky Fighting Words Doctrine." *Harvard Law Review* 106, no. 5 (March 1993): 1129-46.

Mannheinner, Michael J. "The Fighting Words Doctrine." *Columbia Law Review* 93, no. 6 (October 1993): 1527-71.

Charismatic Movement

Charismatic Christians, also called neo-**Pentecostals**, believe in the gifts of the Holy Spirit, which include glossolalia or speaking in tongues, miracle healings, receiving words of knowledge and wisdom, and prophetic utterances. Primarily associated with **Evangelical** Protestants and a **fundamentalist** theology, an expanded Charismatic Movement emerged in the 1960s with the increase of charismatic experiences beyond the traditional Pentecostal denominations. According to Gallup polling, nearly 15 percent of self-identified Charismatic Christians are Catholic and 5 percent represent mainline Protestant denominations and various nondenominational churches. (DD) **See also** Roman Catholicism.

BIBLIOGRAPHY

Synan, Vinson. *The Holiness-Pentecostal Tradition: Charismatic Movements in the 20th Century*. Grand Rapids, MI: William B. Eerdmans Co., 1997.

Cherokee Removal

Occurring between the first and second phases of U.S. territorial expansion, Indian removal from the lands east of the Mississippi to Indian Territory affected many tribes, but the most infamous was the removal of the Cherokee from Georgia. The beginnings of a national removal policy were seen in 1785 with the first Treaty of Hopewell. After the turn of the century, the cessation of lands west of modern-day Georgia and the Louisiana Purchase created the conditions necessary to displace large numbers of Indians in the east. The Cherokee, one of the largest tribes in Georgia, faced pressure from the government to relocate westward as early as 1802. Pressure increased at the conclusion of the War of 1812, and, with the assistance of Secretary of War John C. Calhoun, Major General **Andrew Jackson**, and Governor Lewis Cass of Michigan Territory, an effort was made to formally remove the Indians from the east.

The Cherokee had effectively assimilated into white society by the 1820s. In 1827, the Cherokee adopted a written constitution, but instead of appeasing their neighbors, their efforts only increased the animosity of the state government of Georgia. Missionaries such as **Jeremiah Evarts** led a national campaign to safeguard Cherokee lands, but in 1830, during President Andrew Jackson's second year in office, Congress passed the Indian Removal Act, authorizing the president to set up districts within Indian Territory. After resisting initial efforts, the Cherokee finally signed a removal treaty in 1835, the Treaty of New Echota. However, many of the Cherokee remained on their lands, and General Winfield Scott and his troops forced the Indians to march westward during the winter of 1838-39. The Trail of Tears, as this march became known, had a 25 percent mortality, and many more Cherokee died after resettlement in the Indian Territory in modern Oklahoma because of their malnourished state, lack of food upon arrival and the harsh conditions during the forced march. (GT) **See also** American Indian Religious Freedom Act; Native American Religions; William Penn Essays.

BIBLIOGRAPHY

Evarts, Jeremiah. *Cherokee Removal: The "William Penn" Essays and Other Writings*. Francis Paul Prucha, ed. Knoxville: University of Tennessee Press, 1981.

Lumpkin, Wilson. *The Removal of the Cherokee Indians from Georgia*. New York: Arno Press & the New York Times, 1969.

Wallace, Anthony. *The Long Bitter Trail: Andrew Jackson and the Indians*. New York: Hill and Wang, 1993.

West, John G., Jr. "Evangelicals and Cherokee Removal." In *The Politics of Revelation and Reason: Religion and Civic Life in the New Nation*. Lawrence: University Press of Kansas, 1996.

Lydia Maria Child (1802–1880)

Lydia Child was a successful author and social reformer. In 1833, she and her husband David Lee Child published *An Appeal in Favor of that Class of Americans Called Africans* in which they argued for the education of slaves as a preparation for **abolition**. They continued their abolitionist stance by editing the *National Anti-Slavery Standard*, a weekly New York paper. Child was also an outspoken opponent of **capital punishment** and wrote on **social justice** subjects, including women's suffrage. (MWP) **See also** Women in Religion and Politics.

BIBLIOGRAPHY

Clifford, Deborah P. *Crusader for Freedom*. Boston: Beacon, 1992.

Karcher, Carolyn C. *The First Woman in the Republic*. Durham, NC: Duke University Press, 1994.

Child-Benefit Theory

The U.S. Supreme Court has held that state aid to school children attending private religious schools is constitutionally permissible if the aid is intended to further the educational needs of children and not the sectarian purposes of the schools themselves. Although the Court applied the principle as early as ***Cochran v. Louisiana State Board of Education*** (1930), the best-known case using the child-benefit doctrine is ***Everson v. Board of Education of the Township of Ewing*** (1947), in which Justice **Hugo Black** argued that a New Jersey township could reimburse parents for the cost of their children's bus fare to and from private religious schools. This plan was not a violation of the **Establishment Clause** because the aid went directly to children and their parents, not to schools, and it was available to parents of both private and public school children. Although the Court's application of the doctrine is often confusing and uneven, it has been used to uphold numerous programs benefitting students in religious schools, including textbook lending in *Board of Education v. Allen*

(1968), tax deductions for certain educational expenses in ***Mueller v. Allen*** (1983) and services for disabled religious students in ***Zobrest v. Catalina Foothills School District*** (1993). (KRD) **See also** First Amendment.

BIBLIOGRAPHY

Stilner, Jeffrey. "Rethinking the Wall of Separation." *Capital University Law Review* 23, no. 3 (1994): 823-61.

Christian Coalition

The Christian Coalition was formed in the aftermath of evangelist **Pat Robertson**'s unsuccessful bid for the **Republican Party**'s presidential nomination in 1988. Robertson founded the group in October 1989 because he saw a need for a national grassroots citizens action organization to counter what Robertson called the anti-Christian bias in many areas of American life. The organization advocated what it referred to as family values and **school prayer** while opposing **abortion** and gay rights. It also supported a conservative political agenda.

The approach used by the Christian Coalition was to organize at the county level for the purpose of influencing the policies of the Republican Party. It did this by having members attend Republican Party caucuses and committee meetings. The Coalition's stated objective was to see a working majority of the Republican Party in the hands of conservative Christians by 1996. By 1994, supporters of the Christian Coalition had taken over state caucuses of the Republican Party in five states and had become a major factor in about a dozen other states.

Under the leadership of Executive Director **Ralph Reed**, the Christian Coalition established a sophisticated political operation in the 1990s. This operation included a network of computers, phone banks, direct mail, and fax machines at its Chesapeake, Virginia, headquarters. The Coalition also sponsored Citizen Action Training Schools; set up a governmental affairs office in Washington, DC; established two publications, *Christian American* and *Religious Rights Watch*; and distributed millions of voting guides through churches throughout the United States. By 1997, the Coalition claimed a membership of 1,700,000.

Since the 1996 election, the Christian Coalition has undergone a decline. Ralph Reed resigned as executive director and its contributions fell from over $26 million in 1996 to $17 million in 1997. Some Christian conservatives have transferred their support to the Family Research Council in part because of their disapproval of the Coalition's close ties to the Republican Party. In addition, the Christian Coalition has been sued by the Federal Election Commission, which has accused the nonprofit organization of expressly advocating the election of Republican candidates in violation of its tax exempt status. Despite these problems, the Christian Coalition has the support of approximately 15 percent of the American public, and it has established itself as the dominant Christian conservative group in the United States in the 1990s. (The Christian Coalition's "Contract with the American Family" is reprinted in Appendix 1.) (WVM) **See also** Conservatism; Homosexual Rights; Religious Rights; Televangelism.

BIBLIOGRAPHY

Bruce, Steve, Peter Kivisto and William Swatos, Jr., eds. *The Rapture of Politics*. New Brunswick, NJ: Transaction Books, 1995.

Rozzell, Mark J. and Clyde Wilcox. *God at the Grassroots*. Lanham, MD: Rowman and Littlefield, 1995.

Christian Reconstructionist Movement

The Christian Reconstructionist movement is a political theology advocating the reconstruction of society along strict biblical lines. Often called "dominion theology" or "theonomy," it arose within Reformed Protestantism and frequently parallels the **Puritan** theology of early New England. While not a monolithic movement, Christian Recontructionists share four core beliefs:

Presuppositionalism. Ultimate truth is presupposed. Different presuppositions lead to different conclusions regarding the nature of things, including the political order. The biblical God is the only presupposition that makes the world intelligible.

Biblicism. The Bible contains the necessary blueprint for ordering civil society.

Theonomy. The laws of God revealed to the Old Testament nation of **Israel** are still applicable. A modern theonomic state would, for example, enforce the death penalty against blasphemers, adulterers, and rebellious children.

Postmillennialism. Christians will eventually govern society. This triumphant day may be centuries away, but it will surely come.

The four most influential Christian Reconstructionists are **Rousas Rushdoony** (Chalcedon Foundation), **Gary North** (Institute for Christian Economics), Gary DeMar (AmericaVision), and the late Greg Bahnsen. By all accounts, Rushdoony launched the movement with the publication of his *Institutes of Biblical Law* in 1973. North developed the economic implications of a theonomic state, which include a return to the gold standard, the elimination of property taxes, restrictions on usury, and a 10 percent cap on taxes. DeMar has focused on the political aspects of Reconstructionism, while Bahnsen's writings remain the most erudite defense of the movement.

Politically, Reconstructionists are "Christian libertarians." According to Rushdoony, "The state is limited to a ministry of justice, and free enterprise and individual initiative are given the freedom to develop." Reconstructionists advocate a decentralized, limited, and republican form of government, with the family as the most basic and inviolable governmental unit.

Christian Reconstructionism has been influential. The **fundamentalist** school movement was inspired by Rushdoony's critique of public education, and North influenced a number of **charismatic movements** that forthrightly proclaim the "crown rights of King Jesus." Many New Christian Right activists appreciate the rationale of Reconstructionism, even if they do not accept all its doctrinal assumptions. **Pat Robertson** admitted that he admired many Reconstructionist teachings because they agreed with the Bible teaching that Christians are to "exercise dominion in his name."

Critics of Reconstructionism challenge the assumption that biblical Israel was a model for the modern nation-state. Many have also noted the internal disagreements between Reconstructionists over such things as the applicability of the Sermon on the Mount or even over the use of kosher dietary laws. Others wonder if Reconstructionism can be established peacefully, since many reactionary movements like the New York Patriots have adopted Reconstructionist or semi-Reconstructionist themes. According to these critics, Christian Reconstructionism truncates the Christian gospel and reduces it to an impersonal, and potentially dangerous, legal abstraction. (ARB) **See also** Religious Right; Theonomist.

Bibliography

Barker, William S. and W. Robert Godfrey, eds. *Theonomy: Reformed Critique*. Grand Rapids, MI: Zondervan Publishing, 1990.

Clapp, Rodney. "Democracy as Heresy." *Christianity Today* 31, no. 3 (February 20, 1987): 17-23.

House, H. Wayne and Thomas Ice. *Dominion Theology: Blessing or Curse?* Portland, OR: Multnomah Press, 1988.

Rushdoony, Rousas J. *Institutes of Biblical Law*. Nutley, NJ: Craig Press, 1973.

Christian Science

Founded in 1879 by **Mary Baker Eddy**, Christian Science is a Christian sect that is based upon the healings that Jesus performed in the New Testament. In addition to the Bible, adherents use Eddy's book *Science and Health* (1875) as a guide for living. The theology behind Christian Science contains elements of **Ralph Waldo Emerson**'s **transcendentalism** and **William James**'s pragmatism.

Each local church is a self-governing unit and is run in accordance with the *Manual of the Mother Church*. The Church's headquarters—known as the First Church of Christian, Science—is located in Boston, Massachusetts. In conjunction with its religious activities, the Church publishes the *Christian Science Monitor*, an international daily newspaper, and owns and operates a network of television and radio stations.

One of the most distinctive features of the group is that adherents turn to prayer rather than conventional medicine when they are ill or injured. The Church has full-time practitioners who specialize in the practice of healing. However, this practice of rejecting modern medical treatments has brought members of the Church into conflict with civil authorities, especially when it comes to treating minors who have been seriously injured or who suffer from a serious illness. Several cases in lower courts have sought to give custody to the state or a temporary guardian so as to treat a minor against the wishes of his or her parents.

Bibliography

Hoekema, Anthony A. *Christian Science*. Grand Rapids, MI: Eerdmans, 1974.

Christianity Today

Christianity Today is a magazine of "evangelical conviction" that was founded in 1956 by **Billy Graham**. Published 14 times per year, *Christianity Today* is a forum for Protestant Christians who accept the inerrancy of the Bible and apply its teachings to contemporary problems in society and the church. It supports churches in their primary task of preaching salvation in Christ and addresses the responsibilities Christians have to meet societal needs and to advance public justice. Conservative in its religious perspectives, it is often a counterpoint to liberal Protestant views in *Christian Century*. Christianity Today Incorporated now publishes eight additional magazines. (JVD) **See also** Conservatism; Evangelicals.

Bibliography

Fowler, R.B. *A New Engagement: Evangelical Political Thought, 1966-1976*. Grand Rapids, MI: Eerdmans, 1982.

Church of Jesus Christ of Latter-day Saints

Founded in 1830 by **Joseph Smith** in Palmyra, New York, the Church of Jesus Christ of Latter-day Saints, also known as the LDS or "Mormon" Church, serves as an interesting case study of religion and politics. Because of its peculiar doctrines and practices it was controversial from the beginning and frequently involved in formal legal action. With the discontinuation of its most unusual practice, polygyny, the church began to blend with U.S. society and culture, and has gained wider acceptance in U.S. politics. LDS beliefs, based on the Book of Mormon, the Bible, and other works, represent a distinctly American version of Christianity.

In its early history, the church moved frequently because of persecution, a result of Mormon heterodoxy and Mormon actions that non-Mormons saw as threats to their economic and social life. After Missouri Governor Lilburn Boggs issued an order that all Mormons leave or be "exterminated," the Church settled in Nauvoo, Illinois. Again, the great influx of Mormons and their unusual beliefs and practices, most notably "plural marriage" or polygyny, combined to bring Mormons and non-Mormons into conflict. The strife ended when Smith was murdered in an Illinois jail in 1844, and most Mormons soon after began a trek to Utah under the direction of **Brigham Young**. Most of those who did not follow Young to Utah formed the Reorganized Church of Jesus Christ of Latter-day Saints (RLDS), which is the second largest Mormon body in the country. The RLDS rejected Young's leadership and many of the church's practices including polygyny. Sometimes referred to as the Missouri Mormons, the

RLDS has approximately 250,000 members (the LDS has more than 4.3 million) and is based in Independence, Missouri.

In Utah, the church grew, spreading into Canada and Mexico. During this time, relations between the Church and the federal government were cold. A series of non-Mormon territorial governors, and even federal troops, were sent to watch over the Mormons. Utah statehood was delayed because of polygyny, but granted in 1896 after the Church announced an end to the practice. Despite the announcement, several prominent Mormon men continued polygynous relationships. This adversely affected church-government relations, and subsequent congressional hearings involved prominent Mormons, including the Church's prophet at the time, Joseph F. Smith. These hearings also attempted to prevent Mormons from taking elected office.

During the mid-twentieth century, Mormon political influence grew, at least partly because **Ezra Taft Benson** and others helped the Church to be seen as more mainstream than it had been in the past. Mormons have continued their involvement in national politics by their service in all three branches of the government. Recent Church involvement in elections has been typically limited to positions of neutrality. For example, the church encourages voting, but does not endorse candidates. Its involvement in legal proceedings, however, is worth noting for the political implications. In *Lanner v. Wimmer,* 662 F. 2d 1349 (10th Cir., 1981), the court allowed the continued practice of releasing public school students to obtain religious instruction at LDS seminaries during school hours, but ruled that such students could no longer receive academic credit for those courses. Although the Church was not a direct participant in this litigation between a Utah school district and a private citizen, the case represents the Church's scope of influence in Utah life.

The Angel Moroni gives the plates containing the Book of Mormon to Joseph Smith in September 1827. Founded by Smith, the Church of Jesus Christ of Latter-day Saints (Mormons) suffered persecution in its early days for its unorthodox beliefs and practices, including polygamy. After a drawing by C.C.A. Christensen. Library of Congress.

In a case with broader implications, *Corporation of the Presiding Bishop of the Church of Jesus Christ of Latter-day Saints et al. v. Amos et al.*, 483 U.S. 327 (1987), the U.S. Supreme Court heard the Church defend its practice of requiring employees at Church-owned industries to agree with doctrinal statements and to meet specific standards of behavior. The court ruled that the practice violated neither the Civil Rights Act of 1964, nor the exemption clause of the **First Amendment**.

Not all the church's political activities have been in the courts, nor have they been official. Although Mormons frequently win political office, and their judgments in office tend to reflect Church values, legislators rarely admit even to suspicions of Church involvement or lobbying. The ever-present influence of the Church in Utah reveals itself instead through the mores and values of the state's populace. One exception was the vigorous, and sometimes covert, effort of the Church to ensure that Utah did not pass the **Equal Rights Amendment** in the 1970s.

LDS church growth and expansion in the U.S. has been accompanied by efforts to influence political activities in states other than Utah. These efforts usually take the form of "friend of the court" briefs and announcements in Church services. Hawaii legislation to make homosexual unions equivalent to marriage, and Oregon legislation allowing "doctor-assisted suicide" are two such examples. (MEN) **See also** *Church of Jesus Christ of Latter-day Saints v. United States*; Polygamy.

BIBLIOGRAPHY

Allen, James B. and Glen M. Leonard. *The Story of the Latter-day Saints v United States*. 2nd ed. Salt Lake City: Deseret Books, 1992.

Arrington, Leonard A. and Davis Bitton. *The Mormon Experience: A History of the Latter-day Saints*. New York: Alfred A. Knopf, 1979.

Firmage, Edwin B. and Richard C. Mangrum. *Zion in the Courts: A Legal History of the Church of Jesus Christ of Latter-day Saints, 1830-1900*. Urbana: University of Illinois Press, 1988.

Mauss, Armand. *The Angel and the Beehive*. Urbana: University of Illinois Press, 1994.

Shipps, Jan. *Mormonism: The Story of a New Religious Tradition*. Urbana: University of Illinois Press, 1985.

Church of Jesus Christ of Latter-day Saints v. United States (1890)

In the nineteenth century, the **Church of Jesus Christ of Latter-day Saints** (or Mormon Church), practiced "plural marriage" or polygyny, in which a man married two or more women in an attempt to imitate ancient biblical practices. In an effort to end the Church's polygynous marriages, which were prompting a national outcry, Congress passed a series of increasingly stringent bills to prosecute bigamists. Federal legislation to halt the practice culminated with the Edmunds-Tucker Act (1887), which required the testimony of witnesses at trials, required individuals to sign an oath supporting anti-polygamy laws before voting, claimed most of the Church's assets, and otherwise ended the Church as a legal entity. The provisions of the Edmunds-Tucker Act were challenged but upheld by the U.S. Supreme Court in *Church of Jesus Christ of Latter-day Saints v. United States,* 136 U.S. 1 (1890), and most of the Church's assets were confiscated. Church leaders were forced to go into hiding from the authorities while they tried to obtain support for their cause. After the Church announced an end to polygyny, bills sponsored by legislators sympathetic to Mormonism were passed, helping the Church resume operations. However, the financial hardship imposed on the Church was long-lasting, and polygyny continued surreptitiously. (MEN) **See also** Polygamy; Joseph Smith; Brigham Young.

Bibliography

Firmage, Edwin B. and Richard C. Mangrum. *Zion in the Courts: A Legal History of the Church of Jesus Christ of Latter-day Saints, 1830-1900*. Urbana: University of Illinois Press, 1988.

Hardy, B. Carmen. *Solemn Covenant: The Mormon Polygamous Passage*. Urbana: University of Illinois Press, 1992.

Church of Lukumi Babalu Aye v. City of Hialeah (1993)

A church that included animal sacrifice as part of its ritual appealed to the Supreme Court to overturn ordinances of the City of Hialeah that had the effect of restricting the slaughter of animals. The city argued the ordinances were neutral and generally applicable to the populace, but in *Church of Lukumi Babalu Aye v. City of Hialeah*, 508 U.S. 520 (1993), the Supreme Court held that the ordinances actually barred the killing of animals only for purposes of religious expression. Animal slaughter for purposes of food processing, hunting, or **euthanasia** was not prohibited. Therefore, the asserted governmental interest in disposal of animals and consumption of uninspected meat was actually a ruse to stop religious sacrifices. (FHJ) **See also** Free Exercise Clause; First Amendment.

Bibliography

Cruz, R. Ted. "Animal Sacrifice and Equal Protection Free Exercise. (Case Note)" *Harvard Journal of Law & Public Policy* 17, no. 1 (Winter 1994): 262-73.

Graglia, Lino A. "Church of the Lukumi Babalu Aye: Of Animal Sacrifice and Religious Persecution." *Georgetown Law Journal* 85, no. 1 (November 1996): 1-69.

Church of the Brethren

The Church of the Brethren was a Protestant denomination (with roots in **Pietism** and the Anabaptist tradition) that was founded in 1708 by Alexander Mack in Schwarzenau, Germany. During the 1720s, persecution in Europe led many of the Church's followers to seek refuge in Pennsylvania. Known as German Baptist Brethren, Dunkers, and Dunkards, the denomination formally adopted the name Church of the Brethren in 1908. Like the Friends and **Mennonites**, the Brethren are pacifists. Membership in 1987 was 155,000. A number of smaller denominations share the same roots but differ on how closely they maintain traditional practices. **See also** Baptists; Pacifism; Quakers.

Bibliography

Durnbaugh, Donald F. *The Church of the Brethren Past and Present*. Elgin, IL: Brethren Press, 1971.

Church of the Holy Trinity v. United States (1892)

Early in its history, the U.S. Supreme Court upheld a variety of state laws designed to aid and support religious practice in the United States. The Court rejected arguments that such actions on the part of the states violated the **Establishment Clause**, claiming in *Church of the Holy Trinity v. United States*, 143 U.S. 457 (1892), that "this is a Christian nation," and as long as one sect is not preferred over another, the Constitution has not been violated. The Court explicitly repudiated this approach in ***Engel v. Vitale***, 370 U.S. 421 (1962), rejecting a claim that a **school prayer** was simply an acceptable part of the spiritual heritage of the United States. (JM) **See also** First Amendment.

Bibliography

Frankel, Marvin E. *Faith and Freedom*. New York: Hill and Wang, 1994.

Weber, Paul J., ed. *Equal Protection*. New York: Greenwood, 1990.

City of Boerne v. Flores (1997)

In 1993, Congress passed and President **Bill Clinton** signed the **Religious Freedom Restoration Act (RFRA)**, which was intended to reverse the Supreme Court's decision in ***Employment Division of Oregon v. Smith*** (1990). In the 1997 decision, *City of Boerne v. Flores*, 117 S.Ct. 2157 (1997), the Supreme Court struck down the RFRA. The case involved a Catholic Church in Boerne, Texas, that wanted to expand its building to accommodate the needs of a growing congregation. The Boerne City Council passed an ordinance authorizing its Historic Landmark Commission to prepare a preservation plan. Based upon the plan, the church was denied a building permit to expand. The church challenged the city's decision under the RFRA, claiming that government cannot interfere with religion unless there is a compelling interest.

Instead of limiting its analysis to whether *Boerne* could show a compelling interest in preserving the existing church building, the Court took on the RFRA directly. Justice **Anthony Kennedy** argued that Congress passed the RFRA in direct response to the *Smith* decision under the guise of protecting the **Fourteenth Amendment**. However, he noted that any such legislation must be remedial or preventative in nature. Section five of the Fourteenth Amendment was never designed to permit Congress to amplify or redefine constitutional rights. The effect of *Boerne* is that there is no longer even a statutory shield against the holding in *Smith* that allows government to enforce laws that are neutral on their face even if they conflict with an individual's or denomination's free exercise.

Kennedy's analysis is akin to Justice Robert Jackson's concurring opinion in *Youngstown Sheet & Tube Co. v. Sawyer* (1952). Jackson set up a standard for reviewing presidential action. He suggested that when the president's policy has congressional approval, then it is presumed to be constitutional. When Congress is silent, then the Court must offer greater scrutiny to the presidential action. When the president is at odds with Congress, then his or her action is presumed to be unconstitutional. Kennedy's analysis applies the standard to disputes between Congress and the Court. If Congress is consistent with the Court's constitutional interpretation, then the legislation is likely to be valid. If Congress speaks without the Court, then the justices must look carefully. If Congress acts in opposition to the Court, then it is strongly presumed that its action is unconstitutional. (FG) **See also** First Amendment; Free Exercise Clause.

BIBLIOGRAPHY

Gressman, Eugene and Angela Carmella. "The RFRA Revision of the Free Exercise Clause." *Ohio State Law Journal* 57, no. 65 (1996).

"City on a Hill"

The phrase "city on a hill," long associated with a sense of a unique American mission, is taken from Matthew 5:14: "A city that is set on a hill cannot be hid." It was first applied to the New World by **John Winthrop** in a 1630 sermon, "A Model of Christian Charity," delivered while the ship *Arbella* was crossing the Atlantic. Winthrop was speaking specifically of the religious mission of the "plantation" (i.e., colonies) at **Massachusetts Bay** and of New England, although the language has come to be associated with all of America. In the minds of Winthrop and his **Puritan** companions, they were the new **Israel**, and God had specially chosen and commissioned them to go and build a new Zion in the wilderness; it was in this sense that they were to be a city on a hill, an example for other plantations to follow. Over time, the phrase has become shorthand for the perceived role of the United States as a model and leader on the world stage. American politicians as recent as **Ronald Reagan** have spoken of the United States as a "shining city upon a hill." (JHM) **See also** Manifest Destiny.

BIBLIOGRAPHY

Winthrop, John. "A Model of Christian Charity." In Alan Heimert and Andrew Delbanco, eds. *The Puritans in America: A Narrative Anthology*. Cambridge, MA: Harvard University Press, 1985, pp. 81-92.

Civil Disobedience

Civil disobedience is the intentional violation of a law for a higher moral purpose, often with the aim of affecting social change. Although many ancient and biblical heroes violated the laws of their countries to follow God or their own consciences (Socrates, Moses, and Jesus, for example), the concept of civil disobedience was reborn in the United States among those who ignored the Fugitive Slave Act of 1850 and helped runaway slaves find their freedom. In contrast to the colonial revolutionaries who broke English laws in the 1770s, these dissenters did not deny the legitimacy of their government as a whole; they only rejected the validity of certain laws. This sort of limited resistance reappeared in the 1950s and 1960s when the civil rights movement organized a series of sit-ins, boycotts, and demonstration marches to protest racial segregation.

The writer **Henry David Thoreau** provided one of the first modern expositions of these principled and partial rebellions in his 1849 essay, *Resistance to Civil Government*, later published as *Civil Disobedience*. Thoreau had refused to pay his poll tax to protest the government's tolerance for **slavery** and its prosecution of the Mexican War, and he had spent one night in jail as punishment. In his essay, he maintained that men should follow their consciences rather than the law when the two conflicted. Calling a government of men who blindly follow unjust laws a "machine," he advocated small acts of resistance to hinder its workings: "Let your life be a counter friction to stop the machine. What I have to do is to see, at any rate, that I do not lend myself to the wrong which I condemn." The idea that a principled minority could affect change by "clogging the system" was a strong influence on two twentieth-century **civil rights** leaders, Mahatma Gandhi and **Martin Luther King, Jr**.

Gandhi, the Indian reform leader, read Thoreau's essay in 1906 while defending South Asians against discrimination in South Africa, and found that Thoreau's arguments closely resembled his own ideas about the best way to resist injustice. He stressed even more than Thoreau had the need for protesters to accept the legal punishment for their disobedience, even if that punishment was unjust. Only by experiencing injustice firsthand, he argued, could one combat it effectively. Gandhi also emphasized more than Thoreau the sentiment that civil disobedience must be nonviolent to preserve the dignity of the protesters. He sought to transform the attitudes of the oppressors by appealing to their consciences, and believed that the protesters could only affect this transformation by treating themselves with dignity and their oppressors with love.

That emphasis on nonviolence made a deep impression on the American civil rights leader Martin Luther King, Jr., who encountered Gandhi's writings while studying theology in Pennsylvania. Combining Gandhi's ideas with those of St. Thomas Aquinas, who had written of laws higher than the positive laws of one's country, King forged a strategy for the civil rights movement in the South. He used his considerable oratorical powers to persuade many blacks to disobey unjust laws, to submit peacefully to punishment, and to stand still in the face of insults, threats, and physical violence. Thus gaining the moral high ground, King's protests eventually pressured the federal government into enacting the Civil Rights Act of 1964. While in prison after a march in Birmingham, Alabama, King wrote his *Letter from Birmingham Jail*, in which he justified his civil disobedience as obedience to a higher moral law. King's methods were widely imitated not only by civil rights leaders, but also by those objecting to the **Vietnam War** and by abortion protestors in the 1980s.

The 1970s and 1980s saw a flurry of academic interest in the concept of civil disobedience, addressing, among other questions, the issue of whether the "higher law" that one appeals to must be religious in character, or whether it could refer to a strongly held moral belief. (BDG) **See also** Civil Rights Acts.

BIBLIOGRAPHY

Gandhi, M.K. *Non-Violent Resistance*. New York: Schocken Books, 1961.

King, Martin Luther, Jr. *Letter from Birmingham Jail*. San Francisco: Harper San Francisco, 1994.

Thoreau, Henry David. *Walden, or Life in the Woods, and On the Duty of Civil Disobedience*. New York: New American Library, 1980.

Zashin, Elliot M. *Civil Disobedience and Democracy*. New York: Free Press, 1972.

Civil Religion

Civil Religion is a concept that combines two realms that at first glance seem to be exclusive of one another, the this-worldly and the other-worldy. Religion as such concerns the trans-civil (or trans-political); it demands that believers focus attention on God or the eternal. The civil, on the other hand, concerns, above all, the political community or the secular, the life of human beings as citizens of a given polity. To effect a synthesis between the two, it is necessary for one of the elements to be placed in the service of the other: either politics must serve religion or the religious must be made subordinate to the political. Civil religion, as its name suggests, aims to use religion for political ends. Civil religion sets forth doctrines or teachings of a religious character that are meant to have salutary political effects, often times without regard to the truth of those teachings.

Civil religion comes in a variety of guises. Perhaps the most famous articulation of the concept can be found in the work of the philosopher Jean-Jacques Rousseau. In his treatise *On the Social Contract*, Rousseau defined civil religion as a few, precise dogmas whose sole purpose was to obligate citizens to fulfill their civic duties. These dogmas, which included belief in a just providential God and the afterlife, were set forth by the sovereign without regard to "the fate of subjects in the life hereafter." The sovereign's only business was in seeing that those subjects were good citizens in this life. One hears echoes of Rousseau's teaching in **George Washington**'s Farewell Address in which he spoke of religion as "an indispensable support . . . to political prosperity." Religion and morality were "the great pillars of human happiness" and "the firmest props of the duties of men and citizens." In short, religion was to be cherished as much by the "mere politician" as the believer because "reason and experience both forbid us to expect that National morality can prevail in exclusion of religious principle."

The civil religion advocated by Washington may properly be called instrumental. Such a civil religion is a minimum requirement, a floor, that is required for decent politics in every polity, regardless of its form. (Civil religion is especially necessary in a republic wherein the people have the most liberty and thus the greatest opportunity to lapse into corruption.) Yet there is in the American political tradition a type of civil religion that is more than instrumental, one that springs forth directly from the fundamental principles of the American regime.

More than any other document, the **Declaration of Independence** gives voice to these principles in its articulation of humanity's natural rights: "We hold these Truths to be self-evident, that all Men are Created equal, that they are endowed by their Creator with certain unalienable rights, that among these are life, liberty and the pursuit of happiness." The theory of **natural rights** was originally a philosophic doctrine. That theory was set forth most prominently by the British philosopher **John Locke**, and its principles were meant to be discernible to unassisted human reason. The Declaration begins the process of transforming those rational principles into something that is to be believed as a faith. Those principles are not merely to be thought, but they are to be held. They are as much, if not more, the endowment of God the Creator as they are of nature.

That transformation reached its peak in the beautiful words of **Abraham Lincoln**, who advocated making "reverence for the law"—the laws that stemmed from the Declaration and the Constitution—"the political religion of the nation." He spoke of the principles of the Declaration as our "old" or "ancient Faith." The Founders, according to Lincoln, set forth those principles as "a standard maxim of a free society, which could be familiar to all and revered by all." From the point of view of Lincoln, to believe in those principles is to define oneself as an American. (SJL) **See also** Enlightenment; Thomas Jefferson; Natural Law; Washington's Farewell Address.

BIBLIOGRAPHY

Bellah, Robert N. *Habits of the Heart: Individualism and Commitment in American Life*. Berkeley: University of California Press, 1996.

Lincoln, Abraham. *His Speeches and Writings*. Roy P. Basler, ed. New York: Da Capo Press, 1990.

Rousseau, Jean-Jacques. *On the Social Contract*. Roger D. Masters, ed., Judith R. Masters, trans. New York: St. Martin's Press, 1978.

Tocqueville, Alexis de. *Democracy in America*. J.P. Mayer, ed., George Lawrence, trans. Garden City, NY: Anchor Books, 1969.

Washington, George. *George Washington: A Collection*. W.B. Allen, ed. Indianapolis, IN: Liberty Fund Classics, 1988.

Civil Rights

Civil rights, or equal rights, refer to the rights of every individual to equal protection under the law and equal access to public facilities and opportunities. The U.S. Constitution provides two methods of protecting civil rights. First, it ensures that government itself imposes no discriminatory barriers. Second, it gives both national and state governments the authority to protect civil rights against interference by private individuals.

Equality has been a persistent issue and problem in American society. Historically, disadvantaged groups have had to struggle to achieve legal equality. Segregation laws enacted in the last quarter of the nineteenth century were upheld by the U.S. Supreme Court in cases like *Plessy v. Ferguson* (1896). In that case, the Court ruled that separate facilities were constitutional as long as the facilities were equal.

However, the U.S. Supreme Court was also critical in the struggle for equality. Challenges to segregation focused on the **Fourteenth Amendment** and the equal protection clause of this amendment, designed to prevent discrimination by the government. The clause mandates that no state shall deny any person within its jurisdiction the equal protection of law. The National Association for the Advancement of Colored People (NAACP) challenged segregation in education in a series of

In May 1964, President Lyndon Johnson meets at Georgetown University with Catholic, Protestant, and Jewish leaders who are advocating passage of the civil rights bill. Photo by USIA/Leitz. National Archives.

court cases leading up to the 1954 decision in *Brown v. Board of Education of Topeka*. In Brown, the Court ruled that separate educational facilities created a feeling of inferiority in the minds of African-American children and that separate educational facilities were therefore inherently unequal.

The Civil Rights Acts of 1964 and 1968 were designed to prohibit discrimination by private parties. The 1964 Civil Rights Act entitles all individuals to equal access to businesses serving the general public, such as restaurants, hotels, motels, and sports facilities. It also bars discrimination in hiring based on race, sex, ethnicity, or religion. The 1968 Civil Rights Act prohibited discrimination in housing, in terms of renting or selling property. In 1965, the first Voting Rights Act was passed, which prohibited discrimination in registration and voting. The Act was subsequently renewed in 1970, 1975, and 1982.

Many of the successes in the area of civil rights are tied to the commitment of religious groups and religious leaders. Most abolitionist groups fought against the institution of **slavery** on moral and religious grounds. In more recent times, organizations like the **Southern Christian Leadership Conference (SCLC)** was formed, headed by **Martin Luther King, Jr.** Civil rights leaders like King and **Jesse Jackson** were trained ministers who used their pulpits and religious training to motivate and unite people. The civil rights movement was also heavily supported by Jewish Americans who worked with African-Americans. Jewish Americans felt a common cause with African-Americans because Jews had been persecuted for generations.

Civil rights represent the fundamental principles on which the American political system is based. (WVM) **See also** Abolition; Civil Rights Acts; Judaism.

Bibliography

Stikoff, Harvard. *The Struggle for Black Equality.* New York: Hill and Wang, 1981.

Woodward, C. Vann. *The Strange Career of Jim Crow.* New York: Oxford University Press, 1974.

Civil Rights Acts

From the late 1950s to the late 1960s, the United States Congress passed five Civil Rights Acts to protect minority rights. The 1957 and 1960 Civil Rights Acts had limited impact. The 1957 act created a U.S. Commission on Civil Rights and strengthened the civil rights section of the Justice Department while the 1960 act provided for federal voting referees to enroll voters where local officials denied them the right to suffrage. Neither, however, had a significant impact on minority voting registration.

The 1964 Civil Rights Act was the first law with major substantive and enforcement provisions. It forbade discrimination in public accommodations, such as hotels, restaurants, movie theaters, and sports arenas. Another provision of the act prohibited racial discrimination in any public agency, including schools and hospitals, that received federal grants. It also prohibited discrimination in employment on the basis or race, color, sex, religion, or national origin by private contractors receiving federal funds. If discrimination occurred, the federal government could cut off funds. Also, the federal government or individuals could bring civil suits to force desegregation. Finally, the act extended the life of the U.S. Commission on the Civil Rights, established the Equal Employment Opportunity Commission (EEOC) and created a federal Community Relations Service to mediate racial disputes. The 1964 Civil Rights Act gained support from a national coalition of Jewish, Catholic, and Protestant groups.

The 1965 Voting Rights Act was the most important action concerning minority voting rights. First, it targeted areas where less than 50 percent of the eligible voters were registered or had voted in 1964. In these areas, the U.S. attorney general could send federal examiners to register voters, eliminate literacy tests as a prerequisite for voting, and send observers to watch elections. The act also required state and local governments covered by the act to seek pre-clearance from the Justice Department for proposed changes in voting laws or practices. The Voting Rights Act resulted in an increase in black registration in the South by over 1.3 million in three years, was renewed with expanded coverage in 1970, 1975, and 1982 and now covers the entire United States.

Finally, the Civil Rights Act of 1968 prohibited discrimination in the sale or rental of housing based on race, religion, ethnicity, or sex. As a result of these Civil Rights Acts, African Americans have once again become participants in the political process and the practice of legal segregation has been ended. (WVM) **See also** Civil Rights; Martin Luther King, Jr.

BIBLIOGRAPHY

Bullock, Charles S., III, and Charles M. Lamb, eds. *Implementation of Civil Rights Policy*. Monterey, CA: Brooks Cole, 1984.

Lawson, Steven F. *Black Ballots*. New York: Columbia University Press, 1976.

Civil War (1861–1865)

The American Civil War did not pit religious denominations against one another, such as Catholic versus Protestant, for Catholics, Protestants, and Jews fought on both sides. Yet the

One of the many evangelical missions set up by the U.S. Christian Commission during the Civil War. Library of Congress.

issue that divided the nation and many denominations as well (**Presbyterians**, **Baptists** and Methodists all split) was as powerful and spell-binding as any religious doctrine. **Slavery** stirred convictions with religious intensity, as did the doctrine of states' rights, which justified slavery, and the principles of anti-slavery and devotion to the Union, which ultimately destroyed slavery and its justifying doctrine. Many Confederates saw themselves as latter-day Cavaliers (i.e., the romantic defenders of the royalist cause in the seventeenth-century English civil war), defending ancient traditions and courtliness against an uncivilized foe. Many Unionists perceived themselves as agents of divine wrath against an outworn and iniquitous institution.

Militarily, the economically and numerically superior North faced a difficult strategic decision—occupy Confederate territory or destroy Confederate armies. Only after occupying the bulk of the Confederacy west of the Appalachians did the Union realize that as long as General Robert E. Lee's Army of Northern Virginia was in the field, the war would go on. Not until 1864 did General Ulysses S. Grant fully understand this and have the wherewithal to continuously engage Lee's army. The end came with the fall of Richmond. The capital of the Confederacy had no great strategic value, but Lee had to deplete his army for months to defend it. By April 1865, his army had melted to fewer than 30,000 hungry men surrounded by over three times that number; Lee had to surrender. Grant offered generous terms and Lee responded in kind, refusing to countenance any further resistance to federal authority.

The casualties and suffering wrought by the war shocked the nation and the world. Not since the Napoleonic wars of the early nineteenth century had so many men served in uniform and died in such numbers. Some 25,000 died during the three-day battle at Gettysburg in July 1863, the most in any battle since Waterloo in 1815. As the casualties mounted, especially in the summer of 1864, as Grant forced Lee south, and Lee doggedly resisted, people on both sides began to wonder whether the God they had prayed to for victory had abandoned them, or had given them over to a terrible punishment for some national sin. In his second inaugural address in March 1865, President **Abraham Lincoln** set a religious seal on the conflict with the profoundest theodicy (i.e., a statement defending the goodness and omnipotence of God in view of the existence of great evil in the world) ever uttered by a head of state:

> If we shall suppose that American slavery is one of those offenses which, in the providence of God, must needs come, but which having continued through His appointed time, He now wills to remove, and that He gives both North and South this terrible war as the woe due to those by whom the offense came, shall we discern therein any departure from those divine attributes which the believers in a living God always ascribe to Him? Fondly do we hope, fervently do we pray, that this mighty scourge of war may speedily pass away. Yet, if God wills that it continue until all the wealth piled by the bondsman's 250 years of unrequited toil shall be sunk, and until every drop of blood drawn with the lash shall be paid by another drawn with the sword, as was said 3,000 years ago, so still it must be said, "The judgments of the Lord are sure and righteous altogether."

(RAH) **See also** Abolition; Judaism; Methodism; Roman Catholicism.

BIBLIOGRAPHY

Catton, Bruce. *The Centennial History of the Civil War*. 3 vols. Garden City, NY: Doubleday, 1961-65.

Foote, Shelby. *The Civil War: A Narrative*. 3 vols. New York: Random House, 1958-74.

Wills, Garry. *Lincoln at Gettysburg: The Words that Remade America*. New York: Simon & Schuster, 1992.

John Clarke (1609–1676)

John Clarke originally settled in **Massachusetts Bay** in 1637 but, recognizing the religious intolerance of the **Puritans**, sided with **Anne Hutchinson** in her struggles with the colony's Puritan ministers. By 1638, he had settled in **Rhode Island**. However, during the 1650s, Rhode Island was small, divided, and in danger of being taken over by a larger colony. In 1651,

Clarke and **Roger Williams** sailed to England and obtained a new colonial charter. Clarke remained in England but is still considered one of Rhode Island's founders. (MWP)

BIBLIOGRAPHY

Bicknall, Thomas W. *Story of Dr. John Clarke*. Providence, RI: Thomas W. Bicknall, 1915.

Albert B. Cleage (1911–)

As black political activism shifted from nonviolent **civil rights** protest to black power radicalism in the late 1960s, Albert Cleage was one of the few black pastors to retain influence with the new militants. Pastor of the Shrine of the Black Madonna in Detroit, Cleage published a collection of his sermons entitled, *The Black Messiah*. In the book, Cleage claimed that "Jesus was the non-white leader of a non-white people struggling for national liberation against the rule of a white nation, Rome." **See also** Martin Luther King, Jr.; Malcolm X.

BIBLIOGRAPHY

Cleage, Albert. *The Black Messiah*. New York: Sheed and Ward, 1969.

Ward, Hiley H. *Prophet of the Black Nation*. Philadelphia: Pilgrim Press, 1969.

Clergy in Public Office

The practice of excluding clergy from public office came to the United States in colonial times. Anglican clergy were not permitted to serve in elected positions in the colonial legislatures, a tradition that stemmed from England itself. After the Revolutionary War, the practice of exclusion continued. While the U.S. Constitution prohibited **religious tests or oaths**, most states adopted statues that barred ordained ministers from serving in elected capacities. The theory behind these exclusions was the need for the separation of church and state.

Virginia was the first state to prohibit clergy from serving in public office. Virginia's first independent legislature in 1774 was closed to members of the clergy. At the time, the Anglican Church was the established church of Virginia and politicians feared the undue influence that might be created. By barring clergy, politicians not only prevented Anglican ministers from being elected, but also prevented the backcountry from sending **Baptist** or **Presbyterian** ministers to the state legislature. Other states followed suit in barring ordained ministers. These restrictions did not prevent clergymen from leading efforts for social and political reform during this period. Nor did they keep out of Congress such clergymen as **Manasseh Cutler** and **Frederick Augustus Muhlenberg** (who was the first speaker of the House).

As the number of states with established churches declined in the late eighteenth and early nineteenth centuries, many people began to question the need for prohibiting clergy from public office. Georgia's constitutional disqualification was the first to be repealed in 1798. In 1831, Delaware modified its provision to exclude only ordained ministers. In 1853, it again changed its statute to exclude only ministers holding "pastoral charge."

By the beginning of the twentieth century, only two states maintained clerical disqualification, Maryland and Tennessee. Maryland's exclusion was set aside by the U.S. District Court for Maryland in *Kirkley v. Maryland* (1974), wherein the court ruled that the exclusion violated the **First** and **Fourteenth Amendments** to the Constitution. In 1978, the U.S. Supreme Court came to a similar conclusion in voiding a Tennessee statute in ***McDaniel v. Paty***. In this case, Tennessee argued that the prohibition of clergy was a compelling state interest in maintaining the high wall of separation between church and state. Chief Justice **Warren Burger** wrote that since there was no established church, the need to exclude clergy did not exist.

The issue of clergy in public office did not end with Burger's decision. In 1980, Pope John Paul II ordered Father **Robert Drinan** not to seek re-election to his U.S. House seat. Drinan, a Massachusetts Democrat, had originally been elected to the House as an anti-war candidate in 1970. The pope stated that a priest had no role in partisan politics, adding that "the secular functions are the proper field of action of the laity, who ought to perfect temporal matters with a Christian spirit." Following the pope's directive, Drinan did not seek re-election in 1980 and Father Robert J. Cornell of Wisconsin withdrew from his congressional race.

While Catholic priests have been barred by the pope from running for office, many Protestant leaders have questioned the appropriateness of ministers seeking public office. The presidential candidacies of **Jesse Jackson** and **Pat Robertson** have raised concerns of whether or not ministers can make the kinds of political compromises necessary and still remain faithful to their charge as members of the clergy. Further, candidates like Jackson and Robertson raise concerns about the direct influence religion might have on politics.

Ordained ministers have served in Congress, as governors, and in state and local legislative bodies for most of American history. The basis of their service is the recognition that simply because they have a calling to serve in the ministry, their rights as citizens, including the right to serve in elected office, should not be hampered by the state. **See also** Establishment Clause; Roman Catholicism.

BIBLIOGRAPHY

Hogue, William M. "The Civil Disability of Ministers of Religion in State Constitutions." *The Journal of Church and State* 36, no. 2 (1994): 329-55.

Hyer, Marjorie. "Vatican Directive: Does It Apply to Appointive Positions?" *Washington Post* (May 9, 1980): A48.

McSeveney, Samuel T. "Religious Conflict, Party Politics, and Public Policy in New Jersey, 1874-75." *New Jersey History* 110, no. 1-2 (1992): 18-44.

McTighe, Michael J. "Jesse Jackson and the Dilemmas of a Prophet in Politics." *The Journal of Church and State* 32, no. 3 (1990): 585-607.

Clergy Malpractice

Malpractice is a legal concept which maintains that people with a superior knowledge or skill in a specific area must act in accordance with that knowledge or skill. The application of malpractice law to clergy has been increasing since the late 1970s. At that time, it was reported that a husband and wife had sued the minister who was giving them marriage counseling. Although no such case was filed then, a similar case was filed in 1984.

In the 1984 case, *Nally v. Grace Community Church*, the parents of 24-year old Kenneth Nally sued Grace Community Church and three of its pastors for clergy malpractice after their son committed suicide. The parents claimed that the counselors discouraged their suicidal son from seeking psychiatric or psychological counseling to help him deal with his history of suicidal feelings. The defendants, among other things, argued that the **First Amendment**'s **Free Exercise Clause** prevented such a suit and it was dismissed by the original trial court judge.

Although the case was reinstated on appeal, the trial judge ruled that there was insufficient evidence of malpractice to justify a jury verdict. The Nallys once again appealed and the court announced that, while it could not support the specific claim alleged in the suit, it did find that there was a responsibility on the part of the ministers to refer people like Kenneth Nally to appropriate services. Grace Community Church and the named clergy appealed the appeals court decision to the California Supreme Court. The state supreme court overturned the appeals court decision, writing that the church was engaged in pastoral counselling and not professional counselling. The Nallys appealed to the United States Supreme Court, which declined to review the case.

Nally demonstrated the courts' reluctance to acknowledge that clergy malpractice is a legitimate area of litigation because of the complex church-state issues that would result from such a stand. **See also** Clergy in Public Office.

Bibliography

Ericsson, Samuel E. *Clergy Malpractice: An Illegal Theory.* Merrifield, VA: Center for Law and Religious Freedom, 1986.

McMenanin, Robert W. *Clergy Malpractice.* Buffalo, NY: Hein, 1986.

Grover Cleveland (1837–1908)

Grover Cleveland served as president of the United States from 1885 to 1889 and again from 1893 to 1897. He was the first Democratic president elected since the **Civil War**. As a young man, Cleveland acknowledged that being raised by a minister shaped his outlook as an adult. Cleveland started his political career in Buffalo, New York. He was elected governor of New York in 1882 and president in 1884. In the closing days of the 1884 campaign, a religious slur against Roman Catholics by his opponent's camp helped him carry the important state of New York. When Republican candidate **James G. Blaine** appeared before a meeting of Protestant ministers, Samuel Burchard, one of the speakers, assured Blaine that they would not desert the Grand Old Party for one characterized by "Rum, Romanism and Rebellion." Blaine was slow to repudiate the statement and Cleveland carried the Irish vote and New York State by a slim margin. Cleveland lost to Benjamin Harrison in 1888 and was re-elected in 1892. His second term was marred by an economic depression. (WB) **See also** Democratic Party; Republican Party; Roman Catholicism.

Bibliography

Welch, Richard E. *The Presidency of Grover Cleveland.* Lawrence: University of Kansas Press, 1988.

William Jefferson Clinton (1946–)

In 1992, William Jefferson Clinton was elected the 42nd president of the United States. Calling himself a New Democrat, Clinton espoused more centrist and moderate views than liberal Democrats had held in the past. Although he suffered a number of early legislative defeats, particularly over national health insurance, Clinton won re-election in 1996 and has overseen the passage of the first balanced budget in a generation and the dramatic transformation of the welfare program.

A lifelong Southern Baptist, President Bill Clinton, a Democrat, has attended church regularly since entering the White House. Library of Congress.

Raised a Southern Baptist, Clinton's relationship with religion and its impact on his character are of considerable debate. When Clinton was a student at Georgetown University in the 1960s, a Jesuit, not knowing that Clinton was a Baptist, encouraged him to enter the Jesuit order because the pope allowed Jesuits to be active in both religion and politics. While governor of Arkansas, Clinton developed a close relationship with the conservative Baptist minister Worley Oscar Vaught, and sought Vaught's opinions on such subjects as **capital punishment** and **abortion**.

Since entering the White House in 1993, Clinton and his wife, Hillary Rodham Clinton (a Methodist by upbringing), have regularly attended services. However, various sexual and political scandals, culminating in Clinton's August 1998 admission of an inappropriate sexual relationship with a White House intern, have swirled around Clinton since he entered office. These scandals have called his moral authority into question and have opened him to charges of hypocrisy for his public displays of moral rectitude. **See also** Baptists; Democratic Party; Methodism; Roman Catholicism.

Bibliography

Maraniss, David. *First in His Class.* New York: Simon & Schuster, 1995.

Cochran v. Louisiana State Board of Education (1930)

Citizens and tax-payers of Louisiana challenged a state law that used state tax revenue to provide free school books to all of the state's schools, claiming that taxation for the purchase of these books aided private, religious, sectarian and other schools not embraced in the public educational system of the state and therefore aided those students in violation of the **Establishment Clause** of the **First Amendment**. In *Cochran v. Louisiana State Board of Education*, 281 U.S. 370 (1930), the U.S. Supreme Court disagreed, ruling that the legislation in question operated purely for the public purpose of increasing overall education in the state and therefore did not pose an essentially religious issue. (JM)

BIBLIOGRAPHY

Gaffrey, Edward M., Jr. *Private Schools and the Public Good*. Notre Dame, IN: University of Notre Dame Press, 1981.

Coercion Test

In attempting to determine the limits on government action prescribed by the **Establishment Clause** of the **First Amendment**, the U.S. Supreme Court has developed a number of different tests. The most prominent test was announced in ***Lemon v. Kurtzman*** (1971). The three-fold ***Lemon* Test** required a government program (1) to have a secular legislative purpose, (2) to avoid both advancing or inhibiting religion, and (3) to avoid excessive government entanglement with religion. Over the years, a number of glosses were made on the various parts of the Lemon test, including the coercion test, which was an attempt to elaborate on the second part. Even indirect coercion to follow a certain religious practice would be considered evidence that the government was advancing religion. In ***Lee v. Weisman*** (1992), the Court stated, "Precedents make clear that proof of government coercion is not necessary to prove an Establishment Clause violation. . . . Government pressure to participate in a religious activity is an obvious indication that the government is endorsing or promoting religion." (JM)

BIBLIOGRAPHY

Eastland, Terry. *Religious Liberty in the Supreme Court*. Washington, DC: Ethics and Public Policy Center, 1993.

Stone, Geoffrey R. et. al. *Constitutional Law*. Boston: Little, Brown and Company, 1991.

William Sloan Coffin, Jr. (1924–)

The Reverend William Sloan Coffin, Jr., comes from a long line of Presbyterian preachers. He was chaplain at Yale from 1958 to 1976, becoming famous for supporting the civil rights movement and opposing the **Vietnam War**. He was arrested several times as a freedom rider in the South and was charged, along with Doctor Benjamin Spock, the famous baby doctor, for counseling, aiding, and abetting young men to resist the draft.

While senior minister of Riverside Church in New York City from 1977 to 1987, Coffin sponsored the nuclear freeze campaign and welcomed other activists, such as Cesar Chavez, to his pulpit. An excellent linguist, fluent in Russian and French, Coffin is also a good pianist who studied with Nadia Boulanger in Paris. He was a liaison officer during **World War II** and with the Central Intelligence Agency for three years in the early 1950s.

Coffin continues to travel widely, preaching at a variety of churches and teaching at seminaries and universities. He is a powerful preacher, fond of invoking, as did **Martin Luther King**, the vivid imagery and theology of the prophets to illuminate contemporary circumstances. See also Presbyterian Church. (RAH) **See also** Civil Rights; Nuclear Disarmament; Presbyterian Church.

BIBLIOGRAPHY

Coffin, William Sloan, Jr. *Once to Every Man*. New York: Atheneum, 1977.

——. *A Passion for the Possible: A Message to U.S. Churches*. Louisville, KY: Westminster John Knox, 1993

Colonial America

The colonial period of American history prefigures many of the significant issues in American life today, particularly with respect to religion and the public sphere. These issues include religious diversity and pluralism, religious and civil liberty, religious foundations for civic and public good, and the interpretation of the meaning and purpose of America (including the idea of a Christian America).

The colonial period lasted more than 150 years. (The United States is itself only little more than 220 years old). The colonial years encompassed a complex interaction of profound events, diverse peoples, and a wide variety of religious, social, and political beliefs. The elements and dynamics of the colonial period gave shape to significant issues in the American experience and to the emerging American nation and culture.

Conventionally, the framework for colonial America begins with the founding of the English settlements at Jamestown, Virginia (1607), at Plymouth on Cape Cod (1620), and on **Massachusetts Bay** (1628-29). The end of the colonial period in America comes with the surrender of the British to the colonial revolutionaries and the subsequent establishment of the United States in the 1780s. The earliest English colonial efforts were not simply heroic endeavors for religious and civil freedom, but a mix of religious, political, and commercial purposes. The Jamestown settlement consisted primarily of a commercial venture by the Virginia Company, although the company acknowledged religious purposes and included a minister of the Church of England, who conducted the first Anglican religious service soon after arrival. In contrast, the **Pilgrim** colony in Plymouth and the **Puritan** colony in Massachusetts Bay were fundamentally religious endeavors. The Pilgrims and Puritans left England because they were nonconformists with respect to the Church of England and thus to the Crown, for Church and Crown were explicitly allied in seventeenth-century England. Yet, these nonconformists were also connected with the Virginia Company and other mercantile interests; and a number of those who landed were not themselves Pilgrims or Puritans, but servants or artisans. Throughout the 1600s and 1700s, increasing numbers of those who came to the colonies came for mercantile and other nonreligious reasons or purposes.

English Protestants, moreover, were not the first and only Europeans in the Americas. Following Columbus's 1492 voyage, the Spanish, seeking wealth and power, began a century of vigorous colonizing in the Americas, including southern (Florida) and southwestern (New Mexico, Arizona, California) North America. They brought Spanish Catholicism to the regions they settled. France also engaged in colonial efforts in North America in the 1600s and 1700s. In the early 1600s, the Dutch, with a Reformed Christian heritage, established commercial colonial claims in North America in what is now New York City and up the Hudson River Valley.

New England did not constitute the entire English settlement in North America, although the New England narrative long dominated the shaping of the larger American narrative of national origins. English colonization continued along the eastern seaboard, with the middle and southern colonies evidencing a mix of religious, commercial, and other purposes in their establishment. **Maryland** was founded in the 1630s to establish religious liberty for Catholics, also a restricted group in England. The Carolinas came into being in the 1660s and 1670s chiefly to fulfill the commercial hopes of its proprietors. **William Penn** proceeded in the early 1680s to build Pennsylvania as a place of religious and civic freedom for **Quakers** and all others. Georgia began in the 1730s largely as a penal colony. In 1619, the colonists began importing African slaves. The institution of **slavery**, growing through the 1600s and 1700s, had a profound influence on religion, culture, politics, and economics in the southern colonies, and, to a lesser degree, in the northern colonies. Slavery led to ironic and even cruel religious perspectives, sometimes sanctioned by law, such as that baptism into the Christian faith had no effect on a slave's condition as a slave (i.e., a form of property). By the early 1700s, several colonies had enacted such legislation.

Thus, over the course of the 1600s and 1700s, the colonies experienced the influx of a remarkable variety of religious, class, ethnic, and individual and group aspirations.

> A traveler in 1700 making his way from Boston to the Carolinas would encounter Congregationalists of varying intensity, Baptists of several varieties, Presbyterians, Quakers, and several other forms of Puritan radicalism; Dutch, German, and French Reformed; Swedish, Finnish, and German Lutherans; Mennonites and radical pietists, Anglicans, Roman Catholics; here and there a Jewish congregation, a few Rosicrucians; and, of course, a vast number of the unchurched. . . . (Sydney Ahlstrom, *A Religious History of the American People*, p. 4)

The religious, social, and ethnic situation of colonial America involved more complexity of composition and purposes than suggested by the simple but influential narrative of Pilgrims coming to the New World for religious liberty. This complex variety existed in the colonial period even without detailing the prior and continuing presence of Indian people in North America, with their various religious beliefs and practices.

Complexity also extends to the issue of religious freedom in the colonial period. Religious freedom is one of the fervent tenets we hold concerning the origins of America. Yet the colonial story is not a simple one of principled, unqualified commitment to free exercise of religion. For example, while the Pilgrims and Puritans came for religious freedom, that chiefly meant freedom to practice their religious convictions without constraint from the English authorities. It did not mean religious freedom in general. In Massachusetts, Quakers were outlawed and punished—four were even hanged between 1659 and 1661—for proclaiming a different version of Christian faith. For his dissent from Puritan orthodoxy, **Roger Williams** was banished in 1636 from Massachusetts Bay. Intensely devout, Williams became one of the first to grasp the idea of religious freedom in the sense that we mean it today—freedom to practice any religion or no religion. His **Rhode Island Colony** became the first place of true religious freedom in colonial America. Meanwhile, other colonies had legally established churches, whether the Congregational in Connecticut and Massachusetts, Dutch Reformed in New Netherland, or the Church of England in Virginia. In Maryland, religious toleration came and went. In the 1600s, outside of Rhode Island, only William Penn's "holy experiment" in Pennsylvania was truly a principled attempt to establish religious toleration. Nevertheless, in the course of the 1700s the more odious restrictions on "nonconformist" churches in the various colonies were relaxed by law or in practice, even when establishment of a particular church remained. Part of the reason for those changes had to do with intellectual shifts in England and the colonies in favor of greater toleration and a more rationalistic approach to religion in the currents of the **Enlightenment**. Yet another significant reason for those changes simply had to do with increasing religious pluralism in the colonies.

Although the colonial process toward true religious liberty was fitful and erratic, it led in time to the new and historic constitutional guarantee of free exercise of religion and prohibition of legal establishment of any one church or religion in the United States. The constitutional framework that grew out of the colonial experience marked a genuine, radical break with the alliance of church and ruler that had prevailed for centuries in Christian Europe. This idea was new and revolutionary, a key part of the genius of America—the creation of a nation without an established state church or religion.

Changes toward toleration and religious liberty did not, however, lead to an utter rejection of religion in the civil and public sphere. For many in the 1600s and 1700s, religious foundations were considered necessary and desirable for the commonwealth. Puritans sought not just a place to be left alone for the unfettered exercise of personal beliefs. Activists and visionaries, they considered themselves embarked on an "errand into the wilderness," where they intended to build a new society, a "holy commonwealth," rightly ordered and imbued with individual and social good. Even at the beginning of the national period, the general consensus of the founders of the country, while clearly refusing to establish any one church or religion, was that religion necessarily undergirded a moral people and a virtuous republic. Upon reflection, this idea raises the question of whether a generalized religious sense or a particular religious tradition should serve that moral and civic purpose, a question which would become more acute in the 1800s and 1900s when the United States acquired an even greater diversity of people and beliefs.

The issue of religious foundations leads also to one of the most significant aspects of colonial America: the assertion of a sacred meaning and mission for the American endeavor. With various nuances and in different contexts, such an understanding threads through the colonial period and to the present. This new society, in the words of **John Winthrop** in 1630, is to be "a city on a hill." The Puritans sought to build a New World to be the model and bearer of truth and virtue for the Old World. This idea of a sacred significance, through various permutations, is embedded in American history and culture. America is the New **Israel**, "a new order of the ages," the bearer of **manifest destiny**, the "last best hope of Earth," and still, in the language of comparatively recent politics, "a city on a hill." This element in the American ethos goes far in explaining why Americans view their country as the model for other nations, and why they strive to extend to the world what they hold to be the unique blessings and virtues of the American experiment. (GSS) **See also** American Revolution; Congregationalism; Deism; Judaism; Mennonites; Native American Religions; Presbyterian Church; Roman Catholicism.

Bibliography

Ahlstrom, Sydney E. *A Religious History of the American People*. New Haven, CT: Yale University, 1972.

Bremer, Francis J. *The Puritan Experiment: New England Society from Bradford to Edwards*. New York: St. Martin's, 1976.

Cherry, Conrad, ed. *God's New Israel: Religious Interpretation of American Destiny*. Englewood Cliffs, NJ: Prentice-Hall, 1971.

Gaustad, Edwin Scott. *A Religious History of America*. San Francisco: Harper & Row, 1990.

May, Henry F. *The Enlightenment in America*. New York: Oxford University Press, 1978.

Mead, Sydney E. *The Lively Experiment: The Shaping of Christianity in America*. New York: Harper & Row, 1963.

Mulder, John M. and John F. Wilson. *Religion in American History: Interpretive Essays*. Englewood Cliffs, NJ: Prentice-Hall, 1978.

Raboteau, Albert J. *Slave Religion: The "Invisible Institution" in the Antebellum South*. New York: Oxford University Press, 1978.

Charles Colson (1931–)

Prior to 1973, Charles Colson's career centered on public service. Colson served two years in the Marine Corps, reaching the rank of captain. While completing his law degree at George Washington University, Colson worked as an administrative assistant to Republican Senator Saltonstall. Colson served as special council to President **Richard Nixon** from late 1969 until March 1973, during which time he gained both respect and notoriety as Nixon's "hatchet man." He was forced to resign during the Watergate investigation and plead guilty to one count of obstruction of justice, for which he served over six months in prison.

Colson emerged from prison as a **born-again Evangelical** Christian and committed his life to serving God. In addition to founding Prison Fellowship, Colson has been a prolific writer and commentator speaking out on such issues as criminal justice, the role of the Church in influencing the culture and political change, and ecumenical outreach between Evangelicals and Catholics. Some of his books include *Born Again, Loving God, The Body, Faith on the Line,* and *Evangelicals and Catholics Together*. A leading figure in the Evangelical community, Colson received awards from the National Association of Evangelicals, and the **Salvation Army**, and was awarded the 1993 Templeton Prize for Progress in Religion. (DD) **See also** Roman Catholicism.

Bibliography

Colson, Charles. *Born Again*. New York: Mass Market Paperbacks, 1996.

Committee for Public Education v. Nyquist (1973)

New York amended its **education** and tax laws to establish three financial aid programs for nonpublic schools. The first program provided direct money grants to nonpublic schools to be used for maintenance and repair of facilities and equipment to ensure the students' health, welfare, and safety. The second program established a tuition reimbursement plan for low-income parents of children attending nonpublic schools. The third program gave tax relief to parents failing to qualify for tuition reimbursement, with eligible taxpayer-parents entitled to deduct a certain sum from their gross income for each child attending a nonpublic school. In *Committee for Public Education v. Nyquist*, 413 U.S. 756 (1973), the U.S. Supreme Court ruled that the maintenance and repair program violated the **Establishment Clause** because its "inevitable effect is to subsidize and advance the religious mission of sectarian schools." The Court likewise struck down the tuition reimbursement and tax incentive programs on the grounds that such benefits, if given directly to the schools, would violate the Establishment Clause, and "the fact that they are delivered to the parents rather than the schools" does not change the fact that "the effect of the aid is unmistakably to provide financial support for nonpublic, sectarian institutions." (JM) **See also** First Amendment.

BIBLIOGRAPHY

Bryson, Joseph E. *The Supreme Court and Public Funds for Religious Schools*. Jefferson, NC: McFarland, 1990.

Committee for Public Education v. Regan (1980)

The New York legislature enacted a statute that provided funds for nonpublic schools to pay for costs incurred in the course of complying with state-mandated **education** requirements. The statute was challenged on the grounds that it provided funding to private, religious schools and therefore advanced a religious purpose in violation of the **Establishment Clause** of the **First Amendment**. In *Committee for Public Safety v. Regan*, 444 U.S. 646 (1980), the U.S. Supreme Court, which had earlier struck down a similar New York law, upheld this one because it, unlike the earlier version, provided a means by which state funds were audited to ensure that only the actual costs incurred in providing the covered secular services were reimbursed. (JM)

BIBLIOGRAPHY

Bryson, Joseph E. *The Supreme Court and Public Funds for Religious Schools*. Jefferson, NC: McFarland, 1990.

Common Law and Christianity

A fundamental and enduring church-state question in Anglo-American jurisprudence is whether or not Christianity is part of the common law. Common law is a system of jurisprudence developed in England and transferred to the American colonies. As distinguished from statutory or civil law, the common law comprises the body of laws derived from principles, rules of action, customs, and previous decisions of judicial tribunals. The principal doctrine of the common law is *stare decisis*, which requires judges to adhere to legal principles set forth in prior cases (precedents). The age-old debate concerning whether or not Christianity is part of the common law tradition raises foundational questions about the source and authority of law and the relationship between religion and the legal order.

While debated for centuries in England, the relationship between Christianity and the common law reemerged as a subject of discussion in the United States in the early nineteenth century. Two leading figures in the debate were **Thomas Jefferson** and **Joseph Story**. In a posthumously published essay entitled "Whether Christianity is Part of the Common Law?" Jefferson argued "that Christianity neither is, nor ever was, a part of the common law." In his inaugural address as Harvard's Dane Professor of Law, Justice Story countered that "[t]here never has been a period in which the common law did not recognize Christianity as lying at its foundations."

In a private letter written in June 1824 to the English radical John Cartwright, Jefferson argued that the widely held belief among English and American lawyers that Christianity was a part of the common law was a "judiciary forgery" promulgated by a mistranslation in Sir Henry Finch's influential treatise, *Law, or, A Discourse Thereof* (London, 1613). Finch (1558-1625) cited an earlier judicial opinion by Sir John Prisot (d. 1460). In *Humfrey Bohun v. John Broughton, Bishop of Lincoln* (1458), Prisot said it is proper to give credence to such laws as the people of the Holy Church have in "ancien Scripture," for this is common law on which all manner of laws are founded. Jefferson alleged that Finch, citing Prisot, erroneously construed "ancien scripture" as the Holy Bible, whereas the term should have been translated as the ancient "written laws of the church." According to Jefferson, Finch was thus led to conclude incorrectly that church law having warrant in Christian scriptures was accredited by the common law of England. Finch's point, in short, was that the common law incorporated the Christian scriptures, and nothing in the common law is valid that is not consistent with divine revelation. As Jefferson saw it, however, the issue addressed by Prisot was not whether Christianity was a part of the common law of England, but rather to what extent ecclesiastical law was to be recognized and enforced (i.e., given faith and credit) by common law courts. Jefferson traced Finch's alleged "error" through Sir Matthew Hale, Sir William Blackstone, Lord Mansfield, and other English jurists, who gave this new doctrine respectability, and finally transmitted it to America.

Jefferson's repudiation of the virtually undisputed connection between Christianity and the common law challenged the notion that the United States was in any legal sense a Christian nation. It confirmed to his detractors that he was contemptuous of established judicial, legal, and religious authorities that recognized the Christian basis of the common law. Jefferson's view was rejected not only by Story but also in much nineteenth-century American case law, which affirmed the proposition that general Christianity is and always has been part of the common law, the basis of the American legal system. (DLD)

BIBLIOGRAPHY

Chilton, Bradley S. "Cliobernetics, Christianity, and the Common Law." *Law Library Journal* 83 (1991): 355-62.

Kenny, Courtney. "The Evolution of the Law of Blasphemy." *Cambridge Law Journal* 1, no. 2 (1922): 127-42.

Spiegel, Jayson L. "Christianity as Part of the Common Law." *North Carolina Central Law Journal* 14 (1984): 494-516.

Communitarianism

Throughout the history of the West, like-minded religious believers have banded together to form self-contained communities devoted to a particular way of life. In this context, communitarianism refers to the underlying belief that it is possible to form societies in which every aspect of life can be lived according to shared religious values. In the nineteenth century, Marxists began to form communitarian societies on the basis of shared philosophical, rather than religious, ideas, and in the late twentieth century, the term "communitarianism" has come to refer to a particular body of political and philosophical thought. Communitarians today object to the classic liberal notion that government policies should refrain from supporting any particular set of religious or moral views.

In the United States, a plethora of Protestant communitarian societies sprang up in the open territory of the West during the nineteenth century. One small town in Indiana, for example, was host to two communitarian societies in succession, a Lutheran community called the Rappites and then a society whose members followed **Robert Owen**, a Welsh socialist. Better-known communitarian societies include the Shaker communities, the Mormon towns in Utah, and the Hasidic Jewish neighborhoods in New York City.

In the early 1980s, several intellectuals invoked communitarian ideals to object to a dominant strand of political philosophy, the liberal tradition that requires the government to be neutral among the competing moral beliefs of its citizens. Led by Michael Sandel, **Alasdair MacIntyre** and Charles Taylor, these new communitarian thinkers argued that the liberal tradition was based on an impoverished view of human identity that failed to account for the importance of shared values. Practical attempts to remedy this excess of individualism have recently sprung up in the form of inner city neighborhood centers, small-town revitalization committees, and new attempts to regulate big business. (BGD) **See also** Church of Jesus Christ of Latter-day Saints; Judaism; Liberalism; Lutheran Church; Socialism and Communism; Utopianism.

BIBLIOGRAPHY

Grasso, Kenneth, Gerard V. Bradley and Robert P. Hunt, eds. *Catholicism, Liberalism, and Communitarianism*. Lantham, MD: Rowman and Littlefield Publishing, Inc., 1995.

Hostetler, John A. *Communitarian Societies*. New York: Holt, Rinehart, & Winston, Inc., 1974.

Sandel, Michael J. *Liberalism and the Limits of Justice*. New York: Cambridge University Press, 1982.

James Cone (1938–)

James Cone emerged as a central voice for black **liberation theology** with the publication of *Black Theology and Black Power* in 1969, less than a year after the assassination of **Martin Luther King, Jr**. In that work and his subsequent books, Cone identified the Christian gospel as the story of God's preference for the poor and oppressed. He justified individual and collective social action by appealing to liberation as the central ethical principle of moral life, and he advocated democratic socialism as the fairest and most Christian form of government. Cone believes churches are called to be agents for the liberation of the poor and oppressed throughout the world, and he argues that no one is truly free until all people are liberated.

Cone's early work was criticized by womanist (black feminist) theologians, who believed that his strong emphasis on racial unity in the face of oppression condoned sexism within the black community. His later work responds to this critique with a broader understanding of oppression, even as he continues to focus on developing a theology that gives a Christian context to black identity and an ethical foundation to contemporary black power movements. (KMY) **See also** Feminism; Social Gospel; Social Justice; Socialism and Communism.

Cone, James H. *My Soul Looks Back*. Nashville: Abingdon, 1982.

Kunnie, Julian. *Models of Black Theology: Issues in Class, Culture, and Gender*. Valley Forge, PA: Trinity Press International, 1994.

Congregationalism

Congregationalism is a form of church government whereby the members of the congregation govern all aspects of the church themselves. This form of church government is distinct from episcopacy (rule by bishops) and presbyterianism (rule by ministers elected by church members). Congregationalism developed in the sixteenth century out of the disapproval of English **Puritans** with the episcopal hierarchy of the Anglican Church.

In America, the first example of congregational church government appeared in the **Cambridge Platform** of 1638, which established a system of independent local churches in New England. However, local control led to two major schisms. The first arose during the **First Great Awakening** of the 1730s and 1740s, when those members of Congregational bodies who supported revivalism (New Lights) broke from those who rejected the religious fervor (Old Lights). The New Lights became Baptist congregations. The second schism occurred in 1825 when more than 100 liberal parishes formed the American Unitarian Association (the predecessor to the Unitarian Universalist Association).

Today, the **United Church of Christ**, which was formed in 1957 by the merger of the Congregational Christian Churches and the Evangelical and Reformed Church, is the most direct link with the Puritan founders of congregationalism. The impact of congregationalism in American politics has been extensive. The underlying notion of congregationalism—that the governed choose who will govern them—greatly influenced American notions of self-government and republicanism. Also, the radical nature of congregationalism was a driving force in creating support for the **American Revolution**, especially among New Englanders. **See also** Baptists; Evangelicals; Liberalism; Presbyterian Church; Unitarianism.

BIBLIOGRAPHY

von Rohr, John. *The Shaping of American Congregationalism*. Cleveland: Pilgrim Press, 1992.

Conscientious Objection

For most of American history, Congress has made provisions for exemptions from **military service** for those whose religious beliefs proscribe the taking of human life. While such a status (termed "conscientious objector") has not been held to be a constitutional right by the Supreme Court, such classifications are consistent with the **Free Exercise Clause** of the **First Amendment**. Historically, problems have arisen with respect to the application of measures creating the status of conscientious objector. Two important issues have emerged.

First, it is not clear how "religion" is to be defined for purposes of military exemptions. To what extent do personal moral or religious codes count as protected "religious" scruples? In *Seeger v. U.S.* (380 U.S. 163 [1964]) and *Welsh v. U.S.* (398 U.S. 333 [1970]), the Supreme Court extended the traditional use of conscientious objection to include agnostics and atheists who objected for ethical reasons. Second, must individual beliefs proscribe all killing or participation in warfare to qualify as grounds for conscientious objection, or can objections be more specific to particular military or historical contexts? (TGJ) **See also** Atheism; War.

Bibliography

Schotten, Peter, and Dennis Stevens. *Religion, Politics, and the Law*. New York: Wadsworth, 1996.

Conservatism

Conservatism encompasses a wide variety of practical approaches to, and theoretical articulations of, political action. As its name suggests, conservatism is devoted to the conservation of something thought to be good, be it a tradition or a political order. American conservatism comes in many guises. Among the leading strands of conservatism are traditional or paleo-conservatism, libertarian conservatism, Burkean conservatism, neo-conservatism, Southern conservatism, Christian or religious conservatism, and what one may call "founding conservatism." Within these strands are various sub-strands. For example, founding conservatism, the conservatism that demands adherence to the "original intent" of the Constitution, has as its end the preservation of the principles on which the U.S. was founded. Yet the meaning of those principles is, like conservatism itself, the subject of intense dispute. Are those principles Lockean? Classical? Christian? It is difficult to conserve what one cannot define, or cannot define in a way that is satisfactory to most of the conservers. This dilemma was known to the American Founding Fathers, who universally accepted republicanism, but hotly debated what republicanism demanded. In the *49th Federalist*, Publius (**James Madison**) speaks of the appeal of, and the need to reject, a plan that would have led to frequent conventions designed to reconsider and possibly to amend the Constitution That plan was set forth by none other than **Thomas Jefferson**, the author of the **Declaration of Independence**. Respectfully objecting to Jefferson's scheme, Publius contended, "It may be considered as an objection inherent in the principle [of that plan] that as every appeal to the people would carry an implication of some defect in the government, frequent appeals would, in great measure, deprive the government of that veneration which time bestows on everything, and without which perhaps the wisest and freest governments would not possess the requisite stability."

One can overstate the extent of the divide amongst conservatives. No matter how much their underlying justifications may differ, on a great many practical issues there is considerable overlap amongst the various strands of conservatism. As a rule, American conservatives favor (1) a strong national defense; (2) lower taxes; (3) the promotion of an ethic of individual responsibility and a subsequent decrease in welfare, which is claimed to foster dependency; (4) limited government and; (5) increased federalism. They oppose (1) **abortion** (many libertarians excepted), (2) affirmative action, and (3) judicial activism.

Their practical agreement, however, does not extend to religion. At the far end of the spectrum are libertarians who deny that government (or even society at large) has a legitimate right to attempt to promote morality, to say nothing of religious belief; at the other end are certain Christian conservatives (though by no means a majority of them) who explicitly advocate governmental promotion of what they term "Christian values" (as opposed to "'traditional' values"). Most conservatives in between believe that government should make some attempt to form the character of the citizenry; there is, however, considerable disagreement as to whether the government as such should promote religious activity and belief.

The seeds of this disagreement appeared amongst the Founders themselves, between, for example, the two chief authors of *The Federalist Papers*, **Alexander Hamilton** and James Madison. The former, a hero to most conservatives, saw the need for active, if non-sectarian, governmental promotion of religion. Hamilton was the author of the original draft of **George Washington's** classic statement in his Farewell Address on the need for government to recognize the political importance of religion. Washington's statement, which does not depart in any significant way from Hamilton's draft, reads: "Of all the dispositions which lead to political prosperity, Religion and morality are indispensable supports. In vain would that man claim the tribute of Patriotism, who should labor to subvert these great pillars of human happiness, these firmest props of the duties of Men and citizens. The mere politician, equally with the pious man ought to respect and to cherish them." In other words, a healthy society needs a healthy respect for religion, and those in the government who fail to show that respect, that reverence, are irresponsible to the highest degree. Madison, on the other hand, had a profound fear of the possible despotical consequences of any government entanglement with religion. Often called "the father of the Constitution"—and, as such, a hero to liberals and many conservatives—Madison is the author of perhaps the classic American statement on the theoretical justification for, and the practical necessity of, religious liberty—the "Memorial and Remonstrance Against Religious Assessments." The chief claim of that work is encapsulated in the statement that "as no man's right is abridged by the institution of civil society. . . religion is wholly exempt from its cognizance." Government, according to Madison, has no legitimate role to play in the religious life of a citizen.

Today the mainstream of American conservatism probably stands somewhere between the views of Madison and Hamilton on the problem of religion. Yet, it is difficult to say with whose thoughts conservatives are more comfortable. Or perhaps it would be more precise to say that conservatives are of two minds on the problem. On the one hand, libertarians excepted, the overwhelming majority of conservatives today approve of religious groups playing an active role in the political process. The **Religious Right** has played a major role in recent years in enlisting support for conservative causes and candidates. For example, their support was critical to the election in 1980 of **Ronald Reagan**, a man many conservatives consider the greatest president of the century. The Religious Right has given prominent expression to widespread conservative fears over the collapse of "traditional values." This collapse is seen as a progressive coarsening of societal mores that has resulted in, among other things, unprecedentedly high crime and divorce rates, as well as a general vulgarization of society.

Towards the end of his life, Hamilton advocated the formation of something to be known as "The Christian Constitutional Society," an organization whose two objects were to be "The support of the Christian Religion" and "The support of the Constitution of the United States." And to some extent, the Religious Right has fulfilled the role of the society envisioned by Hamilton. A Madisonian would object that the two objects are, in combination, incompatible. Such a person would claim that even the name of the organization betrays its incoherence: Christianity exists in the realm of "society," and the Constitution is the embodiment of the "state," and it is one of the fundamental assumptions of our regime that the two are meant to be exclusive of one another.

However that may be in theory, in practice there seems to have been a modus vivendi reached by which Christians, or, more generally, the pious, feel they can simultaneously fulfill their responsibilities as believers and as citizens. They do so by transforming their religious convictions into civil opinions. Thus, when they take an active role in politics, they do so first and foremost as citizens, not as members of a specific denomination. That is not to say that they do not let their religious beliefs inform their political views, for it is manifest that they do. It is only to say that when they express those views they tend to do so in secular or "constitutional" terms. The most telling example in this regard is abortion. In large part, the Religious Right arose in reaction to the Supreme Court's decision in ***Roe v. Wade***, a decision that effectively made abortion on demand a constitutional right. Many religious people find this decision intolerable. Yet, whereas their religious beliefs might tell them that abortion is murder, they do not argue that abortion should be outlawed because it is a sin in the eyes of God, but that it should be outlawed because it is wrong, that no self-respecting society should allow such a practice. In short, they make arguments that appeal to Americans as Americans. In this sense, one might say Madison has triumphed.

It is not accidental that the contemporary Religious Right arose in reaction to a Supreme Court decision. **Alexis de Tocqueville** wrote in the nineteenth century that in the United States every political issue eventually becomes a judicial one. Of no issue is this more true than of religion. To the extent that contemporary politics, and therefore contemporary conservatism, addresses directly the issue of the promotion of religion, it almost always becomes a matter for the Supreme Court and the justices' interpretation of the **First Amendment**'s provisions prohibiting the establishment of religion and guaranteeing the free exercise thereof. And no matter how greatly conservatives and liberals differ in regard to their understanding of the proper role of religion within politics, on constitutional matters a broad practical consensus has been formed that effectively denies the state any role in the direct promotion of religion. To see how this is so one only has to look at the character of the issues that have reached the Court over the past few decades. We today argue over such marginal issues as the constitutionality of statutes providing for, among other things, a moment of silence for "voluntary meditation or prayer" (***Wallace v. Jaffree***), and the public display of a creche at Christmas (***Lynch v. Donnelly***). Moreover, conservatives do not seem fundamentally dissatisfied with this state of affairs; it seems almost unthinkable that a conservative today would propose any direct aid to a religious denomination. Given the fears that underlie Madison's passionate call for protecting religious liberty, and given their critique of the state of our society today, conservatives might suspect that Madison's fears were somewhat misplaced. (SJL) **See also** American Revolution; Civil Religion; Clergy in Public Office; Establishment Clause; Free Exercise Clause; Liberalism; John Locke; School Prayer; Washington's Farewell Address.

BIBLIOGRAPHY

Buckley, William F., Jr. and Charles Kesler, eds. *Keeping the Tablets: Modern American Conservative Thought*. New York: Harper and Row, 1988.

Mansfield, Harvey C., Jr. *America's Constitutional Soul*. Baltimore: The Johns Hopkins University Press, 1991.

Nash, George H. *The Conservative Intellectual Movement in America since 1945*. New York: Simon and Schuster, 1976.

Rossiter, Clinton. *Conservatism in America*. Revised second edition with new Foreword by George F. Will. Cambridge, MA: Harvard University Press, 1982.

Will, George F. *Statecraft as Soulcraft: What Government Does*. New York: Simon and Schuster, 1983.

Constitutional Amendments on Religion (Proposed)

From the struggle to pass the Bill of Rights to recent clashes over **abortion** and private **education**, religion has been a recurrent theme among the thousands of proposed amendments to the U.S. Constitution. Many proposals are directed openly toward some aspect of faith, ranging from the exclusion of clergy from elective office to public acknowledgement of the divine. Others do not explicitly invoke religion, but support or opposition for these initiatives often flows from religious sentiments (e.g., Prohibition, the **Equal Rights Amendment**). Although proposals implicating religion, like proposals generally, are likely to fail, they are nevertheless important historical markers of religion's place in society and politics.

Some of the earliest proposals were prompted by Protestant fears of Catholic parochial education. In 1875, for example, House Speaker **James Blaine**, acting with the support of the **Republican Party**, introduced an amendment that would have forbidden teaching religion in the classroom and curtailed the appropriation of public funds by any state for use by sectarian schools. This nineteenth-century scheme, the first of many proposals to focus on the interplay of religion and education, contrasts with dozens of recent attempts to include prayer and Bible reading in public schools through constitutional amendment.

The legal status of marriage has also figured prominently among proposed amendments, especially relating to **polygamy** and the **Church of Jesus Christ of Latter-day Saints** (the "Mormons"). President Ulysses S. Grant, who supported the **Blaine Amendment** by urging that "church and state [remain] forever separate and distinct," formally proposed in 1875 that the Constitution outlaw the Mormon practice of polygamy in the Utah Territory. His recommendation triggered at least 53 similar proposals over the next 54 years. Even after the Church renounced polygamy in 1890, a controversy in 1899 over Representative Brigham Roberts, an "avowed polygamist," set off a spate of amendment proposals to bar Mormons from Congress and other political offices.

Many contemporary proposals result from dissatisfaction with trends in Supreme Court rulings. ***Engel v. Vitale*** (1962), which struck down state-sponsored **school prayer**, was particularly important in mobilizing evangelical support for a constitutional amendment. The so-called "Religious Equality Amendment," proposed in 1995, was a reaction to the Court's controversial free exercise decision in ***Employment Division of Oregon v. Smith*** (1990) and to a series of **Establishment Clause** cases many observers consider too restrictive of faith. The issue of abortion rights also demonstrates the impact of Supreme Court decisions on the frequency and intensity of calls for formal constitutional amendments. After ***Roe v. Wade*** (1973), several proposals by religious groups opposed to abortion rights, among them the Human Life Amendment, made their way into congressional committees. Few of these proposals have traveled far in the legislative process. (KRD) **See also** Clergy in Public Office; Evangelicals; First Amendment; Gospel of Wealth; Roman Catholicism; Temperance and Prohibition.

BIBLIOGRAPHY

Berstein, Richard. *Amending America.* New York: Random House, 1993.

Green, Steven K. "The Blaine Amendment Reconsidered." *American Journal of Legal History* 36, no. 1 (January 1992): 38-69.

——. "Symposium: A Religious Equality Amendment?" *Brigham Young University Law Review* no. 3 (Summer 1996): 561-688.

Continental Congress

Disagreements between the English colonies and the British Parliament increased in intensity and frequency after the French and Indian War (1756-1763). Correspondence between the colonies increased after the 1772 burning of the British customs ship, *Gaspee*. Committees of Correspondence, first established in 1773, provided a means for the colonies to coordinate and expound their grievances against the British government. The greatest incident, however, to spur the colonies to invoke Puritanical motives in their efforts against what they perceived as a morally, ethically, and politically corrupt government, came after the tea party incident in Boston Harbor on December 16, 1773. The resulting conflict between Parliament and the colonies led to the formation of the Continental Congress, first convened in Philadelphia, Pennsylvania, on September 5, 1774. Using **John Locke**'s compact theory of government, the delegates to the convention sought to resolve the relationship between the colonies and the British government and monarchy. Troubles only increased after the Congress convened in 1774, and by its second scheduled session, May 10, 1775, blood had been spilled between the British Army and the citizens of **Massachusetts Bay**. Not all members of the colonies opted for immediate **war**. The Olive Branch Petition, an appeal for conciliation, was rejected in the fall of 1775 by King George III. The governmental body established to prosecute this war was the Continental Congress. The Continental Congress was responsible for the adoption of the **Declaration of Independence,** which calls upon nations to recognize "the laws of Nature" that are derived from God-given inalienable rights. Throughout the Congress's tenure, it called upon colonists to participate in days of "public humiliation, fasting and prayer" to receive God's forgiveness and intervention. Two problems, never completely solved during the war, were how to raise manpower and money to fight the powerful British. Congress was not a centralized, all-powerful body, but merely coordinated requests for action among the 13 colonies. (GT) **See also** American Revolution; Puritans.

BIBLIOGRAPHY

Burnett, Edmund, ed. *Letters of Members of the Continental Congress.* Washington, DC: The Carnegie Institution of Washington, 1921.

Jillson, Calvin and Rick Wilson. *Congressional Dynamics: Structure, Coordination, and Choice in the First American Congress, 1774-1789.* Stanford, CA: Stanford University Press, 1994.

Martson, Jerrilyn. *King and Congress: The Transfer of Political Legitimacy, 1774-1776.* Princeton, NJ: Princeton University Press, 1987.

Rakove, Jack. *The Beginnings of National Politics: An Interpretive History of the Continental Congress.* New York: Knopf Publishing, 1979.

Russell H. Conwell (1843–1925)

Raised in Western Massachusetts, Russell Conwell was wounded in the **Civil War**. After the war, he held a number of jobs, including those of journalist, lawyer and real estate investor. A **Baptist** clergyman who would later found Temple University, Russell Conwell is best known for a lecture, "Acres of Diamonds," which he delivered over 6,000 times. Its theme was based on a classically American one that emphasized self-help and unlimited opportunity. However, Conwell took the

Protestant ethic to extremes. A man of great energy, he revitalized several church congregations and inspired many to capitalist fortunes. (MWP) **See also** Capitalism.

Bibliography

Conwell, Russell H. *Acres of Diamonds: How Men and Women May Become Rich.* 1890.

Smith. Albert H. *The Life of Russell H. Conwell.* Boston, 1899.

Robert L. Cord (1935–)

Robert L. Cord, a political scientist and distinguished professor at Northeastern University, is a leading proponent of the "no preference" or nonpreferentialist interpretation of the **Establishment Clause** of the **First Amendment**. In an influential book, *Separation of Church and State* (1982), and in numerous scholarly articles, Cord argues that the framers of the First Amendment did not erect a high wall of separation between church and state. According to Cord, the historical record indicates that the constitutional concept of church-state separation meant to proscribe the establishment of a national church and to forbid the civil government from giving legal preference or favor to one religious sect, denomination, or tradition. A self-described "non-absolute separationist," Cord concludes that the framers believed the First Amendment permitted the use of nonpreferential sectarian means or activities associated with religion to achieve legitimate secular governmental ends. (DLD)

Bibliography

Cord, Robert L. *Separation of Church and State: Historical Fact and Current Fiction.* New York: Lambeth Press, 1982.

John Cotton (1584–1652)

John Cotton, pastor of the First Boston Church, was the ablest spokesman for the early **Puritan** experiment of building a holy commonwealth in New England. In his political views, church and state were functionally separate but shared a common goal of establishing a Christian community. In his debate with **Roger Williams**, Cotton defended the Puritan vision that civil magistrates should also be responsible for the care of souls and the enforcement of true religious beliefs, basing his appeal on the continued validity of Old Testament injunctions against heretics. Like many Puritans, he assumed that New England would play an important role in establishing the coming millennial kingdom. (ARB) **See also** Colonial America; Massachusetts Bay Colony; Millennialism; Rhode Island Colony.

Bibliography

Ziff, Larzer. *The Career of John Cotton: Puritanism and the American Experience.* Princeton, NJ: Princeton University Press, 1962.

——, ed. *John Cotton on the Churches of New England.* Cambridge, MA: Belknap Press, 1968.

Charles Edward Coughlin (1891–1979)

Roman Catholic priest and political commentator, Charles Coughlin was born on October 25, 1891, in Hamilton, Ontario. Educated at St. Michael's College in Toronto, Coughlin was ordained a priest in 1916. He became pastor of a small suburban church in Royal Oak, Michigan, in 1926 and soon began making Detroit radio sermons. By 1930, these weekly CBS broadcasts criticized **capitalism** and **President Herbert Hoover**.

The strident radio priest used listeners' donations to buy more Sunday afternoon airtime on 60 radio stations. Although he spoke for Franklin D. Roosevelt at the 1932 Democratic national convention, he was criticizing President Roosevelt by 1934. Coughlin founded the National Union for Social Justice, which joined Louisiana Senator Huey P. Long's Share the Wealth movement, headed by Gerald L. K. Smith, and Francis E. Townsend's Union Party to support William Lemke for president in 1936. Coughlin's weekly magazine, *Social Justice*, and his popular weekly "Golden Hour of the Little Flower" criticized bankers, Communists, Jews, and New Dealers. As he became increasingly anti-Semitic and pro-Fascist in 1938, Coughlin drew a private rebuke from the Vatican and attention from government investigators. His popularity waned by 1940 when he ended his radio program. *Social Justice* was barred from the mail under the Espionage Act and ceased publication in 1942 when church superiors imposed silence on Coughlin. He obeyed their orders but remained pastor of his church until retirement in 1966. Father Coughlin, who died on October 27, 1979, in Michigan, was an influential critic of the **New Deal** and a forerunner of **televangelism** and hate radio. (PCH) **See also** Anti-Semitism; Judaism; Roman Catholicism; Social Justice; Socialism and Communism.

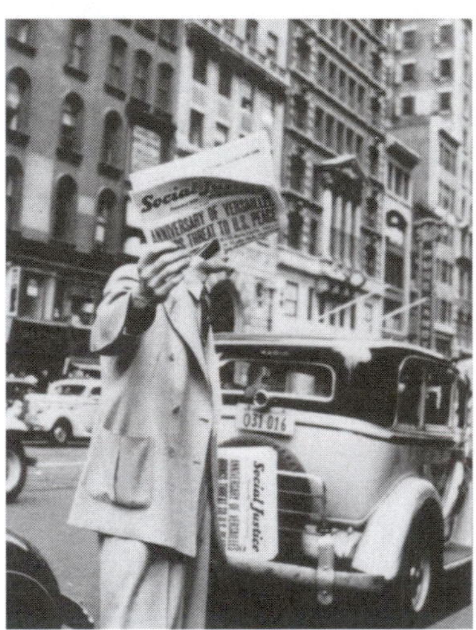

Father Charles E. Coughlin's publication, *Social Justice,* was a strong anti-Roosevelt voice in the 1930s and 1940s. Library of Congress.

Bibliography

Brinkley, Alan. *Voices of Protest: Huey Long, Father Coughlin, and the Great Depression.* New York: Random House, 1982.

Marcus, Sheldon. *Father Coughlin: The Tumultuous Life of the Priest of the Little Flower.* Boston: Little, Brown, 1973.

Warren, David I. *Radio Priest: Charles Coughlin, the Father of Hate Radio.* New York: The Free Press, 1996.

County of Allegheny v. Greater Pittsburgh ACLU (1989)

In *County of Allegheny v. Greater Pittsburgh ACLU*, 492 U.S. 573 (1989), the ACLU challenged the constitutionality of a Christian nativity scene displayed in downtown Pittsburgh on the grounds that the display violated the **Establishment Clause** of the **First Amendment**. The United States Supreme

Court refused to condemn the presence of a nativity scene on public property but did object to this specific holiday display because of the creche angel's words: "Glory to God for the birth of Jesus Christ." According to the Court, this endorsed a patently Christian message, and "Although the government may acknowledge Christmas as a cultural phenomenon, it may not observe it as a Christian holy day by suggesting that people praise God for the birth of Jesus." (JM)

BIBLIOGRAPHY

Pepper, Stephen. "A Brief for the Free Exercise Clause" *The Journal of Law and Religion* 7, no. 2 (Summer 1989): 323-62.

Cox v. New Hampshire (1941)

Five **Jehovah's Witnesses** challenged their conviction for the violation of a New Hampshire state statute prohibiting parades without a special license, claiming that the statute was invalid under the **Fourteenth Amendment** in that it deprived them of their rights of freedom of worship, freedom of speech and press, and freedom of assembly. In *Cox v. New Hampshire*, 312 U.S. 569 (1941), the U.S. Supreme Court affirmed the convictions, stating that the law did not hinder religious practice merely by imposing a licensing condition, particularly since that condition applied to all, regardless of religious beliefs. (JM) **See also** First Amendment.

BIBLIOGRAPHY

Goldberger, David. "Reconsideration of *Cox v. New Hampshire*." *Texas Law Review* 62 no. 3 (November 1983): 403-51.

Wiseman, Gary. "Paying for Free Speech." *Washington University Law Quarterly* 64, no. 3 (Fall 1986): 985-95.

Harvey Gallagher Cox (1929–)

Harvey Cox is a graduate of Yale, Harvard, and the University of Pennsylvania. After work in Berlin and a chaplaincy at Temple and Oberlin, Cox is presently Victor S. Thomas Professor of Divinity at Harvard University. Influenced by his **Baptist** tradition, **James Luther Adams**, Karl Barth, Dietrich Bonhoeffer, **Reinhold Niebuhr, Max Weber,** and **Ernst Troeltsch**, Cox has sought to understand the complex interactions between religion and society. His *Religion in the Secular City* (1984) revised his prognosis on religion first enunciated in his controversial work on secularization, *The Secular City* (1965). His study of the role of religion in politics has led to involvement in, and works upon urbanization, **liberation theologies**, religious pluralism, theological developments in world Christianity, and, most recently, on the political impact of worldwide Pentecostalism. (ISM) **See also** Pentecostals

BIBLIOGRAPHY

Cox, Harvey. *Fire From Heaven: The Rise of Pentecostal Spirituality and the Reshaping of Religion in the Twenty-First Century.* Belmont, MA: Addison-Wesley, 1995.

———. *Religion in the Secular City*. New York: Simon and Schuster, 1984.

———. *The Secular City*. (25th Anniversary Edition) New York: Collier Macmillan, 1990.

———. *The Silencing of Leonardo Boff.* Oak Park, IL: Meyerstone Books, 1988.

Creationism

The theory of creationism holds that all matter and all life was created by God out of nothing in the manner described in the biblical book of Genesis. Creationism contradicts the theory of **evolution** as derived from the work of Charles Darwin. Although Darwin proposed his theory in 1859, creationism held sway with most orthodox Christians for the next 60 years. Except as a justification for ruthless business practices (Social Darwinism), the theory of evolution created little political controversy until 1921, when one of the nation's leading **Fundamentalists**, former Democratic presidential candidate **William Jennings Bryan**, began to speak on "The Menace of Darwinism." Bryan's chief concern was the moral impact of teaching children about the "survival of the fittest." Bryan connected theory with Germany's brutal behavior in **World War I** and with opposition to his populist brand of progressivism. His fears seemed justified when feminist Charlotte Gilman published an article in the liberal magazine *The Nation* in early 1932 that used Darwinian terms to blast "individual fundamentalists" for opposing "sterilizing the unfit" by force.

Recognizing that the Genesis account of creation could not be required reading in public schools, Bryan proposed neutrality, banning all teachings about human origins. His advocacy led to a 1925 Tennessee law against teaching evolution and the famous **Scopes Trial**. Although the law was discredited in the press, the state's argument that the legislature could determine what schools taught was upheld. To avoid controversy, most high school biology textbooks avoided evolution for over three decades.

Evolution began to enter the classroom in the late 1950s when the first Soviet satellite created fears that the country was falling behind in science education. Increased federal funding led to biology textbooks that, unconstrained by any need to make a profit, included evolution. Controversy again resulted, with evolution opponents advancing two legal arguments. Some parents adopted the same argument that the Supreme Court had used to ban **school prayer**. If a few seconds of prayer could be banned as offensive to some, then it seemed reasonable to assume that several weeks of classroom instruction could also. That argument has had little success in courts.

Buttressed by broad public support, some legislatures have passed laws requiring that a scientific form of creationism be taught alongside evolution. Again the courts have been hostile, pointing to the few scientists who accept creationism but ignoring the question of how scientists can be knowledgeable about something that cannot be taught in most of the nation's schools. (MWP) **See also** Education.

BIBLIOGRAPHY

Gilman, Charlotte Perkins "Birth Control, Religion, and the Unfit" *The Nation* 134 (January 27, 1932), 108-09.

Larson, Edward J. *Trial and Error: The American Controversy over Creation and Evolution*. New York: Oxford, 1985.

Alexander Crummell (1819–1898)

Alexander Crummell was ordained an African-American Episcopal minister in 1842, but was refused admission to the Philadelphia diocese because of his race. Active in the Negro Convention Movement and a staunch abolitionist, Crummell went to Europe in 1848 to solicit funds to build **African-American churches** in the United States. In 1853, he went to Liberia in West Africa and founded numerous churches and schools. A mulatto coup in Liberia in 1873 led him to return to the U.S. where he preached the need for increased educational opportunities for African Americans. His call was similar in tone and scope to those of **W.E.B. Du Bois**. **See also** Abolition; African Methodist Episcopal (AME) Church; Education.

BIBLIOGRAPHY

Rigsby, Gregory U. *Alexander Crummell in 19th Century Pan-African Thought*. New York: Greenwood, 1987.

Cruz v. Beto (1972)

A Texas prisoner alleged that the state supported, encouraged, and rewarded prisoner participation in Protestant, Catholic, and Jewish religions. Further, the state even provided materials for these religions, but when the plaintiff requested similar recognition of his Buddhist beliefs, he was placed in solitary confinement. In *Cruz v. Beto*, 405 U.S. 319 (1972), the U.S. Supreme Court held that while the state need not provide the same degree of support to every form of religious expression—regardless of the number of adherents—it must reasonably accommodate the religious beliefs of all prisoners under both the **First Amendment** and the **Civil Rights Acts**. (FHJ) **See also** Buddhism; Judaism; Roman Catholicism.

BIBLIOGRAPHY

Palmer, John W. *Constitutional Rights of Prisoners*. Cincinnati: Anderson Publishing Company, 1997.

Cults

A cult is a religious group that deviates in important ways from a church. Lacking resources, cults generally avoid politics, but in recent decades have sought a measure of relief from political attacks in the courts. In popular use, a cult is any group, particularly one with a charismatic leader, that deviates from the religious mainstream. The term is used imprecisely and its inflammatory connotation often demonstrates prejudice on the part of its user. In scholarly discourse, however, "cult" is one of several related technical terms: religion, church, sect, and cult. In this framework, "religion" is an organization based on some supernatural assumptions; "church" refers to a conventional religious organization; "sects" deviate from a church but have traditional practices and beliefs; and "cults" also deviate from a church but have new or unusual practices and beliefs.

The number of cults is unknown. Depending on the criteria used, several hundred to several thousand cults exist in the United States. The number of adherents is likewise unknown, but believed to be small relative to the rest of the population. Nevertheless, because of their unusual beliefs and practices, cults periodically become the focus of intense public and media scrutiny.

Opposition to cults arises for two general reasons. In some instances, individuals and groups with more traditional religious beliefs are motivated by the cult's heterodoxy. In other instances, the cult gains attention because it advocates a practice that falls outside the norm, as in the case of the **Branch Davidians**, who were accused of stockpiling weapons and mistreating children.

Because of their small size, cults typically have insufficient resources to impact the political landscape. Indeed, their involvement in politics is infrequent and, in some cases, may even be antithetical to the cult's belief system. Cults have also been the focus of legislation, introduced by supporters of anti-cult groups, to restrict a cult's actions or to eliminate it altogether. The **Jehovah's Witnesses** and the **Church of Jesus Christ of Latter-day Saints** are two such cases, having suffered many legislative attacks when they were first developing. As each cult's distinctive beliefs and practices became known, they became the targets of outright persecution, often taking the form of local, state, or federal legislation designed to modify or abolish the group. Such persecution can take either virulent or subtle forms.

Legislative attempts to deal with cults in the nineteenth century reached a height in the case of the ***Church of Jesus Christ of Latter-day Saints v. United States***, (1890) which upheld legislation authorizing the confiscation of the church's assets and prohibiting its members from voting or otherwise participating in the political process. However, political solutions to cults usually occurred at the local or state level until the 1940s, when the U.S. Supreme Court ruled that religion was a national issue. At that time, groups such as the Jehovah's Witnesses found the courts more sympathetic to their needs than Congress, and were thereby able to win relief from onerous local regulations.

In recent years, two controversial issues regarding cults have been examined. The first of these concerns whether individuals who have joined a cult have been "brainwashed" by the group. This issue has arisen because of attempts to treat people, thought to have been brainwashed by cult propaganda, with "deprogramming" techniques, a series of intense and lengthy efforts to persuade the individual to leave the cult. Legal rulings generally have not supported deprogramming attempts. The second issue concerns the taxable nature of gifts to cults. In the case of Scientology, for example, payment for training received at a Scientology center is not considered a tax-exempt gift, suggesting to some that Scientology may not be a religion in the same sense that other religions are. (MEN) **See also** Charismatic Movement.

BIBLIOGRAPHY

Bromely, David G. and Anson Shupe. *Strange Gods: The Great American Cult Scare*. Boston: Beacon, 1981.

Robbins, Thomas and Dick Anthony, eds. *In Gods We Trust: New Patterns of Religious Pluralism in America*. 2nd ed. New Brunswick, NJ: Transaction Publishers, 1990.

Stark, Rodney and William Sims Bainbridge. *A Theory of Religion*. New York: Harcourt Brace Jovanovich, 1987.

Wald, Kenneth. *Religion and Politics in the United States*. Washington, DC: CQ Press, 1992.

Culture War

The term "culture war" was brought into intellectual currency by sociologist **James Davison Hunter**'s 1991 book *Culture Wars: The Stuggle to Define America* and into the popular consciousness by candidate **Pat Buchanan**'s fiery speech at the 1992 Republican convention. Culture war has been used to characterize the social and cultural disputes that divide conservatives and traditionalists, on the one hand, from liberals and progressives, on the other. Thus, issues like **abortion**, **school prayer**, and gay marriage seem to have no middle ground between proponents and opponents: conservatives oppose abortion and gay marriage and support school prayer, while liberals favor choice and gay marriage and oppose school prayer.

This excerpt from Buchanan's 1992 speech captures the flavor of the public rhetoric: "My friends, this election is about . . . what we stand for as Americans. There is a religious war going on in our country for the soul of America. It is a cultural war, as critical to the kind of nation we will one day be as was the Cold War itself. And in that struggle for the soul of America, Clinton and Clinton are on the other side, and George Bush is on our side."

Hunter's analysis is more measured. He argues that in the past few decades a major change has taken place within the ranks of many American religious denominations. Because the old dividing lines were denominational, one could predict much about a person's theological, social, and political positions by simply knowing his or her religious affiliation. Most Catholics could be expected to be on one side of an issue, many Protestants on the other. Among Protestants, one could, for example, expect Episcopalians to hold one set of beliefs and **Baptists** another. In the past few decades, however, many denominations have been split into "orthodox" and "progressivist" wings. Thus, one can find both conservative and liberal Presbyterians, all sitting in the pews of the same church or at least all attending churches in the same presbytery.

Hunter has also discovered that, as a result of this intradenominational split, new alliances have emerged in the public arena. On certain issues, conservative Catholics, Protestants, and Jews have forged alliances, as have their liberal counterparts. If it persists, this development can be significant. American religious pluralism might once have been expected to have a calming and moderating influence, as **Alexis de Tocqueville** argued in the nineteenth century after observing the differences between the political behavior of Roman Catholics in the United States, where they were a minority, and in some European countries, where they constituted a majority. If that pluralism is submerged in the overarching cleavage that Hunter identifies, then we might expect the level of contentiousness in American politics to increase. (JMK) **See also** Conservatism; Episcopal Church; Homosexual Rights; Judaism; Liberalism; Presbyterian Church; Republican Party; Roman Catholicism; War.

Bibliography

Green, John C., James L. Guth, Corwin E. Smidt, and Lyman A. Kellstedt. *Religion and the Culture Wars: Dispatches from the Front*. Lanham, MD.: Rowman and Littlefield, 1996.

Hunter, James Davison. *Culture Wars: The Struggle to Define America*. New York: Basic Books, 1991.

Tocqueville, Alexis de. *Democracy in America*. George Lawrence, trans. J.P. Mayer, ed. Garden City, NY: Doubleday, 1969.

Mario Matthew Cuomo (1932–)

Mario Cuomo, elected governor of New York in 1982, 1986, and 1990, is widely hailed as one of the best political orators of his generation. In contrast with most of his colleagues, the Democratic governor openly acknowledged the importance of his Catholic faith to his political views. Cuomo was sharply criticized by the archbishop of New York, Cardinal **John J. O'Connor**, because of the governor's liberal stance on **abortion**. The governor stated that while his religion was important, he had to uphold the law. This led one Catholic bishop to state that Cuomo was "in serious risk of going to hell." Cuomo also cited his religious beliefs in his reported vetos of death penalty bills from the state legislature. Once considered a rising star and potential presidential candidate, his liberal views seemed out of place in the more conservative **Democratic Party** of the 1990s. (BDG) **See also** Capital Punishment; Liberalism; Roman Catholicism.

Bibliography

McElvaine, Robert S. *Mario Cuomo: A Biography*. New York: Charles Scribner's Sons, 1988.

Manasseh Cutler (1742–1823)

Manasseh Cutler was a Congregational minister and Revolutionary War chaplain who helped found the first permanent white settlement in Ohio. He is credited with being one of the authors of the **Northwest Ordinance** (1787). Among its many provisions, the ordinance guaranteed religious freedom and toleration to all settlers, prohibited **slavery** in the territory, and encouraged the establishment of public schools. From 1801 to 1805, Cutler served in the U.S. House of Representatives from Massachusetts. (MWP) **See also** American Revolution; Congregationalism; Education.

Bibliography

Cutler, William P. *Life, Journals and Correspondences of Rev. Manasseh Cutler*. Temecula, CA: Report Services Corp., 1993.

D

Robert Lewis Dabney (1820–1898)

A Southern Presbyterian clergyman, theologian, and educator, Robert Lewis Dabney also served in the **Civil War** as a Confederate chaplain and later as chief of staff to General Thomas "Stonewall" Jackson, an experience that provided the formative influences for Dabney's subsequent ministerial and professorial careers. Dabney defended the South from both a religious and a political perspective after the Civil War, while also criticizing the prevalent intellectual trends of the nineteenth century. Dabney affirmed a traditional **Calvinism** grounded in the Westminster Confession and Catechism, a theological worldview that he applied to politics by opposing **Reconstruction** and reconciliation with Northern Presbyterians. (HLC) **See also** Chaplaincy; Presbyterian Church.

BIBLIOGRAPHY

Dabney, Robert Lewis. *Discussions, 1890-1897*. Harrisonburg, VA: Sprinkle Publishers, 1982.

Matthews, Merrill. *Robert Lewis Dabney and Conservative Thought in the Nineteenth Century South*. Ph.D. dissertation, University of Texas at Dallas, 1989.

Mary Daly (1928–)

A radical-feminist Catholic writer, Mary Daly is the author of various feminist theological works. In *The Church and the Second Sex*, published in 1968, she criticized the Catholic leaders' views of women throughout history and offered what she called some "modest proposals" for change, centering on the co-education of priests and sisters. In addition to arguing for a greater role for women in the Catholic Church, she has also been a vocal advocate for lesbians and for women's rights. Her views have had little impact on changing the Church's stances but she continues to be active in feminist/theological causes. **See also** Feminism; Homosexual Rights; Roman Catholicism.

BIBLIOGRAPHY

Daly, Mary. *Beyond God the Father: Towards a Philosophy of Women's Liberation*. London: Woman's Press, 1986.

———. *The Church and the Second Sex*. New York: Harper and Row, 1968.

———. *Outercourse*. San Francisco: Harper San Francisco, 1992.

John Nelson Darby (1800–1882)

John Nelson Darby, a leader of the Plymouth Brethren and the English founder of an important Fundamentalist theological system known as dispensationalism, sharply contrasted a heavenly church with a worldly government. Dispensationalism places little value on the accomplishments of human beings and the idea of progress. Instead, it stresses that history is the work of God. Darby's teachings were in sharp contrast to the views of many American Protestants who embraced social progress and **social justice**. His teachings, popularized by J. Scofield's Bible, led many American **Fundamentalists** to abandon political activity as ungodly while encouraging them to support the modern nation of **Israel** as a fulfillment of biblical prophecy. (ARB)

BIBLIOGRAPHY

Brock, Peter. "The Peace Testimony of the Early Plymouth Brethren." *Church History* 53, no. 1 (March 1984): 30–45.

Darby, John Nelson. *The Collected Writings of J. N. Darby*. Sunbury, PA: Believers Bookshelf, 1971.

Clarence Seward Darrow (1857–1938)

After practicing as a small town attorney in Ohio, Clarence Darrow moved to Chicago in 1887 and rose to national prominence in a series of high-profile trials, defending union leaders against conspiracy charges and violent criminals against the death penalty. Quick to deny any religious motivations for his opposition to **capital punishment**, he consistently persuaded juries that the murderers he was defending had acted in response to social and psychological forces beyond their own control. In 1925, Darrow defended the right of John Thomas Scopes to teach **evolution** in Tennessee public schools, sweeping aside arguments by Christian **Fundamentalists** and publicly humiliating their leader, **William Jennings Bryan**, in winning the case. (BDG) **See also** Scopes Trial.

BIBLIOGRAPHY

Darrow, Clarence. *Crime: Its Cause and Treatment*. New York: Thomas Y. Crowell, 1922.

Stone, Irving. *Clarence Darrow for the Defense*. New York: Garden City Publishing Company, 1943.

Samuel Davies (1723–1761)

Presbyterian clergyman and fourth president of the College of New Jersey at Princeton, Samuel Davies was a strong proponent of religious liberty. He opposed the exclusive advantages given the established church in Virginia where he had been pastor, arguing for religious freedom in keeping with the English Toleration Act of 1689. As a younger clergyman, Davies was pivotal in gaining popular support and volunteers to defend the borders of Virginia from "Indian Savages and French Papists" after General Braddock's defeat in 1755.(JHM) **See also** Colonial America; Presbyterian Church.

Bibliography

Pilcher, George William. *Samuel Davies: Apostle of Dissent in Colonial Virginia*. Knoxville: University of Tennessee Press, 1971.

Davis v. Beason (1890)

The U.S. Supreme Court first faced **Free Exercise Clause** challenges in a series of cases dealing with the Mormons, a religious sect that at the time condoned and encouraged **polygamy**. Even though polygamy was illegal in the United States, the Mormons claimed that its criminalization violated their right to freely practice their religion, under the **First Amendment**. In *Davis v. Beason,* 133 U.S. 333 (1890), the Supreme Court ruled that laws prohibiting polygamy were valid exercises of government power, stating that, "crime is not the less odious because sanctioned by what any particular sect may designate as 'religion.'. . . Bigamy and polygamy are crimes by the laws of all civilized and Christian countries. . . to call their advocacy a tenet of religion is to offend the common sense of mankind." Though the Court abandoned such language in subsequent cases, it has maintained the precedent that the government may prohibit certain actions, though not all, even when religious principles dictate the performance of those actions. (JM) **See also** Church of Jesus Christ of Latter-day Saints.

Bibliography

Chopper, Jesse H. *Securing Religious Liberty*. Chicago: University of Chicago Press, 1995.

Cord, Robert I. *Separation of Church and State*. New York: Lambeth Press, 1982.

Davis, Derek. *Original Intent*. Buffalo, NY: Prometheus Books, 1991.

Joseph M. Dawson (1879–1973)

A Texas **Baptist** champion of church-state separation, Joseph Dawson chaired the Southern Baptist Committee on World Peace in 1944. From 1946 to 1953, he headed the Baptist Joint Committee on Public Affairs, a leading Baptist voice on social issues. In 1947, he helped form Protestants and Others United for Separation of Church and State (now called American United) and served as its first executive secretary. Baylor University established the J. M. Dawson Institute of Church-State Studies in 1957, a leading center for the study of religion and politics and publisher of the respected *Journal of Church and State*. (ARB) **See also** Southern Baptist Convention.

Bibliography

Dawson, Joseph Martin. *A Thousand Months to Remember, An Autobiography*. Waco, TX: Baylor University Press, 1964.

_______. *America's Way in Church, State, and Society*. New York: Macmillan, 1953.

Dorothy Day (1897–1980)

Dorothy Day, founder of the **Catholic Worker Movement**, was born in Brooklyn on November 8, 1897, and was raised in Oakland and Chicago. While a student at the University of Illinois in Urbana, she became a socialist. Before converting to **Roman Catholicism**, she was a reporter for some radical New York City newspapers and magazines. The birth of her daughter in 1926 softened her views somewhat. In 1928, she converted to Catholicism and found herself alienated from her lover and bohemian friends.

By 1933, she reconciled radical politics with her religious faith when she joined **Peter Maurin** to found their monthly newspaper, *The Catholic Worker*. Envisioning a nonviolent, just society based on Catholic teachings, Day promoted such unpopular causes as **labor** unions during the Depression and **pacifism** during **World War II**. Later, she supported **conscientious objectors**, critics of nuclear warfare and civilian defense programs, **civil rights** workers, and farm workers' unions. Often jailed, she continued her radical work within the conservative Catholic Church.

Day's most effective work was in creating 30 houses of hospitality in American cities to feed, clothe, and shelter the homeless. She lived in voluntary poverty with her co-workers in these settlement houses and on rural communes. She was a prolific author who published an autobiography, *The Long Loneliness,* in 1952. Her legacy to liberal Catholicism and as a precursor to **liberation theology** cannot be overlooked. Dorothy Day died one of the most influential American Catholic leaders in the twentieth century, an internationally recognized holy woman. (PCH) See also Nuclear Disarmament; Social Justice; Socialism and Communism.

Bibliography

Coles, Robert. *Dorothy Day: A Radical Devotion*. Reading, MA: Addison-Wesley, 1987.

Forest, James H. *Love Is the Measure: A Biography of Dorothy Day*. New York: Paulist Press, 1986.

Declaration of Independence

The delegates to the Second **Continental Congress** appointed a distinguished committee to draft a document that would declare the colonies independent. The committee delegated the task to a subcommittee made up of **John Adams**, **Benjamin Franklin**, and **Thomas Jefferson**, although Jefferson actually wrote the document. His draft was changed only slightly; for example, the section chastising the king for introducing the slave trade into the colonies was deleted. The Congress approved the Declaration unanimously on July 4, 1776.

Jefferson did not claim originality in writing the Declaration. He intended to set forth the common sense of the American people on the subject of political legitimacy. Certainly, the ideas and phrases call to mind **John Locke**. The emphasis on the natural rights of man as the basis of the new political order, and the idea of the necessity of consent, while ultimately justified in the "laws of Nature and Nature's God," had long been acknowledged in the American colonies. Congregational church polity adhered to it, as did many legal writers such as Jean-Jacques Burlamaqui, Samuel Pufendorf, and the authors of Cato's letters.

The universal standard of right established by the Declaration of Independence made the **American Revolution** different from any other in history. The Americans did not appeal to the rights of Englishmen (as had the Whigs in the Glorious Revolution of 1688), but to the self-evident truth that "all men are created equal." The Declaration states that all men are endowed by their Creator with certain unalienable rights, among them "Life, Liberty, and the pursuit of Happiness." The rights are natural, are grounded in **natural law**, and are justified by reason, not by historical use. To secure these rights, "Governments are instituted . . . deriving their just powers from the consent of the governed." For the first time in the history of the human race, a particular political constitution was established that appealed to universal principles applicable to all people everywhere.

The Declaration of Independence enshrined the notion that the United States was founded on the "laws of Nature and Nature's God." National Archives.

The Declaration of Independence was the great constituent act of the American people. It is by this act that they constituted themselves as a people, a nation. The Declaration is the most fundamental constitutional document of the United States. The establishment of the government (whether by the Articles of Confederation or the Constitution) is secondary, and may be attempted, and changed, more than once. But constituting a people on universal grounds of right, with equal liberties, is permanent. And the basis of this new people is not a common history, ties of blood, or even a common language, but the recognition of the natural human rights of equality and liberty. Even though it fell to the new nation to demonstrate to all the world the feasibility of a government based upon the recognition of such rights, these rights remained the rights of all humanity. (PWS) **See also** Civil Religion; Congregationalism; Puritans.

Bibliography

Jaffa, Harry V. "Equality and the Founding." In J. Jackson Barlow, Leonard Levy and Ken Masugi, eds. *The American Founding: Essays on the Formation of the Constitution*. New York: Greenwood Press, 1988.

Mahoney, Dennis J. "The Declaration of Independence as a Constitutional Document." In Leonard W. Levy and Dennis J. Mahoney, eds. *The Framing and Ratification of the Constitution*. New York: Macmillan, 1987.

Maier, Pauline. *American Scripture: Making the Declaration of Independence*. New York: Alfred A. Knopf, 1997

Dedham Case

The Dedham case, a bitter church-state conflict in Massachusetts in the early nineteenth century, ultimately undermined the state's establishment of religion, that is, the support of local churches with tax dollars. The majority of members of the tax-supported church in Dedham parish were orthodox Congregationalists. The majority of voters in the parish, however, were Unitarians who rejected the divinity of Christ. Because voters chose the minister of the tax-supported church, a Unitarian minister was ultimately installed over the objections of church members. In *Baker v. Fales*, 16 Mass. 487 (1821), the Massachusetts supreme court approved the election, declaring that the state bill of rights "secure[d] to towns, not to the churches, the right to elect the minister in last resort." The court also held that voters, not church members, ultimately controlled the property of tax-supported churches. As a result, Congregationalists lost an estimated 81 churches to the Unitarians. Congregationalists subsequently turned against the principle of religious establishment, and in 1823 they joined with Jeffersonian Republicans to elect a reform legislature that significantly liberalized the Massachusetts system of church establishment. In 1833, establishment of religion was abandoned altogether in Massachusetts. (JGW) **See also** Congregationalism; Disestablishment; Establishment Clause; First Amendment; Thomas Jefferson; Unitarianism.

Bibliography

Levy, Leonard. *The Establishment Clause: Religion and the First Amendment*. New York: Macmillan, 1986.

Defense of Marriage Act (1996)

The Defense of Marriage Act amends the federal judicial code to provide that no state, territory, or possession of the United States or Indian tribe shall be required to give effect to any marriage between persons of the same sex under the laws of any other such jurisdiction or to any right or claim arising from such relationship. The act also establishes a federal definition of "marriage" as only a legal union between one man and one woman as husband and wife; and "spouse" as only a person of the opposite sex who is a husband or wife.

Sponsored by Representatives Steve Largent (R-OK) and Bob Barr (R-GA) with a companion bill introduced by Senator Don Nickles (R-OK), the act was introduced to head off a potential federal issue because it was widely believed that the Hawaiian courts would strike down that state's marriage law, which defines marriage as being between two people of the opposite sex. The issue of the definition of marriage is important because under the Constitution's "full faith and credit" clause (Article IV), the decision would jeopardize marriage laws in the other 49 states.

Christian conservatives like **Gary Bauer** of the Family Research Council argued that the act was necessary because the decision in the Hawaiian courts would threaten the traditional family. Bauer argued that "Marriage has been the foundation of civilization for thousands of years in cultures around the world. It is the single most important social institution, and it is the basis for the procreation of children and the heart of family life."

The bill passed overwhelmingly in both Houses and President **Bill Clinton** signed it into law on September 21, 1996. **See also** Homosexual Rights.

Bibliography

Baird, Robert M. and Stuart E. Rosenbaum, eds. *Same-sex Marriage: The Moral and Legal Debate*. Amherst, NY: Prometheus Books, 1997.

Strasser, Mark Philip. *Legally Wed: Same-sex Marriage and the Constitution*. Ithaca, NY: Cornell University Press, 1997.

Deism

Deism was an **Enlightenment** system of natural (rather than formally organized) religion that first appeared in England during the seventeenth and eighteenth centuries. Deism was also popular among educated Americans during the Revolutionary period. While assuming a variety of forms, deism affirms humankind's ability to acquire a knowledge of the Creator through reason alone. By stressing the individual's ability to rationally ascertain the universe's Creator, deists accept reason as the primary guarantee of faith and the sufficiency of religion. Deism also celebrates the adequacy of natural religion, the right of individuals to fulfill their rational capacity for knowledge and their need for toleration. Deists understand the Creator as a deity who has revealed himself in nature and reason, and who is an "absentee" or "watchmaker" Creator, both omnipotent and benevolent, establishing universal and unchanging laws for human life. The deity, however, refrains from further intervention in his creation. Drawing on the humanist impulses of the Renaissance and naturalism, deism celebrated the oneness of humanity and encouraged secularization. Envisioned by some of its advocates as a "reasonable" alternative to orthodox Christianity, the movement tended to denigrate established forms of political obligation and promote the cause of religious and political tolerance. **See also** American Revolution; Civil Religion; Natural Law; Secular Humanism.

Bibliography

May, Henry F. *The Enlightenment in America*. New York: Oxford University Press, 1976.

Democracy

Democracy, a theory and system of government rooted in the basic concept of the rule of the people, is the result of blending earlier political theories and practices. Essential elements of democracy are equality before the law; universal adult suffrage; legislative representation; freedom of speech, press, and assembly; freedom from arbitrary government interference; equal opportunity and freedom of and from religion; and individual freedom. Democracy's founding principles were deeply influenced by religious thought, such as the dignity of men and women, the equality of all, human rights, and human responsibilities.

Democracy appears to have prevailed in the contemporary world, not only because of the greater desire of educated people for greater freedoms, but also because of the failure of its alternatives. According to Samuel Huntingdon, modern democratizing movements have occurred in three historical waves. The first occurred roughly 200 years ago, lasted until **World War II**, and saw democracy established, notably in the United States of America, the United Kingdom, and other European nations. The second wave began after World War II and primarily involved Asian and African colonial nations gaining their independence, instituting democratic polities, and subsequently having them overthrown by military coups. The third wave began with the democratization of Spain and Portugal in the 1970s, continued with the re-democratization of many Latin American nations in the following decade, culminated in the fall of Eastern Europe and the USSR in the late 1980s and early 1990s, and climaxed with the extension of democratic rights to all peoples in South Africa in 1994. Democracy has thus become the most favored form of government worldwide.

Historically, democracy was not always regarded as an ideal form of government, and the concept of democracy evolved slowly over time. Plato, for example, regarded it as nothing but mob rule, as an abasement of the ideal government by rulers and guardians, who would ensure each person would receive his or her due. Aristotle, and many after him, preferred a "mixed" government, comprising monarchical, aristocratic, and popular elements to ensure stability. The medieval period saw the development of key democratic concepts such as individual rights, limitations on supreme power, constitutional limits, and the recognition, inherited from Roman law, that power derives from the people. The post-**Reformation** period witnessed the growth of religious pluralism and theories of toleration limiting government control of religion, one of the keys of democracy. Theories of social contract (Thomas Hobbes and **John Locke**), while not necessarily democratic, contributed the principle that the people should be able to overthrow those governments ruling contrary to natural or constitutional law. Such governments, where representation was by "Estate" (and not by individual) and property and literacy qualifications, dominated Europe until the nineteenth century. Modern democracy, inheriting and modifying earlier concepts, emerged out of the **Enlightenment** and particularly from the American and French revolutionary ideals of the sovereignty of the citizenry. The **French Revolution**, like the slightly earlier **American Revolution**, drew on earlier classical ideals of democracy in its own formulations. In claiming, as Jean-Jacques Rousseau did, a general will of the people for this form of government, a sharp break was made with the earlier medieval concept that rulers were appointed by **divine right** and that a government's task was to ensure the conformity of society to either a divine or **natural law**.

Two historical forms of democracy can be distinguished: representative or indirect democracy and participatory or direct democracy. In a representative democracy, the people elect representatives who are held accountable for the policies they adopt and thus are liable to removal by the electorate if their policies fail to ensure the mutual benefit of all citizens. According to this conception, democracy provides mechanisms to limit the power of the state and abuses of power. This system would include most modern democracies, where because of size, representation is indirect and accomplished by elected representatives who, chosen through a competitive political party process, make the policy and legislative decisions. Proponents of this approach include diverse thinkers such as St. Augustine, James Mill, **James Madison**, **Reinhold Niebuhr**, and most contemporary Western political theorists. The latter approach, direct democracy, regards the government as the provider of opportunity for civic participation at all levels of society. The government thus represents directly the popular will and exists to further the public or common good. While such a polity is only possible in small-scale societies such as classical Greece, **Puritan** New England, the nineteenth-century Orange Free State in southern Africa, or present-day Switzerland, this conception of democracy, advocated by Jean-Jacques Rousseau, Jeremy Bentham, and John Stuart Mill, is supported today by democratic socialists (Norberto Bobbio), communitarians and theologians such as **Paul Tillich**, and liberation theologians. In such democracies, citizens vote directly on all issues, and thus size is critical to their effective functioning. Apart from this basic distinction between representative and direct democracy, twentieth-century democracies exist in many forms, unitary or federal, presidential or parliamentary, or two-party or multi-party systems; most of these systems have rights entrenched in a constitution and bill of rights, as is the case in the United States. Such systems are referred to as constitutional democracies.

The United States is an example of the representative approach in that its Constitution, which divides powers of government into the executive, legislative, and judicial branches, serves to diffuse power and to limit its concentration in any one person or branch of government, thereby providing an institutionalized set of checks and balances. While opinion differs greatly on the extent of theological influence on the specifically American conception of democracy, it is clear that Puritan ideas of law, the divine and social covenant, congregational government, the inherent equality of all humans, and human weakness, all left their imprint upon the founding documents and institutions of the United States. Congregational church government, brought by the Puritans to New England, emphasized the autonomy of local congregations. Individuals made covenants with the church, as God did, and each was responsible for keeping that covenant. The principles of equality, liberty, and reciprocal responsibility overlapped with local governments.

Other examples of theological influences on democracy can be traced as well. The doctrine of original sin and its pessimistic estimation of human capabilities led to the political doctrine of the balance of powers. Behind this conception of democracy lies a particular anthropology, one which, in the Augustinian tradition, assumes a pessimistic view of human nature, a position set out by James Madison in *The Federalist Papers* and reiterated in the twentieth century by the many works of Reinhold Niebuhr. Much of the success of the United States' representative or liberal democracy is attributed (by **Alexis de Tocqueville** and others) to the acceptance of cultural pluralism and the existence of a buzzing profusion of voluntary associations, creating thereby intermediate organizations that mediate between the individual and political society.

A distinctive feature of American democracy is the separation of church and state, set out in the **First Amendment**. It resulted in the **disestablishment** of Congregational Churches in New England and Episcopal Churches in the South and in the development of denominations as purely voluntary associations. Though not initially interpreted as sharply as it is today, this separation is understood as ensuring freedom of religious belief, freedom of worship, and freedom to practice religion in public. Two dominant interpretations of the First Amendment exist at present. The reigning interpretation, being the dominant interpretation of the U.S. Supreme Court since the 1940s, is that of a strict separation that seeks, through application of the ***Lemon* Test**, to rigorously exclude any religious event, instruction, or symbolism from state institutions and schools or from state financial support. However, beginning in the 1980s, this interpretation has been challenged on the grounds that it discriminates against those who hold religious beliefs that do not so sharply separate the public and so-called private spheres. Such challenges, coming from diverse groups such as Orthodox Jews, conservative Christians, liberal religious thinkers, and some feminists, argue that such a neutral or liberal stance violates the actual presumption of liberal freedom upon which democracy is based, for it a priori excludes religious reasons from public decision-making and actions. The debated issue is whether the First Amendment requires the federal government to display neutrality towards religious institutions, seeking no contact and providing no support, or to display impartiality, that is, treating all religions alike and encouraging activities that support the common good. The latter interpretation would provide, for instance, for state support for religious schools.

American Roman Catholics, faced with nineteenth-century papal condemnations of modernism, liberalism, and democracy, as based on an atomized individualism that elevates individual opinion or conscience above revelation, have had to reconcile **Roman Catholicism** with democratic principles. This synthesis was most fully set out in the works of **John Courtney Murray**, S.J.

Philosophically and theologically, democracy is today the preferred form of government because it gives institutional expression to modern liberal understandings of the dignity and autonomy of the individual. An historical argument can also be made, particularly after world events beginning in 1989, that democracies are better able to provide social goods for the greatest number of people. However, political scientists and philosophers are concerned that the contemporary decline of voluntary associations has led to a utilitarian and egocentric individualism that is not connected to public life and thus is disinterested in acquiring civic virtues and pursuing the common goods of a democratic society. Many religious thinkers, while accepting the positive freedoms guaranteed under procedural or liberal democratic systems, would nonetheless seek fuller understanding that includes not just individual liberal rights, but also social rights, such as the rights to work, shelter, medical care, and **education**. The collapse of socialist democracy, they caution, should not be taken as proof of the success of liberal democracy or of **capitalism** as a distributive system. Despite the apparent success of democracy, the burgeoning social problems in newer democratic countries have not disappeared, problems which exacerbate existing inequalities and thus the ability of any representative democracy to function properly. (ISM) **See also** Communitarianism; Civil Religion; Civil Rights; Congregationalism; Episcopal Church; Feminism; Judaism; Liberalism; Liberation Theology; Mayflower Compact; Religious Right; School Prayer; Socialism and Communism.

BIBLIOGRAPHY

Audi, Robert and Nicholas Wolterstoff. *Religion in the Public Square*. New York: Rowman and Littlefield, 1997.

Elshtain, Jean Bethke. *Democracy on Trial*. New York: Basic Books, 1995.

Held, David. *Models of Democracy*. Cambridge: Polity, 1987.

Huntingdon, Samuel P. *The Third Wave: Democratization in the Late Twentieth Century*. Norman: University of Oklahoma Press, 1991.

Lijphart, Arend. *Democracies*. New Haven, CT: Yale University Press, 1984.

Murray, John. *We Hold These Truths: Catholic Reflections on the American Proposition*. New York: Sheed and Ward, 1960.

Nichols, James Hastings. *Democracy and the Churches*. Philadelphia: Westminster Press, 1950.

Niebuhr, Reinhold. *The Children of Light and the Children of Darkness: A Vindication of Democracy and a Critique of Its Traditional Defence*. New York: Charles Scribner's Sons, 1944.

Perry, Ralph B. *Puritanism and Democracy*. New York: The Vanguard Press, 1944.

Provost, James and Knut Wolf, eds. *The Taboo of Democracy within the Church*. Concilium 1992/5. London: SCM Press, 1992.

Regan, Richard J. *American Pluralism and the Catholic Conscience*. New York: Macmillan, 1963.

Theimann, Ronald F. *Religion in Public Life. A Dilemma for Democracy*. Washington, DC: Georgetown University Press, 1996.

Democratic Party

The Democratic Party has long been identified as the party of "outsiders" in American society. This view is particularly reflected in the religious diversity of its constituency. In the nineteenth century, the party enjoyed the consistent support of immigrants, especially Irish and German Catholics, as well as lower-status southern Protestants. This tenuous coalition persisted into the twentieth century with American Jews added to the mix during the presidency of Franklin D. Roosevelt . The last 30 years have witnessed southern Evangelical Protestants defecting to the **Republican Party**, with some gain in liberal northern Protestant support. In its party platforms, the Democratic Party has been conspicuously silent on religious issues, in part to maintain this fragile unity and in part to provide a contrast to the conservative, and historically Protestant, moral crusades of their Republican counterparts.

In **colonial America** and the early United States, the predecessor to the Democratic Party, the Jeffersonian Republicans, enjoyed the support of small farmers and laborers. These groups were often members of lower-status Protestant sects such as **Baptists** and Methodists and were much more likely to identify with the party of **Thomas Jefferson** than were their Congregationalist counterparts. For instance, **John Leland**, the Baptist evangelist and a significant player in the **disestablishment** of the **Episcopal Church** in Virginia, and Peter Cartwright, the Methodist circuit rider, were thoroughgoing Jeffersonians.

Religion was a key factor in the coalition that formed the Democratic Party, culminating in the realignment of the two-party system during the 1830s. Borrowing from its Jeffersonian origins, the Democratic Party became identified as the party of equality. The lower-status Evangelical Protestants, such as Methodists and Baptists, that had previously supported Jeffersonian Republicanism, joined the Democratic Party, as did the increasing number of Catholic immigrants from Ireland and Germany. Despite the fact that the Catholic Church was experiencing one of its most conservative periods worldwide, reflected in its papal denunciations of political liberalism, Catholic immigrants in the U.S. flocked to the Democratic Party and its egalitarian promises.

The religious coalition of the Democratic Party proved to be a fragile one on several occasions. In 1843, an anti-Catholic faction in the party broke ranks and formed the American Republican Party. Characterizing the nativist sentiment spreading through the nation, these individuals were fearful of papal allegiance on the part of some of the party leadership. Some Protestants also defected from the Democratic Party because of the appeal of Christian reform efforts, such as the **temperance** and Sabbatarian laws, that were a prominent part of the Whig Party's agenda. While some Catholics in the Democratic Party were uncomfortable with its political liberalism, the nativist tenor of the Whig Party's rhetoric and the Whigs' distinctly Protestant moral reform efforts assured the Democrats substantial Catholic support. This Whig **nativism** was also unsettling to some Protestants who otherwise found the Whig moral reform agenda appealing. Albeit uncertain, the religious alliance within the Democratic Party was sustained by its commitment to tolerance and equality. This alliance paid political dividends, for the Democrats were the nation's majority party and largely controlled the presidency and the Congress from the 1830s to the **Civil War**.

The issue of **slavery**, however, divided the Democrats—not only regionally, but also religiously. Tensions within the party over the slavery issue were enhanced by the party's appeasement of its increasingly powerful slaveholding southern Protestant members. Consequently, the party lost many of its northern Protestant members to the new Republican Party, assuring a Republican presidential victory in 1860.

Under the leadership of **William Jennings Bryan** during the late nineteenth and early twentieth centuries, the Evangelical Protestant wing of the party imbibed the messages of the **social gospel** and progressive reform. This moralist cast, more often identified with the Republicans, created yet a new religious chasm between the religious elements of the Democratic Party. Bryan frequently advocated the American virtue of rural Protestantism as opposed to the corrupting elements of urban America, alienating the Catholic segment of the party.

The massive European immigration during the early twentieth century brought many more Catholics to the Democratic fold. Catholics, in turn, began to rise in party leadership, as evidenced by the nomination of **Alfred E. Smith** in 1928 as the first non-Protestant to be nominated for president of the United States. Naturally, the presidential campaign and election focused on religious issues, and Smith's candidacy was questioned by Republican partisans. Yet it was the overwhelming opposition to Smith's candidacy from southern Protestants, normally Democratic partisans, that contributed to his lopsided defeat. Certainly Smith's religious identity, along with the highly visible prohibition movement, assured his defeat at the hands of **Herbert Hoover**.

During the next decade, however, these divergent religious elements coalesced to help provide Franklin Roosevelt create a broad and unified Democratic Party. Roosevelt garnered the support of southern Protestants and Catholics. Motivated in part by the Great Depression and prohibition, Jews shifted their support to the Democrats during this period as well. This unity prevailed during the next several decades, culminating in the election of the first non-Protestant to the nation's highest office. The religious rhetoric surrounding the Catholic **John F. Kennedy**'s Democratic campaign for the U.S. presidency hearkened back to the Al Smith campaign of 1928. Unlike the Smith campaign, however, the religious coalition of Catholics, Jews, African-American Protestants, and a mix of northern progressives came together in 1960 to provide a narrow victory for Kennedy. In contrast, **Evangelicals** and **Fundamentalists** were particularly suspicious of a Catholic president. In the South, where the Democratic Party had typically enjoyed strong support, opposition to Kennedy was widespread among Protestants. Despite Kennedy's assurances of his support for the constitutional separation of church and state, the leadership of the **Southern Baptist Convention** and the National Association of Evangelicals warned of the consequences for religious liberty if a Roman Catholic were elected president. Nevertheless, Kennedy was victorious in one of the most closely contested presidential races in history.

The rise of the **Religious Right** during the 1970s reflected the shift of many Evangelical Protestants from the Democratic Party to the Republican Party. This shift was briefly interrupted, however, by the presidential campaign of the Southern Baptist, **Jimmy Carter**, in 1976. Carter's "born again" Christian identity encouraged larger numbers of conservative Evangelicals and Fundamentalists to participate in the electoral process. In Carter, these Protestants believed they had an advocate for their concerns regarding **abortion**, homosexuality, and women's rights. Yet Carter proved to be a disappointment to the Evangelical Protestants because of his administration's moderate to liberal approach to lifestyle issues. Consequently, the conservative Republican **Ronald Reagan** reaped the benefits of a defection of many Evangelical (particularly southern) Protestants to the Republican Party in the 1980 presidential campaign.

With the shift of many southern Evangelical Protestants to the Republican Party, the Democratic religious coalition, although weakened, has maintained an alliance of Catholics, Jews, and some liberal Protestants. The Democratic Party has retained its identity as the party of "outsiders" and as the party of tolerance with regard to moral, social, and religious issues. This identity has been reinforced from within by the desire to maintain the party's diversity and from without by providing a clear alternative to the vocal and influential Religious Right elements of the Republican Party. Ironically, another Southern Baptist, **Bill Clinton**, reclaimed the presidency for the Democrats in 1992, despite the shift of southern Evangelicals to the Republican Party.

Democratic Party platforms have been conspicuously silent on religion for much of the party's history. In 1876, the party platform included a brief statement affirming the separation of church and state, but it would be another 108 years before another statement regarding religion appeared. The Democratic platform of the religiously politicized presidential campaign of 1984 included a statement of protest against the Reagan administration's quest to reverse the long line of

U.S. Supreme Court decisions affirming a high wall of separation between church and state. "We pledge to resist all efforts," the platform stated "to weaken those decisions. . . that preserve our historic commitment to religious tolerance and church/state separation."

In fact, it was a Democratic Court that had adopted and affirmed a strict separationist interpretation of the **First Amendment**. From the ***Everson v. Board of Education of the Township of Ewing*** decision in 1947 to the early 1980s, the Court struck down a variety of forms of support for religion. In particular, statutes that provided for religious exercises and symbols in the public schools as well as public funds for religious schools were found unconstitutional. While overall the Democrats have been supportive of these decisions, there have been some exceptions. The Catholic wing of the party strongly advocated public funds for their massive parochial school system, and some southern Protestants objected to the Court's decisions outlawing **school prayer** and Bible reading. Southern Democrats subsequently supported Republican President Reagan's school prayer amendment proposal 20 years later. In general, however, Democratic lawmakers have more consistently opposed attempts to lower the wall of separation than their Republican counterparts.

The issue of abortion, while a much more divisive issue in the Republican Party, has fostered some skirmishes among Democrats as well. Although a large majority of Democratic candidates and party platforms have supported a woman's right to choose since the 1980s, occasional prominent pro-life voices have been heard. For example, some controversy surrounded the 1992 Democratic National Convention when Governor **Robert P. Casey** of Pennsylvania was not invited to address the convention because of his pro-life stance. Moreover, in the late 1980s, larger numbers of Democrats in the House of Representatives began to question the party's seemingly unqualified support for the pro-choice position and began to support restrictions on the public funding and availability of the abortion procedure.

As long as the religious conservatives continue to play an important role in the Republican Party, the Democratic Party will continue to portray itself as the more tolerant and religiously pluralistic political option. However, the conservative turn in American politics during the last three decades has put many Democratic politicians on the defensive. The current **culture wars** have compelled increasing numbers of Democratic politicians to seek a more moderate identity and to distance themselves from the liberal wing of the party. Nevertheless, the tenuous religious coalition within the party will most likely continue and a platform of religious liberty and toleration will characterize the party's religious pronouncements. (JDH) **See also** Born-Again Christians; Congregationalism; Conservatism; Education; Feminism; Homosexual Rights; Judaism; Know-Nothing Party; Liberalism; Methodism; New Deal; Reconstruction; Roman Catholicism; Sabbatarianism.

BIBLIOGRAPHY

Benson, Peter L. and Dorothy L. Williams. *Religion on Capitol Hill: Myths and Realities*. San Francisco: Harper and Row, 1982.

Fuchs, Lawrence H. *The Political Behavior of American Jews*. Glencoe, IL.: Free Press, 1956.

Hanna, Mary T. *Catholics and American Politics*. Cambridge, MA: Harvard University Press, 1979.

Leege, David C. and Lyman A. Kellstedt, eds. *Rediscovering the Religious Factor in American Politics*. New York: M.E. Sharpe, 1993.

Manza, Jeff and Clem Brooks. "The Religious Factor in U.S. Presidential Elections, 1960–1992." *The American Journal of Sociology* 103, no.1 (July 1997): 38–82.

Menendez, Albert J. *Religion at the Polls*. Philadelphia: The Westminster Press, 1977.

Noll, Mark, ed. *Religion and American Politics*. New York: Oxford University Press, 1990.

Reichley, A. James. *Religion in American Public Life*. Washington, DC: The Brookings Institution, 1985.

Wald, Kenneth D. *Religion and Politics in the United States*. 3rd ed. Washington, DC: Congressional Quarterly Press, 1997.

Wood, James E. Jr. "The Church-State Legacy of John F. Kennedy." *Journal of Church and State* 6 (Winter 1964): 5–11.

Deprogramming

The social ferment of the late 1960s stimulated many new or unusual religions. Because the converts were young and these religions exercised a great deal of control, brainwashing was feared by many parents and families. In the late 1970s, it became common for parents to hire deprogrammers to kidnap their children (typically in their late teens to early twenties) from religious **cults**. The deprogrammer would attempt to pressure and manipulate the children into rejecting their new beliefs. While some courts assisted parents by granting them a conservatorship, the kidnapping and coercion raised serious legal and ethical problems. (MWP)

BIBLIOGRAPHY

Melton, J. Gordon and Robert C. Moore. *The Cult Experience*. New York: Pilgrim Press, 1982.

Detached Memoranda

Written by **James Madison** sometime after his retirement from the presidency, the "Detached Memoranda" has generally been considered a "separationist" document. In this letter, Madison criticized the use of federal money to support congressional or military chaplains, as well as proclamations of days of fast or thanksgiving, as inconsistent with the **Establishment Clause** of the **First Amendment**. Madison argued for a "perfect separation" between religion and government, suggesting that religion is purer and less corrupt when it does not stand in need of government assistance. Madison's arguments in the "Memoranda" may have been inconsistent with earlier Madisonian writings on religion, and they also appear to have been inconsistent with actions taken by Madison during his presidency. For example, when in the Virginia legislature, Madison introduced a bill for days of public fasting and thanksgiving, and as president he issued at least four proclamations for thanksgiving and prayer. (TGJ) **See also** Chaplaincy; Thanksgiving and Fast Days.

BIBLIOGRAPHY

Fleet, Elizabeth. "Madison's 'Detached Memoranda.'" *William and Mary Quarterly* III (1946): 554–62

Levy, Leonard. *The Establishment Clause*. New York: Macmillan, 1986.

Wills, Gary. *Under God.* New York: Simon and Schuster, 1990.

John Dewey (1859–1952)

Born in Burlington, Vermont, to a family of devout New England Congregationalists, John Dewey became one of the most influential American philosophers and educators of the twentieth century. He espoused a pragmatism according to which one should judge the value of an idea not by its relation to a moral intuition or revelation, but by its ability to solve problems in one's practical experience. Though he quietly lost his Christian faith in the early 1890s, Dewey maintained that his pragmatism was compatible with religious sentiments. He also wrote on psychology, **education**, and **democracy**, and in 1896 founded a laboratory school in Chicago to experiment with new pedagogical programs. (BDG) **See also** Congregationalism; Humanist Manifesto.

John Dewey was a leading force behind the "Humanist Manifesto." National Archives.

BIBLIOGRAPHY

Dewey, John. *Democracy and Education.* New York: Free Press, 1966.

Ryan, Alan. *John Dewey and the High Tide of American Liberalism.* New York: W. W. Norton & Co., 1995.

Disciples of Christ

The Disciples of Christ, also known as the Christian Church, was formed in 1832 when the followers of Barton W. Stone (Christians) merged with those of **Alexander Campbell** (Disciples). The newly formed nondenominational body grew rapidly in the mid-nineteenth century, especially in the Midwest and South. Theologically, the group practices baptism by immersion, the celebration of weekly communion, the autonomy of local congregations, and "no creed but the Bible." In 1840, the body founded Bethany College in West Virginia, and in 1849 the American Christian Missionary Society.

While the **Civil War** had an adverse and schismatic impact on many Protestant sects, the Disciples were relatively free from conflict. However, in the early twentieth-century, a growing divide between the Disciples and their more conservative southern elements became a permanent split between the Disciples and the Churches of Christ. This liberal-conservative split was only the first of several that have affected the Disciples. The Disciples have played a central role in the debates between liberal theologians and conservative forces. Their journal, the *Christian Century*, is the most important liberal Protestant publication in the country.

The membership of the Disciples has dropped dramatically in the last 50 years from a high of about 2 million members to fewer than 1 million today. Many scholars suggest that the decline in church membership is because of the Disciples' liberal stances on many theological and social questions. **See also** Conservatism; Liberalism; United Church of Christ.

BIBLIOGRAPHY

Williams, D. Newell, ed. *A Case Study of Mainstream Protestanism: The Disciples' Relation to American Culture, 1880-1989*. Grand Rapids, MI: Eerdmans, 1991.

Disestablishment

Although the U.S. Constitution forbade the establishment of any single religion by the national government, many states continued with their own establishments well into the nineteenth century. Even after these legal establishments were abandoned, de facto establishment of religion, and Protestant Christianity in particular, continued across the country. Bibles were still read in public schools, chaplains continued to offer prayers before legislative sessions, and many members of minority religions were still prevented from full exercise of their **civil rights**. It was not until the early twentieth century that the nation's elites moved decisively to separate church from state. In ***Cantwell v. State of Connecticut*** (1940) and ***Everson v. Board of Education of the Township of Ewing*** (1947), the Supreme Court applied the religion clauses of the Constitution to the states, and so began a series of decisions that have demanded a governmental neutrality toward religion never before experienced in American history. Whether these decisions amount to a wholesale disestablishment of religion is a controversial matter, but taken with shifts in cultural attitudes toward religion, they represent profound changes in the relationship between church and state. (KRD) **See also** Chaplaincy; Establishment Clause; First Amendment; School Prayer.

BIBLIOGRAPHY

Levy, Leonard. *The Establishment Clause: Religion and the First Amendment*. Chapel Hill: University of North Carolina Press, 1994.

Smith, Steven. "Separation and the 'Secular': Reconstructing the Disestablishment Decision." *Texas Law Review* 67, no. 5 (April 1989): 955–1031.

Divine Right of Kings

The divine right of kings is the notion that a hereditary monarch has a God-given right to rule. The monarch was considered responsible for his or her actions to God alone, not to the people he or she governed. To question the right of the monarch to rule, or to attempt to overthrow the regime, was a serious offense against God. The theory also holds that princes should serve as the leaders of their country in accord with the natural authority invested in them by God. Political power, according to divine right, must never be given to the multitude because they have not received a commission to rule from God. The theory, which was used to buttress the English monarchy in the early seventeenth century, was at odds with the Puritan idea that the people should decide who was to rule over them. And it was the **Puritans**, fleeing the pretensions of divine right monarchy in seventeenth-century England, who brought their notions of the proper relationship between governor and governed to America, where those ideas were eventually embodied in the founding documents of the United States. (HLC) **See also** Declaration of Independence.

Bibliography

Filmer, Sir Robert. *Patriarcha and Other Political Works*. Oxford: Basil Blackwell, 1949.

Divorce

The movement to liberalize divorce laws in the United States had two major proponents. The first was the women's liberation movement, which saw the divorce laws as too restrictive and paternalistic in both their content and enforcement. The second group of supporters were Jews who sought to end the restrictive laws that had been passed by Protestant-led state legislatures. Christian divorce laws were far more restrictive than Jewish laws, which allowed a man to divorce a woman for a wide variety of reasons, including some inconsequential ones like burning supper.

Opposition to the liberalization of divorce laws was spearheaded by the Roman Catholic Church. However, the Church was widely criticized for its position, being accused of trying to force its doctrines upon American society. The Church did have a difficult time expanding its own doctrine on marriage and divorce to a more universal application. Unlike its teachings on **abortion**, which are rooted in the **natural law** and therefore binding upon all people, the Church's opposition to divorce is of a more consequential nature in that it prefers whenever possible to retain the integrity of the family and the institution of marriage. The Church feared that liberalized divorce laws would lead to an increase in divorce and the decline of the family.

Divorce reform has become a major movement in the late 1990s. More than 20 states are now considering drastic reforms of the liberalized divorce laws, especially no-fault divorce. Religious conservatives are playing a major role in this movement. The impact of divorce on American society has become a cultural as well as a moral issue. In a 1997 CNN/Time Poll, 50 percent of Americans believed that getting a divorce should be more difficult and 61 percent thought that couples with children should have a more difficult time getting a divorce than the current laws dictate.

The movement for divorce reform will continue as people assess the impact of 30 years of liberalized divorce laws. However, most divorce reform is focused upon tinkering around the edges of no-fault divorce, rather than on a return to more restrictive divorce laws. **See also** Feminism; Judaism; Roman Catholicism.

Bibliography

Gallagher, Maggie. *The Abolition of Marriage.* Washington, DC: Regnery Press, 1997

Pfeffer, Leo. *God, Reason and the Constitution.* Boston: Beacon Press, 1975.

James C. Dobson (1936–)

While eschewing direct political participation, Dr. James Dobson, a conservative psychologist, continues to have an enormous impact on grassroots Evangelical political activity. His Focus on the Family ministry maintains a mailing list of some 3.5 million families, and his daily radio broadcasts are heard on over 2,900 radio stations. According to Dobson, the nation is in the midst of a **culture war**, and conservative Christians must actively participate in the rhetorical and legislative fight. Dobson was a member of the 1980 White House Conference on the Family, and, in 1985, served on Attorney General Edwin Meese's Commission on Pornography. (ARB) **See also** Conservatism; Evangelicals; Republican Party; Televangelism.

Bibliography

Colson, Charles, and James Dobson. "What We're Fighting For." *Focus on the Family Citizen* 11, no. 11 (November 1997): 6–9.

Fisher, Marc. "Dr. Dobson's Political Pill." *Washington Post* (July 2, 1996): D1–D2.

William O. Douglas (1898–1980)

William Douglas served over 36 years on the U.S. Supreme Court. A liberal Democrat, he defended privacy and militant dissent and broadly interpreted free speech to include such actions as burning a draft card. His views on the meaning of the **First Amendment**'s religious clauses were becoming more liberal. He voted with the ***Minersville School District v. Gobitis*** (1940) which upheld State flag salutes but switched his vote when *Gobitis* was reconsidered in ***West Virginia State Board of Education v. Barnette*** (1943). He also believed that the **Establishment Clause** required greater separation between church and state. Through such interpretation he found a right of privacy in *Griswold v. Connecticut* (1965), the basis for striking down a Connecticut law against contraceptives and later a precedent in ***Roe v. Wade*** (1973). He was an avid conservationist and writer on such controversial issues as **school prayer**. (JRV) **See also** Democratic Party.

Bibliography

Countryman, Vern. *The Judicial Record of Justice William O. Douglas.* Cambridge, MA: Harvard University Press, 1974.

Douglas, William O. *The Bible and the Schools.* Boston: Little, Brown and Company, 1966.

Frederick Douglass [Augustus Washington Bailey] (1817–1895)

Frederick Douglass was the most significant black advocate for the **abolition** of **slavery** in the United States in the nineteenth century. Born into slavery in Maryland in 1817, he was sent to Baltimore, where he learned to read and write. He escaped to New York and became an agent of the Massachusetts Anti-Slavery Society.

His abolitionist efforts were primarily accomplished through public speaking tours, publishing, and using political connections. A lay preacher in the **African Methodist Episcopal Church**, his writings are replete with biblical allusions and appeals to Christian themes of justice, redemption, and forgiveness. At the same time, Douglass fiercely criticized what he saw as the religious hypocrisy of Christians who owned slaves. Douglass toured the northeastern United States, Canada, and England before publishing his *Narrative of Frederick Douglass* (1845), one of the most influential abolitionist writings. In 1847, he founded a newspaper, *The North Star*, subsequently published as *Frederick Douglass's Paper*. In 1855, he published *My Bondage and My Freedom* and in 1858, *Douglass's Monthly*. At the outbreak of the **Civil War**, he met with President **Abraham Lincoln** and assisted him in the formation of the 54th and 55th Massachusetts Negro Regiments.

Former slave Frederick Douglass was one of the leading voices for abolition. Library of Congress.

By 1871, he was serving in the territorial legislature for the District of Columbia, and in 1872, he was named a presidential elector for New York. He also served as a member of the Santo Domingo Commission. He held various posts in Washington, DC, until he was appointed minister resident and U.S. consul general to the Republic of Haiti in 1889. (ISM)

Bibliography

Rogers, William B. "We Are All Together Now:" *Frederick Douglass, William Lloyd Garrison, and the Prophetic Tradition*. New York: Garland Publishing, 1995.

Washington, Booker T. *Frederick A. Douglass*. Philadelphia: George W. Jacobs, 1906.

Robert Frederick Drinan (1920–)

A Jesuit priest, Robert Drinan, served as an elected member of the U.S. House of Representatives from Massachusetts from 1971 until 1981. He did not stand for re-election in 1980 because of a Vatican order that priests should not serve in elected political offices. While in Congress, Drinan, a liberal Democrat, was particularly interested in issues of human rights, **social justice**, and civil liberties. Since leaving Congress, Drinan has taught at Georgetown University Law School and serves on the boards of a number of organizations including the World Hunger Education Service. **See also** Democratic Party; Liberalism; Roman Ctholicism.

Bibliography

Drinan, Robert F. *Beyond the Nuclear Freeze*. New York: Seabury Press, 1983.

——. *Cry of the Oppressed: The History and Hope of the Human Rights Revolution*. San Francisco: Harper & Row, 1987.

——. *The Fractured Dream: America's Divisive Moral Choices*. New York: Crossroad, 1991.

——. *Honor the Promise*. Garden City, NY: Doubleday, 1977.

——. *Religion, the Courts, and Public Policy*. New York: McGraw-Hill, 1963.

——. *Vietnam and Armageddon*. New York: Sheed and Ward, 1970.

W.E.B. Du Bois (1868–1963)

An African-American historian, educator, and reformer, William Edward Burghardt Du Bois was born in Great Barrington, Massachusetts, on February 23, 1868. Educated at Fisk and Harvard Universities, he was the first black man to earn a Ph.D. at Harvard. While at Harvard, DuBois became a student of **William James**' secular, liberal theology. While teaching at Atlanta University (1897–1910), he wrote *The Souls of Black Folk* (1903) to announce his intellectual rebellion against **Booker T. Washington**'s conservative leadership of black intellectuals. The book is one of the first volumes on black religious music and black religious life in general. In 1909, Du Bois founded the National Association for the Advancement of Colored People (NAACP).

As editor of the NAACP magazine, *The Crisis* (1909–1932), Du Bois was an influential leader for African Americans and liberal whites. The Pan-African Conferences he organized (1900, 1919, 1921, 1923, 1927, and 1945) called for black pride, independence for African colonies, and recognition of Africa's role in world history. Dubbed a radical by conservative critics, Du Bois fostered the Harlem Renaissance and pioneered the **civil rights** movement.

He returned to Atlanta University from 1932 through 1944, but rejoined the NAACP as director of research and served as editor of the *Encyclopedia of the Negro* from 1933 through 1945. Always an eloquent lecturer and prolific author, Du Bois inspired black people around the world. Disappointed with efforts to end racial discrimination in the United States, he turned to Marxism in the 1940s, was investigated by the federal government, and joined the Communist Party in 1961.

In 1962, a bitter Du Bois emigrated to Africa, becoming a citizen of Ghana and editor of the *Encyclopedia Africana*. He died in Accra on August 27, 1963, and in 1968 his *Autobiography* was published. (PCH) **See also** Education; Socialism and Communism.

BIBLIOGRAPHY

Andrews, William L. *Critical Essays on W. E. B. Du Bois*. Boston: G. K. Hall, 1985.

Reed, Adolph L. *W. E. B. Du Bois and American Political Thought*. New York: Oxford University Press, 1997.

Dueling

Dueling is the practice of resolving disputes of justice or honor by allowing two men to engage in mortal combat, usually with swords or guns. In the United States, the early-nineteenth-century campaign to outlaw duels of honor was one of the first major reform movements spearheaded by religious leaders.

During the Middle Ages, duels were often viewed as appeals to the judgment of God, and their results were trusted because they could not be manipulated by priests. In France, the number of lives lost to dueling quickly became intolerable, and by the twelfth century organized attempts were being made to prohibit duels. The last duel authorized by the French king took place in 1547, and in 1566, Charles IX decreed that anyone found to be participating in a duel would be hanged. In England, where judicial duels had been introduced by William I, the practice was not abolished until 1819, and in Germany, duels were sanctioned by the military code until **World War I**, and then reappeared during the Nazi regime.

Duels of honor were commonly practiced by aristocrats in the early American republic and did not come under serious public scrutiny until the summer of 1804, when Vice President Aaron Burr killed Revolutionary War hero **Alexander Hamilton** in a duel near the banks of the Hudson River in New Jersey. With the attention of the nation focused on Hamilton's death, religious leaders such as **Lyman Beecher** launched a campaign to outlaw the practice that had killed Hamilton. Putting aside their usual squabbling, ministers of different Protestant denominations spoke in similar voices on this issue, proving that evangelical oratory could be mobilized not only to support particular religious doctrines, but also to support general moral positions. Their campaign did not immediately succeed in turning either public opinion or the law against the practice of dueling, but by 1839, Congress had outlawed the practice in the armed forces and in the District of Columbia. Dueling vanished with the Old West later that century. (BDG)

BIBLIOGRAPHY

Setz, Don C. *Famous American Duels*. New York: Thomas Crowell, 1929.

West, John G., Jr. *The Politics of Revelation and Reason: Religion and Civic Life in the New Nation*. Lawrence: University Press of Kansas, 1996.

John Foster Dulles (1888–1959)

The son of a Presbyterian minister and an influential Presbyterian layman, John Foster Dulles began a public service career under President **Woodrow Wilson** in 1917 and eventually served as secretary of state for the Eisenhower administration from 1952 through 1959. Raised in New York State, Dulles attended Princeton University (1908), studied under Henri Bergson at the Sorbonne, and completed a law degree at George Washington University in 1911. He eventually became head of a Wall Street law firm. Dulles served as a Presbyterian elder, and in 1924, he defended **Harry Emerson Fosdick** before the Presbyterian General Assembly, arguing against fundamentalist **William Jennings Bryan**. Involved with the Federal Council of Churches, he chaired the Commission on a Just and Durable Peace (members included **Reinhold Niebuhr** and Harry Fosdick) from 1941 onwards and strongly supported the creation of the United Nations. (ISM) **See also** Dwight Eisenhower; Fundamentalists; Presbyterian Church.

BIBLIOGRAPHY

Immerman, Richard H., ed. *John Foster Dulles and the Diplomacy of the Cold War: A Reappraisal*. Princeton: Princeton University Press, 1989.

Tolouse, Mark G. *The Transformation of John Foster Dulles: From Prophet of Realism to Priest of Nationalism*. Macon, GA: Mercer University Press, 1985.

Timothy Dwight (1752–1817)

Throughout his varied career as Congregational minister (he was the grandson of **Jonathan Edwards**), president of Yale College (1795–1817), author, and state politician, Timothy Dwight applied his enormous mental and physical energies so diligently that he became perhaps the foremost individual in New England during his time. Derided as "Pope Dwight" by his detractors and lauded as second only to the Apostle Paul by his supporters, Dwight was frequently at the nexus of New England religion and politics. He took part in the **Second Great Awakening** and was a leading apologist for Federalism in the Northeast. Dwight served two years as chaplain in the Continental Army, was an acquaintance of **George Washington**, and was considered for appointment to the **Continental Congress**. A Calvinist in religion and a Federalist in politics, Dwight saw **democracy** and infidelity as inevitably linked and throughout his career he preached, wrote, and voted against both. At times, however, his **Calvinism** and Federalism came into conflict. In 1812, Dwight preached a sermon in which he criticized the Constitutional Convention for excluding God from both the Convention and the Consti-

Timothy Dwight was derided as Pope Dwight by his opponents. National Archives.

tution, thus commencing "our national existence under the present system, without God." (JHM) **See also** Chaplaincy; Congregationalism.

Bibliography

Dwight, Timothy. *Travels in New England and New York*. 4 vols. Cambridge, MA: Belknap Press of Harvard University Press, 1969.

Mary Dyer (?–1660)

In 1638, Mary Dyer and her husband William were excommunicated and banished from the **Massachusetts Bay Colony** because of their vocal support of **Anne Hutchinson**. Converting to Quakerism in 1652 while in England, Dyer returned to the colonies and in 1659 was jailed for her religious beliefs. Expelled and warned not to return to Massachusetts, she ignored the warnings repeatedly and was finally executed in 1660. (MWP) **See also** Colonial America; Excommunication; Puritans; Quakers.

Bibliography

Rogers, Horatio. *Mary Dyer: The Quaker Martyr*. Providence, RI: Preston and Rounds, 1896.

E

"Economic Justice for All"

Meeting in Washington, D.C., from November 10 to 13, 1986, the **National Conference of Catholic Bishops** strongly endorsed a pastoral letter entitled "Economic Justice for All." In development for five years, the letter called for both the public and private sectors to work for full employment. It also called for attacks on poverty and supported "judiciously administered affirmative action programs." Additionally, it recommended reducing government expenditures on the military and increasing social spending for such programs as welfare and Medicaid.

Conservative American Catholics were particularly critical of the pastoral letter. Led by William Simon and **Michael Novak**, a group of Catholics publicly criticized the letter in a statement on November 4, 1986. Simon and Novak were concerned that the proposals placed "excessive trust in the state and its officials." Instead, they called for empowering the poor from the bottom up rather than extending political privileges from the top down. ("Economic Justice for All" is reprinted in Appendix 1.) (MWP) **See also** Roman Catholicism.

Bibliography

D'Antonio, William. *Laity, American and Catholic*. Kansas City, MO: Sheed & Ward, 1996.

Gelm, Richard J. *Politics and Religious Authority*. Westport, CT: Greenwood, 1994.

Ecumenical Movement

The ecumenical movement reflects a desire on the part of Christian denominations to join together to form one Christian church and undo some of the splintering of medieval Christianity that occurred with the Protestant **Reformation** of the sixteenth century. The movement has had several manifestations, including attempts by the Roman Catholic Church to reunite with the Eastern Orthodox Churches.

In the United States, most ecumenical efforts have revolved around sects coming together for common purposes. In the nineteenth century, the growth of missionary societies led a number of previously independent bodies to form organizations like the **American Board of Commissioners for Foreign Missions** in 1810 and the **American Sunday School Union** in 1824.

However, despite these efforts, too many doctrinal differences separate the sects to allow them to form a single Christian church. Instead of true reunification, churches have had to settle for the formation of organizations like the National Council of Churches (the successor to the Federal Council of Churches of Christ in America) in 1950 and the World Council of Churches in 1948. The Roman Catholic Church is not a member of either body. Thus, the success of ecumenicalism has been, and likely will remain, limited to cooperation in those areas where the different sects can agree. **See also** Roman Catholicism.

Bibliography

Wainwright, Geoffrey. *The Ecumenical Movement*. Grand Rapids, MI: Eerdmans, 1983.

Mary Baker Eddy (1821–1910)

In 1881, Mary Baker Eddy founded the Church of Christ, Scientist. **Christian Science** is a Christian sect that places special emphasis on the healings that Jesus performed in the New Testament. Always in poor health, Eddy had sought the aid of a mental healer, Phineas Quimby, in 1862. However, she rejected Quimby's methods because he focused upon the powers of the human mind rather than upon the power of God's love. She claimed that she was healed from her afflictions in 1866 while reading the Bible. Over a decade later, she published *Health and Science* (1875), which detailed her religious system. In 1879, she founded the Church of Christ, Scientist and in 1881, moved its headquarters to Boston, Massachusetts. Eddy also authored the *Manual of the Mother Church* (1908) and founded the *Christian*

Mary Baker Eddy was the founder of the Church of Christ, Scientist. Library of Congress.

Science Monitor in 1908. The unorthodox nature of Christian Scientists garnered many critics, most notably Mark Twain, who believed the religion dangerous to the political and religious realms.

BIBLIOGRAPHY

Hoekema, Anthony A. *Christian Science*. Grand Rapids, MI: Eerdmans, 1972.

Education

Much of the controversy over the separation of church and state has centered on education. In fact, the vast majority of Supreme Court cases concerning the religion clauses of the **First Amendment** have involved educational institutions. This fact is not surprising, for the essence of any religion is its promulgation, especially to children, and the school provides an intersection for moral, civic, rational, and social development. Schools are at the crossroads between the family and the state. In the U.S., the main ingredients of the controversy were the disputed meaning of the **Establishment Clause**, the ascendancy of American Protestantism, an assertive community of Catholic immigrants, and the emerging system of public education.

Not until the 1830s did states and municipalities began using tax funds to support public education. Previously, all education had been run by families or churches. But in 1837, Horace Mann founded the first state board of education in New York and attempted to make widespread education a necessary condition for responsible citizenship in a democratic society. Although Mann claimed that he did not want to remove all sectarian influences from the schools, he nonetheless conceded that noncontroversial biblical and moral teachings needed to be the basis of education.

While public education sought to be more nonsectarian, most schools nonetheless taught some variety of Protestantism, used the King James Bible in the classroom, and began and ended each day with prayer. Most schools also required a daily profession of faith that acknowledged God as the omnipotent and omnipresent creator who commanded constant obedience and bestowed every blessing. Such a system met with the approval of most Protestant sects, but it was opposed by the growing Catholic community who saw in these practices an entrenchment of Protestant practices and who were unable to engage in similar Catholic practices (for example, crossing themselves, praying to Mary, or conducting Mass). As a result, Catholic churches began to form their own schools. In the interest of fairness, they sought public funding for their ventures as well. Especially after the **Civil War**, the Catholic Church developed a large-scale effort to put its hands in the public purse. While Catholics were unsuccessful in receiving funds for their schools, they did manage to get tax exemptions and funding for their charitable institutions. As Protestant fears over Catholic attempts to procure government backing increased, Congress and state legislatures moved to block the use of public funds by any religious organization. The move in Congress was instigated by **James G. Blaine**, Republican House leader, who proposed an amendment to the Constitution that would prohibit the use of any public monies by and for any religious organization. Although the House passed the **Blaine Amendment**, it could not muster the necessary votes in the Senate. Nonetheless, the message was clear, and many states began to adopt similar policies.

The Catholic attempt to procure funding for academic endeavors is a classic example of the law of unintended consequences. Instead of developing a more pluralistic funding scheme that supported both the traditional, Protestant-based public education and the Catholic schools, the result was to gradually remove traces of overt Protestantism from the public classroom. In its place, at least temporarily, the states began to substitute a more overt **civil religion** (including use, for example, of the **Pledge of Allegiance**). These reforms were enacted with little resistance from religious groups. Although the early part of the twentieth century saw little controversy over education, the post-**World War I** period saw an explosion of controversy over the religion clauses. This explosion was due in part to the extension of the religion clauses to the states—a move established in ***Cantwell v. State of Connecticut*** (1940)—and Catholic integration into the mainstream of American life. This mix led to the first serious challenge to public funding for private education. Although Catholics had been largely unsuccessful in procuring funding, they had scored marginal victories, particularly in the area of school transportation. The states that had agreed to provide public transportation for parochial schools, such as New York, did so on the premise that these schools provided a useful public service and should enjoy some public benefits. The New York statute provided that the state would bear the transportation costs of the parochial student if the school was remote or such transportation would be in the student's best interest. Generally, these subsidies assumed the form of compensation to the parents.

New Jersey had such a reimbursement system. In November 1946, the Supreme Court heard oral arguments in the case of ***Everson v. Board of Education of the Township of Ewing***, where a taxpayer was granted standing by the Court to sue on the belief that the statute violated the Establishment Clause of the First Amendment by providing public financing in support of religion. The Court concluded that the First Amendment constructed a high and unbreachable wall between church and state, but nonetheless upheld the busing program, a result which, Justice Jackson averred, reminded him of Byron's Julia, who "whispering I will ne'er consent,—consented." The Court allowed the law to stand because it aided the parents and the children and not the institution itself. The dissent argued that it was the character of the school and not the needs of the children that provided the basis for reimbursement. The statute thus constituted, the dissent continued, government aid to a religious institution.

Subsequent decisions involving schools have run into similar contradictions. ***Zorach v. Clauson*** (1952) upheld a released-time, religious instruction program that took place off campus, while in ***McCollum v. Board of Education*** (1948), the Court struck down an identical provision that took place on campus. In ***Tilton v. Richardson*** (1971), the Court upheld a program that funded academic buildings on sectarian campuses, while in ***Lemon v. Kurtzman*** (1971), it struck down a statute that gave direct aid to parochial schools. Most famously, while upholding a tuition tax credit program in ***Mueller v. Allen*** (1983), the Court overturned remedial learning programs taught by public school teachers at parochial schools in ***Aguilar v. Felton*** (1985)—a result that Justice Sandra Day O'Connor labeled "tragic" and that led her to declare the Court's Establishment Test "untenable." *Aguilar* was finally overturned in ***Agostini et al. v. Felton et al.*** (1997).

While the use of public funds in private religious schools has been one side of the controversy, the other side has been the use of religion in public school classrooms. On this issue, the Court has been more consistent. The first important review of religious practices in public schools occurred in ***Engel v. Vitale*** (1962), where the Court ruled that a 22-word nondenominational prayer written for students in the public schools violated the Establishment Clause of the First Amendment. In ***Abington Township v. Schempp*** (1963), the Court ruled that the reading of the Lord's Prayer and reciting Bible verses in public schools should be prohibited. The clash between religious beliefs and scientific theories came to a head in ***Epperson v. Arkansas*** (1968), where the Court overturned an Arkansas statute that forbade the teaching of evolutionary theory, and further in ***Edwards v. Aguillard*** (1987), where the Court ruled that a Louisiana statute that mandated the teaching of **creationism** as a balance to **evolution** was unconstitutional. Other Court cases have forbidden the public posting in schools of the Ten Commandments, [***Stone v. Graham*** (1980)]; allowing a moment of silence for meditation or voluntary prayer [***Wallace v. Jaffree***(1985)]; and praying at commencement ceremonies [***Lee v. Weisman*** (1992)].

The main crux of the problem is that what schools often count as valuable may not necessarily reflect the beliefs of the majority of the parents who send their children to the schools. The schools face the impossible conundrum of not appearing hostile to the beliefs of any people while simultaneously not endorsing those beliefs either. Education has been further complicated by emerging technologies that may, for better or worse, become the driving force of education. Proficiency tests, for example, have gone from being a measure of knowledge to being the criterion of knowledge. States are increasingly restructuring curriculum requirements to ensure increased performance on standardized tests. In such an environment, not only will religious subjects have a difficult time surviving, but so also will many secular subjects. The increased use of computers in the classroom and an emphasis on "distance-learning" also threaten to restructure the traditional classroom.

Critics of the development of American education, particularly as it relates to religion, argue not so much for the establishment of any particular religion within the schools, but rather for a more pluralized educational system that does not establish what they see to be the "faith" of **Enlightenment** rationalism. These critics argue that public funding for private schools allows for a more pluralized educational system that would give parents more genuine choices, and that would satisfy a fundamental requirement of fairness, no longer requiring parents who send their children to private schools to pay tuition as well as taxes. Advocates of the current system argue that it satisfies the requirement of government neutrality that the Court had originally set forward as the test of whether a program constituted an establishment of religion. The First Amendment, they argue, disallows the use of any public funds for sectarian purposes, stating that it threatens religious liberty and coerces support for beliefs to which some people might not adhere. Education will almost undoubtedly continue to be the focal point of such debate. (JP) **See also** Constitutional Amendments on Religion (Proposed); Democracy; Democratic Party; Equal Access Act; Republican Party; Roman Catholicism; School Prayer.

BIBLIOGRAPHY

Berns, Walter. *The First Amendment and the Future of American Democracy*. Chicago: Gateway Editions, 1985.

Carter, Stephen. *The Culture of Disbelief: How American Law and Politics Trivialize Religious Devotion*. New York: Basic Books, 1993.

McCarthy, Rockne, et. al. *Disestablishment a Second Time: Genuine Pluralism for America's Schools*. Grand Rapids, MI: Eerdman's Publishing, 1983.

Nelkin, Dorothy. *The Creation Controversy: Science or Scripture in the Schools*. New York: Norton, 1982.

Jonathan Edwards (1703–1758)

A colonial theologian and preacher in Northampton, Massachusetts (1730–1750), Jonathan Edwards (nicknamed the American Augustine) is recognized as one of the greatest American philosophers and theologians. A leading preacher of the **First Great Awakening**, he is most popularly known as the preacher of the "sermon New England would never forget," namely "Sinners in the Hands of an Angry God." Leaving Northampton in 1750, he served in a Native American mission at Stockbridge, where he wrote his most famous treatises—*The Nature of True Virtue, Freedom of the Will,* and *Original Sin*—before becoming president of the College of New Jersey (precursor of Princeton) in 1758.

His great contribution to theology and social thought was developing a theological aesthetic, defining beauty and sensibility partly in terms of consent, and using the Augustinian concept of love to synthesize private religious experience with social concern. This argument is set out primarily in his series of sermons entitled *Charity and Its Fruits*, preached during 1738 to his congregation, and his two treatises, *The Nature of True Virtue* and *Concerning the End for which God Created the World*. While many modern scholars interpret Edwards's thought as the source of New Englanders' understanding of themselves as a chosen people and thence of the later American self-conception as a "redeemer nation," these conceptions are difficult to sustain fully from his works. Edwards, standing in the Calvinist tradition of the national covenant, understood this conception as being conditional and warned of the danger of losing God's favor. During the **American Revolution**, Edwards's disciples were champions of Revolutionary political ideology. In the twentieth century, his thought influenced the work of the Yale philosopher, John Smith, Princeton ethicist Paul Ramsey, and theologian **H. Richard Niebuhr**, in particular the latter's socio-ethical works, *The Responsible Self* (1963) and *Radical Monotheism and Western Culture* (1960). (ISM) **See also** Calvinism; Civil Religion; Colonial America; Manifest Destiny; Native American Religions; Puritans.

Bibliography

Edwards, Jonathan. "Ethical Writings." In Paul Ramsey, ed. *The Works of Jonathan Edwards*, Vol. 8. New Haven: Yale University Press, 1989.

Fiering, Norman. *Edwards' Moral Thought and Its British Context*. Chapel Hill: University of North Carolina Press, 1981.

McDermott, Gerald. *One Holy and Happy Society: The Public Theology of Jonathan Edwards*. University Park: The Pennsylvania State University Press, 1992.

Edwards v. Aguillard (1987)

In *Edwards v. Aguillard*, 482 U.S. 578 (1987), the Supreme Court ruled that "balanced treatment" laws mandating the teaching of scientific **creationism** along with **evolution** in the public schools were unconstitutional. Scientific creationism seeks to present empirical evidence for the recent, sudden creation of the universe and all that it contains from nothing (creation *ex nihilo*), and to show the insufficiency of mutation and natural selection as an explanation for the development of the various species of life from a single organism. In March 1981, Governor Frank White of Arkansas signed legislation requiring equal time for scientific creationism and evolution in the state's public schools. Over 20 other states soon adopted similar legislation. While the Arkansas statute was overturned in 1982 by a U.S. District Court, the Supreme Court took up the same issue in 1987 in *Edwards v. Aguillard*, overturning a similar "equal time" law in Louisiana. Justice **William Brennan**, writing for the 7-2 majority, argued that by mandating the teaching of scientific creationism, the law served a religious rather than a secular purpose, thus failing the first prong of the ***Lemon* Test** used to adjudicate **Establishment Clause** cases. Brennan added that the court was not forbidding state legislatures from requiring that "scientific critiques of prevailing scientific theories be taught." Indeed, the presentations of scientific alternatives "might be validly done with the clear secular intent of enhancing the effectiveness of science instruction." (ARB) **See also** Education; First Amendment.

Bibliography

Miller, Robert T. and Ronald B. Flowers. *Toward Benevolent Neutrality: Church, State, and the Supreme Court*. vol. 1. 5th ed., Waco, TX: Markham Press Fund of Baylor University Press, 1996.

Eighteenth Amendment

Drawing on the same reforming impulse as the movement to end **slavery**, the drive to prohibit the sale of liquor achieved its first statewide success in Maine in 1846. In the early years of the twentieth century, organizations such as the **Anti-Saloon League** and the **Women's Christian Temperance Union (WCTU)** pushed for national legislation prohibiting the sale of liquor. The result was the Eighteenth Amendment to the Constitution, passed by Congress in 1917, winning approval in state legislatures in a little over a year, and taking effect in January 1920.

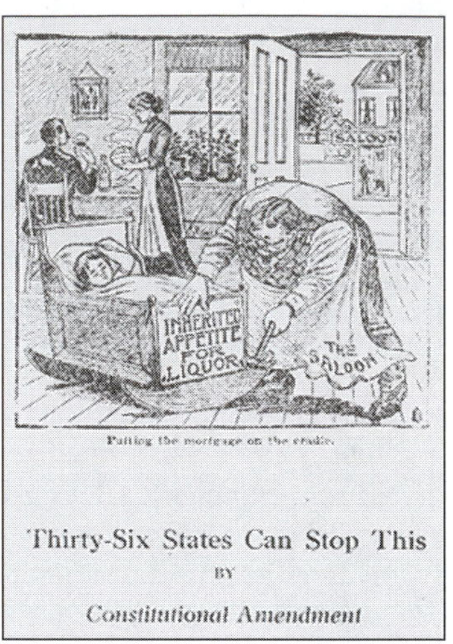

With much support from religious groups and organizations, the Eighteenth Amendment prohibiting the sale and manufacture of alcohol was ratified in 1919. National Archives.

Among Protestants, both conservatives and liberals supported the amendment. Among the non-churchgoers in big cities and Catholics, support was less common. The amendment was not as radical as some have portrayed it. At the time it took effect, some two-thirds of the population lived under some form of local or state prohibition. The problem was that the other one-third lived in areas that had long resisted prohibition, and those areas created enormous enforcement problems. The Eighteenth Amendment was repealed in 1933 with the passage of the Twenty-First Amendment. National prohibition had proven to be a failure. (MWP) **See also** Conservatism; Liberalism; Roman Catholicism; Temperance and Prohibition.

Bibliography

Lee, Henry Walsh. *How Dry We Were*. Englewood Cliffs, NJ: Prentice-Hall, 1963.

Merz, Charles. *The Dry Decade*. Garden City, NY: Doubleday, 1931.

Dwight D. Eisenhower (1890–1969)

Dwight D. Eisenhower was the 34th president of the United States. Born in Denison, Texas, he grew up in Abilene, Kansas, entered West Point in 1911, and, upon graduation, was commissioned a 2nd lieutenant in the United States Army. As a child, he grew up in a deeply religious family of Evangelical Protestants and daily read the Bible. In 1932, he was assigned to the staff of General Douglas MacArthur. During **World War II**, Eisenhower commanded three major Allied invasions, including the assault on Normandy. During the war, Eisenhower regularly attended services. In large part, his understanding of religious pluralism was shaped by the nondenominational army chaplains whom he knew throughout his adult life in the military.

After the war, Eisenhower became the president of Columbia University. In 1952, he defeated Senator Robert Taft for the Republican presidential nomination. He selected **Richard Nixon** as his running mate. Eisenhower easily defeated the Democratic nominee, Adlai Stevenson, garnering 55 percent of the vote. The new president immediately exhibited his deep commitment to **civil religion** and public piety. He began his inauguration with a prayer, a practice that has been followed ever since. Eisenhower was also responsible for adding the phrase "Under God" to the **Pledge of Allegiance**.

President Eisenhower, the first Republican elected since the Depression, did not dismantle the **New Deal** social welfare programs. He carried out his campaign promise to bring an end to the Korean War. Eisenhower suffered a heart attack in 1956, but he was easily re-elected in 1956, defeating Adlai Stevenson with 57 percent of the popular vote and 437 electoral college votes. To handle the growing connection with religious leaders and activities, Eisenhower created an office to coordinate religious affairs. During his second term, efforts to reduce tensions with the Soviet Union were disrupted when the Soviet Union shot down a U.S. U-2 spy plane over its territory. After completing his second term, Eisenhower retired to his home in Gettysburg, Pennsylvania. Eisenhower once stated that "America makes no sense without a deeply held faith in God," and his contemporaries recognized him as the high point of civil religion. (WB) **See also** Chaplaincy; Democratic Party; Evangelicals; Republican Party.

Republican President Dwight D. Eisenhower maintained extensive ties with religious leaders and promoted religion wherever possible. Library of Congress.

Bibliography

Ambrose, Stephen E. *Eisenhower: Soldier and President*. New York: Simon and Schuster, 1990.

Election Sermons

Beginning in the 1630s in **Massachusetts Bay**, a member of the clergy was asked to deliver a sermon to the governor and the legislature after the election of officials. The election sermon subsequently became an annual event that persisted for more than 250 years in Massachusetts and more than 150 years in Connecticut. The practice took root in the late 1700s in Vermont and New Hampshire as well. Election sermons were political in the broadest sense of the term: They solemnized the election results and reinforced republicanism with the sanctions of religion. Typical themes covered in election sermons included the nature of civil and religious liberty, the reasons for **democracy**, the necessity of self-government, and the certainty of God's judgment on societal sins. Usually published, copies were made available to elected officials and to clergymen from the officials' home districts. During the **American Revolution**, clergy used election sermons to fan the flames of the Patriot cause. For example, Massachusetts minister Gad Hitchock declared in his election sermon of 1774 that government "is from the people, who have not only a right, but are bound in duty to lodge it in such hands as they judge best qualified to answer its intention; so when it is misapplied to other purposes they have the same original right to transfer it to others."(JGW) **See also** Civil Religion; Puritans.

Bibliography

Sandoz, Ellis, ed. *Political Sermons of the American Founding Era, 1730-1805*. Indianapolis: LibertyPress, 1991.

Stout, Harry. *The New England Soul*. New York: Oxford University Press, 1986.

Thornton, John Wingate, ed. *The Pulpit of the American Revolution: Political Sermons of the Period of 1776*. New York: Da Capo Press, 1970.

Ezra Stiles Ely (1786–1861)

Ezra Stiles Ely was an influential Philadelphia clergyman. He served as moderator of the Presbyterian General Assembly in the United States, wrote several popular theological treatises, and edited a weekly religious journal. Concerned about the increasing "political atheism" in public life and the declining influence of religious traditionalists, Ely preached a Fourth of July sermon entitled "The Duty of Christian Freeman to Elect Christian Rulers" (1827)." In the sermon, he proposed "a new sort of union," which he called "a Christian party in politics." Ely called for an electoral alliance composed of "three or four of the most numerous denominations of Christians in the United States," including Presbyterians, **Baptists**, Methodists, and Congregationalists. His was to be a party without strict political or sectarian definition and without membership rolls or subscriptions. Rather, he envisioned a loose coalition of Christian political activists united to elect like-minded candidates for public office and to give political voice to Christian values in public life. He believed that if Christian citizens would unite on election day and demonstrate their conscience at the polls, they could dominate every public election. The "Christian Party" was denounced by liberal religionists and freethinkers. They described it as an undemocratic expression of religious intolerance and bigotry that threatened the civil and religious liberties of those who did not share Ely's objectives. (DLD) **See also** Atheism; Congregationalism; Democracy; Freethought; Methodism; Presbyterian Church.

Bibliography

Blau, Joseph L. "The Christian Party in Politics." *Review in Religion* 11 (1946–1947): 18–35.

_______. "The Rev. Dr. Ezra Stiles Ely." *Journal of the Presbyterian Historical Society* 2 (1904): 321–24.

Richard Theodore Ely (1854–1943)

As a social economist and a professor at the University of Wisconsin, Richard Ely influenced the **Social Gospel** movement through such books as his *Social Aspects of Christianity* (1886). He was also influential in producing in his words the economic theory behind many ideas of the progressive movement, including *Monopolies and Trusts* (1900), *Studies in the Evolution of Industrial Society* (1903), and *Foundations of National Prosperity* (1917). Founder of the American Economic Association in 1885, Ely worked to replace the dominant laissez-faire economic mindset with one that focused more on the Christian duty people had for each other. His writings were especially influential with Methodists. (MWP) **See also** Capitalism; Methodism.

BIBLIOGRAPHY

Radar, Benjamin. *The Academic Mind and Reform*. Lexington: University of Kentucky Press, 1966.

Ralph Waldo Emerson (1803–1882)

Essayist, poet, preacher, and philosopher, Ralph Waldo Emerson founded the distinctly American school of thought known as **Transcendentalism**, whose members believed that the soul of each individual should be the final judge in spiritual and ethical matters. Born in Boston of a long line of ministers, he gave his first sermon in 1826, but resigned his ministry in 1832 over disagreements about the Lord's Supper. He then traveled in Europe, meeting the poets William Wordsworth and Samuel Taylor Coleridge, who shared his Romantic-inspired fascination with nature, and Thomas Carlyle, who admired German Idealistic philosophy for its stress on the dignity of the human soul. Soon after returning to the United States, he published his first essay, *Nature* (1936), and delivered two speeches at Harvard University that shocked the more pious members of his audiences: his commencement address, *The American Scholar* (1837), and his *Divinity School Address* (1838), in which he told the young ministers that modern Christianity was a hindrance to their true religious sentiments. Known as "the sage of Concord," Emerson lectured to audiences around the country for the rest of his life. Emerson used his influence to speak out on political issues, including denouncing the removal of the Cherokees from Georgia and opposing **slavery**. A vocal supporter of **Abraham Lincoln**, he also championed early environmental protection. (BDG) See also Cherokee Removal; Freethought.

BIBLIOGRAPHY

Rohler, Lloyd. *Ralph Waldo Emerson: Preacher and Lecturer*. Westport, CT: Greenwood Press, 1995.

Rusk, Ralph. *The Life of Ralph Waldo Emerson*. New York: Charles Scribner's Sons, 1949.

Employment Division of Oregon v. Smith (1990)

Employment Division of Oregon v. Smith, 494 U.S. 872 (1990), involved two Native Americans, Alfred Smith and Galen Black, who were fired from their jobs with a private rehabilitation clinic because they took peyote (a mildly intoxicating drug), which both had ingested for sacramental purposes during religious ceremonies. Peyote, however, had been declared illegal under Oregon's Banned Substance Act. When Smith and Black later applied for unemployment benefits, they were denied by Oregon's Employment Division. The Oregon court, however, ruled in favor of Smith, arguing that the state's interest in the compensation fund did not outweigh the burden imposed on Smith's religious beliefs and practices. In a 6-3 decision, the Supreme Court overturned the ruling of the Oregon court.

In his decision, Justice **Antoin Scalia** argued that the Oregon statute was not specifically targeted toward religious practices and that the restriction of Native American practice was "an incidental effect of a generally applicable and otherwise valid provision." The government, he argued, had a compelling interest in maintaining public order through the restriction of drug use, and such an interest, he continued, would have the "unavoidable consequence" of placing at a "relative disadvantage those religious practices that are not widely engaged in."

Concurring and dissenting opinions averred that the decision was a break with precedent, most notably the Court's earlier decision in ***Sherbert v. Verner*** (1963), where the Court had overturned the denial of unemployment benefits to a **Seventh-Day Adventist** who was fired for refusing to work on the Sabbath. In her concurrence, Justice Sandra Day O'Connor declared the decision hostile to religious liberty by prohibiting religiously motivated conduct. Justice **Harry Blackmun** went even further in his dissent, noting that this case was not an irresponsible use of drugs, and proclaimed the majority decision to be an overreaction to societal drug problems and one that did not protect fundamental religious rights. (JP) **See also** First Amendment; Free Exercise Clause; Native American Religions.

BIBLIOGRAPHY

Eastland, Terry. *Religious Liberty in the Supreme Court*. Washington, DC: Ethics and Public Policy Center, 1993.

Endorsement Test

The portion of the **First Amendment** known as the **Establishment Clause** reads, "Congress shall make no law respecting an establishment of religion." The U.S. Supreme Court has been called on in numerous situations to interpret whether government action constitutes an establishment of religion. To clarify the determination in specific instances, the Court developed a three-prong test known as the ***Lemon* Test**, after the case, ***Lemon v. Kurtzman*** (1971), in which it was first announced. The decision in that case stated, "In the absence of precisely stated constitutional prohibitions, we must draw lines with reference to the three main evils against which the Establishment Clause was intended to afford protection: 'sponsorship, financial support, and active involvement of the sovereign in religious activity.'"

The second prong of the test, which came to be known as the Endorsement Test, stated that to comply with the Establishment Clause, a statute's "principal or primary effect must be one that neither advances nor inhibits religion." This test has been subject to as much difficulty of interpretation as the Establishment Clause itself, and the Court has occasionally abandoned its use in favor of other formulations. (JM)

BIBLIOGRAPHY

Eastland, Terry. *Religious Liberty in the Supreme Court*. Washington, DC: Ethics and Public Policy Center, 1993.

Stone, Geoffrey R. et al. *Constitutional Law*. Boston: Little, Brown and Company, 1991.

Engel v. Vitale (1962)

In *Engel v. Vitale*, 370 U.S. 421 (1962), the Supreme Court ruled 6-1 that it was a violation of the **First Amendment**'s **Establishment Clause** for New York school authorities to compose the following prayer for public school children to recite at the beginning of the school day: "Almighty God, we acknowledge our dependence upon Thee, and we beg Thy blessings upon us, our parents, our teachers and our Country." To this day, it remains one of the most controversial decisions ever rendered by the Court.

Justice **Hugo Black** wrote the opinion for the Court and argued that the Establishment Clause forbids prayers "composed by government officials as a part of a governmental program to further religious beliefs." His opinion included an eloquent defense of religious freedom and a condemnation of past religious persecution, but it is weaker when it seeks to apply the principles garnered from that history to the inclusive—some would say innocuous—prayer at issue in this case, a prayer that the New York authorities sought to make voluntary by allowing children not to participate. Justice **Potter Stewart** dissented, arguing that no official religion is established by "letting those who want to say a prayer say it."

This case gained in significance the following year when its basic reasoning was used to hold that reciting the Lord's Prayer and reading from the Bible without comment were also unconstitutional (***Abington Township v. Schempp***).

Public opinion polls show that clear majorities of the public favor some form of prayer in the public schools; presidential candidates regularly are forced to take stands on the issue, and each session of Congress struggles over proposed amendments to the Constitution designed to allow **school prayer**. To date, proposed amendments have failed to gain the required two-thirds majority in both houses. (SM)

BIBLIOGRAPHY

Pfeffer, Leo. "The New York Regents' Prayer Case (*Engel vs. Vitale*): Its Background, Meaning and Implications." *CLSA Reports*. New York: Commission on Law and Social Action of the American Jewish Congress, 1962.

_______. *Prayer in Public Schools and the Constitution, 1961–1992. Controversies in Constitutional Law*. New York: Garland Publishing, 1993.

Enlightenment

The Enlightenment was an eighteenth-century movement that sought to redefine thinking about politics and religion. One way to grasp the meaning and purpose of the Enlightenment is to contrast it with its opposite, what the English philosopher Thomas Hobbes termed, the "Kingdom of Darkness." By this term, Hobbes meant the medieval and early modern Catholic Church, at whose doorstep he placed the blame for the religious wars that had plagued Europe. Generally speaking, he and his fellow Enlightenment thinkers tried to moderate the political excesses to which an overzealous Christianity had given rise in their view.

Speaking of the Enlightenment as if it were one movement is somewhat problematic. The "Enlightenment" came in various guises: French, Scottish, English, and American. Although all these movements shared the above-named characteristics, they did so to different extents. In its most radical forms, the Enlightenment gave rise to excesses that rivaled those it sought to oppose. In the **French Revolution**, to give only the most prominent example, extreme acts of persecution were committed in the name of the Enlightenment concept of the "Rights of Man."

In America, the Enlightenment came in a much more moderate and politically healthy form. **John Locke**, the English political philosopher upon whose ideas many ideals of the American Enlightenment were based, was a man renowned for his sobriety in both speech and deed. Locke's influence appears in the **Declaration of Independence** as well as in most famous American articulations of the case for religious liberty, namely, **James Madison**'s "Memorial and Remonstrance" and **Thomas Jefferson**'s "Bill for Establishing Religious Freedom." Primary to these last two documents is a commitment to religious toleration and freedom from state dictates.

The Enlightenment is, in all its guises, a modern doctrine that gave rise to modern notions of progress and science. The United States has been able to avoid the Enlightenment's most radical excesses because the Founding Fathers had the good sense to adopt the thought of the most prudent Enlightenment thinkers, not only Locke but David Hume, Montesquieu, and William Blackstone. Perhaps the Founding Father most influenced by Enlightenment thought was Thomas Jefferson, the author of the Declaration. Jefferson said that the Declaration was meant to set forth the shared principles of "the elementary books of public right, as Aristotle, Cicero, Locke, Sydney, etc." Thus, the American heritage is both modern and classical. (SJL) **See also** American Revolution; Deism; Freethought; Roman Catholicism.

BIBLIOGRAPHY

Jefferson, Thomas. *Selected Writings*. Harvey C. Mansfield, Jr., ed. Wheeling, IL: Harlan Davidson, 1979.

Madison, James. *The Mind of the Founder*. Marvin Meyers, ed. Hanover, NH: Brandeis University Press, 1981.

Strauss, Leo. *Natural Right and History*. Chicago: University of Chicago Press, 1953.

Entanglement Test

The Entanglement Test has evolved as one of the standards by which the Supreme Court decides **Establishment Clause** cases. Early articulation of the Entanglement Test occurred in ***Everson v. Board of Education of the Township of Ewing*** (1947), where Justice **Hugo Black** argued that **disestablishment** of religion meant, among other things, that government could not openly or secretly participate in the affairs of religious organizations and groups, and vice versa. The strongest definition of entanglement came in ***Walz v. Tax Commission of the City of New York*** (1970), which rejected a challenge to the tax-exempt status of religious organizations, where Justice **Warren Burger** argued that government support of religion was permissible so long as there was no excessive entanglement between government and religion. This clause became the third prong of the famous ***Lemon* Test** (after ***Lemon v. Kurtzman***). Subsequently, however, the test began to produce anomalous results, and the Court has come to question the usefulness of the Entanglement Test. Justice Sandra Day O'Connor has stated that confusions in Establishment Clause rulings are attributable to the entanglement prong, and that it was ineffectual as a standard if the Court was constantly redefining what was excessive. (JP) **See also** First Amendment.

BIBLIOGRAPHY

Kauper, Paul. *Religion and the Constitution.* Baton Rouge: Louisiana State University Press, 1964.

Levy, Leonard. *The Establishment Clause: Religion and the First Amendment.* New York: Macmillan, 1986.

Episcopal Church

The Episcopal Church in the United States is part of the worldwide Anglican Communion, which originated with the Church of England. In the 1500s, the Church of England, part of the Protestant **Reformation**, separated from the Roman Catholic Church (although the Church of England retained more of the ancient Catholic tradition than most of the Reformation churches).

The Anglican Church was brought to the United States by a colonial minister who arrived in Jamestown in 1607. During the colonial period, the Anglican Church was the established church in some colonies, but a dissenting church in others. The spiritual and organizational health of the Church suffered for various reasons, in part because there were no resident bishops in the colonies. During the **American Revolution**, members of the Anglican Church were often accused of being loyalists. Naturally, the success of the Revolution caused a crisis for the Church. No longer the Church of England in America, it had to reconstitute itself as an indigenous church. Amidst struggles to obtain its own bishops and other issues, it reorganized in 1789 as the Protestant Episcopal Church in the United States—"Protestant" to distinguish it from the Catholic Church, and "Episcopal" (meaning "bishop") to mark its form of church government.

In the 1800s, the Episcopal Church lagged behind the more flexible and revivalistic denominations, particularly **Baptists** and Methodists, in the westward expansion. Also in the 1800s, the Church experienced evangelical and Catholic movements. Each of these invigorated elements of the Church but caused internal controversy. Since the late 1800s, the Episcopal Church has been at the forefront of the **ecumenical movement**. Renewal groups, such as the **charismatic movement**, have been active since the 1960s.

In recent years, the Church has been wracked by controversies over prayer book revision, ordination of women (which it permits), and its stance on homosexuality. Sociologically, it has tended to be associated with the educated, wealthy, and powerful strata of society. While a large number of social and political leaders in American history have been Episcopalians, in recent decades the Church has declined in absolute numbers, and declined considerably as a percentage of the population.

The Episcopal Church shares broad characteristics of the Anglican tradition. Worship is conducted according to a *Book of Common Prayer* (American version). In the Anglican mold, it perceives itself as a via media (middle way) between the more Protestant churches of the Reformation and the Catholic Church. Its theological sources are in Scripture, coupled with reason and tradition. Its theological definition is expressed more in its Articles of Religion and *Book of Common Prayer* than in a detailed confession of faith or corpus of writings by a founding theologian. While expressing commitment to theological essentials, the Episcopal Church aims to be charitably comprehensive and open in membership and outside relations. (GSS) **See also** Colonial America; Evangelicals; Homosexual Rights; Methodism; Roman Catholicism.

BIBLIOGRAPHY

Addison, James Thayer. *The Episcopal Church in the United States, 1789–1931.* New York: Charles Scribner's Sons, 1951.

Holmes, David L. *A Brief History of the Episcopal Church.* Valley Forge, PA: Trinity Press International, 1993.

Epperson v. Arkansas (1968)

In *Epperson v. Arkansas*, 393 U.S. 97 (1968), the Supreme Court ruled on the debate between **creationism** and **evolution** in the public schools. In 1928, Arkansas passed legislation prohibiting public school teachers from teaching "the theory or doctrine that mankind ascended or descended from a lower order of animals," and prohibited the use of any textbooks advocating the same. For the first time in 1965, Little Rock schools adopted a textbook discussing evolution. Susan Epperson, a 10th grade biology teacher, asked the state court to declare the old law void. When the Arkansas Supreme Court failed to do so, the case was appealed to the U.S. Supreme Court in 1968. In the majority decision written by Justice **Abe Fortas**, the Court ruled that law invalid because it did not pass the "Secular Purpose" test used in **Establishment Clause** cases. Furthermore, the law violated the Establishment Clause, because it was based on a particular religious interpretation of the Genesis account of creation. In *Epperson*, the Court reaffirmed its decision that the Establishment Clause clearly forbids public schools from advocating or instructing students in religious dogma or practice. For many conservative Protestants, the ruling was seen as an expression of hostility towards a biblical worldview and contributed to the rise of Fundamentalism as a potent political force in the 1970s. (ARB) **See also** Education; First Amendment; Fundamentalists; *Lemon* Test.

BIBLIOGRAPHY

Miller, Robert T. and Ronald B. Flowers. *Toward Benevolent Neutrality: Church, State, and the Supreme Court*. vol. 1. 5th ed., Waco, TX: Markham Press Fund of Baylor University Press, 1996.

Provenzo, Eugene F. Jr. *Religious Fundamentalism and American Education: The Battle for the Public Schools*. Albany: State University of New York Press, 1990.

Equal Access Act

Generally speaking, the principle of equal access requires that any otherwise available public benefit should not be denied on the basis of a citizen's religious views. The application of this principle in U.S. statutory and constitutional law has been narrowly focused on particular benefits available to students at state-sponsored educational institutions, although it has broader implications for public funding of religious charitable organizations, among other things.

The Supreme Court, in ***Widmar v. Vincent*** (1981), required state-supported universities to allow religious groups to use their facilities on the same basis as non-religious groups. The court said that such equal treatment was mandated by the Constitution's free speech clause. Congress made the logic of *Widmar* applicable to high schools through the Equal Access Act of 1984, an initiative celebrated by those demanding wider latitude for religious expression, especially supporters of **school prayer**. The act required high schools benefiting from federal funds (which includes virtually all public schools) to allow student religious groups to hold meetings on school grounds if other extracurricular groups had the same opportunity. The act is applicable only to high schools, not elementary schools, and in an apparent accommodation to Supreme Court jurisprudence, it only allows student-initiated, voluntary, and nonschool-sponsored meetings. The Supreme Court found the Equal Access Act constitutional in ***Board of Education of the Westside Community Schools v. Mergens*** (1990).

The Equal Access Act applied only to student organizations, but in ***Lamb's Chapel v. Center Moriches Union Free School District*** (1993) the Supreme Court extended its underlying principle to religious groups not associated with a school that seek the same access to facilities as nonreligious groups. Furthermore, the Equal Access principle has been applied beyond simply the use of school facilities; as recently as its ruling in ***Rosenberger v. Rector and Vistors of University of Virginia*** (1995), the Court has held that universities must treat religious and nonreligious activities equally when making certain funding decisions for student groups. (KRD) **See also** Education; Establishment Clause; Free Speech Approach to Religious Liberty.

BIBLIOGRAPHY

Laycock, Douglas. "Equal Access and Moments of Silence: The Equal Status of Religious Speech by Private Speakers." *Northwestern University Law Review* 81, no. 1 (Fall 1986): 1–67.

Monsma, Stephen. *When Sacred and Secular Mix*. Lanham, MD: Rowman and Littlefield, 1996.

West, John G., Jr. "The Changing Battle over Religion in the Public Schools." *Wake Forest Law Review* 26, no. 2 (1991): 361-401.

Equal Rights Amendment

First proposed in 1921, the Equal Rights Amendment sought to ensure that "equality of rights under the law shall not be denied. . . on account of sex." Congress sent the amendment to the states for ratification in 1972, but it failed to gain sufficient support to be enacted despite a three-year extension of the ratification deadline. The amendment was finally declared dead in 1982.

The amendment's strongest supporters were politically liberal groups such as the National Organization for Women (NOW). Its failure was due in large part to Christian conservatives led by Phyllis Schlafly and her National Committee to Stop ERA. Schlafly and her supporters argued that the amendment would actually strip women of their rights by allowing them to be conscripted into battle and by nullifying laws that required husbands to support their wives and children. They further maintained that the amendment attacked inherent gender differences more than gender-based discrimination. (MR) **See also** Constitutional Amendments on Religion (Proposed); Feminism.

BIBLIOGRAPHY

Boles, Janet. *The Politics of the Equal Rights Amendment: Conflict and the Decision Process*. New York, Longmans, 1979.

Felsenthal, Carol. *Phyllis Schlafly: The Sweetheart of the Silent Majority*. Chicago: Regnery Gateway, 1982.

Establishment Clause

After ratification of the Constitution, much debate in Congress centered around a proposed "Bill of Rights" which was widely regarded as an appendage necessary to ensure ratification. On June 8, 1789, **James Madison** proposed for House approval a bill of rights. Among the rights proposed was one that insisted that "the civil rights of none shall be abridged on account of religious belief or worship, nor shall any national religion be established, nor shall the full and equal rights of conscience be in any manner, or under any pretext, abridged." After a series of arguments and changes, the House sent to the Senate an amendment which read: "Congress shall make no law establishing religion, or prohibiting the free exercise thereof, nor shall the rights of conscience be infringed." In the Senate, a number of motions were made to change further the wording of the amendment, including unsuccessful motions that would have narrowed the amendment to prevent the preference of one religion over others. The Senate sent a version back to the House that stated that "Congress shall make no law establishing articles of faith, or a mode of worship, or prohibiting the free exercise of religion." The House refused this version and insisted on a conference that produced the amendment in its final form, which states that "Congress shall make no law respecting an establishment of religion. . . ." The earlier versions do tell us some things, however, about what the amendment intended to accomplish and what it did not.

Leonard Levy has argued that the main purpose of the Establishment Clause was to depoliticize religion and preclude even non-preferential government aid to religion. It was generally felt, he argues, that any kind of intrusion of religion into government would necessarily be dangerous to both religion and the political realm. As a result, the Establishment Clause, particularly in its employment of the word "respecting" (which Levy believes means "not even touching upon"), necessitates a strict separation between church and state. Walter Berns, on the other hand, has argued that most of the framers of the Constitution realized that religion would have to play a role in the formation of the new republic (see, for example, the **Northwest Ordinance** of 1787, already passed by Congress) and therefore could not have meant a strict separation between church and state. In Berns' reading of the Clause, the article "an" receives special attention. Many other authors have argued that the Establishment Clause is subordinate to the **Free Exercise Clause** and its main purpose was to protect people against religious persecution. The struggle for constitutional protection against religious persecution was led by evangelical Protestants. Michael McConnell has written that the purpose and meaning of the Religion Clauses "were not intended as an instrument of secularization, or as a weapon the non-religious and anti-religious could use to suppress the effusions of the religious. The Religion Clauses were intended to guarantee the rights of those whose religious practices seemed to the majority a little odd."

In general, then, reflection on the Establishment Clause has divided into roughly three camps: strict separation, neutrality, or accommodation. There are, of course, varying degrees within each approach (between, for example, strict neutrality and benign neutrality). The U.S. Supreme Court in its jurisprudence has long had a history of strict separation. Its landmark decision in ***Everson v. Board of Education of the Township of Ewing*** insisted on a "high wall of separation" between church and state. The separationists have always had a strong voice on the bench, though there have been periods when neutrality has been ascendant. Recently, accommodationists have made some inroads, especially in the person of Chief Justice **William Rehnquist**. In large part, the Court's difficulty has stemmed from its unwillingness to locate religion within the context of civil society as a whole, or to recognize that its sectarian character can be incidental to its secular effect. (JP) **See also** Civil Religion; Evangelicals; First Amendment.

Bibliography

Berns, Walter. *The First Amendment and the Future of American Democracy.* Chicago: Gateway Editions, 1985.

Curry, Thomas. *The First Freedoms: Church and State in America to the Passage of the First Amendment.* New York: Oxford University Press, 1986.

Levy, Leonard. *The Establishment Clause: Religion and the First Amendment.* New York: Macmillan, 1986.

Madison, James. *The Records of the Federal Convention of 1787.* Max Farrand, ed. 3 vols. New Haven, CT: Yale University Press, 1966.

McConnell, Michael. "Taking Religious Freedom Seriously." *First Things* (May) 1990: 3.

Eugenics

In England, Francis Galton, inspired by Charles Darwin's theory of **evolution** by natural selection, proposed in the 1860s that humans should take control of their own heredity to improve the species. He hoped his drive to promote artificial selection among humans, which he called eugenics, would become a secular religion and supplant Christianity. By the early twentieth century, eugenics had become a prominent movement, advocating legislation to curb reproduction of the mentally ill, criminals, and others deemed "defective." Sterilization legislation became especially popular after Indiana passed the first compulsory sterilization statute in 1907.

Unlike Galton, most American eugenicists, even those who were agnostics or atheists, emphasized the compatibility of eugenics and Christianity, sometimes even claiming religious sanction for eugenics. Eugenics, according to its proponents, placed the common good above individual self-interest and attempted to alleviate suffering, and so embodied Christian virtues.

The religious groups most supportive of eugenics were modernist Protestants, who were impressed by its scientific credentials and progressive tendencies. The prominent Protestant pastor **Harry Emerson Fosdick** and Federal Council of Churches President F. J. McConnell were strong eugenics proponents. When the American Eugenics Society offered cash prizes in 1926 for the best sermons preached on eugenics, they inspired about 300 sermons, most by liberal Protestants.

Catholics were the most effective opponents of eugenics, especially sterilization legislation and immigration restrictions. Even before Pope Pius XI articulated the Catholic Church's opposition to eugenics in his 1930 encyclical, *Casti Connubii*, many American Catholics rallied to oppose eugenics legislation. They were horrified by eugenicists' pronouncements that some human life is valuable, and some is not. Catholic clergy and organizations helped defeat sterilization bills in Pennsylvania, New York, New Jersey, Louisiana, and Colorado. When the Supreme Court ruled in *Buck v. Bell* (1927) that sterilization laws were valid, the only dissenting justice on the Court was Pierce Butler, a Roman Catholic. Catholics also opposed immigration restrictions, which were advocated by many eugenics proponents to keep the white Anglo-Saxon Protestant "Old Stock" from being swamped by the newer immigration, which was largely Catholic. Although not as organized as the Catholics in their efforts, conservative Protestants were often opponents of eugenics, too. Their opposition helped delay the spread of eugenics and concomitant legislation in the southern states.

Religious opposition to eugenics probably played only a minor role in the decline of eugenics after the 1930s. More important in the decline was the replacement of biological determinism by cultural determination (that human nature is defined by environment) in the social sciences and psychology, along with a backlash against the Nazi atrocities perpetrated in the name of eugenics. (RW) **See also** Atheism; Roman Catholicism.

Bibliography

Hasian, Morouf Arif, Jr. *The Rhetoric of Eugenics in Anglo-American Thought.* Athens: University of Georgia Press, 1996.

Kevles, Daniel J. *In the Name of Eugenics: Genetics and the Uses of Human Heredity.* Berkeley: University of California Press, 1985.

Larson, Edward J. *Sex, Race, and Science: Eugenics in the Deep South.* Baltimore: Johns Hopkins University Press, 1995.

Paul, Diane B. *Controlling Human Heredity, 1865 to the Present.* Atlantic Highlands, NJ: Humanities Press, 1995.

Euthanasia

Etymologically, the term "euthanasia" derives, unchanged in form, from the ancient Greek, meaning "good death"–that is, a death without abject suffering. The word has come to mean deliberately killing, or assisting a suicide, for a purported humane purpose or larger social good. In its conservative sense, euthanasia refers to medical intervention that eases or hastens a protracted death agony. In its radical usage, the term is used to describe the killing of abnormal babies, mentally ill, physically handicapped, or those otherwise held to be socially undesirable or unfit.

The opinion that some forms of euthanasia are morally permissible may be traced to Socrates, Plato, and the Stoics, but the practice is strongly condemned in traditional Judeo-Christian belief, chiefly because it is thought to fall under the penumbra of the prohibition of murder in the Ten Commandments. Those opposed to euthanasia on religious grounds have argued that death is inherently and intrinsically a wrong rather than a right, and that pain control is the key to easing suffering at the end of life. Opponents warn as well that legalized assisted suicide may be exploited by avaricious relatives or by state officials eager to rid themselves of patients whose care has become costly or otherwise burdensome. Proponents of assisted suicide, on the other hand, contend that choosing the time and manner of one's death is an essential aspect of self-determination, and that euthanasia is the only hope for those destined to live in extreme pain or under the influence of narcotics that strip identity and dignity.

Organized political action toward the legalization of euthanasia commenced in England in 1935, with the creation of the Voluntary Euthanasia Legalisation Society. The Euthanasia Society of America was founded in 1938. As modern medicine has become more sophisticated, so have techniques for prolonging life, even under conditions of extreme physical or emotional suffering for the patient, and even when the patients are incapable of making conscious choices about their destinies. The debate over euthanasia in the United States has consequently been brought before the courts in a number of guises. Physicians who have declined to take extraordinary measures to prolong life or who have actively withdrawn life-support measures have faced criminal charges. On the other hand, families of comatose or terminally ill patients have taken legal action against medical authorities to withdraw extraordinary life support.

Most religious bodies do not oppose passive euthanasia, that is, the failure to take extraordinary means to prolong life. However, the Roman Catholic, **Lutheran**, and **Episcopal Churches** have all issued formal statements strongly opposing active euthanasia and physician-assisted suicide, as have virtually all Fundamentalist and Evangelical faith groups in the United States. The Rabbinical Council of America and the Orthodox Union have also made extremely strong statements against the practice. Taking a less confident stand, the Unitarian-Universalist Association, a liberal group, issued a statement in 1988 in support of euthanasia and assisted suicide choice, but only given proper precautions to avoid abuse, and the **United Church of Christ** and the Methodist Church have made similar statements. Other churches remain heavily divided on the issue.

Public controversy over euthanasia in the United States has been sharpened acutely in the past decade by the provocative actions of Michigan physician Jack Kevorkian. In the late 1980s, Kevorkian took part in the first of a series of physician-assisted suicides and has since been accused of helping at least 90 others to die by means of a combination of lethal injection and gas. Kevorkian has appeared in court on homicide charges, with some charges still pending.

In 1996, the United States Supreme Court ruled unanimously that terminally ill people have no constitutional right to physician-assisted suicide. In doing so, the Supreme Court overturned two lower-court rulings. The case of *Washington v. Glucksberg* was brought before the court by three patients in the final ravages of terminal disease, four doctors who treat terminally ill patients, and a nonprofit group that counsels the terminally ill. The group challenged the Washington law under which it is a felony for one person to aid another in a suicide attempt. The United States Court of Appeals for the Ninth Circuit had held that individuals have a privacy interest, protected by the Due Process Clause of the Constitution, in choosing how and when to die, a right conceived as being similar to the Supreme Court's understanding of a woman's interest in choosing whether to have an **abortion**. Less than a month later, the Second Circuit Court, across the country in New York, decided a similar case, setting the stage for *Vacco v. Quill*. The New York court reached a similar conclusion, namely, that doctors may prescribe drugs to be self-administered by mentally competent patients who seek to end their lives during the final stages of a terminal illness. The court noted that New York law permitted terminally ill patients on life support to direct that the systems be removed, and argued that by denying terminally ill patients who were not connected to life support the option of ending their lives, the law made an incoherent and illegal distinction.

The 1996, United States Supreme Court decision overturned both circuit courts, with Chief Justice **William Rehnquist** arguing for a critical distinction between respecting a patient's right to refuse treatment for a terminal disease, and actively assisting a patient with suicide. Religious activism was intense during the Court's review of the case. The Union of Orthodox Jewish Congregations of America, for example, through its Institute for Public Affairs, filed an amicus curae brief in support of laws banning physician-assisted suicide. The Rabbinical Council of America joined in the brief, which contended that the Ninth Circuit Court of Appeals erred in striking down Washington's law. The brief contended, among other arguments, that the right to die was not supported by the traditions of the United States legal system, as evidenced by the fact that Jewish legal teaching, one of the roots of American law, is firmly against the active assistance of suicide under any condition. The brief also contended that the Second Circuit Court of Appeals erred in striking down New York's law under the Equal Protection Clause since the state clearly has a rational basis and legitimate interest in banning assisted suicide.

The Supreme Court decision is unlikely to end the controversy, for it leaves states free to construct their own guidelines. Many states are already mired in the debate. In 1994, citizens in Oregon approved a ballot to legalize euthanasia under limited conditions. Under the Death with Dignity Law, a person who sought physician-assisted suicide would have to meet the following criteria: The person must be terminally ill; must have six months or less to live; must make two oral requests for assistance in dying; must make one written request for assistance; must convince two physicians that he or she is not acting on a whim and is acting voluntarily; must not have been influenced by depression; must be informed of "the feasible alternatives, including, but not limited to, comfort care, hospice care and pain control"; and must wait for 15 days. A patient meeting these conditions would be allowed to receive a lethal prescription of barbiturates. Mercy killings by a family member or friend would be forbidden, as would assisted suicides of the type performed by Dr. Kevorkian. Physicians would be prohibited from inducing death by injection or carbon monoxide.

The National Right to Life Committee, supported by the Roman Catholic Church, obtained a court injunction to delay implementation of the measure; the law became stuck in the appeals process and was not enacted. In 1997, conservatives in the Oregon government forced through measures to hold a second public referendum on the issue. The Roman Catholic Church and other conservative religious groups financed the campaign against access to assisted suicide, paying for coordinators, lawn signs, billboards, media ads, and pamphlets. Nonetheless, the vote was 587,778 to 392,070 in favor of access to physician-assisted suicide.

In 1996, nearly half of all state legislatures considered bills dealing with pain treatment for dying patients, and Texas and Minnesota enacted laws allowing doctors to prescribe controlled substances for the terminally ill. As these examples suggest, the debate over euthanasia is still alive and unlikely to reach a concrete legal resolution in the near future.(CB) **See also** Evangelicals; Fundamentalists; Judaism; Methodism; Roman Catholicism; Unitarianism.

BIBLIOGRAPHY

DeSimone, Cathleen. *Death on Demand: Physician-assisted Suicide in the United States*. Buffalo, NY: W.S. Hein, 1996.

Hamel, Ron P. *Choosing Death: Active Euthanasia, Religion, and the Public Debate*. Philadelphia: Trinity Press International, 1991.

Larson, Edward and Darrel Amundsen. *A Different Death: Euthanasia and the Christian Tradition*. Downers Grove, IL: Intervarsity Press, 1998.

Melton, J. Gordon. *The Churches Speak on Euthanasia*. Detroit: Gale Research, 1991.

Tada, Joni Eareckson. *When Is It Right to Die?* Grand Rapids, MI: Zondervan, 1992.

Evangelicals

Evangelicals are conservative Protestants who (1) have a high view of the Bible, (2) believe that personal salvation comes through faith in Jesus Christ, and (3) that Christians must tell others about Jesus. Evangelicals were an important political force throughout most of the nineteenth century, including such reformers as **Lyman Beecher**, **Lewis Tappan**, and **Jeremiah Evarts**. Since the 1970s, Evangelicals have become politically influential once again. Many have become **Republican Party** activists, but the variety of Evangelical political opinion defies simple generalizations.

Although Evangelicalism has deep historical roots, modern Evangelicalism sees itself largely as a corrective to reactionary Fundamentalism. In the 1920s, many Evangelicals took the label "Fundamentalists" in their battles with theological liberals. When the **Fundamentalists** lost control of the major northern denominations in the 1930s, they also withdrew from larger cultural engagements.

With the formation of the National Association of Evangelicals in 1942, moderate Fundamentalists sought to distinguish themselves from both theological liberalism and reactionary Fundamentalism. Carl Henry's influential book, *The Uneasy Conscience of Modern Fundamentalism* (1947), decried Fundamentalism's lack of social concern. These moderates reasserted the name Evangelicals and sought to temper Fundamentalism into a formidable and socially aware force in U.S. culture.

These "new" Evangelicals during the 1940s and 1950s were as conservative politically as the Fundamentalists, but lacked the militant hostility found in Fundamentalist leaders like **Carl McIntire** or **Billy James Hargis**. Through the editorial pages of their flagship journal, ***Christianity Today***, Evangelicals like Henry rose above the callow diatribes of Fundamentalism while still agreeing that communism was a global threat to liberty and that personal transformation was key to remedying society's ills.

Most Evangelicals in the 1960s remained politically conservative, especially in the South. A few, however, sought to unite Evangelical orthodoxy with more progressive social positions. These "young Evangelicals" championed **civil rights**, opposed the **Vietnam War**, and worked for economic justice for the poor. The high point in the development of this social awareness came in 1973, when over 400 Evangelicals gathered in Chicago to write the Declaration of Evangelical Social Concern. The document affirmed the centrality of Christian social witness to the gospel. Notable champions of socially aware Evangelicalism included Jim Wallis (*Sojourners* magazine), theologian **Ronald Sider**, and sociologist **Tony Campolo**. Unlike some, they believed that government should be involved in remedying the effects of poverty, and they advanced what they called a "consistent pro-life ethic," not only opposing **abortion**, but challenging the nuclear arms race and championing the cause of the poor.

Pentecostal Christians are a fast growing segment of modern evangelicalism. Shown here is an evangelical minister preaching at a Pentecostal church in Illinois in 1939. Photo by Arthur Rothestein. Library of Congress.

In 1976, President **Jimmy Carter** galvanized national attention through his open testimony of his Evangelical faith. *Time* magazine reflected society's rediscovery of Evangelicalism and named 1976 "The Year of the Evangelical." Evangelicalism continued to garner national attention as the electorate chose between three self-professed Evangelicals in the 1980 presidential election—Carter, **Ronald Reagan**, and John Anderson.

Despite a growing variety of Evangelical political views, most remained politically conservative throughout the 1970s and 1980s. The abortion issue, the **Equal Rights Amendment**, and the **homosexual rights** movement galvanized conservative Evangelicals into action, as dramatically seen in the rapid rise of the Reverend **Jerry Falwell**'s **Moral Majority** organization. In 1988, many supported the presidential campaign of **Pat Robertson**, who mobilized **Pentecostal** and **Charismatic** Evangelicals in much the same way that Jerry Falwell had mobilized Fundamentalists in 1980.

Even with Robertson running, most Evangelicals in 1988 supported the more mainstream Episcopalian George Bush. In 1992, about a quarter of Evangelicals voted for Democratic (and Southern **Baptist**) candidate **Bill Clinton**. While most opposed his stand on abortion, he was able to attract about an equal percentage of the Evangelical vote in 1996. Evangelicals also remain at the center of many contemporary church-state issues, supporting the recently overturned **Religious Freedom Restoration Act**, but seriously dividing on the issue of prayer in public schools and on tuition vouchers for parochial schools.

The most vigorous Evangelical political organization today is Robertson's **Christian Coalition**. Focusing on local issues and campaigns, the Coalition distributed over 50 million pieces of literature in the 1996 election. Other influential Evangelical conservatives include **James Dobson** (Focus on the Family), **Gary Bauer** (Family Research Council), **Beverly LaHaye** (Concerned Women for America), and **Chuck Colson** (Prison Fellowship International). More reactionary Evangelicals include **Operation Rescue** founder **Randall Terry**, and the proponents of **Christian Reconstructionism** (e.g., **Rousas Rushdoony**, **Gary North**, and Gary DeMar) who advocate a reconstruction of the political order along the lines of the Old Testament theocratic model. Sider, Wallis and Campolo remain the major figures on the Evangelical left.

While generally conservative, the lack of political consensus among Evangelicals remains strong. An accurate understanding of contemporary Evangelical political activity must note this fact. (ARB) **See also** Conservatism; Democratic Party; Liberalism; Nuclear Disarmament; School Prayer; Socialism and Communism.

Bibliography

Cromartie, Michael, ed. *No Longer Exiles: The Religious New Right in American Politics*. Washington, DC: Ethics and Public Policy Center, 1993.

Neuhaus, Richard John and Michael Cromartie, eds. *Piety and Politics: Evangelicals and Fundamentalists Confront the World*. Washington, DC: Ethics and Public Policy Center, 1987.

Smidt, Corwin E., ed. *Contemporary Evangelical Political Involvement: An Analysis and Assessment*. Lanham, MD: University Press of America, 1989.

Wells, David F. and John D. Woodridge, eds. *The Evangelicals: What They Believe, Who They Are, Where They Are Changing*. rev. ed. Grand Rapids, MI: Baker Book House, 1977.

Jeremiah Evarts (1781–1831)

Trained as a lawyer at Yale, Jeremiah Evarts became editor of the orthodox Congregational magazine, *Panoplist,* and was active in numerous religious activities, including advocating the discontinuance of **Sunday mail** and opposition to the relocation of Native American tribes to Western reservations.

Evarts, secretary of the **American Board of Commissioners for Foreign Missions**, led the legal arguments to stop the government from forcing the removal of the Cherokee from Georgia. (MWP) **See also** Cherokee Removal; Congregationalism; Missionaries; Native American Religions; William Penn Essays.

BIBLIOGRAPHY

Spring, G. A. *Tribute to the Memory of the Late Jeremiah Evarts.* New York: Sleight and Robinson, 1831.

Andrews, John A. *From Revivals to Removals: Jeremiah Everts, The Cherokee Nation, and the Search for the Soul of America.* Athens: University of Georgia Press, 1992.

Tracy, E. C. *Memoir of the Life of Jeremiah Evarts*. Boston: Crocker and Brewster, 1845.

Edward Everett (1794–1865)

Edward Everett, a Unitarian clergyman, was first elected to the U.S. House of Representatives in 1825 and served five consecutive terms. In 1836, he was elected governor of Massachusetts from the newly formed Whig Party. As governor he was petitioned to pardon Abner Kneeland who had been convicted of blasphemy. A conservative Unitarian Whig, Everett refused the plea and Kneeland served his sentence. From 1841 to 1845, he was U.S. ambassador to Great Britain and was the president of Harvard from 1846 to 1849. Prior to his election to the U.S. Senate in 1853, he served as secretary of state from 1852 to 1853. He was not re-elected to the Senate in 1854 and began a lecture tour advocating compromise on **slavery**. In 1860, he ran as vice president on the Constitutional Union ticket. He is remembered as one of the great orators during the **Civil War** and is especially remembered for the keynote address he gave prior to **Abraham Lincoln**'s Gettysburg Address. (MWP) **See also** Clergy in Public Office; Unitarianism.

BIBLIOGRAPHY

Bartlett, Irving H. "Edward Everett Reconsidered." *The New England Quarterly* 69 (September 1996): 426–60.

Reid, Ronald F. *Edward Everett: Unionist Orator*. Westport, CT: Greenwood, 1990.

Everson v. Board of Education of the Township of Ewing (1947)

Everson v. Board of Education of the Township of Ewing, 330 U.S. 1 (1947), is a landmark **First Amendment** establishment of religion case. The case not only marked the first time the U.S. Supreme Court gave an authoritative interpretation of the First Amendment prohibition on an establishment of religion, but it also incorporated the nonestablishment provision into the **Fourteenth Amendment** due process of law clause, thereby forcing the states to uphold the prohibition on establishment. It thus initiated a new and comprehensive surveillance of state and local laws and practices dealing with religion.

The case itself revolved around a New Jersey statute that authorized local school districts to provide money to parents for the transportation of pupils to and from school. When the Ewing Township Board of Education approved reimbursement to parents for money they spent transporting their children on public buses to religious schools, a taxpayer filed suit claiming that the reimbursement violated the First Amendment prohibition against any "law respecting an establishment of religion."

While the Court permitted the use of state funds to transport students to religious schools, the most enduring and poignant legacy of *Everson* was the lavish use of strict separationist rhetoric in both the majority and minority opinions. In this regard, there was a remarkable lack of confrontation between the two opinions. Furthermore, all the justices drew on history, especially **Thomas Jefferson** and **James Madison**'s contributions to the dramatic **disestablishment** struggle in revolutionary Virginia, to inform a separationist interpretation of the First Amendment. In defining the nonestablishment provision, Justice **Hugo L. Black**, writing for the majority, declared:

> Neither a state nor the Federal Government can set up a church. Neither can pass laws which aid one religion, aid all religions, or prefer one religion over another. Neither can force nor influence a person to go to or to remain away from church against his will or force him to profess a belief or disbelief in any religion. No person can be punished for entertaining or professing religious beliefs or disbeliefs, for church attendance or nonattendance. No tax in any amount, large or small, can be levied to support any religious activities or institutions, whatever they may be called, or whatever form they may adopt to teach or practice religion. Neither a state nor the Federal Government can, openly or secretly, participate in the affairs of any religious organizations or groups and vice versa. In the words of Jefferson, the clause against establishment of religion by law was intended to erect "a wall of separation between church and State." . . . That wall must be kept high and impregnable. We could not approve the slightest breach.

In even more sweeping terms, Justice Wiley B. Rutledge asserted in a minority opinion that the First Amendment's purpose was "to uproot" all religious establishments and "to create a complete and permanent separation of the spheres of religious activity and civil authority by comprehensively forbidding every form of public aid or support for religion." (DLD) **See also** Establishment Clause.

BIBLIOGRAPHY

Formicola, Jo Renee and Hubert Morken, eds. *Everson Revisited: Religion, Education and Law at the Crossroads*. Lanham, MD: Rowman & Littlefield, 1997.

Evolution

The theory of evolution swept popular imagination in the United States following the publication, in 1859, of the British naturalist Charles Darwin's *Origin of Species*. In its simplest form, the theory postulates that all plants and animals have their origin in other preexisting types, and that differences among them are due to gradual, natural modifications in successive generations. Darwin contended that the animus of evolution resides in two mechanisms, the spontaneous random mutation of organisms and natural selection—an environmental competition in which only the fittest mutations survive. Man's existence is understood to be the product of these two forces; in other words, life is the consequence of chance at work in a purely materialist world. The theory is widely accepted among contemporary biologists, although numerous dissidents within the scientific community consider this account of life's origins both theoretically implausible and inadequately substantiated by empirical evidence.

Darwin's theory directly conflicted with the creationist theories based on the Bible. The theory of special creation holds that the various forms of life on earth were, as the term suggests, created deliberately. In its most extreme form, as embraced particularly among biblical literalists, creationist doctrine holds that all living organisms came into existence abruptly, that the world is only a few thousand years old, and that the Noachian Flood was an actual historical event in which only one pair of each animal species survived. In a less literal incarnation, **creationism** finds Darwinian theory to be inadequate as the sole explanation of the origin of life and argues that certain patterns and complexities in the biological world suggest the signature of an intelligent designer. For example, anti-evolutionists note that the mathematical probability of a chance chemical combination resulting in the emergence of life from inorganic matter is so remote as to be absurd.

Religious authorities have exhibited widely varying reactions to the theory of evolution. The first chapters of the book of Genesis in the Bible describe God's creation of the world, plants, animals, and humans; any literal interpretation of Genesis would, clearly, be at odds with a vision of gradual evolution of life by purely natural processes. Moreover, Christian beliefs in the soul's immortality and in humans as "created in the image of God" do not sit well with a view of humans descended from primates. In 1874, Charles Hodge, a U.S. Protestant theologian, published *What Is Darwinism?*, arguing, as did William Paley before him, that the complexity and integrated functioning of the human eye indicates that "it has been planned by the Creator, like the design of a watch evinces a watchmaker." He concluded that "the denial of design in nature is actually the denial of God." Equally, some religious leaders have feared that a less-than-literal reading of the biblical story of creation would engender widespread loss of faith; **war** and other purported signs of moral degeneracy have been taken by these thinkers as evidence of the damage wrought by the teaching of Darwinian dogma.

On the subject of evolution, organized religion scarcely speaks with a single voice. Other religious leaders have taken a more kindly view of evolutionary theory, seeing a solution to theological discomfiture in the idea that God operates through intermediate causes. By such reasoning, evolution could be seen as the natural process by which a creator brought living beings into existence and developed them according to a plan. Pope Pius XII in his 1950 encyclical *Humani Generis* proposed that evolution was compatible with Christianity, although he argued that divine intervention was necessary to create a human soul. In 1981, Pope John Paul II stated in an address to the Pontifical Academy of Sciences that it would be an error to understand the Bible to be a primer in the natural sciences, an argument clearly directed against Christian **Fundamentalists** who take Genesis literally.

On the U. S. political scene, controversy over the theory of evolution has revolved chiefly around the teaching of Darwinian evolution in public schools. During the 1920s, more than 20 state legislatures debated laws against the teaching of evolution, with four states—Arkansas, Mississippi, Oklahoma, and Tennessee—passing legislation against the teaching of evolutionary theory. **William Jennings Bryan**, three times an unsuccessful Democratic candidate for the presidency, emerged as evolutionary theory's most prominent detractor. In 1925, Bryan led the prosecution of John T. Scopes, a high school teacher from Dayton, Tennessee, who had violated the state's law forbidding the teaching of any doctrine denying the biblical account of the divine creation of humans. The dapper and charismatic **Clarence Darrow** led the defense in the **Scopes Trial**, and the eight-day trial became a sensational global media spectacle. It was the first U.S. trial to be covered by a national radio broadcast, and the first to receive international coverage; commentators and journalists converged on Dayton by the hundreds. In the end, the judge ruled out any test of the law's constitutionality or argument about the validity of Darwinian theory, limiting the trial to the question of whether or not Scopes had taught evolution, which, admittedly, he had. Scopes was convicted and fined $100. On appeal, the state supreme court upheld the constitutionality of the 1925 law but acquitted Scopes on a technicality, noting that he had been fined excessively. The law was repealed in 1967.

Between the 1920s and early 1960s, sentiment against evolution was reflected in public school curricula throughout the United States; generally, textbooks avoided mention of Darwinism and evolution. In 1957, however, the National Science Foundation inaugurated a number of programs designed to reform U.S. science teaching. Among these programs was the Biological Sciences Curriculum Study, which produced a series of biology texts given over in large part to the theory of evolution. These texts were enormously successful in changing the thrust of mainstream **education**, as evidenced by the fact that they are still used by 50 percent of U.S. school children.

In response to this trend in science education and its suggestion of growing secularism in U.S. society at large, Fundamentalist Christians stepped up efforts to counter Darwinian thought. In the 1960s and early 1970s, several Fundamentalist organizations formed to promote the idea that the book of Genesis was supported by scientific observation and data. One such organization was the Institute for Creation Research, affiliated with the Christian Heritage College and supported by the Scott Memorial **Baptist** Church in San Diego, California. Other creation science organizations included the Creation Science Research Center of San Diego and the Bible Science Association of Minneapolis, Minnesota.

In 1968, the Supreme Court of the United States declared unconstitutional any law banning the teaching of evolution in public schools. Since then, Christian Fundamentalists, backed by the organizations named above, have introduced bills in a number of state legislatures ordering that the teaching of "evolution science" be balanced with equal teaching time for "creation science." In the 1980s, both Arkansas and Louisiana passed acts requiring the equivalent treatment of evolution science and creation science in the schools, but opponents successfully challenged the acts as violations of the constitutionally mandated separation of church and state.

In 1981, the governor of Arkansas signed into law Act 590, entitled the "Balanced Treatment for Creation-Science and Evolution-Science Act," which mandated equal treatment in schools for the two theories. Later that year, suit was filed challenging the act's constitutional validity. A number of religious groups joined with the plaintiffs, including the United Methodist Church, the **Episcopal Church**, the **Presbyterian Church**, the Roman Catholic Church, the **African Methodist Episcopal (AME) Church**, and the American Jewish Committee. This alignment clearly indicates that the theory of evolution is not the exclusive darling of secularists.

Biblical creationism suffered a setback, in legal terms, when in 1987 the U.S. Supreme Court ruled that states could not require public schools to teach the creationist theory of human origin alongside evolution if the intention of such instruction was the promotion of religious belief. This requirement, the Court argued, would reflect a violation of the **First Amendment**'s injunction against the mingling of church and state.

At present, a growing challenge to the teaching of evolution comes not from religious activists, but from within the community of biologists and other natural scientists. As biological research at the molecular level has progressed, evolution by Darwinian mechanisms has come increasingly to be seen by many secular scientific figures as wholly implausible. Biochemist Michael Behe and mathematician William Dembski, for example, argue that the best scientific evidence now suggests that the development of life was guided by an "intelligent designer" rather than by a chance process of natural selection. Their proposed paradigm of "intelligent design" holds out the prospect for a new rapprochement between faith and science. The major organization supporting research in this area is the Seattle-based Discovery Institute and its Center for the Renewal of Science and Culture. While Darwinism remains the prevailing academic orthodoxy, objections to the theory are no longer the exclusive provenance of biblical literalists and the attempt to replace Darwinism with a new paradigm will surely be one of the more stimulating intellectual controversies of the new century. (CB) **See also** Judaism; Methodism; Roman Catholicism.

Bibliography

Behe, Michael. *Darwin's Black Box: The Biochemical Challenge to Evolution*. New York: The Free Press, 1996.

Dembski, William. *The Design Inference*. New York: Cambridge University Press, 1998.

———, ed. *Mere Creation*. Downers Grove, IL: Intervarsity Press, 1998.

Larson, Edward J. *Trial and Error: The American Legal Controversy over Creation and Evolution*. New York: Oxford University Press, 1986.

Rachels, James. *Created from Animals: The Moral Implications of Darwinism*. New York: Oxford University Press, 1990.

Toumey, Christopher P. *God's Own Scientists: Creationists in a Secular World*. New Brunswick, NJ: Rutgers University Press, 1994.

Webb, George Ernest. *The Evolution Controversy in America*. Lexington: University Press of Kentucky, 1994.

Excommunication

Excommunication is an official action by a church to exclude notorious sinners and heretics from fellowship and participation in the Sacraments. Such actions, based upon dominical injunctions in the Gospel of Matthew (Chapter 18), have as their intent the return of the excommunicant, through repentance and a process of penance, to full participation in church life. During the Middle Ages, a "greater" and a "lesser" form of excommunication were used. The former included not only separation from all church privileges but also handing the person over to the secular authorities for various punishments, while the latter typically meant suspension from receiving or administering the Sacrament. Excommunication did not affect a person's eternal salvation, as this redemption was the result of God's grace, not the church's activity. In the early American colonies, especially in New England, the **Puritans**, deeply influenced by **John Calvin**'s "third note of the true Church," namely effective discipline, exercised excommunication frequently against theological and social dissenters. These excommunicants either suffered the death penalty, public punishment, or expulsion to **Rhode Island** or elsewhere. Effective excommunication became increasingly difficult to impose, especially after the constitutional separation of church and state. In contemporary society, mainline denominations rarely excommunicate (though the Roman Catholic Church, through its Archbishops, has threatened such penalties to politicians, most notably **Mario Cuomo** when governor of New York, who support **abortion** policies). The practice is more common among **Evangelicals** and **Fundamentalists** and other more sectarian groups such as **Jehovah's Witnesses**. (JRV) **See also** Calvinism; Massachusetts Bay Colony; Roman Catholicism.

Bibliography

Buckley, Thomas J. , S.J. *Church and State in Revolutionary Virginia, 1776–1787*. Charlottesville: University of Virginia Press, 1977.

Catholic Church. *Codex Juris Canonici*. Vatican City: Libreria Editrice Vaticana, 1983.

Miller, Perry. *Orthodoxy in Massachusetts, 1630–1650*. Boston: Beacon Press, (1933) 1959.

Jerry Falwell (1933–)

Jerry Falwell, a Baptist pastor and television evangelist based in Lynchburg, Virginia, brought many U.S. **Fundamentalists** into the political arena in the late 1970s and early 1980s. Earlier in his career, Falwell embodied the long-standing Fundamentalist antipathy towards social and political activity. Starting in the turbulent 1960s, his political views dramatically shifted. As Falwell saw it, the legalized abortion-on-demand following ***Roe v. Wade*** (1973), the government encroachment upon the sovereignty of the church and the family, the perceived threat that the **Equal Rights Amendment** posed for the traditional family, and the growing push for **homosexual rights** forced him to actively assert America's Judeo-Christian moral heritage. In 1976, he staged a number of "I love America" rallies across the United States. In 1979, he organized the **Moral Majority**, which declared itself to be pro-life, pro-family, pro-moral, and pro-American. The Moral Majority mobilized previously inactive Fundamentalists and Evangelicals in support of conservative causes and campaigns. It pushed for prayer in schools, strongly supported the nation of Israel, and opposed big government spending except for national defense. Falwell, a strong anti-communist, supported both President Marcos on the eve of the Philippine Revolution and the South African apartheid regime because of their opposition to communism. While the extent of his political influence is debated, he played a significant role in helping elect **Ronald Reagan** in 1980.

Not all Fundamentalists agreed with Falwell's methods. Because he cooperated with conservative Jews, Mormons, and Roman Catholics, some separatist Fundamentalists like **Bob Jones** III labeled him a "neo-Fundamentalist" and a compromiser. By the end of the 1980s, Falwell himself dropped the Fundamentalist nomenclature and referred to himself as a conservative Evangelical. Though he disbanded the Moral Majority in 1989, Falwell remained in the political spotlight in the 1990s through his adamant support of some dubious videotapes linking President **Bill Clinton** to a conspiracy surrounding the suicide of White House aide Vincent Foster. (ARB) **See also** Abortion and Birth Control Regulation; Americanism; Bible Belt; Conservatism; Evangelicals; Political Participation and Voting Behavior; Religious Right; Televangelism.

Bibliography

D'Souza, Dinesh. *Falwell, Before the Millennium: A Critical Biography*. Chicago: Regnery Gateway, 1984.

Fackre, Gabriel J. *The Religious Right and Christian Faith*. Grand Rapids, MI: Eerdmans, 1982.

Falwell, Jerry. *Listen, America!* Garden City, NY: Doubleday, 1980.

Falwell, Jerry, Ed Dobson, and Ed Hindson, eds. *The Fundamentalist Phenomenon: The Resurgence of Conservative Christianity*. Garden City, NY: Doubleday, 1981.

Snowball, David. *Continuity and Change in the Rhetoric of the Moral Majority*. Praeger Series in Political Communication. New York: Praeger, 1991.

Wallace D. Fard (fl. 1930–1934)

Wallace D. Fard was the founder of the **Nation of Islam**, popularly known as the Black Muslims, a black nationalist organization that rejected Christianity as having enslaved African Americans. Fard appeared in Detroit in 1930, selling silks to ghetto residents and claiming he came from Mecca. He began to be regarded by local people as a prophet sent to bring freedom, justice, and equality to blacks in America. Fard taught that American blacks would found a black nation after the Armageddon of white society, which he said would take place prior to the year 2000. Ordered out of Detroit by city officials in 1933, he moved to Chicago but soon disappeared. Upon Fard's disappearance, **Elijah Muhammad** took over the Nation of Islam and began to teach that Fard had been Allah, and that he, Elijah Muhammad, was the messenger of Allah. (WVM) **See also** African-American Churches; Black Theology; Islam; Race Relations; Slavery.

Bibliography

Lincoln, C. Eric. *The Black Muslims in America*. Revised ed. New York: Kayode Publications, Ltd.,1991.

Louis Eugene Farrakhan (1933–)

Louis Farrakhan, originally named Louis Walcott, has been a member of the **Nation of Islam** since 1955 and its leader since 1978. He joined the Nation of Islam after hearing a speech by **Elijah Muhammad** in 1955. He then became Louis X (the "X" stood for "ex-slave, ex-Christian, ex-smoker, ex-drinker, ex-mainstream power") and was named leader of the Boston Temple in 1957. In 1964, Farrakhan (the last name given to him by Elijah Muhammad) succeeded **Malcolm X** as leader of the New York City Temple after the latter left the movement. After the death of Elijah Muhammad in 1975, Elijah's son, Wallace, moved the Nation of Islam toward the Islamic mainstream and rejected many of the black separatist doctrines of his father. Three years later, Louis Farrakhan broke with Wallace Muhammad and began to promote the teachings of Elijah Muhammad once again.

The ideology of the Nation of Islam is a combination of black pride, black separation, and self-sufficiency. Louis Farrakhan has argued that whites are devils and that blacks are God's chosen people. As such, he maintains that blacks should separate themselves from the larger white society economically, politically, and socially. More recently, however, he has encouraged his followers to register to vote and become involved in politics. In the 1980s, Farrakhan endorsed **Jesse Jackson**'s candidacies for president and the Nation of Islam's security force provided security for Jackson's campaigns.

Louis Farrakhan broadened his focus in 1995 when he organized the **Million Man March** in Washington, D.C., at which black men pledged to improve themselves spiritually, morally, socially, politically, and economically. While Louis Farrakhan has achieved greater national recognition recently, his status as a spokesperson for the larger African-American community has been limited because of his identification with the racial doctrines of the Nation of Islam. He has also attracted criticism because of his disparaging statements about Jews. (WVM) **See also** African-American Churches; Anti-Semitism; Black Theology; Islam; Race Relations; Slavery.

BIBLIOGRAPHY

Lincoln, C. Eric. *The Black Muslims in America*. rev. ed. New York: Kayode, 1991.

Magida, Arthur J. *Prophet of Rage: A Life of Louis Farrakhan and His Nation*. New York: Basic Books, 1996.

Feminism

American Christianity has had an uneasy relationship with feminism. During the women's suffrage movement of the nineteenth century, women like **Elizabeth Cady Stanton**, author of *The Woman's Bible*, were embraced by a few liberals and denigrated by most moderates and conservatives. The second wave of American feminism, which hit in the 1960s, brought pressure on most denominations to ordain women, as well as demands for greater equality in church and social life. While many religious traditions eventually approved women's ordination, female clergy remain a small minority in most denominations, and many local churches still debate the appropriateness of female leadership.

During the eighteenth century, the general legal status of women declined as the Protestant **Reformation** emphasis on the family unit took political form in the United States. Homes were viewed as "little churches," led by the male "spiritual head." Thus, men represented the family in the public realm. Women were admonished to "keep silent" in public in accordance with scripture.

However, the domestic reality by the nineteenth century was that women took responsibility for the religious instruction of children. Evangelical women were also active in benevolent and reform associations. The need for both teachers and missionaries to the frontier provided further opportunities for women and prompted the founding of women's colleges like Mount Holyoke, which began training girls as devout Christian teachers in 1836–1837.

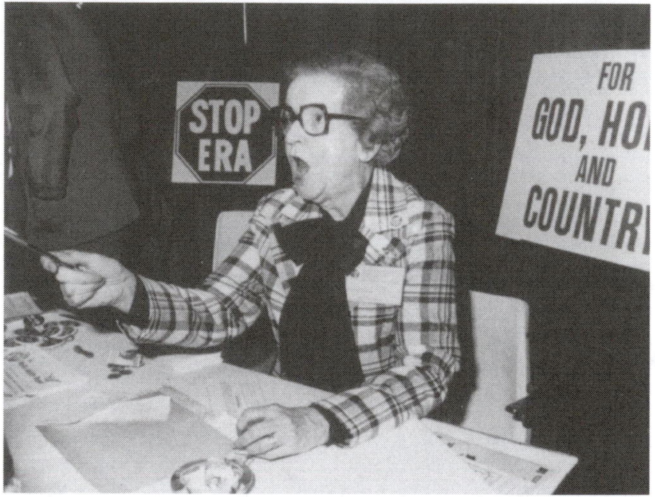

Many leaders of the anti-feminist movement came from Christian women's organizations like STOP ERA. National Archives.

As women moved into these new roles, "women's issues" became national concerns. Margaret Fuller published *Woman in the Nineteenth Century*, the first philosophical statement of feminism by an American, in 1845. Sarah Hale promoted women's issues as the editor of Godey's *Lady's Book*, and her articles were widely quoted in denominational literature. Women made immense contributions to the temperance and anti-slavery movements of the era, and the 1848 Woman's Rights Convention in Seneca Falls brought the women's suffrage movement into the national limelight.

Twentieth-century feminists have raised new questions. In addition to concerns about female leadership, lay and ordained, they have advocated for inclusive language and sexual abuse prevention. Books like **Mary Daly**'s 1973 classic, *Beyond God the Father*, and **Rosemary Radford Ruether**'s *Sexism and God-Talk* challenged the patriarchy of the institutional church. New Testament scholar Elizabeth Schussler Fiorenza has taken on Elizabeth Cady Stanton's role of reinterpreting scripture from a feminist perspective.

Christian Fundamentalism has challenged the feminist interpretation of women's religious roles and has offered its own perspective through the publications of **Tim and Beverly LaHaye** and Maribel Morgan. Many of the leaders of the opposition to the **Equal Rights Amendment (ERA)** were drawn from Christian fundamentalist movements. Women leaders like Phyllis Schlafly and Beverly La Haye challenged the life that would be reached by adoption of the ERA. In the end, they were instrumental in preventing its adoption. **James C. Dobson**'s *Focus on the Family* materials advocate the continuation of the old "family unit" model. But even within such conservative movements as Women Aglow and InterVarsity Christian Fellowship, concern that women follow God first, before any person, has raised issues about how headship and submission properly operate. (KMY) **See also** Abolition; Fundamentalists; Temperance and Prohibition; Women in Religion and Politics.

BIBLIOGRAPHY

Atkinson, Clarissa, Buchanan, Constance H., and Miles, Margaret R., eds. *Shaping New Vision: Gender and Values in American Culture*. Ann Arbor: UMI Research Press, 1987.

Harrison, Beverly Wildung. *Making the Connections: Essays in Feminist Social Ethics*. Boston: Beacon Press, 1985.

Smith-Rosenberg, Carroll. "Women and Religious Revivals." In Leonard Sweet, ed. *The Evangelical Tradition in America*. Macon, GA: Mercer University Press, 1984.

Charles Grandison Finney (1792–1875)

Charles Finney is generally considered to be one of the greatest revivalists of the nineteenth century. He began his career as a lawyer, but he set that aside after a dramatic conversion experience, declaring that he had "a retainer from the Lord Jesus Christ to plead his cause." He labored as a traveling evangelist and pastor until 1835, when he became professor of theology at the newly established Oberlin College in Ohio. Finney later served as president of the college.

Although historians normally do not associate Finney with politics, he greatly influenced two generations with his theology and his views on Christian involvement in politics. Theologically, his starting point was that God is the moral governor of the universe, and that men are subject to his moral government, receiving rewards for obedience and consequences for disobedience. He also advocated the governmental view of the atonement, in which Christ satisfied public justice rather than the wrath of the father. Thus, Finney's theology was also a study in the demands of government.

Charles Grandison Finney was the leading revivalist of the nineteenth century. Library of Congress.

Finney concluded that because God establishes human governments, men should support them. In representative governments, he remarked that men who have a vote are required to use that vote for "the promotion of virtue and happiness." He also called upon men to influence legislation to ensure that the laws enacted are in accord with God's eternal moral laws. Politics was an important part of religion, he felt, and Christians had an obligation to be concerned with the affairs of human government.

Both in his preaching and in his leadership roles at Oberlin College, Finney took stands on certain policy issues, particularly slavery. He was an **abolitionist**, as was all of the Oberlin community, and stressed that God's judgment would fall upon a nation that did not deal righteously with slavery. He believed the United States was hypocritical to legitimize slavery while simultaneously fighting for liberty. (AS) **See also** Evangelicals; Political Participation and Voting Behavior; Public Theology.

BIBLIOGRAPHY

Finney, Charles. *Finney's Systematic Theology: The Complete and Newly Expanded 1878 Edition*. Minneapolis: Bethany House Publishers, 1994.

Finney, Charles. *The Memoirs of Charles G. Finney: The Complete Restored Text*. Grand Rapids, MI: Academic Books, 1989.

Hambrick-Stowe, Charles E. *Charles G. Finney and the Spirit of American Evangelicalism*. Grand Rapids, MI: William B. Eerdmans, 1996.

First Amendment

The religion clauses of the First Amendment have become one of the most controversial areas of constitutional adjudication. Nearly 150 years before the Constitutional Convention, **Roger Williams** had stated the case for religious freedom by arguing that a "**wall of separation**" (a metaphor used later by **Thomas Jefferson**) needed to be erected between "the garden of the church and the wilderness of the world." The purpose of the wall was to protect religion from the meddling and coercive power of government. When Jefferson used the same metaphor in his letter to the Danbury Baptist Association (1802), he intended it to mean that political life should be protected from sectarian strife. These two uses of the wall metaphor reveal the area of agreement that resulted in the religion clauses of the First Amendment.

In the Constitution itself, the only specific mention of religion occurs in Article VI, which forbids the use of religious tests for holding office. Already prior to the convention, debate had occurred over whether government could legitimately fund any religious institution. This debate was taken up most eloquently in 1785 by **James Madison** who, in his "Memorial and Remonstrance on the Rights of Man," argued that religion was primarily an issue of conscience which could be directed only by reason, not by force. On June 8, 1789, in the House of Representatives, Madison introduced an amendment which proposed that the "civil rights of none shall be abridged on account of religious belief or worship, nor shall any national religion be established, nor shall the full and equal rights of conscience be in any manner, or on any pretext, abridged." After a series of stylistic changes, in part prompted by the fact that, at the time, many state laws did provide public support for clergy and churches, many delegates argued that the amendment should apply only to the national government. The amendment was changed to read: "Congress shall make no law establishing religion, or prohibiting the free exercise thereof, nor shall the rights of conscience be infringed." The general assumption appears to have been that neither the federal government nor the states could impinge upon the freedom of conscience (which, since it was removed in the final draft, may have been taken to mean the same as free exercise), and that the federal government could not limit the free exercise of religion nor establish a religion. Although the final wording of the amendment changed, these two restrictions have come to be known as the **Free Exercise Clause** and the **Establishment Clause.**

In this form, the amendment was sent to the Senate. The Establishment Clause, however, continued to be the object of much debate. The Senate entertained a number of unsuccessful motions that would have narrowed the amendment to prevent the preference of one religion or sect over others. The changes were ultimately defeated, however, and the version the Senate sent back to the House stated that "Congress shall make no law establishing articles of faith, or a mode of worship, or prohibiting the free exercise of religion." The regulation of religion and conscience by the states would have been left alone. The House refused this version and insisted on a conference that produced the amendment in its final form. The final version states "Congress shall make no law respecting an establishment of religion . . ." The meaning of the word "respecting" has been the object of considerable debate. The three main positions are the **non-preferentists**, who argue that the clause means that Congress may fund religion, but not in a way that would prefer one religion or sect over another; the strict separationists, who believe that the clause means there can be no government support of religion; and the accommodationists, who believe the amendment means the government should promote and facilitate religious belief.

The issue is made more difficult when one considers the relation between the various clauses. Some have argued that the Establishment and Free Exercise Clauses are independent of one another, while others have argued that the Establishment Clause is the dominant clause. The weight of argument seems to be that the Free Exercise Clause was the most important one, and that the Establishment Clause was regarded as a subordinate clause. Numerous cases have arisen under the amendment's two religion clauses, especially since the Supreme Court's ruling in ***Cantwell v. State of Connecticut*** (1940) which made the clauses applicable to the states. (The First Amendment is reprinted in Appendix 1.) (JP) **See also** Accommodationism; Conscientious Objection; Constitutional Amendments on Religion (Proposed); Fourteenth Amendment; Free Speech Approach to Religious Liberty; Public Aid to Religious Organizations; Religious Tests and Oaths.

BIBLIOGRAPHY

Berns, Walter. *The First Amendment and the Future of American Democracy*. Chicago: Gateway Editions, 1985.

Curry, Thomas. *The First Freedoms: Church and State in America to the Passage of the First Amendment*. New York: Oxford University Press, 1986.

Levy, Leonard. *The Establishment Clause: Religion and the First Amendment*. New York: Macmillan, 1986.

Madison, James. *The Records of the Federal Convention of 1787*. Max Farrand, ed. 3 vols. New Haven: Yale University Press, 1966.

First Great Awakening

In the late 1730s and early 1740s, a religious revival swept through the colonies, from New England to the South, with the height of the revival between 1740 and 1742. It is now referred to as the First Great Awakening, because it was the first widespread religious revival to affect America. Revivals are religious events that occur separately from traditional services. Usually held on a weekday evening, the goal of the revival is to convert those in attendance to accept God's saving grace. Revivals usually last several days and include prayer services, community outreach, and Bible study. In the early 1800s, a **Second Great Awakening** stirred the young country. The First Great Awakening came at a time of significant transition in colonial life. In the early 1700s, in New England in particular, the period of religious fervor and consciousness of purpose of the early colonists was passing. Mercantile perspectives were on the increase. France threatened the western parts of the colonies. Restiveness with British colonial policies grew. Yet, while the awakening had distinctly colonial characteristics and effects, it was not solely a colonial phenomenon. It was part of a greater trans-Atlantic revival, with counterparts in England and Europe.

Leading figures in the revival were **Jonathan Edwards** and **George Whitefield**. Edwards—a Congregationalist theologian and pastor, and one of America's greatest minds—served one church in **Massachusetts Bay** for most

This cartoon shows more conservative religious forces satirizing evangelical preacher George Whitefield. Library of Congress.

of his life. It was in that church in Northampton that early stirrings of revival were experienced in the mid-1730s. Among many pastoral and theological works, he preached and wrote some of the most valuable reflections on revival and religious experience. He is also credited with advancing the notion of America as the redeemer nation. George Whitefield, a young priest in the Church of England (and from England), preached widely in the colonies over a number of years in support of revival. Whitefield was the prime example of a significant phenomenon of the revival—the itinerant preacher, often preaching in the open. A greatly affecting speaker, Whitefield could preach to thousands and be heard by all.

Hundreds of churches and thousands of individuals participated in the revival. The revival also caused controversy and division in individual churches and in whole denominations. "New Lights" and "Old Lights" contended over the origin and character of the revival. New Lights supported the revival. They saw it as of divine origin. Old Lights, fearing enthusiasm—not unreasonable considering the wars of religion in Europe in the 1500s and 1600s—resisted the revival. Each side could point to evidence of its position—New Lights to the renewing effects on individuals and churches; and Old Lights to wildly excessive emotionalism and irrationality.

The First Great Awakening had galvanizing social and political effects on **Colonial America**. Colonists in each region began to experience a new sense of being connected with colonists and colonies from other regions. The First Great Awakening thus played a significant role in the creation of a national consciousness and purpose, giving impetus to forces leading to the **American Revolution** in the 1770s and 1780s. Also of long-lasting significance, the First Great Awakening helped make revival religion a hallmark of Protestantism in America, to the present. (GSS) **See also** Congregationalism.

BIBLIOGRAPHY

Gaustad, Edwin Scott. *The Great Awakening in New England*. New York: Harper & Brothers, 1957.

McLoughlin, William G. *Revivals, Awakenings, and Reform: An Essay in Religion and Social Change in America, 1607–1977*. Chicago: University of Chicago, 1978.

Flag Salute Cases

The Supreme Court performed one of its most dramatic public reversals on the issue of whether laws requiring students in public schools to salute the U.S. flag violated the **First Amendment**. In 1940, a near-unanimous Court declined to strike down such a law in ***Minersville School District v. Gobitis*** (1940), 310 U.S. 586, but just three years later, the Court annulled its own decision and found a similar law unconstitutional in ***West Virginia State Board of Education v. Barnette***, 319 U.S. 624 (1943).

Before the 1930s, few issues of religious freedom had come to the Court, which had decided that the religious freedom of the First Amendment was part of the liberty that the **Fourteenth Amendment** prohibits the states from infringing on. This position opened the way for various religious groups to fight laws that limited their actions or that violated their beliefs. A religious sect known as **Jehovah's Witnesses** pursued its newfound rights particularly zealously, bringing to the Supreme Court a host of cases about religious liberty, including these flag salute cases. Believing that they could not salute the flag without breaking the First Commandment, the Jehovah's Witnesses claimed that laws compelling their children to do so violated their freedom of religion.

Writing for eight of the nine justices in *Minersville*, Justice Felix Frankfurter denied the Jehovah's Witnesses' claim. He argued that religious freedom had to be balanced against the state's rational interest in national unity and claimed that the Court was no more qualified to perform this balancing act than was the school board. The Court's decision surprised the public and was widely criticized. Though Frankfurter did not change his mind, other justices soon did. In a dissent from a related decision two years later—***Jones v. City of Opelika***, 316 U.S. 584 (1942)—Justices **Hugo Black**, **William Douglas**, and Frank Murphy indicated that they had incorrectly decided in the *Minersville* case. The next year, those three justices, newly appointed Justice Wiley Rutledge, and Justice **Harlan F. Stone**, who had been the lone dissenter in 1940, overruled the *Minersville* decision and struck down a flag salute law in *West Virginia State Board of Education v. Barnette*. (BDG) **See also** Conscientious Objection; Pledge of Allegiance.

BIBLIOGRAPHY

Cushman, Robert E. *Leading Constitutional Decisions*. New York: Appleton-Century-Crofts, 1966.

May, Elmer C. *An Investigation of the Relationship between the First Amendment to the United States Constitution and Public School Patriotic Expression (Freedom of), Policy and Practice*. Ann Arbor, MI: University of Michigan, 1995.

Follett v. Town of McCormick, S.C. (1944)

In *Follett v. Town of McCormick, S.C.*, 321 U.S. 573 (1944), Follett, a Jehovah's Witness who went from house to house distributing books, claiming that he offered the books for a contribution, was convicted of violating a town ordinance requiring booksellers to obtain a license. He appealed the conviction on the grounds that the licensing ordinance restricted freedom of worship in violation of the **First Amendment**, which the **Fourteenth Amendment** makes applicable to the states. The U.S. Supreme Court threw out the conviction, claiming that the ordinance contravened freedom of religion and restricted "the exercise of that which the First Amendment has made a high constitutional privilege." (JM) **See also** Free Speech Approach to Religious Liberty; Jehovah's Witnesses.

BIBLIOGRAPHY

Choper, Jesse H. *Securing Religious Liberty*. Chicago: University of Chicago Press, 1995.

Regan, Richard J. *Private Conscience and Public Law*. New York: Fordham University Press, 1972.

Foreign Policy and Religion in Politics

There are two main paradigms or views about the role of religion in U.S. foreign policy. One is a religious liberty view in which the United States sought to hold and preserve freedom of religious expression and worship. The other is a hegemonic determinism view, in which the United States sought world domination (hegemony) whether it wanted to or not, propelled by the forces of history and the "natural" inclination of nation-states to acquire and maintain power (determinism). Both paradigms have corresponding phases.

The phases of the religious liberty paradigm are (1) having religious liberty; (2) preventing the elimination of religious liberty; (3) promoting religious liberty; and (4) preventing religious cleavages.

In the first phase, U.S. foreign policy was generally isolationist—not tending toward intervention in the affairs of other nation-states. The United States remained content to have religious liberty within its own borders. This underpinning of political culture in the United States resulted from the fact that some of the founders of the original 13 colonies had fled to the New World seeking freedom from religious persecution in Europe.

As the country grew into a superpower, its isolationist policy was undermined by forces of history. The United States embraced a superpower role during and immediately following **World War II**. Thereafter, the United States embarked upon a Cold War with the Soviet Union—a **war** propelled by ideological differences, manifested in an expensive arms race and in proxy wars (wars in which certain "proxies"—such as North and South Korea—fought wars supported by the Soviet Union and United States on different sides) as a struggle for influence. United States foreign policy during that period was based on a policy of containment—an effort to contain the influence of communism. The policy of containment had an implicit and sometimes explicit religious dimension. Making the world "safe for democracy" also meant fighting the atheistic ideology of communism, which was inspired by the writings of Karl Marx, who claimed that religion was the "opiate of the masses." In the grand scheme of international politics, capitalism was fighting communism. But in the rhetoric of U.S. politicians and diplomats when nationalistic fervor was necessary to achieve certain foreign policy goals, references to religion were potent symbols. It allowed them to frame the fight as one against an atheistic demon. Thus marked the second phase, when the United States had a policy based in part on the prevention of the elimination of religious liberty.

The third phase emerged as the Soviet Union disintegrated and the Cold War ended. At that point, the policy of enlargement was initiated in which the United States promoted capitalist pluralism. Free markets and freedom of speech and religion were all promoted. When Russia moved toward a state-sponsored Eastern Orthodox religion, U.S.-Russian relations suffered, and the aid provided to Russia from the United States was threatened. In developing and former Eastern-bloc countries, the United States Agency for International Development initiated a civil society program seeking to establish institutions that would promote and preserve pluralism and nondictatorial political processes.

Finally, as the United States matured in its role of being the preeminent superpower, U.S. foreign policy developed more refined approaches to preventing religious cleavages. At the outset of this period considerable concern was expressed over whether the United States might need a new demon to fight against—as if fighting a foreign evil was necessary to garner domestic political support for U.S. diplomatic and military involvement globally. The evil of communism had to be replaced, this argument went, and the most likely "successor demon" would be nation-states composed predominantly of Muslims. Samuel Huntington, a Harvard University professor, warned that a "clash of civilizations" could follow. He foretold that the capitalist, democratic, largely Judeo-Christian West was likely to be in conflict with a substantially feudal, dictatorial, significantly Muslim East. But U.S. foreign policy attempted to forestall such "demonization," perhaps in part due to U.S. economic interest in Persian Gulf oil.

While the United States sought to prevent religion from becoming a new fault line in post–Cold War international politics, religion proved to be more potent in causing cleavages intranationally—such as in the former Yugoslavia. During the fourth phase, the U.S. secretary of state formed the Advisory Committee on Religious Freedom Abroad. In addition to its focus on helping the secretary identify ways of "advancing religious freedom abroad," part of its function was to provide "advice on the role of religious institutions in promoting conflict resolution, reconciliation and human rights." This latter emphasis was necessitated by the increase in "ethnic violence" throughout the world in places where the breakup of the former Soviet Union caused power vacuums. These vacuums resulted in violence between groups of differing identities—ethnic, racial, cultural, and significantly, religious (sometimes called "communal conflict").

In conclusion, the religious liberty view of foreign policy maintains that the United States, from its very inception, had a deep appreciation for freedom of religion. After World War II, it developed a policy of containment that sought to constrain the influence of an atheistic ideology. This approach was replaced after the breakup of the Soviet Union by a policy of enlargement that sought to expand capitalism and pluralism, of which the latter embodied the principles of freedom of religion as a part of strengthening civil society. Finally, in the post–Cold War period, the United States sought to account for the religious dimension of inter- and intranational relations in its diplomatic equation.

The hegemonic determinism view, in contrast, would interpret U.S. foreign policy as having gone through these corresponding phases: (1) assembling power; (2) assertion of power; (3) consolidation of power; and (4) refinement of the exercise of power. According to this paradigm, while the United

States was largely isolationist, it was assembling power. The young country had to build up its industrial and military capacities before it could become a hegemonic force.

During the Cold War, the United States asserted power (phase two). While a clash of ideologies may have been involved, in a deterministic sense the power struggle was the result of a bipolar world in which the head of each pole—the United States of the democratic capitalism pole and the Soviet Union of the centrally-planned communism pole—sought to gain influence in other parts of the world. This view holds that while religion may have been a helpful reference for the purposes of generating nationalistic fervor in speeches of U.S. politicians and diplomats, it was but a facade for domestic consumption. According to this view, the atheistic communistic, demonized Soviet Union was simply in the way of U.S. hegemony.

As the Cold War ended, the United States moved into the third phase, seeking to consolidate its power. This view would see the motivation of making the world safe for capitalist democracy, including religious liberty, as a thin ideological veneer covering the actual impetus—world domination. But "ruling the world" and holding onto hegemonic power required refined diplomatic tools. Hence, the fourth phase began in which the United States sought to employ the influence of religious leaders to keep the peace and thus assist in preserving hegemonic influence.

The religious liberty view interprets U.S. foreign policy priorities as shaped in part by religious considerations, as if religion were of inherent value. The hegemonic determinism paradigm, in contrast, views religion as a force to exploit, regardless of its inherent value, for the purposes of gaining and maintaining power. Some would say that the religious liberty view is naive and simplistic. Others would say the hegemonic determinist view is overly cynical and conspiratorial. The truth probably lies somewhere in-between. (JGB) **See also** Americanism; Atheism; Capitalism; Democracy; First Amendment; Imperialism; Socialism and Communism.

BIBLIOGRAPHY

Huntington, Samuel P. "Religion and the Third Wave." *National Interest* 24 (Summer 1991): 27–38.

Johnston, Douglas and Cynthia Sampson, eds. *Religion, The Missing Dimension of Statecraft*. New York: Oxford University Press, 1994.

Abe Fortas (1910–1982)

As a young lawyer, Abe Fortas served on a number of committees and commissions during the **New Deal**. After returning to private practice, Fortas often took **civil rights** and individual rights cases, including defending suspected communists and the rights of criminals. He became a close advisor to Lyndon B. Johnson, and in 1965, after Johnson became president, he appointed Fortas to the Supreme Court. In 1968, Johnson's attempt to appoint him chief justice was defeated by conservative opposition. The following year, financial irregularities involving Fortas's relationship with someone convicted of stock manipulation caused him to become the first Supreme Court justice to be forced to resign. His resignation in 1969 ended the tradition of the "Jewish seat," on the court which had existed since 1932. (MWP)

BIBLIOGRAPHY

Kalman, Laura. *Abe Fortas: A Biography*. New Haven, CT: Yale University Press, 1990.

Harry Emerson Fosdick (1878–1969)

Harry Fosdick was a Baptist preacher, liberal theologian, and social activist. During the 1920s, he engaged more Fundamentalist clergy in an ongoing debate over the role of Christianity in U.S. society. An advocate of the **Social Gospel** movement, he was pastor of the influential Riverside Church that had members among the elite in New York like John D. Rockefeller. During the Depression, his church acted as a job placement agency in addition to providing many other social services. He conducted a radio broadcast entitled *National Vespers*. Like most liberals, Fosdick had an optimistic view of human progress, believing that human depravity was largely due to unjust institutions and governments. While he was a staunch supporter of the U.S. efforts during **World War I**, he had become a committed pacifist by **World War II** and sought to keep the U.S. out of the European war. The realities of the war, however, modified his beliefs in human progress, leaving him less optimistic than his earlier days. He continued to work for social change until his death in 1969. **See also** Baptists; Liberalism; Pacifism; Social Justice.

BIBLIOGRAPHY

Fosdick, Harry Emerson. *The Living of These Days*. New York: Harper, 1969.

Miller, Robert M. *Harry E. Fosdick: Preacher, Pastor, Prophet*. New York: Oxford University Press, 1985.

Fourteenth Amendment

The Fourteenth Amendment was passed in 1868 following the **Civil War**, largely as a reaction to the Constitution's failure to apply guarantees of rights only to the federal government and not to the states. This lack was remedied with the first section of the amendment, which reads: "No State shall make or enforce any law which shall abridge the privileges or immunities of citizens of the United States; nor shall any State deprive any person of life, liberty, or property, without due process of law; nor deny to any person within its jurisdiction the equal protection of the laws." It was necessary to add this language to the Constitution because the original Bill of Rights referred only to laws made by Congress and as such only limited action on the part of the federal government; thus, states were not prevented by the Constitution from enacting laws that, for example, restricted free speech or the free exercise of religion.

The Fourteenth Amendment, however, did not explicitly incorporate the Bill of Rights guarantees in its language, and much of the controversy surrounding the interpretation of that amendment concerns which aspects of the Bill of Rights are covered by a protection of life, liberty, and property; the due process of law; and equal protection. For a number of years, the U.S. Supreme Court refused to accept that the Fourteenth Amendment fully incorporated all of the protections of the Bill of Rights. Though the **Free Exercise Clause** of the **First Amendment** was considered an inherent part of the "liberty" guaranteed by the Fourteenth Amendment, the Court was not as certain of the status of the **Establishment Clause**, which stated, "Congress shall make no law respecting an establishment of religion." None of the clauses of the Fourteenth Amendment explicitly indicated that the states should not be allowed to aid religious activities and institutions. In recent years, however, the Supreme Court has tended to follow a total incorporation path concerning the religion clauses and has used the same doctrines and tests applied to federal legislation to evaluate state legislation on matters of both free exercise and establishment. (JM) **See also** Accomodationism; Constitutional Amendments on Religion (Proposed).

Bibliography

Berger, Raoul. *Government by Judiciary*. Cambridge, MA: Harvard University Press, 1977.

Fairman, Charles. "Does the Fourteenth Amendment Incorporate the Bill of Rights? The Original Understanding." *Stanford Law Review* 2 (1949): 5–173.

James, Joseph B. *The Framing of the Fourteenth Amendment*. Urbana: University of Illinois Press, 1956.

Fowler v. Rhode Island (1953)

A minister of **Jehovah's Witnesses** was arrested for preaching at a peaceful religious meeting in a public park in the city of Pawtucket, which had an ordinance prohibiting religious meetings in its public parks. The ordinance, however, "shall not be construed to prohibit any [religious group] from visiting any public park in a body, provided that no public address shall be made under the auspices of such [group]." In *Fowler v. Rhode Island*, 345 U.S. 67 (1953), the U.S. Supreme Court judged that the conviction constituted religious discrimination and was therefore invalid, stating that the different nature of worship in different sects meant that other religious leaders "could all preach to their congregations in Pawtucket's parks with impunity [while] the hand of the law would be laid on the shoulder of a minister of this unpopular group for performing the same function." (JM) **See also** First Amendment; Public Aid to Religious Organizations.

Bibliography

Bowser, Anita. "The Meaning of Religion in the Constitution." Unpublished Ph.D. dissertation, The University of Notre Dame, 1976.

Regan, Richard J. *Private Conscience and Public Law*. New York: Fordham University Press, 1972.

Felix Frankfurter (1882–1965)

Associate justice of the Supreme Court and longtime professor of law, Felix Frankfurter consistently endorsed a policy of judicial restraint, leaving legislatures free to experiment with reforms during the **New Deal**, but also free to violate the civil liberties of minorities during **World War II**. As a young lawyer, he supported New Deal labor legislation and defended the civil liberties of immigrants and political radicals. Appointed to the Court in 1939, he argued that judges could not prevent legislatures from compelling flag salutes in public schools, making the Communist Party illegal, or interning Japanese citizens. He wrote the majority opinion in ***Minersville School District v. Gobitis*** (1940) arguing that the state could compel students to salute the flag, and dissented in the case ***West Virgina State Board of Education v. Barnette*** (1943) which reversed *Gobitis*. He also wrote a dissent in ***Everson v. Board of Education of Ewing Township*** (1947) in which he argued reimbursement provisions for bus fare to parochial schools was a violation of the **Establishment Clause**. (BDG) **See also** Civil Rights; Flag Salute Cases.

Bibliography

Parrish, Michael. *Felix Frankfurter and His Times: The Reform Years*. New York: The Free Press, 1982.

Urofsky, Melvin I. *Felix Frankfurter: Judicial Restraint and Individual Liberties*. Boston: Twayne Publishers, 1991.

Benjamin Franklin (1706–1790)

Benjamin Franklin was one of America's greatest statesmen, philosophers, and scientists. A true student of the **Enlightenment**, which stressed reason and scientific methodology, Franklin's religious views reflected his training as a scientist and philosopher. As early as 1735, he defended the Reverend Samuel Hemphill against dismissal because of Hemphill's sermon that Christianity is only an illustration and improvement of the law of nature.

A deist, Franklin placed a strong emphasis on the results of one's actions rather than on the beliefs one held. He believed that public religion was necessary so as "to inspire, promote, or confirm morality." For him, religion was a cultural fact and the differences between religions were unimportant. When it came to doctrinal issues like the divinity of Jesus, Franklin saw no harm in the belief that Jesus was divine because it helped make Jesus's teachings more respected. Even on his deathbed, Franklin refused to speculate on the divine nature of Jesus, saying he would soon know for sure.

In keeping with his belief that religion plays an important role in public affairs, Franklin called for each day of the Constitutional Convention to begin with a prayer. For Franklin, what mattered most was morality and virtue. Religious orthodoxy was not necessary in order to achieve this, though he understood that it could be beneficial. **See also** Colonial America; Deism; Public Theology.

Bibliography

Franklin, Benjamin. *The Autobiography of Benjamin Franklin*. New York: Dover, 1996.

Lopez, Claude-Anne and Eugenia W. Herbert. *The Private Franklin: The Man and His Family*. New York: Norton, 1975.

Van Doren, Carl. *Ben Franklin*. New York: Viking, 1938.

Free Exercise Clause

The **First Amendment** has two separate clauses intended to protect freedom of religion: The **Establishment Clause** (or, better, the "no Establishment" Clause), and the Free Exercise Clause. The two religious liberty clauses have their own personalities. The Establishment Clause is unyielding. The Free Exercise Clause is very flexible. If necessary, it can become almost invisible. It is easy to dismiss the Free Exercise Clause as a second-class citizen in the community of constitutional liberties. When the Supreme Court hears a free exercise case, it first balances the religious liberty claim against the restrictions required by criminal or civil law. More likely than not, the judgment of the elected lawmakers will prevail. Second, the Court will test the liberty claim against the Establishment Clause. Would the state effectuate an establishment by satisfying a particular religious liberty claim? If so, then the free exercise claim must take a back seat. Since the late nineteenth century, the Supreme Court has addressed cases respecting the free exercise of religion. Although most attempts at categorization lead to overgeneralization, the case law might be broken down into three larger areas: The *Reynolds* "caveat," the *Sherbert-Yoder* "directive," and the return to *Reynolds*.

In ***Reynolds v. United States*** (1878), the Court addressed the case of a man convicted of bigamy in the district court of Utah Territory. The Court carefully distinguished religious belief and opinions from religious practices. To prevent regulation of religious practice, noted Chief Justice Waite, would "make the professed doctrines of religious belief superior to the law of the land, and in effect to permit every citizen to become a law unto himself." The *Reynolds* decision indicated the Court's reluctance to protect an absolute right to engage in a course of action because one is compelled by religious duty. In ***Cantwell v. State of Connecticut*** (1940), the Court further distinguished between the free exercise of religion as belief and the free exercise of religion as action. The Court held, "the Amendment embraces two concepts—freedom to believe and freedom to act. The first is absolute but, in the nature of things, the second cannot be. Conduct remains subject to regulation for the protection of society." Thus, the Court permitted the states to regulate anti-social conduct. Government restrictions, when found reasonable by the courts, can be adopted to further the health, safety, morals, and convenience of the community, and they may be enforced against claims of religious liberty. If the state has a valid objective, like preventing suicide, stopping drug use, or ending **polygamy**, then it can enforce its criminal law even over free exercise claims.

Nearly 90 years after *Reynolds*, the Court determined that the Free Exercise Clause meant more than simply the right to believe. In the pivotal decision in ***Sherbert v. Verner*** (1963), the justices deliberated whether a state agency could deny unemployment compensation to those who refused, for religious reasons, any job requiring Saturday work. In *Sherbert*, the Court recognized a new dimension to the Free Exercise Clause. The Court held that the degree to which government can, through pervasive involvement in our lives, indirectly affect religious freedom was limited. Further, the Free Exercise Clause afforded "relatively absolute" protection—only extremely strong interests justify government restrictions on religious conduct. As a result of this ruling, the burden of proof shifted to the government to demonstrate that strong interests exist, and how religious conduct harms those interests. *Sherbert* served much like the Court's equal protection jurisprudence to heighten scrutiny and to establish a two-tiered approach to examining legislation. Just as with racially based legislation, where the government cannot simply provide a rational basis for a law (but must show a compelling reason if the legislation is to pass constitutional muster), the Court held that the government must have an overriding reason to restrict religious liberties. In the ***Wisconsin v. Yoder*** (1972) decision, the Court ruled that a law compelling children to attend school until 16 years of age severely threatened the survival of the **Amish** faith. In *Yoder*, the Court reaffirmed the elements of its decision in *Sherbert*. Moreover, it reinforced the Free Exercise Clause by adding that the state must show a compelling reason to limit state conduct and demonstrate that a less drastic means is available to reach its goal. Thus *Yoder* gave rise to the "least drastic means" component of the balancing test.

But since *Sherbert* and *Yoder*, the Court has had, at best, a mixed record on free exercise claims. Cases such as *United States v. Lee* (1982), ***Bob Jones University v. United States*** (1983), ***Goldman v. Weinberger*** (1986), and ***Lyng v. Northwest Indian Cemetery Protective Association*** (1989) seriously eroded the *Sherbert-Yoder* doctrine. Finally, in 1990, the Court reaffirmed its commitment to the *Reynolds* caveat. In the 5-4 decision in ***Employment Division of Oregon v. Smith*** (1990), the Court reversed a verdict by the Oregon Supreme Court to allow unemployment compensation for two men, members of the Native American Church, fired for ingesting sacramental peyote in violation of the state's controlled substance law. The Oregon Court applied *Sherbert* and held that the men were entitled to unemployment compensation benefits. However, the Supreme Court held that *Sherbert*'s compelling interest test would not apply to free exercise claims requesting exemption from neutral laws of general applicability. Writing for the majority, Justice **Antonin Scalia** argued that one's right of free exercise cannot excuse one from "compliance with an otherwise valid law." Moreover, noted Scalia, there is no disharmony in the Court's free exercise jurisprudence. The only time the Court held that an individual's religious beliefs exempt him or her from neutral, generally applicable law is when the free exercise claim is in conjunction with other constitutional protections. Why did the Court not simply use the compelling interest test to overturn the Oregon Supreme Court? Scalia maintained that with regard to race or free speech, exemptions are permitted to protect societal norms and aspirations. Accommodation is not offered to protect aberrant behavior. "[W]hat it would produce here—a private right to ignore generally applicable laws—is a constitutional anomaly," observes Scalia.

While some jurists and scholars were pleased with the Court's post-*Yoder* treatment of the Free Exercise Clause, others regarded the "return to *Reynolds*" with great alarm. In response to *Smith,* Congress passed the **Religious Freedom Restoration Act (RFRA)** in 1993. This legislation was intended to restore much of the *Sherbert-Yoder* directive via statutory law, but RFRA was held to be unconstitutional in ***City of Boerne v. Flores*** (1997). (FG) **See also** Accommodationism; Native American Religions.

Bibliography

Choper, Jesse. "The Rise and Decline of the Constitutional Protection of Religious Liberty." *Nebraska Law Review* 70, (1991): 651-88.

Laycock, Douglas. "The Remnants of Free Exercise." *Supreme Court Review* 1 (1990): 1 - 68.

Lupu, Ira. "Where Rights Begin: The Problem of Burden on the Free Exercise of Religion." *Harvard Law Review* 102, (1989): 933-90.

Marshall, William. "The Case against the Constitutionality of Compelled Free Exercise Exemptions." *Case Western Law Review* 103, (1990): 357-412.

McConnell, Michael. "The Origins and Historical Understanding of the Free Exercise of Religion." *Harvard Law Review* 103, (1990): 1409-517.

_______. "Free Exercise Revisionism and the Smith Decision." *University of Chicago Law Review* 57 , (1990): 1109-53..

Pepper, Stephen. "Taking the Free Exercise Clause Seriously." *B.Y.U. Law Review* (1986): 299-336.

Tushnet, Mark. "The Rhetoric of Free Exercise Discourse." *B.Y.U. Law Review* (1993): 117-40.

West, Ellis. "The Case against a Right to Religion-Based Exemptions." *Notre Dame Journal of Law, Ethics & Public Policy* 4, (1990): 591-638.

Free Speech Approach to Religious Liberty

The U.S. Supreme Court has developed the principle that governmental constraints on freedom of expression based on the content of the speech itself are unconstitutional, barring some "compelling" state interest in regulating the speech. In ***Widmar v. Vincent*** (1981), the Supreme Court applied this general doctrine to a situation with implications for religious liberty. The Court ruled that once a state university makes its facilities available for use by student groups, it may not forbid a religious student group access to those facilities without compelling reason. The Court argued that the university in this case, which made its decision as part of a general policy prohibiting use of facilities "for purposes of religious worship or religious teaching," was burdening particular forms of expression in violation of the **First Amendment** right to free speech.

The Court's basic reasoning in *Widmar* has been influential in subsequent rulings on religious freedom. The issue in ***Lamb's Chapel v. Center Moriches Union Free School District*** (1993), for example, was a public school board's refusal to grant a church equal access to school property to show a film on family issues. The Court held that the district, which had refused only religious treatments of such topics, had not designed a content-neutral policy toward all types of expression. Even public funding of various groups must maintain neutrality. In ***Rosenberger v. Rector and Visitors of the University of Virginia*** (1995), the Court invalidated the University of Virginia's policy of withholding certain funds for religious student groups (mainly printing costs for a group's publication). The Court argued that the university could not choose which groups to fund solely on the basis of the views expressed by those groups.

As a matter of constitutional jurisprudence, the free speech approach to religious liberty is in its infancy. Yet we might expect greater reliance on the approach if the Court continues to maintain its equal access doctrine. Moreover, the Court recently hinted that certain forms of religious expression count as "symbolic speech," protected by the First Amendment; e.g., ***Capitol Square Review Board v. Pinette*** (1995). (KRD) **See also** Equal Access Act; Public Aid to Religious Organizations.

Bibliography

Greenwalt, Kent. "Viewpoints from Olympus." *Columbia Law Review* 96, no. 3 (April 1996): 697–709.

Paulsen, Michael S. "A Funny Thing Happened on the Way to the Limited Public Forum." *U. C. Davis Law Review* 29, no. 3 (Spring 1996): 653–718.

Freemasonry

Freemasonry is one of the world's oldest secular fraternal organizations, with references to it dating back to the thirteenth century in England. The Freemasons began as members of craft guilds. The first Masonic Lodge in the United States was started in Boston, Massachusetts, in 1733. The primary qualification for membership is a belief in a supreme being. The organization stresses religious toleration, the equality of their male peers, and the themes of classic liberalism and the **Enlightenment**. Its membership is open to all races and religions. It is a nonpolitical organization and is active worldwide. Many prominent Americans have belonged to the Freemasons, including Paul Revere, John Hancock, and at least 15 U.S. presidents beginning with **George Washington**.

Despite these prominent members, allegations of a Freemason conspiracy were circulated in the United States in the late 1700s and early 1800s by people who were suspicious of the Masons, in part because of their religious toleration. The first **anti-Masonic movement** was linked to a 1798 book by John Robison who claimed that a conspiracy against all religions and governments in Europe was being orchestrated by Freemasons, the Illuminati, and reading societies. Those who were attracted to this anti-Masonic movement were generally linked to the preservation of the rights of a single established church, the Congregationalists. The anti-Masonic movement of the 1820s and 1830s attacked the Masons as an infidel society at odds with evangelical Protestantism. This attack resulted in the creation of the Anti-Masonic Party, a cultural preservationist movement. While the immediate impact of the anti-masonic movements was a substantial decline in Freemasonry membership, the organization today has millions of members in the United States. It is a widely recognized worldwide fraternal order that educates its members about philosophical ideas and engages in charitable activities while offering networking opportunities for business and political leaders. (WVM) **See also** Illuminati Controversy.

BIBLIOGRAPHY

Roberts, Allen E. *Freemasonry in American History*. Richmond, VA: Macoy Publishing and Masonic Supply Company, 1985.

Freethought

Freethought is a term used to describe any reaction against conventional religion or theological dogma. Freethought does not define a cohesive group of individuals with an underlying social philosophy, as Jonathan Swift indicated in 1708 when he grouped "atheists, libertines, [and] despisers of religion" as "those who usually pass under the name of freethinkers." Although individual freethinkers run the gamut from liberals to libertarians, some common elements do unite freethinkers of various political and religious persuasions. Freethinkers have a strong belief in the progress of humanity. As intellectual heirs to the **Enlightenment**, they believe that human reason, when freed from the superstition of organized religion, will result in human progress.

In the United States, freethought has never been a serious threat to organized religion. However, it has been a resilient strand that has existed in various forms from **colonial America** to the present. In 1784, Revolutionary War hero **Ethan Allen** wrote a freethought book entitled *Reason the Only Oracle of Man*. Although Allen's work was not influential, at least in part because of it underdeveloped themes, the writings of another Revolutionary freethinker, **Thomas Paine**, were in high demand. Paine's *Age of Reason*, published in 1794, was widely read throughout the U.S. and has become known as the deists' Bible. Paine's work draws upon the Enlightenment and its conclusion that reason and experience are the best guides to truth. The work also argues that any truth found in Christianity was true in nature before it became part of organized religion.

The freethinking of the colonial and early republic periods was diminished by the moral and religious fervor of both **slavery** and the **Civil War**. However, freethought experienced a revitalization in the mid-nineteenth century due in large part to the publication of Charles Darwin's *Origin of Species*. With the propagation of Darwinian science, freethinkers focused upon the scientific method as the only legitimate manner in which to make moral decisions. Freethought took refuge in the belief that Darwin's theory showed that anti-religious ideology could be buttressed with scientific evidence. Leading freethinkers like **Theodore Parker** argued for the scientific study of religion and rejected use of the Bible in schools.

Robert G. Ingersoll, perhaps the most influential freethinker in American history, had an unshakable faith in science. He faulted religion because it had failed to account for natural phenomena. Ingersoll, a gifted orator, traveled the country giving lectures that attempted to debunk Christianity. In 1890, he published a widely read article "Why I am an Agnostic," in which he made an eloquent case for disbelief.

In addition to Ingersoll, **Frances Wright** traveled the country in the only real attempt to inculcate the beliefs of freethought. She lectured widely, trying to spread the gospel of infidelity. **Robert Owen** founded several communities that sought to eliminate all religion and to form a communistic utopia based upon reason and nature.

Several organizations formed to promote freethought in the U.S. In 1876, the National Liberal League was formed with the specific purpose of promoting secularism in the United States. In 1877, it changed its name to the American Secular Union. In addition to organizations, freethinkers published several newspapers, including *The Index,* which was edited by Benjamin F. Underwood, and *The Investigator*. However, in the 1910s, the freethought movement began to decline as a result of a conservative backlash against the growing liberalism within churches.

Freethought is still a part of the American political and religious fabric. In the 1930s, humanists like **John Dewey** signed the **Humanist Manifesto** that relegated God to a passive and inconsequential role in building the American future. Since the 1950s, freethinkers like atheist **Madalyn Murray O'Hair**, who successfully challenged **release times** for religious **education**, have fought an ongoing battle with the **Religious Right**, whose members argue that the United States is a Christian nation. Freethinkers and their associations continue to strive for the secularization of American society and the maintenance of a high **wall of separation** between church and state. **See also** American Revolution; Atheism; Communitarianism; Conservatism; Deism; French Revolution; Abner Kneeland; Liberalism; Religious Right; Secular Humanism; Secularization Thesis; Socialism and Communism; Utopianism.

BIBLIOGRAPHY

Post, Albert. *Popular Freethought in America*. New York: Octagon Books, 1974.

Warren, Sidney. *American Freethought*. New York: Gordian Press, 1966.

Frederick Theodore Frelinghuysen (1817–1885)

Frederick Frelinghuysen, a Republican U.S. senator from New Jersey (1866–1869, 1871–1877) and secretary of state under President Chester A. Arthur (1881–1885), actively supported both the Republican plan for **Reconstruction** of the South, and later, the impeachment of President Andrew Johnson. In the Senate, he successfully introduced legislation outlawing **polygamy**, then being practiced by some Mormons (members of the **Church of Jesus Christ of Latter-day Saints**). A deeply religious man, he was president of the American Bible Society during the last two years of his life. Frelinghuysen University, which until the 1950s educated working-class African Americans in Washington, DC, was named after him. (ARB) **See also** Education; Republican Party.

BIBLIOGRAPHY

Rollins, John Williams. "Frederick Theodore Frelinghuysen, 1817–1885: The Politics and Diplomacy of Stewardship." Unpublished Ph.D. dissertation, University of Wisconsin, 1974.

French Revolution (1789–1799)

From the beginning of European settlement until 1815, the United States was economically, politically, and militarily involved in European wars. These wars spurred independence for America and a revolution in France, and led to dramatic changes in the political system of the United States. The French Revolution began in 1789 and marked dramatic changes in France and for Europe. The events of the Revolution led to the execution of King Louis XVI. During the 10-year course of the Revolution, the divine-right monarchy was replaced with a more democratic government. However, the events had been violent and destructive to French society and led to the rise of Napoleon Bonaparte.

Initial U.S. reaction to the French Revolution was divided. Most Federalists supported the monarchy and trade with Britain, at war once again with France. **Evangelicals** among the Federalists attacked the anti-Christian elements of the French Revolution, including its championing of **Enlightenment** radicalism. **Alexander Hamilton** charged that the Revolution's leaders were trying to exterminate Christianity and "pervert a whole people to Atheism." Others supported the cause of the French revolutionaries and likened the French Revolution to the **American Revolution**. Although President **George Washington** proclaimed neutrality, the U.S. was attacked on the high seas by both countries. The United States soon fought both countries—the French in the Quasi-War (1798–1800), and the British in the War of 1812 (1812–1815). Trying to suppress dissent against the pro-British policies, President **John Adams** pushed for passage of the Alien and Sedition Acts, which were designed to mitigate the influence of recent immigrants and made criminal the publishing of false, scandalous, or malicious writing against the government. In response, Vice President **Thomas Jefferson** and others formed an opposition party, called the Democratic Republicans, which defeated the Federalists in national elections in 1800. (GT) **See also** Democracy; Divine Right of Kings.

BIBLIOGRAPHY

Bowman, Albert. *The Struggle for Neutrality: Franco-American Diplomacy during the Federalist Era*. Knoxville: University of Tennessee Press, 1974.

Doyle, W. *The Oxford History of the French Revolution*. New York: Oxford University Press, 1989.

Hamilton, Alexander. "The Stand No. III." *Papers of Alexander Hamilton*. New York: Columbia University Press, 1961-79, vol. 21: 402-05.

Higonnet, P. *Sister Republics: The Origins of French and American Republicanism*. Cambridge, MA: Harvard University Press, 1988.

Fugitive Slave Laws

In 1793, Congress passed the first fugitive slave law, which sought to facilitate the recapture and return of runaway slaves. Specifically, the law authorized slave owners or their agents to apprehend runaways and then apply for a writ to take custody of the slaves. However, the law did not require local authorities to aid in the capture of runaways. The execution of the law was hampered by the adoption of personal liberty laws by several states. These were laws that specifically sought to prevent the enforcement of the 1793 law. In 1842, the U.S. Supreme Court in *Prigg v. Pennsylvania* ruled that Pennsylvania's citizenship statute was unconstitutional and specifically upheld the constitutionality of the 1793 law. Nevertheless, states continued to enact legislation aimed at curbing the influence of the fugitive slave law and what they perceived as the federal government's interference with state matters. It was clear that the first fugitive slave law was a failure.

An abolitionist addresses a Boston crowd on the evils of the Fugitive Slave Law. National Archives.

The second fugitive slave law, enacted as part of the Compromise of 1850, tried to correct the enforcement problems of the first law. Congress established commissioners who were under the authority of the federal courts and who would be active in the capture of runaway slaves. Congress also enacted severe financial penalties upon U.S. marshals who had slaves escape while in their custody. Additionally, aiding a fugitive slave was now punishable by fines and imprisonment, and ordinary citizens who refused to help capture a fugitive slave could be charged with treason. While the law corrected the enforcement problems, it also helped to solidify opposition to slavery.

Northerners continued to ignore the law, especially **Quakers** who not only refused to acknowledge the legitimacy of the law, but who also were active in aiding runaway slaves. **Harriet Beecher Stowe**'s novel ***Uncle Tom's Cabin*** (1852) recounts both the abuses of the law by slave agents and the conflicts that many Northerners had over cooperating with authorities in the return of slaves. Many devout Christians believed that they could not follow the law and the requirements of their faith. **See also** Abolition; Race Relations; Slavery.

BIBLIOGRAPHY

May, Samuel. *The Fugitive Slave Law and Its Victims*. New York : American Anti-slavery Society, 1861.

Stowe, Harriet Beecher. *Uncle Tom's Cabin*. New York: Bantam Books, 1981.

Fundamental Orders of Connecticut (1639)

The first settlement of **Pilgrims** at Plymouth, Massachusetts, was founded in 1620, and by the next decade, some of the newer **Puritan** immigrants already felt that they were not being allowed enough influence. A pastor named **Thomas Hooker** (who arrived in 1633) believed that political power should not be restricted to a chosen few and that the right to vote should not be limited to church members. He petitioned the Massachusetts government for the right to settle in the Connecticut River valley. His church then provided the core of the first settlement at Hartford (1633), while later settlers (with ties to other churches) went to Saybrook (1635) and New Haven (1638).

The Massachusetts authorities permitted them to go on the condition that they remain under the government of Massachusetts. In 1639, they chose to go their own way, adopting a set of "Fundamental Orders" for their colony that were more democratic than those in Massachusetts. Only the governor was required to be a church member, and anyone who took the proper oath could vote. (The Fundamental Orders of Connecticut are reprinted in Appendix 1.) (MWP) **See also** Colonial America; Massachusetts Bay Colony.

BIBLIOGRAPHY

Kardell, Willmore and George W. Carey. *Basic Symbols*. Baton Rouge: Louisiana State University Press, 1972.

Fundamentalist-Modernist Controversy

The Fundamentalist-Modernist controversy was an extended struggle in the mainline Protestant denominations (Presbyterian, Methodist, Episcopalian, Northern Baptist, and Congregational/United Churches of Christ) between theological conservatives who sought doctrinal conformity and liberals (or Modernists) who sought to accommodate Christianity both to modern culture and to critical and scientific thought. The confrontation was waged from roughly the post-**Civil War** period until the 1930s. The name "Fundamentalist," first used in 1920, came from a series of booklets called *The Fundamentals* (published in 12 volumes between 1910–1915), which stressed the inerrancy of Scripture, premillennialism, and other central doctrines perceived as under threat from Modernism.

After the Civil War, the churches not only faced social challenges such as industrialization, urbanization, and immigration, but they also faced intellectual ones arising from Darwin's evolution theory, which challenged traditional understandings of creation, human nature, and the age of the world; from recent discoveries in the Middle East that challenged the accuracy of biblical accounts; from new advances in biblical criticism; and from the increasing awareness of other peoples and religions which questioned the exclusivity of Christianity. Conservative **Evangelicals** who were to become Fundamentalists reacted to attacks on premillennialism, the issue of commitment to the ecumenical movement of the post-World War I period, and the question of the nature of the church. Major figures in the Fundamentalist-Modernist controversy include, on the Fundamentalist side, **J. Gresham Machen**, Reuben A. Torrey, Isaac A. Haldeman, **William Jennings Bryan**, and James M. Gray, and on the Modernist side, Shailer Mathews and **Harry Emerson Fosdick**.

By the 1930s, the mainline churches had secured institutional unity, permitting doctrinal diversity, a solution that over the following decades was to lead to a loss of theological identity and to a subsequent blurring of the differences between American cultural values and those of the churches. Conservative Evangelicals generally withdrew from their churches at this time to found parallel denominations, complete with their own colleges, seminaries, publishing houses, and mission agencies. They eschewed any socio-political involvement because of their premillenialist beliefs, and adopted various counter-cultural practices. Thus, the end result of the Fundamentalist-Modernist controversy was the formation of a number of splinter Fundamentalist groups. (ISM) **See also** Baptists; Conservatism; Episcopal Church; Fundamentalists; Liberalism; Methodism; Millennialism; Presbyterian Church; United Church of Christ.

BIBLIOGRAPHY

Longstreet, Bradley J. *The Presbyterian Controversy: Fundamentalists, Modernists and Moderates*. New York: Oxford University Press, 1991.

Marsden, George M. *Fundamentalism and American Culture: The Shaping of Twentieth Century Evangelicalism, 1870–1925*. New York: Oxford University Press, 1980.

Sandeen, E. R. *The Roots of Fundamentalism: British and American Millenarianism, 1800–1930*. Chicago: University of Chicago Press, 1970.

Fundamentalists

Scholar George Marsden carefully defines a Fundamentalist as "an evangelical Protestant who is militantly opposed to modern liberal theologies and to some of secularism in modern culture." **Evangelicals** and Fundamentalists both believe three essential doctrines: (1) the supreme authority of the Bible for matters of faith; (2) salvation only through personal faith in the atoning death and resurrection of Jesus Christ; and (3) the Christian imperative to tell others about Jesus. A Fundamentalist regards much of modern society as secular and corrupt, a belief necessitating Fundamentalist withdrawal from mainstream society.

In the 1920s, conservative Protestants appropriated the Fundamentalist label in their struggle against theological liberals in the **Fundamentalist-Modernist controversy**. This coalition of revivalists, pietists, Calvinists, and holiness advocates generally abstained from political activity. Like their liberal Protestant brethren, they supported prohibition and opposed Catholic nominee **Alfred E. Smith** in the 1928 election. However, many Fundamentalists had adopted dispensational theology around the turn of the century and believed that the world was destined for destruction, thus they avoided political activity as a waste of time and resources. Exceptions did occur on the fringe of Fundamentalism; Gerald L. K. Smith, a **Disciples of Christ** minister in Louisiana and political advisor to populist governor Huey Long, and Gerald Winrod, founder of the Defenders of the Christian Faith, championed a number of anti-communist, anti-Semitic, and anti-**New Deal** causes with a limited degree of success.

After **World War II**, most Fundamentalists remained politically uninvolved. A few like **Carl McIntire**, **Billy James Hargis**, and Fred C. Schwartz actively opposed the formation of the United Nations and the World Council of Churches as communist threats to U.S. sovereignty. A number of moderate Fundamentalists began breaking away from the likes of McIntire in 1942. Men like **Carl F. H. Henry**, Harold Ockenga, and E. J. Carnell rejected Fundamentalism's militancy and cultural isolationism. They sought to proactively engage the culture and transform it with the gospel.

In the last half of the 1970s, many Fundamentalists were finally mobilized into political activity by the proposed **Equal Rights Amendment**, legalized **abortion**, the **homosexual rights** movement, and challenges to the independence of church-related schools. Most of the leaders in **Jerry Falwell**'s **Moral Majority** were Fundamentalists. By the 1980s, however, many Fundamentalists were disillusioned with politics because little had been done to advance their agenda on moral issues like abortion and **school prayer**. Some abandoned political activity; others joined the broadly evangelical **Christian Coalition** formed by **Pat Robertson**. Falwell himself disbanded the Moral Majority in 1989, though he continues to oppose President **Bill Clinton**'s social policies.

As a coalition of conservative Protestants, Fundamentalism brings together a number of inconsistent political tendencies. As dispensationalists, Fundamentalists tend to view the United States as wicked Babylon, but as heirs of nineteenth-century revivalism and Calvinism, they maintain the hope that the United States is a New **Israel**—a Christian nation established for the glory of God. Fundamentalism thus swings between isolationist pessimism and activistic triumphalism in its political ideology. While many Fundamentalists have wholeheartedly embraced their role as "players" in **Republican Party** politics, the diversity within the movement makes blanket generalizations somewhat suspect. (ARB) **See also** Anti-Catholicism; Anti-Semitism; Calvinism; Pietism.

BIBLIOGRAPHY

Marsden, George. *Fundamentalism and American Culture: The Shaping of Twentieth Century Evangelicalism, 1870–1925*. New York: Oxford University Press, 1980.

_______. *Religion and American Culture*. San Diego: Harcourt, Brace and Jovanovich, 1990.

Neuhaus, Richard J. and Michael Cromartie, eds. *Piety and Politics: Evangelicals and Fundamentalists Confront the World*. Washington, D.C.: Ethics and Public Policy Center, 1987.

Noll, Mark A., ed. *Religion and American Politics: From the Colonial Period to the 1980s*. New York: Oxford University Press, 1990.

William Lloyd Garrison (1805–1879)

Abolitionist and reformer William Lloyd Garrison used his abilities as a writer and organizer to lead the **American Anti-Slavery Society** in a fight to free American slaves. Deserted at two by an intemperate father, Garrison came under the care of Deacon Ezekiel Bartlett. Apprenticed to a newspaper editor, he learned how to write and publish. Although most famous for his anti-slavery efforts, Garrison also wrote against intemperance, lotteries, **war**, and Sabbath-breaking. He was also publisher of the *Liberator*, an abolitionist newspaper that constantly called for the complete and immediate emancipation of all slaves. He used religion and morality in his arguments against **slavery**. He warned listeners of "the terrible judgment of an incensed God" and attacked American churches for compromising with slavery. Garrison advocated withdrawal from political participation until a more just government was formed. Once the **Civil War** started, however, he saw an opportunity to reform the South through the prosecution of the war. (GT) **See also** Abolition; Sabbatarianism; Temperance and Prohibition.

Bibliography

Cain, William, ed. *William Lloyd Garrison and the Fight Against Slavery: Selections from The Liberator*. Boston: Bedford Books of St. Martin's Press, 1995.

Chapman, John. *William Lloyd Garrison*. New York: Beekman Publishers, 1974.

Marcus Garvey (1887–1940)

Marcus Garvey advocated that blacks return to Africa and establish a black nation. Born in Jamaica, Garvey moved to the United States in 1916 and established chapters of his organization, the United Negro Improvement Association (UNIA), in northern urban ghettos. Using black churches to assemble large audiences, Garvey appealed to his followers by exalting everything black and by insisting that blacks should be proud of their heritage. Garvey founded the African Orthodox Church and encouraged other blacks to form all-black churches with black images of Christ. At its peak, the UNIA had an estimated 500,000 members; however, membership declined quickly after Garvey was convicted of mail fraud. After serving two years in prison, Garvey was deported in 1927. He died in London in 1940. While Garveyism largely fell apart after his deportation, many of his ideas and teachings resurfaced in the black power and black nationalist movements of the **Nation of Islam**. (WVM) **See also** African-American Churches; Race Relations.

Bibliography

Cronon, Edmund D. *Black Moses*. 2nd ed. Madison: University of Wisconsin Press, 1969.

James Gibbons (1834–1921)

As a **Civil War** chaplain, bishop (1868), Baltimore's archbishop (1877), and North America's second cardinal (1886), James Gibbons was one of the most influential Catholics in the U.S. in the nineteeth century. In 1917, former President **Theodore Roosevelt** would number him among the country's most respected citizens, perhaps because of the strong support Gibbons gave Maryland Republicans in 1910 when the state's **Democratic Party** tried to deprive black people of the right to vote. Gibbons also spoke favorably of the compatibility of **Roman Catholicism** and American **democracy**. He also spoke extensively about the declining moral culture he witnessed, including increases in **divorce**, political corruption, and materialism. His 1876 *The Faith of Our Fathers* was enormously popular among Catholics and he devoted much energy to ensuring that the Catholic University of America provided quality **education**. (MWP) **See also** Chaplaincy; Republican Party.

Bibliography

Ellis, John T. *The Life of James Cardinal Gibbons*. Milwaukee: Bruce, 1952.

Girouard v. United States (1946)

Girouard v. United States, 328 U.S. 61 (1946), involved a native of Canada who filed a petition for naturalization and who was willing to take the oath of allegiance, but who replied "No" to the question, "Are you willing to take up arms in defense of this country?" As a **Seventh-Day Adventist**, Girouard's religious convictions did not allow him to bear arms for any reason. Girouard was initially accepted for citizenship, but a court of appeals reversed that decision, citing his unwillingness to serve in the military. However, the U.S. Supreme Court ruled that Girouard should be granted citizenship and that "one could be attached to the principles of our government and could support and defend it even though his religious convictions prevented him from bearing arms." (JM) **See also** Conscientious Objection; Military Service; War.

BIBLIOGRAPHY

Bowser, Anita. "The Meaning of Religion in the Constitution." Unpublished Ph.D. Dissertation, University of Notre Dame, 1976.

Regan, Richard J. *Private Conscience and Public Law*. New York: Fordham University Press, 1972.

Solomon Washington Gladden (1836–1918)

Known as "the father of the **Social Gospel** movement," Solomon Washington Gladden wrote 36 books analyzing the labor and taxation issues of the late nineteenth and early twentieth centuries. He critiqued **capitalism** as overly competitive and socially unjust, and advocated a more socialized economy, with public ownership of utilities, cooperative management of most industries, and profit-sharing among workers and managers.

A Congregational minister in Massachusetts and then Ohio, Gladden argued that churches should hold the American economy to biblical principles of justice, both through their own economic practices and by agitating for social change. In response to the violent **labor** disputes that erupted in 1870, he agitated for the development of strong labor unions. His most famous books, *Applied Christianity* (1886) and *Social Salvation* (1902), argued for a socially conscious Protestant faith that understood the relationship between work and salvation in terms of justice and mercy. Unlike many of his contemporaries, Gladden supported outlawed amusements like dancing, bowling, and card-playing as appropriate recreational activities for laborers and their families. He believed that churches should spend less time judging individual sins and more time addressing social injustice and public corruption. (KMY) **See also** Congregationalism; Social Justice; Socialism and Communism.

BIBLIOGRAPHY

Gladden, Washington. *Applied Christianity: Moral Aspects of Social Questions*. New York: Arno Press, 1976.

Goldman v. Weinberger (1986)

In *Goldman v. Weinberger*, 475 U.S. 503 (1986), the plaintiff was an Orthodox Jew, an ordained rabbi, and an Air Force officer. He requested permission to wear a yarmulke on his head while in uniform. His request was denied because it violated Air Force policy, which stated that anything worn as a form of religious expression must not be visible to the casual observer. The Supreme Court upheld the Air Force policy saying that the courts must give broad professional discretion to the leadership of the military branches in maintaining the discipline and order required for maximum efficiency. (FHJ) **See also** Judaism; Military Service.

BIBLIOGRAPHY

Chazin, Daniel D. "Goldman v. Secretary of State: A New Standard for Free Exercise Claims in the Military?" *National Jewish Law Review Annual* 1 (1986): 13–40.

Gospel of Wealth

The Gospel of Wealth, a theory of God's influence on human progress, was best articulated by industrialist Andrew Carnegie in his June 1889 article, "Wealth." Carnegie argued that it was beneficial to society for wealth to be in the hands of a few who could then be sure that it was spent wisely and on good works. Carnegie believed that it was God's plan that a few have wealth so that they could provide for others. The themes of Carnegie's article were echoed in other writings, including **Russell Conwell**'s sermon *Acres of Diamonds,* which stated that wealth was a sign of godliness. The Gospel of Wealth served two purposes. First, it justified the immense holdings of a few individuals. Second, it called for philanthropy on the part of those few wealthy individuals. (Carnegie's "Gospel of Wealth" is reprinted in Appendix 1.)

BIBLIOGRAPHY

Carnegie, Andrew. *The Gospel of Wealth and Other Timely Essays*. Cambridge MA: Belknap Press, 1962.

Grand Rapids School District v. Ball. See *Aguilar v. Felton*.

Billy Graham (1918–)

A Southern **Baptist** minister, Billy Graham has become one of the most respected figures in the **Evangelical** movement since **World War II**. He is best known for his citywide revival crusades and his influential radio and televisions programs.

He began his career with Youth for Christ in 1945, and by 1956, he was administering a $2 million annual budget for advertising, television and radio programming, and books and videos, all delivering a message of personal salvation and good citizenship. Graham urges Christians to support a strong civil role for religion as a means of developing and supporting an exemplary Christian nation.

Graham regards personal reformation as the primary route to social renewal, and most of his sermons place a great deal of emphasis on the avoidance of personal sins. He regularly preaches against **abortion**, adultery, **divorce**, racial prejudice, and greed. He supports **capital punishment**, opposes **pornography**, and urges parents to place their families above their careers.

During the Cold War years, he characterized communism as the avowed enemy of America, God, and the Bible. The current enemy, according to Graham, is **secular humanism**, which he characterizes as a prevailing belief in the secular self-determination of individuals.

His status as a spokesperson for the Evangelical movement and his public popularity has earned him significant access to every U.S. president since Harry Truman. **Richard Nixon** claimed that praying with Billy Graham prompted him to seek the presidency, and Graham's announcement that he had voted by absentee ballot for Nixon was front-page news prior to the general election in 1968 and may have assisted Nixon in winning. During the 1980s, Graham became controversial among his core constituency because of a trip to the Soviet Union. Allowed to preach at pre-arranged meetings, Graham made comments suggesting that the Soviet Union afforded religious liberty to its citizens. A self-professed Democrat, Graham also sparked controversy in the 1990s due to his warm personal support of President **Bill Clinton**. Congress awarded Graham and his wife Ruth a Congressional Gold Medal in 1996 for their lifetime of service and integrity. (KMY) **See also** Blue Laws; Civil Religion; Homosexual Rights; Sabbatarianism; Socialism and Communism; Southern Baptist Convention; Televangelism.

BIBLIOGRAPHY

Barnhart, Joe E. *The Billy Graham Religion*. Philadelphia: United Church Press, 1972.

Graham, Billy. *Just As I Am: The Autobiography of Billy Graham*. Grand Rapids, MI: Zondervan: 1997.

Andrew Greeley (1928–)

A Roman Catholic priest, Andrew Greeley has focused on Catholics' dissatisfaction with their church. In a 1969 article in *American Ecclesiastical Review*, Greeley pointed out that no systematic research about why priests leave the priesthood had been done and offered his own reasons why. In his 1985 *American Catholics since the Council,* he examined changes in Catholic laity since **Vatican II**. A prolific writer and social critic, Greeley has authored a number of best-selling books, including *Original Sin* and *Cardinal Virtues*, and was instrumental in the controversial television show *Something Sacred*. Greeley hopes through his creative talents to do more than entertain. He seeks to show God's presence even in the lives of his fictional characters. Greeley has been controversial because of his fiction, which is often regarded as "pop porn." A professor emeritus of sociology at the University of Chicago, Greeley continues to study the changing dynamics of the Catholic Church and American vice. (MWP) **See also** Roman Catholicism.

BIBLIOGRAPHY

Greeley, Andrew. *American Catholics since the Council*. Chicago: Thomas Moore Press, 1985.

Shafer, Ingrid H., ed. *The Incarnate Imagination*. Bowling Green, OH: Bowling Green State University Press, 1988.

John Green (1953–)

With colleagues James Guth, Lyman Kellstedt, and Corwin Smidt, John Green has pioneered the quantitative study of how religion shapes American political behavior. As head of the Bliss Institute at the University of Akron, Green has also directed numerous national surveys on religion and politics. Green has argued that the growing political polarization based on religious affiliations is likely to continue because of a collapse of the religious center. (JSF) **See also** Culture War.

BIBLIOGRAPHY

Green, John C., James L. Guth, Corwin Smidt, and Lyman A. Kellstedt. *Religion and the Culture Wars: Dispatches from the Front*. Lanham, MD: Rowman & Littlefield, 1996.

Guth, James L., John C. Green, Corwin E. Smidt, Lyman A Kellstedt, and Margaret M. Poloma. *The Bully Pulpit: The Politics of Protestant Clergy*. Lawrence: University Press of Kansas, 1997.

Sarah Grimke (1792–1873) and Angelina Grimke (1805–1879)

The daughters of a wealthy slave-owning judge in Charleston, South Carolina, Sarah and Angelina Grimke became two of the most important opponents of **slavery** in the antebellum U.S. Because of their first-hand knowledge of the evils of slavery, they were well received in the North as public speakers for **abolition**.

Raised as Anglicans, Sarah became a **Quaker** and moved to Philadelphia in 1821. Angelina joined her sister in 1829, and both siblings adopted the Quaker denomination's opposition to slavery. Angelina's 1836 pamphlet, *Appeal to Christian Women of the South*, and her sister's pamphlet, *An Epistle to the Clergy of the Southern States* (1836), brought the sisters to national attention. Afterwards, they maintained an active schedule, speaking and teaching on behalf of abolition.

In 1837, the General Association of Congregationalist Ministers of Massachusetts attacked the sisters for teaching to mixed audiences. In response to the association, Angelina wrote a series of letters for **William Lloyd Garrison**'s *Liberator* and Sarah published the pamphlet, *Letters on the Equality of the Sexes and the Condition of Woman*, works considered among the most important early defenses of women's rights.

In 1838, Angelina married the abolitionist **Theodore Weld**. Worried by anti-abolitionist rioting, both sisters retired from the lecture circuit, but remained active in a variety of **education** and reform movements. (Angelina Grimke's *Appeal to Christian Women* is reprinted in Appendix 1.) (MDH) **See also** Congregationalism; Feminism; Women in Religion and Politics.

BIBLIOGRAPHY

Lerner, Gerda. *The Grimke Sisters from South Carolina: Rebels against Slavery*. New York: Houghton Mifflin, 1967.

Lumkin, Katharine Du Pre. *The Emancipation of Angelina Grimke*. Chapel Hill: University of North Carolina Press, 1974.

H

Francis Joseph Haas (1889–1953)

A Catholic sociologist and priest, Francis Haas was dean of the Catholic University of America's School of Social Science and held several posts under Franklin Roosevelt's **New Deal**. An expert on **labor**, he was a member of the Labor Advisory Board from 1933 until he moved to the Department of Labor in 1935 as a state mediator. He brought to his labor posts a deep commitment to **social justice**. Writing extensively on labor, he argued that economic **slavery** was the main reason people failed to excercise freedom. In 1943, he was appointed bishop of Grand Rapids, Michigan, where he served until his death. (MWP) **See also** Roman Catholicism.

Bibliography

Haas, Francis Joseph. *Man and Society*. New York: Appleton - Century-Crofts, 1952.

Haas, Francis Joseph. *Shop Collective Bargaining*. Washington, DC: Catholic University of America: 1922.

Alexander Hamilton (1755–1804)

Alexander Hamilton was one of the most influential American Founding Fathers. With **James Madison**, Hamilton was one of the two chief authors of the most famous defense and exposition of the Constitution, *The Federalist Papers*. Hamilton's thought informs almost every aspect of U.S. political life. Although religion was not among the most prominent themes in his work, Hamilton's influence extends into that realm in which politics and religion meet. Hamilton authored what is perhaps the classic American statement on the necessary reliance upon religion of any decent system of politics. In a draft written for **George Washington** to employ in his Farewell Address, Hamilton submitted the following statement, which Washington used almost verbatim: "To all those dispositions which promote political happiness [and] prosperity, Religion and Morality are essential props. In vain does that man claim the praise of patriotism who labors to subvert or undermine these great pillars of human happiness [,] these firmest foundations of the duties of men and citizens." Hamilton returned to the importance of religion for politics in a series of essays entitled *The Stand*, which he wrote to condemn the anti-religious character of the **French Revolution**. Towards the end of his life, he also proposed the formation of a "Christian Constitutional Society" whose objects were to be the simultaneous promotion of Christian and constitutional principles. (SJL) **See also** American Revolution; Civil Religion; Colonial America; Thomas Jefferson; Washington's Farewell Address.

Bibliography

Hamilton, Alexander, John Jay, and James Madison. *The Federalist Papers*. Clinton Rossiter, ed. New York: Mentor Books, 1961.

Hamilton, Alexander. *Selected Writings and Speeches*. Morton J. Frisch, ed. Washington, DC: American Enterprise Institute, 1985.

McDonald, Forrest. *Alexander Hamilton: A Biography*. New York: Norton, 1979.

Hamilton v. Regents of the University of California (1934)

Hamilton v. Regents of the University of California, 293 U.S. 245 (1934), involved a California law that required students at the state university to take a course in military science and tactics. A number of student members of the Methodist Episcopal Church, which renounces violence and military training, refused to take these courses, petitioning unsuccessfully for military training to be made optional so that conscientious and religious objectors to war and military training might not be confronted with the choice of violating and forswearing their beliefs or being denied the right of **education**. The regents refused to make military training optional or to exempt these students, and when they declined to take the course, they were suspended. Although the U.S. Supreme Court accepted that the liberty protected by the Constitution "does include the right to entertain the beliefs, to adhere to the principles, and to teach the doctrines on which these students base their objections to the order prescribing military training," it affirmed the actions of the regents, stating, "There is no ground for the contention that the regents' order, requiring able-bodied male students under the age of twenty-four as a condition of their enrollment to take the prescribed instruction in military science and tactics, transgresses any constitutional right." (JM) **See also** Conscientious Objection; Methodism; Military Service.

Bibliography

Bowser, Anita. "The Meaning of Religion in the Constitution." Unpublished Ph.D. Dissertation, University of Notre Dame, 1976.

Regan, Richard J. *Private Conscience and Public Law*. New York: Fordham University Press, 1972.

Handsome Lake (1735–1815)

Handsome Lake was a Seneca Indian chief who in 1799, after a series of visions, founded a religion blending Christian and Native American beliefs along with bans on alcohol and witchcraft. In one of the visions in 1800, Handsome Lake met **George Washington** and Jesus who advised Lake on how to deal with the pervasive white culture. The religion encouraged farming and family life. Known as the "Longhouse Religion" or "the Old Way of Handsome Lake," the religion is still the basis for Iroquois religious life. It is the oldest prophetic religion in North America. (MWP) **See also** Native American Religions; Temperance and Prohibition.

Bibliography

Wallace, Anthony F. C. *The Death and Rebirth of the Seneca*. New York: Vintage, 1972.

Billy James Hargis (1925–)

A radical **Fundamentalist** preacher from Oklahoma, Billy Hargis founded Christian Echoes National Ministry to mobilize conservative Protestants against atheistic communism in the years following **World War II**. Hargis's motto was, "For Christ and Against Communism." He effectively used television and radio to expand his ministry and published *The Christian Crusade*, a leading anti-communist newspaper. Speaking for many disaffected white Southerners, he combined his anti-communism stance with active opposition to the **civil rights** movement. In 1973, Christian Echoes lost its tax exempt status because of its substantial involvement in political activities, and Hargis's ministry largely disappeared after rumors of personal scandal surfaced in 1974. (ARB) **See also** Atheism; Socialism and Communism; Televangelism.

Bibliography

Hargis, Billy James. *Communist America—Must It Be?* Tulsa, OK: Christian Crusade, 1960.

Redekop, John H. *The American Far Right: A Case Study of Billy James Hargis and Christian Crusade*. Grand Rapids, MI: W. B. Eerdmans, 1968.

Harris v. McRae (1980)

A number of groups, including the Women's Division of the Board of Global Ministries of the United Methodist Church, sought to enjoin enforcement of the **Hyde Amendment**'s prohibition against the use of Medicaid funds to pay for medically necessary abortions on the grounds that the amendment violated the Equal Protection Clause of the Fifth Amendment and the **Free Exercise Clause** of the **First Amendment**. In *Harris v. McRae*, 448 U.S. 297 (1980), the Supreme Court disagreed, claiming that such a prohibition does "not impinge on the 'liberty' protected by the Due Process Clause of the Fifth Amendment held in ***Roe v. Wade***." (JM) **See also** Abortion; Methodism; Women in Religion and Politics.

Bibliography

Bennett, Robert W. "Abortion and Judicial Review" *Northwestern University Law Review* 75, no. 6 (February 1981): 978–1017.

Gold, Jay A. "Does the Hyde Amendment Violate Religious Freedom?" *American Journal of Law and Medicine* 6, no. 3 (Fall 1980): 361–72.

Mark O. Hatfield (1922–)

A devout **Baptist** and Republican U.S. Senator from Oregon from 1967 to 1997, Mark Hatfield's politics were influenced by his deep religious beliefs, which often put him in opposition to his party. During his tenure in the Senate, for example, he opposed U.S. involvement in **Vietnam**, the development of nuclear weapons, and the 1991 Persian Gulf War. In 1996, he cast a historic vote against the Balanced Budget Amendment, which failed to pass the Senate by a single vote. Hatfield has often been at odds with the religious right preferring the more liberal politics of Jim Wallis with whom he served as a contributing editor of *Sojourners*. (JRV) **See also** Nuclear Disarmament; Republican Party; Sojourners.

Bibliography

Hager, George. "Liberal in a Lean Season." *Congressional Quarterly Weekly Report* 53 (May 20, 1995): 1367.

Stanley Hauerwas (1940–)

Stanley Hauerwas is a Christian ethicist at Duke University who argues for a communitarian ethic in reaction against the dominant Protestant liberal tradition of understanding ethics in terms of individual autonomy. His project is undertaken in mutual collaboration with the philosopher, **Alasdair MacIntyre**, with whom he edited *Revisions: Changing Perspectives in Moral Philosophy* (1983). According to Hauerwas, the ethical is only comprehensible through a community's narrative. In his anthropology, individuals do not exist in isolation as modern political liberalism assumes, but rather within formative moral communities whose narrative provides notions of the common good. Thus, he rejects mainline churches' atomistic involvement in the socio-political process. (ISM) **See also** Communitarianism; Liberalism.

Bibliography

Hauerwas, Stanley. *A Community of Character*. Notre Dame, IN: University of Notre Dame Press, 1983.

Rasmusson, Arne. *The Church as Polis: From Political Theology to Theological Politics as Exemplified by Jurgen Moltmann and Stanley Hauerwas*. Studia Theologica Lundensia vol. 49. Lund, Sweden: Lund University Press, 1994.

Rutherford B. Hayes (1822–1893)

Rutherford B. Hayes was the 19th president of the United States. Born in Delaware, Ohio, he graduated from Kenyon College in 1842 and earned a law degree from Harvard. He was one of the activists who helped form the **Republican Party** in Ohio. During the **Civil War**, he served in the 23rd Ohio Volunteer Infantry. As a young officer and devout Christian, Hayes regularly attended prayer meetings. He saw himself as not only a soldier for his country but also as a "soldier of Jesus."

After the war, Hayes was elected to Congress and served from 1865 to 1867. As a congressman, he was aligned with the Radical Republicans. In 1867, he was elected governor of Ohio in a close election. Re-elected in 1869, he followed custom and refused to run for a third term. He was living in Fremont, Ohio, when the Ohio Republicans called on him to run for a third term as governor in 1875, and he was elected.

At the Republican National Convention of 1876, Hayes was nominated on the seventh ballot. He was elected president in one of the most corrupt elections in U.S. history. The Republicans controlled the election boards in three disputed southern states and gave the electoral votes from those states to Hayes. The South accepted Hayes's election because he promised to withdraw federal troops, which he did, and because he brought an end to **Reconstruction**. While in the White House, Hayes's wife—a prohibitionist—earned the nickname "Lemonade Lucy" because she insisted on serving nonalcoholic drinks at official state functions. While in office, Hayes did not regularly attend religious services, although he knelt and prayed every morning at breakfast and held hymn sings on Sunday evenings. Hayes did not seek a second term in 1880 and retired to his home in Fremont. (WB) **See also** Democratic party; Temperance and Prohibition.

During the Civil War, Rutherford B. Hayes, a future Republican president of the United States, wrote that he was a "Soldier of Jesus." Library of Congress.

Bibliography

Hogenboom, Ari. *The Presidency of Rutherford B. Hayes*. Lawrence: University Press of Kansas, 1988.

Isaac Thomas Hecker (1819–1888)

An early spiritual wanderer, Isaac Hecker experimented with many religious denominations, including spending time at Brook Farm, a transcendentalist utopian commune, in 1843 where he experimented with **Transcendentalism**. In 1844, he converted to **Roman Catholicism** and was ordained in 1849. After serving as a missionary, Hecker was offered the post of bishop of Natchez, Mississippi. Infighting within his Redemptionist order led him to found a uniquely American order. In 1857, he traveled to Rome, and with the approval of Pope Pius IX, founded the Paulist Fathers. He was an outspoken advocate of the compatibility of **democracy** and Roman Catholicism. He even considered the founding of an American Catholic Church in response to the **Americanism** problem. (MWP) **See also** Communitarianism; Utopianism.

Bibliography

Farina, John. *An American Experience of God*. New York: Paulist Press, 1981.

Holden, Vincent F. *A Yankee Paul: Isaac Thomas Hecker*. Milwaukee: Bruce, 1958.

Carl F.H. Henry (1913–)

Theologian Carl Henry is a central figure in the twentieth-century resurgence of **Evangelicals** in American politics. In an explosive book, *The Uneasy Conscience of Modern Fundamentalism* (1947), Henry insisted that self-imposed separatism by Evangelicals violated "God's creation-ethic" and the "biblical mandate" to seek justice—a mandate based on the lordship of Christ, the stewardship of creation, and the servanthood of believers. As founding editor of ***Christianity Today***, Henry reiterated this message to an increasingly receptive audience during the 1950s and 1960s.

Henry emphasizes divine revelation rather than **natural law** as the source of enduring principles for a just social order. The scriptural truths that he finds applicable to politics include social problems result from sin; only spiritual regeneration transforms humanity; **social justice** is demanded of all; human rights have a divine source and sanction; church and state are divinely willed institutions with different purposes; and believers are "citizens of two worlds" with a "sacred duty to. . . extend God's purpose of justice and order."

Henry advises political activists to exemplify moderation, toleration, and cooperation and to avoid stridency, intolerance, and fanaticism. Critical of utopian expectations, confrontational tactics, and single-issue campaigns, Henry urges Christians to formulate a persuasive public philosophy and to work through and in obedience to government. (DW) **See also** Utopianism.

Bibliography

Henry, Carl F.H. *Has Democracy Had Its Day?* Nashville, TN: ERLC Publications, 1996.

Weeks, David L. *The Political Thought of Carl F. H. Henry.* Unpublished Ph.D. dissertation, Loyola University of Chicago, 1991.

Patrick Henry (1736–1799)

Patrick Henry is justly famous for his oratory skills, particularly the celebrated climax to a 1775 speech before the Virginia assembly in which he declared, "but as for me, give me liberty, or give me death!" He first gained prominence as a lawyer opposing the Anglican clergy in the "Parsons Cause" (1763). Henry used the case, which concerned the constitutionality of legislation giving the vestry the right to fix the price of tobacco with which the established clergy were paid, to discourse on the proper relationship between the clergy and the community and also to condemn what he perceived to be tyranny in both church and state. Henry proposed to the Virginia legislature "A Bill establishing a provision for Teachers of the

Christian Religion" (1785), which was ultimately defeated by the efforts of **George Mason** and **James Madison** and resulted in the latter's **"Memorial and Remonstrance Against Religious Assessments"** (1785). (JHM) **See also** American Revolution; Colonial America.

BIBLIOGRAPHY

Campbell, N.D. *Patrick Henry: Patriot and Statesman.* Old Greenwich, CT: Devin-Adair, 1969.

Paul B. Henry (1942–1993)

Paul Henry was a Christian political scientist and moderate Michigan Republican congressman who opposed aid to the Nicaraguan Contras and nuclear testing. A leading theologian's son, Henry taught at Calvin College, and served in the U.S. House of Representatives from 1984 to 1993. While in the House, he sought to bar funding of the **National Endowment for the Arts (NEA)** for offensive art, but not all funding. Prior to his service in the House, Henry served in the Michigan state house (1978-1982) and state senate (1982-1984). (JVS) **See also** Evangelicals; Nuclear Disarmament; Republican Party.

BIBLIOGRAPHY

Henry, Paul B. *Politics for Evangelicals.* Valley Forge, PA: Judson Press, 1974.

Hernandez v. Commissioner (1989)

The Church of Scientology provides auditing sessions designed to increase members' spiritual awareness. Pursuant to a central tenet known as the Doctrine of Exchange, the church has mandatory fixed prices for these auditing sessions. Members of the church deducted such payments on their federal income tax returns as charitable contributions. The IRS disallowed these deductions, and the Supreme Court affirmed this ruling in *Hernandez v. Commissioner*, 490 U.S. 680 (1989), on the grounds that there is a difference "between unrequited payments to qualified recipients, which are deductible, and payments made to such recipients with some expectation of a quid pro quo in terms of goods or services, which are not deductible." (JM)

BIBLIOGRAPHY

Eaton, Alison H. "Can the IRS Overrule the Supreme Court?" *Emory Law Journal* 45, no. 3 (Summer 1996): 987–1034.

Geier, Mark. "What the Good Lord Giveth, Uncle Sam Taketh Away." *Hamline Law Review* 13, no. 2 (Spring 1990): 433–61.

Higher Law Theory

The belief that there are moral principles that override human laws can appear in many contexts. In the United States, one of the earliest and most important manifestations of higher law theory occurred during the debate over **slavery**. With revivalistic zeal and ideas derived from Old Testament prophets, some abolitionists denounced the Constitution and any law that supported slavery.

Abolitionists who believed in a higher law did not mince words. In his 1852 *The Higher Law in Its Relation to Civil Government*, William Hosmer wrote that, "the fact that a law is constitutional amounts to nothing" and warned that the only way "to escape the wrath of God" was to deliberately disobey such laws. By polarizing the debate over slavery, the higher law theory gave new vitality to the anti-slavery movement. It also hardened attitudes in the South. President **Abraham Lincoln**'s Second Inaugural Address reflects elements of higher law theory.

Higher law theory has been used in other areas besides slavery. Pacifists rely on higher law to justify their refusal to serve in the military. Pro-life activists also have employed higher law theory to explain their opposition to **abortion**.

Government usually faces the challenge of addressing higher law claims by ignoring them. This has especially been the case in terms of rights or duties based upon religious tenets. The government has generally tried to take the route of neutrality so as to avoid the issue. Neutrality on the part of the government then requires one of two responses by claimants. Either they must suffer the consequencs of breaking the law or they must submit to the law. (MWP) **See also** Abolition; Military Service; Natural Law; Pacifism.

BIBLIOGRAPHY

Cromartie, Michael, ed. *A Preserving Grace: Protestants, Catholics, and Natural Law.* Grand Rapids, MI: Eerdmans, 1997.

Gerber, Scott Douglas. *To Secure These Rights: The Declaration of Independence and Constitutional Interpretation.* New York: New York University Press, 1995.

Hinduism

One of the world's major religions, Hinduism is a complex mixture of social, cultural, and philosophical concepts that originated in India. In the United States, Hinduism has remained a relatively small and largely counter-cultural religion with little impact on politics. American knowledge of Hinduism can be traced back as far as 1721, when **Cotton Mather** wrote *India Christiania*. However, Hinduism did not garner much attention in the United States until the nineteenth century, when transcendentalists like **Ralph Waldo Emerson** and **Henry David Thoreau** reflected some Hindu influence in their works. Hinduism did not attract substantial numbers of American adherents until the 1960s. Largely driven by the counter-culture (which in this case meant counter-Christian culture), many young people were attracted to Hinduism. The two most influential Hindu movements are the transcendental meditation movement (a combination of Hindu philosophy and yoga) of Maharishi Mahesh Yogi and the International Society for Krishna Consciousness (devotees of the Hindu god Krishna) of A.C. Bhaktivedanta Swami Prabhupada.

Religious toleration towards Hinduism has varied. While more than 500,000 Americans have experimented with transcendental meditation and yoga, the number of committed adherents is relatively low. Although more than 60 Krishna temples are found in the U.S., Americans have largely seen

Krishnas as a **cult** because of the striking appearance of adherents (shaved heads and saffron robes) and the group's aggressive recruitment practices.

Perhaps the most direct connection between Hinduism and American politics in recent years has been the effort by followers of Maharishi Mahesh Yogi to found an alternative political party, The Natural Law Party. The Natural Law Party has fielded candidates at the local, state, and national levels, thus far without much success. During the 1970s, the followers of Maharishi Mahesh Yogi became involved in a controversy over the introduction of Transcendental Meditation into public school classrooms. Eventually a federal appellate court struck down the practice as violative of the **Establishment Clause** in *Malnak v. Yogi*, 592 F. 2d 197 (1979). **See also** Transcendentalism.

Bibliography

Fenton, John Y. *Transplanting Religious Traditions*. New York: Praeger, 1988.

Rochford, E. Burke. Hare *Krishna in America*. New Brunswick, NJ: Rutgers University Press, 1985.

Holocaust

The Holocaust is the common term for the systematic persecution and extermination of European Jewry carried out by the Nazis in Germany and its occupied territories from 1933 to 1945. Adolf Hitler created the illusion that the Jewish people were a primary factor in the economic depression Germany suffered in the 1920s and 1930s; as a result, the Jews became one of several Nazi political scapegoats, along with communists, homosexuals, and others.

In the early days of Nazi rule, Jewish citizens had their businesses boycotted, lost their jobs, and, in 1935, lost their German citizenship and the right to marry Germans from other ethnic groups. On the night of November 9–10, 1938, known as *Kristallnacht*, Josef Goebbels led the Nazis in the vandalism and destruction of Jewish synagogues and businesses.

On the eastern front in **World War II**, the Nazis' solution to the "Jewish question" was to have the SS death squads kill entire Polish and Soviet Jewish populations in the towns they conquered. This met with some uneasiness among troops and some sectors of the public. In January 1942, the leading members of the Nazi Party met at the Wannsee conference. The chief result of the conference was the enactment of the "final solution" policy. Jews were rounded up and sent to concentration camps for execution.

The conflict on the European continent ended on May 8, 1945, but by then an estimated 4,000,000 Jews had been murdered in the concentration camps and approximately 6,000,000 (approximately one-third of the world's Jewish population) had been killed during the course of the war.

The staggering loss to the Jewish community in the Holocaust resulted in major political developments. In the aftermath of World War II, the United States and many in the Jewish community supported a Zionist movement that led to the United Nations vote in 1947 to partition the land of Palestine. The state of **Israel** was officially declared on May 14, 1948. The Jewish community and the United Nations has concentrated on bringing Nazi war criminals to justice for crimes committed during the war. The Holocaust also had a profound theological effect on the Jewish community and it has been a major factor in the development of Jewish thought, and to a lesser extent, Christian theology. Jewish responses have ranged from the "death of God" philosophy (Richard Rubenstein), the appeal to the mystery and silence of God (Elie Wiesel), redescription of what God is (Arthur Cohen), and an appeal to a new revelation of God (Emil Fackenheim). Christian theologians have also responded to the Holocaust by condemning **anti-Semitism**, and participating in inter-religious dialogue with the Jewish community. This has been a positive sign for the Christian Church, since the German Christian movement supported Hitler and the responses of the American Churches proved to be ineffective during World War II. (DH) **See also** Homosexual Rights; Judaism; Socialism and Communism; Zionism.

Bibliography

Browning, Christopher R. *Fateful Months: Essays on the Emergence of the Final Solution.* New York: Holmes & Meier, 1985.

Ellis, Mark H., and Roesmary R. Ruether, eds. *Beyond Occupation: American Jewish, Christian, and Palestinian Voices for Peace.* Boston: Beacon, 1990.

Goldhagen, Daniel J. *Hitler's Willing Executioners: Ordinary Germans and the Holocaust.* New York: Vintage, 1996.

Hilberg, Raul. *The Destruction of the European Jews.* New York: Holmes & Meier, 1985.

Wyman, D.S. *The Abandonment of the Jews: America and the Holocaust, 1941–1945.* New York: Pantheon, 1985.

Home Schooling

Home schooling, the practice of educating one's children at home instead of in public or private schools, is a growing trend in U.S. society. In **colonial America**, almost all children were home schooled. When public schools were started, they were often a way of instilling moral as well as intellectual discipline. In the 1880s, the compulsory attendance movement began in conjunction with child **labor** laws. Those promoting this viewpoint argued that the state had a "compelling interest" to assure that all children received an **education** to become productive citizens. Schools also became more secularized at this time as public schools became taxpayer-supported tools for **democracy** and social change.

In the 1960s, the separation of church and state became more formalized, and it became illegal for public schools to provide religious education, including reading the Bible or praying in school. This ruling started a large movement towards Christian schooling, and many private schools began providing this type of education. With the marked increase in enforced, compulsory, state-sponsored secular education came the dissenting viewpoints of people who wanted an educational alternative.

An estimated 1.3 million students are being home schooled in the United States. Reasons for deciding to home school range from wanting to keep the family in close proximity to fear or distrust of public schooling, and personal political or religious beliefs. Parents who want their children raised in a Christian environment often want to educate their children in a more religious manner than that afforded by public schools. It is estimated that over 85 percent of homeschoolers choose to educate their children at home for primarily religious reasons. In 1990, 50 percent of homeschoolers had received some public or private schooling prior to being home schooled, and the average homeschooler tested in the low 80th percentile in national standardized tests.

The Supreme Court ruled that the right to educate one's children is guaranteed by the Bill of Rights and made applicable to the states by the First and **Fourteenth Amendments**. In ***Wisconsin v. Yoder*** (1972), an **Amish** family's **First Amendment** protection from mandatory public education based on their religious orientation was upheld. Subsequent rulings have broadened the legal reasons for home schooling to include other nonreligious belief systems. Home schooling is legal in all 50 states, although it is often heavily regulated with regards to what credentials teachers must have, what educational standards must be met, and the minimum number of days or hours of instruction that is required. (JCW) **See also** School Prayer.

Bibliography

Farris, Michael. *Home Schooling and the Law*. Washington, DC: Home School Legal Defense Association, 1990.

Gorder, Cheryl. *Home Schools: An Alternative*. Columbus, OH: Blue Bird Publishing, 1985.

Klicka, Christopher. *The Right to Homeschool*. Durham, NC: Carolina Academic Press, 1995.

Homosexual Rights

Homosexuals, or gays, have often been the center of controversy with regard to the rights they have or do not have in the United States. The Bill of Rights provides no specific protections for homosexuals, and as a result, they have had to fight for protection against both institutional discrimination and societal discrimination from the **Religious Right** and others. The sociopolitical significance of homosexuals and their impact on U.S. society at large became major issues after **World War II** and are still hotly contested today. Gains have been made in the gay rights movement at large and in the specific areas of religious tolerance, AIDS awareness, and domestic partnerships, but some other areas, such as gay adoption and the privacy to be gay in one's own home or in the military, are still areas of struggle.

Historically, American gays were segregated from each other as discrete sexual minorities in their own towns and cities. With the advent of World War II, many previously isolated gay men met each other through the ranks and formed socially cohesive groups that continued after their members left the service. Women formed similar alliances when the war urged them into the workplace. When the war ended, many of these people gravitated to the cities, specifically areas of large military workforces or disembarkation points such as New York and San Francisco.

In the 1960s, homosexual activism in the United States reached a peak previously unseen. The major turning point in gay politics was an event now called the Stonewall Riots. The gay patrons of the Stonewall Inn in Greenwich Village rebelled against police harassment, common in gay bars at the time. Two days of rioting galvanized the community and began the gay rights movement on a large scale. With the spread of AIDS in the early 1980s , a newer, more militant gay activist contingent formed, including groups like ACT-UP and Queer Nation, whose mission was not only to fight for the rights of homosexuals but also to increase gay visibility.

In terms of legislation, many different attempts have been made to prohibit homosexuality and homosexual behavior. The most widespread of these have been sodomy laws. All states have had laws that prohibit oral and anal sex at one time or another, but many such laws have been recently overturned. In 1986, the U.S. Supreme Court ruled in *Bowers v. Hardwick* that the Constitution does allow states to criminalize sodomy. While the sodomy laws can be applied to either heterosexual or homosexual couples, they are primarily enforced against gay couples. Currently 21 states have sodomy laws, with six states having laws that only apply to same-sex couples.

Workplace discrimination is another large issue for homosexuals because they do not have the same **civil rights** protections as African Americans, religious minorities, or persons of differing ethnic origin. The Employment Non-Discrimination Act currently before Congress would prohibit discrimination on the basis of sexual orientation. Presently, 11 states (and 165 cities) have laws protecting lesbians and gay men from workplace discrimination. Opponents of these laws say that sexual orientation should not be treated like race or gender because it is defined by a person's behavior rather than by an immutable characteristic such as skin color. They also raise religious liberty concerns, arguing that religious day care centers and other businesses should not be compelled to hire employees who have life-styles that employers may find morally problematic.

A recent political movement in the homosexual community has been toward official recognition of domestic partnerships between homosexual couples and a movement towards legalization of homosexual marriages. Major U.S. corporations, such as Microsoft and Disney, have extended standard spousal benefits like health insurance and retirement benefits to domestic partners. This move has caused considerable backlash, including an organized boycott of Disney by the American Family Association. Currently, 18 states have official domestic partnership registries. In addition, 47 municipal or state governments allow some form of domestic partnership registration with varying benefits accorded to the domestic partners.

Homosexuals and gay activists argue that the denial of their right to marry amounts to discrimination and is in violation of the Equal Protection Clause of the Fifth Amendment. They also argue that organizations that object to legal gay marriage as being counter to their religious beliefs are trying to blur the line between church and state; while churches may decline to perform gay marriages in religious ceremonies, the right of citizens to marry in the eyes of the state cannot be countermanded for religious reasons. In the past three years, 49 states have had anti-gay marriage bills introduced. As of January 1998, 24 states had blocked anti-gay marriage bills, and 25 had passed anti-gay marriage laws.

Some of the most active opposition to gay rights and visibility has come from organized religious groups such as the **Christian Coalition**, the American Family Association, and Focus on the Family. Many in these groups cite their interpretations of biblical passages such as Leviticus 18:22, "Thou shalt not lie with mankind, as with womankind: it is an abomination," as supporting their views of homosexuality. They also cite secular reasons, such as disease statistics that show the unhealthiness of the homosexual life-style in their view. These groups typically support the work of "ex-gay" ministries such as Exodus International, which seeks to help homosexuals who want to leave the homosexual life-style. Despite many factions' opposition to the practice of homosexuality, several religious leaders have come out either supporting or not condemning homosexuality, specifically citing the lack of biblical support for an anti-gay agenda, the lack of biblical relevance to contemporary cultures and values, and the importance of loving, committed relationships between members of any gender.

With at least some states recognizing homosexuals' rights to live together in committed domestic relationships, the issue of adoption has become another point of contention. The total number of children nationwide with at least one gay parent ranges from 6 to 14 million. Advocates for homosexual adoption cite the benefits of strengthening the legal relationship between a child and both parents, especially in the event of death or disability of one parent. Opponents of homosexual adoption claim that children in families with gay parents are more likely to be abused, to become gay themselves, and to face greater social stigmas. The American Psychological Association has found no research to support these claims. Currently, 22 states have allowed gay couples to adopt children. Only two, Florida and New Hampshire, have enacted laws barring gays from ever adopting children. State agencies apply a "best interest of the child" standard to determine parental fitness. Using this approach, a parent's sexual orientation cannot be a basis for denying an adoption claim unless it can be demonstrated that this orientation will harm the child.

One of the issues having an enormous impact on gay society has been legislation and public opinion regarding the AIDS epidemic. Despite the fact that AIDS is a disease that affects many different segments of society, it has become part of many gay rights agendas and has been seen by many as a "gay disease." People with AIDS are often subject to a high level of discrimination with regard to employment, housing, and health care, though people with AIDS are somewhat protected under the Americans with Disabilities Act of 1990. Within some religious communities, AIDS education causes faith dilemmas because to make teenagers aware of AIDS prevention methods, one must educate them about birth control and safe needle usage, which are often topics more commonly dealt with by encouraging abstinence or a "just say no" approach. Despite some ideological clashes, over 2,000 AIDS ministries have been organized over the past 15 years, including the umbrella organization, the AIDS National Interfaith Network.

Bill Clinton was the first presidential candidate to actively solicit the gay vote in his campaign when he promised, among other things, to support homosexuals' participation in the military. However, many gay activists cited his Don't Ask Don't Tell policy as a turnaround on this position. The policy, signed into law in 1993 as the National Defense Authorization Act, is a ban on openly gay or lesbian service members in the U.S. armed forces. Presumably, if the service member does not reveal his or her sexual orientation, the military will not investigate it. The rationale for the law is that openly gay service members pose "an unacceptable risk to the high standards of morale, good order and discipline, and unit cohesion that are the essence of military capability" as well as making heterosexual service members uncomfortable. Gay service members have brought lawsuits against the government for impinging on their right to free speech as well as establishing conduct-based regulations that apply to them alone. The rule has since been struck down by a federal judge in New York, and its future is uncertain.

Bill Clinton himself has also been taken to task by the homosexual community for "failing to develop a cure for AIDS, firing Surgeon General Joycelyn Elders for promoting safe sex, and failing to appoint a cabinet-level AIDS czar." While he and the **Democratic Party** are still seen as more gay-friendly than the **Republican Party**, President Clinton is no longer seen as the harbinger of gay rights in the United States.

Many of the issues affecting homosexuals and their legal position in American society have been in flux in recent years. Some states have enacted laws against sexual orientation discrimination, while others have repealed or voted down such laws. At the national level, homosexuals are still without the federal protections afforded to other minority groups. Within various churches, disagreements rage over both the moral and legal status of homosexuality. Although the **Episcopal Church** in the United States contains many leading proponents of gay rights, representatives of Anglican churches from the rest of the world decisively rejected acceptance of homosexuality at the 1998 Lambeth conference. Public schools, meanwhile must struggle with how to cover sexual orientation in sex education classes without opening themselves to accusations of propagandizing for one side or the other. These controversies suggest that the debate over homosexual rights is not likely to be resolved soon. (JCW) **See also** Abortion and Birth Control Regulation; Culture War; James C. Dobson; First Amendment; Military Service; Women in Religion and Politics.

BIBLIOGRAPHY

American Psychological Association. *Lesbian and Gay Parenting: A Resource for Psychologists*. Washington, DC: American Psychological Association, 1995.

Geis, Sally and Donald Messer, eds. *Caught in the Crossfire, Helping Christians Debate Homosexuality*. Nashville: Abingdon Press, 1994.

Marcus, Eric. *Making History, The Struggle for Gay and Lesbian Equal Rights*. New York: Harper Collins, 1990.

Stoddard, Thomas, et al. *The Rights of Gay People*. New York: Bantam Books, 1983.

Yamamoto, J. Isamu. *The Crisis of Homosexuality*. Wheaton, IL: Victor Books, 1990.

Isabella Beecher Hooker (1822–1907)

The daughter of **Lyman Beecher**, Isabella Hooker became one of the leading advocates of women's equality after 1861. In 1868, she founded the Connecticut Woman Suffrage Association, and in 1877, a bill making a husband and wife equal in property rights was drawn up by her husband. With her support, the bill passed the U.S. Congress. (MWP) **See also** Catherine Beecher; Edward Beecher; Henry Ward Beecher; Harriet Beecher Stowe; Women in Religion and Politics.

BIBLIOGRAPHY

Hooker, John. *Some Reminiscences of a Long Life*. Hartford: Belknap & Warfield, 1899.

Thomas Hooker (1586–1647)

Called the "father of American democracy" by some historians, Thomas Hooker fled from England to Holland in 1630 to avoid prosecution for his fervently evangelistic speeches. In 1633, he immigrated to **Massachusetts Bay Colony**, and in 1636, looking for greater political and religious freedom, he helped found Hartford, Connecticut. His role in establishing **democracy** came from his opposition to those who limited the vote to church members and his drafting of the **Fundamental Orders of Connecticut**, which guaranteed freedom of religion to the colony's inhabitants. Hooker strongly believed that legitimacy in both political and religious matters was a function of popular consent. (MWP) **See also** Puritans.

BIBLIOGRAPHY

Kendall, Willmore and George W. Carey. *Basic Symbols*. Baton Rouge: Louisiana State University Press, 1972.

Shuffelton, Frank. *Thomas Hooker, 1586-1647*. Princeton, N.J.: Princeton University Press, 1977.

Walker, George L. *Thomas Hooker: Preacher, Founder, Democrat*. New York: Dodd Mead, 1891.

Herbert C. Hoover (1874–1964)

Herbert Hoover was the 31st president of the United States. He was born in West Branch, Iowa, where he was raised as a **Quaker**, and he was a member of the first graduating class of Stanford University in 1895. During **World War I**, he headed the Commission for Relief and was recognized for his humanitarian acts, most of which had a deep religious basis. He served as secretary of commerce during the administrations of Warren G. Harding and Calvin Coolidge. In 1928, he was nominated by the **Republican Party** and elected president. A dry Protestant, Hoover regularly attended services at a Washington Quaker meetinghouse. His speeches advocating compassion as an antidote to rampant individualism and socialism also reflected his religious beliefs. He had the misfortune of serving as president at the start of the Great Depression and was defeated in 1932 by Democrat Franklin D. Roosevelt. After he was defeated, he headed government reorganization commissions for the administrations of Harry S. Truman and **Dwight D. Eisenhower**. From 1949 until his death, Hoover saw a great evil in communism. He argued that the U.S. should leave the United Nations and form a "cooperative of God-fearing free nations." (WB) **See also** Democratic Party; Socialism and Communism.

The great humanitarianism of Republican President Herbert Hoover can be traced to his devout Quaker upbringing. Library of Congress.

BIBLIOGRAPHY

Burner, David. *Herbert Hoover: A Public Life*. New York: Knopf, 1979.

Robinson, Edgar E. *Herbert Hoover*. Stanford, CA: Stanford University Press, 1975.

How the Other Half Lives (1890)

Jacob Riis's *How the Other Half Lives*, a classic of photojournalism and urban sociology of the 1880s, led to major social reform by exposing the scandalous conditions of immigrants and African Americans living in New York City's tenements.

Drawing partly on his own experience living on the street, Riis recorded in word and picture disease-infested East-Side slums overflowing with humanity, garment-workers toiling in sweatshops, gang members relaxing before their next robbery, and ragged children sleeping in doorways. Before affluent

Christians attempted to meet immigrants' spiritual needs, Riis suggested that such urban **missionaries** should improve the long-term material conditions of the poor.

Despite his compassionate position, Riis nonetheless repeated many of the ethnic prejudices of his day. The book described Jews as greedy, Chinese as lecherous, and African Americans as irresponsible.

The text and especially the illustrations of *How the Other Half Lives* awakened the consciences of many affluent Americans to the plight of the urban poor and spurred many reforms by Progressives and advocates of the **Social Gospel**. The young **Theodore Roosevelt** relied on the book to guide his attacks on sweatshops and substandard police lodging houses. Riis's work also helped convince New York City's government to tear down many of the worst tenements and replace them with public parks. (JSF) **See also** Judaism.

BIBLIOGRAPHY

Gandal, Keith. *The Virtues of the Vicious: Jacob Riis, Stephen Crane, and the Spectacle of the Slum*. New York: Oxford University Press, 1997.

Riis, Jacob A. *How the Other Half Lives: Studies Among the Tenements of New York*. New York: Charles Scribner's Sons, 1890.

Julia Ward Howe (1819–1910)

A committed abolitionist, Julia Ward Howe's lasting fame rests largely on the **Civil War** marching song, "The Battle Hymn of the Republic," which she published in 1862. The song helped expand the North's purpose in fighting the war from just restoring the Union to also ending **slavery**. The Hymn is a millennial-based work that calls upon the Union armies to defend the gospel by "crush[ing] the serpent [slavery and its defense]". Like many abolitionists, Howe saw slavery as proof of human sinfulness and the need for atonement. After the war, she was so disturbed by the plight of the war's many widows that she campaigned for improved educational and employment opportunities for women. (The lyrics to Howe's "Battle Hymn of the Republic" are reprinted in Appendix 1.) (MWP) **See also** Abolition; Education; Millennialism; Women in Religion and Politics.

BIBLIOGRAPHY

Clifford, Deborah Pickman. *Mine Eyes Have Seen the Glory*. Boston: Little Brown, 1979.

Charles Evans Hughes (1862–1948)

Raised in a strong **Baptist** family, Charles Evans Hughes had decided early in his life to pursue the ministry but later chose law, graduating from Columbia Law School in 1884. His life of public service began in 1905, when he served on a special committee investigating gas and utility rations in New York. In 1906, he was elected governor of New York, where he pursued progressive policies. In 1910, he was appointed to the U.S. Supreme Court, where he remained until his nomination for president by the **Republican Party** in 1916. He lost in a close election to **Woodrow Wilson**. After Hughes served as secretary of state in the administrations of Warren G. Harding and Calvin Coolidge, President **Herbert Hoover** appointed him chief justice of the Supreme Court, where, among other accomplishments, he helped uphold much of the **New Deal** legislation of Franklin D. Roosevelt. Hughes was also instrumental in extending the Constitution's religious clauses to the states. In ***Lovell v. City of Griffin, Georgia*** (1938), Hughes wrote the opinion that struck down a ban on distributing leaflets without a permit. He also sided with the majority in ***Cantwell v. State of Connecticut*** (1940). However, in ***Cox v. New Hampshire*** (1941), he upheld the convictions of **Jehovah Witnesses** for parading without a permit. (MWP) **See also** Democratic Party; First Amendment.

While chief justice of the U.S. Supreme Court, Charles Evans Hughes, the Republican presidential candidate in 1916, oversaw the application of the free exercise and establishment clauses of the First Amendment to the states. Library of Congress.

BIBLIOGRAPHY

Pusey, Merlo J. *Charles Evans Hughes*. New York: Macmillan, 1951.

Wesser, Robert F. *Charles Evans Hughes*. Ithaca, NY: Cornell University Press, 1967.

Humanist Manifesto I (1933) and II (1973)

During the 1920s, some Unitarians began to reject theism and to advocate humanism, which they saw as an alternative to the more conventional religions. The universe, they said, was not created and humans were merely a product of **evolution**. The humanists believed that there was no distinction between mind and body, miracles did not occur, and no personal God existed. They even rejected the traditional deism of **Unitarianism**.

The first humanist societies began in 1929 in New York City under the leadership of Charles Francis Potter and in Hollywood under Theodore C. Abell. In 1933, 11 of the movement's most prominent leaders issued "A Humanist Manifesto," which also drew on the pragmatism taught by one of its signers, **John Dewey**. It said that the goal of life should be the development of the human personality and that scientific, social control will make the world a better place, theories that have been embraced by many liberal programs of the **New Deal** and Great Society. Humanists argued that the course of evil in the world was not humanity's innate sinfulness, but rather the faulty institutions of society. Therefore the solution to many problems was to be found in redesigning government. In 1941, the American Humanist Association was founded to coordinate humanist activities. In 1973, the manifesto was amended to place more stress on human responsibility for humanity. (The 1933 Humanist Manifesto is reprinted in Appendix 1.) (MWP) **See also** Liberalism; Secular Humanism.

Bibliography

Kurtz, Paul, ed. *The Humanist Alternative*. Buffalo, NY: Prometheus Books, 1973.

_______. *The Humanist Manifesto I and II*. Buffalo, NY: Prometheus Books, 1973.

James Hunter (1955–)

University of Virginia sociologist James Hunter has studied **Evangelicals** and other politically active religious conservatives. His writings argue that the sharp division between social conservatives and liberals, as revealed in current political debates, will ultimately endanger **democracy**. (ARB) **See also** Conservatism; Culture War; Liberalism.

Bibliography

Hunter, James. *Before the Shooting Begins: Searching for Democracy in America's Culture War*. New York: Free Press, 1994.

_______. *Culture Wars: The Struggle to Define America*. New York: Basic Books, 1991.

Anne Hutchinson (1591–1643)

Anne Hutchinson founded Portsmouth, **Rhode Island**, in 1638, after she was banished from the **Massachusetts Bay Colony** as a religious heretic. A member of **John Cotton**'s Boston congregation, Hutchinson took Cotton's emphasis on the role of grace in salvation to an extreme and criticized those who argued for good works as part of the salvation process. Her claim to have received special revelations from God infuriated the religious hierarchy, as did her charges that they were preaching a "Covenant of Works" that let people think they were saved because their ministers and others saw their good works.

Her opponents labeled her anti-works position "slothful," and condemned her as anti-clerical. Her supporters, including William Coddington, who co-founded Portsmouth, eventually hailed her as a prophet. **Quakers** view her as a forerunner, for her emphasis on the inner signs of saving grace anticipated the Quaker concept of an "inner light." As her notoriety waned, she moved to New York, where, despite her advocacy of friendly relations with the displaced Native Americans of the region, she was killed in a Siwanoy raid of her farm. (KMY) **See also** Puritans.

Bibliography

Bremer, Francis J., ed. *Anne Hutchinson: Troubler of the Puritan Zion*. Huntington, NY: Robert E. Krieger Publishing Company, 1981.

Dunlea, William. *Anne Hutchinson and the Puritans: An Early American Tragedy*. Pittsburgh: Dorrance Publishing Company, 1993.

Hyde Amendment

Sponsored by Representative **Henry J. Hyde**, the Hyde amendment bans using federal funds to pay for abortions. Hyde succeeded in placing his amendment, with exceptions for rape, incest, or to protect the health of the mother, on the Medicaid provision of the Social Security Act. Hyde, a Roman Catholic Republican from suburban Chicago, came to Congress wanting to restrain the effects of the ***Roe v. Wade*** (1973) decision, which legalized **abortion**. Hyde argued that whatever the merits of that right, the American taxpayers should not subsidize its exercise. The amendment has been applied to expenditures by various agencies with domestic and foreign responsibilities. Critics challenged the provision for denying equal protection to poor and minority women. In ***Harris v. McRae*** (1980), the Supreme Court said the right to an abortion does not obligate government payment for it. The Hyde Amendment does support indigent women who give birth to children. (JRV) **See also** Republican Party; Roman Catholicism.

Bibliography

Yarnold, Barbara M. *Abortion Politics in the Federal Courts: Right Versus Rights*. Westport, CT: Praeger, 1995.

Henry J. Hyde (1924–)

In the 1980s, representative Henry Hyde authored the **Hyde Amendment**, which forbids spending federal funds for abortions. A devout Roman Catholic, he has served in the Illinois state house (1967–1974) and the U.S. House of Representatives (1975–present). He is chairman of the House Judiciary Committee. (JRV) **See also** Abortion and Birth Control; Republican Party; Roman Catholicism.

Bibliography

Yarnold, Barbara M. *Abortion Politics in the Federal Courts: Right vs. Rights*. Westport, CT: Praeger, 1996.

I

Illuminati Controversy

The Illuminati, a secret Masonic society founded in Bavaria in 1778 by Dr. Adam Weishaupt, a Jesuit-trained professor of canon law at the University of Ingolstadt, spread throughout Germany after its founding. Its goal, nominally, was to "perfect and ennoble mankind." Rumors that the Illuminati were attempting to wipe out Christianity and become world dictators surrounded the order and created much controversy about it. The controversy was further fueled by the Illuminati's secret ceremonies, nicknames, signs, and passwords. Weishaupt was removed from his post and all original papers concerning the order were destroyed, thus adding to its mystery. Despite Weishaupt's removal, the order persevered, even after being condemned by Pope Pius VII. The society faded from the limelight after 1820 and, besides a brief revival in Dresden in 1898, never again enjoyed significant prominence. In the early United States, rumors that the Illuminati planned to create their own government were common. (JCW) **See also** Freemasonry.

Bibliography

Robison, John. *Proofs of a Conspiracy Against All the Religions and Governments of Europe Carried On in the Secret Meetings of Free Masons, Illuminati, and Reading Societies*. New York: George Forman Publisher, 1798.

Vivian, Herbert. *Secret Societies, Old and New*. London: Thornton Butterworth Limited, 1927.

Imperialism

Imperialism is the "effective domination by a relatively strong state over a weaker people." Imperialism in the Western hemisphere entailed both Europe's conquest of America and the expansion of the United States across the continent and beyond. Religion has been one among many indirect incentives and sanctions for American imperial activity.

Modern imperialism has passed through four stages: (1) "New World" imperialism, c. 1500–1820: the colonization of expatriate Europeans to dominions in the Americas; (2) early "Old World" imperialism concurrent with American "continentalism," c. 1820–1860: expansion by Europeans into Africa and Asia and by the United States in North America; (3) later "Old World" imperialism, c. 1860–1920: competitive acquisition of classic colonial empires by both Europeans and Americans; (4) "neo-imperialism," c. 1920–1990: competition between rival global hegemonic systems.

Before American independence, European imperial states vied for control of the Americas, motivated in part by religion (including Protestant-Catholic rivalry). With the founding of the American Republic came an enduring, religiously based conviction that the U.S. held a special place in human history, a national mission as a "Redeemer Nation," a duty as custodian of a system of free government to preserve the "blessings of liberty." On occasion, this vision compelled restraint, at other times an unabashed imperial enterprise.

Perhaps the most important religious dimension of American imperialism was the **Northwest Ordinance** of 1787, which explicitly extended freedom of worship to western lands. Subsequently, the antebellum U.S., heavily influenced by millennialist and perfectionist impulses drawn from revivalistic Protestantism, looked even farther westward. Indeed, Protestant **missionaries** were the vanguard of the Oregon settlement. Nevertheless, commercial opportunity, strategic advantage, and land hunger weighed more heavily on continental expansion.

The same more pragmatic factors dominated the acquisition of overseas possessions in the late 1890s. **Josiah Strong**'s *Our Country* might conjoin Christian civilization and the Anglo-Saxon race, and a devout President **William McKinley** might prayerfully consider religious factors as he pondered the Philippines, but the burgeoning foreign missionary movement accompanied more than activated the imperialist thrust.

Similarly, in the twentieth century, American civilization, still woven with religious strands, reached outward both protectively and proactively to shape a stable, democratic, commercially open world. Religious sentiment remained a cultural buttress to global action motivated mostly by more traditional justifications.

In sum, religious motivations and rationalizations contributed to American imperialism, but, couched more often in terms of "**civil religion**" than explicit Christian missionary or millennialist imperatives, they served mostly to reinforce more direct rationales for empire. Nevertheless, periodically religious arguments were, ironically, marshalled against imperialism. (WW) **See also** Democracy; Manifest Destiny; Millennialism; Roman Catholicism.

Bibliography

McDougall, Walter. *Promised Land, Crusader State: The American Encounter with the World since 1776.* Boston: Houghton Mifflin, 1997.

Smith, Tony. *The Pattern of Imperialism: The United States, Great Britain, and the Late-Industrializing World since 1815.* New York: Cambridge University Press, 1981.

Tuveson, Ernest. *Redeemer Nation: The Idea of America's Millennial Role.* Chicago: University of Chicago Press, 1968.

In God We Trust

In 1861, Secretary of the Treasury Salmon Chase received numerous appeals asking the government to recognize God on U.S. coins. Chase asked James Pollock, director of the mint at Philadelphia, to prepare a motto that expressed the belief that "no nation can be strong except in the strength of God, or safe except in his defense." Congress approved the motto in April 1864. Since 1938, all U.S. coins bear the inscription, and since 1955, all U.S. currency. In July 1956, **President Dwight Eisenhower** approved a Joint Resolution of Congress declaring "In God We Trust" the national motto of the United States.

A number of challenges have argued that the use of such overtly religious language violates the **Establishment Clause** of the **First Amendment**, but none has been successful. In his dissent in ***Lynch v. Donnelly*** (1984), Justice **William Brennan** stated "the designation 'In God We Trust' as our national motto . . . can be best understood as a form of 'ceremonial deism,' protected from Establishment Clause scrutiny chiefly because [it has] lost through rote repetition any significant religious content." A 1996 ruling by the 10th Circuit Court of Appeals upholding use of the motto was refused review by the Supreme Court. (JP) **See also** Deism.

Bibliography

Jones, Richard H. "'In God We Trust' and the Establishment Clause." *Journal of Church and State* 31, no. 3 (Autumn 1989): 381–417.

In His Steps (1897)

Written by Congregational Minister **Charles Sheldon**, *In His Steps* tells the story of a minister, Reverend Maxwell, who challenges his church to pledge that for one year they make no major decisions without first asking, "What would Jesus do?" The story recounts the church members' experiences as well as the impact that their commitment has at home, at work, and in the community. The **social gospel** thrust of the book emphasized the socio-political input of individual conversion.The book was enormously successful, selling more than eight million copies in its first 60 years of publication. **See also** Congregationalism.

Bibliography

Ferre, John P. *A Social Gospel for Millions.* Bowling Green, OH: Bowling Green University Press, 1988.

Henrichs, Henry Frederick, ed. *In His Steps Today.* Litchfield, IL: Sunshine Press, 1948.

Inaugural Prayer

At his first inauguration in 1953, President **Dwight D. Eisenhower** began the tradition of opening the inaugural ceremony with a prayer, a tradition that has been followed by presidents ever since. The inaugural prayer is generally not considered a violation of the Constitution's prohibition against the establishment of religion because the oath of office has traditionally been taken by swearing on a Bible and because legislative sessions, both at the federal and state level, have long been opened with a prayer. (JM) **See also** Establishment Clause; First Amendment; *Marsh v. Chambers.*

Bibliography

Alley, Robert S. *So Help Me God.* Richmond, VA: John Know Press, 1972.

Hutchinson, Richard G. *God in the White House.* New York: Macmillan, 1988.

Robert Green Ingersoll (1833–1899)

As a politician, Robert Ingersoll served as Illinois attorney general. As an orator, he was a talented and well-paid public speaker. His agnosticism and outspoken attacks on traditional religion kept him from achieving greater political accomplishments. In the heyday of **freethought**, he earned renown as the "great agnostic" for his attacks on orthodox Christianity. Like a crusader, he sought to debunk religion of its oppressive myths and replace it with the light of reason. (MWP) **See also** Secular Humanism.

Bibliography

Anderson, David R. *Robert Ingersoll.* Boston: Twayne, 1972.

Farrell, Clinton P., ed. *The Works of Robert Ingersoll.* New York: Dresden, 1907.

Larson, Orvin. *American Infidel: Robert G. Ingersoll.* New York: The Citadel, 1962.

International Society for Krishna Consciousness v. Lee (1992)

The Port Authority of New York and New Jersey barred solicitation inside its airport terminals, although it permitted solicitation on the surrounding sidewalks. A nonprofit religious group protested the solicitation ban in the terminals. In *International Society for Krishna Consciousness v. Lee*, 505 U.S. 672 (1992), the Supreme Court upheld the ban for three reasons. First, the terminals were not free expression areas—public fora—either by tradition or purpose. Second, when government is acting as a proprietor managing the airport's internal operations, regulations need only be reasonable and justifiable. Third, the Port Authority was not attempting to censor speech based on its content. (FHJ) **See also** Hinduism.

BIBLIOGRAPHY

Schutte, Stephen K. "*International Society for Krishna Consciousness, Inc. v. Lee*: The Public Forum Doctrine Falls to a Government Intent Standard. (Symposium: First Amendment Law)" *Golden Gate University Law Review* 23, no. 1-2 (Spring 1993): 563–98.

John Ireland (1838–1918)

Born in Ireland, John Ireland immigrated to the United States in 1849 and became a bishop (1884) and then the first archbishop (1888) in St. Paul, Minnesota. As a political and religious liberal, he pushed for the integration of Catholics into American life. He also was active in the **temperance** movement, believing that Protestant criticism and stereotyping of Catholics as drunkards prevented them from fully participating in American society. His views put him in conflict with conservative Catholics who wanted to retain their ethnicity and traditional church practices. Along with American Catholic reformers like **James Gibbons** and **Isaac Hecker**, Ireland sought a more cohesive fit between American **democracy** and the Church. His activities were, however, brought under direct criticism in the papal encyclical *Testem Benevolentae*. (MWP) **See also** Liberalism; Roman Catholicism.

BIBLIOGRAPHY

Ireland, John. *The Church and Modern Society*. Chicago: D. H. McBride, 1896.

O'Connell, Marvin R. *John Ireland and the American Catholic Church*. St. Paul: Minnesota Historical Society Press, 1988.

Islam

Islam, the religion of submission to the will of God, is embraced by one billion of the world's people, and today numbers an estimated five to six million adherents in the United States. Like its predecessors **Judaism** and Christianity, it is uncompromisingly monotheistic, and, also like them, it arose in the Middle East. Islam teaches that after God (in Arabic, "Allah," linguistically related to the Hebrew words "El" and "Elohim") had spoken through a series of prophets, he brought his final and perfect revelation through his messenger, Muhammad (570–632). Islam teaches that this supreme revelation is the Koran, a book divinely unfolded over some 20 years to Muhammad through the angel Gabriel. Comprising 114 suras, or chapters, and regarded as the infallible expression of God's character and will for humankind, the Koran forms the basis for Islamic doctrine. Islam teaches the oneness, justice, and mercy of God; the importance of a life of obedience (Islam means "submission"); and a final judgment predicated on the believer's deeds, with rewards or punishments to follow. Additionally, Muslims regard (among others) Abraham, Moses, and Jesus as important prophets, with Muhammad as the last prophet, a man fully submitted to God but in no sense divine. Central to Islamic practice are five pillars: the *shahada*, (the confession: "There is no god but God, and Muhammad is His messenger"); *salat* (prayer; traditionally observed as a community five times daily); *zakat* (alms); *saum* (fasting during the lunar month Ramadan); and the *hajj* (pilgrimage to Mecca in Saudi Arabia). After the death of Muhammad, Islam spread rapidly in the region, easily defeating the weakened armies of the Byzantines and the Persians. What followed was an era of extraordinary development in government, jurisprudence, science and mathematics, medicine, literature, and certain arts like calligraphy.

Islam came to the Americas at least as early as the sixteenth century following the expulsion of Jews and Muslims from Spain in 1492. Additionally, some African Americans brought into the United States as slaves were Muslim. Regular emigration began in the 1870s and 1880s, with Muslims coming especially from the Levant and later from Pakistan, many of whom took blue collar positions. A change of immigration laws in the 1960s, which stipulated ability to contribute to society as a precondition for immigration rather than simply permitting chain migration, has brought a marked influx of Islamic professionals. As an indigenous phenomenon in the United States, the rise of Islam occurred first among African Americans. The **Nation of Islam**, founded by **Wallace Fard** and developed after his disappearance in 1934 by **Elijah Muhammad**, drew from several earlier quasi-religious black nationalist organizations. After **World War II**, the Nation of Islam grew rapidly, more because of its political overtures and appeal to a frustrated and suffering black community, than for Islamic orthodoxy. Later, however, **Malcolm X**, Nation of Islam's articulate spokesman, went on a *hajj* and had revelations about the tolerant nature of Islam that marked a significant turn for many of its members. Before his assassination in 1965, Malcolm repudiated the position that all members of the white race are inherently evil and pointed the way to a more orthodox approach to the religion. Following his death, many of the group followed the lead of Elijah Muhammad's son, Warithuddin, and embraced Islamic orthodoxy, while others have remained in a revitalized Nation of Islam under the sometimes controversial leadership of **Louis Farrakhan**.

Islam represents one of the fastest growing faiths in the United States. Ethnographically, American Muslims now comprise 40 percent blacks and 25 percent Indo-Pakistanis, with the remaining one-third distributed mostly among Africans, Arabs, Turks, and Caucasians. The number of mosques and Islamic centers has increased from approximately 50 after World War II to over 1,200 today, with a roughly equal number of Islamic organizations, schools, publishers, and radio stations. Web sites dedicated to Islam abound on the Internet, and Islamic lobbies, like the American Muslim Council, address Congress with issues that range from **school prayer** to foreign policy. With over 9,000 service personnel identifying themselves as Muslims, the Department of Defense now accepts Islamic chaplains. Following intervention by the courts, public schools have begun to recognize particular needs of Islamic students, even as the penal system has begun to accommodate free exercise rights of Muslim prisoners with respect to worship and diet during Ramadan. The recognition of Islam in the larger American society has not been altogether easy. Yet older stereotypes are being broken down, and American Muslims have had the opportunity, in a broadly democratic culture, to re-examine the meaning of their Islamic faith, one that challenges conventions even as it asserts the abiding primacy of the Koran. Islam is helping reshape the character of a pluralistic American national society. (JML) **See also** Chaplaincy; First Amendment; Free Exercise Clause; Slavery.

BIBLIOGRAPHY

Esposito, John. *Islam: The Straight Path*. New York: Oxford University Press, 1991.

Haddad, Yvonne. *Muslim Communities in North America*. Albany: State University of New York, Press, 1994.

Haddad, Yvonne, John Voll, and John Esposito. *The Contemporary Islamic Revival: A Critical Survey and Bibliography*. Westport, CT: Greenwood Press, 1991.

Hourani, Albert. *A History of the Arab Peoples*. Cambridge, MA: Harvard University Press, 1991.

Israel

The country of Israel, founded by Jews as a safe haven in the aftermath of the **Holocaust**, has played a role of singular importance in the last half-century of American politics. More than any other issue, support of a strong, democratic Israel unites American Jews. Toward that end, they urge their fellow Americans to offer whatever assistance they can to Israel, both privately and publicly. And for the most part—especially over the past 30 or so years—that aid has been forthcoming. Though not without exception, leading Democrats and Republicans alike accept the arguments that favor American aid to Israel. Those arguments come in two forms, moral and strategic. It is contended that offering such aid is in the moral interest of the U.S. because Israel is a liberal **democracy** and the U.S. has a responsibility to promote liberal democratic principles both at home and abroad. Israel, it is argued further, offers the U.S. a healthy example of the often necessary sacrifices a democratic people must make to remain free. Supporters of American aid claim that it is also in our strategic interest to support a strong Israel, which is the leading military power in the Middle East. Israel has proven to be an ally that the United States can confidently rely upon for support in times of crisis.

The American role in Israeli affairs runs deep. For example, within 30 minutes of Israel's declaration of statehood on May 14, 1948, President Harry S. Truman offered de facto American recognition to the new country. This act, which Truman took much to the dismay of many State Department officials, offered immediate legitimacy to a country whose very being generated immense hostility from many. The United States, during the administration of President **Jimmy Carter**, also played a crucial role in helping facilitate the Camp David accords whereby Egypt became the first Arab country to officially recognize the state of Israel. (SJL) **See also** Democratic Party; Islam; Judaism; Liberalism; Republican Party.

BIBLIOGRAPHY

Grose, Peter. *Israel in the Mind of America*. New York: Alfred A. Knopf, 1984.

Lipset, Seymour Martin and Earl Raab. *Jews in the New American State*. Cambridge, MA: Harvard University Press, 1984.

Netanyahu, Benjamin. *A Place Among the Nations: Israel and the World*. New York: Bantam, 1993.

J

Andrew Jackson (1767–1845)

The seventh president of the United States, Andrew Jackson lost his Irish father shortly before his birth and the rest of his family during the **American Revolution**. During Tennessee's constitutional convention, he opposed amendments requiring officials to believe in God and in the divine authority of the Old and New Testaments. While he opposed these measures, he was a Christian who read the Bible daily. Best known for his Indian removal policy, political appeal to the masses, and fight against the Bank of the United States, Jackson established a great military reputation at the Battle of New Orleans during the War of 1812. He was a controversial figure among many **Evangelicals** because he killed a man in a duel and because of his harsh treatment of the Cherokee. (GT) **See also** Cherokee Removal.

BIBLIOGRAPHY

Remini, Robert. *Andrew Jackson and the Course of American Empire, 1767–1821*. New York: Harper & Row, 1977.

———. *Andrew Jackson and the Course of American Empire, 1822–1832*. New York: Harper & Row, 1981.

———. *The Legacy of Andrew Jackson: Essays on Democracy, Indian Removal, and Slavery*. Baton Rouge: Louisiana State University Press, 1988.

Jesse Jackson (1941–)

As a **civil rights** activist, **Baptist** minister, and Democratic presidential candidate, Jesse Jackson has sought to continue the work of his one-time colleague **Martin Luther King, Jr**. Born in Greenville, South Carolina, Jackson turned down an offer to play baseball for the Chicago White Sox and instead attended the Agricultural and Technical College of North Carolina, where he helped lead protests that ended segregation in local restaurants. He then moved to Chicago, studied at the Chicago Theological Seminary, and worked with King in the **Southern Christian Leadership Conference (SCLC)**. In 1966, he started the Chicago Freedom Movement, which worked to integrate schools and housing markets; he also led the local branch (and eventually the national headquarters) of Operation Breadbasket, an organization devoted to persuading businesses to hire black workers. In 1968, he was ordained a Baptist minister. Three years later, he resigned from the SCLC and founded PUSH (Push United to Save Humanity) to promote economic advancement for black Americans.

Collecting the support of various minority groups into what he called a "Rainbow Coalition," Jackson ran for the Democratic presidential nomination in 1984 and won one-fifth of the delegate votes. Between that election and the next, his activities expanded to include extensive lobbying for divestment from apartheid South Africa, a campaign that earned him praise from many circles. In 1988, he again ran for the Democratic presidential nomination and came in second to the eventual nominee, Michael Dukakis, with twice as many delegates as he had won four years earlier. This achievement made him the first black presidential candidate to command serious attention at a national political convention. Jackson continues to be a leading voice for **social justice** and racial integration in the United States. (BDG) See also Democratic Party; Race Relations.

BIBLIOGRAPHY

Frady, Marshall. *Jesse: The Life and Pilgrimage of Jesse Jackson*. New York: Random House, 1996.

Henry, Charles P. *Jesse Jackson: The Search for Common Ground*. Oakland, CA: Black Scholar Press, 1991.

Harry V(ictor) Jaffa (1918–)

Harry V. Jaffa is a political philosopher, teacher of politics, and Lincoln scholar. From his early work on the divergences between Aristotle and Thomas Aquinas to his current scholarship, Jaffa celebrates the positive tension between reason and revelation in Western tradition, and affirms politics as a moral enterprise. He has argued that human equality must serve as the foundation of morality, and as the basis for our rights and duties as citizens. (HLC) **See also** Abraham Lincoln.

BIBLIOGRAPHY

Jaffa, Harry V. *Thomism and Aristotelianism: A Study of the Commentary of Thomas Aquinas on the Nicomachean Ethics*. Chicago: University of Chicago Press, 1952.

Schrems, John J. "Harry V. Jaffa's Thomism and Aristotelianism." *The Political Science Reviewer* XVIII (Fall 1988): 163-95.

Kay Coles James (1949–)

A dean at Regent University, Kay James is a black woman who grew up in poverty and under segregation. In the upper grades, she experienced the initial school integration in Richmond, Virginia. Despite this background, after a spiritual conversion, she took on conservative views about equality and racial quotas; sexual, alcohol, and drug abuse issues; and related government programs. As a result of these beliefs, she rose through positions in the Reagan and Bush administrations and was spokesperson for Right to Life. She directed the Health and Human Services Department for Virginia under Governor George Allen. In a Christian university, she does scholarly work and writing, including *Kay James* (1995) and *Transforming America from the Inside Out* (1995). (JRV) **See also** Abortion and Birth Control; Civil Rights; Conservatism; Ronald Reagan; Women in Religion and Politics.

BIBLIOGRAPHY

James, Kay C. and Jacqueline C. Fuller. *Kay James*. Grand Rapids, MI: Zondervan, 1995.

James, Kay C. and David Kou. *Transforming America from the Inside Out*. Grand Rapids, MI: Zondervan, 1995.

William James (1842–1910)

William James rejected a medical career and developed an interest in literature (an avenue pursued by his brother Henry), psychology, and religion. In particular, he became concerned whether religious conviction could be maintained in the face of Darwinian science. James wanted to show that respect for religion was not inconsistent with philosophical empiricism, and thus attended, in his own studies, to the varieties of the manifestations of religion without searching for a common essence. Religion, he argued, refers to the feelings of people in their solitude as they understand them in relation to whatever they consider to be divine. His thoughts became the foundation for pragmatic thought in both American politics and religion. When combined with idealism and a belief in progress, James' philosophy has had a large role in shaping the political viewpoint of twentieth-century **liberalism**. (JP)

BIBLIOGRAPHY

James, William. *The Varieties of Religious Experience*. New York: Mentor Books, 1958.

Jamison v. State of Texas (1943)

A member of the **Jehovah's Witnesses** was charged with distributing handbills on the streets of Dallas, Texas, in violation of a city ordinance that prohibited such distribution. The Supreme Court reversed the conviction in *Jamison v. State of Texas*, 318 U.S. 413 (1943), stating that the Dallas ordinance denied the freedom of press and of religion guaranteed by the First and **Fourteenth Amendments**. The Court also said that while "the state can prohibit the use of the street for the distribution of purely commercial leaflets," it "may not prohibit the distribution of handbills in the pursuit of a clearly religious activity." The handbills were thus protected by the **Free Exercise Clause** of the **First Amendment**. (JM)

BIBLIOGRAPHY

Regan, Richard J. *Private Conscience and Public Law*. New York: Fordham University Press, 1972.

Weber, Paul J., ed. *Equal Separation*. New York: Greenwood, 1990.

John Jay (1745–1829)

John Jay is best known as one of the authors of the *Federalist Papers* and as first chief justice of the Supreme Court (1789–1795). He also served as a delegate to the **Continental Congress**, as a negotiator of the Treaty of Paris, and as secretary of foreign affairs in the Articles of Confederation government. In 1795, he was elected governor of New York, a position he held until his retirement from active politics in 1801.

Jay's Huguenot (Protestant) family left Catholic France because of religious persecution. Consequently, Jay developed a great appreciation for religious liberty. Throughout his career, Jay was greatly influenced by his Christian beliefs. As a jurist, Jay commented that the laws by which nations deal with one another come from God. As governor, based upon his Christian convictions, he signed the bill that provided for the eventual abolition of **slavery** in New York. His son, **William Jay**, commented, "His patriotism, prompted and guided by the precepts of Christianity, ever refused to make the smallest sacrifice of truth or justice to the cause of his country." One biographer notes, "Jay believed the Bible. He knew every word of it to be completely and literally true." This devotion to the Bible led Jay, in the 1820s, to accept the presidency of the American Bible Society. (KAS) **See also** American Revolution; Alexander Hamilton; Thomas Jefferson; James Madison; Roman Catholicism.

After retiring from politics, John Jay, the first chief justice of the U.S. Supreme Court, became the president of the American Bible Society. Library of Congress.

BIBLIOGRAPHY

Monaghan, Frank. *John Jay: Defender of Liberty*. Indianapolis: Bobbs-Merrill, 1935.

Morris, Richard B. *Witnesses at the Creation: Hamilton, Madison, Jay and the Constitution*. New York: New American Library, 1985.

William Jay (1789–1858)

Like many nineteenth-century **Evangelicals**, William Jay, the son of **John Jay**, led a life that blended Evangelism with social action. A judge and writer, he helped found the American Bible Society, was for many years the president of the American Tract Society, and served as secretary for the Society for the Suppression of Vice. He criticized his fellow Episcopalians for defending **slavery** and regarded plans to return freed slaves to Africa as immoral. (MWP) **See also** Episcopal Church.

BIBLIOGRAPHY

Lerski, Hanna H. *William Jay*. Lantham, MD: University Press of America, 1983.

Tuckerman, Bayard. *William Jay and the Constitutional Movement for the Abolition of Slavery*. Westport, CT: Greenwood, 1969.

Thomas Jefferson (1743–1826)

Thomas Jefferson, third president of the United States, was an ardent proponent of religious liberty and church-state separation in Virginia and the new nation. He was the driving force behind sweeping resolutions adopted by the Virginia legislature in November 1776 that called for repeal of all acts of the British Parliament that criminalized religious opinion, the refusal to attend religious services, or modes of worship. His proposed legislation also exempted dissenters from all taxation or forced contributions to the established church. A bill was written in conformity with the resolutions, but before its enactment in December 1776, Jefferson and his allies were forced to accept compromise language that stopped short of complete **disestablishment** of the **Episcopal Church**. In the late 1770s, Jefferson drafted the Virginia "Bill for Establishing Religious Freedom," one of the most eloquent and influential American pronouncements on religious liberty. The bill was eventually enacted in 1786, following the demise of a proposed general assessment for the support of teachers of the Christian religion.

In an 1802 letter to the Danbury Baptist Association of Connecticut, President Jefferson used the celebrated metaphor, "wall of separation between church and state." In the twentieth century, Jefferson's metaphor has profoundly influenced discourse and policy on church-state relations. The "wall" metaphorically represented the **First Amendment**, which in Jefferson's day imposed its limitations on the federal government only.

While he supported church-state separation, during his public career Jefferson adopted policies that used religious means to achieve secular governmental ends. For example, he was the chief architect of a legislative package in Virginia's revised code that included, along with his "Bill for Establishing Religious Freedom," a "Bill for Punishing Disturbers of Religious Worship and Sabbath Breakers" and a "Bill for Appointing Days of Public Fasting and Thanksgiving." In 1779, as Virginia's governor, he issued a proclamation decreeing a day "of publick and solemn thanksgiving and prayer to Almighty God." As U.S. president, he pursued a policy of building churches through Indian treaties.

Thomas Jefferson, third president of the United States, worked for a greater separation of church and state. Library of Congress.

Jefferson believed that religion is a matter between humans and their God—beyond the control of civil magistrates and the state. He advocated sect equality and free religious expression in the public marketplace of ideas. An exclusive religious establishment, he thought, threatened religious liberty. Church-state separation, however, was not an end in itself; rather, it was a means toward achieving religious freedom. If free religious exercise was advanced by limited interaction between the institutions of church and state, Jefferson occasionally accepted such a cooperative arrangement. (Jefferson's letter to the Danbury Baptist Association is reprinted in Appendix 1.) (DD) **See also** Baptists; Civil Religion; Free Exercise Clause; James Madison; Thanksgiving and Fast Days.

BIBLIOGRAPHY

Gaustad, Edwin S. *Sworn on the Altar of God: A Religious Biography of Thomas Jefferson*. Grand Rapids, MI: William B. Eerdmans, 1996.

Peterson, Merrill D. and Robert C. Vaughan, eds. *The Virginia Statute for Religious Freedom: Its Evolution and Consequences in American History*. New York: Cambridge University Press, 1988.

Jehovah's Witnesses

The Jehovah's Witnesses, who have also been known as The Watchtower and Tract Society, Millennial Dawnists, and Russellites before formally adopting the current name in 1931, are a religious sect founded by **Charles Taze Russell** in Pittsburgh, Pennsylvania. Russell preached that Jesus Christ would return in 1914 and mark the beginning of a 1,000-year reign on Earth. Russell's successor, Joseph Franklin Rutherford, was left to change the sect's teachings when the cataclysm of 1914 did not happen and Russell died in 1916. Jehovah's Witnesses avoid as much worldly and political participation as possible. Members of the group do not vote, refuse to salute the flag, and are pacifists. During **World War I**, many Jehovah's Witnesses were harassed for their unwillingness to enlist in the military. Despite this retreat from public life, Jehovah's Witnesses have played a major role in politics and American life. The sect's controversial preaching methods have made it party to numerous Supreme Court cases challenging local restrictions on door-to-door proselytism and public prayer in schools, and other cases have involved the members' aforementioned refusal to salute the flag or serve in the military. Jehovah's Witnesses are one of America's fastest growing denominations with more than 850,000 members. **See also** Military Service; Pacifism; School Prayer.

BIBLIOGRAPHY

Penton, M. James. *Apocalypse Delayed*. Toronto: University of Toronto Press, 1985.

White, Timothy. *A People for His Name*. New York: Vantage Press, 1968.

Jimmy Swaggart Ministries v. Board of Equalization of California (1990)

Jimmy Swaggart Ministries, an evangelistic organization, claimed an exemption to a sales tax on religious materials sold in California, arguing that the tax was an unconstitutional burden on the free exercise of religion. In *Jimmy Swaggart Ministries v. Board of Equalization of California*, 294 U.S. 378 (1990), the U.S. Supreme Court ruled that a generally applicable tax assessed on religious organizations or materials is constitutional if it does not target those organizations and does not act as a "prior restraint" on religious exercise. The California sales tax, the Court concluded in an unanimous ruling, met both of these criteria. (KRD) **See also** Evangelicals; Tax-Exempt Status; Televangelism.

BIBLIOGRAPHY

Laycock, Douglas. "The Remnants of Free Exercise." In Gerhard Casper, Dennis A. Hutchinson, and David Strauss, eds. *Supreme Court Review: 1990*. Chicago: University of Chicago Press, 1990.

Richard M. Johnson (1780–1850)

A Kentuckyian, Richard Johnson led a long campaign that brought an end to imprisonment for debt in that state in 1832. Johnson served in a number of elected offices, including the Kentucky state legislature (1804–1807), the U.S. House of Representatives (1807–1819), and the U.S. Senate (1819–1829). While in the Senate, he issued a controversial 1829 committee report supporting the delivery of mail on Sundays that set off a public debate over the operation of Post Offices on Sunday. In 1836, he ran as Martin Van Buren's running mate, but because none of the vice-presidential candidates received a majority of the vote, he was elected by the U.S. Senate, the only vice president to hold this distinction. (MWP) **See also** Democratic Party; Sunday Mail.

BIBLIOGRAPHY

Meyer, Leland W. *Life and Times of Colonel Richard M. Johnson of Kentucky*. New York: AMS Press, 1983.

West, John G., Jr. *The Politics of Reason and Revelation*. Lawrence: University Press of Kansas, 1996.

Bob Jones (1883–1968)

Bob Jones, an influential southern evangelist and educator, championed a brand of Fundamentalism that generally disdained Christian involvement in politics. In an important free exercise case in 1983, Bob Jones University, which Jones founded, lost its **tax-exempt status** over the school's policy forbidding interracial dating on religious grounds. The university claimed that it could not be denied its tax-exempt status because of its policy because the policy was part of its religious teachings and therefore protected by the **Free Exercise Clause**. (ARB) **See also** Education; First Amendment; Fundamentalists; Race Relations.

BIBLIOGRAPHY

Dalhouse, Mark Taylor. *An Island in the Lake of Fire: Bob Jones University, Fundamentalism, and the Separation Movement*. Athens: University of Georgia Press, 1996.

Charles Colcock Jones (1804–1863)

As a Presbyterian minister in Georgia, Charles Jones served as a missionary and teacher to slaves. Jones, a plantation owner and slaveholder, was known as the "Apostle to the Blacks." In 1837, he wrote *A Catechism of Scripture, Doctrine and Practice* that served as a basic primer for the instruction of slaves. He was the also author of the *The Religious Instruction of the Negroes in the United States* (1842), which he wrote to supplement his 1837 book. In 1850, he published *The Southern Presbyterian,* which challenged many of the criticisms of northern abolitionists concerning the treatment of slaves and the morality of slavery. (MWP) **See also** Abolition; Missionaries; Presbyterian Church.

BIBLIOGRAPHY

Myers, Robert M., ed. *The Children of Pride*. New Haven, CT: Yale University Press, 1972.

James Warren (Jim) Jones (1931–1978)

Jim Jones, a charismatic preacher on topics such as social and racial equality in the 1950s and 1960s, moved to California in 1965, where he formed a **cult**, The People's Temple, which was aligned with the Christian Church (**Disciples of Christ**). In 1976, Jones was appointed to the San Francisco Housing Authority by the mayor because of Jones's commitment to social activism. However, after allegations about his misuse of church money and abuses of power circulated in the press, he moved with hundreds of followers to Guyana in 1977 to set up the insulated agricultural commune, Jonestown. In 1978, Jonestown was the scene of a mass suicide in which 913 members of Jones's cult, including Jones himself, died after drinking cyanide-laced Kool Aid. The mass suicide occurred after U.S. House Representative Leo Ryan (D-CA) visited the compound and sought to bring back an ex-member's child. Jones's guards attacked the Congressman's delegation, killing several members including Ryan, as it was preparing to return to the United States. The events at Jonestown led to increased suspicion in the U.S. of cults or "new religions." (JCW) **See also** Charismatic Movement; Race Relations.

BIBLIOGRAPHY

Reston, James. *Our Father, Who Art in Hell*. New York: Times Books, 1981.

J[ohn] William Jones (1836–1909)

A southern-born clergyman, J.William Jones was known as the "fighting parson" for his **Civil War** service under Confederate General A. P. Hill. He later wrote numerous books about the war, including his account of the religious revival in the Confederate armies, *Christ in the Camp* (1887). He was also one of the leading proponents of the **lost cause myth,** which argued that despite the South's loss, their political and spiritual goals were lofty ones. (MWP) **See also** Slavery; War.

BIBLIOGRAPHY

Jones, J. William. *Christ in the Camp; or, Religion in the Confederate Army*. Harrisonburg, VA: Sprinkle Publications, 1986.

Wilson, Charles Reagan. *Baptized in Blood: The Religion of the Lost Cause, 1865–1920.* Athens: University of Georgia Press, 1980.

Jones v. City of Opelika (1942)

The City of Opelika, Alabama, charged a number of **Jehovah's Witnesses** with violating its licensing ordinance by selling books without a license. In *Jones v. City of Opelika*, 316 U.S. 584 (1942), the convictions were appealed on the grounds that the ordinance violated the **Free Exercise Clause** of the **First Amendment**, as applied to the states by the **Fourteenth Amendment**. The U.S. Supreme Court rejected the First Amendment challenge and upheld the convictions, affirming the legitimacy of statutes aimed at regulating the orderly conduct of business and social interactions, stating that a person's "actions rest subject to necessary accommodation to the competing needs of his fellows." (JM)

Bibliography

Newton, Merlin. *Armed with the Constitution.* Tuscaloosa: University of Alabama Press, 1995.

Swancara, Frank. *Obstruction of Justice by Religion.* New York: Da Capo Press, 1971.

Jones v. Wolf (1979)

In *Jones v. Wolf*, 443 U.S. 595 (1979), the Supreme Court held that a court may resolve disputes within a church if secular legal principles apply, even if the court's ruling contradicts the decision of an ecclesiastical authority. The *Jones* decision represents an important exception to the Supreme Court's general rule requiring deference to church governing authority in conflicts of religious doctrine. *Jones* involved a dispute over ownership of church property following the withdrawal of a local congregation from the **Presbyterian Church** in the United States. (KRD) **See also** *Kedroff v. St. Nicholas Cathedral.*

Bibliography

Adams, Arlin and William Harlon. "*Jones v. Wolf.* Church Autonomy and the Religion Clauses of the First Amendment." *University of Pennsylvania Law Review* 128, no. 6 (June 1980): 1291–1339.

Gerstenblith, Patty. "Civil Court Resolution of Property Disputes among Religious Organizations." *American University Law Review* 39, no. 3 (Spring 1990): 512–72.

Judaism

Judaism, the religion of God's chosen people as set forth in the Torah (the Old Testament), has a profoundly ambiguous status in the United States, religiously and, to a lesser extent, politically. Despite this ambiguous status, no country, **Israel** excepted, has been as hospitable to the Jewish people as the United States has been. From the outset, at least in principle (and largely so in practice), Jews in the United States have enjoyed the blessings of religious liberty. Perhaps the most beautiful expression of the American principle of religious liberty occurs in a letter from **George Washington** to the Hebrew Congregation in Newport. Therein Washington, with a justifiable pride, lauded the example that the United States was providing to humanity of "an enlarged and liberal policy [of religious freedom]—a policy worthy of imitation." Given their history as the victims of persecution, Jews have reason to be grateful for the freedoms they enjoy as citizens of the United States. This is not to deny the existence of a number of ugly anti-Jewish movements within U.S. history (nor even the small number that remain today). It is only to say that to the extent such movements have or do exist, they are in no way representative of the character of the regime.

A rabbi teaches students in a synagogue. National Archives.

Why then is the Jewish religious status in the United States ambiguous or problematic? Judaism as a religion is defined by its adherence to the laws given to Moses by God at Sinai. A strictly observant Jew—an Orthodox Jew—must obey those laws fully. It is difficult, bordering on impossible, for Orthodox Jews to observe the Jewish law while simultaneously participating in American society, perhaps the most dynamic and secular society in human history. As a result, Orthodox Jews often choose a form of self-segregation from American society. The overwhelming number of Jews in the U.S. are not Orthodox, but either Conservative or Reformed. Conservative and especially Reformed Jews are, more or less, fully assimilated into American society. Assimilation, however, presents difficulties of its own for American Jews, many of whom have lost their identity as Jews, both figuratively and literally. A number of thoughtful Jews have expressed dismay at the lack of knowledge of things Jewish—the Bible, Hebrew, and Jewish heritage and history—displayed by even well-educated American Jews. To some, even more alarming is the number of Jews who simply give up their identification as Jews. One recent survey showed that since 1985 about 52 percent of Jews married non-Jews, and that in only 5 percent of the cases did the non-Jewish partner convert to Judaism.

Yet it would be wrong to speak simply of the effect that the American regime—American politics understood in its broadest sense—has had on the character of Judaism in the U.S. Jews have played and continue to play a significant role in American political life. One could speak at length of individual Jews who have had a profound effect in shaping American self-understanding in this century, such men as Supreme Court Justices **Louis Brandeis** and **Felix Frankfurter**. Yet to do so would be to restrict narrowly the contribution of the Jewish people as a whole to American political life. It would also obscure the overall character of Jews as political actors in the United States.

In this country, as a group, Jews have tended to be overwhelmingly liberal in their politics. This tendency has changed to some extent in recent years. Understandably fearful of persecution, Jews have first and foremost been staunch advocates of **civil rights** and liberties. The best known Jewish "political" organization in the United States is the **Anti-Defamation League of B'nai B'rith**. However, it would be unjust to reduce Jewish support of civil liberties to a narrow self-interest. Jews were, for example, one of the most prominent groups in the civil rights movement of the 1960s.

The other political issue American Jews have consistently shown concern with is the plight of the state of Israel. Since witnessing its founding in 1948, American Jews have constantly urged the American government to support Israel, both for our own sake as well as for Israel's. In recent years, a small but significant number of Jews have begun to move away from their traditional liberalism. These are the neo-conservatives, a small band of influential intellectuals. Neo-conservatives argue that contemporary liberalism is unhealthy both for Jewish and American interests because it weakens the political will of the U.S., and because a strong Israel needs a strong U.S. (SJL) **See also** Anti-Semitism; Holocaust; Liberalism; Washington's Letter to the Hebrew Congregation; Zionism.

Bibliography

Abrams, Eliot. *Faith or Fear: How Jews Can Survive in a Christian America*. New York: The Free Press, 1997.

Borden, Morton. *Jews, Turks and Infidels*. Chapel Hill: University of North Carolina, 1984.

Lipset, Seymour Martin and Earl Raab. *Jews in the New American State*. Cambridge, MA: Harvard University Press, 1984.

Neusner, Jacob, ed. *The Challenge of America: Can Judaism Survive in Freedom?* New York: Garland, 1993.

Neusner, Jacob, ed. *The Religious Renewal of Jewry*. New York: Garland, 1993.

Just War Theory

The Western theory that some wars could be just is first clearly articulated by St. Augustine (354 A.D.–430 A.D.). He defended Christian participation in war by arguing that war serves as a temporal form of punishment for evil-doers. The theory of just war was systematically set out by St. Thomas Aquinas (1225–1274), who argued that a just war required proper authority, just cause, and right intention in its prosecution. The later refinements to the Thomistic theory by Francisco de Vitoria, Francisco Suarez, and Hugo Grotius made just war theory part of international law and politics by the eighteenth century, though it was not actually codified until this century.

In its traditional formulations, just war theory is composed of two separate though connected parts. One part deals with the causes leading to war (*jus ad bellum*) while the other deals with the just prosecution of war (*jus in bello*) once begun. The just war theory typically comprises five principles, namely, that war is declared by competent and legitimate authorities, for only just causes, by appropriate means, as the only alternative, and with the right intentions. These ideals, part of a continuously developing set of principles for regulating combatants' conduct, were set out in the 1864 Geneva and the 1868 St. Petersburg Conventions and were further refined at the 1899 and 1907 Hague and 1949 Geneva Conventions.

The concept of a just war has been called into question in an age when nuclear weapons of mass destruction can potentially eliminate whole populations, combatants and noncombatants, as well as pollute and contaminate the environment. Such scenarios raise the issues of proportionality (the concept that the force used should be proportional to the situation, i.e., excessive force is immoral) and of the discrimination of legitimate targets—in modern societies it is increasingly difficult to distinguish combatants from noncombatants. The critical issue was and remains who arbitrates precisely which wars are just and which combatants are justified? Just war theory and its dilemmas have been examined by such American ethicists and philosophers as **John Courtney Murray**, James Johnson, Paul Ramsey, **Michael Walzer**, and Gabriel Palmer-Fernandez. (ISM) **See also** Conscientious Objection; Military Service; Nuclear Disarmament; War.

Bibliography

Johnson, James T. *Just War Tradition and the Restraint of War*. Princeton, NJ: Princeton University Press, 1982.

Palmer-Fernandez, Gabriel. *Deterrence and Crisis in Moral Theory: An Analysis of the Moral Literature on the Nuclear Arms Debate*. New York: Peter Lang, 1996.

Murray, John Courtney. *Morality and War*. New York: Church Peace Union, 1959.

Ramsey, Paul. *The Just War*. New York: Scribner's, 1968.

Walzer, Michael. *Just and Unjust Wars*. New York: Basic Books, 1977.

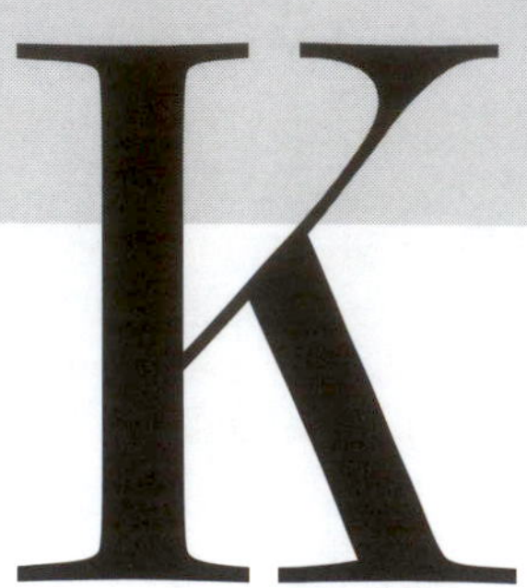

Horace Meyer Kallen (1882–1974)

The Prussian-born son of a rabbi, Horace Meyer Kallen elaborated one of the earliest philosophies of cultural pluralism and held that secularism was the religion most compatible with democracy. Kallen was influenced by William Jones, under whom he earned a Ph.D. in 1908, and his philosophy of pragmatism. He argued that democracy was the best form of government to protect individual differences. He taught at various universities and was instrumental in the founding of the new School for Social Research in 1919 where he remained until 1969. Kallen's arguments for a Jewish homeland appear to have influenced **Louis Brandeis**'s defense of **Zionism**. Kallen argued that a Jewish state in Palestine should be small, egalitarian, agrarian, and open, and protective of Jews and non-Jews alike. (JSF) **See also** Democracy; Israel; Judaism; Public Theology; Secular Humanism.

BIBLIOGRAPHY

Kallen, Horace Meyer. *Culture and Democracy in the United States: Studies in the Group Psychology of the American Peoples*. New York: Boni & Liveright, 1924.

Kallen, Horace Meyer. *Zionism and World Politics: A Study in History and Social Psychology*. Garden City, NY: Doubleday, Page & Co., 1921.

Kedroff v. St. Nicholas Cathedral (1952)

A New York court—convened to determine which prelate was entitled to the use and occupancy of a cathedral of the Russian Orthodox Church in New York City—held that New York law required the transfer of administrative control of the Russian Orthodox churches in North America from the Supreme Church Authority in Moscow to the authorities selected by a convention of the North American churches. In *Kedroff v. St. Nicholas Cathedral*, 344 U.S. 94 (1952), the U.S. Supreme Court held that the statute violated the **First Amendment**, stating that "Legislation which determines, in an hierarchical church, ecclesiastical administration or the appointment of the clergy, or transfers control of churches from one group to another, interferes with the free exercise of religion." (JM) **See also** Free Exercise Clause; *Jones v. Wolf* (1979).

BIBLIOGRAPHY

Sirico, Louis J., Jr., "The Constitutional Dimensions of Church Property Disputes." *Washington University Law Quarterly* 59, no. 1 (Spring 1981): 1–79.

Dean M. Kelley (1926–)

A liberal Methodist with ties to the National Council of Churches, Dean Kelley surprised the religious world with his 1972 scientific study, *Why Conservative Churches Are Growing*. In it, he concluded that the very attitudes that the liberal churches were counting on to attract more members were making them less appealing. Specifically, Kelley noted that churches which focused on issues of social justice rather than on giving meaning to human existence were more likely to be shrinking. He found that conservative or evangelical denominations were more concerned with "making sense of life." Kelley's survey was seminal in the study of religion and politics. It highlighted what religion did for most people and the political context of it. The growing religious conservatism that Kelley chronicled may be, according to him, a positive force in curbing "the continued atomization and destruction of this culture." (MWP) **See also** Conservatism; Evangelicals; Liberalism; Methodism; Social Justice.

BIBLIOGRAPHY

Kelley, Dean M. *Why Conservative Churches Are Growing*. New York: Harper & Row, 1972.

Anthony M. Kennedy (1936–)

An associate justice of the U.S. Supreme Court since 1988, Anthony Kennedy argues that the appropriate test for separation of church and state questions is whether the governmental act coerces individuals. Using this standard, he has reached divergent results, from supporting (in dissent) the constitutionality of a creche on public property to writing the opinion of the Court striking down nonsectarian prayer at public school graduations. Kennedy is perhaps best known for his change on the abortion issue. Having first voted to restrict abortion, he later voted to uphold it, co-authoring a broad opinion affirming an individual's constitutional liberty "to define one's own concept of existence, of meaning, of the universe, and of the mystery of human life." (RA) **See also** Abortion and Birth Control Regulation; First Amendment; *Lee v. Weisman*; *Planned Parenthood of Southeastern Pennsylvania v. Casey*; Publicly Funded Religious Displays; Religious Tests and Oaths; School Prayer; Wall of Separation.

BIBLIOGRAPHY

Greenhouse, Linda. "The Supreme Court: A Telling Court Opinion; The Ruling's Words Are About Abortion, but They Reveal Much About the Authors," *New York Times* (July 1, 1992): A1.

John Fitzgerald Kennedy (1917–1963)

John F. Kennedy, the 35th president of the United States, was born in Brookline, Massachusetts, on May 29, 1917. He was a descendant of Irish Catholics who had migrated to Boston. After graduating from Harvard, he entered the navy and saw combat duty in the Pacific theater. Following **World War II**, he was elected to the U.S. House of Representatives in 1946 and the U.S. Senate in 1952. In 1956, Adlai Stevenson, the **Democratic Party**'s presidential candidate, allowed the convention to choose his running mate, and Kennedy lost the vice presidential nomination to Estes Kefauver of Tennessee. In 1960, John Kennedy won the Democratic Party's nomination for president. In the general election, Kennedy faced opposition from some conservative Christian groups and **Fundamentalists**, especially in the southern states, because he was Roman Catholic. In the November election, however, his Catholicism helped him in the industrial east where large numbers of Catholics lived. He narrowly defeated **Richard Nixon**, and at age 43 became the youngest man and the first Roman Catholic elected president of the United States. As president, Kennedy proved that anti-Catholic concerns that he would be dominated by his religious commitments to Rome were unfounded. Kennedy created a public-personal barrier and firmly placed his Catholic ideology in the realm of private. On November 22, 1963, John F. Kennedy was assassinated in Dallas, Texas. (WVM) **See also** Anti-Catholicism; Conservatism; Political Participation and Voter Behavior; Roman Catholicism.

John F. Kennedy was the first Roman Catholic president of the United States. Library of Congress.

BIBLIOGRAPHY

Sorensen, Theodore C. *The Kennedy Legacy*. New York: Macmillan, 1969.

White, Theodore. *The Making of the President 1960*. New York: Antheneum, 1961.

Robert Samuel Kerr (1896–1961)

Robert Kerr, Democratic U.S. Senator from Oklahoma from 1948 through 1961, was proclaimed "uncrowned king" of the Senate during his tenure there. Earlier, he served as governor of Oklahoma from 1943 until 1947. Also noted as founder of Kerr-McGee Oil Industries, Inc., he was a leading Baptist layman who regularly taught Sunday School while he was governor and was a major contributor to denominational causes. (AOT) **See also** Baptists; Clergy in Public Office; Political Participation and Voting Behavior.

BIBLIOGRAPHY

Morgan, Anne H. *Robert S. Kerr: The Senate Years*. Norman: University of Oklahoma Press, 1977.

Martin Luther King, Jr. (1929–1968)

A **civil rights** leader and Baptist minister, Martin Luther King Jr. ignited a mass movement that demanded an end to racial prejudice and eventually compelled Congress to outlaw racial segregation in the United States. By organizing a series of nonviolent protests in strategically selected southern cities during the 1950s and 1960s, King brought the brutality of southern segregation into plain view of the nation. By persuading the black protesters to demonstrate peacefully, he instilled in them a sense of discipline and dignity, and allowed no observer to doubt that they occupied the higher moral ground.

Born in Atlanta, Georgia, to a Baptist pastor, King was himself ordained in 1947, and appointed assistant pastor at his father's church. He went on to study theology at Crozer Theological Seminary in Pennsylvania and Boston University. While at Crozer, he discovered Gandhi's doctrine of nonviolent resistance, a philosophy that he later had a chance to put into action in Montgomery, Alabama, where a black woman had been arrested in 1955 for refusing to give her bus seat to a white man. King led the enraged black population through a peaceful boycott of the city buses, inspiring the protesters with powerful sermons that drew upon biblical themes and images that soon earned him national attention. In 1956, the Supreme Court nullified the Alabama law that had segregated the buses.

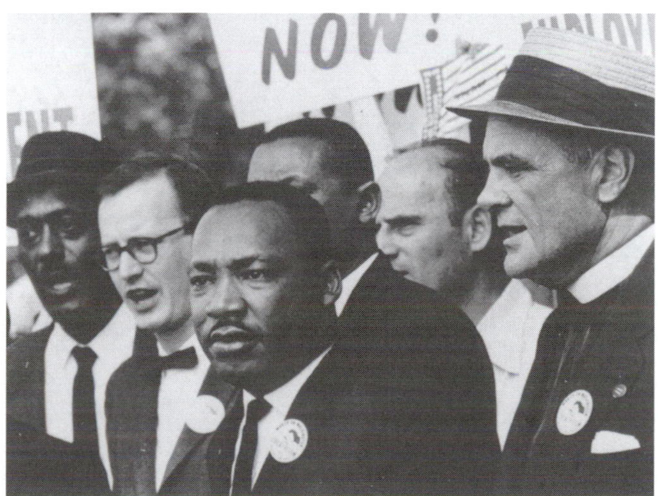

Martin Luther King, Jr., pictured here at the 1963 March on Washington, was a leader of the civil rights movement and a founder of the Southern Christian Leadership Conference. National Archives.

The following year King brought sympathetic Southern ministers together into the **Southern Christian Leadership Conference (SCLC)**, which organized Montgomery-style protests across the South. In choosing towns where racial tensions were high, such as Birmingham (1963) and Selma (1965), Alabama, King's strategy was to provoke white Southerners into publicly using violence against peaceful black protesters, and thus pressure the federal government into action. In 1963, he delivered his famous "I have a dream" speech to a crowd of 250,000 in front of the Lincoln Memorial in Washington, DC, and the following year Congress desegregated all public facilities with the Civil Rights Act of 1964. King won the Nobel Peace Prize that year, but encountered new opposition when he turned his attention to broader issues of black poverty in the north and the war in Vietnam. He was assassinated in Memphis, Tennessee, on April 4, 1968. (BDG) **See also** African-American Churches; Black Theology; Civil Rights Acts; Pacifism; Race Relations; Social Justice.

BIBLIOGRAPHY

Branch, Taylor. *Parting the Waters: America in the King Years, 1954–1963*. New York: Simon & Schuster, 1988.

King, Martin Luther Jr. *Letter from the Birmingham Jail*. San Francisco: Harper San Francisco, 1994.

Lewis, David L. *King: A Critical Biography*. New York: Praeger, 1971.

Oates, Steven B. *Let the Trumpet Sound: The Life of Martin Luther King, Jr.* New York: Harper & Row, 1982.

Russell Amos Kirk (1918–1994)

Historian, political philosopher, and novelist Russell Kirk attempted to invigorate the "moral imagination" or inherited wisdom of human beings in an effort to guide contemporary politics. A convert to **Roman Catholicism** in middle age, Kirk argued that Christianity was the primary influence in the development of the American political tradition. The decay of religious belief was, according to Kirk, the great affliction of modern civilization. Kirk is often described as the "father" of modern American conservatism. (HLC) **See also** Conservatism; Public Theology.

BIBLIOGRAPHY

Kirk, Russell. *The Conservative Mind*. Chicago: Regnery, 1995.

——. *The Roots of American Order*. Washington, DC: Regnery, 1992.

Abner Kneeland (1774–1844)

Abner Kneeland was one of the nineteenth century's better-known freethinkers. Initially a Baptist, in 1803 he became a Universalist, preaching and writing for them until 1829 when his increasingly radical views led them to ask him to leave. From then until his death, he was a leader in the First Society of Free-Inquirers, sometimes entering politics on the "infidel ticket." In a number of trials in the mid-1830s, he was charged with blasphemy for the contents of his newspaper. In the fourth trial in November 1835 Kneeland was convicted and sentenced to 60 days in jail. His passionate appeal before the State Supreme Court ended with his sentence being upheld. (MWP) **See also** Freethought.

BIBLIOGRAPHY

Kneeland, Stillman F. *Seven Centuries of the Kneeland Family*. New York: S. F. Kneeland, 1897.

Levy, Leonard. *Blasphemy*. New York: Knopf, 1993.

Know-Nothing Party

The Know-Nothing Party was also known by its formal name: the American Party. The party was made up of a number of secretive societies, one of which was named the Supreme Order of the Star Spangled Banner. Newspaperman Horace Greeley named them "know-nothing" because they concealed the identity of their members and the candidates they were backing, and when members were asked about the party, they answered, "I don't know."

Anti-Catholic and anti-immigrant, the Know- Nothing Party was a short-lived third party that was active before the Civil War. Shown here is former President Millard Fillmore, the party's presidential candidate in 1856. Library of Congress.

The party, developed in reaction to the large waves of immigration beginning in the 1830s, was anti-Catholic and anti-immigrant. In the election of 1854, it captured almost all of the state offices in Massachusetts and was also active in New York, Maryland, Kentucky, and California. The party's platform included demands that aliens live in the United States 21 years before being allowed to vote and that immigrants should never be allowed to hold office. After the 1856 election, the party collapsed over the issue of **slavery**, although most members supported the newly emergent **Republican Party**. **See also** Anti-Catholicism; Democratic Party; Political Participation and Voting Behavior.

BIBLIOGRAPHY

Holt, Michael. "The Politics of Impatience: The Origins of Know Nothingism." *Journal of American History* 60, no. 2 (September 1973).

C. Everett Koop (1916–)

Noted especially as a visible spokesman about public health issues, C. Everett Koop, a deeply religious man and friend of **Francis Schaeffer**, was appointed surgeon general by President **Ronald Reagan**, serving from 1981 to 1989. Koop's appointment generated considerable opposition because of his outspoken views against **abortion** and **euthanasia**. While surgeon general, he spoke for healthy lifestyles to prevent AIDS, teen pregnancy, and drug and tobacco addiction, and he emphasized needs of children, including disabled infants who were denied medical care based on their disabilities. Koop worked hard to balance his Christian views with the demands of his job as surgeon general. Prior to his executive appointment, he trained in medicine at the University of Pennsylvania, practiced surgery, taught pediatrics, and edited the *Journal of Pediatric Surgery* (1964–1976). He has received many honors including the Presidential Medal of Freedom in 1995. He has also served as professor of surgery at Dartmouth-Hitchcock Medical Center in Hanover, New Hampshire. (JRV)

BIBLIOGRAPHY

Koop, C. Everett. *Koop: The Memoirs of America's Family Doctor*. New York: Random House, 1991.

Schaeffer, Francis and C. Everett Koop. *Whatever Happened to the Human Race?* Old Tappan, NJ: Fleming Revell, 1979.

Ku Klux Klan

The original Klan was started in 1865 in Pulaski, Tennessee. In the post-**Civil War** South it became a vigilante and terrorist group opposed to **Reconstruction**. With the end of Reconstruction, it disappeared.

The Klan was revived by William Joseph Simmons in 1915 as the Knights of the Ku Klux Klan. In the 1920s, the organization had a membership of over 2,000,000 with its greatest number of members coming from the Midwest. The Klan appealed to Anglo-Saxon Protestants who felt threatened by immigrants who had migrated to the United States between the Civil War and **World War I**. These immigrants were generally from southern and eastern Europe and were primarily Catholic and Jewish. The Klan portrayed itself as a patriotic group while attacking foreigners and as a supporter of Protestantism against Catholics and Jews. The Klan also proclaimed itself to be the defender of traditional American values while attacking the immorality of urban America where the immigrants lived. It did achieve a victory with the passage of the National Origins Act in 1924, which severely limited immigration into the country.

Anti-black, anti-Catholic, and anti-Semitic, the Ku Klux Klan sees itself as the protector of white Protestant Americans. Shown here is a Klan group in Port Arthur, Texas, in 1924. Photo by W.D. Post. Library of Congress.

In the mid-1920s, the Knights of the Ku Klux Klan began to decline because of internal splits, scandals, and criticism of its policies by groups ranging from the American Legion to church organizations. In 1944, it was formally disbanded.

As a response to the **civil rights** movement in the 1960s, the Klan was revived in the South, attracting 50,000 members; however, by the early 1970s, Klan membership dropped to less than 5,000. In the late 1970s, new Klan leaders appeared, and some Klan groups began to admit Catholics; however, the Klan quickly declined once again, and in the mid-1990s, membership in various Klan groups totaled approximately 5,000. (WVM) **See also** Americanism; Anti-Catholicism; Anti-Semitism; Race Relations; Terrorism.

BIBLIOGRAPHY

Chalmers, David M. *Hooded Americanism*. New York: Franklin Watts, 1981.

Wade, Wyn Craig. *The Fiery Cross*. New York: Simon & Schuster, 1987.

Kunz v. New York (1951)

The New York City police commissioner granted Kunz, a member of the **Jehovah's Witness**, a permit to hold religious meetings on the streets of New York City, but the permit was revoked on evidence that Kunz had ridiculed and denounced other religious beliefs, in violation of a criminal provision of the ordinance under which the permit was issued. The following year, Kunz's application for a similar permit was denied. He continued to preach and was arrested and convicted for holding a religious meeting on the streets without a permit. In *Kunz v. New York*, 340 U.S. 290 (1951), the U.S. Supreme Court reversed the conviction on the grounds that the ordinance violated the Freedom of Speech and Freedom of Religion Clauses of the **First Amendment**. (JM) **See also** Fourteenth Amendment; Free Speech Approach to Religious Liberty.

BIBLIOGRAPHY

Choper, Jesse H. *Securing Religious Liberty*. Chicago: University Press of Chicago, 1995.

Ivers, Greg. *Redefining the First Freedom*. New Brunswick, NJ: Transaction Publishers, 1993.

L

Labor

The term "labor" refers to people employed in but not owning or managing industries, manufacturing facilities, shops, and other places of employment. "Organized labor" refers to associations of workers, distinct from owners and managers. An association of workers may exist for a variety of purposes, such as ethnic solidarity and social community. A chief purpose is to enhance the employment conditions and economic situation of its members through collective strength and action.

The relationship between religion and organized labor in the United States has been complex. Religious structures and individuals have at times supported organized labor and at times opposed it. For its part, organized labor, in its various expressions, has at times seen religion as a friend and at times as an enemy. In looking at labor in America, we will examine this ambiguous relationship between religion and labor, which persists into the present.

Organized labor has historical roots in the craft guilds of medieval Europe. The impetus for the rise of modern workers' associations came with the onset of the industrial age of England, Europe, and North America at the end of the 1700s and into the 1900s. For the first time in history, large numbers of people worked in settings outside of the home, the farm, or small shops. Industrialization led to unprecedented numbers of working people who did not own their places and means of production, who worked for long hours in large factories and shops apart from their homes, and who gradually saw machines doing more and more work that had previously been labor- and skill-intensive. Additionally, the 1800s and early 1900s witnessed growing economic and class divides between those who owned the means of production (for example, land, buildings, machines) and those who worked for those who owned. The **Civil War**, with its urgent needs for massive quantities of supplies, greatly spurred industrialization and, consequently, development of organized labor in the Knights of Labor (1869) and later the American Federation of Labor (1886), to name but two of the biggest labor organizations.

Labor and social issues intensified with massive waves of immigration in the 1800s and early 1900s. Immigrants entered the work force at the bottom, putting pressure on jobs and wages. They came from foreign ethnic groups and cultures, often with religious heritages different from what was common in America at the time. They included Irish and German Catholics, Eastern Orthodox and Jews from eastern Europe, and Asians, with cultures religiously and philosophically rooted in Buddhism and Confucianism. Thus immigration, particularly in its non-Protestant and non-Anglo-Saxon characteristics, raised fears among Americans. That led to prejudice and backlash against immigrants, workers and labor associations (that often consisted largely of immigrants).

Numerous social and economic problems resulted. For example, men and women labored in dangerous and wearying conditions. They lived in crowded, inadequate housing in increasingly urbanized areas. Many children worked in mills and mines for long hours in dangerous conditions with little pay, undermining their health, minds, and spirits. **Education** for working and working class children was erratic or non-existent.

As indicated above, the response of many workers from the eighteenth century to now has been to organize to enhance their strength for the purpose of improving their working and living conditions. However, organized labor has not been a simple, unified movement from strength to strength. It has been a complex, dynamic of people, movements, and aspirations. Its fortunes have ebbed and flowed. Workers and labor organizations have acted in unity at times, but they also found themselves a bitter odds wit each other. For example, skilled and unskilled laborers were often with each other in terms of organization and goals. Much of the organization of labor in the 1800s and early 1900s occurred among skilled workers and along trade lines. Unskilled workers were of the far less conservative American Federation of Labor, which emphasized trade or craftworkers and unions, and the more socialistic and radical Industrial Workers of the World, also known as the Wobblies, which sought to organize all workers, especially the unskilled, into "one big union." Additionally ethnic and racial differences and antagonsims afflicted and profoundly shaped structures and goals of labor organizations.

Opposition to organized labor from society and from industrial and political leaders was common and vigorous. Unions were viewed as secret societies (which they sometimes were), subversive and injurious to commercial interests. Hence, government authorities often used judicial, police, and military force to suppress unions and labor strikes. The conflict between labor and capital in the United States had often been violent and bloody.

Many religious people and structures have sided with industry and capitalists over immigrants and workers. William Lawrence, Episcopal bishop of Massachusetts in the first quarter of the 1900s, was an unblinking apologist for the essential compatibility of the accumulation of wealth with morality and Christianity. Suspicious of the moral character of the poor and working class, he declared in *The Relation of Wealth to Morals* the "Godliness is in league with riches." The strong individualism of American culture, which pervaded much of American religion, made the cultural and religious climates hostile to organized labor. A further hindrance to acceptance of organized labor by many religious people and structures was the specter of **socialism and communism** in the unionism. Even the major papal encyclicals that supported many of the rights and interests of labor—*Rerum Novarum* in 1891 and *Quadragesimo anno* in 1931—warned against the dangers of socialism and communism in labor agitation. This struggle between socialists and non-socialists was even played out among union members themselves, with the non-socialists winning in the dominant American Federation of Labor. Yet organized labor remained tainted with socialist associations for many in America.

Other religious people and organizations responded with greater charity to the social and economic issues of capitalism, industrialization, and the laboring class. In the middle 1800s, and especially after the Civil War, numerous Protestant voluntary organizations came into being to ameliorate social need and reform social ills. For example, YMCAs and YWCAs ran religious, educational, and social programs in cities for workers and their families.

Still others provided formal support for the rights and interests of labor. A notable instance is the **Social Gospel** movement in America, a largely Protestant movement in the late 19th century and early 20th century. Religious leaders in this movement urged government assistance and organized churches to provide programs to remedy the needs of workers and their families. They developed critical analyses of social and economic realities and advocated new social and economic attitudes, practices, and structures. Adherents of the Social Gospel movement supported workers' associations and concurred with organized labor on many issues and goals, such as collective bargaining, the abolition of child labor, and the eight-hour day. We must qualify this somewhat, however, by noting Henry May's point on page 216 of *Protestant Churches and Industrial America* that the "Social Gospel did not succeed in abating the anti-clericalism developed in the American labor movement by several generations of church opposition."

Further examples of religious interest in economic issues and support for labor can be found. In the early 1900s the **Presbyterian Church** established a Department of Church and Labor. The Presbyterians even seated a minister from the Department, Charles Stelzle, as a fraternal delegate at a convention of the American Federation of Labor in 1906. In 1923 the Federal Council of Churches was joined by the Central Conference of American Rabbis and the **National Catholic Welfare Conference** in formally denouncing the oppressive work conditions in the steel industry.

The Labor and Religion Forward movement conducted a joint religious revival and union recruiting campaign between 1911 and 1916 in 150 cities. This movement was largely but not exclusively **Protestant**. Also, like the American Federation of Labor itself, it was decidedly anti-socialist. David Montgomery notes in *The Fall of the House of Labor,* "Evangelical rallies for Christianity were coupled with celebration of the virtues of union craftsmen, promotion of union-label products, and often systematic canvassing of working-class neighborhoods by AFL recruiters."

Another, more radical example of a supportive religious response to workers and their families was the **Catholic Worker movement** begun by **Dorothy Day**. She was a concerned lay person who initiated the Catholic Worker movement, with its hospitality houses, in response to the great need she saw among workers and others in New York City.

Montgomery also points out that American Catholic thinkers developed the concept of the "living wage" in support of the legitimate needs of working people. This notion had two important elements. First, a living wage, to which each worker was entitled as a "natural right," was based not on his productivity but on what was necessary for "reasonable and frugal comfort." Second, it had to be an amount sufficient for him to provide for his family without financial contribution by his wife or children.

In 1996, the **National Conference of Catholic Bishops** issued "A Catholic Framework for Economic Life." In it they explicitly state, "The economy exists for the person, not the person for the economy." They go on to declare the inescapable moral dimensions of economic structures and processes, concern for the welfare of the poor and vulnerable in the economy, and the right of workers to organize in unions and other associations. Yet it is difficult to say what influence such a document might have on Catholic business people and laborers, much less on the larger population in business and work.

Following decades of often bloody struggle, with victories and defeats, the strength of organized labor in American reached its zenith in the middle decades of this century. It reached one of its lowest points in the 1980s, but it has definitely not expired. The future of organized labor remains uncertain. It also remains uncertain what role or roles organized religion in America will choose to play in the future of labor as businesses and workers move into the changes ahead. (GSS) **See also** Capitalism; "Economic Justice for All"; Gospel of Wealth; Race Relations.

BIBLIOGRAPHY

Ahlstrom, Sydney E. *A Religious History of the American People.* New Haven, CT: Yale University, 1972.

Colman, Penny. *Strike! The Bitter Struggle of American Workers from Colonial Times to the Present.* Brookfield, CT: Millbrook Press, 1995.

Forell, George W., ed. *Christian Social Teachings: A Reader in Christian Social Ethics from the Bible to the Present.* Minneapolis: Augsburg, 1971.

Geoghegan, Thomas. *Which Side Are You On? Trying to Be for Labor When It's Flat on Its Back.* New York: Farrar, Straus, & Giroux, 1991.

Glazer, Nathan. *American Judaism.* Chicago: University of Chicago Press, 1957.

May, Henry. *Protestant Churches and Industrial America.* New York: Harper, 1949.

Meltzer, Milton. *Bread—and Roses: The Struggle of American Labor, 1865-1915.* New York: Facts On File, 1991.

Montgomery, David. *The Fall of the House of Labor: The Workplace, the State, and American Labor Activism, 1864-1924.* Cambridge: Cambridge University Press, 1987.

Willis, James F. and Martin L. Primack. *An Economic History of the United States.* 2nd ed. Englewood Cliffs, NJ: Prentice Hall, 1989.

William Ladd (1778–1841)

Called the "Apostle of Peace," William Ladd was one of the nineteenth century's most prominent pacifists, sometimes creating controversy by opposing both offensive and defensive wars. In 1828, he founded the American Peace Society to promote his views. (The organization ceased operation with the founding of the United Nations in 1945.) In his book, *Essay on a Congress of Nations* (1840), he advocated the passing of international laws and the setting up of an international court to settle disputes. (MWP) **See also** Pacifism; War.

BIBLIOGRAPHY

Hemmenway, John. *A Review of the Life of William Ladd.* New Vienna, OH: Peace Association of Friends in America, 1875.

Timothy LaHaye (1926–) and Beverly Jean LaHaye (1929–)

Tim and Beverly LaHaye are two of the leading critics of **secular humanism** and the moral decline of the United States. Beginning in 1956 on a syndicated television program called "LaHayes on Family Life," the couple's national ministry has expanded to include articles, books, and a 1972 national lecture series called "Family Life Seminars."

Tim LaHaye is a **Baptist** minister who met his wife Beverly while both were attending Bob Jones University in 1946. During his ministry, which included several pastorates in Minnesota and California, LaHaye founded several educational and research institutes, including Christian Heritage College and the Institute for Creation Research. He gained national attention with his 1966 best-selling book, *Spirit-Controlled Temperament.* His 1980 book, *The Battle for the Mind,* was a critical attack on secular humanism that was highly regarded in Fundamentalist circles. His other books, including *The Battle for the Family* (1982) and *The Battle for the Public Schools* (1983), were also widely read in conservative circles. Understanding the growing link between his ministry and politics, he organized leaders of the **Religious Right** to form the American Coalition for Traditional Values, a political lobbying organization. He has authored more than 20 books and continues to be a popular Christian author and speaker.

Beverly LaHaye, who had dropped out of college after her marriage to Tim in 1947, played an important role in their joint ministry. Author of more than a half dozen books, Beverly organized Concerned Women for America in 1979 as an anti-**Equal Rights Amendment** and anti-**abortion** organization to counter the political effects of the National Organization for Women. The group's membership has surpassed that of NOW and Concerned Women for America is currently the largest women's organization in the United States. Beverly continues as the organization's leader and also hosts a nationally syndicated radio program, "Beverly LaHaye Live." **See also** Conservatism; Fundamentalists; Bob Jones; Televangelism.

BIBLIOGRAPHY

Clouse, R.G. "The New Christian Right, America and the Kingdom of God." *Christian Scholar's Review* 12 (1983): 3-16

"Tim LaHaye—DOOR Interview." *Wittenberg Door* 55 (June/July 1980): 8-12.

Lamb's Chapel v. Center Moriches Union Free School District (1993)

A school district permitted public groups to use its facilities after regular school hours, but when a religious organization sought permission to use a theater to show a religious movie, its request was rejected. The school district reasoned that to allow a religious group to use a public school building would represent an unconstitutional support of religion by the state. However, in *Lamb's Chapel v. Center Moriches Union Free School District,* 508 U.S. 384 (1993), the U.S. Supreme Court held that once a public forum is created, all groups must be treated equally. To bar a religious group based on its message would represent an unconstitutional form of public censorship. (FHJ) **See also** First Amendment; Public Aid to Religious Organizations.

BIBLIOGRAPHY

Salmone, Rosemary C. "Public Forum Doctrine and the Perils of Categorical Thinking: Lessons From Lamb's Chapel." *New Mexico Law Review* 24, no. 1 (Winter 1994): 1-26.

Sekulow, Jay Alan, Keith A. Fournier, and John D. Etheriedge. "*Lamb's Chapel v. Center Moriches Union Free School District:* An End to Religious Apartheid." *Mississippi College Law Review* 14 no. 1 (Fall 1993): 27-53.

Larson v. Valente (1982)

A Minnesota statute imposed a reporting requirement on religious organizations that solicited more than 50 percent of their funds from non-members. *In Larson v. Valente,* 456 U.S. 228 (1982), the U.S. Supreme Court invalidated the statute on the grounds that it violated the **Establishment Clause** of the **First Amendment**, largely on the grounds that the legislative history indicated that the law was tailored specifically to regulate the Moonies, the followers of the Rev. **Sun Myung Moon**, (*see* **Unification Church**). The Court stated that the law violated "the clearest command of the Establishment Clause, that one religious denomination cannot be officially preferred over another." (JM) **See also** Fourteenth Amendment; Wall of Separation.

BIBLIOGRAPHY

Boles, Donald E. "Religion and the Public Sector in Judicial Review." *Journal of Church and State.* 26, no. 1 (Winter 1984): 55-71.

Levinson, Rosalie Beger. "Separation of Church and State: And the Wall Came Tumbling Down." *Valparaiso University Law Review* 18, no. 4 (Summer 1984): 707-39.

Norman Lear (1922–)

Norman Lear, best known as a television writer and producer, is the most prominent founder of **People for the American Way**, an organization formed in 1980 to counter the political efforts of the **Religious Right**. After military service in World War II, Lear began a career as a Hollywood comedy writer and eventually created such popular television shows as "All in the Family" and "Mary Hartman, Mary Hartman." In recent years, he has stressed that his political beliefs are not anti-religious and he has emphasized the need for restoring spirituality and moral responsibility in American society. (KRD) **See also** Conservatism; Liberalism.

BIBLIOGRAPHY

Landy, Thomas. "What's Missing from this Picture? Norman Lear Explains." *Commonweal* 69, no. 17 (October 9, 1992): 17-20.

Lee v. Weisman (1992)

A middle school principal in Providence, Rhode Island, invited a rabbi to give a nonsectarian prayer at graduation ceremonies. A member of the graduating class went to court to get an injunction against prayers at public graduation exercises. In *Lee v. Weisman*, 505 U.S. 577 (1992), the U.S. Supreme Court, in a 5-4 decision, ruled that the principal was a representative of the state. When he selected a member of the clergy to offer a prayer and provided him with instructions as to the prayer's content, he was endorsing a civic religion and subjecting a group of students and their families to state-selected religion on one of the most important days of the students' lives. This action represented unconstitutional state involvement with religion in clear violation of the **Establishment Clause**.

Given the significance of the event, the unconstitutional nature of public prayer is not overcome by excusing an offended student from graduation exercises. Likewise, constitutional ills are not cured by permitting a student to leave the room during the prayer, because children would feel strong peer pressure to stay in the auditorium during the prayer. (FHJ) **See also** First Amendment; Fourteenth Amendment; School Prayer; Wall of Separation.

BIBLIOGRAPHY

Pershing, Stephen B. "Graduation Prayer After *Lee v. Weisman*: A Cautionary Tale. (Religious Speech in the Public Schools)" *Mercer Law Review* 46, no. 3 (Spring 1995): 1097-1121.

Schweitzer, Thomas A. "The Progeny of *Lee v. Weisman*: Can Student-Invited Prayer at Public School Graduation Still be Constitutional?" *BYU Journal of Public Law* 9, no. 2 (Fall 1995): 291-307.

Isaac Leeser (1806–1868)

When Isaac Meyer Wise attempted to unite nineteenth-century American Jews in non-traditional Reform **Judaism**, the German-born Isaac Leeser led the traditionalist opposition and thus helped to define conservative Judaism in the United States. In 1843, he became editor of *The Occident and American Jewish Advocate*, a conservative monthly newspaper that reflected his own political opinions. He was also responsible for establishing several schools and for an English translation of the Hebrew Bible. (MWP)

Isaac Leeser was a religious leader of traditional Jews in the nineteenth century. Library of Congress.

BIBLIOGRAPHY

Leeser, Isaac. *The Claims of the Jews to an Equality of Rights.* 1842.

Morias, Henry S. *Eminent Israelites of the Nineteenth Century.* 1880.

Sussman, Lance J. *Isaac Leeser and the Making of American Judaism*, Detroit: Wayne State University Press, 1995.

John Leland (1754–1841)

John Leland was an itinerant Baptist minister and ardent proponent of religious liberty in post-colonial America. Born in Massachusetts, he moved to Virginia in 1776 and emerged a leader among the Commonwealth's **Baptists** with a ministry that spanned nearly 15 years. He was instrumental in allying the Baptists with **Thomas Jefferson** and **James Madison** in the struggle to disestablish the **Episcopal Church** and secure freedom for religious dissenters. In 1791 Leland returned to his native New England, where he fought successfully for **disestablishment** and religious liberty in Connecticut and Massachusetts. The most celebrated episode of Leland's life was his presentation to President Jefferson on New Year's Day, 1802, of a "mammoth cheese" weighing 1,235 pounds as a token of support for Jefferson's politics. According to biographer L. H. Butterfield, Leland "was as courageous and resourceful a champion of the rights of conscience as America has produced." (DLD)

BIBLIOGRAPHY

Butterfield, L.H. "Elder John Leland, Jeffersonian Itinerant." *Proceedings of the American Antiquarian Society* 62 (October 1952): 155-242.

Green, L.F., ed. *The Writings of the Late Elder John Leland.* New York, 1845.

Lemon Test

In 1971, the U.S. Supreme Court laid down a legal standard for other courts when interpreting the **Establishment Clause** of the **First Amendment**, which states: "Congress shall make no law respecting an establishment of religion. . . ." The "*Lemon* Test" is named for Chief Justice **Warren E. Burger**'s opinion in the Supreme Court case, ***Lemon v. Kurtzman,*** 403 U.S. 602 (1971) and is comprised of three parts. Appropriate regulations and laws must (1) have a secular purpose, (2) have a principal effect that neither advances nor inhibits religion, and (3) not bring about an excessive entanglement with religion.

The Establishment Clause was first applied to the states in ***Everson v. Board of Education of the Township of Ewing*** 330 U.S. 1 (1947). Originally the clause applied only to Congress, but citing the "Equal Protection" clause of the **Fourteenth Amendment**, the Court applied it to the states and substate governments ("creatures of the state," such as public schools).

The first of the tests is "secular purpose." In *Everson*, the court found that New Jersey fulfilled a secular purpose by reimbursing parents for the costs of sending their children to either private or public schools on public transportation. In ***Abington Township v. Schempp***, 374 U.S. 203 (1963), the court struck down mandatory Bible reading in school, saying governments may neither "advance or inhibit religion," the second test. The third element in *Lemon* was taken from ***Walz v. Tax Commission of the City of New York*** 397 U.S. 664 (1970), upholding the New York City's property tax exemptions to religious organizations as "not an excessive entanglement with religion." In *Lemon*, state financial supplements to non-public schools were challenged. The court pulled together these three criteria and found that state supplements to non-public schools for secular subjects created an entangling relationship between church and state, thereby violating separation of church and state.

Whether the *Lemon* Test will continue to serve as a sufficient standard has been questioned by several current Supreme Court justices, but it has not been overruled by a Supreme Court decision. (JRV) **See also** Entanglement Test; Public Aid to Religious Organizations; Tax-Exempt Status; Wall of Separation.

BIBLIOGRAPHY

Lee, Francis Graham, ed. *All Imaginable Liberty: The Religious Liberty Clauses of the First Amendment.* Lanham, MD: University Press of America, 1995.

Lemon v. Kurtzman (1971)

In *Lemon v. Kurtzman*, 403 U.S. 602 (1971), the U.S. Supreme Court, deciding that a state could not pay non-public school teachers for teaching secular subjects, nor reimburse a non-public school for its expenses in teaching secular subjects, established the ***Lemon* Test**. Rhode Island provided a supplemental salary for state-certified teachers in non-public schools teaching secular courses using the same instructional materials as were used in the public schools. One-fourth of the school population was served by non-public schools, mostly Catholic schools. Pennsylvania reimbursed non-public schools for costs of instruction, including books and other material, used in secular courses. Chief Justice **Warren E. Burger**, who wrote the Court's opinion in the case, derived this triple test for interpreting the **Establishment Clause** of the **First Amendment**: Any law or regulation must have a secular, not a religious purpose; its principal effect may neither advance not inhibit religion; and it must not bring about "an excessive government entanglement with religion." Subsequent cases have applied and elaborated on the "*Lemon* Test." Its principles have been effectuated in public school procedures across the United States. (JRV)

BIBLIOGRAPHY

Levy, Leonard Williams. *The Establishment Clause: Religion and the First Amendment. 2nd ed. rev.* Chapel Hill: University of North Carolina Press, 1994.

A Letter Concerning Toleration (John Locke)

The British political philosopher John Locke's *A Letter Concerning Tolerance* is considered by many to be the most influential document ever written in support of religious tolerance. Locke's *Letter* had a profound impact upon **Thomas Jefferson**, one of America's greatest advocates for religious liberty. Locke's argument proceeded on two grounds: the theological and the philosophical. These two grounds, if not naturally compatible, can be made to be politically complementary. In the *Letter*, Locke proclaims, "I esteem that Tolerance to be the Chief Characteristical mark of the True Church." Yet in the same work—relying upon the reasoning set forth in his *Second Treatise*, a work that abounds with anti-theological implications—Locke restricts the end of society to the protection of what he terms men's "Civil Interests." Chief among these interests are life, liberty, and property. (SJL)

Bibliography

Locke, John. *A Letter Concerning Toleration.* James H. Tully, ed. Indianapolis: Hackett, 1983.

Marshall, John. *John Locke: Resistance, Religion and Responsibility.* New York: Cambridge University Press, 1994.

Levitt v. Committee for Public Education (1973)

A New York law appropriated $28,000,000 to reimburse non-public schools for the expense of state-mandated services. While the statute stated that it did not authorize payments for religious worship or instruction, church-sponsored schools were eligible to receive payments. The statute was challenged as a violation of the **Establishment Clause** of the **First Amendment**. In *Levitt v. Committee for Public Education*, 413 U.S. 472 (1973), the U.S. Supreme Court ruled that it represented an impermissible aid to religion because no attempt was made to ensure that funded activities were free of religious instruction and avoided inculcating students in the religious precepts of the church sponsoring the school. (JM) **See also** Public Aid to Religious Organizations.

Bibliography

Bryson, Joseph E. *The Supreme Court and Public Funds for Religious Schools.* Jefferson, NC: McFarland, 1990.

Leonard W. Levy (1923–)

A Pulitzer Prize–winning constitutional historian, Levy is a former professor at Brandeis University and Claremont Graduate University. He has written extensively on the meaning of the **First Amendment**'s **Establishment Clause**, arguing that its ban on laws "respecting an establishment of religion" was intended to prevent even non-preferential federal aid to religion. A defender of the principle of church-state separation, Levy points out that separation safeguards religion as much as it does the state. Levy also has written a legal history of the crime of blasphemy. (JGW)

Bibliography

Levy, Leonard W. *The Establishment Clause: Religion and the First Amendment.* 2nd rev. ed. Chapel Hill: University of North Carolina Press, 1994.

Levy, Leonard W. *Blasphemy: Verbal Offense Against the Sacred, from Moses to Salman Rushdie.* Chapel Hill: University of North Carolina Press, 1995.

Liberalism

Today to say that someone is "liberal" is to place him or her on the left of the political spectrum. Priding themselves on their compassion, liberals disapprove strenuously of "greed" and "elitism"; for them wealth and status are suspect goals. Perhaps what liberals today most passionately disapprove of is what they see as a certain type of invidious discrimination, one that denies equal recognition to a person because of an inherent or natural characteristic. Above all, racism and sexism are evils that must be eradicated. So circumscribed, liberalism is a type of democratic egalitarianism. However, this definition does not take into account the distinctions that exist between various kinds of liberalism, e.g., welfare-state liberalism and neo-liberalism. Yet unlike their conservative counterparts, liberals are largely united on the goals of society. Liberals are confident that **democracy** and equality are good things, and they seek to ensure that we have increasing amounts of each. The term "liberalism" has today been largely supplanted by "progressivism." President **Bill Clinton**, whose views closely correspond to those of the self-identified liberalism of the last half-century, prefers to call himself a "progressive." Recently, liberalism as a term has even fallen into disrepute; in the 1988 presidential election, the "L"-word became synonymous with a type of fuzzy-headed idealism. Yet this was not always the case. Liberalism was once a term of approbation in the U.S. To be an American was to be liberal. Even the most conservative of our Founders would have been insulted had they been accused of harboring principles that were not liberal. How is it that liberalism has gone from being a term of strong approval to one of dubious repute?

The original meaning of liberalism is to some extent captured today, if negatively, by the term "illiberal." To be illiberal is to be mean and narrow. Liberalism in the U.S. was originally associated with, among other things, a certain generosity of spirit. Citizens were proud to be liberal democrats, "liberal" democracy being a term that denoted the American way of life as a society. The most famous expression of American liberalism is the **Declaration of Independence**, whose most celebrated statement is the following: "We hold these Truths to be self-evident, that all Men are Created equal, that they are endowed by their Creator with certain unalienable rights, that among these are life, liberty and the pursuit of happiness." But standing up for these rights required the signers of the Declaration to pledge their lives, their fortunes, and their sacred honor. Thus, from the Founders' perspective, the possession of liberty in the contemporary sense is seen to depend on generosity or liberality of spirit in the older sense. Ironically, the character of this dependence seems to indicate that the very victory of the liberal principles set forth by the Declaration would make less necessary the liberality of spirit needed to win such a victory, for one does not need admirable qualities of soul to embrace principles that are more or less universally accepted.

Perhaps nowhere is the difficulty into which this paradox leads more clearly exhibited than in the issue of religious liberty, an issue that is noteworthy in its absence from contemporary liberalism's list of pressing concerns. Modern liberals are not indifferent to religious liberty. If and when called upon, they are zealous defenders of "the **wall of separation** between church and state," to employ **Thomas Jefferson**'s famous metaphor. It is only that they are almost never called upon. Religious liberty is largely taken for granted. When we turn to the writings of Jefferson and of **James Madison**, the other great advocate of religious liberty during the Founding era, it is generally with a view to determining a legalistic fine point, or—perhaps more often—to finding support for a particular opinion on a legalistic fine point. One recent Supreme Court decision serves as an example, ***Employment Division of Oregon v. Smith*** (1990). The issue at stake in this case, whether or not members of the Native American Church of Oregon should be allowed to smoke peyote as part of their religious rituals, is not fundamental from the point of view of the original advocates for religious liberty; it is simply a question of how far religious liberty should extend in the face of considerable conflict with civil interests. There is no question as to whether the Indians should be compelled to become Christian. The principle of religious liberty itself is a given. Much the same could be said of the Supreme Court's activity in this realm within the past half-century.

Though no one today would question the blessings we owe to our heritage of religious liberty, one might wonder whether there is not a price we pay in taking this freedom for granted. Liberalism as a theoretical teaching largely grew out of the felt need to overcome, not merely religious intolerance, but religious persecution. The aspiration for religious liberty—perhaps more than any other good—animated the liberalism of the Founders. When Madison attempted to define the term "property," he listed five types of property to which people have rights. The only one he singled out as having a "peculiar value" was religious liberty.

Why, then, was this question of particular concern to the Founders and to other early liberals? Religious intolerance and persecution, for all of their ugliness, bespeak a strong faith in one's religion, a belief that it teaches the one right way to live. The principles of liberalism, as set forth in the Declaration of Independence, assert that all people have a natural right to liberty. From the point of view of religion, this means that government smiles equally upon those who live the one right way and all those who live the wrong way—for liberals were in favor not only of religious toleration, but of religious freedom. To tolerate is to grant sufferance; it is to make allowances for others' failings. Thus a government that practices religious tolerance need not be silent on the question of which religion is the true one; it merely chooses not to force its views onto those who will not willingly accept them. Religious freedom, on the other hand, means that the government is silent on the question of the true religion. It implies a neutral stance towards the various religions. Thus a government that establishes religious liberty appears to be indifferent to the fundamental question that is the concern of religion. Before the unquestioned triumph of liberal principles, one had to confront the adamant claim of believers that they knew the right way for all to live. One had to take this claim seriously and ultimately to accept or to reject it. One had no choice but to consider seriously whether the truth or falsity of these claims should be the concern of government. Early liberals' support for religious freedom presupposed such a consideration, and they tried to convince others that their conclusion was the right one.

Today, by contrast, liberals take this freedom for granted; they assume from the outset that government should be indifferent to the truth or falsity of citizens' beliefs, and that it should only concern itself with protecting the right to these beliefs. But the failure to raise the question as to the goodness of religious freedom bespeaks a failure seriously to consider whether or not there is one right way of life, and, if so, what that life might demand of us. In other words, religious liberty is an answer to a question of fundamental importance, but the unthinking acceptance of that answer tends to make one oblivious of the question itself.

The results of a recent Gallup poll illustrate the character of such oblivion and indicate its presence in the U.S. today. According to this survey, 77 percent of the American people claimed to accept "the full authority of the Bible." At the same time, the survey found that only 42 percent of Americans can identify the author of the Sermon on the Mount or even name the four gospels. What is most striking in these statistics is not the number of Americans who profess belief or disbelief, but rather the apparent lack of awareness of what genuine religious belief would entail. This lack of awareness may be the price to be paid for the unequivocal victory of the principle of religious freedom. The Founders themselves were not unaware that the establishment of religious liberty could have such an effect. In his *Notes on the State of Virginia* (Query XVII), Jefferson praises New York and Pennsylvania, two pre-Revolutionary states that had "long subsisted without any [religious] establishment at all," for making "the happy discovery, that the way to silence religious disputes, is to take no notice of them." The indifference begotten by religious liberty may then be desirable insofar as it is needed to preserve peace and order. Yet, at the same time, this fostering of indifference to religion may be problematic not only from the point of view of religion, but from that of liberty as well, as Jefferson himself emphasized. For in the same work, he raises a question that even contemporary liberals may find troubling: "And can the liberties of a nation be thought secure when we have removed their only firm basis, a conviction in the minds of the people that these liberties are the gift of God? That they are not to be violated but with his wrath?"

If it is true that religious liberty is no longer foremost in the hearts of today's liberals, it is by no means true that contemporary liberalism as a political creed has entirely divorced itself from religion, or at the very least, from certain religious organizations and congregations. The Catholic Bishops of America periodically issue letters that call for, among other things, greater social and economic justice ("justice" understood as economic equality—for man must have bread to live). The "nuclear freeze" movement of the 1980s found solace and support from many churches. In the past decades there has even arisen from certain left-liberal churches an ideology known as "**liberation theology**," which preaches against any American intervention in the internal affairs of our "progressive" neighbors to the south. What is peculiar about many of these church-led efforts is that they do not try to use the moral authority of their creeds to promote the cause or aims of religion (unlike, e.g., the **Religious Right**), but that they use the moral authority of religion to promote ends that are, for the most part, religiously indifferent. But whatever one may think of these efforts, one cannot overlook the crucial role that the church played in twentieth-century liberalism's greatest domestic achievement: the **civil rights** movement of the 1950s and 1960s. That movement gained much of its impetus from black churches, as well as other religious organizations. The movement might be held up as the model of how church-led opinions can be made, not simply to avoid conflict with, but to complement classically liberal principles in the U.S. (KES) **See also** Abortion and Birth Control Regulation; African-American Churches; Americanism; Atheism; Capital Punishment; Conservatism; Democratic Party; Equal Rights Amendment; Euthanasia; Evolution; Labor; Native American Religions; New Deal; Nuclear Disarmament; Race Relations; Republican Party; Secular Humanism; Social Justice; Women in Religion and Politics.

Bibliography

Croly, Herbert. *The Promise of American Life.* New York: Macmillan, 1911.

Galston, William. *Liberal Purposes: Goods, Virtues and Diversity in the Liberal State.* New York: Cambridge University Press, 1991.

Hartz, Louis. *The Liberal Tradition in American Political Thought since the Revolution.* New York: Harcourt, Brace, 1955.

Mansfield, Harvey C. Jr. *The Spirit of Liberalism.* Cambridge, MA: Harvard University Press, 1978.

Rawls, John. *Political Liberalism.* New York: Columbia University Press, 1996.

Sandel, Michael, ed. *Liberalism and its Critics.* Oxford: Blackwell Press, 1984.

Strauss, Leo. *Liberalism: Ancient and Modern.* New York: Basic Books, 1968.

Walzer, Michael. *Spheres of Justice: A Defense of Pluralism and Equality.* New York: Basic Books, 1983.

Liberation Theology

Liberation theology emerged in the post-**World War II** world as a hybrid of Protestant and Catholic thinking, synthesized with Marxism. In the wake of the failure of many of the churches to address the rise of Hitler, some theologians began to move theological reflection away from speculative pursuits toward a more practical theology. Foremost among these was the Protestant theologian Jurgen Moltmann, who attempted to demonstrate that **Max Weber** erred in linking **Calvinism** to **capitalism**, arguing, by stressing the common eschatological element in each, that Calvinism was more closely attuned to socialism.

The convergence of Christianity and socialism took on a more revolutionary flavor when transplanted to the Latin American context, where Liberation Theology has fomented. Most of the theologians in Latin America were educated in Europe, and more than half of the clergy—who form the backbone of the liberation theology movement (although only 19 percent consider themselves such)—are foreign missionaries. Nearly all are Catholic. Liberation theology draws the strength of its appeal from its analysis of poverty. This analysis is twofold: first, by turning more to scriptural theology rather than systematic theology, Liberation Theologians focused on the book of Exodus and various Gospel sayings to conclude that God "was on the side of the poor and oppressed" and desired their liberation from their status as victims; and, second, by drawing on their interpretation of Marxism to show that the impoverished state of the third world was due to its dependency on the developed nations, and political and economic liberation could only come if the underdeveloped nations would assert their autonomy. Liberation theologians argue that social problems are derived from social conditions, most notably the nature of power relationships in society, and that the gospel teaches a form of consciousness-raising which makes people aware of their oppressed state and recognize that revolution against their oppressors is a divine mandate and a historical necessity. (JP) **See also** Imperialism; Liberalism; Roman Catholicism; Social Justice; Socialism and Communism.

Bibliography

Gutierrez, Gustavo. *A Theology of Liberation.* Trans. Sr. Caridad Inda and John Eagleson. Maryknoll, NY: Orbis Books, 1973.

Miranda, Jose. *Marx and the Bible.* Trans. John Eagleson. Maryknoll, NY: Orbis Books, 1974.

Liberty Party

Formed in 1840, the Liberty Party was an outgrowth of the American and Foreign Anti-Slavery Society and was the first political party in the United States dedicated to the **abolition** of **slavery**. The formation of this party resulted in a split among abolitionists, many of whom believed that their cause was better served by remaining within the major parties. But when the Whig Party nominated William Henry Harrison, a slavery supporter, for president in 1840, many abolitionists were angered, and the Liberty Party ran James G. Birney as a presidential candidate. The platform, however, was a moderate one, calling only for the elimination of slavery in federally administered areas and the prohibition of the interstate slave trade. The party did not regard the abolition of slavery within a state a matter over which the federal government had any authority.

The Liberty Party initially had little impact, as abolitionists had feared. Both the Whigs and Democrats were ignoring the slavery issue in 1840, and the newspapers barely mentioned that an abolitionist party had been formed. Even abolitionists failed to strongly support the party, preferring to use their influence on banking and tariff issues. In the end, the party garnered only 7,000 votes, which was a mere 0.3 percent of the vote. The party ran Birney again in 1844, this time garnering 2.3 percent of the vote. Birney had a major impact on the election, however, but not in the way the party had hoped; his 15,812 votes in New York gave Birney that state's 36 electoral votes, swinging the election to Democrat James K. Polk, a Tennessee slave-owner. Following this disappointing and counter-productive showing, the party split into three factions, with some of its leaders creating a new party with even more moderate views on slavery, the Free Soil Party, while the remaining members split into two groups that disagreed over the direction of the party's platform. In 1848, one of these factions, headed by **Gerrit Smith**, split off to form the Liberty League, which addressed other issues in addition to slavery. The now-purified Liberty Party, in its last election, ran a reluctant New Hampshire Senator, John Hale. (JM)

Bibliography

Rosenstone, Steven J. *Third Parties in America.* Princeton: Princeton University Press, 1984.

Abraham Lincoln (1809–1865)

Abraham Lincoln was the sixteenth president of the United States and is considered by many to be its greatest. Lincoln's religious beliefs are a matter of controversy. By his own admission he was "not a member of any Christian Church," but his speeches have an undeniably religious, even Biblical, resonance to them. Few, if any, Americans have used the language and imagery of religion in as beautiful and as profound a way as Lincoln did. His most famous speeches and statements abound in words, Biblical and otherwise, that elevate the principles enunciated in the **Declaration of Independence** into an American civil religion. It is not an accident that some have spoken of Lincoln as an American prophet.

According to Lincoln, it is the principles of the Declaration—especially the "proposition" that "all men are created equal"—that animate our way of life as a society. The Declaration "meant to set up a standard maxim for a free society, which should be familiar to all, and revered by all." By Lincoln's account, to be an American, to be fully American, is to aspire to live up to the demands that naturally follow from the holding of the Declaration's self-evident truths.

Perhaps nowhere did Lincoln use religious language in as meaningful way as in his Second Inaugural Address. Therein, he broached the possibility that the **Civil War** was Providential punishment visited upon all Americans, North as well as South, for their complicity in the evil of **slavery**. By noting the peculiarity of a war in which both sides "read the same Bible, and pray to the same God," Lincoln brought forth the necessarily problematic character of an appeal to divine justice, as opposed to divine mercy; justice may demand that both sides be punished. Though he found it particularly strange "that any man should dare to ask assistance in wringing their bread from the sweat of other men's faces," he resisted the temptation to moralize: "Let us judge not that we be not judged." (Lincoln's Second Inaugural Address is reprinted in Appendix 1.) (SJL) **See also** Abolition; Civil Religion; Race Relations.

Abraham Lincoln helped promote the strand of American civil religion that is based on the Declaration of Independence. National Archives.

Bibliography

Jaffa, Harry V. *Crisis of the House Divided.* Chicago: University of Chicago Press, 1959.

Lincoln, Abraham. *His Speeches and Writings.* Roy P. Basler, ed. New York: Da Capo Press, 1990.

John Locke (1632–1704)

John Locke has been called the philosopher of the **American Revolution**. Perhaps more than any other thinker, Locke defined the terms of the Revolutionary debate. His writings, especially his *Two Treatises of Government* and his ***A Letter Concerning Toleration***, are preeminent sources of classical **liberalism**. One cannot help but notice the

Lockean provenance of many of the most weighty thoughts and statements of the Founding period. To give just one telling example, in his *Second Treatise*, Locke speaks of men's natural rights to "life, liberty, and property"; the **Declaration of Independence** speaks of men's unalienable rights to "life, liberty, and the pursuit of happiness." (The term "the pursuit of happiness" also has a Lockean origin.) **Thomas Jefferson**'s praise for Locke was almost unlimited. The author of the Declaration included Locke among his "trinity of the three greatest men the world has ever seen" and called his *Second Treatise* "perfect as far as it goes." Among other places, one can see Locke's influence in two great American works devoted to the defense of religious liberty, Jefferson's "A Bill for Establishing Religious Freedom" and **James Madison**'s "Memorial and Remonstrance." Put briefly, Locke argued for removing the concern with the other-worldly from the political realm so as to preserve peace in this world. (SJL) **See also** Colonial America.

The political philosophy of English writer John Locke shaped the views of many American Founding Fathers on politics and religion. Library of Congress.

BIBLIOGRAPHY

Locke, John. *A Letter Concerning Toleration.* James H. Tully, ed. Indianapolis: Hackett, 1983.

Locke, John. *Two Treatises of Government.* Peter Laslett, ed. New York: Mentor Books, 1965.

Simmons, A. John. *The Lockean Theory of Rights.* Princeton, NJ: Princeton University Press, 1997.

Lost Cause Myth

After the **Civil War**, both North and South needed to find a meaning for the hundreds of thousands of young men killed or crippled by the fighting. For the winning side, an end to **slavery** and the restoration of the union provided relatively easy answers. Southerners found explaining their lost cause far more difficult. The answer could not lie in slavery or independence, since one had been abolished and the other had been lost. They found answers in their religion and a belief in the superiority of their culture. No longer about slavery or states' rights, the war became a defense of the Southern way of life.

In a deeply religious South, the myth took on the aura of religion. Those who had led the South, Jefferson Davis, Robert E. Lee, and Stonewall Jackson became saints revered more for their moral character than their military abilities. Those who had died in the fighting were martyrs. Relics of the **war** became sacred objects and graves of soldiers were decorated with flowers on a uniquely Southern Memorial Day, June 3. Even a distinctive literature grew up, finding its most powerful expression in the book, and later the film, *Gone with the Wind.*

The myth was strongest in parts of the South that had borne the brunt of the fighting, from Tennessee and Georgia through Virginia. It was also most powerful in the half-century after the war when memories were strongest. Today the myth survives among history buffs with a particularly Southern way of looking at what they called the War of Northern Aggression. (MWP) **See also** Reconstruction.

BIBLIOGRAPHY

Osterweis, Rollin G. *The Myth of the Lost Cause, 1865–1900.* Hamden, CT: Shoe String Press, 1973.

Wilson, Charles R. "The Religion of the Lost Cause." David G. Hackett, ed. *Religion and American Culture.* New York: Routledge, 1995.

Lovell v. City of Griffin, Georgia (1938)

Alma Lovell was convicted in the city of Griffin, Georgia, for violating a city ordinance that required written permission from the city manager before distributing circulars, handbooks, advertising, or literature of any kind. The conviction was based on distribution, free of charge, of a religious pamphlet setting forth the gospel of the "Kingdom of Jehovah." The conviction was challenged as an abridgment of freedom of the press and freedom of religious exercise. In *Lovell v. City of Griffin, Georgia*, 303 U.S. 444 (1938), the U.S. Supreme Court invalidated the ordinance, stating that it "strikes at the very foundation of the freedom of the press by subjecting it to license and censorship." (JM) **See also** First Amendment; Fourteenth Amendment; Jehovah's Witnesses.

BIBLIOGRAPHY

Chopper, Jesse H. *Securing Religious Liberty.* Chicago: University of Chicago Press, 1995.

Martin Luther (1483–1546)

German theologian Martin Luther was an ordained Catholic priest and Augustinian monk. His protest against the theology and practices of the Roman Catholic Church led to the formation of the Protestant churches, including the **Lutheran Church**.

Luther rejected the notion that the church was superior to the state, believing instead that both church and state were created by God to fulfill different functions.

Martin Luther was a leader of the sixteenth-century Protestant Reformation. National Archives.

The church was to preach the word of God, the state was to provide for order and some measure of justice in society. This view is often called the "two kingdoms" theory. Luther also rejected the idea that the clerical or religious life was superior to other occupations and saw involvement in the secular, political realm as an honorable Christian vocation. (MJH) **See also** Reformation.

Bibliography

Thompson, W. D. J. Cargill. *The Political Thought of Martin Luther.* Sussex, NJ: Barnes & Noble Books, 1984.

Lutheran Church

The Lutheran Church began in the religious **reformation** led by **Martin Luther** in the sixteenth century. Lutherans first arrived in the United States in the seventeenth century and settled in the middle colonies. The first important leader was Henry Melchior Muhlenberg, an immigrant German pastor who organized the Lutheran church among the Germans in Pennsylvania in the mid-eighteenth century. During the nineteenth century, Lutheran immigrants continued to arrive from Germany and were joined by others from Scandinavia, eastern Europe, and Russia. Church bodies tended to be organized initially along ethnic lines, but as generations passed and English became the common language, some merged with others. Currently the two major Lutheran bodies in the United States are the Evangelical Lutheran Church of America (ELCA), baptized membership 5,180,000, headquartered in Chicago, and the Lutheran Church-Missouri Synod (LCMS), baptized membership 2,600,000, headquartered in St. Louis. Several smaller Lutheran bodies also exist. Lutherans tend to be concentrated in Pennsylvania, the Midwest, the Northern Plains, and the Pacific Northwest.

The Lutheran confessions, especially the Augsburg Confession (1530), articles 16 and 28, set forth the Lutheran view of government's role. The Lutheran tradition, following the "two kingdoms" theory developed by Martin Luther, holds that government has been created by God for the purpose of curbing evil and upholding justice in this world; it is not a step or a means to the Kingdom of God or some other utopia. The function of government is good and necessary; however, this does not mean that governments always act properly. Disobedience may be necessary when a government commands something which cannot be obeyed without sin. The distinction between the civil and spiritual orders (or kingdom) cannot be reduced to an absolute separation between church and state. Both kingdoms are God's, each has a purpose, and their purposes complement each other. Interaction is inevitable and desirable. For example, the church is expected to call the state to account before God's law for all humans. The state is expected to govern in accordance with God's law written into creation and accessible to the reason of all humans. A Christian should participate in the civil order but should not claim superior knowledge of how to run civic affairs based on the Christian faith. All human efforts to discern and fulfill the law are clouded by sin. The Lutheran tradition recognizes that a measure of civil righteousness can be achieved but ultimately all human efforts require correction. However, this is not a cause for despair; it frees individuals and societies to seek and value the relative goods or relative justice which humans can achieve.

Lutheran church bodies have varied in the degree to which they engage in advocacy on socio-political issues. The ELCA maintains an Office for Governmental Affairs and the LCMS maintains an Office of Government Information. Both of these are located in Washington, DC. (MJH)

Bibliography

Benne, Robert. *The Paradoxical Vision: A Public Theology for the Twenty-First Century.* Minneapolis: Augsburg Fortress, 1995.

Nelson, E. Clifford, ed. *The Lutheran in North America.* Philadelphia: Fortress Press, 1975.

Tappert, Theodore G., ed. *The Book of Concord: The Confessions of the Evangelical Lutheran Church.* Philadelphia: Fortress Press, 1959.

Lynch v. Donnelly (1984)

The city of Pawtucket, Rhode Island, annually erected a "Season's Greetings" display on public property, which included a Christian creche and to which a group of citizens objected. In *Lynch v. Donnelly*, 465 U.S. 668 (1984), the U.S. Supreme Court held that, while government cannot endorse or coerce participation in religious expression, government must not be hostile toward religion nor treat it with "callous indifference." The Constitution requires reasonable accommodation of all religious beliefs. Here, the Court noted the creche was part of a larger seasonal display, it had historical as well as religious significance, and it was not a surreptitious attempt by government to support a particular religious belief. (FHJ) **See also** Establishment Clause; First Amendment; Fourteenth Amendment; Publicly Funded Religious Displays; Wall of Separation.

BIBLIOGRAPHY

Fairchild, David C. "*Lynch v. Donnelly*: The Case for the Creche." *Saint Louis University Law Journal* 29, no. 2 (March 1985): 459-488.

Myers, Richard S. "The Establishment Clause and the Nativity Scene: A Reassessment of Lynch v. Donnelly." *The Kentucky Law Journal* 77, no. 1 (Fall 1988): 61-115.

Lyng v. Northwest Indian Cemetery Protection Association (1988)

In 1982, the U.S. Forest Service announced plans to construct a highway through an area of the Six Rivers National Forest and also allow timber harvesting there. The area in question had historically been used by certain American Indians for religious rituals that depended upon privacy, silence, and an undisturbed natural setting. In *Lyng v. Northwest Indian Cemetery Protection Association*, 485 U.S. 439 (1988), the U.S. Supreme Court rejected a challenge to these actions based on the claim that they would violate Indians' rights under the **Free Exercise Clause** of the **First Amendment**, stating, "Even assuming that the Government's actions here will virtually destroy the Indians' ability to practice their religion, the Constitution simply does not provide a principle that could justify upholding respondents' legal claims." (JM) **See also** Native American Religions.

BIBLIOGRAPHY

Brooks, Samuel D. "Native Americans' Fruitless Search for First Amendment Protection of their Sacred Religious Sites." *Valparaiso University Law Review* 24, no. 3 (Spring 1990): 521-51.

Crain, Christopher A. "Free Exercise of Religion and Indian Burial Grounds." *Harvard Journal of Law and Public Policy* 12, no. 1 (Winter 1989): 246-51.

M

J. Gresham Machen (1881–1937)

J. Machen was a staunch Calvinist minister and theologian in the **Presbyterian Church** in the United States. He was deposed from a professorship at Princeton Theological Seminary, the leading Presbyterian seminary of the day, because he opposed liberalizing changes in the Westminster confession and in denominational missionary activities during the **Fundamentalist-Modernist Controversy**. He defended historic interpretations of the Bible and doctrine, founded and taught at Westminster Theological Seminary in Philadelphia, and led in the establishment of the Presbyterian Church in America (later known as the Orthodox Presbyterian Church). He wrote widely for both scholarly and popular audiences, and is remembered for the concise definitions in his *Christianity and Liberalism* (1923). (JRV) **See also** Calvinism; Liberalism.

BIBLIOGRAPHY

Hart, Darryl G. *Defending the Faith: J. Gresham Machen and the Crisis of Conservative Protestantism in Modern America.* Baltimore, MD: Johns Hopkins Press, 1994.

Alasdair MacIntyre (1929–)

Born in Glasgow, Scotland, professor of philosophy Alasdair MacIntyre is an influential critic of twentieth-century **liberalism**, often placed in the intellectual company of contemporary communitarian thinkers Charles Taylor and Michael Sandel. He has taught at universities in the United States since 1969. Unlike other philosophical communitarians, he draws upon and refers to theological traditions and has influenced contemporary theologians and ethicists. (BDG) **See also** Communitarianism.

BIBLIOGRAPHY

MacIntyre, Alasdair. *After Virtue: A Study in Moral Theory.* Indiana: University of Notre Dame Press, 1984.

MacIntyre, Alasdair. *Marxism and Christianity.* London: Duckworth, 1995.

James Madison (1751–1836)

James Madison was an untiring advocate for the rights of conscience and a leading architect of the American constitutional approach to church-state relations. As a delegate to the Virginia Convention of 1776, he proposed amending **George Mason**'s draft of Article XVI of the **Virginia Declaration of Rights**, from a statement of religious toleration to the first official legislative pronouncement that all men are equally entitled to the free exercise of religion. The adoption of Madison's amendment reoriented American thinking on religious exercise from mere tolerance to liberty and equality in religious exercise.

In mid-1785, Madison drafted the **"Memorial and Remonstrance Against Religious Assessments"** in a successful campaign to mobilize opposition to a proposed general assessment for the support of teachers of the Christian religion. The "Memorial and Remonstrance," a succinct statement of Madison's church-state views, is one of the most powerful American defenses of religious liberty and **disestablishment**. Encouraged by the defeat of the general assessment proposal, Madison introduced and guided to passage in the Virginia legislature **Thomas Jefferson**'s "Bill for Establishing Religious Freedom."

James Madison, the future fourth president of the United States, played a key role in the drafting and ratification of the First Amendment. Library of Congress.

Madison was a leading figure in the Philadelphia convention of 1787 that drafted the U.S. Constitution. In the subsequent ratification debate, Madison reluctantly acceded to antifederalist demands for a national bill of rights in order to neutralize opposition to the Constitution. As a member of the First Congress, he orchestrated the framing of a bill of rights. In June 1789 he proposed the following article that, after much revision and ratification, became the **First Amendment** religion clause: "The civil rights of none shall be abridged on account of religious belief or worship, nor shall any national religion be established, nor shall the full and equal rights of conscience be in any manner, or on any pretext, infringed."

As U.S. president, he vetoed congressional measures "incorporating the Protestant **Episcopal Church** in the Town of Alexandria in the District of Columbia" and setting apart federal land in the Mississippi territory for a Baptist church, because he said they violated the constitutional prohibition on religious establishment. Late in life Madison expressed the separationist opinion that legislative chaplains paid from public funds and executive proclamations of days for public thanksgiving and prayer violated the ban on religious establishment. This view was not wholly consistent with his actions as an elected official. For example, as a Virginia legislator in 1785, he introduced bills from Virginia's revised code that included, along with Jefferson's "Bill for Establishing Religious Freedom," a "Bill for Punishing Disturbers of Religious Worship and Sabbath Breakers" and a "Bill for Appointing Days of Public Fasting and Thanksgiving." As U.S. president, on at least four occasions, he issued proclamations designating days for public thanksgiving and prayer.

Madison believed that the civil government must treat all religious sects equally; thus, he fervently opposed the establishment of a national church or any arrangement that gave one religion legal preference. He also thought that the best and only security for religious liberty is a multiplicity of contending religious sects that would check one sect or group of sects from establishing a religion to which all others would be compelled to conform. (DLD) **See also** Baptists; Colonial America; Constitutional Amendments on Religion (Proposed); Establishment Clause; Public Aid to Religious Organizations; Thanksgiving and Fast Days; Wall of Separation.

Bibliography

Alley, Robert S., ed. *James Madison on Religious Liberty.* Buffalo, NY: Prometheus, 1985.

Asa Mahan (1799–1889)

Asa Mahan was one of the nineteenth century's leading advocates of the Wesleyan/holiness doctrine of sanctification. He had a varied career as a pastor, writer, and university president. His outspoken condemnation of **slavery** included a call for social reform and complete equality for African Americans. In fact, he accepted the presidency of Oberlin College on the grounds that it would be open to African Americans. (MWP) **See also** Civil Rights; Methodism; Race Relations.

Bibliography

Maddan, Edward H. and James E. Hamilton. *Freedom and Grace.* Metuchen, NJ: Scarecrow Press, 1982.

Malcolm X (1925–1965)

A Muslim cleric, social activist, and theorist of black nationalism, Malcolm Little was born in Omaha, Nebraska, the son of an itinerant Baptist minister who died in an accident when Malcolm was six. Little spent a number of years in foster homes as child, and during his teenage and young adult years he lived in Boston and New York, where he sold drugs and committed burglaries. Arrested and convicted of burglary, Malcolm was imprisoned from 1946 to 1952. While in prison, he read the works of **Elijah Muhammad** and eventually converted to **Islam**. After prison, Malcolm followed Muhammad's counsel and changed his name from Malcolm Little to Malcolm X. He quickly became a major spokesman for the **Nation of Islam**.

Conflicts soon arose between Malcolm and the more traditionalist Elijah Muhammad, who suspended Malcolm's ministerial status in 1963. Malcolm X traveled to Mecca in Saudi Arabia in 1964 and proclaimed himself an orthodox Muslim. Upon his return to the United States, Malcolm X founded the Organization of Afro-American Unity, which signalled a change in strategy and worldview from his earlier days. Instead of promoting black nationalism, Malcolm X began to advocate racial toleration and international socialism. He was assassinated in New York in 1965 by members of the Nation of Islam. Malcolm X's complex legacy as a religious and political leader can be witnessed in a variety of contemporary movements. (HLC) **See also** African-American Churches; Baptists; Black Theology; Civil Rights; Wallace D. Fard; Louis Eugene Farrakhan; Martin Luther King, Jr.; Race Relations; Socialism and Communism.

Bibliography

Dyson, Michael Eric. *Making Malcolm: The Myth and Meaning of Malcolm X.* New York: Oxford University Press, 1995.

Malcolm X. *The Autobiography of Malcolm X.* New York: Ballantine, 1992.

Manifest Destiny

The belief that Americans were destined, by Providence and for the good of soon-to-be-conquered societies, to spread westward to the Pacific Ocean, came in waves, created by domestic and foreign opportunities, and reached an almost feverish zeal in the 1840s. The first wave occurred from 1803 to 1819 with the acquisition of the Louisiana Territory, the Floridas, and lands as far west as modern-day Canada, Washington, and Oregon. The second wave came during the 1840s and was driven by the concept of Manifest Destiny. Simply stated, this was the belief that Americans had a God-given right to develop the lands of neighboring countries. Although the term was first used in the summer of 1845 to justify annexing Texas, the concept soon spread to include the lands recently won as a result of the Mexican-American War (1846–1848). With a relative balance of power achieved on the European Continent after the Napoleonic Wars, the United States could turn its attention towards its weaker neighbors, Canada and Mexico. The controversy over Oregon between Britain and the United States ended when President James K. Polk, elected in 1844 and a strong supporter of the **Democratic Party**'s belief in territorial expansion, resolved the boundary dispute with Britain in order to prosecute a war with Mexico after his attempts to purchase the Mexican lands failed. The Treaty of Guadalupe Hidalgo (1848) granted the northern half of Mexico to the United States. The issue of Manifest Destiny was resurrected in the 1890s, by Republicans, to justify the third wave of territorial expansion that included Guam, Hawaii, and the Philippines, among others. (GT) **See also** Imperialism; War.

BIBLIOGRAPHY

Brown, Charles. *Agents of Manifest Destiny: The Lives and Times of the Filibusters.* Chapel Hill: University of North Carolina Press, 1979.

Graebner, Norman, ed. *Manifest Destiny.* Indianapolis: Bobbs-Merrill, 1968.

Haynes, Sam. *James K. Polk and the Expansionist Impulse.* New York: Longman, 1997.

Morrison, Michael. *Slavery and the American West: The Eclipse of Manifest Destiny and the Coming of the Civil War.* Chapel Hill: University of North Carolina Press, 1997.

Stephanson, Anders. *Manifest Destiny: American Expansionism and the Empire of Right.* New York: Hill and Wang, 1995.

Marsh v. Chambers (1983)

In *Marsh v. Chambers*, 463 U.S. 783 (1983), the Supreme Court ruled 6-3 that the Nebraska legislature's practice of having a paid chaplain open its sessions with prayer was constitutional. The opinion, written by Chief Justice **Warren E. Burger**, stressed that opening legislative sessions "with a prayer is deeply embedded in the history and traditions of this country" and "has become part of the fabric of our society." He did not apply the three-part ***Lemon* Test** the court had earlier developed.

Marsh v. Chambers helped signal that the Supreme Court was moving away from its strict church-state separation stance articulated in a number of decisions in the 1960s and 1970s, but by not seeking a principled basis on which to reconcile the results in this case with the previously enunciated strict church-state separation principles, it left legislative prayer appearing to be an exception to be allowed because of its long history and popularity. It thereby did little to resolve—and may have added to—the uncertainty and confusion in church-state law. **See also** Clergy in Public Office; Establishment Clause; School Prayer; Wall of Separation.

BIBLIOGRAPHY

Levy, Leonard Williams. *The Establishment Clause: Religion and the First Amendment.* 2nd ed. rev. Chapel Hill: University of North Carolina Press, 1994.

Marsh v. State of Alabama (1946)

In *Marsh v. State of Alabama*, 326 U.S. 501 (1946), the U.S. Supreme Court was asked to rule on whether or not it was consistent with the **First Amendment** and the **Fourteenth Amendment** for a state to impose criminal punishment on a person who undertook to distribute religious literature on the premises of a company-owned town against the wishes of the company's owners. The Court ruled that it was not Constitutionally permissible to impose such sanctions, stating, "When we balance the Constitutional rights of owners of property against those of the people to enjoy freedom of press and religion, as we must here, we remain mindful of the fact that the latter occupy a preferred position." (JM)

BIBLIOGRAPHY

Newton, Merlin. *Armed with the Constitution.* Tuscaloosa: University of Alabama Press, 1995.

Regan, Richard J. *Private Conscience and Public Law.* New York: Fordham University Press, 1972.

Martin v. City of Struthers (1943)

A Jehovah's Witness was convicted of violating an ordinance of the City of Struthers, Ohio, for going to the homes of strangers and distributing leaflets advertising a religious meeting. The ordinance forbade this traditional method of distribution, even to homes where the caller was welcome. In *Martin v. City of Struthers*, 319 U.S. 141 (1943), the U.S. Supreme Court invalidated the ordinance, stating, "Freedom to distribute information to every citizen wherever he desires to receive it is so clearly vital to the preservation of a free society that . . . it must be fully preserved." (JM) **See also** First Amendment; Fourteenth Amendment; Free Speech Approach to Religious Liberty; Jehovah's Witnesses.

BIBLIOGRAPHY

Bowser, Anita. *The Meaning of Religion in the Constitution.* Ph.D. Dissertation. The University of Notre Dame, 1976.

Regan, Richard J. *Private Conscience and Public Law.* New York: Fordham University Press, 1972.

Martin E. Marty (1928–)

Martin Marty is a prolific author, especially in American religious history. An ordained Lutheran minister, he was a distinguished professor in the Divinity School of the University of Chicago from 1963 to 1998. He continues, since 1956, as a senior editor of *Christian Century* and contributes to other church-related journals. In award-winning books, he has chronicled American Protestantism from its early beginnings to the diversity of the present. With R. Scott Appleby, he recently completed co-editing a five-volume study of religious fundamentalism throughout the world. (JRV) **See also** Fundamentalists; Lutheran Church.

BIBLIOGRAPHY

Marty, Martin E. *By Way of Response.* Nashville, TN: Abingdon Press, 1981.

Maryland Colony

When his first colony in the new world, located in Newfoundland and established specifically for Roman Catholics, failed because of severe weather, **George Calvert**, first Lord Baltimore, sought to move further south. King Charles I granted territory in what is today the states of Maryland and Delaware to Calvert who named it St. Mary's in honor of Henrietta Maria, queen consort of Charles I. However, Calvert died before the charter was issued and his son, **Cecilius Calvert**, second Lord Baltimore, pursued his father's work by sending his brother, Leonard Calvert, to the territory in 1633 to serve as the colony's governor. The first settlers arrived with Leonard Calvert at St. Mary's in 1634.

The colonial history of Maryland is one of religious unrest between Catholics and Protestants. While the colony was settled as a safe haven for English Catholics, Protestants made up a large number of the initial settlers and soon were a majority in the colony. Catholics were directed by Calvert to be tolerant of others and not to encourage any conflict by practicing too publicly. By 1645, Protestants, under the leadership of William Claiborne, had taken control of the colony by force and it took nearly two years for Governor Calvert to re-assert his authority. The 1649 Act of Toleration guaranteed religious freedom and citizenship to all who professed a belief in the Trinity, did little to settle matters. Even the creation of specifically controlled Puritan areas did not end the growing conflicts between Catholics and Protestants.

In 1654, Protestants once again took control of the colony and disenfranchised Catholics. Oliver Cromwell, Lord Protector of England, recognized Lord Baltimore's title and by 1658 the colony was once again under the control of the Calvert family. The colony remained relatively peaceful for the duration of Cecilius Calvert's life, but upon his death in 1675, unrest resumed. Charles Calvert, third Lord Baltimore and son of Cecilius, enacted a number of undemocratic and pro-Catholic measures. He was also involved in a boundary dispute with **William Penn** over the territory of Delaware which was decided in Penn's favor in 1685. One year after the Glorious Revolution (1688), Protestant forces once again took control of the colony and in 1691 William II revoked the Calvert charter, making Maryland a royal colony. By 1692, the Protestant leaders of the colony were enacting laws that limited the citizenship rights of Catholics. In 1715, the colony was returned to Charles Calvert, fifth Lord Baltimore and a Protestant. Catholics were excluded from the right to vote and forbidden to worship in public.

The remainder of colonial Maryland's history involved a protracted dispute over its northern boundary with Pennsylvania. This dispute was settled between 1763 and 1767 by the British surveyors Charles Mason and Jeremiah Dixon. Maryland was also a center of revolutionary sentiment during the period leading up to its declaration of independence and adoption of a state constitution in 1776. **See also** Anti-Catholicism; Colonial America; Pennsylvania Colony; Puritans; Roman Catholicism.

BIBLIOGRAPHY

Dolan, Jay P. *The American Catholic Experience.* Notre Dame, IN: University of Notre Dame Press, 1992.

Land, Aubrey C. *Colonial Maryland.* Millwood, NY: KTO Press, 1981.

Hennesey, James. *American Catholics.* New York: Oxford University Press, 1981.

Maryland Jew Bill

The Jew Bill, which was officially titled "An Act to extend to the sect of people professing the Jewish religion the same rights and privileges enjoyed by Christians," was passed by the Maryland general assembly in 1826. It annulled the test oath in Maryland's state constitution that required state officeholders to be Christian. The bill was originally introduced by state senator Thomas Kennedy in 1818. Following the passage of the bill, Jewish businessmen Solomon Etting and Jacob I. Cohen were elected to the Baltimore city council. (JCW) **See also** Anti-Semitism; Judaism; Religious Tests and Oaths.

BIBLIOGRAPHY

Eitches, Edward. "Maryland's Jew Bill." *American Jewish Historical Quarterly* 60, no. 3 (1971): 258-79.

George Mason (1725–1792)

George Mason, a Virginia planter, was the principal craftsman of the Declaration of Rights adopted by the Virginia Convention on June 12, 1776. Article XVI of the Declaration is a seminal, post-colonial statement on the rights of conscience. Throughout a distinguished public career as a Virginia legislator and delegate to the Constitutional Convention, Mason championed the rights of conscience. He paid to print and distribute for popular endorsement **James Madison**'s **"Memorial and Remonstrance Against Religious Assessments"** (1785), which was instrumental in defeating "A Bill Establishing a Provision for Teachers of the Christian Religion" (1784) and in enacting the Virginia "Statute for Establishing Religious Freedom" (1786). Mason was a leading anti-federalist critic of the U.S. Constitution and advocate for a national bill of rights. (DLD) **See also** Colonial America; Virginia Declaration of Rights.

BIBLIOGRAPHY

Miller, Helen Hill. *George Mason: Gentleman Revolutionary.* Chapel Hill: University of North Carolina Press, 1975.

Rutland, Robert A., ed. *The Papers of George Mason, 1725–1792.* 3 vols. Chapel Hill: University of North Carolina Press, 1970.

Massachusetts Bay Colony

Massachusetts Bay, early New England's primary settlement, was established by English **Puritans** in 1630, first at Salem, then at Boston. At once religious and commercial, the colony was the outgrowth of the Massachusetts Bay Company, chartered in 1629 in England as a joint stock trading venture. The charter stipulated that the stockholders (known as "freemen") could elect a governor and others who would manage company affairs. Under the leadership of **John Winthrop** and with royal charter in hand, the first group left for New England in March 1630.

Aboard the flagship *Arbella*, Governor Winthrop set forth his vision for the new colony. This would be a godly community established by mutual consent, a new **Israel** crossing its own sea, to "seek out a place of cohabitation and consortship, under a due form of government both civil and ecclesiastical," where, Winthrop concluded, "we shall be as a city upon a hill." The Puritans set about in earnest to build such a city, making a commonwealth out of the corporation, and seeking to erect, not a theocracy, but a rule of the regenerate.

In the colony's new towns, all built around a central meeting house where both church services and civic affairs were conducted, local ministers carried enormous personal authority, and magistrates were seen as "nursing fathers." Urian Oakes (1631–1681), president of Harvard and a Cambridge minister, described the pattern: "According to the design of our founders and the frame of things laid by them, the interest of righteousness in the commonwealth and holiness in the churches are inseparable. . . .I look upon this as a little model of the glorious kingdom of Christ on earth." But the pattern could not last. With an extremely limited franchise (only male church members could vote or hold office), fearful intolerance of dissenting doctrine, and failure to keep separate civic and religious realms, the "New England way" began to change. Yet, in its wake, Massachusetts Bay permanently contributed to a growing national identity, one that would stress individual moral and civic responsibility, reformist social movements, and a sense of American exceptionalism. (JML) **See also** Americanism; City on a Hill; Colonial America; Salem Witchcraft Trials.

Bibliography

Ahlstrom, Sydney. *A Religious History of the American People.* New Haven, CT: Yale University Press, 1972.

Hudson, Winthrop. *Religion in America.* New York: Charles Scribner's Sons, 1973.

Noll, Mark A., Nathan O. Hatch, and George M. Marsden. *The Search for Christian America.* Colorado Springs, CO: Helmers and Howard, 1989.

Noll, Mark A. *A History of Christianity in the United States and Canada.* Grand Rapids, MI: William B. Eerdman's Publishing Company, 1992.

Cotton Mather (1663–1728)

Scion of the illustrious Mather family, Cotton was the son of **Increase Mather** (1639–1723) and, like his father, was a Congregational minister, prolific author, scientist, and educator. He was ordained at the Second Church in Boston (1685) where he worked alongside his father until the latter's death in 1723. While his father was in England petitioning the king for restoration of the original **Massachusetts Bay** charter, Mather opposed the royal governor Sir William Andros and, when actual rebellion against Andros broke out, wrote *The Declaration of the Gentlemen, Merchants, and Inhabitants of Boston* (1689), a proto-declaration of Massachusetts independence. When his father returned in 1692 bringing with him a Mather protégé, Sir William Phipps, as the new governor, Cotton's political influence increased substantially. However, because of his role (although passive) in the **Salem Witchcraft Trials** of that year, and because of his identification with the Phipps government and the new royal charter, the rise in Mather's popularity was rather quickly checked. His later years were devoted to ministry and to the founding and growth of Yale College, which he saw as a necessary corrective to the theological liberalism at Harvard. (JHM) **See also** Colonial America; Congregationalism; Puritans.

Coming from an influential religious family, Cotton Mather was a powerful figure in colonial America. Library of Congress.

Bibliography

Mather, Cotton. *Magnalia Christi Americana; or, The Ecclesiastical History of New England.* Raymond J. Cunningham, ed. New York: F. Ungar, 1970.

Middlekauff, Robert. *The Mathers: Three Generations of Puritan Intellectuals, 1596–1728.* New York: Oxford University Press, 1971.

Increase Mather (1639–1723)

When the crown revoked the charter of the **Massachusetts Bay Colony** in 1688, thereby denying the colony the right to select its own governors, the Congregational minister Increase Mather was sent to England to petition the king. The eventual result of the petition was a new compromise charter in which the restriction of the vote to church members was abolished, as was popular appointment of the governor, but most of the powers of the colonial assembly were retained. For his efforts, Mather was granted the privilege of nominating the new governor, which gave him unique political influence for a time in Massachusetts. (JHM) **See also** Colonial America; Congregationalism; Cotton Mather; Puritans.

When its charter was revoked, Massachusetts Bay Colony sent Increase Mather to England as its envoy. Library of Congress.

Bibliography

Middlekauff, Robert. *The Mathers: Three Generations of Puritan Intellectuals, 1596–1728.* New York: Oxford University Press, 1971.

Aristide Peter Maurin (1877–1949)

The son of French peasants, Aristide Maurin immigrated to the United States in 1909. He adopted a life of voluntary poverty, teaching that labor was a gift rather than a commodity to be sold. In 1933, with the help of **Dorothy Day**, he started

The Catholic Worker to spread their ideas of **social justice**. (MWP) **See also** Capitalism; Catholic Worker Movement; Labor; Roman Catholicism; Socialism and Communism.

Bibliography

Piehl, Mel. *Breaking Bread: The Catholic Worker and the Origin of Catholic Radicalism in America.* Philadelphia: Temple University Press, 1982.

Sheehan, Arthur. *Peter Maurin.* Garden City, NY: Doubleday, 1959.

Mayflower Compact

The first European settlement in modern-day New England was led by Puritan separatists (known in American history as the **Pilgrims**) who rejected the official Anglican Church as too unreformed to be tolerated. They left England in 1608 seeking freedom of worship in Holland. However, they soon came to fear that their children were growing up more Dutch than English and so sought permission to establish a settlement in North America. In 1620, 102 travelers—36 **Puritans** and 66 non-Puritans referred to as "Strangers," set sail on the *Mayflower* from Plymouth, England. Bound for Virginia, the *Mayflower* was blown far to the north by a storm, a deviation that the Puritans believed was God's will. Because the expedition's royal charter specified a settlement in Virginia, not New England, the Puritans realized that they had no legal document laying out how the colony should be governed and so required a new political contract. The Mayflower Compact was drafted and signed before they landed, thus meeting their needs. The first social contract written to institute a voluntary approach to government by men of equal rights, the Compact clearly differentiated these settlers from the earlier English settlers at Jamestown, and from the many other settlers still to come to America. (The Mayflower Compact is reprinted in Appendix 1.) (GT) **See also** Colonial America; Massachusetts Bay Colony.

Bibliography

Caffrey, Kate. *The Mayflower.* New York: Stein and Day, 1974.

Wood, Herbert and J. Rendel Harris. *Venturers for the Kingdom: A Study in the History of the Pilgrim Fathers.* London: Hodder and Stoughton, 1920.

Jonathan Mayhew (1720–1766)

Jonathan Mayhew, a liberal Congregational minister, vigorously propagated ecclesiastical and political anti-authoritarianism in pre-revolutionary New England. He opposed both the Stamp Act and Anglican (see **Episcopal Church**) efforts to establish an American episcopate and was a pioneer Unitarian. (PV) **See also** Colonial America; Congregationalism; Unitarianism.

Bibliography

Akers, Charles W. *Called Unto Liberty: A Life of Jonathan Mayhew, 1720–1766.* Cambridge, MA: Harvard University Press, 1964.

Vashti Cromwell McCollum (1910–)

Vashti McCollum challenged the legality of the **release time** religious instruction program conducted in her son's school in Champaign, Illinois. In ***McCollum v. Board of Education*** in 1948, the U.S. Supreme Court agreed that such religious teaching on public school property violated the **Establishment Clause** of the **First Amendment**. After that decision, McCollum remained active in church-state relations, arguing for a high **wall of separation**. (ARB)

Bibliography

McCollum, Vashti Cromwell. *One Woman's Fight.* rev. ed. Boston: Beacon Press, 1961.

Miller, Robert T. and Ronald B. Flowers. *Toward Benevolent Neutrality: Church, State, and the Supreme Court.* Vol. 1. 5th ed. Waco, TX: Markham Press Fund of Baylor University Press, 1996.

McCollum v. Board of Education (1948)

In Illinois ex rel. *McCollum v. Board of Education,* 333 U.S. 203 (1948), the U.S. Supreme Court ruled unconstitutional the Champaign, Illinois, school board's **release-time** program. Under the program, religious instructors conducted weekly religion classes in public school buildings during regular school hours. A private council comprised of Jews, Roman Catholics, and Protestants employed the religious teachers at no expense to the public schools; the instructors, however, were subject to the school superintendent's approval and supervision. Students whose parents so requested were excused from regular classes to attend religion classes. Nonparticipating students remained in public school buildings for secular study. The public school kept an attendance record of pupils in both instructional tracks. The Court held that "[t]his is beyond all question a utilization of the tax-established and tax-supported public school system to aid religious groups to spread their faith. . . . The State also affords sectarian groups an invaluable aid in that it helps to provide pupils for their religious classes through use of the State's compulsory public school machinery. This is not separation of Church and State." In some respects, *McCollum* was more significant than the landmark separationist opinions in ***Everson v. Board of Education of the Township of Ewing*** (1947), the New Jersey bus transportation case decided the previous term. The narrow 5-4 decision in *Everson* gave way to an 8-1 majority in *McCollum*, thereby solidifying a strict separationist bloc on the Court. More significantly, *McCollum* differed from *Everson* in that minimal funds from the public treasury were expended in the challenged release-time program. (DLD) **See also** Education; Establishment Clause; First Amendment; Vashti Cromwell McCollum; Public Aid to Religious Organizations; School Prayer.

Bibliography

Levy, Leonard W. *The Establishment Clause.* Chapel Hill: University of North Carolina Press, 1995.

McCollum, Vashti Cromwell. *One Woman's Fight.* rev. ed. Boston: Beacon Press, 1961.

Miller, Robert T. and Ronald B. Flowers. *Toward Benevolent Neutrality: Church, State, and the Supreme Court.* Vol. 1. 5th ed. Waco, TX: Markham Press Fund of Baylor University Press, 1996.

McDaniel v. Paty (1978)

A Tennessee constitutional revision barred "ministers of the Gospel or priests of any denominational" from running for the position of delegate to a state constitutional convention. The Tennessee Supreme Court ruled that clergy disqualification imposed no burden on religious belief, but in *McDaniel v. Paty*, 435 U.S. 618 (1978), the U.S. Supreme Court overturned that decision. The High Court held that the challenged constitutional provision violated a minister's **First Amendment** right to the free exercise of his religion by forcing him to choose between exercising his religious beliefs and exercising his political right to seek public office. (FHJ) **See also** Clergy in Public Office; Fourteenth Amendment; Free Exercise Clause; Political Participation in Voting Behavior.

BIBLIOGRAPHY

Chopper, Jesse H. *Securing Religious Liberty.* Chicago: University of Chicago Press, 1995.

Ivers, Gregg. *Redefining the First Freedom.* New Brunswick, NJ: Transaction Press, 1993.

William Holmes McGuffey (1800–1873)

Few people in American history have had as much impact on American education as William McGuffey, an ordained Presbyterian minister. Much of his knowledge of teaching came from practical experience. While teaching at Miami University in Ohio, he helped local school teachers and taught neighborhood children in his home. In 1836 a publisher asked him to develop four readers for school children. He eventually developed six "McGuffey's Readers," and they, along with a speller developed by his brother, became the standard textbooks of the era (especially in the Midwest and South) with over 120 million copies sold. "McGuffey's Readers" provided lessons in morality as part of the curriculum. (MWP) **See also** Education; Presbyterian Church.

BIBLIOGRAPHY

Minnich, Harvey C. *William Holmes McGuffey and His Readers.* New York: American Book Co., 1936.

Vail, Harry H. *A History of the McGuffey Readers.* Cleveland: Burrows Brothers, 1911.

Carl McIntire (1906–)

Fundamentalist Presbyterian, anti-Communist crusader, and author, Carl McIntire opposed **liberalism** in religion, economics, and politics. He once declared, "The capitalistic system . . . comes from no other person than the Lord Jesus Christ." In the 1960s he organized a number of "Marches for Victory" in support of the **Vietnam** War. (ARB) **See also** Capitalism; Presbyterian Church; Socialism and Communism.

BIBLIOGRAPHY

Fea, John. "Carl McIntire: From Fundamentalist Presbyterian to Presbyterian Fundamentalist." *American Presbyterian* 72 (Winter 1994): 253-268.

McIntire, Carl. *Author of Liberty.* Collinswood, NJ: Christian Beacon Press, 1946.

William McKinley (1843–1901)

William McKinley, a Republican from Ohio, ran successfully for the presidency against Democrat **William Jennings Bryan** on a platform of high tariffs to protect industry and opposition to the free coinage of silver to prevent inflation. As president, he maintained a high tariff and prevented the free coinage of silver, but he also found himself forced into a **war** with Spain over Cuba. The result was the creation of an American empire that included Guam, Puerto Rico, and the Philippines. McKinley was criticized by some religious and political leaders for his imperialist policies, and he responded by stating that there were no imperialistic designs in his plans. However, he did call upon religious leaders to send forth **missionaries** to the Philippines and "civilize and Christianize" them. Re-elected in 1900, with **imperialism** as one of the major campaign issues, McKinley would not serve out his term. He was assassinated by avowed anarchist Leon Czolgosz in Buffalo, New York, on September 6, 1901. His last words, prior to his death on September 14, were reported to have been "It is God's will. His will, not ours, be done." Vice President **Theodore Roosevelt** succeeded to the presidency. **See also** Democratic Party; Republican Party.

William McKinley, a Republican president of the United States, saw that the U.S. could be a positive Christianizing force in the world. Library of Congress.

BIBLIOGRAPHY

Damini, Brian P. *Advocates of Empire: William McKinley, the Senate, and American Expansion, 1889–1901.* New York: Garland, 1987.

Gould, Lewis L. *The Presidency of William McKinley.* Lawrence: University Press of Kansas, 1986.

Meek v. Pittenger (1975)

Pennsylvania passed two acts authorizing aid to nonpublic schools that included the loan of textbooks used in public schools, the loan of instructional materials and equipment, and the provision of auxiliary services such as counseling, testing, psychological services, speech and hearing therapy, and related services for exceptional, remedial, or educationally disadvantaged students. These acts were challenged as violations of the **Establishment Clause** of the **First Amendment.** Although in *Meek v. Pittenger*, 421 U.S. 349 (1975), the U.S. Supreme Court upheld the constitutionality of the textbook loan programs, it ruled that the instructional materials loan programs and the auxiliary services program were unconstitutional. Instructional materials and auxiliary services were ruled unconstitutional because the Court believed that they offered too great a possibility of entanglement between church and state. This decision is a precursor to the Court's ruling in ***Aguilar v. Felton*** (1985). (JM) **See also** Education; Entanglement Test; Public Aid to Religious Organizations.

Bibliography

Bryson, Joseph E. *The Supreme Court and Public Funds for Religious Schools.* Jefferson, NC: McFarland, 1990.

Memorial and Remonstrance Against Religious Assessments (1785)

The "Memorial and Remonstrance Against Religious Assessments" is **James Madison**'s most eloquent and passionate statement on religious liberty and church-state relations. Drafted in 1785, the "Memorial and Remonstrance" was a forceful response to a proposal in the Virginia legislature to levy a tax or general assessment to support "teachers of the Christian religion." The document is presented in the form of a "memorial" and "remonstrance," that is, a formal petition or complaint addressed to the legislature with an attached declaration of reasons. Thus, each of the document's 15 numbered paragraphs begins with the word "because." The "Memorial and Remonstrance" was printed and distributed throughout Virginia for popular endorsement. It effectively galvanized anti-assessment sentiment. Madison reported in an 1826 letter that the "Memorial and Remonstrance" was "so extensively signed by the people of every religious denomination, that at the ensuing [legislative] session the projected [assessment] measure was entirely frustrated."

Madison argued that religion, or the duty owed the Creator, is a matter for individual conscience and not within the cognizance of civil government. All citizens are entitled to the full, equal, and natural right to exercise religion according to the dictates of conscience. "[T]he same authority which can establish Christianity, in exclusion of all other Religions," Madison warned, "may establish with the same ease any particular sect of Christians, in exclusion of all other Sects." The establishment of a particular church "violates that equality which ought to be the basis of every law." Furthermore, it is "an arrogant pretention" to believe "that the Civil Magistrate is a competent Judge of Religious Truths; or that he may employ Religion as an engine of Civil policy." Experience confirms that "ecclesiastical establishments, instead of maintaining the purity and efficacy of Religion, have had a contrary operation." The fruits of ecclesiastical establishment, Madison reported, have been "pride and indolence in the Clergy, ignorance and servility in the laity, in both, superstition, bigotry and persecution." Religious establishment in Virginia would be an unfortunate "departure from that generous policy, which, offering an Asylum to the persecuted and oppressed of every Nation and Religion, promised a lustre to our country, and an accession to the number of its citizens."

Madison rejected the view that religion could not survive without the sustaining aid of civil government, nor the civil government preserve social order and stability without the support of an established church. He believed, to the contrary, that true religion prospered in the public marketplace of ideas unrestrained by the monopolistic control of the civil authority. He thought it a contradiction to argue that discontinuing state support for Christianity would precipitate its demise, since "this Religion both existed and flourished, not only without the support of human laws, but in spite of every opposition from them. . . . [A] Religion not invented by human policy, must have pre-existed and been supported, before it was established by human policy." If Christianity depends on the support of civil government, the "pious confidence" of the faithful in its "innate excellence and the patronage of its Author" will be undermined. The best and purest religion, Madison thus concluded, relied on the voluntary support of those who profess it, without entanglements of any sort of civil government—including those fostered by financial support, regulation, or compulsion. (The "Memorial and Remonstrance" is reprinted in Appendix 1.) (DLD) **See also** Colonial America; Establishment Clause; First Amendment; Public Aid to Religious Organizations; Wall of Separation.

Bibliography

Braun, Eva T. H. "Madison's *'Memorial and Remonstrance':* A Model of American Eloquence." Glen E. Thurow and Jeffrey D. Wallin, eds. *Rhetoric and American Statesmanship.* Durham, NC: Carolina Academic Press, 1984.

Rutland, Robert A., William M. E. Rachal, et al., eds. *The Papers of James Madison. Vol. 8.* Chicago: University of Chicago Press, 1973.

Henry Louis Mencken (1880–1956)

H.L. Mencken was a widely-read essayist, columnist, and satirist, as well as editor of the *Baltimore Herald.* Mencken used his talents to attack both Puritanism and Fundamentalism in American society. He advocated a philosophy of individualism and liberty against what he saw as the destructive forces of both the puritanical heritage and evangelicals like **Billy Sunday.** While a committed capitalist, he also wrote against America's growing consumerism. His coverage of the **Scopes Trial** in 1925 brought him a national reading audience. He was author of several influential books including *The American Language* (1919). **See also** Capitalism; Conservatism; Evangelicals; Fundamentalists; Puritans.

Bibliography

Bode, Carl. *Mencken.* Carbondale: Southern Illinois University Press, 1969.

Rogers, Marion B., ed. *The Impossible H.L. Mencken: A Selection of His Best Newspaper Stories.* New York: Doubleday, 1991.

Mennonites

A Christian denomination, Mennonites are spiritual heirs of the sixteenth-century Protestant Reformation's Anabaptist movement, which had sought to recreate the life of the early church. Mennonites reject infant baptism, restricting church membership to confessing adults who willingly claim faith and assume its ethical implications. They espouse nonviolence and insist on the separation of church and state, in addition to stressing mutual aid, community, and accountability within the church. Mennonites have not always agreed on how to put their beliefs into practice, and have consequently divided into a number of groups representing a continuum ranging from highly sectarian to more broadly acculturated. The oldest American Mennonite community dates to 1683, and European Mennonite immigrants arrived in North America in several different waves, notably during the mid-1700s and in the 1870s. Closely related groups include the culturally conservative **Amish** and the communal Hutterites.

Given their sectarian sensibilities and experience of persecution at the hands of European authorities, Mennonites who arrived in America were understandably wary of political involvement. In addition, their refusal to swear oaths and their belief that the church alone represented God's redeemed order in the midst of a "fallen" world, worked against their easy assimilation into American political life. As a result, Mennonites have traditionally been seen as an apolitical group, aloof from much meaningful civic participation. Certain conservative and so-called Old Order Mennonites have maintained this sectarian apolitical stance to the present.

Nevertheless, some American Mennonites have always engaged the political sphere. During the Colonial period, for example, Pennsylvania's **Quaker**-led government drew Mennonite support. During times of war, Mennonites have joined other "historic peace churches" (Quakers, Brethren) to obtain conscientious objection privileges or to negotiate alternative service arrangements in lieu of military conscription.

Moreover, since the mid-twentieth century, increasing numbers of Mennonites have seen "witness to the state" as a significant part of Christian faithfulness. Many now view government—and not only the church—as an agent of God for good in the world. Even so, they typically continue to believe that the threat of violence which underlies much governmental authority warrants the church's constant critique and prophetic protest. As a result of this shift in attitude, Mennonites have begun speaking politically on a range of issues, including poverty, social justice, abortion, arms reduction, the environment, and international policy. In 1970, the Mennonite Central Committee, a denominational relief and development agency that seeks to convey constituency convictions to federal officials and heighten Mennonite awareness of public policy issues and implications, opened a Washington (D.C.) Office.

In a 1972 survey, more than one-third of Mennonites reported that they refrained from voting. By 1989, this rate had dropped to 23 percent as Mennonites continue to acculturate to the American political scene. (SMN) **See also** Abortion and Birth Control Regulation; Colonial America; Pacifism; Pennsylvania Colony; Political Participation and Voting Behavior; Reformation; Social Justice.

BIBLIOGRAPHY

Driedger, Leo and Donald B. Kraybill. *Mennonite Peacemaking: From Quietism to Activism.* Scottdale, PA: Herald Press, 1994.

Graber-Miller, Keith. *Wise as Serpents, Innocent as Doves: American Mennonites Engage Washington.* Knoxville: University of Tennessee Press, 1996.

Peachey, Urbane, ed. *Mennonite Statements on Peace and Social Concerns, 1900–1978.* Akron, PA: Mennonite Central Committee, 1980.

________. *Washington Memo.* Akron, PA: Mennonite Central Committee, 1970–present [bimonthly newsletter].

Methodism

Methodism is a religious and social movement that originated in John and Charles Wesley's attempt to reform the Church of England during the eighteenth century. The sons of Samuel Wesley, a Church of England cleric, John and Charles attended Oxford, where they formed a "Holy Club" to encourage greater spirituality. The title "Methodists" was originally given to the group as a term of derision. Both John and Charles were ordained by the Church of England, and retained this affiliation throughout their lives. After an unsuccessful missionary journey to America in the 1730s, during which he met with and was influenced by a group of Moravian colonists, John returned to England and experienced a spiritual transformation after attending a religious service held on Aldersgate Street in London in 1738. Wesley claimed he was "strangely warmed," and his subsequent ministry promoted spiritual and social renewal.

The Wesleys' Methodist movement quickly spread from England to America, where, under the early leadership of **Francis Asbury**, Thomas Coke, and others, it became the larg-

Methodists have been active in a number of church-state issues, including abortion and prohibition. Pictured here is the Methodist Church in Linworth, Ohio, in 1938. Photo by Ben Shahn/WPA. Library of Congress.

est Protestant denomination in the country by the middle of the nineteenth century. The church assumed the name Methodist Episcopal Church (MEC), sending traveling preachers known as "circuit riders" throughout the country. The influence of these clergy, who stressed personal holiness and moral restraint, was tremendous. The MEC established annual conferences, a form of church polity that continues to serve as the model for most Methodist-related denominations today.

From its beginnings, Methodism in America was involved with civil affairs, including disputes over church polity, **slavery**, and prohibition. By 1830, a serious division arose within the MEC over the authority of bishops and the role of the laity. This dispute resulted in the establishment of the Methodist Protestant Church (MPC). In 1844, the slavery crisis provoked MEC conferences in the South to separate and form the Methodist Episcopal Church, South (MECS). At a Uniting Conference held in 1939, the MPC, the MEC, and the MECS joined to form the Methodist Church. In 1968, The Methodist Church merged with the Evangelical United Brethren Church to form the United Methodist Church (UMC), which is today the largest body of Methodists in North America.

Black Methodists, who were denied access to worship, formed the Free African Society in 1787 under the leadership of **Richard Allen**. This action led to the establishment of a separate denomination in 1816, the **African Methodist Episcopal Church (AME).** The African Methodist Episcopal Zion Church (AMEZ) was created in 1796, and the Christian Methodist Episcopal Church (CME) (known as the Colored Methodist Episcopal Church before 1954) was established in 1870 by blacks who left the MECS. The rise of the Holiness Movement in the nineteenth century promoted additional divisions among Methodists, and resulted in the establishment of the Wesleyan Methodists and Free Methodists, as well as other minor Methodist groups.

In the nineteenth century, Methodism's relationship to the political system was strained by its promotion of the temperance cause. Methodist clergy and laity, Sunday school literature, and various Methodist organizations, including the **Women's Christian Temperance Union (WCTU)**, supported total abstinence for many years. The ground swell of support among Methodists eventually aided the 1919 ratification of the **Eighteenth Amendment**, which prohibited the manufacture, sale, or transportation of alcohol. The amendment was subsequently repealed by the adoption of the Twenty-first Amendment in 1933. In the twentieth century, Methodism has also become increasing embroiled in debates over **pacifism** and the limits of **capitalism**, as well as a myriad of social issues that continue to threaten schism. (HLC) **See also** African-American Churches; Episcopal Church; Temperance and Prohibition.

Bibliography

Richey, Russell, et al. *The Methodists*. Greenwood Press, 1996.

Mexican-American War (1846–1848)

During America's second wave of expansion, President James K. Polk pursued his policy of **Manifest Destiny** by waging **war** against Mexico. The predominantly Protestant Americans fought the Roman Catholic Mexicans over border disputes, diplomatic controversies, and the annexation of the Republic of Texas. The **Democratic Party**'s mantra of expansion after the election of 1844, the need for new territories

The notion of Manifest Destiny played a large role in the motivations behind the Mexican-American War. National Archives.

for settlement, and the desire to increase slave-holding states within the United States, all led to the desire for **war** with Mexico. The fledgling Mexican government had officially received its independence from Spain only two decades earlier, and could not economically, politically, or militarily defend itself against its northern neighbor. American opposition to this war, and to territorial expansion based on the will of Providence, was fragmented. After defeats in California, New Mexico, and Mexico City, the Mexicans surrendered the northern half of their country with the Treaty of Guadalupe Hidalgo, on February 2, 1848. (GT) **See also** Henry David Thoreau.

Bibliography

Eisenhower, John. *So Far From God: The U.S. War with Mexico, 1846–1848.* New York: Random House, 1989.

Johannsen, Robert. *To the Halls of the Montezumas: The Mexican War in the American Imagination.* New York: Oxford University Press, 1985.

Meyer v. State of Nebraska (1923)

A teacher at the Zion Parochial School was convicted for unlawfully teaching the subject of reading in the German language to a 10-year-old student, in violation of a Nebraska act forbidding the teaching of foreign languages to students prior to the eighth grade, an act passed largely to prevent Catholic schools from teaching the native language of its members. The Supreme Court of Nebraska upheld the law, stating that it was a valid exercise of the police power of the state. But in

Meyer v. State of Nebraska, 262 U.S. 390 (1923), the U.S. Supreme Court overruled that decision, invalidating the law on the grounds that "the statute as applied is arbitrary and without reasonable relation to any end within the competency of the state." (JM) **See also** Anti-Catholicism; Education; First Amendment; Roman Catholicism.

BIBLIOGRAPHY

Bowser, Anita. *The Meaning of Religion in the Constitution.* Ph.D. dissertation, University of Notre Dame, 1976.

Cord, Richard I. *Separation of Church and State.* New York: Lambeth Press, 1982.

Military Service

Because of the church-state issues it raises, military service has, for centuries, been vigorously debated. Prior to the time of Constantine, early Christians were almost uniformly pacifist and eschewed military service. That changed, however, with the political enfranchisement of the church; thereafter, only smaller sects (generally) maintained pacifism. Pivotal in the church's changed stance was St. Augustine's "just war" doctrine, a doctrine that has been refined and debated, but largely maintained by nations in the West.

The United States has been a venue for the on-going debate, as well as for intense discussion of **conscientious objection** (CO). Historically, military service, when called for, has been seen as a key obligation of citizens. The U.S. Constitution, which gives Congress sole power to "raise and support armies," takes the necessity of service as a given, and does so without debate. (During the drafting of the Bill of Rights, there was some discussion about inclusion of a provision for COs.) But questions about military service were part of the national conversation from the beginning, with **Quakers** prominent among those who refused service. During the **American Revolution**, the **Continental Congress** made some allowance for men of "tender conscience." The **Civil War** offered the first national measure for exemption of COs, but it extended only to those who were members of well-recognized pacifist churches. Most litigation in the courts about military service has occurred in the twentieth century, with several significant rulings by the U.S. Supreme Court during the **Vietnam** era. In *United States v. Seeger*, 380 U.S. 163 (1965) and *Welsh v. United States*, 398 U.S. 333 (1970), the Court enlarged the warranted basis for CO, adopting a "parallel belief" test: Does an individual's belief system occupy in his life a moral force parallel to that furnished by traditional religious tenets? After the United States went to an all-volunteer force in 1973, the debate diminished; but its military history adds importance to any contemporary discussion of the obligations of citizenship and the formation of ethical systems in a pluralistic society. (JML) **See also** Just War Theory; Liberalism; Mexican-American War; Pacifism; Peace Movements; Persian Golf Conflict; Spanish-American War; War; World War I; World War II.

BIBLIOGRAPHY

Brock, Peter. *A Brief History of Pacifism from Jesus to Tolstoy.* Syracuse, NY: Syracuse University Press, 1992.

Greenawalt, Kent. "Conscientious Objection and the Liberal State." James E. Wood, Jr., ed. *Religion and the State.* Waco: Baylor University Press, 1985.

Miller, Robert T. and Ronald B. Flowers. *Toward Benevolent Neutrality: Church, State, and the Supreme Court.* 4th ed. Waco: Baylor University Press, 1992.

Schlissel, Lillian, ed. *Conscience in America: A Documentary History, 1757–1967.* New York: E.P. Dutton, 1968.

Millennialism

The millennium, an element of Christian eschatology (branch of theology dealing with the Second Coming), is derived from Revelation 20:4, where it is asserted that Christ, at the end of time, will rule upon the earth, thereby ensuring peace and justice, for a thousand years (the Latin is *mille annis*). St. Augustine (A.D. 354–430) identified the millennium with the rule of the Church in the world, an interpretation that would dominate Roman Catholic and Protestant theology until the nineteenth century. During the Middle Ages and the **Reformation** period, millenarianism, typically linked to apocalyptic critiques of Church and State which sought **social justice**, was propounded by radicals, the most notable example being the Peasants' Revolt (1524–1525) in Germany. Millennialism in differing forms played a prominent role among the English and American **Puritans** and the continental Pietists. It appears in the thought of **Jonathan Edwards** (1703–1758) and in the work of the Chilean Jesuit, Manuel de Lacunza (1731–1801). The latter's interpretation shifted the millennium to the distant future to refute Protestant interpretations. His works, translated by Edward Irving, become sources for later dispensationalist pre-millennialist views. Today three interpretations of millennialism exist, the pre-millennial, the post-millennial and the amillennial. Only one, the pre-millennial, takes the verse literally as a 1,000 year rule after the eschatological return of Christ. The amillennial interpretation understands the millennium as a figurative way of describing Christ's rule in and through the Church. The post-millennial interpretation argues that the Church, by its work in advancing the rule of God, culminates in an actual millennium of peace on earth, at the end of which Christ returns. This last, theocratic interpretation dominated among the Puritan settlers of New England and later in American **Calvinism**. The early Puritans believed that they had been sent "into the wilderness" to establish a "city set upon a hill," while the later Calvinist, Jonathan Edwards, in witnessing the **First Great Awakening**, thought that the millennium was imminent and beginning in America. Such belief fostered the growth of an American nationalism and popular notions of a **Manifest Destiny**.

Millenarian beliefs in an alternative and more equitable society revived during the period of American industrialization of the nineteenth century among groups such as the

Shakers (1770s), **Joseph Smith** and the Mormons (1830s), William Miller and the **Seventh-Day Adventists** (1830s), and **John Humphrey Noyes**' Oneida Community (1840s). After the shocks of the Civil War and World War I, optimistic post-millennial views tended to be displaced by a pessimistic pre-millennialism which reinforced Fundamentalist and Evangelical withdrawal from societal and political involvement. Recent dramatic confrontations between the federal government and the **Branch Davidians** in Waco, Texas, have underlined the role of millennialist beliefs in radical critiques of American society. Millennialism is a significant marker for the identification of militant counter-cultural religious movements. (ISM) **See also** Americanism; Church of Jesus Christ of Latter-day Saints; "City on a Hill"; Evangelism; Fundamentalists; Pietism; Roman Catholicism.

BIBLIOGRAPHY

Boyer, Paul. *When Time Shall Be No More: Prophecy Belief in Modern American Culture.* Cambridge: Harvard University Press, 1992.

Kaplan, Jeffrey. *Radical Religion in America: Millenarian Movements from the Far Right to the Children of Noah.* Syracuse, NY: Syracuse University Press, 1997.

Marsden, George. *Fundamentalism and American Culture: The Shaping of Twentieth Century Evangelicalism.* New York: Oxford University Press, 1980.

Sandeen, Ernest R. *The Roots of Fundamentalism: British and American Millenarianism, 1800–1930.* Chicago: University of Chicago Press, 1970.

Perry Gilbert Eddy Miller (1905–1963)

A Harvard historian and literary critic, Perry Miller was widely respected for his books on New England history, especially those about the **Puritans** and **Jonathan Edwards**. He is credited with dispelling many false impressions of the Puritans as well as reinvigorating interest in the study of Puritanism. *The Puritans* (1938), *Roger Williams* (1953), and *The New England Mind* are numbered among his many books. (MWP) **See also** Colonial America; Massachusetts Bay Colony; Pilgrims; Rhode Island Colony; Roger Williams.

BIBLIOGRAPHY

Levin, David. "Perry Miller at Harvard." *The Southern Review* 19 (October 1983): 802-816.

Million Man March

Held on the Mall in Washington, DC on October 16, 1995, this 12-hour-long rally was organized by **Nation of Islam** leader **Louis Farrakhan**. It was to provide "a holy day of atonement and reconciliation" for black men to unite and take responsibility for their lives, families, and communities.

Almost every aspect of the rally stirred controversy. Jewish leaders criticized the role of Farrakhan, who had called **Judaism** a "gutter religion" in a 1984 speech. The **Southern Christian Leadership Conference (SCLC)** and the Congressional Black Caucus endorsed the rally, but, due to Farrakhan's involvement, the NAACP, the National Urban League and the National Black Convention did not. Black feminist Angela Davis also attacked the rally for its focus on men, calling it "retrograde politics."

Controversy also surrounded the number who attended. National Park Service figures placed attendance at 400,000 (150,000 more than attended the 1963 **civil rights** march). March organizers protested those figures and, using overhead photos, a Boston University study concluded that 837,000 people (plus or minus 20 percent) had attended. (MWP) **See also** Black Theology; Feminism; Promise Keepers; Race Relations.

BIBLIOGRAPHY

Cottman, Michael H. *Million Man March.* New York: Crown, 1995.

Minersville School District v. Gobitis (1940)

In *Minersville School District v. Gobitis,* 310 U.S. 586 (1940), the U.S. Supreme Court decided that a law requiring students at public schools to salute the flag did not unconstitutionally restrict freedom of religion. Members of the religious sect known as **Jehovah's Witnesses** had argued that the law infringed on the separation of church and state guaranteed by the **First Amendment**. The group believed that they could not salute the flag without breaking the First Commandment, which provides for allegiance to God above all others. Associate Justice **Felix Frankfurter**, writing for all but one member of the Court, denied their claim. Frankfurter argued that religious freedom had to be balanced against the state's rational interest in national unity, and claimed that the Court was no more qualified to perform this balancing act than was the school board. The Court's decision surprised the public and was widely criticized. Though Frankfurter did not change his mind, other Justices soon did, and the Court reversed itself three years later in ***West Virginia State Board of Education v. Barnette*** (1943). (BDG) **See aslo** Education; Flag Salute Cases; Religious Tests and Oaths.

BIBLIOGRAPHY

Cushman, Robert E. *Leading Constitutional Decisions.* New York: Appleton-Century-Crofts, 1966.

Missionaries

Missionaries served a dual purpose in American life. By spreading the news of a particular faith tradition to people who were previously unaware of it, they presented the American way of life to immigrants, native peoples, and foreigners with whom the United States wished to establish economic and political relationships. In so doing, they inculcated many into a Christianity that marries **democracy** and **capitalism** with theology.

One of the earliest missionary groups was the Connecticut Missionary Society, formed in 1798 to Christianize the "heathen" (primarily Native Americans) and promote biblical literacy in New England. As the frontier moved farther west, the missionaries followed, serving as educators, civic leaders, and exponents of culture. The introduction of black slave trade in the Southern states attracted missionaries—both white and free black—who sought to teach the newcomers the religion and cultural values of American life. However, white landowners rebuffed missionary activity because they feared insurrections, like the one led by **Nat Turner** in 1831, would follow evangelism. Following the **Civil War**, many missionaries were sent from New England to assist in the reconstruction of southern society and the training of African Americans in proper Christian virtues. Missionaries are still active in the United States among poor populations, especially in rural areas and Native American communities.

The formation in 1806 of the first American foreign mission board took American **civil religion** throughout the world. The foreign missionary movement reached its peak from 1890 through **World War I**. Motivated by a passionate desire to "save souls" and a sense that the United States was meant to be a beacon to the world, young men and women dedicated themselves to serving God in remote villages in Asia, Africa, Latin America, and elsewhere. They optimistically believed that all people could be saved before the Judgment Day, and that ignorance, not rejection, was the basis for so many unconverted people. It was not until after World War I that foreign missionaries shifted their emphasis from individual salvation to the current focus on social services offered with a faith perspective. (KMY) **See also** Buddhism; Church of Jesus Christ of Latter-day Saints; Evangelism; Hinduism; Imperialism; Islam; Liberation Theology; Persecution of Christians Overseas; Reconstruction; Slavery; Society for the Propagation of the Gospel.

Bibliography

Marty, Martin E., ed. *Missions and Ecumenical Expressions.* New York: K.G. Saur, 1993.

Walls, Andrew F. *The Missionary Movement in Christian History.* Maryknoll: Orbis Books, 1996.

Dwight Lyman Moody (1837–1899)

One of the foremost evangelists of the nineteenth century, Dwight Moody had an enormous impact on the spiritual lives of people in both Britain and the United States. Although he was reared a nominal Unitarian, as a young man in Boston he converted to **Evangelical** Christianity. Moody moved to Chicago, where he was soon spending his time in Christian work. In 1870 he joined with Ira Sankey, a singer and hymn writer, and held evangelistic meetings in the United States and in Britain. He stressed the Bible, avoiding the doctrinal differences; criticized **evolution**; and believed that social problems could be solved by conversion. (MWP) **See also** Evangelism; Unitarianism.

Bibliography

Findlay, James F. Jr. *Dwight L. Moody: American Evangelist, 1837–1899.* Chicago: University of Chicago Press, 1969.

Sun Myung Moon (1920–)

Korean-born Sun Myung Moon founded the **Unification Church** in Seoul, Korea, in 1954, claiming that he had seen a vision of Jesus calling him to complete Christ's Messianic mission. Despite hostility from traditional Christians, Reverend Moon's movement grew rapidly.

Moon had developed conservative, strongly anti-communist politics as a result of undergoing, and barely surviving, torture by North Korean jailers in 1946. After coming to the United States in 1972, he held patriotic rallies calling the nation to return to God and to forgive President **Richard Nixon** for Watergate. In 1982 he founded the *Washington Times*, a daily newspaper, to compete with the liberal establishment of the *Washington Post*.

At the same time, Moon was accused of preaching heresy, living extravagantly, and "brainwashing" converts, popularly known as "Moonies." In 1982, following a prosecution marked by alleged irregularities, Moon was convicted of tax evasion and sentenced to prison. A host of American religious leaders and civil libertarians vigorously protested this verdict, even though they often disagreed with his teachings. Appeals courts nevertheless refused to overturn the conviction, and Moon spent 13 months behind bars. Upon his release in 1985, he resumed active leadership of the Unification Church. (JSF) **See also** Conservatism; Cults.

Bibliography

Sherwood, Carlton. *Inquisition: The Persecution and Prosecution of the Reverend Sun Myung Moon.* Washington, DC: Regnery Gateway, 1991.

Sonntag, Frederick. *Sun Myung Moon and the Unification Church.* Nashville, TN: Abington, 1977.

Moral Majority

Moral Majority was founded in 1979 by Rev. **Jerry Falwell**, pastor of Thomas Road Baptist Church in Lynchburg, Virginia, and host of a popular cable television program, *The Old Time Gospel Hour*. During the 1980s, the organization was perhaps the most visible manifestation of what was known as the New Christian Right.

Moral Majority represented a clear strategic change for evangelical Christians, who had traditionally participated in politics at very low levels. Many evangelicals were initially mobilized by the presidential candidacy of Southern Baptist **Jimmy Carter**, who publicly identified himself as an evangelical. However, many white evangelicals became disillusioned with Carter's social liberalism. Two of the specific grievances were the policy of the IRS under Carter to deny religious schools tax exemptions if such institutions engaged in racial discrimination, and the 1979 White House Conference on Families. The latter event became controversial because the Carter White House defined "family" quite inclusively, to cover a variety of alternative living arrangements. Many evangelicals were angered by the apparent refusal of President Carter to endorse the "traditional" family.

Falwell's organization consisted of local and state chapters throughout the nation. While Falwell was quite clear that Moral Majority was a political organization with an ecumenical base rather than a religious organization, a large number of Moral Majority activists were members of Baptist churches. The purposes of Moral Majority were to engage in grassroots mobilization (including voter registration) of evangelical Christians, to educate voters on issues of interest to the organization, and to lobby at the state and national levels to forward the organization's goals.

Falwell claimed credit for **Ronald Reagan**'s victory in the 1980 presidential election, as well as the defeat of several venerable Senate liberals. While the actual extent of Moral Majority influence remains controversial, it is generally believed that the organization's electoral influence was actually quite limited. Moreover, Moral Majority quickly became one of the most unpopular political groups in the nation, and was eventually unfavorably regarded by even its core target constituency of white evangelical Christians. The movement was also limited by the effects of religious particularism, in that Moral Majority failed to attract support from Roman Catholics or charismatic Protestants. The failure of Falwell to support charismatic minister **Pat Robertson**'s presidential campaign revealed the narrow base from which Moral Majority operated.

In 1988, Falwell folded Moral Majority into a larger organization, known as the Liberty Federation, and terminated Moral Majority completely in June of 1989. But for almost a decade, Moral Majority symbolized the renewed political activism of evangelical Protestants. (TGJ) **See also** Abortion and Birth Control Regulation; Baptists; Charismatic Movement; Evangelism; Liberalism; Political Participation and Voting Behavior; Race Relations; Religious Right; Roman Catholicism; Southern Baptist Convention; Tax-Exempt Status; Televangelism.

Bibliography

Martin, William. *With God on Our Side: The Rise of the Religious Right in America.* New York: Broadway Books, 1996.

Moen, Matthew C. *The Transformation of the Christian Right.* Tuscaloosa: University of Alabama Press, 1992.

Wilcox, Clyde. *God's Warriors: The Christian Right in Twentieth Century America.* Baltimore: Johns Hopkins University Press, 1992.

Moral Re-Armament

A religious movement based upon acceptance of Jesus Christ as one's personal savior followed by living a life of purity, unselfishness, and honesty, Moral Re-Armament was founded at Princeton University in 1922 by Lutheran pastor **Frank Buchman**. After generating controversy at Princeton University, it moved to Oxford University where it became a worldwide movement known as the Oxford Group. In 1938, it adopted the name Moral Re-Armament as part of an effort to avoid the approaching **war** by individual spiritual awakenings. The movement was effective in reaching affluent, educated people. Many critics believe that it influenced the appeasement policies at the beginning of **World War II**. (MWP) **See also** Lutheran Church.

Bibliography

Howard, Peter. *Frank Buchman's Secret.* Garden City, NY: Doubleday, 1962.

Lean, Garth. *Frank Buchman.* London: Constable, 1985.

Mormon Church. See Church of Jesus Christ of Latter-day Saints.

Jedidiah Morse (1761–1826)

Jedidiah Morse was a Massachusetts Congregational clergyman who actively opposed **Thomas Jefferson** in the 1800 election, concerned that Jefferson's unorthodox religious views would be detrimental to the nation. Jefferson's view of religion discounted much of Christianity's belief in the divinity of Jesus and the strength of revelation. Morse, who had been battling **Unitarinism** in Massachusetts, believed that Jefferson's view of religion would undermine the Christian nature of the nation. Morse, an Orthodox **Calvinist**, believed that the tendency of republicanism was morally corrupt. (AS) **See also** Colonial America; Congregationalism.

Bibliography

Morse, James King. *Jedidiah Morse: A Champion of New England Orthodoxy.* New York: Columbia University Press, 1939; reprinted New York: Harper and Row, 1971.

Sprague, William B. *The Life of Jedidiah Morse.* New York: Anson D. F. Randolph, 1874.

Mueller v. Allen (1983)

A 1982 Minnesota statute allowed taxpayers to deduct up to $500 for each child in the sixth grade or below, and up to $700 for each child in seventh grade or above, based on payments the parents made to nonprofit private schools or to out-of-district public schools for tuition, textbooks, and transportation. The statute further stipulated that the books could not be religious in content and the schools had to adhere to **civil rights** laws.

In the U.S. Supreme Court's 5-4 decision on *Mueller v. Allen*, 463 U.S. 388 (1983), Justice **William H. Rehnquist**, writing for the majority, noted that the Minnesota program served a plausible secular purpose, namely, ensuring a well-educated citizenry, and relieving the public schools of the burden of too many students. Additionally, the benefits were going to parents rather than to the schools themselves. The question remained, however, whether the program would have the primary effect of promoting one religious belief, inasmuch as the overwhelming majority of beneficiaries were parochial school parents. In fact, 85,000 parochial school students benefited, as opposed to only 79 public school students, leading Justice Marshall to remark in dissent "the effect of the aid is unmistakably to provide desired financial support for nonpublic, sectarian institutions." (JP) **See also** Public Aid to Religious Organizations.

BIBLIOGRAPHY

Bryson, Joseph E. *The Supreme Court and Public Funds for Religious Schools.* Jefferson, NC: McFarland, 1990.

Elijah Muhammad (1897–1975)

Elijah Muhammad was born Elijah Poole in Sandersville, Georgia. He succeeded **Wallace D. Fard** as the leader of the black separatist religious movement, the **Nation of Islam.** Muhammad claimed that Fard was Allah, and he was Allah's messenger. In 1936, he established Nation of Islam headquarters in Chicago. He called for the establishment of a separate nation for black Americans, and a religion based on the worship of Allah with the belief that blacks were Allah's chosen people. In later years he moderated his strident anti-white tone and advocated self-help among black people. (JCW) **See also** African-American Churches; Black Theology; Islam; Louis Eugene Farrakhan; Malcolm X; Race Relations; Slavery.

BIBLIOGRAPHY

Clegg, Claude Andrew. *An Original Man: The Life and Times of Elijah Muhammad.* New York: St. Martin's Press, 1997.

Frederick Augustus Conrad Muhlenberg (1750–1801)

Frederick Muhlenberg, son of the leader of the **Lutheran Church** in **colonial America**, was born in Pennsylvania, educated in Halle, Germany, and ordained a Lutheran pastor in 1770. Elected to the **Continental Congress** in 1779, he also served in the Pennsylvania assembly. He presided over the Pennsylvania convention called to ratify the federal constitution and was elected to the first four congresses as a Federalist from Philadelphia. He served as speaker of the House of the first and third Congresses and cast the decisive vote on a resolution supporting the Jay Treaty (1796), an action which ended his political career. The Jay Treaty, negotiated by **John Jay** at the request of **George Washington**, was an attempt to end growing hostilities between the United States and Great Britain. The treaty combined several unpopular concessions including trade restrictions and the repayment of prerevolutionary debts. (MLH) **See also** Clergy in Public Office; Pennsylvania Colony.

BIBLIOGRAPHY

Wallace, Paul A. W. *The Muhlenbergs of Pennsylvania.* Philadelphia: University of Pennsylvania Press, 1950.

John Muir (1838–1914)

John Muir was a Scottish-born American naturalist whose writings spurred the modern conservation movement and the resultant national parks and forests. After attending the University of Wisconsin (1860–1863), he journeyed throughout North America, observing nature. Eventually settling in California, he devoted his life to conservation after 1890. His efforts led to the creation of Yosemite and Sequoia National Parks and his publications stimulated public demand for national conservation policies. A meticulous observer, his writings are notable for their detailed and rhapsodic advocacy of nature as an expression of God. (AOL)

John Muir's writings were instrumental in starting the modern conservation movement. Muir (right) is shown here in California's Yosemite Valley with Theodore Roosevelt. National Archives.

BIBLIOGRAPHY

Austin, Richard C. "Baptized into Wilderness: A Christian Perspective on John Muir." *Environmental Theology Series.* vol. 1. Creekside, VA: 1991.

Wilkins, Thurman. "John Muir: Apostle of Nature." *Western Biographies Series,* vol. 8. University of Oklahoma Press, 1995.

Murdock v. Commonwealth of Pennsylvania (1943)

A number of **Jehovah's Witnesses** were arrested and convicted of violating a City of Jeannette, Pennsylvania, ordinance that required paying a license tax in order to engage in canvassing and solicitation within the town. The convictions were sustained by the Superior Court of Pennsylvania against the contention that the ordinance deprived them of the freedom of speech, press, and religion guaranteed by the **First Amendment.** In *Murdock v. Commonwealth of Pennsylvania*, 319 U.S. 105 (1943), the U.S. Supreme Court reversed that decision, stating that "It could hardly be denied that a tax laid specifically on the exercise of those freedoms would be unconstitutional. Yet the license tax imposed by this ordinance is in substance just that." (JM) **See also** Fourteenth Amendment; Free Speech Approach to Religious Liberty.

BIBLIOGRAPHY

Chopper, Jesse H. *Securing Religious Liberty.* Chicago: University of Chicago Press, 1995.

Ivers, Greg. *Redefining the First Amendment.* New Brunswick NJ: Transaction, 1993.

John Courtney Murray (1904–1967)

John Murray, a Jesuit theologian, was one of the most prominent American Roman Catholic proponents of the compatibility of Catholicism with a secular democratic state.

During **Vatican II** (1962–1965), Murray was the principal author of the Council's "Declaration on Religious Freedom." Murray entered the Jesuit order in 1920; studied at Weston College (B.A. 1926), Boston College (1927), Woodstock College (1934), and the Gregorian (S.T.D. 1937); and was ordained in 1933. Appointed professor of theology at Woodstock, he served as editor of *Theological Studies,* a religious editor for *America,* as well as an advisor to **John Fitzgerald Kennedy**'s 1960 presidential campaign. In his seminal work, *We Hold These Truths: Catholic Reflections on the American Proposition* (1960), Murray argued that Catholic thought and American democracy were compatible. (ISM) **See also** Democracy; Roman Catholicism.

BIBLIOGRAPHY

Ferguson, Thomas P. *Catholic and American: The Political Theology of John Courtney Murray.* Kansas City, MO: Sheed and Ward, 1993.

McElroy, Robert W. *The Search for an American Public Theology: The Contribution of John Courtney Murray.* New York: Paulist Press, 1989.

Naked Public Square

A number of analysts, beginning perhaps with **Alexis de Tocqueville**, have argued that democratic politics requires a consensus on matters of ethics and morality. For most societies, such a consensus is thought to have involved general agreement on certain basic religious beliefs and principles. In such a society, politics may appear to be quite secular, in that religious values may never be made an explicit part of the debate. However, religion is thought to provide a framework within which political controversies are negotiated. Indeed, some observers (most recently, Peter Berger) have suggested that a societal consensus on religious or moral matters provides a "sacred canopy," which sets boundaries for acceptable political discourse.

In recent years, it has been suggested that the public role of religion has declined, and, correspondingly, so has political civility and community. In part, the breakdown of political religion is attributable to the general secularization of society. However, it is also argued that government policies, including the decisions of the U.S. Supreme Court, have played a major role in reducing the influence of transcendent beliefs in American politics. **Richard Neuhaus** has suggested that this state of affairs has led to a "naked public square," in which there is no generally accepted moral framework for political discussion. Political agreement, compromise, and civility, it is argued, are thought to become rarer in the absence of generally shared religious values. (TGJ) **See also** Civil Religion; Communitarianism; Democracy; Moral Majority; Moral Re-Armament; Secularization Thesis; Social Gospel; Transcendentalism.

Bibliography

Berger, Peter. *The Sacred Canopy: Elements of a Sociological Theory of Religion.* New York: Doubleday, 1967.

Neuhaus, Richard John. *The Naked Public Square.* Grand Rapids, MI: Eerdmans, 1984.

Nation of Islam

The Black Muslims, formally known as the Nation of Islam, was started by **Wallace D. Fard** in Detroit in 1930. From 1934 until his death, **Elijah Muhammad** headed the movement, which preached that whites were devils and that blacks should separate themselves from the larger white society and become self-sufficient. The Muslims rejected Christianity, saying it was the religion of their slave masters and that blacks should follow **Islam**. The movement attracts primarily African Americans living in urban ghettoes. Since 1978, the Nation of Islam has been led by **Louis Farrakhan** and in the mid-1990s, it had an estimated membership of 20,000. (WVM) **See also** African-American Churches; Million Man March; Race Relations; Religion and Urban Issues; Slavery.

Bibliography

Lincoln, E. Eric. *The Black Muslims in America.* Revised Edition. New York: Kayode Publications, Ltd., 1991.

Magida, Arthur J. *Prophet of Rage.* New York: Basic Books, 1996.

Carry Amelia Moore Nation (1846–1911)

Carry Nation was born in Kentucky in 1846 to a poor family. Her first husband was an alcoholic who died early in their marriage, which left her as the sole support for their child. After her second marriage deteriorated, Nation began to believe that she was put on earth not to be personally happy at home, but to be a "home defender" for other women. In 1892 she established a local chapter of the **Women's Christian Temperance Union (WCTU)** in Kansas and became their "jail evangelist." Although Kansas was a dry state, liquor was readily available. Believing it her duty to fight illegal liquor consumption, Nation began what she called her "hatchetation" of local saloons, destroying property and bottles of liquor with an ax, while accompanied by psalm-singing followers. She was frequently arrested and eventually was rejected by the WCTU. Unable to support herself, she turned to the vaudeville circuit to promote her message. She published her autobiography *The Use and Need of the Life of Carry A. Nation* in 1904 and died in 1911 in Leavenworth, Kansas. (JCW) **See also** Anti-Saloon League; Temperance and Prohibition; Women in Religion and Politics.

Bibliography

Ross, Ishbel. Charmers and Cranks: *Twelve Famous American Women who Defied the Conventions.* New York: Harper & Row, 1965.

Taylor, Robert Lewis. *Vessel of Wrath: The Life and Times of Carry Nation.* New York: New American Library, 1966.

National Catholic Welfare Conference

Begun in 1917 the National Catholic Welfare Conference was organized to coordinate the religious and social services of Roman Catholics during **World War I**. Encouraged to continue its efforts after the **war** by Pope Benedict XV, the group became involved in international peace and justice movements and entered into the debate of a series of government-sponsored social programs, including health care and child labor. The group changed its name to NCW Council and stated that the organization held no ecclesiastical jurisdiction. It was divided into two bodies in 1966: the **National Conference of Catholic Bishops** and a lobbying arm, the United States Catholic Conference. (MWP) **See also** Labor; Pacifism; Peace Movements; Roman Catholicism; Social Justice; Vatican, Diplomatic Relations; Welfare.

BIBLIOGRAPHY

Dolan, Jay P. *The American Catholic Experience.* Notre Dame, IN: Notre Dame University Press, 1992.

McKeown, E. K. *War and Welfare: American Catholics and World War I.* New York: Garland, 1988.

National Conference of Catholic Bishops

The conference was established in 1966 in response to **Vatican II**'s call for each nation to have a national organization representing its bishops. The new organization took over some of the roles of the **National Catholic Welfare Conference**. It coordinates the activities of the nation's 320 bishops in internal church matters such as liturgy, worship, and the training of clergy. Its counterpart for political and social issues involving the general public is the United States Catholic Conference. (MWP) **See also** Clergy Malpractice; Clergy in Public Office; Public Theology; Religious Tests and Oaths; Roman Catholicism; Vatican, Diplomatic Relations; Welfare.

BIBLIOGRAPHY

Reese, Thomas J. *A Flock of Shepherds.* Washington, DC: FADICA, 1992.

National Endowment for the Arts (NEA)

The National Endowment for the Arts (NEA) was created in 1965 as part of President Lyndon Johnson's "Great Society" programs. Although federal funding of the arts did occur prior to its creation, the NEA was the first agency to encourage and develop the arts in a systematic manner. Johnson sought to create the NEA—and met little congressional resistance—because of his belief that art should be available to all members of a society, regardless of income. With an original budget of $5 million, the NEA has grown to its current budget of $99 million. The NEA funds many civic organizations, arts training in the schools, local theater groups, orchestras and opera companies, and traveling theater groups. It also provides more controversial individual grants to particular artists. The latter grants have been a source of difficulty for the NEA, particularly the grants that helped underwrite Robert Mapplethorpe's photo exhibit (considered "obscene"), Andres Serrano's "Piss Christ" (subversive of morals and antagonistic to religion), and Karen Finley's performance art (smearing herself with chocolate sauce). Republicans, after taking over the Congress in 1994, vowed to eliminate the NEA, but have so far been unsuccessful.

Supporters of the NEA have argued that, comparatively speaking, Americans spend a far smaller portion of their budget on public arts funding than any other developed nation. They also argue that funding provides access to art that people might otherwise not enjoy, helps build local communities, encourages instruction in the arts, and helps ensure that art that piques nonetheless can be created. Critics have argued that the NEA forces Americans to spend their money on art that they do not like or that offends, subjects artistic creation to bureaucratic regulation, and is not a necessary expenditure of government funds. Several large church organizations like the **Christian Coalition** and Focus on the Family have made repeated calls for the defunding of the NEA. They argue that the organization purposely funds projects that are anti-religion and immoral. Other critics have been concerned that government funding of the arts would discourage private donations, which have long been the backbone of artistic support. (JP) **See also** Censorship; Education; First Amendment; Free Speech Approach to Religious Liberty; Liberalism; Publicly Funded Religious Displays; Religion and Politics in Film.

BIBLIOGRAPHY

Moen, Matthew. "Congress and the National Endowment for the Arts: Institutional Patterns and Art Funding, 1965–1994." *The Social Science Journal.* 34 no. 2 (April 1997).

O'Sullivan, John, et. al. "The Nation vs. The National Review." *American Theatre.* 14 no. 7 (September 1997).

Native American Religions

The history behind Native American religious freedom within the American political scene is complex because issues involving religious freedom are inextricably tied to the founding of the United States. The U.S. was founded on principles of religious freedom embodied in two clauses of the **First Amendment** to the Constitution—the **Establishment Clause** and the **Free Exercise Clause**. The constitutional protection of religion is based on the language of the Establishment Clause: "Congress shall make no law respecting an establishment of religion, or prohibiting the free exercise thereof." Although Indian religions are entitled to the same protection under the First Amendment as any other religion or belief, past federal policy has tended to repress Native American religious practices. This repression was one of the ways the United States government attempted to assimilate Indians into the larger society.

Federal regulations passed at the turn of the century outlawed tribal religions and punished their practitioners with confinement in agency prisons or loss of government rations. Although this religious ban was lifted in 1934, the federal government continued to inhibit tribal religious practices by cutting the hair of Indian children and by arresting Indians for possession of such sacred objects as peyote and eagle feathers. Federal agents also prohibited schoolchildren from speaking their native languages, prevented Native American access to holy places on public lands, destroyed sacred sites, and interfered with tribal ceremonies.

Congress finally responded to the religious needs of Native Americans by passing the **American Indian Religious Freedom Act** in 1978 (Public Law 95-341) The act recognizes the fundamental right of all persons to have religious freedom. The act's broad policy statement recognizes the religious practices of American Indians, Native Alaskans, and Hawaiians as integral parts of each culture's tradition and heritage. These religious practices, according to the act, form the basis of Indian identity and value systems and are indispensable and irreplaceable components of Indian life.

Among other things, the act guarantees access to religious sites, use and possession of sacred objects, and freedom to worship through traditional ceremonial rites. In addition to articulating a general policy promoting and preserving traditional Indian religious practices, the act calls for an examination of current federal policy by the relevant government agencies to determine what appropriate changes should be made to implement the spirit of the law.

Native American religious freedom often involves questions of property rights. To the native peoples of America, certain places and lands are sacred. The journey to these lands and places is a spiritual journey, and much preparation and thought is necessary to make such a journey. A significant number of Indian tribal religions rely upon the performance of ceremonies and rituals in specific locations. Because a particular mountain, lake, butte, or river is the center of a tribe's religious history, that places also forms the core of the tribe's identity. These site-specific locations are used for vision quests, sweat lodge ceremonies, and places of isolation.

Native American religious values are inherently different from Judeo-Christian values. Because Native American religious practices are often site-specific, Native Americans have a fundamental need for a pristine environment in which to exercise their religious traditions. This pristine environment requires large areas of undisturbed land. Protecting these lands is an issue that has gone to the United States Supreme Court. In ***Lyng v. Northwest Indian Cemetery Protection Association***, 108 S.Ct. 1319(1988), the issue was whether the First Amendment's Free Exercise clause forbids the government from permitting timber harvesting in, or road construction through, a portion of a national forest that has traditionally been used for religious purposes by members of three American Indian tribes in northwestern California. In an opinion written by Justice Sandra Day O'Connor, the Court concluded that the First Amendment guarantee only provides protection against laws that coerce citizens to violate their religion or punishes them for practicing their beliefs. As a result of *Lyng*, a growing number of irreplaceable and sacred tribal sites are no longer under government protection and are in danger of being destroyed.

The Free Exercise Clause has been invoked by Native Americans to protect their right to ingest sacred peyote, to practice their spirituality at sacred sites, to gather and keep sacred objects, to hunt and fish, to protect the spirits of their children, and to express their spirituality through traditional dress while in prison. An analysis of the history and development of free exercise jurisprudence, focusing especially on the conflicts that arise between the government and Native Americans, reveals that the Indians almost always lose. Sometimes the government refuses to recognize the religious character of Indian religious claims. Other times the government recognizes that Native American interests are religious but does not acknowledge that the government actions at issue actually burden religious practice. In other instances, the government acknowledges its burden on Native Americans' religious practices but believes that the interests of the majority culture trump the religious rights of Indians. In all these types of cases, the courts have largely failed to protect the religious exercise claims of Native Americans. (PAP) **See also** Cherokee Removal; Handsome Lake; *Quick Bear v. Leupp*.

BIBLIOGRAPHY

Deloria, Vine, Jr., ed. *American Indian Policy in the Twentieth Century*. Norman: University of Oklahoma Press, 1992.

Deloria, Vine, Jr. and Clifford M. Lytle. *American Indians, American Justice*. Austin: University of Texas Press, 1983.

Inouye, Daniel K. "Discrimination and Native American Religious Rights." In John R. Wunder, ed. *Native Americans and the Law*. Lincoln: University of Nebraska Press, 1990.

Prucha, Francis Paul, ed. *Documents of United States Indian Policy*. Lincoln: University of Nebraska Press, 1990.

Wunder, John R. *Native American Cultural and Religious Freedoms*. New York: Garland Publishing, Inc, 1996.

Nativism

Throughout U.S. history, there have been instances of Americans hating and persecuting immigrants and trying to restrict further immigration. Such stances, termed "nativism," have targeted various nationalities and religions, especially non-Protestant immigrants.

Early nativists particularly opposed immigration by Irish- and German-born Roman Catholics, who they feared would turn the United States into a "Papist" tyranny. Protestant mobs destroyed many Catholic churches and convents from the 1830s to 1850s, and a semi-pornographic literature of anti-Catholic "escape-from-the-nunnery" tales enjoyed widespread popularity. Pre-**Civil War** nativists formed the American, or **"Know-Nothing" Party**, which primarily targeted Catholic immigrants. In the 1890s the anti-Catholic "American Protective Association" lobbied to restrict largely Catholic immigration from Southern Europe. Catholic newcomers from Quebec also faced some hostility from Protestant New Englanders in the late nineteenth and early twentieth centuries.

Jewish immigrants have been another favorite target of American nativists. As thousands of Eastern-European Jews fled the pogroms of the late nineteenth and early twentieth centuries, many Americans began calling for an end to Jewish immigration. These sentiments led to the Literacy Test Act of 1917, which aimed to restrict migration from Eastern Europe. Following a new wave of pogrom-induced Jewish immigration in 1920–1921, nativist politician Albert Johnson stirred up enough congressional **Anti-Semitism** to win passage of the Quota Act of 1921. Unlike the 1917 legislation, the 1921 act and its 1924 successor dramatically reduced immigration by Eastern-European Jews as well as by Southern- and Eastern-European Catholics. This restrictive policy and the anti-Semitism behind it continued during much of the Nazi era, making the admission of Jewish refugees extremely difficult. In 1939, for example, over 900 Jews fleeing the Nazis attempted to come ashore in Miami, Florida. The U.S. government forced their ship to return to Europe, where many eventually perished in the **Holocaust**.

Today's nativists seem most likely to object to immigration by Latin Americans, most of whom are Catholics. Yet recent anti-immigration rhetoric has tended to focus more on migrants' economic condition and native language than on their religion. During the Gulf War, however, hate crimes against Muslim immigrants to the United States increased dramatically, and xenophobes have also attacked foreign-born Hindus in New Jersey.

The causes of nativism are diverse, but cultural antagonism appears to drive hostility to immigrants at least as much as do economic privations. Among the nativists, belonging to the religious majority generally increases anti-immigrant sentiments, but being unemployed almost never has any effect. Over time, however, declines in the amount of money people have to spend usually coincide with greater overall support for nativist measures. (JSF) **See also** Anti-Catholicism; Hinduism; Islam; Judaism; Persian Gulf Conflict; Pornography; Race Relations; Roman Catholicism; War; World War II.

Bibliography

Billington, Ray Allen. *The Protestant Crusade, 1800–1860: A Study of the Origins of American Nativism.* New York: Macmillan, 1938.

Higham, John. *Strangers in the Land: Patterns of American Nativism, 1860–1925.* New Brunswick, NJ: Rutgers University Press, 1955.

Perea, Juan F., ed. *Immigrants Out!: The New Nativism and the Anti-Immigrant Impulse in the United States.* New York: New York University Press, 1997.

Smith, Rogers M. *Civic Ideals: Conflicting Visions of Citizenship in U.S. History.* New Haven, CT: Yale University Press, 1997.

Natural Law

Natural law comprises a set of rules or a body of perceptions that is accessible through human reason, independent of convention or positive law. Within human nature, rationality provides the basis for natural law. The capability of humans to appreciate natural law separates humankind from all other life forms.

Natural law has assumed various forms, although two primary views of the concept are distinguishable. The ancient and medieval philosophers argued natural law could be derived from a higher or divine law. For St. Thomas Aquinas, natural law was the outgrowth of eternal law. Natural law was also understood as the unfolding of universal experience and common sense, aided by right reason.

The Renaissance and the **Reformation** produced a view of natural law grounded exclusively upon human reason. Hugo Grotius, Immanuel Kant, and Baron Pufendorf are representatives of this understanding. Grotius, a seventeenth-century Dutch legal theorist, argued that the precepts of natural law were provided by human reason alone, and that through human interaction natural law would receive greater definition. On the other hand, Kant rejected the idea that all natural law had its origins in divine law. In the nineteenth and twentieth centuries, the philosophies of utilitarianism and legal positivism expanded upon these earlier efforts, and the secularized concept of natural law became the prevailing view. The older understanding of natural law survived in various forms, including in the works of Edmund Burke and in Roman Catholic social thought. In the latter half of the twentieth century, interest in natural law theories has revived. (HLC) **See also** Roman Catholicism; Secular Humanism; Secularization Thesis.

Bibliography

Budziszewski, J. *Written on the Heart: The Case for Natural Law.* Downers Grove, IL: Intervarsity Press, 1997.

Cromartie, Michael, ed. *A Preserving Grace: Protestants, Catholics, and Natural Law.* Grand Rapids, MI: Eerdmans, 1997.

Rommen, Heinrich. *The Natural Law.* Indianapolis: Liberty Fund, 1998.

Natural Rights

Rights may be defined as claims to some good that others must respect, for example, the right to a "free exercise of religion." Natural rights are rights that one possesses independent of all human authority or convention. They are the gift of nature. No human being can legitimately infringe upon another's natural rights. The most influential articulation of the doctrine of natural rights can be found in the British philosopher **John Locke**'s *Second Treatise of Government*, in which Locke attempts to show that a person's' natural condition is one of radical freedom, independence, and equality. People exist in a "state of nature" in which they are absolutely free to appropriate from nature whatever they need for their own self-preservation. Yet, according to Locke's teaching, a person is not only radically free by nature but radically insecure. To say the least, in the state of nature people do not always respect other people's lives: people are equally subject to violent death. Therefore, via their own consent, they are compelled to form governments to protect their natural rights, insofar as that is possible. Natural rights are thereby turned into **civil rights**, rights to be protected by a government to which one has consented. One must consent to a government because one can only give up part of one's natural freedom, which is shared equally with all others, voluntarily. Yet no matter how much of one's natural freedom one voluntarily cedes to a government, there are natural rights that cannot be alienated. The most basic of these are the rights to life and to liberty. One cannot voluntarily consent to be a slave. One may say that a government, a constitution, is legitimate in proportion, and to the degree that it protects these natural rights.

The **Declaration of Independence** pronounces that by "the laws of nature and of nature's God" the American colonies had a right to revolt from the tyranny of King George III of England. Its most famous and weighty sentence asserts a version of Locke's natural rights teachings. "We hold these truths to be self-evident that all men are created equal; that they are endowed by their Creator with certain unalienable rights; that among these rights are life, liberty, and the pursuit of happiness." To the extent that those rights are the product of the "laws of nature," they are natural rights. It is necessary to add that one cannot, and should not, confuse the doctrine proclaimed in the Declaration with Locke's teaching. Though **Thomas Jefferson**, the author of the Declaration, was a great student of Locke, and the Declaration at a number of places appropriates Locke's language (e.g., the phrase "a long train of abuses" is taken from the Second Treatise), the Declaration is not simply a Lockean document, and it should not be assumed to be one. It is undeniable, however, that the doctrine of natural rights, Lockean or not, has powerfully shaped the American way of life. (SJL) **See also** Civil Rights Acts; Equal Rights Amendment; First Amendment; Free Exercise Clause; Free Speech Approach to Religious Liberty; Fourteenth Amendment; Natural Law; Slavery.

BIBLIOGRAPHY

Locke, John. *Two Treatises of Government.* Peter Laslett, ed. New York: Mentor Books, 1965.

Strauss, Leo. *Natural Right and History.* Chicago: University of Chicago Press, 1953.

Tuck, Richard. *Natural Rights Theories: Their Origin and Development.* New York: Cambridge University Press, 1979.

Richard John Neuhaus (1936–)

President of the Institute on Religion and Public Life, based in New York City, Father Richard John Neuhaus is best known as the editor-in-chief of the Institute's publication, *First Things: A Monthly Journal of Religion and Public Life.* Through this vehicle, Neuhaus has become one of the country's foremost authorities on the role of religion in contemporary politics and culture.

He has popularized the concepts of the "public square," where the concerns of **democracy** and religion intersect—thus recognizing and protecting the deepest moral convictions of a people—and the "**naked public square**," in which an unbounded and anti-democratic government violates the separation of church and state, acknowledging no higher authority or moral realm other than the state. With other distinguished thinkers, he has advocated a "Catholic moment" as the foundation for a politically and socially renewed America. Pope John Paul II has identified Neuhaus, **Michael Novak**, and **George Weigel** as the three most important Roman Catholic intellectuals in American politics.

Neuhaus particularly has addressed issues of ecumenism, international justice, and **civil rights**. His many publications include treatments of the relationship between Jews and Christians in the modern world, religious and social bonds between Catholics and **Evangelicals**, the moral challenge of a free economy, and the role of religion in South Africa.

In a postmodern context, he has examined the American experiment in self-government and the country's ability to perpetuate its people, principles, and institutions in the face of a judiciary that has overstepped its constitutional authority. The essays in a 1996 First Things symposium entitled "The End of Democracy?" set off a debate, often acrimonious, among leading American intellectuals of all faiths and resulted in the resignation of several prominent persons from the journal's editorial board. Neuhaus maintains that the debate was necessary at a critical time, that discussions about judicial arrogance were not new in American discourse, and that most critics ignored the question mark in the symposium's title.

Neuhaus was born in Canada and educated there and in the United States. Before being ordained a Catholic priest in 1991, he was a **Lutheran** clergyman and, for almost 20 years, was senior pastor of a low-income, largely black parish in Brooklyn. He also held presidential appointments in the **Jimmy Carter**, **Ronald Reagan**, and George Bush administrations. (EES) **See also** Capitalism; Ecumenical Movement; First Amendment; Fourteenth Amendment; Roman Catholicism; Social Justice.

BIBLIOGRAPHY

Neuhaus, Richard John. *The Naked Public Square: Religion and Democracy in America.* College Park, MD: Washington Institute for Contemporary Issues, 1986.

——. *The Catholic Moment: The Paradox of the Church in the Postmodern World.* San Francisco: Harper & Row, 1987.

——. *Doing Well & Doing Good: The Moral Challenge of the Free Economy.* New York: Doubleday, 1992.

——. and Leon Klinichi. *Believing Today: Jew and Christian in Conversation.* Grand Rapids, MI: Eerdmans, 1989.

——. and Charles Colson, eds. *Evangelicals & Catholics Together: Toward a Common Mission.* Dallas: Word, 1995

New Age Movement

In the early 1970s, ideas from spiritualism, theosophy, and similar mystical traditions began to merge with then-popular ideas from Eastern religions such as **Hinduism**. The result was a loosely organized, non-creedal set of beliefs and practices that acquired the name New Age. One of its first popular books was the 1971 *Be Here Now* by Baba Ram Dass. Another example of New Age thinking was the popular song, "The Age of Aquarius."

Beliefs vary, but common to all is the idea that humanity is undergoing a radical transformation in consciousness. Individuals are acquiring a mystical awareness that allows them to see God as the unifying principle binding humanity to nature (pantheism). When enough individuals are changed, society will be transformed and a new age of peace and harmony will begin.

Practices differ even more widely, ranging from a loose, do-it-yourself approach to religion to strongly authoritarian **cults** controlling every aspect of the lives of their followers. Common to many are practices such as vegetarianism, meditation, and yoga. (MWP)

Bibliography

Ferguson, Marilyn. *The Aquarian Conspiracy.* Los Angeles: J. B. Tarcher, 1980.

Satin, Mark. *New Age Politics.* New York: Delta, 1979.

New Deal

The New Deal is the name given to the political and economic policies pursued by the administration of President Franklin D. Roosevelt in the 1930s. The New Deal included a large number of economic stimulus packages as well as the creation of a larger, more powerful federal government. The New Deal was controversial for many reasons. It shifted power from states to the federal government, opened whole new areas of the economy to federal regulation, and created a number of programs that were socialistic in nature.

Religious supporters of the New Deal saw it as a way to achieve many of the goals of the **social gospel**. Some argued that the program's general terms were modeled upon Father **John A. Ryan**'s Bishops Program for Social Reconstruction (1919), which Father Ryan wrote on behalf of the **National Catholic Welfare Conference**. The Bishops Program included the establishment of a guaranteed wage, health, unemployment, and old age insurance, and stricter labor laws that protected workers, unions, and children. However, the forces behind the New Deal were largely secular. Roosevelt's advisors and the architects of the plan were largely secular humanists who saw the policies they advocated as a means of progress and humanitarianism.

Religious critics attacked the plan as socialism. The leading critic, Father **Charles E. Coughlin** originally was a supporter of Roosevelt's policies. However, by 1934 he had become convinced that the policies were not in the best interests of the United States. He used his widely listened to radio show to attack Roosevelt. He also formed the National Union for Social Justice, which at its peak had more than 500,000 members. Coughlin's influence declined when the Roman Catholic Church intervened and put a stop to his broadcasts because they were anti-Semitic and too vitriolic. **See also** Anti-Semitism; Roman Catholicism; Secular Humanism; Socialism and Communism.

Bibliography

Tull, Charles J. *Father Coughlin and the New Deal.* Syracuse, NY: Syracuse University Press, 1965.

H. Richard Niebuhr (1894–1962)

H. Richard Niebuhr was a professor of theology at Yale, counted among the leading theological interpreters of the interrelation between Christianity and American culture and politics. His thought represents a synthesis of **Ernst Troeltsch**'s sociological analysis of religion, especially its recognition of the historicity and relativity of all religious institutions, and the **Calvinist** emphasis on the absolute sovereignty of God. Niebuhr's basic theological focus is the relation between faith and culture, the question of how the commitment to ultimate reality is worked out in the context of less than ultimate ecclesiastical, cultural, and political structures. This issue and his concern that all too often God's ultimacy is identified with human institutions inform his evaluation of American religious life and history.

Niebuhr's first book, *The Social Sources of Denominationalism* (1929), argues that sociological rather than doctrinal factors account for America's denominational diversity. *The Kingdom of God in America* (1937) identifies the idea of "God's Kingdom" as a unifying motif of American Protestantism and influential concept for American civilization at large. *Christ and Culture* (1951) outlines five basic types of Christian attitudes toward the world, ranging from radical separation to conformism. Finally, *Radical Monotheism and Western Culture* (1960) proposes a strict theocentric vision over against the implicit "polytheism" within church, politics, and culture.

Notable in Niebuhr's thought is his appreciation of America's political ideal of religious liberty, which prevents the absolutization of either church or state, and his ethics of responsibility and relationality. Ethical behavior is the "fitting response" to the constellation of one's relation to God and neighbor in a given situation; ethical values derive less from abstract principles than from the life of human community. (PV) **See also** John Calvin; Communitarianism; First Amendment; Fourteenth Amendment; Free Exercise Clause; Political Participation and Voting Behavior; Theocracy; Wall of Separation.

Bibliography

Diefenthaler, Jon. *H. Richard Niebuhr: A Lifetime of Reflections on the Church and the World.* Macon, GA: Mercer University Press, 1986.

Keiser, R. Melvin. *Roots of Relational Ethics: Responsibility in Origin and Maturity in H. Richard Niebuhr.* Atlanta, GA: Scholars Press, 1996.

Karl Paul Reinhold Niebuhr (1892–1971)

One of the most influential American Protestant theologians and ethicists of the twentieth century, Karl Niebuhr was a renowned author, founder, and editor of *Christianity and Crisis* (1941–), and advocate of a "Christian realism" that sought to combine Christian teaching on love with the political demands of **social justice**. Deeply influenced by the "**Social Gospel**" while a pastor in Detroit (1915–1928), he advocated socialism and even ran as a socialist candidate for congressional office. However, his experiences with striking Ford Motor Company workers and management led to disillusionment regarding social progress, and the advocacy of a realism that recognized human finitude or limitations. He then became a professor at Union Theological Seminary in New York where he was to write his most influential works, *Moral Man and Immoral Society* (1932) and his Gifford lectures, *The Nature and Destiny of Man* (1941–1943).

Christian realism consisted of three basic principles. Based upon an Augustinian anthropology that recognized the paradoxical confluence of freedom and sin in individuals and society, Niebuhr argued that powers need to be held in balance to ensure peace. This approach influenced figures such as **John Foster Dulles**, Hans Morgenthau, and Kenneth Thompson. Also, in light of the future Kingdom of God, Niebuhr held that love is at best an "impossible possibility," which nonetheless remains as the telos of human striving. This realism, in combining love and justice, reflected his deep pessimism regarding the human situation and the ambiguity of human intentions and actions. Finally, despite human finitude, Niebuhr believed that one is compelled to act in the political sphere, to bring public policies into harmony with the principles of love and denominations. The resulting political theory is a moderate one that was attacked during the 1970s and 1980s by liberation theologians who saw it as a support of the status quo. (ISM) **See also** Liberation Theology; Socialism and Communism.

Bibliography

Fox, Richard. *Reinhold Niebuhr: A Biography.* New York: Harper & Row, 1985.

Kegley, Charles W. and Robert W. Bretall, eds. *Reinhold Niebuhr: His Religious, Social, and Political Thought.* New York: Macmillan, 1956.

McCann, Dennis P. *Christian Realism and Liberation Theology.* Maryknoll, NY: Orbis Books, 1982.

Niebuhr, Reinhold. *Christian Realism and Political Problems.* New York: Charles Scribner's Sons, 1953.

Niebuhr, Reinhold and Paul Sigmund. *Democracy.* Berkeley: University of California Press, 1960.

Niemotko v. Maryland (1951)

The applications of a group of **Jehovah's Witnesses** for permits to use a Havre de Grace, Maryland, city park for Bible talks were denied, although the city had routinely granted permits to other religious and fraternal organizations. The Jehovah's Witnesses attempted to hold a meeting and make speeches in the park, and although there was no evidence of disorder or threat of violence or riot, they were arrested on charges of disorderly conduct and convicted. In *Niemotko v. Maryland*, 340 U.S. 268 (1951), the U.S. Supreme Court overturned the convictions, finding that the group was denied equal protection of the laws and the freedoms of speech and religion in violation of the **First** and **Fourteenth Amendments**. (JM)

Bibliography

Choper, Jesse H. *Securing Religious Liberty.* Chicago: University of Chicago Press, 1995.

Regan, Richard J. *Private Conscience and Public Law.* New York: Fordham University Press, 1972.

Richard Nixon (1913–1994)

The 37th president of the United States, Richard Nixon was born on January 9, 1913, in Yorba Linda, California, in humble circumstances. Raised a Quaker, his religious beliefs were deep and led him to form a great tolerance of others and great intellectual understanding. His father, Frank, would take him to revivals, including those of **Billy Sunday**. He graduated from Whittier College in 1934, and earned his law degree from Duke University. During **World War II** he served in the Navy in the Pacific Theater of Operations.

After the **war**, Nixon entered politics and was elected to Congress in 1946 as a strong anti-Communist candidate. He gained national attention by pursuing the Alger Hiss case and was elected to the United States Senate in 1950. Selected as **Dwight Eisenhower's** running mate in 1952, the ticket of "Ike and Dick" was successful in 1952 and 1956. However, in 1960 Nixon ran for president and was defeated by **John F. Kennedy** in the general election. At this time a deep and lasting friendship was formed with Reverend **Billy Graham** who acted as an advisor to Nixon. Graham was to have formally endorsed Nixon in 1960 in *Life* magazine, but the piece had been pulled. Nixon sought and lost the governorship of California in 1962. In 1968 he again ran for president and defeated Hubert Humphrey. In his first term, Nixon successfully brought an end to the **Vietnam** War and opened U.S. relations with Communist China. Graham and other religious leaders continued to influence Nixon. During the first two years of his first term, Nixon held 26 White House religious services. The number dropped off as criticism of the practice and those in attendance mounted. In 1970, Religious Heritage of America named Nixon "Churchman of the Year" for his efforts at "creating an atmosphere for a return to the spiritual, moral, and ethical values of our Founding Fathers."

Republican President Richard M. Nixon enjoyed the support of many religious leaders, including the Rev. Billy Graham. Library of Congress.

Nixon was easily re-elected in 1972 against George McGovern, but during that campaign, Nixon's political operatives broke into **Democratic Party** headquarters at the

Watergate Hotel. The revelation of the break-in, and Nixon's subsequent White House cover-up, led to his resignation in August 1974. (WB) **See also** Quakers; Republican Party; Socialism and Communism.

BIBLIOGRAPHY

Ambrose, Stephen E. *Nixon: The Education of a Politician, 1913–1962.* New York: Simon and Schuster, 1988.

Pierard, R. V. and R. D. Linder. *Civil Religion and the Presidency.* Grand Rapids, MI: Eerdmans, 1988.

Non-Preferentialism

Scholars have long debated the relation of the **Establishment Clause** to the **Free Exercise Clause** and have wondered what might be meant by the **First Amendment**'s phrasing "respecting" an establishment of religion. The most significant debate is between those who say that the clause means no state support of religion, and those who say the clause means the state may not favor one sect to the exclusion of others. This latter view is known as non-preferentialism, or the belief that government aid to religion is permissible so long as it does not prefer one religion or sect over others. Non-preferentialists argue that the alternative position effectively gives more aid and protection to organized **atheism** than to organized religion—a result, they argue, clearly at odds with the Founders' intent, since most of them recognized religion to be indispensable to the preservation of the constitutional system. Non-preferentialists have found a champion on the U.S. Supreme Court in the person of Chief Justice **William H. Rehnquist**. (JP) **See also** Fourteenth Amendment; Public Aid to Religious Organizations; Wall of Separation.

BIBLIOGRAPHY

Berns, Walter. *The First Amendment and the Future of American Democracy.* Chicago: Gateway Editions, 1985.

Levy, Leonard. *The Establishment Clause: Religion and the First Amendment.* New York: Macmillan, 1986.

John Franklyn Norris (1877–1952)

Born in rural Texas poverty, John Norris became a Southern Baptist preacher and one of Fundamentalism's most flamboyant speakers. Active in politics, in the 1930s he became fiercely anti-Communist. In 1939 he advocated U.S. intervention against Hitler, and in later life, he was a strong supporter of **Zionism**. (MWP) **See also** Baptists; Fundamentalists; Socialism and Communism; Southern Baptist Convention.

BIBLIOGRAPHY

Hankins, Barry. *God's Rascal: J. Frank Norris and the Beginnings of Southern Fundamentalism.* Lexington: University Press of Kentucky, 1996.

Gary North (1942–)

As director of the Institute for Christian Economics (I.C.E.) in Tyler, Texas, Gary North, originally a disciple of **Rousas J. Rushdoony**, remains a controversial yet influential popularizer of Christian Reconstructionism. Through his numerous books and articles, he brought Reconstructionism to an audience beyond the Calvinistic circles that gave it birth. In particular, he did much to unite **Reconstruction**'s triumphalist post-**millennialism** with the dominion theology of many charismatics in the word-of-faith movement. His ideas include advocacy for free markets, private property rights, hard currency, and an end to the **welfare** state. (ARB) **See also** John Calvin; Calvinism; Capitalism; Charismatic Movement; Christian Reconstructionist Movement; "Economic Justice for All."

BIBLIOGRAPHY

House, H. Wayne and Thomas Ice. *Dominion Theology: Blessing or Curse?* Portland, OR: Multnomah Press, 1988.

North, Gary and Gary DeMar. *Christian Reconstruction: What it is, What it isn't?* Tyler, TX: Institute for Christian Economics, 1991.

Oliver North (1943–)

A decorated veteran of the **Vietnam War**, Marine Lieutenant Colonel Oliver North led an undercover counterterrorism group within the National Security Council during the **Ronald Reagan** administration. He was dismissed for his role in the Iran-contra affair, but he electrified the nation with his charismatic testimony before a congressional committee investigating the matter. A controversial figure, North subsequently wrote an autobiography that stressed the formative role of Christianity in his life, and in 1994 he gained the support of many Christian conservatives in his unsuccessful bid for a U.S. Senate seat from Virginia. (MR) **See also** Conservatism; Religious Right; Terrorism.

BIBLIOGRAPHY

North, Oliver. *Under Fire.* San Francisco: HarperCollins Publishers, 1991.

Northwest Ordinance

Passed by the United States Congress in 1787 under the Articles of Confederation and repassed in 1789 by the First Congress under the new Constitution, the Northwest Ordinance provides for the government and organization of the Northwest Territory. One of its articles reads, in part: "Religion, morality, and knowledge being necessary to good government and the happiness of mankind, schools and the means of education shall forever be encouraged." Opponents of the U.S. Supreme Court's "strict separationist" reading of the First Amendment **Establishment Clause**—classically articulated by Mr. Justice **Hugo L. Black**'s opinion for the majority in ***Everson v. Board of Education the Township of Ewing***, 330 U.S. 1 (1947)—have used this section of the ordinance to argue that the establishment clause does not prohibit all public aid to religious schools.

As stated by Mr. Justice **William H. Rehnquist** in his dissent in ***Wallace v. Jaffree***, 472 U.S. 38 (1985), the argument goes something like this: The Northwest Ordinance provided for land grants to support not only secular public schools, but also religious schools, a practice not ended by Congress until 1845. "The House of Representatives took up the Northwest Ordinance on the same day as **[James] Madison** introduced his proposed amendments which became the

Bill of Rights.... [I]t seems highly unlikely that the House...would simultaneously consider proposed amendments to the Constitution and enact an important piece of territorial legislation which conflicted with the intent of these proposals." Taken together, these two legislative actions by the first Congress amount to evidence for an endorsement of "multiple establishment" or "**non-preferentialism**," that is, nondiscriminatory governmental aid to all religions, at least with respect to religious education. What the authors and enactors of the **First Amendment** intended to prohibit, on this reading, is the exclusive establishment of a single national religion. They did not intend for government necessarily to be neutral between religion and irreligion, as some have interpreted the Establishment Clause to require.

Defenders of separationism often respond to this line of argument in much the same way as **Dean M. Kelley** did in an article published in 1987: "It is the function of the Supreme Court not only to apply the founders' broad principles to changing conditions through the centuries but to explore and plumb the fuller implications of those principles, which may not have been grasped by the founders themselves in the few years allotted to them." The authors and enactors of the First Amendment may either not have understood its full implications or may not have been thinking about it when they repassed the Northwest Ordinance.

In any event, no one relies on this piece of evidence alone. To settle the original meaning of the First Amendment requires an extensive examination, both of the debates in the First Congress and of the debates in the states that voted to ratify the Bill of Rights. After the meaning of the historical record is settled, if indeed it can be settled, there remains a question of whether and to what extent the "framers' intentions" matter in the contemporary application of the Constitution. (The Northwest Ordinance is reprinted in Appendix 1.) (JMK) **See also** Education; Public Aid to Religious Organizations.

Bibliography

Berns, Walter. *The First Amendment and the Future of Democracy.* New York: Basic Books, 1976.

Goldwin, Robert A. and Art Kaufman. *How Does the Constitution Protect Religious Freedom?* Washington, DC: American Enterprise Institute, 1987.

Levy, Leonard. *The Establishment Clause: Religion and the First Amendment.* New York: Macmillan, 1986.

Malbin, Michael J. *Religion and Politics: The Intentions of the Authors of the First Amendment.* Washington, DC: American Enterprise Institute, 1978.

Michael Novak (1933–)

Michael Novak is a Roman Catholic thinker whose work focuses on the moral and religious implications of democratic **capitalism**. Awarded the Templeton Prize for Progress in Religion in 1994, Novak's most influential work is *The Spirit of Democratic Capitalism*, published in 1982. He is also credited with influencing Pope John Paul II's 1991 draft of *Centesimus Annus*, an encyclical on Catholic social teaching, which calls for the establishment of a free economy.

Novak argues that democratic capitalism fosters morality because virtuous habits facilitate economic success in a free economy. He believes that creativity, the building of community, and the practice of realism are the most important benefits of a free market. He has also found that businessmen are among the most religious social groups. While he is generally opposed to government regulation of business, he has admonished corporations to remember that their purpose should be to promote the good of society as a whole. (MR) **See also** Democracy; Roman Catholicism.

Bibliography

Novak, Michael. *The Spirit of Democratic Capitalism.* New York: Simon and Schuster, 1982.

——. *Catholic Social Thought and Liberal Institutions: Freedom with Justice.* 2d edition. New York: Transaction, 1989.

John Humphrey Noyes (1811–1886)

John Humphrey Noyes founded Oneida, a utopian commune that combined religious perfectionism with socialist ideals. The concepts of "theocratic democracy," "Bible communism," and "complex marriage" (**polygamy**) summarize his proposals for reform in the areas of politics, economics, and sexual ethics. (PV) **See also** Socialism and Communism; Theocracy; Utopianism.

Bibliography

Mandelker, Ira L. *Religion, Society, and Utopia in Nineteenth-Century America.* Amherst: University of Massachusetts Press, 1984.

Nuclear Disarmament

Nuclear disarmament is the term given to the movement that sought the removal of nuclear weapons from nations who possess them. This movement was largely sparked by the fear that nuclear proliferation could lead to a devestating nuclear holocaust. Taking the holocaust threat seriously, the **National Conference of Catholic Bishops**, in response to heightened public concern in the early years of **Ronald Reagan**'s presidency, released a long pastoral letter. This letter, ***The***

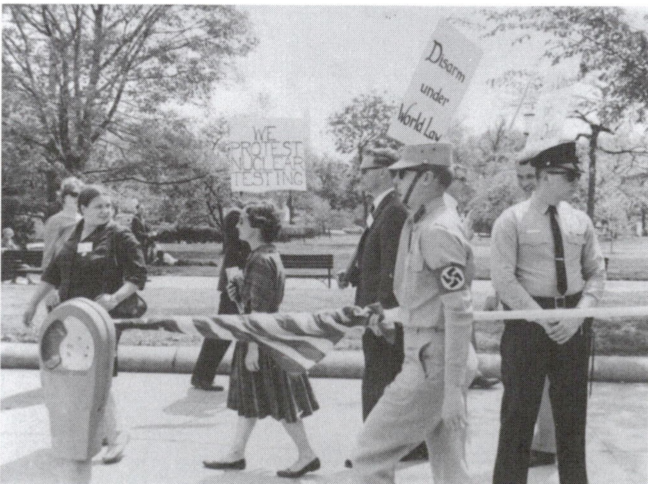

Quakers demonstrate for peace in 1962; a member of the Neo-Nazi party marches with them (foreground). National Archives.

Challenge of Peace, made the case for "negotiations to halt the testing, production, and deployment of new nuclear weapons systems"; in other words, arms control and multilateral disarmament—not unilateral disarmament. Drawing on biblical and Catholic just war teachings, the bishops followed a middle course: "'no' to nuclear conflict" but yes to "verifiable agreements especially between two superpowers." Protestants and even non-Christians could embrace their logic: agreeing to the goal but prescribing only careful, negotiated steps toward nuclear disarmament. (SW) **See also** Just War Theory; War.

Bibliography

Bundy, McGeorge. *Danger and Survival: The Political History of the Nuclear Weapon.* New York: Random House, 1988.

Gardner, Gary T. *Nuclear Nonproliferation: A Primer.* Boulder, CO: Lynne Rienner Publishers, 1994.

Lee, Steven P. *Morality, Prudence, and Nuclear Weapons.* New York: Cambridge University Press, 1993.

National Conference of Catholic Bishops. *The Challenge of Peace: God's Promise and Our Response.* Washington, DC: United States Catholic Conference, 1983.

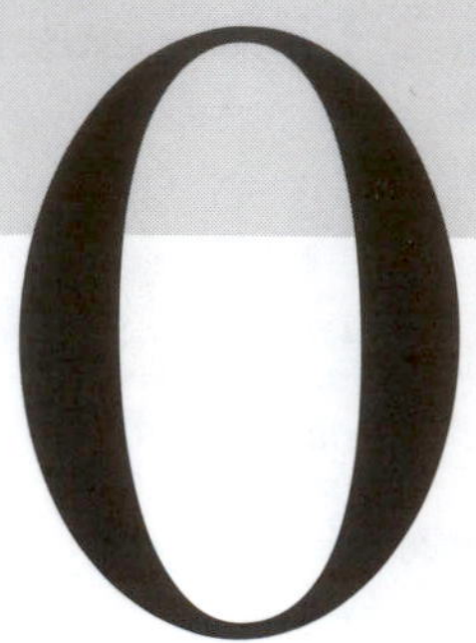

John J. O'Connor (1920–)

Ordained a Roman Catholic priest in 1945, the future Cardinal John J. O'Connor responded to a call in 1952 by then Cardinal **Francis Joseph Spellman** for priests to serve as military chaplains. For the next 27 years, O'Connor would serve as a navy and marine chaplain. In 1968, he wrote a book entitled *A Chaplain Looks at Vietnam* in which he defended the U.S. military action as a just war. (He would later state that it was a bad book.) In 1979 he was appointed a bishop in the New York Diocese. In June 1983 he was appointed bishop of Scranton where he served for only nine months before being appointed the archbishop of New York. During his installment ceremony, O'Connor vowed to "raise the stakes" in the abortion debate. As cardinal of New York, he has challenged two of the most prominent New York Democrats—Governor **Mario Matthew Cuomo** and vice presidential candidate Geraldine Ferraro—when they asserted that they could be pro-choice as a public policy stance and good Catholics at the same time. **See also** Abortion and Birth Control Regulation; Just War Theory; Military Service; Political Participation and Voting Behavior; Roman Catholicism; Vietnam.

BIBLIOGRAPHY

Faulhaber, Gregory M. *Politics, Law and the Church.* San Francisco: ISP, 1996.

O'Hair v. Blumenthal (1978)

Madalyn Murray O'Hair, a well-known atheist, alleged that the motto, **"In God We Trust,"** on the coins and currency of the United States, violated both the **Free Exercise Clause** and **Establishment Clause** of the **First Amendment**. To be valid, the court in Texas applied a three-prong test: the statute requiring the currency motto would have to reflect a secular purpose, have a primary effect that neither advanced nor inhibited religion, and would have to avoid unnecessary entanglement of government with religion. In *O'Hair v. Blumenthal*, 462 F. Supp. 19 (WD Texas 1978), the court of appeals, following earlier statements by the U.S. Supreme Court that held the use of such mottos was ceremonial and patriotic and not an expression of a national religion, upheld the constitutionality of the phrase. On appeal the Supreme Court declined to review the case. (FHJ) **See also** Atheism; Entanglement Test; One Nation under God.

BIBLIOGRAPHY

Jones, Richard H. "'In God We Trust' and the Establishment Clause." *Journal of Church and State*. 31 no. 3 (Autumn 1989): 381-417.

Madalyn Murray O'Hair (1919–)

One of America's best-known atheists, O'Hair was propelled to fame in 1963 when the U.S. Supreme Court in *Murray v. Curlett* upheld her lawsuit against prayer in public schools, a suit filed on behalf of her son, William Murray (who later became a Christian and wrote a book about his life). In 1969, she founded the American Atheists Inc. She continued her attack on religion and religious symbols by challenging "under God" in the **Pledge of Allegiance**. In 1986, O'Hair resigned as president of American Atheists but continued to serve on its board of directors. **See also** Atheism; Establishment Clause; First Amendment; Fourteenth Amendment; Free Exercise Clause; In God We Trust; *O'Hair v. Blumenthal*; One Nation under God; School Prayer; Wall of Separation.

BIBLIOGRAPHY

Murray, William J. *My Life without God.* Nashville, TN: Thomas Nelson, 1982.

O'Hair, Madalyn M. *Bill Murray, the Bible and the Baltimore Board of Education.* Austin: American Atheists Press, 1970.

O'Lone v. Estate of Shabazz (1987)

Inmates of a New Jersey prison who were of the Islamic faith brought suit against prison officials for adopting policies that prevented them from attending Muslim congregational services, claiming that the policies violated their rights under the **Free Exercise Clause** of the **First Amendment**. In *O'Lone v. Estate of Shabazz*, 482 U.S. 342 (1987), the U.S. Supreme Court rejected the prisoners' challenge, accepting the prison officials' claims that the policies were necessary for the security of the prison. The Court refused to put First Amendment claims ahead of "the determinations of those charged with the formidable task of running a prison." (JM) **See also** Islam; Prisoners, Religious Rights of.

BIBLIOGRAPHY

Blischak, Matthew P. "The State of Prisoners' Religious Free Exercise Rights." *American University Law Review.* 37 no. 2 (Winter 1988): 453–86.

Solove, Daniel. "Faith Profaned: The Religious Freedom Restoration Act and Religion in the Prisons." *Yale Law Journal* 106 no. 2 (November 1996): 459–91.

One Nation under God

The original pledge of allegiance, written in 1892 by Baptist minister and Christian Socialist Francis Bellamy, ended with the words "one nation, indivisible, with liberty, and justice for all." The words "under God" were added by an act of Congress introduced by Congressman Louis C. Rabaut of Michigan, House Joint Resolution 243, and signed into law on Flag Day, June 14, 1954. This addition was made at the request of President **Dwight D. Eisenhower**, who had heard the words in a sermon at a Lincoln Day Observance Service and felt they would be "reaffirming the transcendence of religious faith in America's heritage and future." He had also been very heavily lobbied by the Knights of Columbus, a Catholic lay fraternal society, who had been using the amended version of the pledge in their meetings. President **Abraham Lincoln** had originally used the concept of a nation under God in his Gettysburg Address where he stated "That this nation, under God, shall have a new birth of freedom." (JCW) **See also** Flag Salute Cases; Jehovah's Witnesses; Madalyn Murray O'Hair; Roman Catholicism.

BIBLIOGRAPHY

Miller, Margarette. *Twenty-three Words.* Portsmouth, VA: Printcraft Press, 1976.

Operation Rescue

Operation Rescue is a militant anti-abortion group founded by **Randall Terry** on November 28, 1987. On that day, 300 "rescuers" blockaded an abortion clinic in Cherry Hill, New Jersey, beginning a pattern of peaceful **civil disobedience** that would become the hallmark of the organization. Operation Rescue remains a loose coalition of **evangelicals, fundamentalists**, and mainline Protestants. Their tactic of civil disobedience, disdained by most other anti-abortion groups, intentionally hearkens back to the work of nineteenth-century abolitionists and more recent **civil rights** protesters. By 1990, Operation Rescue estimated that there had been more than 35,000 arrests of its members across the country.

The confrontational tactics used by the organization have garnered national attention, though not necessarily national support. A National Day of Rescue in 1988 led to the arrest of 2,631 in 32 cities. In the presidential campaign of 1992, one Operation Rescue member handed Governor **Bill Clinton** an aborted fetus in an attempt to challenge the candidate's support of abortion rights. Norma McCorvey, the Jane Roe of ***Roe v. Wade*** (1973), became associated with Operation Rescue in 1995. She changed her views on abortion after the anti-abortion group moved its headquarters next door to the abortion clinic where she worked. In 1997, Operation Rescue sought to focus attention on the sale of alleged child **pornography** by Barnes and Noble and other national bookstores. Today, the group seems to eschew its earlier "rescue" strategy, perhaps due to the severe financial penalties leveled against the practice.

Beginning in 1989, the federal courts allowed abortion rights activists to sue Operation Rescue under federal antitrust and racketeering laws (RICO). The large financial judgments against it effectively bankrupted the organization and forced it to go underground. Judicial motions against the rescue movement have continued. Flip Benham, the current director of Operation Rescue, was given a six-month prison sentence in February 1998 for trespassing during a pro-life protest at a Lynchburg, Virginia, high school.

Abortion rights proponents are adamant that Operation Rescue is a criminal organization impeding access to a constitutionally guaranteed right. Many anti-abortion groups have criticized the group for shifting the debate away from abortion onto the issue of tactics and civil disobedience. (ARB) **See also** Abolition; Abortion and Birth Control Regulation.

BIBLIOGRAPHY

Ginsburg, Faye. "Saving America's Souls: Operation Rescue's Crusade Against Abortion." Martin Marty and R. Scott Appleby, eds. *Fundamentalisms and the State.* Chicago: University of Chicago Press, 1993.

Terry, Randall. "OR Founder Terry Unabashed." *Christianity Today.* 34 (September 19, 1990): 49.

Orthodox Christianity

The Orthodox Christian sects, which include Russian Orthodox, Greek Orthodox, and other Eastern rites, began to separate from the Roman Catholic Church during the medieval period. The separation involved two key issues: the authority of the pope, the bishop of Rome, and the role that the Holy Spirit played in the Trinity. The final separation occurred in 1054 and was known as the Great Schism. Since that time, several unsuccessful attempts have been made at reuniting the groups under the authority of the pope.

In America, the various sects that constitute Orthodox Christianity have had little impact on either society at large or politics in general. The first Orthodox practitioners in what would become the United States were Russian monks who formed a church on Kodiak Island in Alaska in 1793. From the late 1800s to the outbreak of **World War I** in 1914, large numbers of Orthodox Christians arrived in the U.S. During this period, immigrants from Greece and such Slavic countries as Romania and Russia came to the U.S. for economic reasons and brought Orthodox Christianity with them. During this period, the Russian Orthodox Church attempted to unify the various Orthodox sects under its structure. These efforts were supported both politically and financially by the Russian czars. However, the Russian Revolution of 1917 ended such unification efforts.

Orthodox Christians have faced issues of acculturalization as their religion is seen largely as one of immigrants and Eastern European ethnic groups. The sects, however, have relied on conversion in the last few decades to increase their membership. The largest denomination is the Greek Orthodox Archdiocese of North and South America, with approximately two million members in the U.S. The Orthodox Church in America (Russian Orthodox Church) is the second largest with about one million members. There are about another one million members in a dozen smaller sects in the United States.

Orthodox groups in the U.S. have been active in the **ecumenical movement**, reaching out to other Christian denominations when common goals can be met. They have also been cautious members of the World Council of Churches. **See also** Roman Catholicism.

Bibliography

Harakas, Stanley S. The Orthodox Church. Minneapolis: Light & Life Publishing Co., 1987.

Smith, Barbara S. Russian Orthodoxy in Alaska. Anchorage: Alaska Historical Commission, 1980.

Robert Dale Owen (1801–1877)

The Scottish-born son of the English reformer Robert Owen, Robert Dale Owen immigrated to the United States with his father in 1825, to the socialistic community his father had begun at New Harmony, Indiana. New Harmony was based upon the egalitarian and formal anti-religious views of Robert Owen. When the community failed in 1827, he moved to New York City where he worked for the reforms his father had sought for working-class people. Editor of *The Free Enquirer*, Owen was an advocate of women's rights and free public education. Throughout his life he participated in politics and practical reform, helping to found the Smithsonian Institution. From 1858 on, he strongly opposed **slavery** but following the **Civil War**, he opposed giving the vote to blacks until they had been free for 10 years. (MWP) **See also** Education; Socialism and Communism.

Bibliography

Leopold, Richard W. *Robert Dale Owen: A Biography.* Cambridge, MA: Harvard University Press, 1940.

Taylor, Anne. *Visions of Harmony.* New York: Oxford University Press, 1987.

P

Pacifism

Pacifism is commonly defined as opposition to participation in and preparation for warfare, although many pacifists themselves would construe its meaning in larger terms, suggesting a broadly nonviolent approach to all facets of life. In American history pacifism has often, though not always, been connected to religious belief. Pacifism has intersected with the world of politics chiefly at two points: efforts to direct public policy in more pacifistic directions and attempts to obtain **conscientious objection** exemptions from **military service**.

Members of the Religious Society of Friends (**Quakers**) were the most notable proponents of pacifism in early America. Quaker officials in colonial Pennsylvania operated the province without a militia and sought to maintain peaceful relations with Native Americans. Although losing their governing majority after 1756, Quakers continued to believe that pacifism was a politically relevant ideal and sought to limit state violence.

James Madison's original 1789 draft of the Bill of Rights included the provision that "No person religiously scrupulous of bearing arms shall be compelled to render military service in person." However, members of Congress deleted this clause, arguing that conscientious objection was not a natural right protected by the state, but a privilege dispensed by governments. During the early national period, Quaker and German sectarian pacifists in Pennsylvania had some legislative success in limiting the legal demand for state militia participation.

During the antebellum period, liberal religious thinkers, evangelical revivalists and social reformers spawned a variety of popular and utopian peace groups, such as the American Peace Society (1828), which flourished until the **Civil War**. In the mid-nineteenth to early twentieth centuries, pacifism became an important theological commitment for a variety of newly emergent American denominations in the Adventist, Holiness, and Pentecostal traditions. Although these convictions withered somewhat under the public patriotism of **World War I**, in most cases it was the popular justification of **World War II** that deflated pacifist sentiments in these churches. However, several small and highly sectarian Holiness and Pentecostal groups remain pacifist at the end of the twentieth century.

During the first half of the twentieth century, the pacifist banner was most closely associated with mainline Protestantism, and its **Social Gospel** ideal expressed by groups such as the Fellowship of Reconciliation (1915), which pressed not only for an end to international hostilities, but also was an early advocate (1942) of domestic policy to promote racial equality and harmony. A 1935 gathering of so-called historic peace churches (Quakers, **Mennonites**, Brethren) launched an ongoing cooperative effort to secure provisions for conscientious objectors. Eventually forming what would come to be known as the National Service Board for Conscientious Objectors, the historic peace church-led movement became more broadly ecumenical in the post-World War II era.

The broadening was most apparent during the **Vietnam War** when student protests, peace marches, and other activities highlighted anti-war sentiments. Often, political ideology animated pacifism as much as, or more than, religious conviction. In the context of opposition to conscription during the Vietnam era, several United States Supreme Court cases gave pacifism more precise legal definition. In *Welsh v. United States* (1970) the high court expanded the basis of conscientious objection from deeply held religious belief to "deeply held moral and ethical conviction." In *United States v. Sisson* (1970) the Court held that conscientious objectors must oppose all warfare, they cannot be selective objectors to particular military conflicts.

A significant recent development in the area of religion and pacifism has been the post-**Vatican II** American Catholic Church's acknowledgment of conscientious objection as a theologically valid and worthy moral stance toward war. The **National Conference of Catholic Bishops**' 1976 condemnation of nuclear weapons as beyond the bounds of traditional Catholic teaching on justifiable means of war signaled a step in this direction. The 1983 pastoral document *The Challenge of Peace: God's Promise and Our Response*, however, went further, presenting pacifism as an equally valid Catholic moral teaching alongside the "just war" tradition.

During the last quarter of the twentieth century, religiously informed pacifism has also addressed concerns beyond conscientious objection. Some pacifists worked for arms reduction and actively opposed United States military involvement in Central America and elsewhere. Other pacifists have refused to pay the Defense Department portion of their federal income tax, and have spearheaded an effort to pass the National Peace Tax Fund legislation that would allow designated tax payment to nonlethal federal projects. (SMN) **See also** Daniel Berrigan; Philip Berrigan; Civil Disobedience; Colonial America; Evangelicals; Just War Theory; Liberalism; Mexican-American War; Natural Rights; Nuclear Disarmament; Peace Movements; Pennsylvania Colony; Pentecostals; Persian Gulf Conflict; Seventh-Day Adventists; Spanish-American War; Utopianism; War.

BIBLIOGRAPHY

Brock, Peter. *Freedom from Violence: Sectarian Nonresistance.* Toronto: University of Toronto Press, 1991.

Brock, Peter. *Freedom from War: Nonsectarian Pacifism.* Toronto: University of Toronto Press, 1991.

Keim, Albert N. and Grant M. Stoltzfus. *The Politics of Conscience: The Historic Peace Churches and America at War, 1917–1955.* Scottdale, PA: Herald Press, 1988.

Hughes, Richard T. and Theron F. Schlabach, eds. *Proclaim Peace: Christian Pacifism for Unexpected Quarters.* Urbana, IL: University of Illinois Press, 1997.

Thomas Paine (1737–1809)

Although best remembered as the writer whose small pamphlet, *Common Sense*, sparked revolutionary fever among the American colonists in 1776, Thomas Paine launched irreverent attacks on political and religious hierarchies in England and France as well as the United States. Like many of the American founders, Paine was a Deist. He claimed to find evidence of God in the orderliness of nature, but he thought that all organized religions were pompous attempts to monopolize the truth about God, and that all religious disagreements were masked battles for power. He may have acquired his distaste for religious fervor as a boy, noticing that his father, a **Quaker**, had been cast out by other Quakers because he had married an Anglican (see **Episcopal Church**). After working as a corset maker with his father in England, Paine immigrated to America in 1774 where he supported the revolutionary cause with the extremely influential *Common Sense* (1776) and *The Crisis Papers* (1776–1783). He then sailed to France, where he wrote *The Age of Reason* (1794) and was imprisoned by the Jacobins during their Reign of Terror. When he returned to the United States, the religious fervor of the **Second Great Awakening** had turned popular opinion against him; only six people attended his funeral in 1809. (BDG) **See also** American Revolution; Colonial America; Deism.

A Deist, Thomas Paine, the author of "Common Sense," did not trust the religious fervor of the Second Great Awakening. Library of Congress.

BIBLIOGRAPHY

Foner, Eric. *Tom Paine and Revolutionary America.* New York: Oxford University Press, 1977.

Keane, John. *Tom Paine: A Political Life.* Boston: Little, Brown & Co., 1995.

Theodore Parker (1810–1860)

Theodore Parker, a New England pastor whose belief that all theological doctrine was transitory, created a controversy that proved too liberal for his Unitarian congregation, and he was forced to resign. In a sermon entitled, "The Transient and Permanent in Christianity," he claimed that the moral truths of Christianity would remain long after the dogmas had faded, a popular idea in the late nineteenth century. He used his influence to champion many reform causes including the temperance movement, prison reform, and women's education. He was also part of a secret committee that aided the revolutionary abolitionist **John Brown**. (MWP) **See also** Abolition; Education; Temperance and Abolition; Unitarianism.

A leading nineteenth-century reformer, Theodore Parker aided the abolitionist efforts of John Brown. Library of Congress.

BIBLIOGRAPHY

Commager, Henry S. *Theodore Parker: Yankee Crusader.* Boston: Little, Brown and Company, 1936.

Parker, Theodore. *Collected Works,* 15 vols. Boston: Centenary, 1907–1911.

Charles Henry Parkhurst (1842–1933)

A studious and little-noticed pastor at New York City's Madison Square **Presbyterian Church**, Charles Parkhurst was propelled to fame when his February 14, 1892, sermon denouncing corruption in the city's Tammany Hall administration was unexpectedly picked up by a reporter, creating a firestorm of controversy. Forced to defend his remarks, he and some friends began to research a sermon that he delivered on March 13. This unleashed a still greater furor, eventually leading to the 1894 Lexow investigation and political reform. For the rest of his life, Parkhurst remained a critic of political corruption. (MWP) **See also** Political Participation and Voting Behavior.

BIBLIOGRAPHY

Parkhurst, Charles H. *Our Fight with Tammany.* New York: Scribners, 1895.

Francis Greenwood Peabody (1847–1936)

As a **Unitarian** theologian who taught social ethics at Harvard Divinity School, Frances Peabody was one of the leading advocates of the **Social Gospel**, an American movement that emphasized economic and social reform in a changing society. He was also an outspoken critic of the growing commercialism and materialism of American society. (MWP)

BIBLIOGRAPHY

Peabody, Francis. *The Christian Life in the Modern World.* 1914.

———. *Jesus Christ and the Social Question.* 1900.

Peace Movements

In the colonial period, **pacifism** was largely confined to sectarian church groups. Widespread populist peace movements first emerged in the democratic atmosphere that developed in America in the early 1800s.

The antebellum peace movements of the 1820s through the 1840s grew out of the popular reformist sentiments that imbued early nineteenth-century society. Seen as the "ultimate reform," peace captured the imagination of both liberal religious thinkers and evangelical revivalists and led to the 1828 organization of the American Peace Society. Ten years later, abolitionist **William Lloyd Garrison** split from the Society and founded the New England Non-Resistance Society, which advocated more radical anarchist ideals. Both groups eventually collapsed under the growing militancy and justification of force that accompanied the coming of the **Civil War**.

The turn-of-the-century progressivist spirit that accompanied another round of reformism in the United States also produced a small group of public peace activists, such as **Jane Addams**, while the profound disillusionment following **World War I** ("the war to end all wars") sparked renewed peace interest in the interwar years. Encouraged by developments such as the 1929 Kellogg-Briand Pact in which 59 nations renounced warfare, groups such as the Women's International League for Peace and Freedom campaigned to end global violence. Portions of the interwar peace movement also turned to isolationism.

Religious pacifists often had broader social concerns. Founded in 1933, **Dorothy Day**'s **Catholic Worker Movement** united pacifism with action on behalf of the nation's poor. Formed in 1915, the Fellowship of Reconciliation became a leading nondenominational pacifist voice during the interwar years. Its executive secretary A.J. Musts pioneered the theory and practice of nonviolent direct action as a means of social change. In 1942, the Fellowship spawned the Congress of Racial Equality and linked peace activists with the emergent **civil rights** movement. Later, Civil Rights leaders such as **Martin Luther King, Jr.** would make nonviolence both a tactic and a goal of that effort, and involve Christian, Jewish, and other religiously oriented pacifists.

Perhaps the most widespread American peace movement was the one that developed in opposition to the **Vietnam War**, producing massive protests against military conscription and the general conduct of the war. In the late 1960s, many Protestant groups and the Union of American Hebrew Congregations passed resolutions against the **war**, as did Roman Catholic bishops in 1971. Catholic brothers **Philip Berrigan** and **Daniel Berrigan** were already well-known in the peace movement, especially after their 1968 involvement in the destruction of the Catonsville, Maryland, draft board.

In recent years, peace activists have launched efforts against nuclear weapons, American military intervention overseas, and the size of Defense Department appropriations.

Peace movements have always been caught between their impulse to be prophetic and uncompromising and their desire to be effective and relevant. (SMN) **See also** Abolition; Civil Disobedience; Colonial America; Conscientious Objection; Evangelicals; Judaism; Just War Theory; Liberalism; Mexican-American War; Military Service; Nuclear Disarmament; Pacifism; Persian Gulf Conflict; Quakers; Roman Catholicism; Social Justice; Spanish-American War; Utopianism; War; World War I; World War II.

BIBLIOGRAPHY

Brock, Peter. *Pacifism in the United States from the Colonial Era to the First World War.* Princeton: Princeton University Press, 1968.

Chatfield, Charles. *For Peace and Justice: Pacifism in America, 1914–1941.* Knoxville, TN: University of Tennessee Press, 1971.

DeBenedetti, Charles. *An American Ordeal: The Antiwar Movement of the Vietnam Era.* Syracuse, NY: Syracuse University Press, 1990.

McNeal, Patricia F. *Harder than War; Catholic Peacemaking in Twentieth-Century America.* New Brunswick, NJ: Rutgers University Press, 1992.

William Penn (1644–1718)

William Penn was expelled from Oxford University in 1662 because of his controversial religious beliefs and jailed in 1669 for his views, which had moved from Puritanism to Quakerism. His 1670 trial ended in a not-guilty verdict despite the judge's instructions to the jury to return a guilty verdict. In 1681, King Charles II deeded Penn land in the new

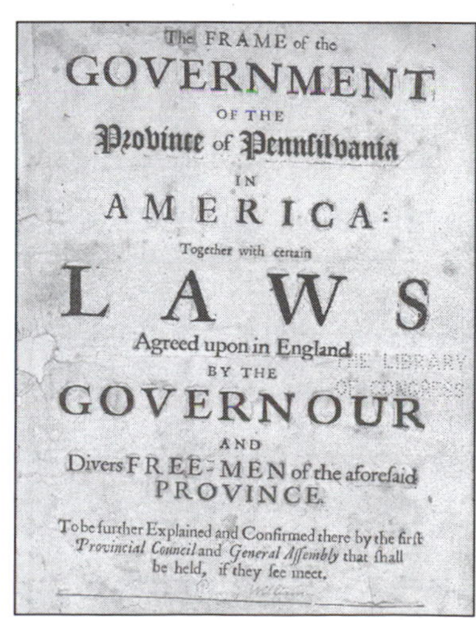

The FRAME of the
GOVERNMENT
OF THE
Province of Pennsilvania
IN
AMERICA:
Together with certain
LAWS
Agreed upon in England
BY THE
GOVERNOUR
AND
Divers FREE-MEN of the aforesaid
PROVINCE.
To be further Explained and Confirmed there by the first *Provincial Council* and *General Assembly* that shall be held, if they see meet.

William Penn, the Quaker founder of the colony of Pennsylvania, published this work on the nature of government in his colony. Library of Congress.

world as repayment of a family debt, and Penn subsequently founded the **Pennsylvania Colony**, which was open to all religions. His ideas of government are outlined in his 1682 work, *Frame of Government.* In 1701 the colony elected its first assembly as the colonists wanted greater management of the colony. Besides extending religious toleration to Europeans, Penn was also remarkable for his ethical treatment of Native Americans. **See also** Colonial America; Puritans; Quakers.

BIBLIOGRAPHY

Dunn, Mary M. *William Penn: Politics and Conscience.* Princeton, NJ: Princeton University Press, 1967.

Hull, William T. *William Penn: A Topical Biography.* London: Oxford University Press, 1937.

Pennsylvania Colony

In 1681, **William Penn**, a Quaker, sought a charter from King Charles II to form a colony out of the land that lay between the New Jersey Colony and that of **Maryland**. Calling the colony Penn's Woods, or Pennsylvania, Penn established a written plan of government that articulated the relationship between him as proprietor and the colonists. Penn's *Frame of Government* (1682) guaranteed freedom of worship as an integral part of the colony.

Penn's charter was revoked in 1692 by King William III, but it was restored two years later. In 1701, the colony changed its structure of government from the original Frame of Government to a Charter of Privileges. As part of the change, the colonists elected their first legislative assembly. The Charter of Privileges remained Pennsylvania's governing document until 1776 when the colony adopted its first constitution.

In addition to his success in securing religious liberty, Penn was also noteworthy for his ethical dealings with the native populations. However, westward expansion and the growing conflicts between the French and British that led to the French and Indian War (1754–1763) ended that legacy.

By the time of the **American Revolution**, Pennsylvania's capital, Philadelphia, was recognized as the most important city in the colonies. Additionally, drawn by the sincere guarantee of religious freedom, the colony grew rapidly to encompass new immigrants, including a large number of German-speaking **Mennonites**, **Amish,** and Moravians who formed the group known as the Pennsylvania Dutch ("Dutch" being a derivative of Deutsch, or German). In 1767, an ongoing boarder dispute between Maryland and Pennsylvania was settled by English surveyors, Charles Mason and Jeremiah Dixon. **See also** Colonial America; Quakers.

BIBLIOGRAPHY

Bronner, Edwin B. *William Penn's Holy Experiment.* Westport, CT: Greenwood, 1963.

Kelley, Joseph J. *Pennsylvania: The Colonial Years, 1681–1776.* Garden City, NY: Doubleday, 1980.

Pentecostals

During the mid-nineteenth century, some Christians protested the church's conformity to middle-class ideas of respectability and self-improvement, and the claims of many that church membership was their birthright. These Christians, called Pentecostals because of their identification with the spirit-filled events of the Christian Pentecost celebration, believed that a dramatic conversion experience was essential to salvation.

While the first evidence of Pentecostalism emerged from the Holiness movement in **Methodism**, the largest Pentecostal movement—the **Assemblies of God**—traces its roots to 1901. In that year, several students at Bethel Bible College had spontaneous ecstatic experiences of speaking in tongues or unfamiliar prayer languages. Similar experiences occurred among African-American worshippers at the Azusa Street Mission in Los Angeles in 1906. These events spawned a movement that now claims eight major denominations and over 1.5 million members.

Pentecostals can be identified by their belief in speaking in tongues, their emphasis on divine healing through a ritual of laying on hands, and their strict behavioral code of conduct. They hold that the days of judgment are near, and that their close relationship with God's Spirit results in special revelations from the Spirit. With the 1942 founding of the National Association of Evangelicals, Pentecostals gained an effective public voice in the church-state debate, particularly as that debate concerned military chaplaincies in the 1940s and prayer in school in the late twentieth century.

The largest group of black Pentecostals is the Church of God in Christ, founded in the 1890s. The strict moral demands of this and like movements contributed to the upward social mobility of its members, because their ideals corresponded with white middle-class virtues. Black Pentecostalism was closely tied to black politics in the beginning, but the two moved apart when the 1960s black power movement took a more militant approach.

Pentecostalism is also strong among Spanish-speaking Americans, who were introduced to it through Protestant **missionaries** in Latin America. (KMY) **See also** School Prayer.

BIBLIOGRAPHY

Ox, Harvey. *Fire from Heaven: The Rise of Pentecostal Spirituality and the Reshaping of Religion in the Twenty-First Century.* Reading, MA: Addison-Wesley Publishing, 1995.

Hummel, Charles E. *Fire in the Fireplace: Charismatic Renewal in the Nineties.* Downers Grove, IL: InterVarsity Press, 1993.

Suurmond, Jean-Jacques. *Word & Spirit at Play: Towards a Charismatic Theology.* Grand Rapids, MI: William B. Eerdmans Publishing Company, 1995.

People for the American Way

In 1980, a group of political, religious and media figures, led by television producer and writer **Norman Lear**, formed People for the American Way in opposition to the political efforts of the **Moral Majority** and other groups on the **Reli-**

gious Right. The organization has not been an antagonist of religious conservatives at every turn, however; it joined an unusual coalition of evangelical Christians and **civil rights** organizations in supporting the **Religious Freedom Restoration Act** of 1993. Claiming a membership of over 300,000, People for the American Way has also supported a variety of other causes, including public education and resistance to **censorship**. The group employs tactics ranging from litigation to citizen education and maintains its own political action committee. The group's high-water mark was its opposition to Judge Robert Bork's nomination to the U.S. Supreme Court in 1987. It expended nearly 10 percent of its annual budget in its anti-Bork campaign, although it likely made up for the expenditures through donations which arrived after the successful effort. Recently, however, leadership changes and internal problems have weakened its influence. (KRD) **See also** Conservatism; Education; Evangelicals; Liberalism.

Bibliography

Pertschuk, Michael and Wendy Schaetzel. *The People Rising: The Campaign Against the Bork Nomination.* New York: Thunder's Mouth Press, 1989.

Victor, Kirk. "Feeling Its Way." *National Journal.* 28, no. 49 (December 1996): 2641–45.

Percival Affair (1826)

In the early decades of the nineteenth century, missionary efforts among native Hawaiians were so successful that tribal chiefs began to enact laws based on the Ten Commandments. A law banning prostitution was especially disliked by foreigners.

In 1826 a U.S. naval schooner named the *Dolphin* arrived in the islands, skippered by Lieutenant John "Mad Jack" Percival. Hearing of the ban on prostitution, Percival protested to Hawaiian leaders. The next Sunday, a mob of sailors from his boat and other vessels broke into church worship services, smashing windows and attacking the houses of **missionaries**. The missionaries wrote to their mission board in Massachusetts, which in turn demanded a government investigation. A court of inquiry held in Boston in 1828 cleared Percival, but the next vessel reaching the island carried a letter of apology from President **John Quincy Adams**. (MWP)

Bibliography

West, John G. *The Politics of Revelation and Reason.* Lawrence: University of Kansas, 1996.

Permoli v. Municipality No. 1 of the City of New Orleans (1845)

In *Permoli v. Municipality No. 1 of the City of New Orleans,* 44 U.S. (3 Howard) 589 (1845), the U.S. Supreme Court held that the **First Amendment** to the U.S. Constitution did not apply to the states. In 1827 the City of New Orleans adopted an ordinance that, purportedly for public health reasons, made it unlawful "to convey and expose into the parochial church of St. Louis any dead person." Charged with conducting a funeral service in a Roman Catholic church in violation of the ordinance, the Reverend Bernard Permoli, a Roman Catholic priest, responded that the ordinance was null and void since it was contrary to the U.S. Constitution and laws, "which prevent the enactment of any law prohibiting the free exercise of any religion." In an opinion delivered by Justice John Catron, the Supreme Court rejected Permoli's claim, ruling unanimously that "[t]he Constitution makes no provision for protecting the citizens of the respective States in their religious liberties; this is left to the state constitution and laws: nor is there any inhibition imposed by the Constitution of the United States in this respect on the states. . . . [T]he question presented by the record is exclusively of State cognizance." (DLD) **See also** Fourteenth Amendment; Free Exercise Clause; Roman Catholicism.

Bibliography

Drakeman, Donald. *Church-State Constitutional Issues.* New York: Greenwood Press, 1991.

Miller, William Lee. *The First Liberty: Religion and the American Republic.* New York: Knopf, 1986.

Persecution of Christians Overseas

This type of persecution, while more common than generally recognized, has achieved higher visibility in the closing years of the twentieth century and has the potential to become a major foreign policy issue in the United States. Persecution can be understood as occurring at at least three ascending levels of severity. It can occur simply as discrimination of various kinds, escalate into the loss of civic freedoms and the denial of certain human rights, and ultimately result in violent actions and death. The Judeo-Christian tradition is replete with examples of adherents being persecuted for their religion; from the biblical accounts of the Hebrews enslaved in Egypt, through the trials of the prophets, to Stephen, the first Christian martyr (a person who is put to death specifically for witnessing to the faith). Within the Roman Empire, Christians and Jews were persecuted by the authorities up to the Edict of Toleration in A.D. 312, which finally ended public religious persecution within the Roman Empire.

In the twentieth century, Western human rights activists have largely focused on issues of political rights. While not ignoring the phenomenon of religious persecution, human rights groups have had difficulty in persuading Western nations to act on religious persecution since it occurs primarily in non-Western countries which contain about two-thirds of world Christianity. This is despite the fact that such persecution contravenes stipulations of the 1948 United Nations Convention on the Prevention and Punishment of the Crime of Genocide, the 12th Article of the 1969 American Convention on Human Rights, and the 1981 United Nations Declaration on the Elimination of All Forms of Intolerance and of Discrimination Based on Religion or Belief. While the case of the persecution of Soviet Jews presented a clear-cut and well-publicized example of religious persecution from the 1960s to the 1980s, little attention was devoted to the persecution of Christians until the 1990s. It should be noted that the persecution of Christians, like much religious persecution, is a controversial subject because religion is often not the only criterion or cause of persecution. The religious identity is often intertwined with nationalist, ethnic, or economic factors which are perceived as a whole by the persecutors. The contemporary persecution of overseas Christians occurs in one of four contexts; under **Islam**, under communism, by differing ethnic or national groups, or by other Christians.

Historically, Islam has been known to be generally more tolerant than Christianity. However, this changed in the twentieth century. The first modern genocide was that of the Armenian Christian minority by the Turks within the Ottoman Empire (an area now encompassed by Turkey) in a series of massacres from 1894 onwards and reaching a climax during **World War I**. Today, in an area stretching from West Africa to Indonesia, Muslim states such as Saudi Arabia, Sudan, and Comoros employ direct state power against their Christian populations. In Sudan, for instance, this practice resulted in over a million deaths and enslavements of women and children and forced conversion to Islam. Iran and Pakistan encourage mob violence against Christians, while in Egypt, Nigeria, and Ghana mob violence, though not state-sanctioned, nonetheless exists. East Timor, invaded by Muslim-dominated Indonesia in December 1975 and illegally annexed in 1976, has witnessed government atrocities on an unprecedented scale, with over 200,000 murders committed by the Indonesian military. While out of the public eye for the last two decades, East Timor came to prominence in 1996 when its Roman Catholic bishop, Carlos Filipe Ximenes Belo, and the exiled leader of East Timorese resistance, Jose Ramos Horta, were awarded the Nobel Peace Prize.

The Communist revolution in Russia led to the active persecution of all religions (Christianity, **Judaism,** Islam, and **Buddhism**), a fate suffered by post-**World War II** Eastern Europe, though levels of persecution differed by country. Communist persecution of religion, especially Christianity, followed political triumphs in China (1948), Cuba (1959), Vietnam (1974), and North Korea (1953) and remains state policy in these nations. This situation is fast becoming a major foreign policy issue as the United States seeks to expand trade with China.

Persecution of Christians as minority groups of differing ethnic or linguistic origins is also common. Although sometimes such persecution is state policy, more often it is the result of mob violence, as is the case in Uzbekistan, India, Sri Lanka, Burma, and various African nations.

Finally, we have instances of Christians being persecuted by other Christians. The Ethiopian Orthodox Church has persecuted non-orthodox groups, primarily Protestants and Muslims, while in Russia a bill "On Freedom of Conscience and Religious Associations," strongly supported by both houses of the Russian parliament and the Russian Orthodox Church, was vetoed by President Yeltsin on July 22, 1997. Yeltsin cited international pressure and the potential damage to Russia's image if it were passed. (It subsequently passed on September 20, 1997, by a 358 to 6 vote which overrode Yeltsin's veto.) The bill protects the Russian Orthodox Church and gives recognition only to religious minorities recognized earlier than 15 years ago. Thus, the Russian Orthodox Church is recognized as are Islam, Buddhism, and Judaism. Although aimed at limiting the activity of popular religious cults such as Aum Shinri Kyo and the influx of Western Protestant missions and cultists, the bill also limits Roman Catholics, Russian **Baptists**, and dissident Orthodox splinter groups. Such groups are denied recognition, and thus forbidden to worship publicly, operate religious schools, distribute literature, or proselytize. In Latin America, discrimination and persecution of Protestants by Roman Catholics has been widespread.

Beginning in the 1990s, conservative Christian groups such as the National Association of **Evangelicals**, the **Southern Baptist Convention**, the **Christian Coalition**, and the Family Research Council have highlighted the issue of religious persecution in foreign countries and built up a constituency to pressure the Clinton administration. In July of 1997, the State Department released a report which noted problems of religious persecution in 78 countries, largely against Christians, but also against other religions, such as Bahai in Iran and Buddhism in China. The report also accused China of limiting religious rights and in many cases, of actively persecuting members of Roman Catholic and Protestant churches. Such widespread persecution of Christians was brought sharply to the attention of the American public when this State Department report was followed by the proposed "Freedom from Religious Persecution Act." Supported by **Fundamentalist** and Evangelical Christian denominations, the **Christian Coalition**, the National Jewish Coalition, the National Association of Evangelicals, Campus Crusade, the Institute on Religion and Democracy, Concerned Women for America, and over 30 other religious organizations, this act was endorsed in September 1997 by Republican leaders in the House (Newt Gingrich) and in the Senate (Trent Lott). The act, sponsored by Senator Arlen Specter and Representative Frank Wolf, would set up an Office of Religious Persecution Monitoring in the White House, independent of the State Department. Any infringement of religious rights would lead to automatic economic sanctions and anyone claiming religious persecution would have priority in the immigration process. Other significant promoters of this act are Nina Shea, Director of the Center for Religious Freedom at Freedom House, and J. A. Rosenthal, columnist for the *New York Times*. Shea has actively mobilized human rights groups on the issue of religious persecution and the 1997 bill. She authored *In the Lion's Den*, which recounts the current persecution of Christians in 11 countries. Rosenthal has called sharply for action in his *New York Times*' columns. The act would focus American foreign policy on religious persecution primarily in countries such as China, Sudan, Iran, Egypt, Vietnam, and Indonesia, and would seek to ensure that accepted human rights law includes a ban on religious persecution.

Mainline religious groups such as the National Council of Churches and national human rights organizations such as Amnesty International have responded uncertainly to this new movement and its advocacy of the Specter-Wolf Bill. On the one hand, they value support for human rights in the foreign policy arena, but on the other, they are concerned that the focus might be primarily on persecution of Christians, to the exclusion of other religious groups. (It should be noted that the bill is supported, as is the issue, by prominent members of other faiths, such as Judaism, represented by Rabbi Irving Greenberg, President of the Jewish Life Network and the aforementioned columnist J. A. Rosenthal.) Further, such groups fear that focusing on religious persecution could deflect attention away from significant political issues such as democracy in China, the rights of imprisoned dissidents such as Wei Jinsheng, and the broader human rights issues.

The publicity and interest generated by this largely conservative Christian movement is drawing some conservatives and liberals into a common political stance. The issue has united political conservatives, Evangelicals, labor activists, and veterans of the Soviet Jewry movement. It holds the potential to revive the human rights movement, seeking direction both in the United States and internationally, after the collapse of European communism and South African apartheid in the early 1990s. However, this movement and the proposed bill illuminates the growing political power of conservative religious groups and could prove divisive for the **Republican Party**, since the bill, if successful in 1998, could create a wedge between those groups, who support it, and the Republican business leaders, who oppose it. (ISM) **See also** Anti-Catholicism; Anti-Semitism; Baptists; Cults; Foreign Policy and Religion in Politics; Missionaries; Roman Catholicism; Socialism and Communism.

BIBLIOGRAPHY

Deng, Francis M. "The Sudan: Stop the Carnage." *Brookings Review.* 12 no. 1 (Winter 1994): 6–12.

Goldberg, Jeffrey. "Washington Discovers Christian Persecution." *The New York Times Magazine.* (December 21, 1997).

Gordon, Michael R. "Russians Pass Bill Sharply Favoring Orthodox Church." *The New York Times.*(September 20, 1997): Sec. 1, 1.6.

Holmes, Stephen A. "GOP Leaders Back Bill on Religious Persecution." *The New York Times.* (September 11, 1997): A3.

Linden, Ian. *East Timor: The Continuing Betrayal.* London: Catholic Institute for International Relations, 1996.

Ramet, S., ed. *Catholicism and Politics in Communist Societies.* Durham, NC: Duke University Press, 1990.

Toynbee, Arnold. *Armenian Atrocities: The Murder of a Nation.* London: Hodder and Stoughton, 1915.

United States Congress. House. Committee on International Relations. *The History of the Armenian Genocide: Hearing before the Committee on International Relations, House of Representatives. 104 Congress, 2nd Session, May 15, 1996.* Washington, DC: GPO, 1996.

Persian Gulf Conflict

The Persian Gulf Conflict, 1990–1991, which reversed the Iraqi occupation of Kuwait, had far-reaching political and religious implications for the Middle East and international politics. The war began when Iraq invaded Kuwait on August 2, 1990, largely due to oil, boundary, and financial disputes. In the following months, the United States—under the auspices of the United Nations—built a massive coalition, 540,000 of whom were U.S. troops; and UN resolutions called for restoring the status quo ante, including UNR 678 which specified "all necessary means" to expel Iraq. The U.S. Congress did not formally declare **war** but did pass a joint resolution authorizing the use of force. Allied military action began on January 16, and the cease-fire was called March 3, 1991.

The war rekindled some anti-war protests in the United States; but because of the relatively small number of casualties (146 U.S. personnel killed in action) and the brevity of combat, the protests did not approach the level of those that took place during the **Vietnam War**. There was, additionally, some debate on whether "just war" criteria had been met, with both churches and the scholarly community taking part. But the debate tended to stay there; 86 percent of the public, by early February, approved of President Bush's action as necessary. The Middle East was not as enthusiastic, and massive demonstrations occurred in several Arab capitals. This reflected a pent-up anger which Iraqi leader Saddam Hussein shaped to his own ends, casting U.S. forces as new crusaders who had come to reassert dominance. Saddam drew attention to the presence of over a half-million non-Muslims in the Arabian peninsula, claiming this defiled the holy cities of Mecca and Medina. What followed was a "war of fatwas" (a fatwa is a religious opinion or decision given by recognized authority) that debated the proper response to Saddam and the issue of western involvement, with numerous Islamic jurists taking part, and Muslim masses responding. In fact, the conflict exacerbated existing political and religious enmities in the region, and made the U.S. presence much more problematic. Subsequent difficulties with the Iraqi sanctions and the inspection regime, as well as terrorist attacks on U.S. forces, have borne this out. (JML) **See also** Imperialism; Islam; Just War Theory; Military Service.

BIBLIOGRAPHY

Conduct of the Persian Gulf War: Final Report to the Congress. Washington, DC: Department of Defense [available through the U.S. Government Printing Office], 1992.

Haddad, Yvonne. "Operation Desert Storm and the War of Fatwas. Muhammad Khalid Masud, ed. *Islamic Legal Interpretation: Muftis and Their Fatwas.* Cambridge: Harvard University Press, 1996.

Piscatori, James, ed. *Islamic Fundamentalisms and the Gulf Crisis.* Chicago: American Academy of Arts and Sciences, 1991.

Summers, Harry G. *Persian Gulf War Almanac.* New York: Facts on File, 1995.

Leo Pfeffer (1910–)

Leo Pfeffer has been among the most prolific constitutional scholars of the late twentieth century. Pfeffer has analyzed the **Establishment Clause** of the **First Amendment** from a "separationist" standpoint, arguing that this constitutional provision requires strict separation between church and state. From this perspective, government may offer no assistance to specific religions or religion in general. (TGJ) **See also** Flag Salute Cases; In God We Trust; One Nation under God; Public Aid to Religious Organizations; Publicly Funded Religious Displays; School Prayer; Wall of Separation.

Bibliography

Pfeffer, Leo. *Church, State, and Freedom.* Boston: Beacon Press, 1967.

Pfeffer, Leo. *Religious Freedom.* Lincolnwood, IL: National Textbook Company, 1983.

Pfeffer, Leo. *Religion, State, and the Burger Court.* Buffalo, NY: Prometheus Books, 1984.

Pierce v. Society of Sisters (1925)

Oregon passed a law compelling general attendance at public schools by children between 8 and 16, the effect of which was to make it illegal for parents to send their children to religious schools. The Society of Sisters, a Catholic religious order that ran a parochial school in Oregon, challenged the law, claiming that it violated the rights of parents to choose schools where their children will receive appropriate mental and religious training, and the rights of schools and teachers to engage in a useful business or profession. In *Pierce v. Society of Sisters*, 268 U.S. 510 (1925), the U.S. Supreme Court struck down the Oregon law, though the ruling dealt mostly with Oregon's interference with the schools' right to do business and little with the issues of religious freedom and parental control. The Court stated that the nonpublic schools of Oregon were "threatened with destruction through the unwarranted compulsion which [the state was] exercising over present and prospective patrons of their schools. And this Court has gone very far to protect against loss threatened by such action." (JM) **See also** Education; Home Schooling; Roman Catholicism.

Bibliography

Holsinger, M. Paul. "The Oregon School Controversy, 1922–1925." *Pacific Historical Review. XXXVII* (August 1968): 327–41.

Tyack, D. B. "Perils of Pluralism: The Background of the Pierce Case." *American Historical Review* 75 (October 1968): 74–98.

Pietism

Pietism originated as a reform movement in the German **Lutheran Church** during the seventeenth century, but quickly spread to other parts of Europe. Possessing characteristics of both the original and radical phases of the **Reformation**, pietism stressed spiritual growth and devotion, Bible study, and personal religious experience. As a movement, pietism was a reaction against social decadence and a merely formal and intellectual practice of religion. Through the influence of Lutheran, Reformed, and Methodist churches, pietism became a vital influence upon American life, encouraging a deeper spirituality, the pursuit of societal holiness, and the expansion of missionary activities. (HLC) **See also** Americanism; Methodism; Missionaries; Social Justice.

Bibliography

Erb, Peter, ed. *The Pietists: Selected Writings*. New York: Paulist Press, 1983.

Pilgrims

The Pilgrims were the early English settlers who founded the first permanent colony in New England at Plymouth in 1620. The Pilgrims are often confused with the **Puritans** who founded the **Massachusetts Bay Colony** in 1628. The term Pilgrim was used to describe the group by one of the colony's founders, **William Bradford,** who served as governor almost continuously from 1621 to 1656. Bradford wrote a book *The History of Plymouth Plantation, 1620–1640* that details the early struggles and achievements of the colony.

Many of the first settlers were separatists who sought a radical break from the established Church of England. These Pilgrims had initially left England for the Netherlands because of religious persecution. After more than 10 years of living in the Netherlands, the group decided to emigrate to the New World, and they left Plymouth, England, on September 16, 1620, with 102 men, women, and children aboard the *Mayflower*. On November 21, they arrived in the harbor of what is now known as Provincetown, Massachusetts, and on December 21, they landed at Plymouth.

In addition to being the first colony specifically formed for religious reasons, the Pilgrims also gave America its first written constitution, the **Mayflower Compact**. Among the provisions of the Compact were two important principles, the right to self-government and the guarantee of freedom of religion. **See also** Americanism; "City on a Hill"; Colonial America; Salem Witchcraft Trials.

Bibliography

Kendall, Willmoore and George W. Carey. *Basic Symbols.* Baton Rouge: Louisiana State University Press, 1971

Stratton, Eugene Aubrey. *Plymouth Colony: Its History & People, 1620–1691.* Salt Lake City, UT : Ancestry Publishers, 1986.

Planned Parenthood of Southeastern Pennsylvania v. Casey (1992)

The Commonwealth of Pennsylvania passed a number of restrictions on a woman's right to have an abortion. Among the restrictions were required **education** about abortion, knowledge of health risks, alternatives to abortion, parental or court consent, spousal consent, and a 24-hour waiting period. All of these restrictions, except the spousal consent requirement, were upheld by the U.S. Supreme Court in *Planned Parenthood of Southeastern Pennsylvania v. Casey*, 505 U.S. 833 (1992).

The Court noted that the principles it laid out in ***Roe v. Wade*** (1973) were still good law. The state has to balance the interests of the mother against society's interest in the welfare of the fetus. However, as long as the fetus in not capable of independent existence outside the mother, the mother's choice to terminate the pregnancy remains superior to the interests of the state. While the state can place restrictions on a woman's right to terminate her pregnancy, such as required education and time to consider carefully her decision, it cannot place unreasonable obstacles in the way of her ultimate choice. The spousal consent provision was struck down because it would give a husband an effective veto over his wife's choice. (FHJ) **See also** Abortion and Birth Control Regulation; Anthony Kennedy; Liberalism; Religious Right.

BIBLIOGRAPHY

Bigel, Alan I. "Planned Parenthood of Southeastern Pennsylvania v. Casey: Constitutional Principles and Political Turbulence." *University of Dayton Law Review.* 18 no. 3 (Spring 1993): 733–62.

Pledge of Allegiance

The Pledge of Allegiance was originally written in 1892 by a socialist named Francis Bellamy, who penned the pledge for *Youth's Companion*, a national family magazine for youths. Bellamy was commissioned to write the pledge as part of the magazine's campaign to sell American flags to public schools, which at that time did not typically fly them in classrooms. Publicists for the flag campaign succeeded in getting the National Education Association to support *Youth's Companion* as a sponsor of the national public schools' observance of Columbus Day, which was to include the use of the American flag. Bellamy helped arrange for Congress and President Benjamin Harrison to issue a national proclamation making the public school ceremony the center of the national Columbus Day celebrations for 1892. Bellamy wrote the program for the celebration, which included the flag salute that would, with minor modification, become the Pledge of Allegiance. The phrase "under God" was added by Congress and President **Dwight Eisenhower** in 1954, at the urging of the Knights of Columbus, a lay Catholic fraternal society. (JM) **See also** Flag Salute Cases; Jehovah's Witnesses; One Nation under God; Religious Tests and Oaths; Roman Catholicism.

BIBLIOGRAPHY

Miller, Margarette S. *Twenty-three Words.* Portsmouth, VA: Printcraft Press, 1976.

Political Participation and Voting Behavior

An intellectual tradition that can be traced back at least to Karl Marx has suggested that religion (perhaps especially Christianity) is unfavorable to political mobilization and participation. The otherworldliness of orthodox Christianity is thought to distract attention from the immediacy of political action, and the promise of an afterlife has been regarded as a source of acceptance for earthly tribulations. However, recent American history has shown that religious beliefs and memberships can often have the effect of mobilizing and empowering ordinary citizens, and altering the direction of vote choices.

Recent research has suggested that involvement in religious organizations can have a positive effect on political participation. This sort of "spillover effect" can be attributed to two distinct processes. First, in certain circumstances, churches can be places in which direct political socialization occurs. In some instances, pastors will preach on explicitly political themes, and such "pulpit politics" are occasionally quite effective. Churches have also been arenas in which political participation has been directly mobilized by serving as meeting sites for political organizations or voter registration. Since there is often considerable overlap between the subject areas of religion and politics, pastors and churches are often sources of political learning. Second, political mobilization occurs indirectly in churches as well. Participation in religious organizations allows church members to acquire political skills, such as public speaking, debating, coalition-building, etc., which can be applied to more manifestly political organizations. Such latent political learning appears to occur most readily in certain evangelical churches, with low levels of organizational hierarchy and highly egalitarian, participatory organizational structures. Indeed, it has been suggested that such pietistic churches are among the few organizations that impart political skills to American citizens who are otherwise disadvantaged in this area. While most agents of political socialization in the United States appear to exacerbate inequality between politically advantaged and disadvantaged citizens, churches appear to enhance prospects for equality.

The mobilizing effect of church participation can be seen most clearly in the African-American community. For much of American history, the black church was one of the very few autonomous organizations available to the descendants of African slaves. While black churches were often criticized for encouraging compliance with the practices of racial segregation, such congregations provided organizational resources for the **civil rights** movement of the 1950s and 1960s. Indeed, it is worth noting how many civil rights leaders, such as **Martin Luther King, Jr.**, **Andrew Young**, **Ralph David Abernathy**, and **Jesse Jackson**, were Protestant (usually Baptist) ministers. More recently, while church participation has not affected the direction of African-American political participation (most U.S. blacks remain steadfast Democrats), it has affected (positively) the extent of such activity.

During the 1980s, church participation appears to have had a similar mobilizing effect among white evangelical Christians. This group, which had traditionally been characterized by relatively low levels of electoral participation, increased its turnout in response to the 1976 presidential candidacy of **Jimmy Carter**. Carter's explicit identification as an evangelical Christian, as well as his highly public religious activity, appears to have attracted a number of white evangelicals to the polls for the first time. However, many socially conservative evangelicals became disillusioned with the Carter presidency and supported the candidacy of **Ronald Reagan** in 1980. Several evangelically oriented political organizations (most visibly, **Jerry Falwell**'s **Moral Majority**) offered the possibility of political mobilization (including voter registration in churches) as well as tacit support for the Republican ticket. Since 1980, the Moral Majority and, more recently, the **Christian Coalition** have attempted to encourage the electoral participation of doctrinally and politically conservative Christians.

Religion has not only affected the extent of political participation, but has also affected the direction of vote choices and partisan self-images. At various points in American history, religious affiliation has been a durable source of party identification. In the twentieth century, religion has often been an important short-term force in American elections. For example, the Presidential candidacies of Democrats **Alfred E. Smith** (1928) and **John F. Kennedy** (1960) were defined to a large extent by the religious affiliation (**Roman Catholicism**) of each candidate. Smith's Catholicism was in large measure responsible for the fact that the **Republican Party** candidate gained southern electoral votes in 1928 for the first time since the **Civil War**, and Kennedy's affiliation may have cost him several percentage points in the popular vote in his narrow victory in 1960.

More recently, religious values have appeared to serve as the basis of an emerging partisan difference between social traditionalists and progressives. The presidential election of 1972 is often considered something of a watershed in this regard. The social liberalism of Democratic candidate George McGovern (who was characterized by opponents as the candidate of "amnesty, acid, and abortion") appears to have accelerated the movement of some traditional Democratic constituencies (notably, Southern whites) to the GOP. While social issues alone cannot account for this partisan realignment among some white evangelicals (the politics of race have had a large impact on the party identification of some whites), the association of the **Democratic Party** with the "permissiveness" of the 1960s on issues like crime, sexual morality, and drug use provided an important swing constituency for Republican candidates in the 1970s and 1980s. Although the movement of white evangelicals to the GOP appeared to have been interrupted by the Carter candidacy of 1976, the realignment of socially conservative white evangelicals is among the most important trends of recent American political history. White evangelicals have been an extremely reliable source of support for Republican presidential candidates in the 1980s and 1990s, and have extended their Republicanism to lower offices as well. It is also noteworthy that the Republican trend among evangelicals has been most pronounced among the most religiously orthodox and observant evangelical Christians.

The partisan movement among white evangelicals is all the more impressive when contrasted to the partisan stability of other major religious groups. Mainline Protestants have retained their status as the most Republican religious group in the United States, despite the increasing policy liberalism of some mainline clergy (mainline clergy involves Congregationalists, Presbyterians, and Episcopalians). In general, attempts at political socialization by Mainline pastors have not been as successful as those of their evangelical counterparts. Conversely, American Jews (a relatively small religious group) have retained their liberal issue attitudes and Democratic identification. Perhaps the most interesting religious facet of the American electorate has been the partisan inertia of white Catholics. Traditionally, American Catholics have identified with the Democratic Party. Many Catholics, as the descendants of relatively recent immigrants, have tended to reside in ethnically and religiously homogeneous urban neighborhoods. Many urban Catholics had been mobilized by Democratic political organizations in large Northern cities, and some immigrants had benefited from social services offered by such organizations.

While many American Catholics hold conservative attitudes on social issues (perhaps especially on issues of sexual morality, such as abortion and homosexuality), there has been no large Catholic movement toward the Republican Party corresponding to the realignment of evangelical Protestants. Indeed, despite a great deal of assimilation, intermarriage and social mobility, Roman Catholics remain among the most Democratic of religious groups in the United States. Indeed, whatever movement has taken place toward the Republican Party has occurred among younger, less religious Catholics, who seem attracted to Republican liberatarianism on economic issues, rather than to the GOP's conservatism on social issues. Despite long-term and apparently stable attachments to the Democratic Party, Catholics have constituted an important swing vote in recent presidential elections. (TGJ) **See also** Abortion and Birth Control Regulation; African-American Churches; Baptists; Black Theology; Clergy in Public Office; Congregationalism; Episcopal Church; Equal Rights Amendment; Evangelicals; Homosexual Rights; Jehovah's Witnesses; Judaism; Liberalism; Liberation Theology; Mennonites; People for the American Way; Pietism; Presbyterian Church; Social Justice; Socialism and Communism; Women in Religion and Politics.

Bibliography

Jelen, Ted G. *The Political World of the Clergy.* Westport, CT: Praeger, 1993.

Jelen, Ted G. "Culture Wars and the Party System: Religion and Realignment, 1972–1993." Rhys H. Williams, ed. *Culture Wars in American Politics: Critical Reviews of a Popular Myth.* New York: Aldine de Gruyter, 1997.

Kleppner, Paul. *The Cross of Culture.* New York: Free Press, 1970.

Leege, David C. "The Catholic Vote: Can It Be Found in Church?" *Commonweal.* 123 (September 27): 11–18.

Leege, David C. and Lyman A. Kellstedt. *Rediscovering the Religious Factor in American Politics.* Armonk, NY: M. E. Sharpe, 1993.

Verba, Sidney, Kay Lehman Scholzman and Henry E. Brady. *Voice and Equality: Civic Voluntarism in American Politics.* Cambridge: Harvard University Press, 1995.

Wald, Kenneth D. *Religion and Politics in the United States. 3rd ed.* Washington, DC: CQ Press, 1997.

Wilcox, Clyde. *God's Warriors; The Christian Right in Twentieth Century America.* Baltimore: Johns Hopkins University Press, 1992.

Polygamy

Polygamy is the inclusive term for both polygyny (the taking of more than one wife) and polyandry (the taking of more than one husband). While Americans had encountered polyandry among Hawaiians, and polygyny among Africans and Asians, polygamy only became a political issue with the rise of Mormonism (or the **Church of Jesus Christ of Latter-day Saints**) in the 1830s. Its founder **Joseph Smith** instituted the secret practice of polygamy while in Nauvoo, Illinois (1839–1844). **Brigham Young**, his successor, established the State of Deseret and applied unsuccessfully in 1849 for admission to the Union. The territory of Utah was then established as part of the Compromise of 1850. In 1852, Smith's earlier sanction of polygamy was revealed, the practice of which led to confrontation with the federal administration of President James Buchanan and the brief "Mormon War" of the late 1850s. Polygamy remained the primary reason for the failure of the territory of Utah to achieve statehood. Congress passed laws in 1862 (Anti-Bigamy Law), 1883 (Edmunds' Law), and 1887 (Edmunds-Tucker Bill) prohibiting the practice. Further, in 1879 President **Rutherford B. Hayes** warned that citizenship rights would be withdrawn from practicing polygamists. His successors, President James A. Garfield and Chester A. Arthur upheld these positions. Finally, on the 25th of September, 1890, the Mormon Church, by issuing the Woodruff Manifesto, rejected the practice, though small Mormon splinter groups still continue it to this day. The Enabling Bill became law in 1894 and in 1896 President **Grover Cleveland** signed the proclamation of Utah's statehood. This had depended upon the State's Constitutional Convention, dominated by Republicans, adopting the Constitution of the United States, accepting a Republican constitution and women's suffrage, and guaranteeing religious freedom (provided that polygamy was forbidden). The federal government's opposition to polygamy was vigorously supported by the Protestant **Episcopal Church**, the Methodist Episcopal Church, the **Presbyterian** Church, and the Baptist Home Mission Board in their respective legislative bodies during 1880–1881. This period also witnessed anti-polygamy crusades by women's groups, especially the National Women's Anti-Polygamy Society. (ISM) **See also** Baptists; Civil Disobedience; Divorce.

BIBLIOGRAPHY

Driggs, Ken. "After the Manifest: Modern Polygamy and Fundamentalist Mormons." *Journal of Church and State.* 32 (Spring 1990): 367–89.

Iverson, Joan Smyth. *The Anti-Polygamy Controversy in U.S. Women's Movements, 1880–1925: A Debate on the American Home.* New York: Garland Publishing, 1997.

Lyman, Edward L. *Political Deliverance: The Mormon Quest for Utah Statehood.* Urbana: University of Illinois, 1986.

Pornography

Pornography is loosely defined as written or pictorial matter intended to arouse sexual feelings. It is often confused with obscenity, which is a term with specific legal meaning. Much material that could be considered pornographic is not legally obscene and as such falls outside current areas of legislation and is protected by the **First Amendment** right to freedom of speech. Pornography is the subject of intense debate primarily because it is not currently legislated against at a federal level and because its definition is so vague. Different experts have argued that pornography can be harmful to minors, can exploit women, or is harmful to society as a whole. With the advent of the Internet as a readily available means of distribution, many groups have attempted to enforce stricter legislation against pornography and have encountered strong resistance.

Obscenity refers to the legal concept of prohibited sexual materials. The currently binding definition of obscenity was determined by the U.S. Supreme Court in the case *Miller v. California* in 1973. It establishes that for a work to be considered obscene, and hence legally restrictable, it must: (1) appeal to a prurient interest in sex, (2) be patently offensive under contemporary community standards, and (3) lack significant scientific, literary, artistic, or political ("SLAP") value.

Cases in recent decades have indicated that only visual images—photographs and films—will be held obscene under this standard, as pure text is always found to have at least minimal literary value. If material is deemed to be obscene, its transmission, sale, or possession can be prohibited.

The modern concept of pornography was developed in the nineteenth century by European men who were mainly concerned with keeping such material away from women and the lower classes. With the spread of literacy and **education**, pornography became available to anybody who could read. Pornography in the United States occupied a legal gray area for most of its early history. An early British case, *Regina v. Hicklin*, stated that a work could be declared pornographic if even one page could be considered offensive. This was the primary criterion for determining obscenity in pornographic works until 1933 in the case *United States v. One Book Entitled Ulysses*, where it was determined that a work must be evaluated as a whole. In the 1957 case *Roth v. United States*, the Supreme Court attempted to provide standards for judging pornography when it determined that for a pornographic work to be considered obscene it must appeal to unwholesome interests and be utterly devoid of redeeming social importance. This case set the standard for evaluation of pornographic works until the Miller case became the standard in 1973.

In 1967, Denmark became the first Western country in the world to abolish all pornography laws. The next year, two films by a Swedish director *I Am Curious (Yellow)* and *I Am Curious (Blue)* were shown in the United States to audiences that were more mainstream than those that usually viewed the traditional pornographic films of the time. In 1972 the first full-length, 35 millimeter, hard-core pornographic movie—*Deep Throat*—premiered in cinemas. Unlike previous porn films, this one became popular with the general public and its star, Linda Lovelace, became something of a celebrity. Lovelace even appeared on the *Tonight Show*, thus pushing the pornography debate into the arena of popular culture.

Presidential administrations have attempted to define pornography and determine its effects on the population to determine how to effectively legislate it. In 1967, the Johnson Commission on Pornography and Obscenity was formed, with a mandate to explore the legislation affecting pornography; study the effects of pornography on the public, particularly minors; and explore the relation, if any, to criminal and other anti-social behaviors. The determination of that commission was that while some pornography reflects acts that are harmful, such as child molestation and rape, ultimately there was no link found between exposure to explicit sexual material and criminal behavior, so the commission urged the repeal of obscenity laws. In fact, the commission stated that the actual problem associated with pornography came from "the inability or reluctance of people in our society to be open and direct in dealing with sexual matters."

In 1985, at the request of President **Ronald Reagan**, Attorney General Edwin Meese appointed a panel to update the findings of the 1967 panel. President Reagan had been receiving pressure from **Jerry Falwell**'s **Moral Majority** and an association of Catholic bishops who had been imploring him to appoint a federal coordinator to monitor enforcement of obscenity laws. The commission had one year and half a million dollars to "determine the nature, extent, and impact on society of pornography in the United States." **Civil Rights** activists argued that the supposedly objective commission was comprised primarily of criminologists and people with strong religious convictions. The Meese Commission Report, released in July 1986, divided pornography into four categories: (1) sexually violent material; (2) nonviolent explicit sexual material depicting humiliation, degradation, submission, or dominance; (3) explicit sexual material not fitting into category two; and (4) nudity. The commission determined that all types of pornography were harmful and it made broad recommendations urging more vigilant enforcement of obscenity laws and more stringent regulation of certain forms of pornography that it considered harmful, but not legally obscene.

The debate over pornography often comes down to differing opinions concerning the values of individual freedom versus social control. Americans' opinions on the usefulness and legitimacy of pornography vary widely. Opponents of pornography come from varying backgrounds—from Christian family-oriented organizations to feminist activists. They claim that pornography is degrading to women, encouraging unrealistic sexual expectations and maltreatment of women. The Family Research Council, a large non-profit organization committed to protecting Judeo-Christian values in the United States, argues that "Pornography has a corrupting influence on individuals, turns natural desires into unnatural cravings, and reduces human beings to anonymous tools for the stimulation and gratification of those cravings." Anti-pornography activists have been involved in recent cases attempting to get pornographic material, such as *The Joy of Sex* removed from public libraries, and boycotting merchants who sell pornographic material.

People opposed to further legislation of pornography range from non-consumers of pornography concerned with infringement of **First Amendment** rights, to "sex positive" feminists and others who argue that pornography can satisfy a healthy sexual curiosity, provides a means of sexual education and information, and is a safe way to experience sexual alternatives. They claim that, since child pornography and violence against women are already illegal, further legislation would only serve to censor legal material to the disadvantage of people's rights to enjoy free expression and to choose what to do with their own bodies.

Despite the large-scale growth of the pornography industry, means of distribution were often more effectively regulated than the actual product itself. Boycotts of large retail stores selling pornography—by groups such as the American Family Association—have often proven effective in limiting pornographic content available in those stores. However, the Internet provides many small scale dealers of pornography with an easy and inexpensive means of dissemination, as well as a captive audience for their product. In 1995, a study which detailed the availability of pornography in images and text on the Internet was published in the *Georgetown Law Review Journal*. Entitled "Marketing Pornography on the Information Superhighway" by Marty Rimm, this study concluded that 83.5 percent of the material on the Internet could be deemed pornographic. The study, later found to be severely flawed, was used as the basis of an article in *Time* Magazine on "cyberporn" and immediately a furor began to pass legislation to address this issue.

In 1994, in response to a review copy of Rimm's study, Senator Jim Exon (D-NE) sponsored a bill known as the Communications Decency Act as part of the Telecommunications Act of 1996. The intent of this act was to make transmission of "indecent" or "patently offensive" speech via the Internet a felony. The bill, intended primarily to protect children but applying to adults as well, was signed into law in 1996 and was immediately protested against as being too vague, and criminalizing speech that is protected by the **First Amendment**. It also received criticism from conservative members of Congress, including Newt Gingrich, who objected to it as unconstitutional. The act was immediately challenged and overturned in June, 1997, in the case *ACLU v. Reno.*

The pornography debate in the United States is still heated on both sides. Though recent cases seem to indicate a legislative trend away from further pornography legislation, well-organized groups with anti-pornography agendas are still attempting to pass legislation at the state and local levels to limit people's access to pornography. (JCW) **See also** American Civil Liberties Union (ACLU); Censorship; Conservatism; Culture Wars; Feminism; Liberalism; Religious Right; Roman Catholicism; Women in Religion and Politics.

Bibliography

Califia, Pat. *Public Sex: The Culture of Radical Sex*. San Francisco: Cleis Press, 1995.

Dwyer, Susan. *The Problem of Pornography.* Belmont, CA: Wadsworth Publishing Company, 1995.

Elmer-Dewitt, Phillip. "On a Screen Near You: Cyberporn." *Time.* 146 (July 3, 1995).

Kendrick, Walter M. *The Secret Museum: Pornography in Modern Culture.* New York: Viking, 1987.

Kuh, Richard. *Foolish Figleaves? Pornography in and out of Court.* New York: Macmillan, 1967.

McElroy, Wendy. "A Feminist Defense of Pornography." *Free Inquiry Magazine.* 17 no. 4 (November 1997).

Nobile, Philip and Eric Nadler. *United States of America vs. Sex.* New York: Minotaur Press, 1988.

Rimm, Marty. "Marketing Pornography on the Information Superhighway." *Georgetown Law Review Journal.* 83 no. 5 (1995).

Adam Clayton Powell, Jr. (1908–1972)

Adam Clayton Powell, Jr. succeeded his father as the pastor of the Abyssinian Baptist Church in New York City's Harlem. A talented leader and speaker, he became the first black New York City councilman in 1941. He was elected to the U.S. House of Representatives in 1944, eventually becoming head of the powerful Education and Labor Committee. His behavior and extravagent lifestyle, however, led some to question his ethics, and he was disciplined by the House for financial corruption and successfully sued for libel. (He refused to pay the judgment, incurring contempt charges.) In 1970, his voters, who had stood by him previously, no longer supported him and his political career ended. (MWP) **See also** African-American Churches; Baptists; Clergy in Public Office; Adam Clayton Powell, Sr.; Race Relations.

Bibliography

Hamilton, Charles V. *Adam Clayton Powell Jr.: The Political Biography of an American Dilemma.* New York: Macmillan, 1991.

Powell, Adam Clayton Jr. *Adam by Adam.* New York: Dial, 1971.

Adam Clayton Powell, Sr. (1865–1953)

Adam Clayton Powell, Sr. was one of America's leading African-American clergymen. He was the pastor of the Abyssinian **Baptist** Church, which was relocated from Manhattan to Harlem. This move reflected the growing political and social importance of Harlem. During Powell's tenure, the congregation grew from 1,600 to more than 14,000 members and it provided community services, including soup kitchens, job placement, and job skills training. A popular and effective lecturer, he often spoke out on **race relations** in America. He also served as vice president of the National Association for the Advancement of Colored People (NAACP). **See also** African-American Churches; Baptists; Adam Clayton Powell, Jr.

Bibliography

Powell Sr., Adam Clayton. *Palestine and Saints in Caesar's Household.* New York: R.R. Smith, 1939.

Presbyterian Church

There are three major Presbyterian denominations in the United States. The largest is the Presbyterian Church USA (or PCUSA), formed in 1983 from a union between the Northern United Presbyterian Church in the USA and the Southern Presbyterian Church in the United States. Next in size is the Presbyterian Church in America, which was formed in 1983 by the withdrawal of those Southern Presbyterian Churches that opposed union with the Northern United Presbyterian Church. The Orthodox Presbyterian Church, which emerged from the Northern Church during the **Fundamentalist-Modernist controversy**, is the smallest.

While individual Presbyterian congregations existed before the **American Revolution**, the first synod was formed in 1716, and the General Assembly constituted in Philadelphia in 1788, the same year in which the Synod of Philadelphia approved the separation of church and state. Divided by theological issues arising out of the **First and Second Great Awakenings**, the church was further divided by the **Civil War** and again by the Fundamentalist-Modernist controversy. The latter set the agenda for much of the first half of the twentieth century, as prominent Presbyterians were embroiled in theological controversy. These included **Harry Emerson Fosdick; William Sloane Coffin**; biblical scholar Charles Augustus Briggs; **William Jennings Bryan**, participant in the famous John T. **Scopes Trial** of 1925; and the Princeton scholar **J. Gresham Machen**, who left his position in 1929 to found Westminister Theological Seminary and, in 1936, the Orthodox Presbyterian Church.

Named for its conciliar form of government by elders in a hierarchy of courts (Greek for elder is *presbuteros*), Presbyterianism has generally followed **John Calvin**'s teaching in favoring conciliar forms of government and in supporting the rights of citizens over/against unjust rulers. But it has also exhibited diverse political attitudes. Like members of other reformed churches, Presbyterians do not believe that the separation of church and state denies the church's ethical responsibility for social and political justice. Thus, they recognize the duty to both support the state and to challenge unjust laws and social structures. From the time that **John Witherspoon** signed the **Declaration of Independence** (the only clergyman to do so), Presbyterian churches have been involved in socio-political issues, from forming voluntary societies for the **abolition** of **slavery** and the maintenance of various charities, to supporting legislation promoting Sabbath-keeping and the regulation of alcohol. The 1960s and 1970s saw active involvement in the **civil rights** movement and in anti-apartheid campaigns.

True to Calvin's stress on the catholicity of the church, Presbyterian Churches (with some conservative exceptions) are members of the World Council of Churches, the National Council of Churches, and various Reformed Councils. Like other mainline denominations, the PCUSA has witnessed dramatic membership decline since the 1960s, variously attributed to historical, theological, or sociological factors. As of 1996, the PCUSA had 2,631,466 members and 11,328 congregations. Despite its relatively small numbers, the Presbyterian Church has been influential in American politics, counting a large number of presidents and members of Congress among its constituents. (ISM) **See also** Blue Laws; Social Justice; Temperance and Prohibition.

Bibliography

Longfield, Bradley J. *The Presbyterian Controversy: Fundamentalists, Modernists and Moderates.* New York: Oxford University Press, 1991.

Roof, Wade Clark and William McKinney. *American Mainline Religion.* New Brunswick, NJ: Rutgers University Press, 1987.

Stone, Ronald H., ed. *Reformed Faith and Politics.* Washington, DC: University Press of America, 1983.
Thompson, Ernest T. *Presbyterians in the South.* Richmond: John Knox, 1963–1973.
Trinterud, L. J. *The Forming of an American Tradition.* North Stratford, NH: Ayer, 1970.
Wuthnow, Robert. *Restructuring Mainline American Religion.* Princeton: Princeton University Press, 1992.

Priest-Penitent Privilege

The priest-penitent privilege derives its origins from Roman Catholic theology in which the priest is obliged to maintain secrecy about information received in sacramental confession. The practical reason for the seal of the confessional, as it is known, is the peace of mind it gives to the penitent that comments will be kept private. The theological basis rests in the fact that the priest is merely acting in place of Christ. While the doctrine developed gradually, it was formally established in the ninth century and was part of the Fourth Lateran Council in 1215. Within the Roman Catholic Church, the seal of the confessional is part of **canon law** (CIC C. 889.1f) and violation is punishable by **excommunication**.

In the United States, communication between a priest and a penitent receives special protection under the laws of all 50 states and the District of Columbia. The laws, however, vary from state to state. In most states, the privilege is given to the penitent, who can prevent a priest from revealing what he was told in confidence. In 11 states, the privilege is given to the priest, whose church may require him to keep such communications confidential. Two states, Alabama and Ohio, allow either priest or penitent to refuse to disclose and prevent the other from disclosing the communication. (MWP) **See also** Roman Catholicism.

Bibliography

Horner, Chad. "Beyond the Confines of the Confessional." *Drake Law Review.* 45 (March 15, 1997): 697–732.
Sippel, Julie Ann. "Priest-Penitent Privilege Statutes." *Catholic University Law Review.* 43 (Summer 1994): 1127–64.

Prince v. Commonwealth of Massachusetts (1944)

Sarah Prince was convicted of violating Massachusetts' child labor laws by furnishing her nine-year-old niece with magazines to sell on the street. She appealed the conviction on the grounds that the application of these laws in this case violated the free exercise of religion. In *Prince v. Commonwealth of Massachusetts*, 321 U.S. 158 (1944), the U.S. Supreme Court, while recognizing the importance of family control and religious freedom, affirmed the conviction, stating that "the family itself is not beyond regulation in the public interest, as against a claim of religious liberty." (JM) **See also** First Amendment.

Bibliography

Ivers, Gregg. *Redefining the First Freedom.* New Brunswick, NJ: Transaction, 1993.
Regan, Richard J. *Private Conscience and Public Law.* New York: Fordham University Press, 1972.

Prison Fellowship

Prison Fellowship operates as a non-profit, para-church organization with the stated mission to minister to prisoners, former prisoners, and their families. Founded in 1976 by **Charles Colson** with proceeds from his book *Born Again*, Prison Fellowship was expanded to include a ministry to victims of crime, and subsidiary organizations such as Angel Tree, an outreach to children of prisoners, and Justice Fellowship, which advocates reforms of criminal justice policies. Advocated policy reforms are based on restorative justice that includes victim-offender reconciliation programs, restitution requirements for convicted criminals, crime victims' rights, and prison industries programs. (DD) **See also** Born-Again Christians; Prisoners, Religious Rights of.

Bibliography

Loux, Gordon. *Uncommon Courage: The Story of Prison Fellowship International.* New York: Vine Books, 1988.

Prisoners, Religious Rights of

The **First Amendment** to the United States Constitution states that "Congress shall make no law respecting an establishment of religion, or prohibiting the free exercise thereof." Prison inmates do not lose this right once they become incarcerated, but considerations such as prison security, deterrence of crime, and rehabilitation occasionally necessitate limits on their freedoms, including religious freedom.

An important distinction regarding prisoners' rights to religious freedom involves the difference between the freedom to believe in a given religion, assumed to be absolute, and the freedom to exercise that same belief, which can be regulated by the state. With prisoners, there is also a variation of the "clear-and-present danger" test, which allows for restrictions on religious expression in cases where the restrictions are "clearly and immediately necessary to protect an interest far more important to democratic society than the unrestricted exercise of religion."

To assess the validity of inmates' claims of restriction of religious freedom practices by institutions, courts must first have a method of determining valid religious beliefs. Since prisoners practice a variety of traditional and alternative religions, courts must assess these on a case-by-case basis to determine their validity. There are many tests and criteria for determining this, but two are essential: (1) sincerity of belief—the prisoner must be a sincere adherent to the belief system, and (2) nature of belief—the belief system must constitute a religion.

Sincerity of belief does not include evaluating the merits of the prisoner's belief structure, but simply determining whether the beliefs are sincerely held. To do this, the courts will interview witnesses, including the prisoner, and make an assessment. If the religion is a commonly practiced one with an organized church, evaluations can be made as to the level of the inmate's knowledge and adherence to the practices of the church. If, however, the religion is of a more alternative nature, the courts must make more subjective assessments of adherence.

Nature of belief primarily involves determining and eliminating belief structures that are purely moral, political, secular, or created for the sole purpose of avoiding governmental interference. There are no strict guidelines for this process, but two tests are the 3rd Circuit's "objective test" and the 2nd Circuit's more "subjective test."

The objective test, originally constructed in *Africa v. Pennsylvania*, employs three criteria that must be met for a belief system to qualify as a religion: (1) it must "address fundamental and ultimate questions having to do with deep and imponderable matters"; (2) it must be comprehensive, usually including some form of creation theory or supreme being; and (3) it must have external signs and symbols by which it can be recognized.

The subjective test involves examining an inmate's personal state of mind and attitude towards the belief system. This is difficult to assess, but necessary—the court in *Patrick v. LeFevre* believed—to ensure protection of religious rights and freedoms. Courts may choose to apply one or both of these tests; the subjective test is the one more commonly applied.

There are two different tests that have been used to determine whether prison regulations are legitimately limiting a prisoner's free exercise of religion. The stricter test, known as the "compelling interest standard," mandates that any limitation of a prisoner's right to religious expression must "further a compelling state interest in the least restrictive way possible." The looser test, the "reasonableness standard," gives more benefit of the doubt to prison officials as to how they treat the inmates. The decision regarding which standard to use can often determine the outcome of a particular case, since the compelling interest standard favors the rights of prisoners and the reasonableness standard gives more authority to the prison officials.

Prior to the 1970s, most freedom-of-religion cases involving prisoners were decided in favor of the prison institutions. In 1987, the Supreme Court set criteria by which future free-exercise claims of prisoners could be reviewed. Under this four-part test, prisons had the burden of proving that the restrictions imposed on prisoners' constitutional rights were related to a legitimate penalogical interest and were reasonable. The four parts of the test were (1) the need for a clear connection between the regulation and the government interest served by the regulation, (2) reasonableness depends in part on whether there are alternatives for prisoners' exercise of their rights, (3) the effect that accommodation of the prisoners will have on other prisoners, guards, and prison resources, the "cost" of the accommodation, and, (4) "the existence of easy, obvious alternatives at little cost may indicate that the regulation is unreasonable." (In the latter case, the prisoner is often called upon to determine a less burdensome alternative.)

This standard, known as the Turner/O'Lone standard, reflects a balancing between the rights of prisoners and the legitimate interests of penal institutions. Instead of requiring prisons to regulate prisoners' religious freedom in the least restrictive way possible, they now must simply try to be reasonable in accordance with specific guidelines. The institutions must, however, have specific reasons behind the restrictions they choose to impose and must show how they are necessary to further penalogical interests, such as safety and security, rehabilitation, or discipline.

In ***Employment Division of Oregon v. Smith*** (1990), the U.S. Supreme Court altered the standards used for the review of limitations to religious free exercise and effectively removed the requirement of the institutions to prove a "compelling government interest" in determining what restrictions to free expression were acceptable. As long as the policies in question were neutrally stated and generally applicable, they would hold up under constitutional attack unless they were targeting a specific religious group. This ruling made it difficult to challenge incidental infringements on personal religious liberty.

In 1993 Congress enacted the **Religious Freedom Restoration Act (RFRA)**, which stated that government may not substantially burden a citizen's right to freedom of religion unless that burden serves a compelling government interest and is the least restrictive means of furthering that interest. The RFRA substantially increased the ability of prisoners to raise **First Amendment** challenges to their free expression of religion by essentially reinstating the government's need to show a compelling interest. It also applied to laws and regulations that were not specifically designed to apply to religion but that have effects on religious expression. However, the U.S. Supreme Court struck down RFRA in the case of ***City of Boerne v. Flores*** (1997).

Prison officials also need to determine which religious activities to allow and which to disallow. Penal institutions are often generally in favor of the exercise of religion since it is seen as a rehabilitative tool. Adherents to less traditional religions often argue that their religion is being singled out for unequal treatment while others are given chapel space, Bibles, or dietary accommodations. In general, prisons may limit free expression of religion, but may not do so discriminatorily against members of certain religions or sects. Thus, if adherents to a specific religion are given meeting space, all religious groups within the institution must have similar accommodations made for them, but not necessarily in different spaces or with state-provided clergy.

Prisons have in the past successfully prohibited the wearing of yarmulkes, long hair and beards, and religious jewelry. Dietary restrictions are another point of contention because special food for a prisoner with dietary restrictions can place administrative or financial burdens on an institution. In *Kahane v. Carlson*, the 2nd Circuit court ruled that unless there are prohibitive costs associated with providing religious diets, the prison should be required to provide them. This rule applies specifically to diets that are required by a religion and not those that are ceremonial.

The right of inmates to congregate for the purpose of worship is contentious because there can be legitimate security risks when groups of prisoners are involved. Prison administrators can fear an inmate-leadership structure dynamic, which hampers their ability to discipline the inmates. Generally, services are encouraged, but can be logistically problematic, specifically because all religious groups must have access to the same quality services. An interesting limitation to this is that prisons may limit the purpose for which inmates may congregate to specifically prohibit religious worship because religious worship involves "an organized, functioning alternative authority structure among inmates"—whereas a boxing match does not.

The practice of religious freedom by prisoners has been a hotly contested issue that contrasts a citizen's right to freedom of religion with the penal institution's need to maintain security, discipline and a rehabilitative atmosphere. With the court's decision striking down the Religious Freedom Restoration Act, the future expansion of prisoners" rights in light of the lowered court threshold of *Employment Division v. Smith* is unlikely. (JCW) **See also** American Civil Liberties Union (ACLU); Islam; Judaism; *O'Lone v. Estate of Shabazz* (1987).

Bibliography

Branham, Lynn S. *Sentencing, Corrections, and Prisoners' Rights in a Nutshell.* St. Paul, MN: West Publishing Co., 1994.

Knight, Barbara B. *Prisoners' Rights in America.* Chicago: Nelson-Hall, 1986.

Lynn, Barry et al. *The Right to Religious Liberty, the Basic ACLU Guide to Religious Rights.* Carbondale: Southern Illinois University Press, 1995.

Palmer, John W. *Constitutional Rights of Prisoners.* Cincinnati, OH: Anderson Publishing Company, 1996.

Rudovsky, David. *The Rights of Prisoners, the Basic ACLU Guide to a Prisoner's Rights.* New York: Avon Books, 1973.

Zimmerman, Roy. *Jurisprudence, Rights & Treatments in Prisons: Index of New Information with Authors, Subjects & Bibliography.* Washington, DC: ABBE Publishers Association, 1995.

Promise Keepers

Promise Keepers is a non-denominational evangelical Christian organization founded in 1990 and aimed at spiritual renewal of and by men. Its founder and chief executive is William McCartney, former University of Colorado football coach who was a major participant in the Fellowship of Christian Athletes, a nondenominational organization of coaches and players who seek to bring prayer and other public displays of religion onto the playing field. In 1996, over one million men attended 22 stadium events. On October 4, 1997, several hundred thousand men attended its "stand in the gap" revival event in Washington, D.C. They prayed for forgiveness in putting personal ambitions before God, church, and family. Critics say the group encourages sexism and a conservative political agenda. The charge of sexism stems largely from its male only focus. Its conservative political perception is because of the group's emphasis on traditional family values and the father as head of house. The group, however, does not publically advocate any specific political agenda. (JRV) **See also** Conservatism; Divorce; Evangelicals; Feminism; Million Man March; Publicly Funded Religious Displays.

Bibliography

Abraham, Ken. *Who Are the Promise Keepers?: Understanding the Christian Men's Movement.* New York: Doubleday, 1997.

McCartney, Bill. *Sold Out: God's Strategy for the Game of Life.* Dallas: Word Publishing, 1997.

Providential History

The idea that God has uniquely blessed the New World has been an explicit and implicit theme in many histories written about the United States. Providential history sanctified American nationalism by giving a distinct and transcendent identity to a diverse and divided people. School textbooks early in the nineteenth century were thoroughly nationalistic and providential. The **Pilgrim** settlement was the exodus of a New Israel; the founding fathers were the biblical patriarchs born again.

Providentialism was a powerful impetus for moral reform and territorial expansion. To maintain the covenant with God, the nation had to purge itself of such sins as **slavery**, ignorance, and intemperance. And when a more secular outlook finally prevailed, Providentialism was transformed into a national sense of **Manifest Destiny**.

While academic historians have now abandoned providentialism and the belief that the United States is the bearer of a special universal hope, popular historians continue to write providential history. The bicentennial celebrations brought forth a flurry of providential histories, especially from evangelical and fundamentalist publishers. The most enduring modern example remains *The Light and the Glory*, written by Peter Marshall and David Manuel. Politically, many religious conservatives have enlisted providential history books to support their thesis that America was once a "Christian nation." (ARB) **See also** "City on a Hill"; Democracy; Evangelicals; Fundamentalists; Imperialism.

Bibliography

Berens, John F. *Providence and Patriotism in Early America, 1640–1815.* Charlottesville: University Press of Virginia, 1978.

Noll, Mark, Nathan Hatch and George Marsden. *The Search for Christian America.* Westchester, IL: Crossway Books, 1983.

Public Aid to Religious Organizations

The issue of public aid to religious organizations hinges largely on the interpretation of the **Establishment Clause** of the Constitution. In general, advocates of the strict separation of church and state have long argued that this separation entails a complete absence of government funds going to religious organizations. Generally speaking, however, the U.S. Supreme Court, as well as the bulk of scholarly opinion, has adopted a position of loose **accommodationism**, that is, that public aid may go to religious organizations that serve a public purpose.

All governments—federal, state, and local—funnel a great deal of financial aid to religious organizations. These organizations include not only churches, but religious hospitals, clinics, orphanages, halfway houses, and a variety of other social service programs. (See *Bradfield v. Roberts* [1899], where the Court ruled in favor of public funding for these organizations.) The main focus of controversy in this area, however, has been public funding for private schools. Here, the Court's jurisprudence has been less than a model of consistency. Typically, the Court has tried to navigate its way between accommodationism and the limiting of free exercise (but giving religious groups less public support than private organizations motivated by something other than religion) by distinguishing between direct and indirect aid. The Court has argued that aid that goes to the student directly accrues to the institution indirectly, and that certain public benefits enjoyed by a religious organization (such as police protection) also constitute indirect aid. In ***Everson v. Board of Education of the Township of Ewing*** (1947), the landmark ruling on Establishment Clause cases, a deeply divided Court ruled, despite the logic of its "high **wall of separation**" metaphor, that a New Jersey program for busing students to parochial schools did not constitute an establishment of religion.

Subsequent cases have faced similar difficulties. In ***Zorach v. Clauson*** (1952) the Court ruled that a **release time** program to provide religious instruction for public school students, off school grounds, was constitutionally permissible. The key ruling, however, came in ***Lemon v. Kurtzman*** (1971), where the Court struck down a "direct aid" program that used public funds to supplement the salaries of private school teachers. In this case, the Court developed the famous ***Lemon* Test**, which mandated that for any piece of legislation to be constitutionally acceptable, it had to have a primarily secular purpose, its primary effect could neither promote nor inhibit religion, and it could not entail an excessive entanglement of church and state. Because the first two prongs of the test have proven difficult to determine, cases have typically rested on the third prong; but this too has proved an elusive standard, since few can agree on what might be considered "excessive." Thus, for example, *Lemon*'s companion case, ***Tilton v. Richardson*** (1971), upheld a $240 million federal funding program for the construction of academic buildings on private sectarian and secular colleges, under the understanding that such grants did not create "excessive" entanglement. Likewise, in *Hunt v. McNair* (1973), the Court upheld a South Carolina state bond issue which provided for the construction of buildings which served nonreligious purposes on religious campuses. These cases seem to go beyond the indirect aid standard the Court had set forward in *Everson* by giving aid directly to the religious institution.

At the same time, the Court has (with more consistency) upheld programs that give aid directly to the student. In ***Meek v. Pittenger*** (1975) the Court upheld the loan of secular subject textbooks from public schools to private schools. In *Bowen v. Kendrick* (1988), the Court gave its imprimatur to the authorization of federal funds for public and private organizations, including those affiliated with organized churches, which provided premarital counseling. In this case, the Court's decision was made more difficult because the aid went directly to the organization, and this difficulty manifested itself in the Court's 5-4 decision. The determining factor, undoubtedly, was that the actions of the organization were in part mandated by the state, in compliance with the **Adolescent Family Life Act** (1981). Where religious institutions are operating in compliance with state mandated activities, they are more likely to receive public funds. In a similar case, ***Committee for Public Education v. Regan*** (1980), again a 5-4 Court decided that reimbursement for certain expenses for record keeping and testing incurred by private schools following state regulations should be upheld. The Court has similarly ruled that programs providing for diagnostic and therapeutic testing services for private school students and a program providing sign-language interpreters for deaf students at private schools would both pass constitutional muster.

At the same time, certain programs of a similar nature have not been approved by the Court. *Meek v. Pittenger* (1975) struck down a program that provided counseling, testing, remedial classes, equipment, and other auxiliary services to schools affiliated with religious organizations, the key distinction evidently being that the schools received the aid directly. In ***Wolman v. Walter*** (1977), the Court struck down, by a 5-4 margin, a statute that provided financial aid for field trips and class paraphernalia to private religious schools. This decision seemed particularly peculiar to some since it meant that government could provide textbooks to private schools, but not maps. This provoked Senator Daniel Moynihan to quip: "What about atlases?" A series of cases in 1973 also struck down numerous attempts to provide services and educational equipment to religiously affiliated schools. While the Court upheld reimbursement of certain testing costs in *Regan*, it struck down direct reimbursement for record keeping and testing services in *New York v. Cathedral Academy* (1977). Contrasting to the Court's earlier decision in *Wolman*, in ***Aguilar v. Felton*** and *Grand Rapids School District v. Ball* (1985), the Court struck down two successful remedial learning programs for public school students, taught by public school teachers, because they were held in parochial schools. In dissenting from the Court's decision, Justice Sandra Day O'Connor stated "it is difficult to understand why a remedial learning class offered on parochial school premises is any more likely to supplant the secular course offerings of the parochial school than the same class offered in a portable classroom next door to the school." She continued to argue that concern over indoctrination because one was on the premises of a parochial school would "require us to close our public schools, for there is always some chance that a public school teacher will bring religion into the classroom, regardless of its location. . . . To a great extent, the anomalous results in our **Establishment Clause** cases are 'attributable to the entanglement prong.'"

A good example of such confusion can be seen in the Court's decisions regarding tuition reimbursement programs. In *Essex v. Wolman* (1972), the Court struck down a program providing an annual tuition rebate of $90 per child attending religiously affiliated schools. Likewise, in ***Levitt v. Committee for Public Education*** (1973) and ***Committee for Public Education v. Nyquist*** (1973) the Court overturned statutes which provided financial aid for parochial schools, including tuition reimbursement and tax exemptions. However, 10 years later, the Court, in a decision penned by Justice **William H. Rehnquist**, the leader of the "**non-preferentist**" school on the bench, upheld a Minnesota program which allowed taxpayers, in computing their state income tax, to deduct up to either $500 or $700 a year for tuition, transportation, or textbook expenses. Rehnquist reasoned that such deductions were allowed by state law, had a plausible secular purpose, went to the parents rather than to the school directly, and actually helped prevent the inhibition of religion by relieving some of the additional burden placed upon parents who send their children to these schools. Again, the Court was divided 5-4, with the dissent arguing that the statute had a primary effect of promoting religion.

Finally, the question of financial aid for religious institutions emerges in the issue of granting **tax-exempt status** to religious institutions. The most important case here is ***Walz v. Tax Commission of the City of New York*** (1970), where the Court upheld the tax-exempt status. Here, the Court ruled that government must possess a "benevolent neutrality" with regard to religion, and ruled that any institution that fosters mental or moral improvement and generally helps the community should not be inhibited in their activity by taxation. Furthermore, the Court's ruling that buttressed by the long-standing tradition of granting tax-exempt status to these institutions. Subsequent challenges to this status have failed, though the Court did overturn a Texas law giving tax-exempt status to religious periodicals in *Texas Monthly, Inc. v. Bullock* (1989). (JP) **See also** Education; Entanglement Clause; Free Exercise Clause; Publicly Funded Religious Displays; School Prayer; Tuition Tax Credits.

BIBLIOGRAPHY

Berns, Walter. *The First Amendment and the Future of American Democracy.* Chicago: Gateway Editions, 1985.

Carter, Stephen. *The Culture of Disbelief: How American Law and Politics Trivialize Religious Devotion.* New York: Basic Books, 1993.

Fowler, Robert Booth and Allen Hertzke. *Religion and Politics in America: Faith, Culture, and Strategic Choices.* Boulder: Westview, 1995.

Levy, Leonard. *The Establishment Clause.* Chapel Hill: The University of North Carolina Press, 1995.

Public Theology

Public Theology, a recent movement among mainline theologians, ethicists, and social scientists such as Peter Berger, **Richard John Neuhaus**, Max Stackhouse, **Ronald Frank Thiemann**, and **Glenn Tinder**, responding to the privatization of religion in the public sphere (secularization), seeks to recover the communal and public voice of religious communities without advocating relativism or the adoption of specific policies (the conservative Christian approach). They seek to avoid the "world-denying" sectarian approach of **Stanley Hauerwas** and the liberal stance of the "early" **John Rawls**. Public theology argues on both theological and legal grounds for active ecumenical participation in the formation of public policy. Rejecting narrow and exclusionary interpretations of the **First Amendment**, Thiemann argues for a new conceptual framework that includes both neutrality and cooperation. The old state-church dichotomy needs revision, and religious groups, rather than being excluded, need to be understood as part of the vast voluntary associational movement. He argues that contemporary religion is not irrational, does not separate the private from the public, and is compatible with democratic values. However, such participation should be subject to the criteria of publicly accessible norms, mutual respect for difference and moral integrity. Though advocated by a diverse body of scholars (Protestant, Jewish, Catholic, Evangelical), public theology itself reflects that pluralistic dialogue in which religious communities engage their own beliefs and practices with the broader society. (ISM) **See also** Democracy; Evangelicals; Roman Catholicism.

BIBLIOGRAPHY

Stackhouse, Max L. *Public Theology and Political Economy: Christian Stewardship in Modern Society.* Grand Rapids: Eerdmans, 1987.

Thiemann, Ronald F. *Constructing a Public Theology: The Church in a Pluralistic Culture.* Louisville: Westminster/John Knox Press, 1991.

Publicly Funded Religious Displays

Every holiday season there are disputes about whether nativity scenes displayed on public property or supported by public funds violate the **First Amendment** restriction against laws "respecting an establishment of religion." The 1997 season was no different: in at least five cities, observers took notice of, and in some cases threatened litigation over, nativity scenes in public places. While some city governments, like that of Oklahoma City, affirmed their intentions to continue sponsoring such displays, others, like those of St. Ann, Missouri, and Jersey City, New Jersey, backed down in the face of judicial decisions and threats of litigation. At issue in every case is how far government may go to accommodate or acknowledge the religious dimension of the holiday season without crossing over the line into sponsoring or establishing religion.

All of these disputes are framed by three recent decisions of the United States Supreme Court: ***Lynch v. Donnelly*** 465 U.S. 668 (1984), ***County of Allegheny v. Greater Pittsburgh ACLU*** 492 U.S. 573 (1989), and ***Capitol Square Review Board v. Pinette*** 115 S. Ct. 2440 (1995). The first decision permitted a publicly sponsored nativity scene in a private park in downtown Pawtucket, Rhode Island. The second ruled unconstitutional a privately sponsored nativity scene at the

Allegheny County (Pennsylvania) Courthouse and constitutional a large menorah placed outside the city-county building in Pittsburgh. The third permitted a privately sponsored cross erected on publicly owned land close to the Ohio state capital in Columbus. It is important to examine these decisions closely to gain coherent guidance from them.

In *Lynch*, a narrow majority (five justices) found in favor of the publicly owned and erected nativity scene. Applying a relaxed version of the ***Lemon* Test**—so named because it was first articulated in the ***Lemon v. Kurtzman*** (1971) decision—the majority found that the sponsorship of the nativity scene carried out a secular purpose, did not have the principal or primary effect of advancing religion, and did not involve excessive entanglement with religion. It identified the secular purposes as "celebrat[ing] the Holiday and…depict[ing] the origins of that Holiday." The premise underlying this argument is that, despite its religious origins, Christmas has become a largely secular holiday. A depiction of its origins can be regarded as merely cultural or historical and need not principally be religious. The majority also insisted that the aid the nativity scene gives to religion is "indirect, remote, and incidental," far less, in any event, than many other forms of assistance to religion the Court has found constitutional over the years. The dissenters argued, however, that secular purposes (such as "celebrating the holiday season and promoting retail commerce") can be accomplished by the other facets of the park's holiday display (such as Santa and reindeer). They also rejected the majority's view that the benefit of public sponsorship that the nativity scene provides is minimal: "The effect on minority religious groups, as well as on those who may reject all religion, is to convey the message that their views are not similarly worthy of public recognition nor entitled to public support." Finally, the minority sought to limit the effect of the ruling by calling attention to the broader setting of the nativity scene: it was a part of a significantly larger holiday display that contained many secular elements and so could be regarded as serving the secular purpose and conveying the secular message the majority attributed to it. The question of the fate of a publicly sponsored nativity scene standing on its own remained to be settled.

Another ruling determined by a bare majority of five justices, *Allegheny* addressed a somewhat different set of facts. Here the religious holiday displays were privately owned, but placed on public property in such a way that their position might be understood to convey some message of public endorsement or sponsorship. According to the majority, the differing fates of the nativity scene (unconstitutional) and the menorah (constitutional) had everything to do with the setting and the context in which they were placed. What mattered about the nativity scene was its prominent placement in the county courthouse, a setting not regularly available to other displays, and its context, which did nothing to secularize or detract from the religious message it might send. Despite the fact that the display bore a sign indicating its private sponsorship, everything else seemed to suggest that the government endorsed the efforts of the private organization to celebrate the exclusively religious dimension of the Christmas holiday. In the case of the menorah, its juxtaposition with a much larger Christmas tree (understood by the Court as a secular symbol of Christmas) and a sign indicating the city's celebration of liberty served effectively to secularize and render constitutional the overall message. The minority contended that in ruling unconstitutional the nativity scene the majority abandoned the accommodation or acknowledgment of religion that had been the hallmark of previous Supreme Court decisions. In this case, the governments were merely passively acknowledging the religious dimension of the holidays, not engaging in the kind of active coercion or proselytizing that is required to run afoul of the First Amendment **Establishment Clause**.

The *Allegheny* ruling is significant for another reason: in it, the majority adopted for the first time an interpretation of the First Amendment doctrine offered by Justice Sandra Day O'Connor in her concurrence in *Lynch*. There she suggested that the best way to make sense of the logic of the *Lemon* Test is to consider the question of whether the government action serves as an "endorsement" of religion. As the *Allegheny* majority understands the endorsement doctrine, it is no longer relevant how significant the governmental support for religion is; any endorsement is invalid. Furthermore, the doctrine offers a method for ascertaining whether or not the display conveys a message of endorsement: how do its viewers understand it? While in *Lynch* Justice O'Connor sided with the majority, the other members of the *Allegheny* majority dissented in that case. Their disagreement in the earlier case turned not on the understanding of the constitutional doctrine, but rather on the assessment of the particular facts of the case. It would thus be fair to conclude that, so far as the *Allegheny* majority is concerned, everything now depends upon how observers understand a holiday display. If it seems to them to endorse religion, it is constitutionally impermissible. If it does not, it is permissible.

This doctrine is refined by Justice O'Connor in her partial concurrence in *Capitol Square* and supported by a majority of the justices in that case, but rejected by the plurality opinion. In this case, which concerns a cross erected by the **Ku Klux Klan** during the holiday season on the square surrounding the Ohio state capitol (traditionally regarded as a public forum open to all sorts of private speech), there are three camps: a plurality of four justices (the *Allegheny* dissenters with Justice **Clarence Thomas** replacing Justice Byron White) who focused on the character of *Capitol Square* as a public forum; a group of three justices led by O'Connor who applied the "endorsement" doctrine and concluded that a "reasonable observer" would not in this instance regard the proximity of the private religious display to a government building as an endorsement of religion; and two who judged that the character of the setting—especially the close proximity to statues and other symbols clearly belonging to the government—would convey endorsement to a reasonable observer. The plurality contends that closing a public forum to religious expression on these grounds is not neutral and actually discriminates against religion.

At the moment, then, there are five justices on the Supreme Court willing to apply the **endorsement test** and ask what a hypothetical reasonable observer would conclude about the message sent by the display. Of course, they might disagree about how to interpret the facts of a particular case, so that, with the support of the justices in the *Capitol Square* plurality, certain publicly sponsored religious displays might still pass constitutional muster. Privately sponsored religious displays on public property pose a different issue. Where the property is deemed a public forum—generally and genuinely open to all forms of private expression, which are subject only to neutral regulation of time, place, and manner (absent a demonstrably compelling state interest in further restriction)—there is a presumption in favor of freedom of religious expression. Four current members of the Supreme Court would go no further than this: all things being equal, religious expression in a public forum is defended by the **Free Exercise Clause** and not subject to the establishment clause. Five current members might be open to challenges based on the context of the display and the appearance of governmental endorsement associated with it.

A recent nativity scene case, *Elewski v. City of Syracuse*, indicates the current state of the law. In 1997, the 2nd Circuit Court of Appeals, by a 2-1 vote, turned back a challenge to a city-owned nativity scene in a public park. Relying on the endorsement doctrine, the majority decided that a reasonable observer would not regard the display as a governmental endorsement of religion. The city articulated a secular purpose similar to that offered by Pawtucket in *Lynch*, erected a wide variety of other secular holiday decorations, and assisted in the erection of a privately owned menorah in the same park. The dissenting judge disputed the majority's assessment of what a reasonable observer would conclude, but suggested that there was an alternative to the city's action. Following the *Capitol Square* plurality, he recommended that the city permit a private organization to place the nativity scene in the park, which was a public forum. In March 1998, the Supreme Court declined to hear a challenge to this decision.

In sum, at the moment governments must be careful to convey a non-religious message in the overall context of the religious displays they sponsor. Private organizations cannot readily be denied access to public forums on establishment grounds but, here too, everything depends on the context. Five current justices are willing under certain circumstances to close a public forum to religious expression. Given the pattern of Supreme Court nominations and appointments, the balance of power on this issue depends upon whether a Democratic or a Republican president is in office when the next justice retires. While not every Republican appointee favors on principle maximal accommodation of religion, every recent Democratic appointee has been devoted to the endorsement test. (JMK) **See also** Accommodationism; Democratic Party; Entanglement Test; Judaism; Republican Party.

Bibliography

Adams, Arlin M. *A Nation Dedicated to Religious Liberty.* Philadelphia: University of Pennsylvania Press, 1990.

Gedicks, Frederick Mark. *The Rhetoric of Church and State.* Durham, NC: Duke University Press, 1995.

Lee, Francis Graham, ed. *All Imaginable Liberty.* Lanham, MD: University Press of America, 1995.

Levy, Leonard W. *The Establishment Clause.* Chapel Hill: University of North Carolina Press, 1994.

Lynn, Barry W. *The Right to Religious Liberty: The Basic ACLU Guide to Religious Rights.* Carbondale: Southern Illinois University Press, 1995.

Smith, Steven D. *Foreordained Failure.* New York: Oxford University Press, 1995.

Weber, Paul J., ed. *Equal Separation.* New York: Greenwood Press, 1990.

Puritans

The Puritans, who had sought unsuccessfully to purify and revive English religion, migrated to the New World in order to form "holy commonwealths": religiously organized civil societies that would transform the old country by their example. The first immigrants arrived in the **Massachusetts Bay** area in the early and mid-seventeenth century, and by 1641, 20,000 English Puritans had relocated in New England.

Although under British rule, the Puritans in Massachusetts were at liberty to organize parochial governments to oversee their religious and civil affairs. They viewed both governmental structures and laws as God-ordained restraints on human sin, and thus necessary for salvation as well as social well-being. They advocated a strict ordering of personal and social life, and thus set about creating precise laws for every circumstance and clear consequences for every infraction. They rejected idleness and recreation as frivolous, and required that all citizens adopt somber dress and a sober countenance. They were concerned primarily with living dutifully, which for them meant engaging in productive work, practicing frugality in all things, and obeying all laws and social conventions.

Puritan theology emphasized an inward experience of conversion, or sense that God had saved one. They trained their children and themselves to prepare for God's grace, even as they proclaimed the remoteness and inscrutability of God. Puritans took seriously the doctrine of predestination, which states that God—and only God—determines who will be saved and who will be damned in the final judgment. Human works have no bearing on God's decision, according to predestinarians, because God predetermined the saved, or "elect," before time began. For Puritans, this meant that they organized their lives around preparing for and living in God's grace in the face of unresolvable uncertainty about their own election. Even a conversion experience was no guarantee of God's favor, although testifying to such an experience was a prerequisite to church membership.

Under these theological conditions, fewer and fewer Puritans met the criteria for full church membership. Young adults, baptized as children but not converted, formed families of their own and could not present their children for baptism because they were not full members of a congregation. Fear for the damnation of their children led to the creation of a "Halfway Covenant," through which children could be baptized even if their parents were not full communicants. While this assuaged the immediate social concerns for inclusion and recognition as upstanding parents, it undermined the importance of full church membership to the success of the commonwealth concept. The presumption had been that adult members of the commonwealth would correspondingly be full communicants of the church, and thus speed the Second Coming of Christ through the creation of a godly society. Instead, most adults participated in the civil religion of the commonwealth without expectation of full church membership or the creation of anything more than a dutiful society.

Early Puritans also sought to speed the Second Coming through their evangelization of Native Americans. They believed that the conversion of the "heathen" pleased God and contributed to the creation of a truly Christian commonwealth in which God would be willing to dwell. However, the Puritans' lack of respect for Native American rights and lands more often led to violence than conversion.

What the commonwealth did benefit from was the Puritan emphasis on work and frugality. This strong work ethic influenced farming production and commercial development, acting as a spur to economic growth in New England. The Puritans' heavy emphasis on law and civil responsibility contributed to the creation of good moral citizens who upheld the commonwealth through their labor. New England prospered, and new waves of immigrants came to enjoy the wealth of the commonwealths. While the Puritans did not succeed in converting the world to their ways of thinking, they did succeed in forming a new nation that still claims to believe in a Protestant work ethic similar to their own. Even the 1960s rejection of Puritan stereotypes did little to shake the dominant cultural emphasis on duty and responsibility that is the Puritan legacy. (KMY) **See also** "City on a Hill"; Colonial America; Episcopal Church; Mayflower Compact; Perry Miller; Pilgrims.

Bibliography

Hambrick-Stowe, Charles E. *The Practice of Piety: Puritan Devotional Disciplines in Seventeenth-Century New England.* Chapel Hill: The University of North Carolina Press, 1982.

Morgan, Edmund S. *Visible Saints: The History of a Puritan Idea.* Ithaca: Cornell University Press, 1963.

Porterfield, Amanda. *Female Piety in Puritan New England.* New York: Oxford University Press, 1992.

Vaughan, Alden T. and Francis J. Bremer, eds. *Puritan New England: Essays on Religion, Society, and Culture.* New York: St. Martin's Press, 1977.

Quakers

Quakerism originated in England about 1660. It was started after the Protestant **Reformation** by George Fox and others, as a religious protest against the excessive formalism of the Established Church of England. The Quakers' official name is the Religious Society of Friends and the members are referred to as Quakers or simply Friends. Many doctrines of the Society of Friends were borrowed from other, earlier religious groups, specifically the Anabaptists and Independents, who believed in independent congregations, complete separation of church and state, and lay leadership. The Friends' original intent was to unify the splintered Christian churches—not necessarily to start a separate sect. They were originally called Children of Light, or Friends of the Truth, and were said to quake with religious zeal.

Persecuted in Massachusetts, colonial Quakers found safe havens in Rhode Island and Pennsylvania. National Archives.

Friends were active in the American colonies as early as 1654. They were persecuted by the Puritans in Massachusetts for their unpopular anti-**war** beliefs as well as their refusal to defer to authority. They were seen as a threat to the hard-won organized religion of the colonies and often jailed or exiled from the colonies under threat of death. The sole exception to this was **Rhode Island Colony**, which had been founded in the spirit of religious tolerance. During the eighteenth century, the Quakers were perceived as controversial because of their abolitionist beliefs, and their persecution continued. Nonetheless, they formed strong communities in many Eastern states, particularly Pennsylvania and New Jersey.

The Society of Friends has undergone many schisms in beliefs since the 1800s, particularly regarding adherence to customs of dress and speech, resulting in many smaller Quaker factions with some differences in doctrines. Overall, this is in keeping with the Quakers' belief in a decentralized institutional structure and in not adhering to one specific creed or dogma but rather "seeking for the leadings of God" or "Inner Light" within themselves. Quakers believe that they can commune with God directly without the aid of church or clergy, and as such all have spiritual equality regardless of race or gender. Some commonly held Quaker beliefs are **pacifism**, refusal to take oaths of any kind including loyalty oaths and pledges of allegiance, and aversion to the death penalty. Many Quakers are activists on these topics.

Quaker worship services are called meetings. At these meetings, members sit silently until they are moved by the Spirit to speak at which point they stand up, speak, and then return to sitting. There is no clergy and no formal structure. There are also business meetings, known as Monthly Meetings, in which the business of the membership such as marriages, rental payments, and administrative tasks are dealt with. World membership of Quakers has been estimated at 200,000 Friends, spanning 30 countries. (JCW) **See also** Abolition; Capital Punishment; Colonial America; Establishment Clause; First Amendment; Pledge of Allegiance; Religious Tests and Oaths; Wall of Separation.

BIBLIOGRAPHY

Brinton, Howard Haines. *Friends for 300 Years: The History and Beliefs of the Society of Friends Since George Fox Started the Quaker Movement.* New York: Harper, 1952.

Quebec Act of 1774

In 1774, after years of vacillation, the British decided to deal harshly with their rebellious American colonies by passing four acts that became known in the colonies as the Intolerable Acts. One of those was the Quebec Act. Building on a Royal Proclamation the previous year, the act expanded the crown colony of Quebec to include all land from the Allegheny mountains to the Mississippi and Ohio Rivers. While French Canadians were delighted, Americans were outraged, viewing the land as their own and fearing the growth of an undemocratic, French-speaking, Catholic power to their west.

The act was partly the result of lobbying efforts by General Guy Carlson. Upon becoming the British governor of Quebec in 1766, Carlson decided that the existing policy of making Quebec culturally English was a mistake, that its population should be used as a check on the growing power of the American colonies. In 1770 he returned to England to promote this idea and in 1774, with support from liberals, he achieved it. Far from intimidating Americans, the four acts made them even more rebellious. (MWP) **See also** Colonial America; Democracy; Liberalism; Roman Catholicism.

BIBLIOGRAPHY

Coffin, Victor. *The Province of Quebec and the Early American Revolution.* Madison: University of Wisconsin, 1896.

Quick Bear v. Leupp (1908)

Members of the Sioux Indian Tribe attempted to block the use of treaty funds, held in trust and administered by the Commissioner of Indian Affairs, to pay for Roman Catholic schools for Sioux children. The tribe claimed that the government, in paying for religious schooling, violated the **Establishment Clause** of the **First Amendment**. In *Reuben Quick Bear v. Leupp*, 210 U.S. 50 (1908), the U.S. Supreme Court ruled that whereas the government could not legitimately pay for Catholic schooling with its own funds, the money being used to pay for the schools actually belonged to the Sioux Tribe and not the government, and therefore there was no constitutional violation. (JM) **See also** Education; Native American Religions; Public Aid to Religious Organizations; Roman Catholicism.

BIBLIOGRAPHY

Cord, Robert I. *Separation of Church and State.* New York: Lambeth Press, 1982.

R

Race Relations

Current interest in race relations, or minority relationships, developed after **World War II** and coincided with the end of colonialism and the rise of new nation states in Africa and Asia. The Swedish social scientist Gunnar Myrdal had already, in his magnum opus, *The American Dilemma* (1944), described race as a dilemma for America and the West because their embedded racism contradicted the common Western and American belief, bolstered by religion, that all people were equal.

Race relations, as a a social science subdiscipline, derives largely from the work of Robert Park, Lloyd Warner, and Gunnar Myrdal during the 1930s, 1940s, and 1950s. Park, Warner, and Myrdal argued that such a category of social relations served to explain and thereby possibly overcome discrimination and racism. More recently, however, the rise of critical sociological theory, drawing from Marxist categories of social analysis, has suggested that the categories of "race" and "race relations" are not only conceptually troublesome, but are in fact the reification of historical and cultural forces and thus are no different from other social relationships. Despite the differences noted above, social scientists accept the category of "race relations" as a referent to the relations between whites and blacks and/or Hispanics in the United States. In the early 1800s, the French traveler and social observer **Alexis de Tocqueville** noted that, in America, the liabilities of race and caste are different from those that pertain to ethnic or other minority status. These effects were as noticeable on blacks—in terms of self-esteem, life chances, and opportunity, as they were on whites—in terms of expectations and prerogatives. Race relations can be explored historically through an examination of the terms with which they are most closely associated, segregation and integration.

Segregation refers to the separation of people by restricting one group to certain defined residential areas, separated institutions, or facilities. The basis for segregation is typically race, ethnicity, color, religion, and culture, or a combination of these. Segregation has been, and often still is, a public policy (if not de jure, then de facto), a social system, and an ideology that discriminates against the segregated group, is imposed by force, and is often claimed to be beneficial for the segregated group, since it enables them to maintain their distinctive cultural values. Segregation inevitably functions to preserve the economic, political, and social advantages of those in power, i.e., the politically dominant group.

In the twentieth century, segregation has primarily been understood in terms of white population groups attempting to preserve dominance over others through social and legal color bars. Surprisingly, the use of the term segregation for such a racial color bar is comparatively recent, first coming into widespread use in the United States after 1890. The most prominent forms of segregation are modern phenomena, associated with modernization, economic specialization, and urbanization, processes that, according to modernization theory, were supposed to eradicate such discriminatory practices. One of these, South African apartheid, ended with the release of Nelson Mandela from prison and the election victory of his African National Congress in 1994. Another, segregation in the American South, ended in 1964 when President Johnson signed the Civil Rights Act, which forbade discrimination on the basis of race in federal programs, voting, education, and public institutions.

The mechanisms of such segregation vary widely. By 1876, the Hayes-Tilden Compromise settling the dispute over the outcome of the 1876 presidential election had made segregation the norm in the American South, despite the Emancipation Proclamation (January 1, 1863). Although the period of **Reconstruction** (1865-1877) following the **Civil War** saw passage of a Civil Rights Bill in 1866 and the Sumner Act in 1875, the former was vetoed by President Andrew Johnson and the latter was declared unconstitutional by the Supreme Court in 1883. This led to the practical denial of the Fourteenth (granting citizenship to blacks) and Fifteenth (the right to vote) Amendments, and to the passage of many discriminatory state laws. These were the infamous "Jim Crow" enactments that divided Southern society in two along racial lines, reducing blacks to second-class citizenship, segregating public institutions, and prohibiting intermarriage. The Southern states' continuous enactment of segregation laws was subsequently encouraged by the decision of the U.S. Supreme Court, in *Plessy v. Ferguson* 163 U.S. 537, (1896), declaring that the provision of separate but equal facilities was not a violation of the right to equal protection under the law, according to the **Fourteenth Amendment**.

This de jure segregation remained in force in the American South until the 1950s, when the **civil rights** movement was triggered by opposition to segregated public transportation. Thus, from 1955 to circa 1965, the goals of the Civil Rights Movement were largely defined in terms of overcoming segregation and promoting integration and enfranchisement. This applied to blacks as well as other minorities under the rubric of civil rights. By the mid-1960s **Martin Luther King, Jr.**, recognizing the international scope of segregation, spoke out on apartheid at the United Nations, initiating a further struggle which accelerated into divestment and disinvestment campaigns throughout the 1980s and culminated in the imposition of U.S. economic sanctions against South Africa. This campaign was widely supported by most major religious institutions.

The decade from 1970–1980 saw the social consequences of the Civil Rights Movement being hammered out. Unfortunately this led, particularly in the North, to further de facto segregation. All minority groups, but particularly blacks, are, when compared to Asians and Hispanics, residentially segregated in large metropolitan areas. This has clear class and economic bases, although most researchers still would attribute significant weight to white prejudice and fear.

In general, minorities have had two options open to them, separation from, or integration into, the mainstream. The former option has generally not been viewed as realistic, though it has sometimes been advocated by black nationalists (see below). The latter option, the assertion and exercise of social, political, and economic rights guaranteed under the U.S. Constitution, or integration, has been understood and actualized in three basic ways. The earliest and dominant option was that of assimilation (or "anglo-conformity"), one that was, of course, taken up by white national (ethnic) minorities. This option largely excluded racial minorities such as African Americans. The second option was to be both part of the larger society and at the same time preserve one's ethnic identity and culture, an approach described as "integration-at-a-distance," or as amalgamation. This involves the integration of the "best features" of the various peoples into a new nation, an approach often associated with the French-American Hector St. John de Crevecoeur who, in his *Letters from an American Farmer* (1782), wrote of "individuals of all nations ...melted into a new race of men." The third method, that of accommodation, or cultural pluralism, probably always existed, but has only become prominent recently as society and immigrants themselves reject the "melting pot" thesis and seek to preserve their own cultures and traditions. This approach recognizes the diversity of peoples and cultures and views society as a mosaic or patchwork quilt of nations within a nation. This is the official approach in Canada. In the United States, while historically this option only envisioned the European nations as participants, it is presently undergoing a revival and expansion

Integration has had diverse meanings. The move for integration as assimilation reached its zenith during the years from 1954 to 1963, with a coalition of black and white reformers calling for the United States to live up to its constitutional ideals. The climax of this movement for integration came with the 1963 Emancipation Proclamation centennial anniversary march on Washington, and Martin Luther King, Jr.'s "I have a dream" speech, and its consequences, the Civil Rights legislation enacted in 1964, 1967, 1968, and amended in 1982. While King's efforts caused controversy among southern white Protestant churches (and this gave occasion for King's celebrated "Letter from a Birmingham Jail"), many northern denominations and individuals from their southern counterparts actively supported the Civil Rights Movement.

Integration as amalgamation has not expanded to include involuntary immigrants such as African Americans or recent dark-skinned immigrants from the Caribbean. Prior to the 1980s, most attempts made to redress the effects of segregation were aimed at promoting integration in these first two senses. However, these attempts were predicated on the assumption that American society would and could see beyond race. When it became apparent that this was not so, black radicalism grew in tandem with black pride and culture movements as in fact did similar Hispanic and Asian movements.

Despite various Civil Rights Acts passed during the 1960s, the slow pace of change and the failure of political movements to change the socio-economic position of the poor African American led to a conscious abandonment of integration as a goal. As black-white reformist coalitions crumbled, militant African-American leadership emerged; the focus now was on "Black Pride" and "Black Power," and many urban ghettoes erupted in violence by the decade's end. Meanwhile, college enrollment of African Americans was increasing and African-American Studies departments were being founded. From some of these would emerge theories of the Afro-centric origins of Western civilization.

Arguments for racial separation and solidarity tend to emerge when racial equality is perceived to have failed. The ideas of self-acceptance and racial solidarity were old ones, powerfully advocated a century ago by **Booker Taliaferro Washington**. His self-help philosophy was carried by lower-class blacks in northern cities who flocked to **Marcus Garvey**'s "Back-to-Africa" movement during the 1920s; by independent black churches during the 1930s and 1940s, and in recent times, by the **Nation of Islam**. Such separatism had been encouraged by the apparent inability of the dominant Churches, both Protestant and Roman Catholic, to effectively promote integration on the local parish level. Local congregations tended to follow the racial mores of their immediate contexts. On the national level by contrast, both the Protestant National Council of Churches and the **National Conference of Catholic Bishops** have repeatedly spoken out on issues involving race relations. As the African-American middle class expanded, the lower classes remained or fell back, leading sociologist William Julius Wilson to speak of the existence of a growing underclass of minorities, particularly of African Americans. This was the scenario during the 1970s and 1980s. However, while great advances were made during these decades in dealing with racial and ethnic prejudice, African Americans (together with other minorities) were divided on how to approach the broader structural issues created by segregation and integration. Should equality be attained through group-based, that is, affirmative action programs or by the impartial application of already existing laws? Such questions arose from the mixed results of federal attempts to enforce desegregation programs. These attempts resulted in backlash, particularly in working-class white suburbs, to enforced school integration and to the reversal of affirmative action university application processes in the Allan Bakke case. More recently, a 1996 California election resulted in the acceptance of Proposition 209, a measure that overturned affirmative action programs in that state.

Race relations have also been made more complex by a growing awareness of multiculturalism, a term coined during the last decade in response to vocal African-American, Hispanic, and Asian political pressure groups. This expression of racial, ethnic, national, and cultural awareness is in reaction to the perceived failure of liberal integrationist visions and to the persistent racist belief that others needed to integrate by conforming to, and accepting, the norm of the majority. (ISM) **See also** African-American Churches; Civil Rights Acts; Colonial America; Culture Wars; Education; Equal Rights Amendment; Louis Eugene Farrakhan; Islam; Ku Klux Klan; Liberalism; Malcolm X; Religious and Urban Issues; Roman Catholicism.

BIBLIOGRAPHY

Gordon, Milton, ed. "America as a Multicultural Society." *The Annals of the American Academy of Political and Social Science,* 454 (March, 1981): 1–205.

Gates, William, ed. *Race and Writing.* Cambridge: Harvard University Press, 1984.

Kelsey, George D. *Racism and Christian Understanding of Man.* New York: Charles Scribner's Sons, 1965.

Massie, Robert Kinloch. *Loosing the Bonds: The United States and South Africa in the Apartheid Years.* New York: Doubleday, 1997.

Myrdal, Gunnar. *The American Dilemma: The Negro Problem and American Democracy.* New York: Harper, 1944.

Osborne, William A. *The Segregated Covenant: Race Relations and American Catholics.* New York: Herder and Herder, 1967.

Schlesinger, Arthur. *The Disuniting of America.* New York: Norton, 1992.

Smith, Shelton H. *In his Image But...* Durham, NC: Duke University Press, 1972.

Takaki, Ronald. *A Different Mirror: A History of Multicultural America.* Boston: Little, Brown, 1993.

Wilson, Julius. *The Declining Significance of Race.* Chicago: University of Chicago Press, 1978.

Walter Rauschenbusch (1861–1918)

Walter Rauschenbusch, a Baptist minister and church history professor in New York, was a major proponent of the **Social Gospel** movement from the late nineteenth century through **World War I**. Rauschenbusch insisted that religion and ethics were inseparable. He believed in the centrality of the Bible and the example of Jesus as the foundation and model of ethical behavior. He criticized **capitalism** and advocated socialist solutions to economic and social problems like unemployment and industrial corruption. With other activists and clergy, he formed the Brotherhood of the Kingdom, which set up day care centers and soup kitchens for the working poor and the homeless in Hell's Kitchen, a notorious section of New York City that bordered his parish. He denounced the opulence of the wealthy, and scorned inherited wealth as a threat to the Protestant work ethic.

He became nationally famous with the publication of *Christianity and the Social Crisis* in 1907. He advocated the establishment of the Kingdom of God on earth, rather than upholding the common Christian belief that God's Kingdom would be heavenly. He articulated a strong doctrine of a kingdom of evil, opposed to God's power. He saw this kingdom of evil at work both in Germany's initiation of world **war** and in American **imperialism**. Despite his support of American action against Germany in World War I, most of his friends and colleagues shunned him because of his German heritage and his advocacy of Christian socialism.

His last book, *A Theology for the Social Gospel* (1917), was an attempt to provide the Social Gospel movement with a theological justification for social action. His work serves as a precursor to the **liberation theology** movements of the late twentieth century. (KMY) **See also** Baptists; Labor; Socialism and Communism.

BIBLIOGRAPHY

Minus, Paul M. *Walter Rauschenbusch: American Reformer.* New York: Macmillan Publishing Company, 1988.

Rauschenbusch, Walter. *A Theology for the Social Gospel.* Nashville: Abingdon, 1981.

Smucker, Donovan E. *The Origins of Walter Rauschenbusch's Social Ethics.* Buffalo: McGill-Queen's University Press, 1994.

John Rawls (1921–)

John Rawls is generally regarded as being among the most important of contemporary political theorists. Rawls' general project has been the justification of political authority among autonomous individuals who may not share substantive conceptions of justice or virtue, a position elaborated in his *A Theory of Justice* (1971). While he has emphasized the importance of fairness and procedure as a source of legitimacy in liberal politics, he has been criticized by communitarians and religious thinkers for failing to include other voices, criticism he has sought to address in later works such as *Political Liberalism* (1993). (TGJ) **See also** Communitarianism; Liberalism; Social Justice.

BIBLIOGRAPHY

Daniels, Norman, ed. *Reading Rawls: Critical Studies on Rawls' "A Theory of Justice."* Stanford: Stanford University Press, 1989.

Rawls, John. *Political Liberalism.* New York: Columbia University Press, 1993.

Rawls, John. *A Theory of Justice.* Cambridge: Harvard University Press, 1971.

Sandel, Michael J. *Liberalism and the Limits of Justice.* New York: Cambridge University Press, 1986.

Ronald Reagan (1911–)

The 40th president of the United States, Ronald Reagan emphasized the important role of faith in public life throughout his public career. Religious conservatives were among his strongest supporters, and he achieved success during the 1980s in large part because he was able to unite religious and economic conservatives under a single banner of limited government and traditional family values.

Religious conservatives strongly supported Republican President Ronald Reagan. Library of Congress.

Reagan regularly cultivated the support of religious groups. He frequently spoke about issues important to religious conservatives such as voluntary **school prayer**, the threat of communism, and **abortion**. His opposition to abortion on demand led him to publish a lengthy essay explaining his views in 1983, *Abortion and the Conscience of the Nation.*

Though he was criticized for having been divorced and for not attending church regularly while in office (for stated reasons of security), his White House aides noted the fact that he sometimes kneeled to pray with visitors in the Oval Office. By his own account, his faith in God deepened when he survived an assassination attempt in 1981 shortly after he took office. (MR) **See also** Conservatism; Religious Right; Socialism and Communism.

Bibliography

D'Souza, Dinesh. *Ronald Reagan: How an Ordinary Man Became an Extraordinary Leader.* New York: Free Press, 1997.

Reagan, Ronald. *Abortion and the Conscience of the Nation.* Nashville: Thomas Nelson Publishers, 1984.

Shepherd, David, ed. *Ronald Reagan: In God I Trust.* Wheaton, IL: Tyndale House Publishers, 1984.

Reconstruction (1865-1877)

Reconstruction, the effort to rebuild the Union after the **Civil War**, went through several iterations based on who held national power. President **Abraham Lincoln** offered to welcome back the secessionist states as early as March 1861 in his first inaugural address. In *A Proclamation of Amnesty*, Lincoln's December 1863 blueprint for accepting the Confederate states back into the Union, he proposed that as soon as 10 percent of the individual state's population took an oath of future loyalty, the state could re-enter the Union. Lincoln's death in April 1865, put Vice President Andrew Johnson in charge of Reconstruction, and southern states were accepted back into the Union by the time Congress reconvened on December 4, 1865.

In January 1866, Congress began its own Reconstruction by throwing out the southern politicians, approving the Freedmen's Bureau in March 1866, and passing the Civil Rights Act of 1866. Reconstruction came to an end with the election of 1876 and the removal of federal troops the following year. (GT) **See also** Civil Rights Acts.

Bibliography

Foner, Eric. *A Short History of Reconstruction, 1863–1877.* New York: Harper & Row, 1990.

McPherson, James. *Ordeal By Fire: The Civil War and Reconstruction.* New York: McGraw-Hill, 1982.

Ralph Reed (1961–)

Ralph Reed's entry into national politics came as an operative of the National College Republican Committee, where he learned the skills of local political organization. Early in life, Reed also demonstrated a propensity for academic pursuits, publishing an essay in a respectable journal of history as a college senior at the University of Georgia. After a number of years as a political activist, Reed experienced a spiritual awakening. He left **Methodism**, the ancestral faith of his family, and turned to an evangelical church. This new faith commitment encouraged Reed to found Students for America, a national student forum. Following his scholarly interests, he entered a doctoral program in history at Emory University. As Reed was completing his dissertation, **Pat Robertson** asked him to become the executive director of the **Christian Coalition**, a grassroots interest group. Under his leadership, the Christian Coalition became an active force in American politics, claiming millions of members and establishing political organizations at the state and local levels. In 1997, Reed resigned as executive director to pursue a new career as a political consultant. See also Evangelicals. (HLC)

Bibliography

Reed, Ralph. *Active Faith.* New York: Free Press, 1996.

——. *Politically Incorrect.* Dallas: Word Publishing, 1994.

Reformation

The Reformation of the sixteenth century was a confluence of people, ideas, and religious reorganization attempting to reform doctrine and practices in Western Christianity. The first great fissure in Christendom occurred in 1054 with the Great Schism, when the Eastern and Western Churches severed relations. The Reformation was the second, fracturing the Western Church. From the Reformation emerged the two branches of Western Christianity—Catholicism and Protestantism, with Protestantism dividing into numerous branches since the 1500s. Also, the Reformation occurred along with other profound transitions in Europe that began shaping the modern world, particularly the Renaissance and the rise of nationalism.

By the beginning of the sixteenth century, Catholicism was rife with corruption in the hierarchy, poor-quality clergy, dubious practices, and doctrinal confusion. Indeed, the Reformation had antecedents in reform-minded men such as John

Wycliffe (1300s) and John Huss (early 1400s). Even after the Reformation began, some Catholics, such as Erasmus, stood for at least moderate reforms.

Two of the major figures of the Reformation were **Martin Luther** and **John Calvin**. The Reformation is often considered as dating from 1517, when Luther nailed his Ninety-five Theses to a church door to urge reform. Major ideas of the Reformation included an emphasis on faith—not good works—as the basis of salvation, and the Bible—not the Church—as the authority for doctrine. Because of differences among Luther, Calvin, and other reformers, and because of the variety of settings, the configuration of the Reformation varied from region to region.

The Reformation consisted of conservative, moderate, and radical wings. Lutherans tended toward more conservative reform, retaining more of Catholic doctrine and practice. Calvinists tended to be more aggressive and bold. Anabaptists went furthest in breaking with Catholicism and forging new theological and ecclesiological directions. The Catholic Church responded with what has been called the Counter-Reformation. It included the Council of Trent, which repudiated Protestant doctrines and clarified Catholic positions and greatly influenced subsequent Catholicism.

In modern times, beginning with the Protestant churches, then between Protestant and Catholic churches, and ultimately including Eastern orthodox churches, much effort has gone into ecumenical initiatives, to understand, reconcile, and even reunite, to the greatest extent possible, the churches of Christianity divided by the Great Schism and the Reformation. (GSS) **See also** Calvinism; Ecumenical Movement; Lutheran Church; Roman Catholicism.

BIBLIOGRAPHY

Bainton, Roland H. *The Reformation of the Sixteenth Century.* Boston: Beacon Press, 1952; enlarged ed., 1985.

Chaunu, Pierre, ed. *The Reformation.* New York: St. Martin's Press, 1990.

Nauert, Charles G., Jr. *The Age of Renaissance and Reformation.* New York: University Press, 1981.

Ozment, Steven. *Protestants: The Birth of a Revolution.* New York: Doubleday, 1992.

William H. Rehnquist (1924–)

William Rehnquist's jurisprudence as both associate justice (1972–1986) and now chief justice (1986–) of the U.S. Supreme Court supports government accommodation of religion and discourages judicially created rights. Justice Rehnquist argues that the religion clause of the **First Amendment**—like all of the U.S. Constitution—must be read in historical context, and that such a reading requires the government to accommodate the religious practices and heritage of the people. Rehnquist therefore supports the constitutionality of moments of silence in public schools, the placement of religious symbols (such as creches and crosses) on public property, equal access for religious groups to public facilities, and allocation of state funds and services to religious individuals and groups for legitimate governmental purposes. At the same time, Justice Rehnquist is opposed to the creation of new rights by judicial caveat. He dissented from the court's opinion in ***Roe v. Wade*** (1973), and wrote the opinion of the court upholding the constitutionality of state laws prohibiting assisted suicide. (RA) **See also** Abortion and Birth Control Regulation; Education; Establishment Clause; Free Speech Approach to Liberty; *Mueller v. Allen*; Public Aid to Religious Organizations; Publicly Funded Religious Displays; School Prayer; Wall of Separation; *Wallace v. Jaffree*; *Zobrest v. Catalina Foothills School District.*

BIBLIOGRAPHY

Davis, Derek. *Original Intent: Chief Justice Rehnquist and the Course of American Church-State Relations.* Buffalo, NY: Prometheus Books, 1991.

Release Time

In 1914, the Gary, Indiana, school system established the first "release time" program. Students were released from their regular classes to attend religious classes conducted in nearby churches or synagogues. To prevent truancy, religious teachers took attendance and reported any absences to school officials. For many, the release time program seemed to be the answer to the often-repeated complaint that the public schools lacked sufficient religious and moral instruction. The apparent success of the Gary plan encouraged educators across the country to adopt similar release time programs. By 1947, nearly two million students in over 2,200 communities were involved in release-time activities.

Champaign, Illinois, adopted the Gary plan in 1940, but authorized religious instruction to be given in the school buildings themselves. Religious classes were taught by either a Catholic priest, a Jewish rabbi, or a Protestant teacher, and pupils who did not attend were sent to another part of the school to pursue some other instructional task or duty.

In ***McCollum v. Board of Education*** (1948), Mrs. **Vashti Cromwell McCollum** challenged Champaign's release time program as a violation of the **Establishment Clause**. When the case reached the U.S. Supreme Court, the justices ruled 8-1 in favor of Mrs. McCollum. Justice **Hugo L. Black**, writing for the majority, declared, "This is beyond all question a utilization of the tax-established and tax-supported public school system to aid religious groups to spread their faith. And it falls squarely under the ban of the **First Amendment**."

A few years later, in ***Zorach v. Clauson*** (1952), a divided Supreme Court distinguished between on-campus and off-campus religious instruction. In *Zorach*, the Court found off-campus programs constitutionally acceptable. Justice Black wrote for the 6-3 majority that, "The First Amendment . . . does not say that in every and all respects there shall be a separation of Church and State. . . .We would have to press the concept of separation of Church and State to . . . extremes to condemn the present law on constitutional grounds." The precedent established in *Zorach* allowing off-campus religious instruction still stands. (ARB) **See also** Education; School Prayer; Wall of Separation.

BIBLIOGRAPHY

Boles, Donald E. *The Bible, Religion, and the Public Schools.* Ames, Iowa: Iowa State University Press, 1965.

Dierenfield, Richard H. *Religion in American Public Schools.* Washington, DC: Public Affairs Press, 1962.

Miller, Robert T. and Ronald B. Flowers. *Toward Benevolent Neutrality: Church, State, and the Supreme Court.* Vol. 1 5th ed. Waco, TX: Markham Press Fund of Baylor University Press, 1996.

Religion and Politics in Film

Some of the earliest American films took religion as their theme. Silent films of the 1910s and 1920s, when they were not pursuing love or humor, sought to recreate Bible stories. As such, Cecil B. DeMille's 1926 *King of Kings* served as a prototype for his later biblical epic, *The Ten Commandments* (1956), and for contemporary films like Franco Zeffirelli's *Jesus of Nazareth.* All these films focus on the humanness of their central characters and the religious transformations of these men. Some of them, for example Martin Scorsese's *The Last Temptation of Christ* (1988), drew protests from Christian **Fundamentalists** because of the interpretive liberties taken with the biblical texts.

In other films, Christ figures or personal transformations call to mind the intersection of religion and politics in nonbiblical stories. John Ford's *The Fugitive* and Alfred Hitchcock's *I Confess* both explore the question of morally motivated self-sacrifice in politically charged contexts. Frank Capra probes the crucifixion/resurrection motif in the class-based suffering and triumph of the James Stewart characters in *Mr. Smith Goes to Washington* and *It's a Wonderful Life*. Class novels like John Steinbeck's *The Grapes of Wrath* and Ernest Hemingway's *The Old Man and the Sea* have been translated into cinemagraphic versions of Jesus-like transformation stories. In both films, the central characters endure and rise above suffering. They shoulder the crosses that life gives them and are transformed in the process.

George Lucas' *Star Wars* trilogy serves as an example of contemporary films that engage the religious through an apocalyptic portrayal of the battle between good and evil. Obi-Wan Kenobi, the wise teacher, holds the Christ figure role against the Prince of Evil, Darth Vader. Han Solo and Luke Skywalker function as classic disciples, and the phrase, "The Force be with you!" resounds as a traditional benediction. Star Wars does not limit itself to Christian symbols only; its use of light imagery and sometimes sympathetic portrayal of Darth Vader trades in Eastern religious philosophy as well.

The religious problem of evil has received much attention in films, especially in the horror genre. William Friedkin's *The Exorcist*, Richard Donner's *The Omen* trilogy, and Roman Polanski's *Rosemary's Baby* play out the challenge of evil against human presumptions of goodness. *The Omen*, released in 1976, explores the theme of the Antichrist as political figure. Less classic portrayals of evil abound in films like Steven Spielberg's *Jaws* and in the natural disaster flicks popular in the 1970s and 1980s.

Science fiction films almost always use religious imagery in their attempts to create a picture of the future. The box office family hit *E.T.*, directed by Steven Spielberg, offers an extra-terrestrial Christ figure who transforms at least one family and points the way to heaven for thousands of moviegoers. Public authorities are portrayed as self-serving and ultimately impotent in the face of a transcendent being. *Close Encounters of the Third Kind* and *2001: A Space Odyssey* play on the religious desire for human transcendence and the hope of becoming omnipotent like God. *The Handmaid's Tale* probes the politics of **theocracy** as a means of critiquing both religion and American notions of gender, power, and authority.

Lengthy and explicit representations of religions other than Christianity are uncommon in American film, although such themes are appearing with greater frequency in the 1990s. *The Chosen*, adapted from a Chaim Potok novel in 1982, explores the conflicts between a conservative Jewish sect, Hasidism, and the Zionist movement of the 1940s. It is a sympathetic portrayal of the religious and political implications of faith and its ethical demands. Barbara Streisand's *Yentl* uses a fantasy tale to highlight the social limitations of Jewish women in 1904 America. *Not Without My Daughter* is a political drama that uses a sensationalized caricature of Islamic fundamentalism as its primary plot device.

While religion is not the primary theme of most contemporary films, many do feature popularly understood images of religion such as backdrop characters in religious attire, church facades, or crosses. These images underscore the **civil religion** that common people identify with American life. Even parodies of religious claims or symbols work in film because of the embeddedness of religion in the American psyche. To describe and make sense of the politics of American communities, films rely on religious metaphor and common civil religious experience. (KMY) **See also** Disciples of Christ; Islam; Judaism; Transcendentalism; Zionism.

BIBLIOGRAPHY

May, John R., and Bird, Michael. *Religion in Film.* Knoxville: The University of Tennessee Press, 1982.

Miles, Margaret R. *Seeing and Believing: Religion and Values in the Movies.* Boston: Beacon Press, 1996.

O'Brien, Tom. *The Screening of America: Movies and Values from "Rocky" to "Rain Man."* New York: Continuum, 1990.

Walsh, Frank. *Sin and Censorship: The Catholic Church and the Motion Picture Industry.* New Haven: Yale University Press, 1996.

Religion and Urban Issues

Cities are not new. Humans have long congregated for sociability, commerce, and other reasons. However, the substantial urbanization of industrial and post-industrial societies is new and fraught with complex issues. A fundamental issue, especially from a religious perspective, is the very meaning of the city. We find ambiguity about cities in **Judaism** and Christianity. The first mention of a city in the Bible occurs when Cain, the slayer of Abel, founds one. Yet later, Jerusalem becomes for Jews the city of hope, "the city of God." For Christianity, the Book of Revelation envisions the new Jerusalem, where God dwells and humans live in perfection.

This ambiguity pervades urbanization and the religious response to it in America. For one thing, the sense of space—wilderness or agricultural—has been foundational to American culture. Thomas Jefferson held forth the vision of agrarian, and thus virtuous, America. The structures of American Protestantism were predominantly small town and rural up to the mid-1800s. These have been powerful, shaping perspectives. Yet urbanization spelled the end of that agrarian and small town vision.

The end began with industrialization, requiring the massing of workers and resources, and transforming America in the time between the **Civil War** and **World War I**. Immigration in the late 1800s and early 1900s rapidly swelled cities. In the last 100 years, the United States has become industrial and urban, then post-industrial but still urban. With urbanization has come major problems, including crime, ethnic and **race relations**, pollution, over-crowding, disparities in wealth, loss of open land, and tensions between community and anonymity. These forces have radically challenged political, social, and religious systems.

The response of religious leaders and communities has been ambivalent. Some have decried urbanization as destructive of American culture, of morals and religion. Some have fled urbanization. In the 1950s and 1960s in particular, many urban churches, with largely white congregations, relocated to suburban areas. Some sought other approaches. The moderately progressive **Social Gospel** movement developed remedial programs and proposed structural reforms. Reformed Judaism urged Jews to seek social justice in industry and city. The Catholic Church organized offices and programs to respond to the cities. Some more radical Protestants and Catholics aligned with socialist aims or became socialists in the late 1800s through the 1930s. While some fled the cities in the 1950s and 1960s, others launched urban ministries and programs. **Harvey Gallagher Cox** published *The Secular City* (1965), in which he wrote of the human-centered city, with its potential for human freedom and maturity through the forces of urbanization and secularization.

The city is in one sense quintessentially human, in that humankind is essentially social. As such, the city intensifies the ills of human existence. Yet the city permits, for example, the fostering of arts, entertainment, and educational resources. In this ambiguity of curse and blessing, the city remains a challenge for people of faith. (GSS) **See also** Education; Roman Catholicism; Secular Humanism; Secularization Thesis; Socialism and Communism.

Bibliography

Ahlstrom, Sydney E. *A Religious History of the American People.* New Haven: Yale University, 1972.

Cox, Harvey. *The Secular City: Secularization and Urbanization in Theological Perspective.* London: SCM Press, 1965.

Pasquariello, Ronald D.; Donald W. Shriver, Jr.; and Alan Geyer. *Redeeming the City: Theology, Politics, and Urban Policy.* New York: Pilgrim Press, 1982.

Green, Constance McLaughlin. *The Rise of Urban America.* New York: Harper & Row, 1965.

Religious Apartheid

A provocative allusion to the South African coercive policy of racial separation, "religious apartheid" is a term that refers to laws and public policies that separate religion and religious expression from public life. The phrase was coined by Douglas Laycock and popularized by John W. Whitehead in the late 1980s. According to Whitehead, "the term describes the increasing hostility of secular concerns toward religious interests. Religion, especially public manifestations of Christianity, is being systematically separated from American society." A critic of strict separation between religion and public life, Whitehead cites the "forced, systematic removal of religious symbols from public places, of Christmas pageants from public schools, of the Ten Commandments from classroom walls as evidence of coercive secularization of public life or religious apartheid." A similarly pejorative term, borrowed from "ethnic cleansing," is "religious cleansing." Keith A. Fournier has used the term "to describe the current hostility and bigotry toward religion and people of faith that are leading to covert and overt attempts to remove any religious influences from the public arena." (DLD) **See also** Establishment Clause; First Amendment; Public Aid of Religious Organizations; Publicly Funded Religious Displays; School Prayer; Secular Humanism; Secularization Thesis; Wall of Separation.

Bibliography

Fournier, Keith A. *Religious Cleansing in the American Republic.* Nashville, TN: Thomas Nelson, 1993.

Whitehead, John W. "Avoiding Religious Apartheid: Affording Equal Treatment for Student-Initiated Religious Expression in Public Schools." *Pepperdine Law Review.* 16 (1989): 229–58.

Whitehead, John W. *Religious Apartheid: The Separation of Religion from American Public Life.* Chicago: Moody Press, 1994.

Religious Freedom Restoration Act (1993–1997)

In an effort to supplant the Supreme Court's decision, ***Employment Division of Oregon v. Smith*** (1990), Congress passed the Religious Freedom Restoration Act (RFRA). On November 16, 1993, President **Bill Clinton** signed RFRA into law. Specifically, RFRA dictated that government shall not substantially burden a person's exercise of religion even if the burden results from a rule of general applicability, unless the government demonstrates that application of the burden to the person furthers a compelling government interest and is the least restrictive means of furthering that compelling government interest.

Proponents of the RFRA argued that by the act Congress asserted its obligation to protect individual liberties and declared that religious freedom is a substantive liberty. The effect of RFRA, they claimed, was to reinstitute, as a matter of statutory law, the tests articulated in *Sherbert v. Verner* (1963) and

Wisconsin v. Yoder (1972). Thus, they held that religious liberty is not simply a recapitulation of the freedom of speech. Regulations that impacted upon sincerely held religious beliefs faced a heightened level of scrutiny by the judiciary. Further, RFRA required government to demonstrate an actuality rather than a potential harm before it could regulate religious people. Finally, the government had to prove that there was no less drastic means of accomplishing its goals.

Some critics of the RFRA argued that it could not provide balance in cases pitting the **Free Exercise Clause** against the **Establishment Clause**, and questioned how extensively RFRA could shield free exercise claims from the will of the majority, as articulated through the criminal law. Others insisted that the judiciary could effectively undermine the legislation by simply defining "compelling interest" very broadly. A number of scholars argued that RFRA was an unconstitutional exercise of congressional authority. One practical consequence of RFRA was that it paved the way for prisoners to assert what seemed to the public to be outrageous demands including special gourmet meals, frequent conjugal visits, and guns and knives for their worship services.

Whether over time RFRA would have fulfilled its promise—or would have been largely ineffective—is no longer relevant. In ***City of Boerne v. Flores*** (1997), the U.S. Supreme Court struck down RFRA. Justice **Anthony M. Kennedy** argued that Congress passed RFRA in direct response to the *Smith* decision under the guise of protecting the **Fourteenth Amendment**. However, he noted that any such legislation must be remedial or preventative in nature. The Court maintained that section five of the Fourteenth Amendment was never designed to permit Congress to amplify or redefine constitutional rights. (FG) **See also** Free Speech Approach to Religious Liberty; Prison Fellowship; Prisoners, Religious Rights of.

BIBLIOGRAPHY

Berg, Thomas. "What Hath Congress Wrought? An Interpretive Guide to the Religious Freedom Restoration Act." *Villanova Law Review.* 39 no. 1 (1994).

Bybee, Jay. "Taking Liberties With the First Amendment: Congress, Section 5, and the Religious Freedom Restoration Act." *Vanderbilt Law Review.* 48 no. 1539 (1995).

Conkle, Daniel. "The Religious Freedom Restoration Act: The Constitutional Significance of an Unconstitutional Statute." *Montana Law Review.* 56 no. 39 (1995).

Eisgruber, Christopher and Lawrence Sager. "Why the Religious Freedom Restoration Act is Unconstitutional." *NYU Law Review.* 69 no. 437 (1994).

Gressman, Eugene and Angela Carmella. "The RFRA Revision of the Free Exercise Clause." *Ohio State Law Journal.* 57 no. 65 (1996).

Hamilton, Marci. "The Religious Freedom Restoration Act: Letting the Fox into the Henhouse Under Cover of Section 5 of the Fourteenth Amendment." *Cardozo Law Review.* 16 no. 357 (1994).

Idleman, Scott. "The Religious Freedom Restoration Act: Pushing the Limits of Legislative Power." *Texas Law Review.* 73 no. 247 (1994).

Laycock, Douglas. "Free Exercise and the Religious Freedom Restoration Act." *Fordham Law Review.* 62 no. 883 (1994).

_______. "RFRA, Congress, and the Ratchet." *Montana Law Review.* 56 no. 145 (1995).

Robin-Vergeer, Bonnie. "Disposing of the Red Herrings: A Defense of the Religious Freedom Restoration Act." *Southern California Law Review.* 69 no. 589 (1996).

Whitehead, John and Alexis Crow. "The Religious Freedom Restoration Act: Implications for Religiously-Based Civil Disobedience and Free Exercise Claims." *Washburn Law Review.* 33 no. 383 (1994).

Religious Right

The Religious Right refers to Christian conservatives who have become involved in the American political process. The phenomenon is not new. Evangelical activism occurred in the 1920s in opposition to alcohol, Catholicism, and the teaching of evolution. During the Cold War era of the 1950s and 1960s, conservative Christian organizations such as **Billy James Hargis**'s Christian Crusade and **Carl McIntire**'s Twentieth-Century Reformation Hour led anti-communist crusades. The most recent revival of the Religious Right began in the late 1970s. These religious conservatives have worked through a variety of organizations and extensively used new technology, such as direct mail and cable television, to communicate with their supporters and sympathizers. The groups have generally aligned themselves with the conservative wing of the **Republican Party** and have focused on issues such as anti-communism, conservative economic reforms; opposition to abortion, homosexuality; and **pornography**; and support for **school prayer**.

The first organization to appear was Christian Voice, which was created by Robert Grant and Richard Zone in 1979. This group was a merger of several preexisting anti-gay, anti-pornography, and pro-family groups on the west coast. By the mid-1980s the organization had a mailing list of 150,000 laymen and 37,000 ministers including 3,000 Catholic priests. While the group claimed to have membership from 37 denominations, most came from independent Baptist, Bible, and Assembly of God churches in the Southwest and West. The approach used by Christian Voice was to set up a lobbying organization in Washington, DC, to try to influence national policy.

The best known organization was **Moral Majority**, which was founded by Lynchburg, Virginia, minister **Jerry Falwell** in July, 1979. Falwell used the computer list of the "Old Time Gospel Hour" donors to raise money and traveled throughout the United States holding "I Love America" rallies. The Moral Majority operated in a decentralized manner and focused on local issues and getting **Fundamentalists** registered to vote. It was concentrated in 18 states, generally in the South and Southwest. Membership was approximately 300,000 in the mid-1980s and consisted primarily of ministers and laymen from independent Baptist churches and small fundamentalist sects. In 1986 Falwell changed the name of the group to the Liberty Federation and in 1989 he abolished it after spending an estimated $69 million on the organization.

A third major Christian right organization was Religious Roundtable. This was created by Ed McAteer, a Southern Baptist and field organizer for the conservative caucus. This group was designed to appeal to mainline Southern Baptist, Presbyterian, and Methodist ministers who did not feel comfortable with either the Christian Voice or the Moral Majority. It was primarily a forum for political discussion and education using a variety of conservative figures. It also sponsored workshops throughout the United States instructing ministers on mobilization of their congregations on behalf of conservative candidates and causes.

In October 1989, television Evangelist **Pat Robertson** created the **Christian Coalition**. This organization became involved in a variety of activities designed to get conservative activists involved in politics. It also distributed millions of voter guides through churches prior to major elections. The Christian Coalition also worked through the Republican Party and became the dominant Christian right group in the 1990s. In the mid-1990s it had a membership of 1,700,000 and a budget of $26,400,000.

In assessing the Religious Right, it is important to understand that it is a social movement that stems from a set of religious and political beliefs and values. Its involvement in politics has been cyclical and its approach to politics has focused on protest, personalism, as well as pluralism. Most writers agree that the Religious Right's major shortcoming has been its inability to plan a long-term strategy, which has resulted in its periodic decline in involvement and influence in politics. (WVM) **See also** Abortion and Birth Control Regulation; Americanism; Assemblies of God; Baptists; Conservatism; Homosexual Rights; Methodism; Presbyterian Church; Roman Catholicism; Socialism and Communism.

BIBLIOGRAPHY

Lienesch, Michael. *Piety and Politics in the New Christian Right.* Chapel Hill: University of North Carolina Press, 1993.

Wilcox, Clyde. *God's Warriors: The Christian Right in 20th Century America.* Baltimore: Johns Hopkins University Press, 1992.

Religious Tests and Oaths

Requiring oaths affirming belief in religious doctrine or allegiance to a particular church as a prerequisite to holding public office, voting, or exercising other civic duties has long been an instrument for preserving the political power of established churches and denying equal opportunity to religious dissenters. Religious test oaths were common in English law and were incorporated into American colonial charters and practices. Departing from this tradition, Article VI, clause 3 of the U.S. Constitution of 1787 provided that "no religious Test shall ever be required as a Qualification to any Office or public Trust under the United States." This provision followed language instructing all state and federal officeholders to take an oath or affirmation to support the Constitution. The constitutional framers believed the religious test ban would prevent any plausible prospect of a national religious establishment by removing a mechanism by which a religious sect could dominate the political process.

Religious test oaths were included in many state constitutions and laws in the founding era. State laws, however, were not always free of ambiguity. For example, the Tennessee Constitution of 1796 included the language of the Article VI test ban; however, the same constitution provided that "[n]o person who denies the being of God, or a future state of rewards and punishments, shall hold office in the civil department of this State." Adopting a standard definition of oaths, the Kentucky Constitution of 1792, which omitted an express religious test but prescribed a basic oath of office, state that required oaths and affirmations "shall be esteemed by the legislature [as] the most solemn appeal to God." This late-eighteenth-century understanding of oaths, which was widely embraced in the founding era, suggests that the U.S. Constitution was not entirely devoid of religious affirmations and did not create a wholly secular polity. The argument was made in state ratifying conventions that the several oath clauses in the U.S. Constitution implicitly countenanced an acknowledgment of God (which, in a sense, constituted a general, nondenominational religious "test"), while the Article VI test ban proscribed sect-specific oaths for federal officeholders.

Anti-federalist critics of the U.S. Constitution complained that the Article VI test ban, coupled with the Constitution's lack of explicit Christian designation, indicated, at best, indifference or, at worst, hostility toward the Christian religion. Modern commentators have typically viewed Article VI as the cornerstone of a secular, nonreligious civil policy. In reality, the religious test ban (applicable to federal office holders only) was not driven by a general renunciation of religious tests as a matter of principle. Religious tests actually accorded with popular wishes, a fact confirmed by their inclusion in many revolutionary era state constitutions. Significantly, religious liberty and nonestablishment provisions coexisted with religious tests in numerous state constitutions written between 1776 and 1787. This suggests that the founding generation did not consider these concepts incompatible. Also, some delegates at the Constitutional Convention who endorsed the federal test ban had previously participated in framing religious tests in their respective state constitutions. The framers believed, as a matter of federalism, that the U.S. Constitution denied the national government all jurisdiction over religion, including the authority to administer religious tests. Many in the founding generation supported a federal test ban because they valued religious tests required under state laws, and they feared that a federal test might displace existing state test oaths and religious establishments. It was thus generally understood that Article VI deferred to the states when it came to framing and implementing religious test oaths. As a political matter, it is doubtful the state ratifying conventions would have approved any provision in the proposed U.S. Constitution that nullified existing tests and establishments under state laws.

While many state constitutions written after 1787 followed the federal model, others retained religious tests well into the nineteenth and twentieth centuries. In ***Torcaso v. Watkins* (1961)**, the U.S. Supreme Court ruled that a Maryland requirement that public officials affirm belief in the existence of God violated the **First Amendment.** (DLD) **See also** Civil Rights; Colonial America; Establishment Clause; Wall of Separation.

BIBLIOGRAPHY

Dreisbach, Daniel L. "The Constitution's Forgotten Religion Clause: Reflections on the Article VI Religious Test Ban." *Journal of Church and State.* 38 (1996): 261–95.

Reorganized Church of Jesus Christ of Latter-day Saints. See Church of Jesus Christ of Latter-day Saints.

Republican Party

The Republican Party was founded in the 1850s by opponents to the expansion of **slavery**, who were outraged by the Kansas-Nebraska Act. The Republican Party eclipsed the declining Whig Party, which had enjoyed the support of native Protestants, many of whom had moved to support the **Know-Nothing Party**, or American Party, which wanted to restrict the influx of Catholic immigrants. The Know-Nothings also favored free public schools and the prohibition of liquor. The Know-Nothings were divided over the issue of slavery, and many of them gravitated to the newly emergent Republican Party. The Republican Party issues of **abolition** and prohibition reflected the values of moralistic Protestantism of this period. In 1856, the Republican Party nominated John C. Fremont, who was the new party's first presidential nominee. Fremont lost that election to Democrat James Buchanan.

In 1860, the Republicans defeated the divided Democrats with their nominee from Illinois, **Abraham Lincoln.** The Republicans broadened their appeal in 1860, and also won both houses of Congress. Nevertheless, Lincoln received only 40 percent of the vote in that election. The election of the Republicans caused the southern states to secede from the Union, which ignited the **Civil War**.

For decades after the Civil War, the Republican Party—also known as the "Grand Old Party" or "GOP"—enjoyed the electoral support of the North and the enmity of the South. At the end of the nineteenth century, the party, under the leadership of President **William McKinley**, became a promoter of protectionism for the emerging industries in the North.

The Republican Party lost its preeminent position with the onset of the Great Depression. The role of majority party was taken by the New Deal Democrats under the leadership of Franklin D. Roosevelt.

After **World War II**, the GOP reemerged as a presidential party, capturing the White House in the 1950s with General **Dwight D. Eisenhower**; in the 1970s, with **Richard Nixon**; and in the 1980s, with **Ronald Reagan** and George Bush. The party made very few gains in the national legislature during this period.

The party of Lincoln became divided over **Civil Rights**. In 1964, the party's presidential nominee, Barry Goldwater, had voted against the Civil Rights bills, and the Republican Party began to make inroads into the South. This sectoral realignment of the South was not complete until the 1990s.

The post-war presidential victories were partially based on the strong anti-communist views of the party, which was religious in the sense that communism was equated with **atheism**. Richard Nixon epitomized the post-war Republican Party. Nixon gained prominence by pursuing the Alger Hiss espionage case, and casting his Democratic opponents as soft on communism. In the 1980s, President Ronald Reagan is credited with contributing to the collapse of the Soviet Union by promoting heavy defense spending in the United States, which forced the Soviet Union to keep pace, straining its economy.

With the election of Ronald Reagan, who enjoyed the support of the newly mobilized evangelical Protestant coalition and their political organizations, such as the **Moral Majority**, the Republican Party began to focus on wedge social issues such as **abortion**. Abortion has been a symbolic issue of the modern Republican Party. It has been used as a litmus test to determine the outcome of Republican primaries. The language of the 1996 Republican National Convention platform, like past platforms, supported a constitutional amendment that would outlaw abortion in all circumstances. In 1996, GOP presidential nominee Bob Dole wanted to insert language providing tolerance on the abortion issue, but that was rejected by the conservative delegates at the Republican National Convention. Abortion symbolized the concern by church members with the breakdown of the two-parent family, growing sexual promiscuity, illegitimacy, and many other moral social ills in late-twentieth-century America. The Republicans have been ardent proponents of "family values."

In recent years, several issues have topped the agenda of the Republicans. In 1996 a great deal of attention was given to illegal immigration and the 1996 Republican platform opposed public **welfare** benefits to illegal aliens. Affirmative action had been promoted in the federal government by the Nixon administration. The Republicans, in their 1996 platform, expressed support for Proposition 209, the California Civil Rights Initiative. This ballot initiative, which passed, effectively eliminated affirmative action in California.

In dealing with crime, the Republicans have advocated harsh penalties for law breakers, and in the 1996 platform they focused on juveniles, calling for adult trials for juveniles who commit adult crimes. The Republicans long enjoyed an advantage with voters on the crime issue.

The Republicans also oppose federal involvement in the field of **education**. In their 1996 platform, they once again pledged to abolish the Department of Education and asserted that they would return control of education to parents, teachers, local school boards, and local communities. Republicans generally favor market solutions to problems. They favor vouchers, charter schools, and **home schooling**. Republicans are concerned about, and oppose, excessive federal control over curriculum in public schools.

The Republicans favor voluntary prayer in school and have promoted the idea of a constitutional amendment allowing it.

The GOP has long been the party of limited government and deregulation of the economy and a promoter of unfettered **capitalism** and a balanced budget.

Additionally, the Republican Party gave up its nineteenth-century protectionist stance long ago, and it has held to a free-trade doctrine in recent decades. In its 1996 platform, the GOP called for free and fair trade. There are a few Republicans, such as **Patrick Buchanan**, who continue to advocate protectionism, but his views on trade are held by a minority in the current make-up of the Republican Party. Clinton was able to pass the North American Free Trade Agreement with Republican votes in Congress.

The Republicans became the majority party in Congress in the stunning general election of 1994. Fifty-two new Republican members of Congress were elected. This was the first time the Republicans took majority in the House since 1952. The Republicans held their majorities in the House and the Senate in the 1996 election. This was the first time a Republican majority was reelected to the House since the 1920s. The architect of this surprising development was Newt Gingrich of Georgia, who became the Speaker. The switch to the Republicans in the South and especially the political activity of the **Religious Right** contributed significantly to these new majorities in Congress. In the 1994 election, the Republicans put forward their Contract with America, which was a national platform articulating a list of policy proposals. They offered a list of ten bills and three resolutions, positions that they promised to vote on. They focused on the line item veto, welfare reform, a balanced budget amendment, a crime bill, tax reform, and deregulation. A number of these provisions were adopted and all of them were voted on, which was a promise of the Contract. The Republicans effectively redefined the national agenda in 1994.

There has been tension in the party between religious, social conservatives and economic conservatives. The former promote religious-based views designed to restrain and discourage social behavior such as abortion. The latter often hold a more libertarian position on government and do not favor restricting social behavior.

Political scientists are divided on whether the success of the Republicans in the late twentieth century constitutes a true realignment. Certainly, there has been a realignment in the South. The Republicans have enjoyed tremendous electoral success in the 1980s and 1990s. The political activism of fundamentalist, evangelical Christians has played a major role in the electoral success of the Republicans, and they have reshaped the party. (WB) **See also** Abortion and Birth Control Regulation; Christian Coalition; Civil Rights Acts; Conservatism; Democratic Party; Evangelicals; Fundamentalists; School Prayer; Socialism and Communism; Temperance and Prohibition.

BIBLIOGRAPHY

Gienapp, William E. *The Origins of the Republican Party, 1852–1856.* New York: Oxford University Press, 1987.

Maisel, Louis and Joseph Cooper, eds. *Political Parties: Development and Decay.* Beverly Hills, CA: Sage, 1978.

Mayer, George H. *The Republican Party: 1854–1964.* New York: Oxford University Press, 1964.

Wald, Kenneth. *Religion and Politics in the United States.* Washington, DC: CQ Press, 1997.

Wilcox, Clyde. *God's Warriors.* Baltimore: Johns Hopkins University Press, 1992.

Reynolds v. United States (1878)

In *Reynolds v. United States*, 98 U.S. 145 (1878), the U.S. Supreme Court first announced the distinction that the **First Amendment**'s **Free Exercise Clause** protects beliefs, not behaviors. The 1878 case involved a Mormon named George Reynolds who was convicted of **polygamy** under an act passed by Congress regulating the Utah Territory. Reynolds argued that because his practice was based on his religious convictions, the law was unconstitutional. However, the Court decided that the law was constitutional because it had been passed with a compelling interest.

According to the Court, the First Amendment meant that "Congress was deprived of all legislative power over mere opinion, but was left free to reach actions which were in violation of social duties or subversive of good order." In effect, the Court upheld the position that the majority may limit the exercise of individual rights if there was a compelling state interest involved. To have decided otherwise, the Court argued, would have been to make "professed doctrines of religious beliefs superior to the law of the land, and in effect to permit every citizen to become a law unto himself. Government could exist only in name under such circumstances." While the Court in much of the twentieth century chipped away at the idea of compelling state interest, it has returned to it in the 1990s with its decisions in ***Employment Division of Oregon v. Smith*** (1990) and ***City of Boerne v. Flores*** (1997).

BIBLIOGRAPHY

Stronks, Julia K. "The Court's Definition of Religious Activity," *Religion, Public Life, and the American Polity.* Edited by Louis E. Lugo. Knoxville: University of Tennessee Press, 1994.

Rhode Island Colony

Rhode Island was one of the 13 original colonies and one of the most liberal in terms of religious toleration. An English clergyman, **Roger Williams**, founded the colony of Rhode Island and Providence Plantations in 1636 after he had been banished from the **Massachusetts Bay Colony** for advocating rigid separatism, or the disassociation of church and state. In Massachusetts, **Puritans** had established a **theocracy**, a government in which religious leaders claimed divine guidance and not all religious groups were granted religious freedom. Dissenters, such as Roger Williams and **Anne Hutchinson**, were required to leave the Massachusetts Bay Colony.

Williams selected the name Providence in gratitude for "God's merciful providence" since the Narragansett Indians granted him title to the site. Under Williams' direction, the colony became a refuge where all could come and worship as they pleased without interference from the government of the colony. In 1838, when Anne Hutchinson was banned from the Massachusetts Bay Colony, she started Pocasselt, now Portsmouth, where she preached that each person should follow their own inner light and not depend on ministers for their salvation. With its liberal views on religion, the Rhode Island Colony also had the first Baptist church, the first Jewish synagogue, and one of the first Quaker meeting houses in the New World.

Roger Williams also argued against the forced conversion of the Indians to Christianity because he believed forced conversion violated Christian principles. He referred to it as Anti-Christian Conversion. Williams also advocated that the European settlers respect the land claims of Native Americans and live and trade with them as neighbors.

Under the direction and leadership of Roger Williams, the Rhode Island Colony became the first genuine **democracy** and the first church-divorced and conscience-free colony in the New World. (WVM) **See also** Baptists; Colonial America; Establishment Clause; First Amendment; Judaism; Liberalism; Native American Religions; Quakers; Wall of Separation.

Bibliography

Gaustad, Edwin S. *Liberty of Conscience: Roger Williams in America.* Grand Rapids: W. B. Eerdmans Publishing.

Gabriel Richard (1767–1832)

French-born and ordained a Sulpician priest, Gabriel Richard fled the **French Revolution** in 1792 and came to the United States where Bishop **John Carroll** assigned him to frontier mission work in the Northwest Territory. In 1798 he was sent to Detroit where he became a pastor, publisher, and reformer. As a minister in the territory, he balanced a number of competing interests including those of the native populations and French traders. He opened both an elementary school and an academy for young ladies to train teachers. Taken prisoner in the War of 1812 by British forces, his release was secured by Tecumseh. In 1817 he was one of 10 founders of the University of Michigan. In 1822 he became the first priest elected to the U.S. House of Representatives from Michigan Territory, where he served from 1823 to 1825. Defeated for re-election in 1824, he returned to Detroit and continued his work on behalf of the church in civic and ecclesiastical offices. (MWP) **See also** Missionaries; Native American Religions.

Bibliography

Elliot, Richard R. *Sketch of the Life and Times of Rev. Gabriel Richard of Detroit, Michigan.* Philadelphia, 1899.

Dargellis, Stanley M. *Father Gabriel Richard.* Detroit, MI: Wayne State University Press, 1950.

Jacob Riis (1849–1914)

In *How the Other Half Lives*, Danish-born photojournalist and social reformer Jacob Riis documented the appalling conditions of late-nineteenth-century immigrants living in New York City's slums. A progressive and advocate of the **Social Gospel**, Riis believed practical Christianity meant seeking justice for the poor. Riis was active in progressive politics both nationally and in New York State. In 1912, he campaigned for **Theodore Roosevelt** whom he had known and campaigned for when Roosevelt was running for governor of New York. Riis, like **Jane Addams**, believed that human goodness could be achieved by all if a healthy environment could be created by the powerful force of government. (JSF) **See also** Secular Humanism; Social Justice.

Bibliography

Lane, James B. *Jacob A. Riis and the American City.* Port Washington, NY: Kennikat Press, 1974.

Riis, Jacob A. *How the Other Half Lives: Studies Among the Tenements of New York.* New York: Charles Scribner's Sons, 1890.

Pat Robertson (1930–)

Pat Robertson has been a leading figure for the **Religious Right** in the United States in the 1990s. Marion Gordon "Pat" Robertson was born March 22, 1930, in Lexington, Virginia. His father, A. Willis Robertson, served in the United States House of Representatives and the United States Senate for 30 years. Robertson graduated from Washington and Lee University in 1946, Yale University Law School in 1955, and received a master's degree from New York Theological Seminary in 1959. In 1961 he was ordained a Southern Baptist minister.

In 1959 Robertson bought a bankrupt UHF television station in Portsmouth, Virginia, and two years later started the Christian Broadcasting Network. By the mid-1990s, CBN's programs were broadcast throughout the United States and in 90 foreign countries. Its flagship program, the "700 Club," is hosted by Robertson and has been on the air continuously since 1966.

Robertson also created Regent University, a Christian conservative institution, and the American Center for Law and Justice, a Christian conservative public interest law firm and educational association. Following his unsuccessful attempt to win the **Republican Party**'s presidential nomination in 1988, Robertson started the **Christian Coalition**. In the 1990s the Christian Coalition became the dominant Christian Right organization in the United States. The organization established a sophisticated political operation at its Chesapeake, Virginia, headquarters and by the mid-1990s it claimed a membership of 1,700,000. While claiming to be nonpartisan, the Christian Coalition became a significant force within the Republican Party as Coalition members became active in Republican Party politics throughout the United States and Pat Robertson became the acknowledged leader of the Christian Right. (WVM) **See also** Baptists; Conservatism; Moral Majority; Televangelism.

Bibliography

Rozell, Mark J. and Clyde Wilcox. *God at the Grassroots.* Lanham, MD: Rowman and Littlefield, 1995.

Wilcox, Clyde. *Onward Christian Soldiers? The Religious Right in American Politics.* Boulder: Westview, 1996.

Roe v. Wade (1973)

In *Roe v. Wade*, 410 U.S. 113 (1973), the U.S. Supreme Court asserted that a woman has a fundamental right to terminate pregnancy by **abortion**. A highly controversial decision by the **Warren E. Burger** Court (1969–1986), it lifted widely practiced limits on abortion previously defined in the laws of the states. The 7-2 opinion of the court was written by Justice **Harry Andrew Blackmun**. Jane Roe (a fictitious name to protect her privacy) was an unmarried woman prevented from choosing abortion by Texas law, which only permitted abortion to save the life of the mother.

The Court found the Texas law unconstitutional for violating the woman's right to privacy, as protected by the Due Process Clause of the **Fourteenth Amendment**. However, states could have some capacity to regulate abortion. The Court distinguished three trimesters, or periods, of a pregnancy. In the first, her right to terminate is fundamental and protected. In the second, with risks to a woman's health increased, states may regulate to protect her. In the third, the state has a compelling interest to protect an unborn, except when necessary to preserve "the life or health of the mother." The opinion was criticized in dissents by Justices White and **William H. Rehnquist** for finding a right not specified in the Constitution and applying it to laws like those in force when the Fourteenth Amendment was enacted.

The decision brought about an increase in abortions as well as the beginning of a vigorous "right to life" movement. Subsequent cases have upheld restrictions on choice: Congress may prohibit Medicaid funds for non-therapeutic abortions, and states need not fund abortions for indigent women. Later, the Court approved additional state restrictions on the practice, but upheld early pregnancy abortions in ***Planned Parenthood of Southeastern Pennsylvania v. Casey***, 505 U.S. 833 (1992). (JRV)

Bibliography

Faux, Marian. *Roe v. Wade: The Untold Story of the Landmark Supreme Court Decision that Made Abortion Legal.* New York: Macmillan, 1988.

_______. *A Documentary History of the Legal Aspects of Abortion in the United States: Roe v. Wade.* Littleton, CO: F. B. Rothman, 1993.

_______. *Origins and Scope of Roe v. Wade: Hearing Before the Subcommittee on the Constitution of the Committee on the Judiciary, House of Representatives, 104 Congress. 2nd Session.* Washington, DC: U.S. Government Printing Office, 1996.

Roemer v. Maryland Public Works Board (1976)

A Maryland statute authorized the payment of an annual fiscal year subsidy to qualifying colleges and universities based upon the number of students. The statute prohibited subsidies to schools that awarded only seminarian or theological degrees and excluded—for purposes of calculating the amount of the subsidy—students in seminarian or theological academic programs. Maryland citizens and taxpayers challenged the statutory scheme as a violation of the **Establishment Clause** of the **First Amendment**. In *Roemer v. Maryland Public Works Board*, 426 U.S. 736 (1976), the U.S. Supreme Court upheld the law, asserting that the aid was narrowly drawn to avoid advancing religion and therefore did not violate the Constitution. (JM) **See also** Education; Public Aid to Religious Organizations; Wall of Separation.

Bibliography

Bryson, Joseph E. *The Supreme Court and Public Funds for Religious Schools.* Jefferson, NC: McFarland, 1990.

Roman Catholicism

The term "Roman Catholicism" refers to the Christian church headed by the pope, the bishop of Rome. The sixteenth-century **Reformation** split the church, creating many Protestant Christian denominations that rejected the authority of the pope, as well as various other Catholic doctrines and practices. By the seventeenth century, the Anglican Church, the established church in England, was Protestant, and the civil and religious rights of English Catholics had been restricted by law. As a result, only one English colony, Maryland, established in 1634, allowed Catholics freedom of worship. Several Maryland Catholics signed the **Declaration of Independence** and the Constitution in the eighteenth century. With immigration and natural increase in the nineteenth and twentieth centuries, Catholics became about quarter of the American population.

The American Constitution and Bill of Rights provided freedom of religion for all citizens of the country, including Catholics. This freedom represented something unusual in the history of relations between Christians and politics. The Constitution proposed that religion and politics, by understanding their own proper missions, could exist side by side and be helpful to one another. Although American Catholics were often subject to various sorts of prejudice or persecution, such as nineteenth-century nativist attacks on Catholic immigrants and the **Ku Klux Klan**'s oppostion to blacks, Jews, and Catholics in the early twentieth century, Catholicism generally prospered in the United States.

Catholics have actively participated in the American political system by voting for public officials at all levels of government, by serving in the armed forces and various civil bureaucracies, and by participating in all sectors of the economy. Catholics have also run for and held all manner of public offices. When **Alfred E. Smith**, a Catholic, ran for the presidency in 1928, Protestant fears that his victory would mean handing the American government over to the pope helped bring about Smith's defeat. When another Catholic, **John Fitzgerald Kennedy**, ran successfully for the presidency in 1960, his Catholicism was still a political issue, but not nearly the liability it had been for Smith three decades earlier.

Today a candidate's Catholicism is of little political significance except as it may shape his or her stance on a number of controversial social issues, such as abortion, birth control, and **capital punishment**. While not all politically active American Catholics adhere rigidly to the Church's positions, the Church itself has spoken out on numerous contentious issues. For instance, the American Catholic bishops were among the first groups to speak against the Supreme Court's ***Roe v. Wade*** (1973) decision guaranteeing abortion rights.(JVS) **See also** Abortion and Birth Control; Anti-Catholicism; Anti-Semitism; Colonial America; Judaism; National Conference of Catholic Bishops; Nativism; Vatican I; Vatican II; Vatican, Diplomatic Relations with.

BIBLIOGRAPHY

Dolan, Jay P. *The American Catholic Experience*. Notre Dame, IN: University of Notre Dame Press, 1992.

Ferguson, Thomas P. *Catholic and American*. Kansas City: Sheed and Ward, 1993.

Hennesey, James. *American Catholics*. New York: Oxford University Press, 1981.

Theodore Roosevelt (1858–1919)

Theodore Roosevelt was the 26th president of the United States (1901–1909). Elected to the New York Assembly at the age of 23, he also served six years on the federal Civil Service Commission during the administration of Benjamin Harrison. In 1895 he became the police commissioner of New York City. In 1898, he resigned his post as assistant secretary of the Navy in the McKinley administration to form an all-volunteer cavalry troop named the Rough Riders. Recognized for his exceptional courage in Cuba during the **Spanish-American War** (1898), Roosevelt was elected governor of New York in 1898. Roosevelt was a firm adherant to the nation of **manifest destiny**, an expansionist policy that argued the United States should extend its power and influence to bring Christian civilization to other areas of the world. At the Republican Convention of 1900, Roosevelt was chosen as **William McKinley**'s running mate, becoming president when McKinley was assassinated in 1901. Roosevelt was elected president in his own right in 1904. He promoted active social programs and attempted to break up large business trusts. An environmentalist, Roosevelt was responsible for preserving many of the nation's natural treasures through the national park system.

Roosevelt used the authority of the presidency as, in his words, a "Bully Pulpit," an instrument to persuade the country to needed action and to advance his vision of the United States. He would often make use of his bully pulpit to make moral judgments. A devout member of the Dutch Reformed Church, Roosevelt believed that the religious convictions of one man could make a difference. A boisterous hymn singer, Theodore Roosevelt would gather friends at the White House on Sunday evenings for singing. In 1906, he won the Nobel Prize for Peace for his efforts at resolving the Russo-Japanese War. Roosevelt stumbled into a religious controversy in 1905 when noted American sculptor Augustus Sant-Garders designed a new penny and 10- and 20-dollar bills without the words "**In God We Trust**." The controversy resulted in a bill passed in 1908 that restored the motto.

He did not seek re-election in 1908 and grew unhappy with the Republican administration of his hand-picked successor William H. Taft. In 1912, he launched his own third party, the Bull Moose Party, which split the Republican vote and led to the election of Democrat **Woodrow Wilson**. (WB) **See also** Democratic Party; Republican Party.

BIBLIOGRAPHY

Gould, Lewis L. *The Presidency of Theodore Roosevelt.* Lawrence: University Press of Kansas, 1991.

Harbaugh, W. H. *The Life and Times of Theodore Roosevelt.* New York: Collier, 1966.

Rosenberger v. Rector and Visitors of the University of Virginia (1995)

A University of Virginia student organization was denied university funding for its publication, despite the fact that the university funded the activities and publications of a large number of other student organizations out of student activity fees. The university claimed that the refusal was due to the religious nature of the publication in question and that to fund it would represent unconstitutional state support and endorsement of religion.

In *Rosenberger v. Rector and Visitors of the University of Virginia*, 515 U.S. 819 (1995), the U.S. Supreme Court noted that by funding student organizations the university had created a public forum. Once a governmental agency creates such a forum, it can only restrict access for compelling reasons, and the beliefs of the organization cannot constitute such a reason. Since the Constitution requires neutrality towards religious expression, not hostility, to permit the government to decide which viewpoints it will fund and which it will not represents an unconstitutional form of **censorship**. Therefore, once the university funded one viewpoint, it was required to fund all viewpoints, including religious ones. (FHJ) **See also** Education; Establishment Clause; First Amendment; Free Speech Approach to Religious Liberty; Public Aid to Religious Organizations; Wall of Separation.

BIBLIOGRAPHY

Manhire, John T. Jr. "*Rosenberger* Effectively Harmonizes First Amendment Tensions, but Fails to Lay the Specter of *Lemon* to Rest. (Case Note)" *Regent University Law Review.* 7 (Fall 1996): 145–64.

Rosemary Radford Ruether (1930–)

Rosemary Ruether is a radical feminist theologian who attempts to bridge the gap in her activism between the religious left and feminists. Author of several books, she has fought sexist language in the churches and religion, focusing especially on **Roman Catholicism**. Believing that countercultural movements have been central to the development of Christian thought, she seeks to counter the conservative religious mainstream with a radical form of Christianity. Critical of the use of **civil religion** to ensure what she sees as the ruling gender, race, and class, she has sought through her social activism to give alternative meaning to it. (MWP) **See also** Conservatism; Feminism; Liberalism; Religious Right; Women in Religion and Politics.

BIBLIOGRAPHY

Ruether, Rosemary R. *The Church Against Itself.* New York: Herder and Herder, 1967.

——. *Faith and Fratricide: The Theological Roots of Anti-Semitism.* Boston: The Seabury Press, 1974.

——. *New Woman, New Earth: Sexist Ideologies and Human Liberation.* Boston: Beacon Press, 1975.

——. *Sexism and God-Talk: Toward a Feminist Theology.* Boston: Beacon Press, 1983.

——. *Women-Church: Theology & Practice.* San Francisco: Harper & Row, 1985.

Benjamin Rush (1745–1813)

A native Philadelphian, Benjamin Rush was a physician and humanitarian. Devout if non-sectarian and unconventional, he was nevertheless a professing Christian at his death. Rush was the author of a *Defence of the Use of the Bible as a School-Book* (1806) in which he assumed that "Christianity is the only true and perfect religion, and that in proportion as mankind adopt its principles, and obey its precepts, they will be wise and happy." Rush spent his professional career trying to put his religious convictions into practice by treating the poor and by advancing the cause of virtue in America. Having been affected by **George Whitefield** and the **First Great Awakening** as a youth, Rush was a continual champion of humanitarian causes and reforms including the **abolition** of **slavery**; temperance; and reforms in **education**, the penal system, and hospital care.

In 1806, Benjamin Rush wrote a defense of the Bible as a school text. Library of Congress.

During the Revolutionary era, Rush was a pamphleteer; a volunteer and surgeon-general in the colonial army; Continental congressman; and signer of the **Declaration of Independence**. In 1787, he returned to politics and served as a leading member of the Pennsylvania convention that ratified the Constitution. Rush was appointed treasurer of the United States Mint by President **John Adams**. (JHM) **See also** American Revolution; Temperance and Prohibition.

BIBLIOGRAPHY

Kloos, John M. Jr. *A Sense of Deity: The Republican Spirituality of Dr. Benjamin Rush.* Brooklyn, NY: Carlson Publishing, 1991.

Rousas J. Rushdoony (1916–)

The publication of Rousas Rushdoony's *Institutes of Biblical Law* in 1973 is often seen as the beginning of the **Christian Reconstructionist Movement**. As head of the California-based Chalcedon Foundation, Rushdoony, a conservative reformist, has promoted the continued validity of Old Testament judicial and civil sanctions as a rule for all nations. An influential populizer of Rushdoony's position is **Gary North**'s Institute for Christian Economics in Texas. (ARB) **See also** Conservatism.

BIBLIOGRAPHY

Barker, William S. and W. Robert Godfrey, eds. *Theonomy: A Reformed Critique.* Grand Rapids, MI: Zondervan, 1990.

Rushdoony, Rousas J. *Institutes of Biblical Law.* Nutley, NJ: Craig Press, 1973.

Charles Taze Russell (1852–1916)

Charles Russell was the founder of the Watch Tower Bible and Tract Society **(Jehovah's Witnesses)**. He denied the Trinity and the existence of Hell while claiming that Christ would return in 1914. Russell and his followers have been a controversial sect in America and the focus of a number of important U.S. Supreme Court decisions on issues such as prayer in school and free speech. (MWP) **See also** Establishment Clause; First Amendment; Free Speech Approach to Religious Liberty; School Prayer; Wall of Separation.

BIBLIOGRAPHY

Penton, M. James. *Apocalypse Delayed: The Story of Jehovah's Witnesses.* Toronto: University of Toronto Press, 1985.

John Augustine Ryan (1869–1945)

As one of the best known Catholic social commentators of the first half of the twentieth century, John Ryan advocated an enlarged role for government in dealing with social problems, such as the need for a legal minimum wage, which would enable people to earn enough money to support themselves and their families. His vocal support of Franklin Roosevelt earned him the nickname, "Right Reverend **New Deal**." Though he played a prominent role in many liberal organizations, he also clashed with liberals over issues such as religious freedom and personal morality. (MWP) **See also** First Amendment; Labor; Liberalism; Roman Catholicism; Social Justice.

BIBLIOGRAPHY

Broderick, Francis C. *Right Reverend New Dealer: John A. Ryan.* New York: Macmillan, 1963.

Ryan, John A. *A Living Wage: Its Ethical and Economic Aspects.* New York: Arno, 1971.

Ryan, John A. *Social Doctrines in Action: A Personal History.* New York: Harper, 1941.

Sabbatarianism

Generally, Sabbatarianism refers to religious observance of a weekly day of worship and respite from normal activities. Specifically, Sabbatarianism refers to strict observance of Sabbath worship and rest, including advocacy of legislation to enforce the uniqueness of the Sabbath throughout society. The Sabbath is rooted in Jewish antiquity. The account of creation at the beginning of Genesis establishes the origin of the Sabbath: God created the universe in six days, and, on the seventh day, God rested. The fourth commandment given to Moses in Chapter 20 of Exodus 20 is to keep the Sabbath day holy. Following Genesis, **Judaism** observes the Sabbath on Saturday, the seventh day of the week.

The first Christians were Jews who acknowledged Jesus as the Messiah. They, too, observed the seventh-day Sabbath. Yet, they also began the weekly commemoration of the resurrection of Jesus on the morning after the Jewish Sabbath. They called Sunday, the first day of the week, "the Lord's Day"; Sunday was otherwise a normal working day. By the ninth century, the Christian Church had largely transferred the Sabbath to Sunday, which became the Christian day for worship and rest, although acts of mercy and even suitable (i.e., nonlicentious) recreational activities were considered appropriate for the Sabbath.

Following the **Reformation** in the sixteenth century, Sabbatarianism in the specific sense came into being among certain groups. In particular, English Puritans advocated strict Sabbath-keeping for Christians and the entire society. Following this Puritan tradition, the Sunday Sabbath in the United States has occupied a special religious and cultural significance since colonial times. Strict observance of Sunday worship and rest came to be viewed by the Protestant churches as essential to true religion and to national character and identity. Through individual efforts and moral societies, American Protestants influenced legislation in the states to inhibit much commercial and other activity on Sunday. The Protestant churches denounced different approaches to Sunday, especially as these increased with immigration from non-Protestant and even non-Christian nations in the nineteenth and early twentieth centuries. The growing pluralism of American society eroded the Protestant tradition of strict Sabbath-keeping. Even so, despite pluralism and the constitutional prohibition of laws respecting establishment of a particular religion or religious practice, a special cultural and legal status for Sunday persisted until the last generation or two of the twentieth century. (GSS) **See also** Colonial America; Sunday Mails.

BIBLIOGRAPHY

Edwards, Tilden. *Sabbath Time: Understanding and Practice for Contemporary Christians*. New York: Seabury Press, 1982.

John, Richard. "Taking Sabbatarianism Seriously: The Postal System, the Sabbath, and the Transformation of the American Political Culture." *Journal of the Early Republic* 10 (Winter 1990): 517-67.

Strand, Kenneth A., ed. *The Sabbath in Scripture and History*. Washington, DC: Review and Herald Publishing Association, 1982.

Salem Witchcraft Trials

The Salem Witchcraft Trials occurred in the early 1690s in the town of Salem, a settlement in Massachusetts Bay, one of England's North American colonies. The trials began when a group of girls were caught playing with a crystal ball. To avoid punishment, the girls claimed that witches made them do it. The accusations of witchcraft were fueled by the court's acceptance of spectral evidence, sensory evidence offered by witnesses without corroborating physical proof. The trials reached their peak in 1692, but quickly died out once Governor William Phipps banned spectral evidence. In all, 150 people were imprisoned, 50 confessed to being witches, and 20 were executed (19 were hanged and one was pressed to death). Most of the victims of the trials were middle-aged women with little or no family to protect them from the charges. Twenty years after the trials reached their peak, all the convictions were annulled and reparations were paid. **See also** Colonial America; Massachusetts Bay Colony; Puritans.

BIBLIOGRAPHY

Boyer, Paul and Steven Nissenbaum. *Salem Possessed*. Cambridge, MA: Harvard University Press, 1974.

——, eds. *Salem Witchcraft Papers*. New York: Da Capo Press, 1977.

Salvation Army

A Protestant denomination, the Salvation Army was founded in London in 1865 by Methodist minister William Booth. The evangelical group adopted its current name and military attire and hierarchy in 1878 to distinguish itself. The group focuses on two main goals. First, it seeks to convince others to recognize Jesus Christ as their savior. Second, it does deeds of **social justice** in recognition of God's love for the downtrodden. At its heart, the Salvation Army focuses on a group of people often ignored by other Christian denominations.

The Salvation Army came to the United States in 1880, but did not prosper until Evangeline Booth, daughter of William Booth, became field commissioner in 1904. Evangeline's brother, Ballington, who preceded her as field commissioner, formed his own group, the Volunteers of America.

The Salvation Army is the largest organization of its type in the United States, with nearly 500,000 members in more than 1,000 congregations. It continues to serve the poor by collecting foodstuffs, furniture, and money. The Salvation Army continues to be an important evangelical force in the United States. **See also** Evangelicals; Methodism.

Bibliography

McKinley, Edward H. *Marching in Glory: The History of the Salvation Army in the United States, 1880-1980.* San Francisco: Harper & Row, 1980.

Sanctuary Movement

Suspecting that the **Ronald Reagan** administration was systematically denying asylum to Salvadorans and Guatemalans fleeing political violence in their homelands, Quaker Jim Corbett and Presbyterian minister John Fife started the Sanctuary Movement in 1981 by hiding undocumented Central Americans in churches and homes. Although founded in Arizona, the Sanctuary Movement grew to include over 500 congregations and localities throughout the country. After infiltrating the movement, the U.S. government obtained criminal convictions against eight activists, including Fife, in 1986. From the late 1980s until its demise in the mid-1990s, the movement declined as leaders quarreled over aims, potential workers feared further prosecution, and the United States stopped deporting most Central Americans. (JSF) **See also** Presbyterians; Quakers.

Bibliography

Davidson, Miriam. *Convictions of the Heart: Jim Corbett and the Sanctuary Movement.* Tucson: University of Arizona Press, 1988.

Golden, Renny and Michael McConnell. *Sanctuary: The New Underground Railroad.* Maryknoll, NY: Orbis, 1986.

Antonin Scalia (1936–)

Antonin Scalia, the second Roman Catholic appointed to the U.S. Supreme Court (**William J. Brennan** was the first in 1957) was nominated by President **Ronald Reagan** in 1986. Although often described as a staunch conservative, his judicial opinions on the **First Amendment**'s religion clauses have vexed conservatives and liberals alike. For instance, his controversial opinion in the free-exercise-of-religion case, ***Employment Division of Oregon v. Smith*** (1990), held that the ritual use of hallucinogens (peyote) by Native Americans is not exempt from generally applicable state drug laws. Scalia has also urged his colleagues to abandon the so-called ***Lemon* test**, which the Court has often used to determine whether governmental actions violate the **Establishment Clause**. Scalia has argued that many laws will conflict with one religious practice or another, but as long as the law is generally applicable then it does not interfere with free exercise. His scathing dissents in ***Edwards v. Aguillard*** (1987), ***Lee v. Weisman*** (1992), and ***Lamb's Chapel v. Center Moriches Union Free School District*** (1993), among others, illustrate his mode of textual analysis to Establishment Clause jurisprudence. (KRD) **See also** Conservatism; Free Exercise Clause; Native American Religions; Roman Catholicism.

Bibliography

Brisbin, Richard A., Jr. *Justice Antonin Scalia and the Conservative Revival.* Baltimore: The Johns Hopkins University Press, 1997.

Francis Schaeffer (1912–1984)

Although this noted evangelical apologist lived most of his life in Switzerland, his writings profoundly affected many politically active American Christians, including **Charles Colson**, **Jerry Falwell**, Jack Kemp, and **Randall Terry**. Schaeffer argued that **Reformation** Christianity was essential to maintaining political freedom. Without orthodox, Protestant Christianity circumscribing liberty, freedom necessarily leads to chaos, which, in turn, leads to authoritarianism. The decline of Western society was thus rooted in a contemporary humanistic outlook that lacked the intellectual and moral absolutes of Protestant Christianity. According to Schaeffer, the modern acceptance of **abortion**, infanticide, and **euthanasia** resulted from the loss of the biblical concept that humanity was created in the image of God. The remedy for the current predicament of human society was to return to biblical absolutes. (ARB) **See also** Evangelicals; Secular Humanism.

Bibliography

Ruegsegger, Ronald W., ed. *Reflections on Francis Schaeffer.* Grand Rapids, MI: Zondervan, 1986.

Schaeffer, Francis A. *The Complete Works of Francis A. Schaeffer: A Christian Worldview.* 2nd ed. Westchester, IL: Crossway Books, 1995.

Philip Schaff (1819–1893)

Philip Schaff was a leading Protestant theologian and church historian of the nineteenth century. He came to the United States in 1844 to teach at a small German Reformed seminary, and he later taught at New York's Union Theological Seminary. In a brief treatise, *Church and State in the United States* (1888), Schaff celebrated the American approach to church-state relations, which he said was characterized by voluntarism, equality among sects, and religious liberty based on an amicable separation between the institutions of church and civil government. (Schaff's speech on "The Idea of Religious Freedom" is reprinted in Appendix 1.) (DLD) **See also** Establishment Clause; First Amendment; Wall of Separation.

Bibliography

Graham, Stephen R. *Cosmos in the Chaos: Philip Schaff's Interpretation of Nineteenth-Century American Religion.* Grand Rapids, MI: William B. Eerdmans, 1995.

Schaff, Philip. *Church and State in the United States; or, The American Idea of Religious Liberty and Its Practical Effects*. New York: G. P. Putnam's Sons, 1888.

Schneider v. Irvington, New Jersey (1939)

A Jehovah's Witness was arrested in Irvington, New Jersey, and charged with canvassing without a permit, a violation of a town ordinance that required a written permit from the chief of police for such activities. In *Schneider v. Irvington, New Jersey*, 308 U.S. 147 (1939), the U.S. Supreme Court invalidated the ordinance, stating, "To require a **censorship** through license which makes impossible the free and unhampered distribution of pamphlets strikes at the very heart of the constitutional guarantees." (JM) **See also** First Amendment; Free Exercise Clause; Free Speech Approach to Religious Liberty; Jehovah's Witnesses.

BIBLIOGRAPHY

Choper, Jesse H. *Securing Religious Liberty*. Chicago: University of Chicago Press, 1995.

School Prayer

The issue of whether or not organized prayer in public schools is constitutionally permissible has been among the most divisive issues in American politics for the past generation. In 1962, in the case ***Engel v. Vitale***, the U.S. Supreme Court held that the ritual of beginning each school day with a brief, nondenominational prayer, which was then a common practice, violated the **Establishment Clause** of the **First Amendment** and was unconstitutional. The Court held that having public employees (in this instance, schoolteachers) lead organized prayers was tantamount to government endorsement of religion, which the Court regarded as historically forbidden. To reach this conclusion, the Court made two controversial assumptions: First, the *Engel* decision required the Court to apply the First Amendment (initially, a restriction on the federal government) to the actions of state governments. This step was warranted through the doctrine of selective incorporation, wherein the provisions of the Bill of Rights were applied to the states via the Due Process Clause of the **Fourteenth Amendment**. Second, the Court (following its earlier precedent in the 1947 case of ***Everson v. Board of Education of the township of Ewing*** [1947]) asserted that the Establishment Clause required government at all levels to be neutral between religion and irreligion. That is, the Establishment Clause not only proscribes government endorsement of a particular religion, but also enjoins government from promoting religion in general.

Since *Engel*, and despite numerous changes in the Court's personnel over time, the Supreme Court has been consistent in applying this broad view of the Establishment Clause to the question of religious observance in public schools. In the year following the *Engel* decision, the Court ruled that the reading of Bible verses in public schools was unconstitutional (***Abington Township v. Schempp*** [1963]). In 1985, the Court ruled a mandated "moment of silence" unconstitutional if prayer was explicitly mentioned to students as an option (***Wallace v. Jaffree*** [1985]), and, a "voluntary" prayer recited at a high school graduation was also struck down on Establishment Clause grounds (***Lee v. Weisman*** [1992]). In the three decades since the original decision, the Court has not modified or qualified its opposition to organized religious observance in public schools.

Such consistency is remarkable when one considers the enormous popularity of the idea of school prayer. In virtually every major public poll taken on the subject, large majorities have favored the notion of prayer in public schools. Perhaps in response to public opinion, over 100 constitutional amendments have been proposed in Congress to restore the right to school districts to encourage public religious observance, and several presidential candidates have made school prayer an important rhetorical issue. For example, in his 1980 campaign for president, Republican **Ronald Reagan** frequently observed that "If we could just get government out of the classroom, we might get God back in."

Proponents of school prayer have argued that the Court's reading of the Establishment Clause in *Everson* and *Engel* was fundamentally misguided. "Accommodationists" have argued that the First Amendment simply proscribes government endorsement of particular religions, but permits a "benevolent neutrality," in which government may encourage religion in general. They also argue that the Court's "separationist" reading of the Establishment Clause not only misrepresents the meaning of that clause, but also distorts the meaning of the **Free Exercise Clause**. By interpreting the Establishment Clause so broadly, the Court has arguably interfered with the right of citizens to exercise their religious freedom by limiting the opportunity to express their religious beliefs in a public setting (such prohibitions might also violate the Free Speech Clause of the First Amendment). While this Free Exercise argument can be traced at least to Justice **Potter Stewart**'s dissenting opinion in *Schempp*, the "voluntary" nature of school prayer has been emphasized with increasing frequency by advocates of religious accommodation.

Supporters of the Court's decisions have argued that the Free Exercise Clause does not justify state endorsement of religious observance, and have questioned how "voluntary" organized school prayer might be. Some have suggested that the social pressure nonparticipating children might experience is a form of subtle, yet forbidden, government coercion. (TGJ) **See also** Accomodationism; Education; Equal Access Act; Free Speech Approach to Religious Liberty; Release Time; Wall of Separation.

BIBLIOGRAPHY

Jelen, Ted G. and Clyde Wilcox. *Public Attitudes Toward Church and State*. Armonk, NY: M.E. Sharpe, 1995.

Levy, Leonard. *The Establishment Clause*. New York: Macmillan, 1986.

Monsma, Stephen V. *Positive Neutrality: Letting Religious Freedom Ring*. Westport, CT: Praeger, 1993.

Murley, John A. "School Prayer: Free Exercise of Religion or Establishment of Religion?" In Raymond Tatalovich and Bryon Daynes, eds. *Social Regulatory Policy: Moral Controversies in American Politics*. Boulder, CO: Westview, 1988.

Schotten, Peter and Dennis Stevens. *Religion, Politics, and the Law*. New York: Wadsworth, 1996.

Scopes Trial (1925)

Known as "The Great Monkey Trial," this 1925 high-profile courtroom spectacle in Dayton, Tennessee, dramatized the decline of religious fundamentalism as a force in American culture in the 1920s. The defendant, a schoolteacher named John Thomas Scopes, had taught Charles Darwin's theory of **evolution** to his science class and thus violated a state law that had made it illegal for a teacher "to teach any theory that denies the story of the Divine Creation of man as taught in the Bible, and to teach instead that man has descended from a lower order of animals." Scopes volunteered himself to the **American Civil Liberties Union (ACLU)** as a case on which to challenge the constitutionality of Tennessee's law, and the famous Chicago attorney **Clarence Seward Darrow** volunteered to defend him. The state was represented by an even greater celebrity, religious fundamentalist and three-time populist presidential candidate for the Democrats, **William Jennings Bryan**, who was both a lawyer and a Presbyterian

Pictured here are Clarence Darrow (left) and Judge John Roultston, two key figures in the 1925 Scopes Trial. Library of Congress.

elder. More than 900 spectators filled the courtroom from July 10-25, 1925, to watch what Bryan had promised would be "a duel to the death" between evolution and Christianity. The climax of the trial came when Darrow, in a surprise move, called Bryan to the stand as an expert on the Bible. After getting Bryan to say that he believed every word in the Bible to be the literal truth, Darrow wove the usually dignified orator into a web of self-contradiction by pointing out the impossibilities in the story of Genesis. He asked, for example, how Cain could have found a wife if the only people alive then were Adam, Eve, Abel, and Cain himself. Bryan eventually admitted that he did not think the earth had been made in six days of 24 hours, thus alienating his followers who were devoted to the literal reading of the Bible. Although Scopes was found guilty and fined $100, the verdict was overturned on a legal technicality and the case was never retried. The Tennessee law was finally repealed in 1967, and the following year the U.S. Supreme Court held a similar law in Arkansas to be an unconstitutional infringement of the separation of church and state. (BDG) **See also** Creationism; Establishment Clause; First Amendment; Fundamentalism; Presbyterian Church; Wall of Separation.

Bibliography

De Camp, L. Sprague. *The Great Monkey Trial*. Garden City, NY: Doubleday, 1968.

Edwards v. Aguillard, 482 U.S. 578 (1987).

Larson, Edward. *Summer for the Gods: The Scopes Trial and America's Continuing Debate over Science and Religion*. New York: Basic Books, 1997.

Second Great Awakening

The Second Great Awakening was a series of Christian revivals in the U.S. in the late eighteenth and early nineteenth centuries. The revivals brought to their participants a heightened interest in spirituality, evangelism, and social reform. Most historians place the beginning of the revivals in the late 1790s in the pulpits of New England and the camp meetings on the southern frontier. Led by such Populist preachers as **Timothy Dwight**, **Lyman Beecher**, **Nathaniel W. Taylor**, and **Charles Grandison Finney**, the revivals continued in one form or another, in one section or another, right up until the **Civil War**. In many ways, the movement can be seen as an extension and adaptation of the themes first articulated by the itinerant preachers associated with the **First Great Awakening** (1740–1743) of the previous century. Both Awakenings emphasized the importance of the immediate action of the Holy Spirit upon the soul; both movements placed the focus of ministerial activity not on abstract analysis of covenant theology but on the experiential heart of religion. Of particular importance during the Second Great Awakening, however, was the perception among many that the new nation lacked a clear sense of its own identity, a problem compounded by the growing influence of **Enlightenment** rationalism and materialism, the rise of new religious sects, and the various social stresses and anxieties associated with a growing nation. Through the evocation of the familiar themes of human depravity and divine redemption, the evangelists were able to resurrect not only the spiritual life of the nation but the familiar set of ordering myths and symbols first articulated in the "chosen people" imagery of their Puritan ancestors.

The impact of the Second Great Awakening can hardly be overemphasized, for its dramatic cultural symbolism and nationalizing tendencies affected directly or indirectly just about every major social, political, and religious issue in the antebellum United States. The movement's ability to organize the American people for charitable works led to the founding of missionary organizations, interdenominational

The Second Great Awakening began in New England, but also had a great impact on the frontier West. Library of Congress.

Bible and tract societies, Sunday school unions, and relief agencies for the poor. The enthusiasm of the era ushered in the new language of "**manifest destiny**" in the 1840s, as Americans once again became confident in their belief that the American republic would be the primary redemptive agent in history, chosen by God to perfect themselves and the world. The movement's reformist component gave birth to the nativist, anti-Catholic, anti-slavery, temperance, and feminist movements, and the movement's experientialist component gave rise to new forms of art, literature, architecture, spirituality, and even political organization. The development of Jacksonian **democracy** in the 1830s and the populist impulse of the early nineteenth century owes a great deal to the faith in the common citizen that emerged from the leveling forces of widespread religious enthusiasm that affected all social classes during the Second Great Awakening. (GSB) **See also** Abolition; Anti-Catholicism; Evangelicals; Feminism; Missionaries; Nativism; Puritans; Social Justice; Sunday School Movement; Temperance and Prohibition.

Bibliography

Keller, Charles R. *The Second Great Awakening in Connecticut*. New Haven, CT: Yale University Press, 1942.

McLoughlin, William G. *Revivals, Awakenings and Reform*. Chicago: University of Chicago Press, 1978.

Miller, Perry. *The Life of the Mind in America: From the Revolution to the Civil War*. New York: Harcourt, Brace, 1965.

Secular Humanism

Secular humanism has its intellectual roots in the Renaissance and the **Enlightenment** when an increased emphasis was placed on humans, and on their ability to reason and their dominant position in nature. Although the early form of humanism—classical humanism—stressed the study of ancient Greek and Roman literature and philosophy, it was not hostile to Christianity. Leading classical humanists such as Erasmus and Sir Thomas More were explicitly Christian in their humanism.

Modern humanism has broken that tie with Christianity. Secular humanism has three important elements: (1) the belief that human reason is superior to divine revelation when the two come into conflict, (2) the belief that human solutions are enough for human problems, and (3) a growing belief in ethical relativism or situational ethics as distinct from moral precepts.

The most dramatic public statement of American secular humanism was the 1933 **Humanist Manifesto** issued by 11 prominent university professors, including **John Dewey**. However, a strand of humanism, either classical or secular, has run through American thought from the time of the Founders to the present. Some scholars have claimed that the most important of the Founding Fathers—**George Washington**, **Benjamin Franklin**, and **Thomas Jefferson**, among others—were humanists. Additionally, rationalism and human-centered ethical theories are reflected in many American freethinkers, including transcendentalists like **Henry David Thoreau**.

Some critics of secular humanism and its accompanying political **liberalism**, like conservative scholar **J. Gresham Machen**, the author of *Christianity and Liberalism* (1923), have even argued that one could not be a liberal and a Christian. More recently, the debate over humanism has centered on public schools, where critics of secular humanism say that its dominance is undercutting the moral values of children and, ultimately, of the United States. **See also** Conservatism; Education; Freethought; Secularization Thesis; Transcendentalism.

Bibliography

Gaddy, Barbara B. *School Wars: Resolving Our Conflicts Over Religion and Values*. San Francisco: Jossey-Bass Publishers, 1996.

Hook, Sidney. *On the Barricades*. Buffalo, NY: Prometheus Books, 1989.

Murrin, John M. "Religion and Politics in America from the First Settlements to the Civil War." In Mark A. Noll, ed. *Religion and American Politics*. New York: Oxford University Press, 1990.

Secularization Thesis

"Secularization" and the related term "secular" come from the Latin word meaning "world." While historically secularization was a technical legal term for the reversion of ecclesiastical property to lay or secular status, today, in popular and social scientific language, secularization refers to the process of separating social, political, and economic institutions from religious institutions and influences. Thus, secularization refers to religion's loss of influence over a particular society through the marginalization of the society's beliefs and ethics. Both religious and philosophical scholars locate the origins of Western secularization in the Renaissance, **Reformation**, and **Enlightenment**, a complex of European historical movements running from the fifteenth to the eighteenth centuries. In particular, the Peace of Westphalia (1648) is taken to initiate the modern separation of politics from religion, leading eventually to the rise of two secularized polities, namely France and the United States. Social scientists have tended to understand the process of secularization as an inevitable result of modernity, one resulting paradoxically not in human freedom, but in the rationalized and dehumanizing *Eisenstahlgehause* or "iron cage" of modernity predicted by **Max Weber** in his *The Protestant Ethic and the Spirit of Capitalism* (1904). Thus increasing modernization in the West, with its concommitant rationalization, has withdrawn religion from the public domain and restricted it to the private domain. Due to its increased specialization, and the differentiation of roles into specific tasks, society has become increasingly impersonal and humans have become depersonalized. Such interpretations tend to identify religion only with its institutional forms and have been criticized by philosophers, such as Karl Lowith and Leo Strauss, by sociologists, such as David Martin, and by theologians, such as Karl Barth, Edward Schillebeeckx, and **Harvey Gallagher Cox**.

The secularization thesis has been challenged because according to Weber's thesis and indeed all secularization theories, modernity, and thus secularization, should have led to the "demagification" of the world, that is, the separation of religion from societal institutions and the eventual demise of religion itself. Yet the last quarter of the twentieth century has witnessed the dramatic growth of religion in both the West and the East and the resurgence of fundamentalist movements. In the United States, institutionalized mainline denominations have declined, but evangelical and pentecostal churches, as well as new age religions, have grown dramatically. Some modern evangelical and fundamentalist groups, contrary to their original founding impetus and to versions of the secularization thesis, are now active in the political arena, a phenomenon that began with Reverend **Jerry Falwell** and the **Moral Majority** in 1979, and has continued into the 1990s with the **Christian Coalition**. (ISM) **See also** Establishment Clause; Evangelicals; First Amendment; Fundamentalist; New Age Movement; Pentecostals; Secular Humanism; Wall of Separation.

Bibliography

Bruce, Steve, ed. *Religion and Modernization: Sociologists and Historians Debate the Secularization Thesis*. New York: Oxford University Press, 1992.

Cox, Harvey G. *Religion in the Secular City*. New York: Schuster and Son, 1984.

——. *The Secular City*. New York: Macmillan, 1965.

Martin, David. *The Religious and the Secular.* Studies in Secularization. New York: Shocken Books, 1969.

Weber, Max. *The Protestant Ethic and the Spirit of Capitalism*. New York: Charles Scribner's Sons, 1920.

Gershom Mendes Seixas (1746–1816)

An orthodox Jewish rabbi of Portuguese descent, Gershom Seixas, an early spokesman for Jews in America, preached the first English-language sermons in an American synagogue. He was a strong supporter of the new American **democracy**, arguing for full participation by Jews, and in 1798 delivered one of the first Thanksgiving sermons. When British forces invaded New York during the **American Revolution**, Seixas left for Connecticut while most of his congregation went to Philadelphia. In 1780, he moved to Philadelphia and helped found a new synagogue there. While a strong proponent of Jewish support for American democracy, he was not mute regarding discrimination. When Pennsylvania made belief in Christ a requirement to hold a seat in the assembly, Seixas formally protested this unconstitutional religious test. (MWP) **See also** Judaism; Religious Tests and Oaths; Thanksgiving and Fast Days.

Bibliography

Phillips, Naphtali. *An Eulogium to the Memory of the Rev. Greshom M. Seixas*. New York: J. H. Sherman, 1816.

Jay Alan Sekulow (1956–)

As the chief counsel for the American Center for Law and Justice, Jay Sekulow has argued numerous religious rights cases before the U.S. Supreme Court. Sekulow describes himself as a Messianic Jew who believes in Jesus. Jewish leaders, however, argue that Sekulow is a Christian. With strong ties to **Pat Robertson**, Sekulow has been an important force in helping to shape recent **First Amendment** law. His agenda includes guaranteeing that free religious literature can be distributed at airports, stadiums, and parks; that public schools cannot ban Bible and prayer clubs; and that pro-life protests cannot be discriminated against. (MWP) **See also** Abortion and Birth Control Regulation; Education; Free Exercise Clause; Free Speech Approach to Religious Liberty; Judaism.

Bibliography

Sekulow, Jay. *And Nothing But the Truth*. Nashville, TN: Thomas Nelson, 1966.

Elizabeth Ann Seton (1774–1821)

Declared a saint by the Roman Catholic Church in 1975, Elizabeth Seton was the first native-born American to be canonized. Once an Anglican, married, and the mother of five children, Seton seemed an unlikely candidate for Catholic sainthood. But the death of her husband in 1803 and her conversion to Catholicism in 1805 led her to found an elementary school in 1809 to which she attracted a group of young women who, in 1813, became the Sisters of Charity. Together, Seton and the Sisters of Charity helped establish the Catholic parochial school system in the United States. (MWP) **See also** Canon Law; Education; Roman Catholicism; Women in Religion and Politics.

Bibliography

Kelly, Ellin M. and Annabelle M. Melville, eds. *Elizabeth Seton: Selected Writings*. New York: Parlist Press, 1987.

Stone, Elaine Murray. *Elizabeth Bayley Seton: An American Saint*. New York: Parlist Press, 1993.

Seventh-Day Adventists

The Advent movement began in the United States in the 1840s with the preaching of William Miller (1782-1849). With quasi-scientific calculations and a literal interpretation of the Bible, Miller predicted that Christ would return between March 21,

1843, and March 21, 1844. When his original prediction failed, Miller recalculated and anticipated the second coming on October 22, 1844. When Christ again failed to appear, Miller's followers fell into confusion and disorder and suffered local persecution. Seventh-Day Adventism emerged in the years following Miller's failed predictions as the largest faction to branch off from the Millerite movement. With an organization similar to the **Presbyterian Church**, the Seventh-Day Adventists accept the teachings of Ellen G. White (1827–1915), an early leader of the Seventh-Day Adventist faction, and observe the Sabbath on the seventh day rather than on Sunday. White revived many despairing followers of Miller through her prophetic visions and explanations.

White's leadership played a critical role in developing the philosophical position of the Adventist church in American society. She encouraged members to avoid conflict over political issues wherever possible. When members encountered Sunday legislation in the 1880s, the church used the **First Amendment** in a struggle to protect religious liberties. However, as proponents of the separation of church and state, Adventists largely strove to create peaceable solutions. For example, Adventists worked around the difficult issue of military drafts by creating the Medical Cadet Corps to provide acceptable military service on Saturdays.

Adventists have created microcosms within society rather than openly attacking mainstream institutions. Adventist schools are one example of this desire to quietly exist on the periphery. Self-supporting movements have led to various independent communities and are actually an area of growth within the Seventh-Day Adventist church. These independent societies offer a sanctuary from mainstream American society. (CH) **See also** Establishment Clause; Free Speech Approach to Religious Liberty; Sabbatarianism.

BIBLIOGRAPHY

Bull, Malcolm and Keith Lockhart. *Seeking a Sanctuary*. San Francisco: Harper and Row, 1989.

Dick, Everett N. *William Miller and the Advent Crisis*. Berrien Springs, MI: Andrews University Press, 1994.

Marsden, George M. *Religion and American Culture*. Orlando, FL: Harcourt Brace, 1990.

Al Sharpton (1954–)

Born in Brooklyn, New York, Al Sharpton began preaching at age four and was ordained a minister at age 10. He ran unsuccessfully for the New York State Senate in 1978 and became an outspoken community activist for the rights of African Americans. He ran in the Democratic primary for the U.S. Senate in 1992 and finished third. In 1994, he ran for the Senate again and lost, but attracted 25 percent of the vote. In 1996, he ran an unsuccessful campaign to be the Democratic nominee for mayor of New York City. He is widely known as the leader of protests that followed the murder of a black as he was fleeing a group of white youths in 1986 in Howard Beach, New York. A vocal agitator, Sharpton gained national attention again in 1988 when he became spokesman/advisor for Tawana Brawley, an African-American teenager who claimed she had been abducted and repeatedly raped by six white men. The story proved to be untrue. This event, however, has not kept Sharpton from tackling other controversial issues. (JCW) **See also** African-American Churches; Democratic Party; Race Relations.

BIBLIOGRAPHY

Klein, Michael. *The Man Behind the Soundbite: The Real Story of Reverend Al Sharpton*. New York: Castillo, 1991.

Sharpton, Al and Anthony Walton. *Go and Tell Pharaoh: The Autobiography of the Reverend Al Sharpton*. New York: Doubleday, 1996.

Charles Monroe Sheldon (1857–1946)

The pastor of Congregational churches in Waterbury, Vermont (1886–88), and Topeka, Kansas (1889–1912), Charles Sheldon preached a unique sort of sermon. Like a magazine story that continues from issue to issue, each of his sermons built on the previous. One of his sermon series described life in a small town after the residents made a promise to live for a year exactly like Jesus. Published as a book entitled ***In His Steps*** (1897), Sheldon's sermon series became one of the best-selling books in U.S. history with over 8 million copies sold in the next 60 years. *In His Steps* was dramatized in 1923. Sheldon published several other volumes, including *Richard Bruce* (1891), *The Narrow Gate* (1902), *The Heart of the World* (1905), *In His Steps Today* (1921), and *He Is Here* (1931). Sheldon was the editor of the *Christian Herald* in New York City from 1920 to 1925, and was also active in the temperance movement and on behalf of **pacifism**. (MWP) **See also** Congregationalism; Temperance and Prohibition.

BIBLIOGRAPHY

Elzey, Wayne. "What Would Jesus Do?" *Soundings* 58 (Winter 1975): 463-89.

Sheldon, Charles M. *In His Steps*. Nashville, TN: Broadman, 1966.

Sherbert v. Verner (1963)

In *Sherbert v. Verner*, the Supreme Court directly addressed the concerns of sabbatarians who refused to work on the Sabbath. A member of the Seventh-Day Adventist Church was discharged by her South Carolina employer because she would not work on Saturday, the Sabbath Day of her faith. She was unable to obtain other employment because she would not work on Saturday, and she was denied a claim for unemployment compensation benefits under the South Carolina Unemployment Compensation Act, which provided that claimants were ineligible for benefits if they have failed, without good cause, to accept available suitable work when offered. In *Sherbert v. Verner*, 374 U.S. 398 (1963), the U.S. Supreme Court overturned this ruling on the grounds that it violated the **Free Exercise Clause** of the **First Amendment**, stating that "Disqualification. . . for unemployment compensation benefits, solely because of her refusal to accept employment in which she would have to work on Saturday contrary to her religious belief, imposes an unconstitutional burden on the free exercise of her religion. . . . There is no compelling state interest enforced in the eligibility provisions of the South Carolina statute which justifies the substantial infringement of appellant's right to religious freedom." (JM) **See also** Labor; Sabbatarianism; Seventh-Day Adventists

BIBLIOGRAPHY

Eastland, Terry. *Religious Liberty in the Supreme Court*. Washington, DC: Ethics and Public Policy Center, 1993.

Ronald J. Sider (1939–)

Stressing God's special concern for the poor, Ronald Sider, an Eastern Baptist Theological Seminary professor has tried to reconnect modern evangelical theology with the social dimensions of the gospel. His writings have encouraged many **Evangelicals** to live simply and to uphold individual and structural justice for the oppressed. Having been named one of the 12 most influential Christians in America, Sider is a controversial figure because he argues that wealth is a sin. His book, *Rich Christians in an Age of Hunger*, has sold more than 350,000 copies and has been called a "modern classic" by *Christianity Today*. While conservative Christians dislike his contempt for **capitalism**, liberals are put off by his opposition to abortion and homosexuality. (ARB) **See also** Abortion and Birth Control Regulation; Baptists; Gospel of Wealth; Homosexual Rights; Liberalism; Social Gospel; Social Justice.

BIBLIOGRAPHY

Sider, Ronald J. *Genuine Christianity: Essentials for Living Your Faith*. Grand Rapids, MI: Zondervan Publishing, 1996.

——. *Rich Christians in an Age of Hunger*. 2nd ed. Downers Grove, IL: Inter-Varsity Press, 1984.

Yves Simon (1903–1961)

Yves Simon was a French born and educated Roman Catholic philosopher and political thinker who taught at Notre Dame and the University of Chicago from 1938 to 1961. He helped expand the influence of Thomism, the philosophical thoughts of St. Thomas Aquinas, which includes among other things adherance to **natural law** and the compatibility of reason and revelation beyond Catholic circles. His political works contain important insights into the nature of **democracy**, freedom, authority, and the common good tradition. (MDH) **See also** First Amendment; Roman Catholicism.

BIBLIOGRAPHY

Rourke, Thomas. *A Conscience as Large as the World: Yves R. Simon versus the Catholic Neoconservatives*. Lanham MD: Rowman and Littlefield, 1997.

Simon, Yves. *Philosophy of Democratic Government*. Notre Dame, IN: University of Notre Dame Press, 1993.

Slavery

Organized religion and American slavery have had important influences on one another. The most important early development was the **First Great Awakening** of the mid-eighteenth century, which saw an increased spreading of Christianity to slaves, often times by masters who themselves were recently converted by the growing religious enthusiasm of the period. Slaves often blended Christianity with the traditional religious beliefs they brought with them from Africa and the West Indies.

By the 1830s, however, ministers like the Methodist **Charles Colcock Jones** were making a more concerted effort to evangelize slaves. The missionary efforts of these preachers were conducted for various reasons. The missions were a legitimate outgrowth of the belief that Christians had a duty to teach about Christ to all, including slaves. However, **missionaries** (and masters) often hoped that conversion to Christianity would make slaves more docile. To this end, the texts of the Apostle Paul that called upon slaves to obey their masters, and other texts promising rewards in the next life, were often stressed. Many masters refrained from teaching Christianity to slaves because it raised serious questions of morality that they preferred not to face. Some religious groups even went so far as to argue that slavery was a positive good because it helped Christianize slaves. Or, they adopted positions similar to the one held by Presbyterian minister **James Henley Thornwell** of South Carolina, who argued that the church should concern itself only with spiritual matters and leave societal issues alone.

Abolitionists countered with tracts like **Theodore Dwight Weld**'s *The Bible Against Slavery* (1837), which showed that slavery was a moral evil and condemned by the Bible and God. **Harriet Beecher Stowe**'s monumental work, ***Uncle Tom's Cabin* (1852)** argued against slavery in the most compelling terms. The work, which sold more than 300,000 copies in its first year of print, drew upon religious symbols and called upon Americans to act as Christians in the battle against slavery.

Evangelizing slaves made some slaveowners concerned. The slave uprisings led by **Denmark Vesey** and **Nat Turner** had religious roots. Vesey, a freed slave, decided to use the religious liberty many slaves exercised in South Carolina to organize a revolt that would occur on Sunday morning when large numbers of slaves could gather without much suspicion. However, on June 17, 1821, the authorities were informed of the plot by several houseslaves and arrested the leaders, including Vesey. On July 2, 1821, Vesey was hanged. Because of Vesey's activities, white authorities no longer allowed slaves to congregate for religious worship without white supervision.

Nat Turner claimed he had seen visions in which God told him he would be the leader of a revolt against the sin of slavery. On August 22, 1831, Turner led a group of slaves to carry out his visions. By the time Turner and his men were captured, more than 60 whites had been killed. More than 100 slaves and free blacks were executed for having taken part in the plot. Turner, seeing himself as a Christ-figure, welcomed his punishment. The revolt led many slaveowners to more closely supervise the religious activities of their slaves.

Individual denominations addressed the issue of slavery in different manners. The **Episcopal Church** avoided any formal stance on the morality of slavery, and its conservative structure and worship did not attract many slaves or many free black members. However, the outbreak of the **Civil War** led the Southern Episcopal Churches to form the Episcopal Churches of the Confederate States of America. Methodists suffered a number of schisms over the issues of slavery and **abolition**, including the formation of the Wesleyan Methodist Church in 1843. While **Baptists** and Presbyterians split along regional lines, the Roman Catholic and Lutheran churches, which had few southern members, were largely unaffected by the issue of slavery. However, many Irish Catholics saw a large free black population as a threat to their own economic security. **See also** African-American Churches; American Anti-Slavery Society; American and Foreign Anti-Slavery Society; Amistad Case; Susan Brownell Anthony; Henry Ward Beecher; Black Theology; John Brown; Lydia Maria Child; William Lloyd Garrison; Sarah Grimke and Angelina Grimke; Lutheran Church; Methodism; Robert Dale Owen; Presbyterian Church; Race Relations; Social Justice; Sojourner Truth; Elizabeth Cady Stanton; Roman Catholicism; Albert Tappan; Lewis Tappan; Frances Wright.

Bibliography

Genovese, Eugene D. *Roll Jordan Roll*. New York: Partheon, 1974.

Lofton, John. *Denmark Vesey's Revolt*. Kent, OH: Kent State University Press, 1984.

Matthews, Donald G. *Slavery and Methodism*. Princeton, NJ: Princton University Press, 1965.

——. *Slavery in the Old South*. Chicago: University of Chicago Press, 1977.

Quarles, Benjamin. *The Black Abolitionists*. New York: Oxford University Press, 1969

Oates, Stephen B. *The Fires of Jubilee*. New York: Harper & Row, 1975.

Alfred E. Smith (1873–1944)

Al Smith was the Democratic presidential nominee in 1928, an election he lost to Republican **Herbert C. Hoover**. Al Smith's parents were Irish Catholic immigrants. He served in the New York state assembly for 12 years before being elected governor of New York in 1918. Smith was defeated in 1920, and was then re-elected three times. He was succeeded as governor of New York by Franklin D. Roosevelt. He was the first Catholic nominee of a major American political party. His religion and his opposition to Prohibition created considerable opposition to his candidacy in the normally Democratic South. The mobilization of the urban Catholic vote for Smith in 1928 contributed to the building of the **New Deal** coalition that elected Franklin D. Roosevelt to the presidency in 1932. (WB) **See also** Democratic Party; Religion and Urban Issues; Roman Catholicism; Temperance and Prohibition.

Bibliography

Josephson, Matthew and Hannah Josefson. *Al Smith: Hero of the Cities*. Boston: Houghton Mifflin, 1969.

Gerrit Smith (1797–1874)

One of the wealthiest men in the early United States, Gerrit Smith used his money to support such causes as **Sabbatarianism**, prison reform, women's rights, and anti-**slavery**. He was active in founding the anti-slavery **Liberty Party** and ran as governor of New York on the party's ticket in 1840. Elected as an independent in 1858, he served one term in the U.S. House of Representatives before retiring. Smith continued his advocacy for **abolition** and supported the use of force against pro-slavery forces in Kansas. Because he was a supporter of the radical abolitionist **John Brown**, Smith may have had prior knowledge of Brown's intention to seize the federal arsenal at Harper's Ferry, Virginia, in October 1859, an action that Brown believed would lead to a slave uprising. (MWP) **See also** Liberalism.

Bibliography

Smith, Gerrit. *Sermons and Speeches of Gerrit Smith*. Stratford, NH: Ayer Company Publishers, 1978.

Joseph Smith, Jr. (1805–1844)

Founder of the **Church of Jesus Christ of Latter-day Saints**, Joseph Smith was a prophet who led a theocratic community onto the U.S. frontier. His unorthodox beliefs gathered both converts and animosity, which forced the church to move from New York to Ohio, Missouri, and then Illinois, where Smith was assassinated in 1844.

Born in Sharon, Vermont, Smith lived in Palmyra, New York, during a time of religious revival. After claiming that God appeared to him to reveal that all existing churches were in error, Smith described angelic visitations that culminated in his reception from the angel of ancient gold plates inscribed with a record to be known as the Book of Mormon. In 1830, Smith established the Church of Jesus Christ of Latter-day Saints, becoming its first "prophet, seer, and revelator."

Smith's teaching of continuing revelation from God was seen by outsiders as a threat to **democracy** because citizens would have little input into the running of a community whose

Growing anti-Mormon sentiment led to the murder of Joseph Smith and several of his followers in Illinois in 1844. Library of Congress.

leader was guided directly by God. Also troubling to outsiders were allegations of Smith's involvement in improper business dealings and the church's practice of "plural marriage" or polygyny (i.e., having more than one wife at a time). Smith, however, saw the financial problems as a result of bad advice, and the theocratic community and polygyny as the restoration of biblical practices.

After settling in Nauvoo, Illinois, Smith attempted to complete his theocratic vision. In addition to leading the church, he served as city mayor, justice of the peace, and general of the Nauvoo Legion. Smith also ran for president in 1844 in an effort to publicize the mistreatment of his followers. Because of increasing violence between Mormons (as church members were called) and non-Mormons, Smith used the Nauvoo Legion to protect the city. When a division occurred over polygyny, Smith drove out his opponents and destroyed their printing press. This act led to charges of treason, and Smith was jailed in nearby Carthage, where he and his brother Hiram were murdered by a mob from surrounding communities. (MEN) **See also** Polygamy; Theocracy.

Bibliography

Brodie, Fawn M. *No Man Knows My History: The Life of Joseph Smith, the Mormon Prophet.* 2nd ed. Rev. New York: Alfred A. Knopf, 1971.

Hill, Donna. *Joseph Smith: The First Mormon.* New York: Doubleday, 1971.

Hill, Marvin S., ed. *The Essential Joseph Smith.* Salt Lake City: Signature Books, 1995.

Quinn, D. Michael. *The Mormon Hierarchy: Origins of Power.* Salt Lake City: Signature Books, 1994.

Samuel Stanhope Smith (1750–1819)

A Presbyterian clergyman born in Pequea, Pennsylvania, in 1750, Samuel Smith in 1795 succeed his father-in-law **John Witherspoon** as the president of his alma mater, the College of New Jersey at Princeton. After ministering in Virginia where he helped found what became the College of Hampden-Sydney, Smith returned to Princeton in 1779 as an administrator and professor of moral philosophy. His *Lectures . . . on the Subjects of Moral and Political Philosophy* (1812), in both their spoken and printed forms, had a lasting impact on American political thought. Smith's opposition to **slavery**, which was rooted in both the Bible and American political ideals of the **Declaration of Independence**, influenced many in the years leading to the **Civil War**. However, doubts about Smith's administration caused some of the more orthodox Princeton trustees to found Princeton Theological Seminary in 1812 as an alternative to the College. (JHM) **See also** Abolition; Education; Presbyterian Church.

Bibliography

Noll, Mark A. *Princeton and the Republic, 1768-1822.* Princeton, NJ: Princeton University Press, 1989.

Social Gospel

The Social Gospel movement captured the imagination of liberal Christians between the **Civil War** and **World War I**. A response to the increasing urban poverty that accompanied industrialization, the Social Gospel sought to bring a faith perspective to the social issues of its era. Pastors and theologians, such as **Solomon Washington Gladden** and **Walter Rauschenbusch**, called attention to biblical references about the Kingdom of God, and argued that it was the responsibility of Christians to help bring that Kingdom into being on earth.

The optimism of the Social Gospel rested on its liberal assumption that both individuals and societies are progressive, that both are evolving into ever better examples of what they might be ideally. In many ways, the Social Gospel movement was a religious version of the socio-political progressive movement of the era. Unlike secular liberals and utopians, however, the leaders of the Social Gospel identified God as the source of these improvements. They pointed to the eventual Second Coming of Christ promised in scripture, and urged individuals and communities to prepare a fit place for Christ's return. Complete perfection would not occur until the Second Coming, but diligent preparation would hasten that event. Thus, Social Gospel leaders called on Christians and churches to direct religious faith and moral strength to the social tasks of gaining control of unregulated social forces and combating evil.

The social work of this movement took several forms. Liberal denominations set up **labor** commissions that advocated shorter (10-hour) workdays and Sunday closing laws. They preached a message of compassion and mutual respect between employers and employees, and labeled as "sin" business practices that favored the wealthy owners without properly valuing the contributions of the laborer. They set up day care centers for the working poor and soup kitchens for both the poor and the homeless. They promoted a model of family relationships that stressed cooperation, companionship, and accessible parents, and urged businesses to provide for and respect family time. They held Jesus up as a model for aspiring young men to imitate as they strove to balance individual responsibility and achievement with cooperation and giving to others.

Cooperation between liberal denominations led to the founding of the Federal Council of Churches in 1918, which quickly issued a lengthy report on *The Church and Modern Industry*. This report documented the unsafe labor conditions, long hours, and low pay that most laborers faced. But the Social Gospel never gained broad public appeal because evangelical Christians were more inclined to equate religious ideals with the business-oriented values of American **capitalism** and **democracy**. The movement suffered from accusations that it was "socialist" and therefore anti-American. Also, many urban churches were themselves struggling for survival, and thus saw themselves as—and indeed often were—incapable of wider social ministry.

The Social Gospel movement developed alongside the **Salvation Army**, the Young Men's and Women's Christian Associations (the YMCA/YWCA), and revivalism. Because these movements addressed personal piety and behavior more than social structures, they were accepted more readily. The Social Gospel also faced difficulty establishing itself in the South, where it was limited primarily to the work of Methodists, who admonished former slaveholders to face their responsibilities toward their black neighbors.

The advent of World War I and the Great Depression shattered the faith of even the most optimistic supporters, and the Social Gospel languished in silence during those periods. The 1930s, however, brought a revival of the movement. This reincarnated Social Gospel advocated social planning and lobbied for government action to promote economic recovery after the Depression. This time the rallying concern was class struggle and the fear of class war if the inequities became too severe. Neo-orthodox religious leaders, such as **Karl Paul Reinhold Niebuhr**, picked up the Social Gospel themes and talked about the need for the gospel to critique culture and transform the world. Both versions of the Social Gospel would eventually shape the development of liberation theologies in the second half of the twentieth century. (KMY) **See also** Evangelicals; Liberalism; Liberation Theology; Methodism; Race Relations; Religion and Urban Issues; Social Justice; Socialism and Communism; Utopianism.

Bibliography

Antonides, Harry. *Stones for Bread: The Social Gospel and its Contemporary Legacy*. Jordan Station, Ontario, Canada: Paideia Press, 1985.

Curtis, Susan. *A Consuming Faith: The Social Gospel and Modern American Culture*. Baltimore: The Johns Hopkins University Press, 1991.

Hutchison, William. *The Modernist Impulse in American Protestantism*. New York: Oxford University Press, 1982.

White, Ronald. *The Social Gospel*. Philadelphia: Temple University Press, 1976.

Social Justice

Social justice is a concept with an ancient and rich lineage of many variations. In the eighth century B.C., the Hebrew prophets Isaiah, Amos, and Micah proclaimed the justice of God and its requirements. In *The Republic,* Plato (427–347 B.C.) detailed his vision of the good society. Aristotle, once a student of Plato, expounded his own analysis of justice and injustice in his *Nichomachean Ethics*. In the thirteenth century, Thomas Aquinas, interpreting Aristotle through a Christian perspective, examined the elements of general or legal justice in his *Summa Theologica*. These few examples suggest the long tradition of inquiry into the nature of justice.

In the United States, the notion of social justice, as it is phrased, has gained currency only in the last 100 years. In American religion, attention to social justice has been more applied than theoretical, manifesting itself largely in a concern for issues in industry, **labor**, economic fairness, race, gender, and politics.

Certain characteristics distinguish a focus on social justice from a focus on the ethical life of the individual. The inquiry into social justice assumes and focuses on the intrinsically social or relational nature of the human being. Thus, examination of the good leads naturally to examination of the social good. At its most basic, social justice refers to the good of the whole community or society. In classic Catholic thought, social justice is the virtue that motivates and structures all human acts toward the common good. Social good—justice—can in this sense be characterized as a higher good than individual good, because social good is more complete. It perfects individual good.

This social approach to the good can be expressed in two ways. One way is to speak of the organic character of human society. The individual person is irreducibly significant, but human society is more than an aggregate of individuals. The "life" and bond of human society both incorporate and transcend the individual. Hence, a social justice approach to the good involves more than just the aggregate or sum of right-acting individuals, more than just the sum of individual right acts, or more than the sum of discrete right relations between individuals. Social justice envisions an organic whole or "community of the good." In this organic sense, social justice catches up right-acting individuals and particular instances of virtue into an encompassing general good or virtue.

In a social justice perspective, the sphere and concern of ethics are as much systemic as personal (or individual). Hence, while social justice is irreducibly personal in nature, it also highlights the supra-personal and supra-individual aspects of social existence in which our individual lives are embedded, such as race, gender, class, politics, and economics. Social justice examines the nature of the good in those kinds of systems.

Up to the **Civil War**, responses to social problems tended toward exhortation of individual virtue and remedial assistance, although the seventeenth-century **Puritans**, with their vision of a "holy commonwealth," had a strong sense of the social good. Additionally, many Protestants in the middle 1800s, struck by various social ills, organized into benevolent and reform societies to assist those in need and remedy the ills of the period. A notable example of that social zeal was the abolitionist movement among the churches. Abolitionists saw **slavery** not simply as a set of wrongs to individuals, though it was that at least. They saw it as an unjust institution, and they sought to sweep away the entire institution and reform society of that social evil.

Nevertheless, a divide between the private and personal and the public and social existed, in various forms, in Catholicism, Judaism, and Protestantism. What Michael Meyer says of **Judaism** after the Civil War in *Response to Modernity* applies in general to the Christian churches in the United States as well: "If American society had its problems, they lay not in the system itself, but in individual lack of character. Rabbis preached personal morality rather than public action, social service rather than social justice." The strong individualism in American culture disposed clergy and others to view moral and social issues almost completely in terms of personal responsibility. Not until the late 1800s and early 1900s did social justice and action become more explicit and acceptable among all these groups. The changes occurred to a large degree as religious people, among others, were distressed by industrialism, labor conditions, socialism, urbanization, and immigration following the Civil War.

In American Protestantism, the propellant of social justice thought and action was the **Social Gospel** movement, which had significant roots in the benevolent and reform movements of the middle 1800s. **Solomon Washington Gladden** (1836–1918) and **Walter Rauschenbusch** (1861–1918), pastors and writers of theology and social analysis, were prominent shapers of this movement. Adherents of the Social Gospel engaged in critical analysis of social and economic realities. They outlined and advocated reforms in social and economic attitudes, practices, and structures. This movement laid a greater emphasis on the communal themes in the teachings of Jesus, especially the Kingdom of God, which played a profound role in shaping their social thought and hopes. The Social Gospel movement influenced many people in the Protestant churches into the 1930s and beyond, even when those people diverged from its optimistic progressivism. A chief example was the pastor and theologian **Karl Paul Reinhold Niebuhr**, who extensively applied the notion of justice to social and political issues in the United States and in the international sphere. Niebuhr in turn had profound influence for years on Protestant ethicists and even statesmen.

For American Catholics disturbed by the social tumult of the day, Pope Leo XIII's 1891 encyclical *Rerum novarum* gave explicit support to social justice. Catholic congresses in Baltimore in 1889 and in Chicago in 1893 issued statements on pressing social issues (e.g., communism and socialism, **capitalism**, and the right of labor to organize) and urged the Church to be active in social reform. In the 1910s, the American Federation of Catholic Societies pressed for specific measures to improve social structures (e.g., abolition of child labor, adequate wages, and humane working conditions). Pope Pius XI referred to social justice numerous times in his 1931 encyclical *Quadragesimo anno*, which was also very influential among American Catholics for its social teachings. It applied criteria of social justice to the social character of economic life, particularly with respect to fair distribution of goods, adequate workers' wages, respect for human dignity in capital's employment of labor, and institutions of social assistance.

A singular manifestation of social justice action among Catholics was the **Catholic Worker Movement**, founded by **Dorothy Day** and **Aristide Peter Maurin** in the 1930s. They opened hospitality centers in New York City and other urban areas to assist homeless and jobless men and women. The Catholic Worker was a more radical movement, centering especially on issues of poverty, the working class, and **pacifism**. It nurtured many young Catholics in social thought and action, and continues to do so even to the present.

Reform Judaism, emerging in the United States in the latter half of the nineteenth century, generally went further in terms of advocating social thought and justice than the more theologically conservative communities in American Judaism. Reform rabbis gathered in 1885 and issued the Pittsburgh Platform, which, among other things, urged American Jews to participate for justice in the social problems of the day. In 1923, the Central Conference of American Rabbis joined the Federal Council of Churches (a Protestant organization) in speaking out against harmful labor conditions.

Nevertheless, among Protestants in the 1900s, the divide continued between what was seen as social Christianity and conservative Christianity. Theologically conservative Christians often had deep suspicion of and even hostility to attempts to extend ideas of faith beyond the strictly individual sphere to the public and social sphere. The suspicion and hostility had both a theological and a socio-political component. Theologically, the suspicion has been based on the perceived religious liberalism of the Social Gospel movement in the early 1900s and its later heirs. As to the socio-political element, many Protestants and Catholics have long had a deep suspicion of and hostility to anything that suggested **socialism and communism**. Social thought and action came to be identified in the 1950s and 1960s with liberal Protestantism and even liberal or socialistic politics.

In that same period, other religious people—Protestant, Catholic and Jewish—were raising issues of social justice and working against the systems of racial segregation and the lack of **civil rights**. In recent decades, liberation theologies, with roots in Catholic Latin America's engagement with Marxist thought, have advocated visions of social justice, especially with respect to rights and opportunities for women, ethnic minorities, working class people, and dispossessed and poor people.

More contemporary Protestant groups have sought to overcome the divide between social Christianity and conservative Christianity. Evangelicals for Social Action, founded in the 1970s, aims to bridge the divide between liberal and conservative Protestants over religion as either a matter of social witness and this-worldly salvation or a matter of individual evangelism and other-worldly salvation. Similar to this group, though less an organization and more a community of similarly convinced people, is a group called **Sojourners**. Sojourners, arising out of a theologically conservative seminary in the late 1960s, is intentionally evangelical in theology and communitarian and systemic in ethical thought, action, and lifestyle.

The history of this divide makes all the more remarkable the emergence in the 1980s of conservative Protestantism's vigorous engagement with the public and social sphere through numerous leaders and organizations, such as **Jerry Falwell** and the **Moral Majority** and **Pat Robertson** and the **Christian Coalition**. Motivated by a strong perception of the sorry state of the social good, and no longer eschewing the political realm, but with very different analyses and agendas from religious liberals or even social **Evangelicals**, they look forward to a spiritual renewal of individuals and the social realm.

These various perspectives on social good in our contemporary situation reveal vast differences in analysis and prescription. They show that merely having a concern for public and social good does not guarantee commonality in analysis of what is wrong or in prescription of what would be right in the search for the good society. (GSS) **See also** Abolition; Communitarianism; Conservatism; "Economic Justice for All"; Liberalism; Liberation Theology; Race Relations; Religion and Urban Issues; Roman Catholicism; Welfare; Women in Religion and Politics.

BIBLIOGRAPHY

Ahlstrom, Sydney E. *A Religious History of the American People*. New Haven, CT: Yale University Press, 1972.

Aristotle. *The Ethics of Aristotle: The Nichomachean Ethics Translated*. J. A. K. Thomson, translator. Baltimore: Penguin Books, 1955; Penguin Classics reprint, 1971.

Bellah, Robert N., Richard Madsen, William N. Sullivan, Ann Swidler, Steven M. Tipton. *The Good Society*. New York: Alfred A. Knopf, 1991.

Cohen, Ronald L., ed. *Justice: Views from the Social Sciences*. New York: Plenum, 1986.

Forell, George W., ed. *Christian Social Teachings: A Reader in Christian Social Ethics from the Bible to the Present*. Minneapolis: Augsburg, 1971.

Meyer, Michael A. *Response to Modernity: A History of the Reform Movement in Judaism*. New York: Oxford University Press, 1988.

Plato. *The Republic of Plato*. Francis MacDonald Cornford, translator. Oxford: Oxford University Press, 1970.

Rawls, John. *A Theory of Justice*. Oxford: Oxford University Press, 1978.

Smith, Timothy L. *Revivalism and Social Reform in Mid-Nineteenth-Century America*. New York: Abingdon, 1957.

Troeltsch, Ernst. *The Social Teachings of the Christian Churches*. 2 vols. Olive Wyon, translator. Chicago: University of Chicago, 1976.

Socialism and Communism

Socialism and communism involve a complex of movements, perspectives, and goals from the late 1700s to the present. Some forms of socialism and communism emphasize the economic; some, the social; and some, the political. Historically and ideologically, socialism and communism consist of a continuum from comparatively conservative and evolutionary reform, to radical and revolutionary change, and even to anarchistic or totalitarian forms. Moreover, religious people have variously advocated, qualified, or vilified socialism and communism. In turn, socialists and communists have variously appropriated, qualified, or vilified religious ideas and patterns.

The terms "socialism" and "communism" are sometimes used interchangeably. There is some warrant for this. Adherents of communism have at times referred to the system they pursue as socialism or the end stage of socialism. Nevertheless, socialism and communism can also be meaningfully distinguished. At its most basic, socialism refers to common ownership of the means of production and distribution. Communism more narrowly refers to particular social, economic, and political applications of Karl Marx's materialist philosophy and theory of economic struggle, especially as carried out in Russia following the 1917 revolution. Some socialists argue that communism in Russia and other countries deviates from and even perverts socialism. Antecedent to communism, socialism encompasses a broader variety of ideas and goals.

In considering socialism and communism in the United States, we will concentrate on socialism. For many reasons, socialism has been stronger and more popular than communism in the U.S. American communism, in itself and in its support for Russian communism, tended toward a more ideological and intransigent opposition to religion and to American democratic perspectives. Such characteristics have made it anathema to the majority of Americans, even those skeptical about American **capitalism** and society.

Some religious leaders have embraced communism and socialism as remedies for the evils they see in capitalism. Shown here is a meeting of the Michigan Branch of the American Communist Party. Photo by Arthur Siegel. Library of Congress.

Broadly speaking, many antecedents to socialism can be found. In Plato's *Republic*, the guardians or rulers of society were not to own property. Chapter four of the New Testament Book of Acts describes the early Christian community in Jerusalem. Those Christians disclaimed private ownership, gave property and proceeds from sale of property to be held in common, and distributed their goods to each according to need. Thomas More's *Utopia* (1516) projected a society in which all land is owned in common. Radical Protestants (Anabaptists) in the European Reformation—such as the Hutterites, originating in the 1530s and continuing to this day even in Canada and the United States—instituted communal ownership and life.

Utopian visions, usually with common ownership, communal lifestyles, and perfectionist impulses, thread throughout history as antecedents to or outgrowths of socialist notions and hopes. Such visions gained great impetus in reaction to the Industrial Revolution and modern capitalism in the late 1700s and the 1800s. Utopian socialist experiments in England and America sprang up from several sources—religious, philosophical, political, and economic. A few that practiced, in various forms, common ownership of goods and communal lifestyles include the Shakers in England and New England (late 1700s and 1800s), New Harmony in Indiana (early 1800s), the Oneida Community in upper New York State (from 1848 to around 1880), and the transcendentalist utopian experiment at Brook Farm in Massachusetts (1840s).

The beginnings of socialism date chiefly from this fertile period of utopian experiments, the first half of the 1800s. Additionally, revolutions in France and elsewhere in 1848 promoted egalitarian and socialist ideas. Marx and Engels published the *Communist Manifesto* in 1848, arguing in terms of economic struggle and change (dialectical materialism) and urging workers (the proletariat) to unite against capitalism. They helped organize the First International (Congress) of the International Workingmen's Association in 1866. While the history is too vast and varied to detail here, socialist and communist organization continued through the later 1800s and into the 1900s, with the Second International in 1889, the Russian Revolution in 1917, and the spread of socialist and communist movements and parties. One example was the Christian socialists in England in the mid-1800s and early 1900s (notable leaders were F. D. Maurice and Charles Kingsley, clergy in the Church of England). The Fabian Society, founded in England in 1884, dissented from Marxism and revolution, yet clearly stood for progressive socialist reforms and goals.

In the United States, the **Civil War** accelerated industrialization, capitalism, and urbanization. **Social justice** took on greater urgency in this post-war period. For example, the **Social Gospel** movement arose in the late 1800s and early 1900s, with prominent Protestant clergy among its proponents, such as **Josiah Strong**, **Solomon Washington Gladden**, and **Walter Rauschenbusch**. This social Christianity provided a critique of individualistic and exploitative capitalism, and urged structural reforms in **labor**, industry, and urban life. At points, Reformed **Judaism** in the late 1800s issued appeals for social justice, and in 1923 the Central Conference of American Rabbis joined the Protestant churches in formally denouncing certain industrial practices and advocating reforms. Catholic and Protestant churches instituted agencies and programs to ameliorate the troubles of the poor and working class. Much of what they did paralleled and approximated socialist goals for a just society.

Also in the post-Civil War period, socialists of various backgrounds (often with European socialist backgrounds, and often connected with organized labor) began organizing into the Socialist Labor Party (1877) and the Social Democracy Party (1898). Representatives from those groups and others inaugurated the Socialist Party of America in 1901. Eugene V. Debs—labor organizer, visionary, and presidential candidate—was the leading socialist of this period. The Socialist Party reached its zenith of membership and electoral successes in the years before the **World War I**, which, along with the Russian Revolution and fears of communism—seriously damaged the party. The American Communist Party formed in 1919 and aligned with the Russian communist model. Socialists and communists in the United States began struggling with each other, to each other's detriment.

Some religious people became actual socialists. In the late 1880s through the 1930s, a number of Christians joined the Socialist Party, organized societies of Christian socialists, or identified themselves with socialist views and goals. Many were influenced by Christian socialism in England. Among them were the Episcopal priest William Dwight Porter Bliss and the lay theologian Vida Scudder. Prominent for a time as a Christian socialist was the prolific and influential pastor and theologian, **Karl Paul Reinhold Niebuhr** (though he later turned from socialism). In 1934, the National Council of Methodist Youth circulated a pledge that began, "I surrender my life to Christ. I renounce the Capitalist system." The **Catholic Worker Movement**, begun in the 1930s, had strong connections with socialism and nurtured numerous Catholics in radical critiques of American capitalism and "bourgeois" culture.

Yet, in general, mainstream religious leaders and people have shied from or denounced socialism and communism, even when they sought goals that bore affinities to socialist aims. The papal encyclicals *Rerum novarum* (1891) and *Quadragesimo anno* (1932), important for spurring social justice thought among Catholics, explicitly condemned socialism and communism. In 1938, the **Southern Baptist Convention** declared the American economic system the best in the world, and said there "ought to be no room for radical Socialism and for atheistic Communism in the United States." Socialism and communism have been rejected as materialist and atheistic. Also, the collectivist approach of socialism and communism runs directly counter to the deeply ingrained, sacrosanct individualism of American culture. For the most part, religion in the United States has found capitalism more congenial to faith and American life.

Many in the socialist and communist movements have also been suspicious of or hostile to religion. For example, immigrants from Germany brought socialist ideas with them, including a rejection of churches as aligned with the capitalist system. The radical Industrial Workers of the World (the "Wobblies") was basically a socialist labor organization oriented toward the unskilled and non-unionized working class, and skeptical at best of religion.

During the 1930s, the Great Depression and Franklin Roosevelt's **New Deal** greatly affected socialism, capitalism, and religion. This period was a high point for socialism among Christians. Yet, many socialists derided the New Deal as insufficiently socialistic, whereas conservatives attacked the New Deal as too socialistic. In reality, the New Deal did not overthrow or even threaten the democratic, capitalist system; yet it ushered in long-lasting changes toward a mixed economy—

capitalism with socialistic elements, such as more government intervention in the economy and government guarantees of some social **welfare** systems (e.g., Social Security).

Since then, the long-term social welfare effects of the New Deal on American government and culture have come under severe criticism from theologically and politically conservative religious quarters. Coupled with this attack has been a resurgence in the 1980s and 1990s of strong defenses of democratic capitalism by influential religious thinkers, such as **Michael Novak** and **Richard John Neuhaus**. However, socialism has not died out in the United States, despite Americans' fears of communism in Eastern Europe and Russia at its height and now relief at its collapse. Socialists, such as Michael Harrington (himself once an editor at *The Catholic Worker*) and Irving Howe, and socialist groups continue to advance socialist views.

Certain religious movements and groups also continue to pursue ideas with significant affinities to socialism. The Bruderhof (Society of Brothers), formed in 1953, carries on something of the Anabaptist tradition with farm and light industry communes in the United States and elsewhere. Aspects of the "Jesus" movement in the 1960s were socialistic and communal in nature. Groups like **Sojourners** and The Other Side share many socialist perspectives and goals. An important movement in other countries and in the United States in the last 30 years is **liberation theology**, much imbued with socialist and even Marxist analysis. Of the variety of liberation theologies, some emphasize political and economic issues, and some emphasize gender or ethnic issues, though all usually have some mix of such concerns. Thus, the encounter between Christ and Marx, or religion and socialism, begun more than 150 years ago, still engages both religious and nonreligious people in vigorous and challenging ways. (GSS) **See also** Atheism; Conservatism; Democracy; Race Relations; Religion and Urban Issues; Roman Catholicism; Trancendentalism; Utopianism.

BIBLIOGRAPHY

Ahlstrom, Sydney E. *A Religious History of the American People*. New Haven, CT: Yale University Press, 1972.

Dombrowski, James. *The Early Days of Christian Socialism in America*. New York: Columbia University, 1936.

Harrington, Michael. *Socialism: Past and Future*. New York: Arcade Publishing, 1989.

Howe, Irving. *Socialism and America*. New York: Harcourt Brace Jovanovich, 1985.

Kipnis, Ira. *The American Socialist Movement, 1897-1912*. New York: Columbia University Press, 1952.

Laslett, John H. M., and Seymour M. Lipset, eds. *Failure of a Dream? Essays in the History of American Socialism*. Los Angeles: University of California, 1984.

Tabb, William K., ed. *Churches in Struggle: Liberation Theologies and Social Change in North America*. New York: Monthly Review Press, 1986.

Wells, Harold. *A Future for Socialism? Political Theology and the "Triumph of Capitalism."* Valley Forge, PA: Trinity Press International, 1996.

Society for the Propagation of the Gospel

The Society for the Propagation of the Gospel was formed in 1701 by Thomas Bray to supply the colonies with ministers. Based in England, the Society trained Anglican ministers to go to the New World and fill the growing need for properly trained clergy among the growing colonial population. The Society was especially effective in both North and South Carolina where their influence made the Anglican Church the established church. **See also** Colonial America.

BIBLIOGRAPHY

Curry, Thomas J. *The First Freedoms*. New York Oxford University Press, 1986.

Sojourners

The Sojourners form a community of Christians, who are basically evangelical in theology and committed to the **social justice** dimensions of the gospel of Jesus. The community takes its name from the biblical idea that the people of God are merely sojourners in this world. It began in the early 1970s with a group of seminary students at Trinity Evangelical Divinity School in Deerfield, Illinois. In word and action, that small group of students protested numerous issues, including American involvement in **Vietnam**, racism, and the captivity (in their view) of the Christian churches to American culture. They initiated a journal called *The Post-American*, which eventually became *Sojourners* magazine, which is still in publication. One of the group's original leaders, Jim Wallis, continues in an influential role in the Sojourners' community and in the wider Christian world.

The Sojourners' vision is influenced by the Anabaptist movement, especially its peace witness, and the social thought and action of the **Catholic Worker Movement**. Many who affiliate with the Sojourners live in simplicity and community in an urban setting in Washington, D.C. Through the magazine, activism, neighborhood service, and networks with other Christian groups, the Sojourners seek to be a faithful, prophetic community in the often hard realities of modern life. (GSS) **See also** Evangelicals; Mark O. Hatfield; Race Relations; Religion and Urban Issues; Roman Catholicism.

BIBLIOGRAPHY

Wallis, Jim. *The Soul of Politics: A Practical and Prophetic Vision for Change*. New York: The New Press, 1994.

——. *Agenda for Biblical People*. New York: Harper & Row, 1976.

Southern Baptist Convention

The Southern Baptist Convention is the largest Baptist organization in the world with over 35,000 churches, 16,000,000 members, and **missionaries** in over 120 countries. Split from the General Missionary Convention in 1845 over disagreements that mirrored deeper regional divisions over **slavery**, the denomination retained its southern character until the mid-twentieth century. That regional linkage weakened in the second half of the century as the denomination's churches spread to every state.

The Convention has often struggled to maintain unity; protracted tensions over biblical inaccuracy and other fundamental issues of faith after 1980 increased denominational conservatism and spawned more liberal divisions such as the Cooperating Baptist Fellowship. In 1996, the four highest offices in the constitutional order of succession to the presidency, though contested, were held by conservative Southern **Baptists**. The conservatives have used their ascendency to enforce prohibitions of the ordination of women and to take such controversial actions as the boycott of the Walt Disney Company for films perceived to be anti-Christian and its willingness to extend benefits to the partners of its gay and lesbian employees. (AOT) **See also** Conservatism; Homosexual Rights; Women in Religion and Politics.

BIBLIOGRAPHY

Ammerman, Nancy T., ed. *Southern Baptists Observed: Multiple Perspectives on a Changing Denomination.* Knoxville: University of Tennessee Press, 1993.

Smith, Oran P. *The Rise of Baptist Republicanism.* New York: New York University Press, 1997.

Southern Christian Leadership Conference (SCLC)

The Southern Christian Leadership Conference (SCLC) was organized in Atlanta, Georgia, in December 1952 following the successful boycott of the segregated bus system in Montgomery, Alabama. The boycott, which had been led by the Reverend **Martin Luther King, Jr.**, represented the emergence of African-American ministers as leaders in the **civil rights** movement. Their leadership was a result of their status in the African-American community as well as their economic independence from the white power structure in the South.

The SCLC was led by Martin Luther King, Jr. from its origin until his assassination in Memphis, Tennessee, on April 4, 1968. The primary strategy of the SCLC was the use of nonviolent direct action techniques, including marches, demonstrations, boycotts, and **civil disobedience** as a way of protesting racial discrimination and segregation. The activities of the Southern Christian Leadership Conference were instrumental in securing the passage of the Civil Rights Act of 1964 and the Voting Rights Act of 1965 and establishing the role of Dr. Martin Luther King, Jr. as the most prominent spokesperson for the civil rights movement until his death. (WVM) **See also** African-American Churches; Civil Rights Acts; Race Relations.

BIBLIOGRAPHY

Fairclough, Adam. *To Redeem the South of America: The Southern Christian Leadership Conference and Martin Luther King, Jr.* Athens: University of Georgia Press, 1987.

Garrow, David J. *Bearing the Cross: Martin Luther King, Jr., and the Southern Christian Leadership Conference.* New York: W. Morrow, 1986.

Spanish-American War (1898)

The Spanish-American War of 1898 made the United States a global naval power, illustrated the ability of the press to shape public opinion, and thrust Americans into a moral debate over **imperialism**. Newspaper coverage of the 1895 Cuban revolt against Spain created great sympathy for the Cuban cause. In December 1897, rioting in Havana led the United States to send the battleship *Maine* to the city's harbor. On February 15, 1898, an explosion of unknown origins sunk the battleship and killed its crew of 260 men. Despite Spanish efforts to investigate the sinking, the yellow press in the United States, led by William Randolph Hearst and Joseph Pulitzer, called for **war** by repeating the slogan, "Remember the Maine, to hell with Spain."

Newspaperman William Randolph Hearst helped fuel the flames of war after the USS *Maine* was sunk in Havana Harbor. National Archives.

Driven by public opinion, Congress demanded that Spain leave Cuba. On April 24, 1898, Spain declared war and the United States followed suit the following day. A series of one-sided naval battles in Cuba and the Pacific, and a largely successful land campaign in Cuba, left Spain defeated. On December 10, the two countries signed the Treaty of Paris. Spain withdrew from Cuba and received $20 million and the United States acquired the Spanish colonies of Guam, Puerto Rico, and the Philippines.

There was considerable disagreement about the impact of the newly acquired territories. Some churches supported Republican President **William McKinley** and his call "to educate the Filipinos, and uplift and civilize and Christianize them." Although McKinley denied that the United States had any "imperial designs," many religious and political leaders, like Senator George F. Hoar of Massachusetts, objected to what they saw as the country's growing imperialistic tendencies. Though, McKinley denied that there was any "imperial designs lurk[ing] in the American mind." **See also** William Jennings Bryan; Theodore Roosevelt.

BIBLIOGRAPHY

Karraker, William Archibald. *The American Churches and the Spanish-American War.* Chicago: The University of Chicago Press, 1940.

Samuels, Peggy. *Remembering the Maine.* Washington, DC: Smithsonian Institution Press, 1995.

Francis Joseph Spellman (1889–1967)

Cardinal Francis Spellman was one of the most influential Catholic prelates in the United States. Ordained in 1917, Spellman became Archbishop of New York in 1939 and a member of the College of Cardinals in 1946. Spellman was the first American attaché to the Vatican Secretary of State, Cardinal Pacelli. During his tenure in the Vatican, Spellman was responsible for smuggling out Pope Pius XI's condemnation of Nazism, which was published by the Associated Press in 1937. At Spellman's urging, Franklin D. Roosevelt became the first American president to appoint a personal representative to the Vatican. An outspoken anti-Communist, Spellman was a strong supporter of American efforts in **World War II**, Korea, and **Vietnam**. **See also** Roman Catholicism; Socialism and Communism; Vatican, Diplomatic Relations with.

Cardinal Francis Joseph Spellman, shown here reviewing a St. Patrick's Day parade in New York City in 1965, was one of the most important prelates of the American Catholic Church. Library of Congress.

BIBLIOGRAPHY

Cooney, James. *The American Pope*. New York: Time Books, 1984.

Gannon, Robert I. *The Cardinal Spellman Story*. Garden City, NY: Doubleday, 1962.

Elizabeth Cady Stanton (1815–1902)

One of the most important advocates of women's rights in the nineteenth century, Elizabeth Cady Stanton was remarkable among early feminists for her conclusion that Christianity is antithetical to the rights of women.

Initially active in the temperance and abolitionist movements, Stanton began to focus on the rights of women after she was denied a seat at the World Anti-Slavery Conference in London in 1840. In 1848, Stanton and Lucretia Mott organized the first women's rights convention in Seneca Falls, New York, where Stanton drafted the famous Declaration of Sentiments demanding equal rights for women.

In 1851, Stanton formed an important partnership with **Susan Brownell Anthony**. With Stanton doing most of the speaking and writing and Anthony doing most of the organizing, the two lobbied unceasingly for women's rights. In 1869, they founded the National Woman Suffrage Association and in 1890 the National American Woman Suffrage Association.

The two friends also published a suffrage newspaper, *The Revolution* (1868–1870), and they collaborated with their colleague Matilda Gage on the compilation and publication of the first three volumes of *The History of Woman Suffrage*, 6 vols. (1881–1922).

Unlike many of her colleagues, Stanton became convinced the "Bible and the Church have been the greatest stumbling blocks in the way of woman's emancipation." To help remedy the problem, Stanton published the *Woman's Bible* (1895), an unorthodox reinterpretation of the Bible that embarrassed many of her colleagues. (MDH) **See also** Abolition; Feminism; Slavery; Temperance and Prohibition; Women in Religion and Politics.

BIBLIOGRAPHY

Griffith, Elizabeth. *In Her Own Right: The Life of Elizabeth Cady Stanton*. New York: Oxford University Press, 1984.

Stanton, Elizabeth Cady. *Eighty Years and More: Reminiscences 1815-1897*. New York: Schocken Books, 1971.

Rodney Stark (1934–)

Born in Jamestown, North Dakota, Rodney Stark obtained his doctorate from the University of California, Berkeley. Teaching first at the Center for the Study of Law and Society, Stark then became professor of sociology at the University of Washington. Known for his research on church growth, Stark has explained how religious groups change from new religious movements on society's fringe to culturally supported institutions supported by society. This evolution occurs as the group accommodates modernity while maintaining cultural and theological distinctiveness. In 1968, he published with Charles Glock, *American Piety*, which became a seminal work in the sociological study of religion. A pioneer, he helped lay much of the theoretical groundwork for an experimental study of religion and politics. (MEN)

BIBLIOGRAPHY

Finke, Roger and Rodney Stark. *The Churching of America, 1776-1990: Winners and Losers in Our Religious Economy*. Brunswick, NJ: Rutgers University Press, 1992.

Stark, Rodney and Charles Y. Glock. *American Piety: The Nature of Religious Commitment*. Berkeley: University of California Press, 1968.

Potter Stewart (1915–1985)

Appointed to the U.S. Supreme Court by in 1958 by President Dwight D. Eisenhower, Potter Stewart became one of the Court's conservatives and was the lone dissenter to the Court's decision in ***Engel v. Vitale*** (1962), the important case banning **school prayer**. Stewart also wrote dissents *in Griswold v. Connecticut* (1965), in which the Court struck down a state law banning contraceptives. He retired from the Court in 1981, having established himself as a vocal opponent of justices who read their own political and moral opinions into the Constitution. Stewart practiced judicial restraint, believing that it was the role of the legislature to prescribe specific practices and to define social mores. Accordingly, he gave greater deference to laws than his liberal colleagues. (MWP) **See also** Abortion and Birth Control Regulation; Conservatism; Pornography.

Bibliography

Bendiner, Robert. "The Law and Potter Stewart." *American Heritage* 35 (December 1983): 98.

Binion, Gayle. "An Assessment of Potter Stewart." *Center Magazine* 14 (September-October 1981): 2.

Ezra Stiles (1727–1795)

Ezra Stiles was the pastor of the Second Congregational Church in Newport, Rhode Island, from 1755 to 1786. Instrumental in founding Brown University in 1764, Stiles was also a staunch supporter of the **American Revolution**. He was elected president of Yale College in 1778, and served as professor of ecclesiastical history and an instructor in Hebrew, theology, and the sciences. Stiles combined a life of extraordinary scholarship with active involvment in New England's struggles for ecclesiastical and political liberty. He also promoted, on religious grounds, a conciliatory attitude towards the Jews and the **abolition** of **slavery**. (PV) **See also** Congregationalism; Judaism.

Bibliography

Morgan, Edmund Sears. *The Gentle Puritan: A Life of Ezra Stiles, 1727-1795.* New Haven, CT: Yale University Press, 1962.

Anson Phelps Stokes (1874–1958)

Son of the millionaire banker by the same name, Anson Phelps Stokes was a leading educator and Episcopal Priest. In 1950, he published his monumental three-volume study, *Church and State in the United States*. The work details the relations of church and state from colonial times to the mid-twentieth century. Almost instantly upon publication, the book became the classic work (one reviewer called it "absolutely essential to every student of American religious history.") on the subject. **See also** Episcopal Church; Establishment Clause; First Amendment; Wall of Separation.

Bibliography

Stokes, Anson Phelps. *Church and State in the United States.* New York: Harper & Row, 1964.

Stone v. Graham (1980)

A Kentucky statute required the posting of a copy of the Ten Commandments on the wall of each public school classroom in the state. The copies were required to be purchased with private contributions, and the statute mandated the following notation in small print at the bottom of each display: "The secular application of the Ten Commandments is clearly seen in its adoption as the fundamental legal code of Western Civilization and the Common Law of the United States." In *Stone v. Graham*, 449 U.S. 39 (1980), the U.S. Supreme Court ruled that such an avowed purpose was not sufficient to avoid conflict with the **First Amendment**. Since the preeminent purpose of posting the Ten Commandments was religious in nature, the posting did not serve a solely secular educational function and therefore violated the **Establishment Clause** of the First Amendment. The Court went on to note that the fact "that the posted copies are financed by voluntary private contributions is immaterial, for the mere posting under the auspices of the legislature provides the official support of the state government that the Establishment Clause prohibits." (JM) **See also** Education; Wall of Separation.

Bibliography

Eastland, Terry. *Religious Liberty in the Supreme Court.* Washington, DC: Ethics and Public Policy Center, 1993.

Harlan Fiske Stone (1872–1946)

Although appointed to the Supreme Court in 1925 by Republican Calvin Coolidge, Harlan Fiske Stone upheld many of the **New Deal** reforms of Democrat Franklin Roosevelt. In *United States v. Butler* (1936) he opposed the majority when it declared Franklin Roosevelt's Agriculture Adjustment Act unconstitutional, warning that judicial power was more difficult to restrain than legislative power. He took part in a number of important Supreme Court cases involving religion including ***Cantwell v. State of Connecticut*** (1940), ***Minersville School District v. Gobitis*** (1940), and ***West Virginia State Board of Education v. Barnette*** (1943). He wrote an important and memorable dissent in *Gobitis* arguing that state could not compel people against their religious beliefs to say the **pledge of allegiance**. His dissent in the **Jehovah's Witness** flag salute case would become the court's opinion in *Barnette*. Roosevelt appointed Stone chief justice in 1941, a position he held until his death. (MWP) **See also** Conservatism; Flag Salute Cases; Liberalism.

Bibliography

Konefsky, Samuel J. *Chief Justice Stone and the Supreme Court.* New York: Macmillan, 1945.

Mason, Alpheus T. *Harlan Fiske Stone: Pillar of the Law.* New York: Viking Press, 1956.

Joseph Story (1779–1845)

A preeminent American jurist, Joseph Story was an associate justice of the U.S. Supreme Court, Harvard University's Dane Professor of Law, and a prolific legal commentator. A member of the House of Representatives from Massachusetts in 1808–09, Story was appointed to the Supreme Court in 1811 by President **James Madison**. During his 33-year tenure on the Supreme Court, Story authored important church-state opinions. In ***Terrett v. Taylor*** (1815), he ruled that the Virginia legislature lacked authority to expropriate the property of the **Episcopal Church**, the former established church of Virginia. In *Vidal v. Girard's Executors* (1844), Story upheld Stephen Girard's will establishing a college for poor white orphans who were to be taught "the purest principles of morality" but without the benefit of clergy. Heirs contested the will, arguing that it was "derogatory and hostile to the Christian religion, and so is void, as being against the common law and public policy of Pennsylvania." While upholding the will, Story stated that in accord with the principle that Christianity is part of the common law, the college must respect the Christian religion. His influential three-volume *Commentaries on the Constitution of the United States* (1833) provided an authoritative interpretation of the constitutional principles governing church-state relations. He argued that the **First Amendment** permits the civil state to encourage Christianity in general but forbids the promotion of any one particular denomination or limitation on the private rights of conscience. (Selections from Joseph Story's *Commentaries* are reprinted in Appendix 1.) (DLD) **See also** Common Law and Christianity; Establishment Clause; Wall of Separation.

BIBLIOGRAPHY

McClellan, James. *Joseph Story and the American Constitution: A Study in Political and Legal Thought*. Norman: University of Oklahoma Press, 1971.

Harriet Beecher Stowe (1811–1896)

One of the best-known female authors in the United States in the nineteenth century, Harriet Beecher Stowe is most famous for her anti-**slavery** novel ***Uncle Tom's Cabin***, which, like many of her works, was clearly informed by her evangelical convictions. One of 13 children of **Lyman Beecher**, a Congregational (later Presbyterian) minister, Harriet Beecher was raised as an evangelical Calvinist. Many of her works, such as *The Mayflower; or Sketches of Scenes and Characters among the Descendants of the Pilgrims* (1843) and *The Minister's Wooing* (1859), have clear religious themes. Stowe lived in Cincinnati, Ohio, for 18 years, first with her father's family and then with her husband, the Bible scholar Calvin Ellis Stowe, whom she married in 1836. Her first-hand experiences living next to the slave state of Kentucky, when combined with the evangelical impulse to reform society, led her to become a strong abolitionist. Encouraged by her husband and her brother, **Henry Ward Beecher**, she wrote her anti-slavery work, *Uncle Tom's Cabin* or *Life Among the Lowly*, which was first published in serial form in 1851–52 in the *National Era*, an anti-slavery paper in Washington, D.C. Published in book form in 1852, *Uncle Tom's Cabin* greatly aroused anti-slavery sentiment in the North and helped make slavery as much a moral issue as a political one. The book is often considered a cause of the **Civil War**, a view reinforced by **Abraham Lincoln** who, upon meeting Stowe during the war, reportedly asked if she was "the little woman who started this great war?" (MDH) **See also** Abolition; Catherine Beecher; Edward Beecher; Calvinism; Congregationalism; Evangelicals; Isabella Beecher Hooker; Presbyterian Church; Women in Religion and Politics.

(Left to right) Harriet Beecher Stowe with her father Lyman Beecher and her brother Henry Ward Beecher. Library of Congress.

BIBLIOGRAPHY

Hendrick, Joan. *Harriet Beecher Stowe: A Life*. New York: Oxford University Press, 1994.

Wilson, Forrest. *Crusader in Crinoline: The Life of Harriet Beecher Stowe*. Philadelphia: J.B. Lippincott, 1941.

Josiah Strong (1847–1916)

In 1885, the American clergyman Josiah Strong published *Our Country*, which called for religious solutions for the growing social problems of industrialization. From 1886 to 1898, Strong served as secretary of the American Branch of the Evangelical Alliance (founded 1867), an organization begun in London in 1846 to promote the unification of Protestant churches. A strong proponent of the **Social Gospel** and of the need to Christianize society, Strong published *The New Era* in 1893 to argue that the Christian church could expand the Kingdom of God on earth by involvement in social work for the good of society. In 1898, Strong resigned his secretaryship and founded the League for Social Service. He also began to work on what became the Federal Council of Churches of Christ (1908), which, thanks to Strong's influence, developed a stress on social issues. (MWP) **See also** Evangelicals; Social Justice.

BIBLIOGRAPHY

Strong, Josiah. *Our Country: Its Possible Future and Its Present Crisis*. New York: Baker & Taylor, 1885.

——. *Religious Movements for Social Betterment*. New York: Baker & Taylor, 1900.

——. *The Challenge of the City*. New York: Young People's Missionary Movement, 1907.

——. *My Religion in Every-Day Life*. New York: Baker & Taylor, 1910.

In Re Summers (1945)

Illinois denied Clyde Wilson Summers admission to the practice of law. Applicants for admission to the bar are required to take an oath to support the Constitution of Illinois. Summers' religious convictions prevented him from serving in the Illinois militia, and he declared that he could not in good faith take the prescribed oath. Summers challenged this decision on the grounds that it violated the First and Fourteenth Amendments. In the case *In Re Summers*, 325 U.S. 561 (1945), the Supreme Court rejected this challenge, stating that it was within the legitimate powers of a state to place such qualifications upon admission to the bar. (JM) **See also** First Amendment; Fourteenth Amendment.

BIBLIOGRAPHY

Regan, Richard J. *Private Conscience and Public Law*. New York: Fordham University Press, 1972.

Sunday Law Cases (1961)

In 1961, so-called **Blue Laws** were challenged in two states, Pennsylvania and Maryland. The Pennsylvania law requiring that businesses be closed on Sundays was challenged on free exercise grounds by Orthodox Jews whose religion required that they close their stores on Saturdays. The Maryland law was challenged as a violation of the **Establishment Clause** of the **First Amendment**. In both cases, the U.S. Supreme Court upheld the Sunday closing laws, arguing that the Constitution did not prohibit state legislation "whose reason or effect merely happens to coincide with the tenets of some or all religions." In *McGovern v. Maryland* (1961), the Court stated, "The present purpose and effect of most of our Sunday Closing Laws is to provide a uniform day of rest for all citizens; and the fact that this day is Sunday, a day of particular significance for the dominant Christian sects, does not bar the State from achieving its secular goals." In *Braunfeld v. Brown* (1961), the Court stated that statutes were valid if "the State regulates conduct by enacting a general law within its power, the purpose and effect of which is to advance the State's secular goals." (JM) **See also** Free Exercise Clause; Judaism; Sabbatarianism.

BIBLIOGRAPHY

Stone, Geoffrey R. et. al. *Constitutional Law*. Boston: Little, Brown and Company, 1991.

West, John G. *The Politics of Revelation and Reason*. Lawrence: University Press of Kansas, 1996.

Sunday Mail

The **First Amendment** prohibits Congress from making laws "respecting an establishment of religion." Hence, as a matter of law ("de jure"), it is unconstitutional to make legislation with the primary purpose of advancing the religious beliefs of one group. However, as a matter of fact ("de facto"), Protestant Christianity has throughout American history pursued, enjoyed, and defended a privileged position within Christian beliefs and practices. Generally, this "establishment" has been largely informal, embedded in the structures of American culture. Yet at times legislation has been sought and enacted to give privileged positions to certain Christian beliefs or practices. Supporters of such efforts believe that they are permissible because they facilitate the **free exercise** rights of the majority of Americans.

One example of the favorable treatment of Protestant Christianity in American history is the status of Sunday. While **Judaism** observes its Sabbath on Saturday, and **Islam** observes its Sabbath on Friday, the majority of Christians observe the Sabbath on Sunday. Since the colonial period, Sunday has occupied a special status, culturally and even legally. Much of the cultural and legal heritage of Sunday's special status stems from the **Puritans**, who enforced a strict observance of Sunday as a day kept holy through worship and avoidance of "worldly" pursuits. Protestant Christianity has sought ever since to maintain a sacred character for Sunday as vital and necessary for believers and for the whole nation. Only in the last generation or two have the **Blue Laws** restricting commerce and certain other activities on Sunday been largely dismantled.

An interesting controversy in the early 1800s highlighted these issues. In 1810, Congress legislated that mail be delivered every day, including Sunday. Unsuccessfully at first, many **Evangelical** Protestants opposed Sunday delivery, denouncing it as pernicious to morality, Christian civilization, and local control. They also argued that Sunday mails infringed on religious liberty by compelling Christian postal workers to work on Sunday against their conscience and by lending government support to sabbath-breaking. After hundreds of petitions flooded Congress urging the repeal of Sunday mails in 1829, **Richard M. Johnson**, then chairman of the Senate Committee on Post Offices and Post Roads, attacked "religious combinations to effect a political object" and claimed that shutting down the post office on Sundays would force the government to decide the theological question of which day was the true sabbath. Even so, Johnson acknowledged that people needed a day of rest and did not object to the fact that the rest of the federal government's "public business" was generally suspended on Sundays. While today we may not have Sunday mail delivery, we remain entangled with similar issues of religion, pluralism, public policy, and the Constitution. (GS) **See also** Establishment Clause; First Amendment; Sabbatarianism; Wall of Separation.

BIBLIOGRAPHY

John, Richard. "Taking Sabbatarianism Seriously: The Postal System, the Sabbath, and the Transformation of American Political Culture." *Journal of the Early Republic* 10 (Winter 1990): 517-67.

West, John G. *The Politics of Revelation and Reason*. Lawrence: University of Kansas, 1996.

Sunday School Movement

The Sunday school movement began in England in 1780 when Anglican clergymen working with poor children in the city were appalled by their impiety and illiteracy. These free voluntary schools to educate young children on Sunday mornings spread to the United States in 1791. The teachers, often young men and women from established congregations familiar with charity work, recruited boys and girls from city streets by promising games, music, food, and clothing.

By the 1830s, only one-third of American children attended school, so many public officials cooperated with Sunday schools to rid the streets of truant and disorderly youngsters, often in tacit support of the schools' proselytization efforts. Most antebellum Protestant churches adopted the Sunday school as a necessary moral instruction method for all children in the era of the expanding secular public school. Publishers provided specialized tracts and books with hymns and biblical stories appropriate for juveniles, and young women found suitable careers as teachers. Sunday school superintendents formed denominational and regional organizations to promote this work by the 1840s and the first national Sunday School Convention was held in 1875.

Some evangelical Protestant churches opened Sunday schools as a mission for poor children, arousing opposition from Catholics who feared Sunday schools as child-stealing. In 1864, Lower East Side missions also prompted New York City Jews to open free Sabbath schools for poor Jewish children much as Catholic Sunday schools were established. Nonetheless, Congregational and Methodist middle-class congregations invented the Sunday school mite box to collect pennies in support of these missionary Sunday schools in slum districts.

By the 1880s, the Sunday school movement had become an American institution common in most Protestant, Catholic, and Jewish neighborhoods. The fourth World Sunday School Convention in Jerusalem in 1904 aroused interest in missionary Sunday schools abroad, and American progressives adopted the ecumenical Religious Education Association as a liberal reform. Sunday schools continued to expand from 13 million pupils in 1906 to 37 million in 1960, and they may be the most influential educational innovation since the Protestant **Reformation**. (PCH) **See also** Congregationalism; Ecumenical Movement; Education; Judaism; Liberalism; Methodism; Missionaries; Roman Catholicism; Social Justice.

Bibliography

Boylan, Anne M. *Sunday School: The Formation of an American Institution*. New Haven: Yale University Press, 1988.

Dunstan, J. Leslie. *A Light to the City: 150 Years of the City Missionary Society of Boston, 1816-1966*. Boston: Beacon Press, 1966.

Holloran, Peter C. *Boston's Wayward Children: Social Services for Homeless Children*. Boston: Northeastern University Press, 1994.

Billy Sunday (1863–1935)

William A. ("Billy") Sunday was one of the best-known evangelists in history, speaking to an amazing 100 million people in over 300 revival campaigns during his 39-year career. Growing up an orphan and becoming a professional baseball player in 1883, Sunday, a fundamentalist Presbyterian, left sports in 1891 to become a Young Men's Christian Association (YMCA) worker. In 1896, Sunday, following in the footsteps of **Dwight Moody**, began holding evangelistic meetings in large cities, including a New York City crusade in 1917. Some 1 million people are said to have accepted his message. Sunday used his influence to help advance the temperance movement and to rally support for American participation in **World War I**. (MWP) **See also** Evangelicals; Fundamentalists; Presbyterian Church; Temperance and Prohibition.

Bibliography

Dorsett, Lyle W. *Billy Sunday and the Redemption of Urban America*. Grand Rapids, MI: Eerdmans, 1991.

William W. Sweet (1881–1959)

Historian William Sweet wrote numerous books on American church history, including *The Story of Religion in America* and *Revivalism in America*. He taught at several schools, including the University of Chicago and Perkins School of Theology. Sweet linked American Christianity and reform movements like temperance and **abolition** to a uniquely American frontier ethos. He also credited the frontiers with the development of religious toleration in the United States. (MWP) **See also** Temperance and Prohibition.

Bibliography

Sweet, William W. *Revivalism in America*. Boston: Peter Smith, 1944.

——. *Religion on the American Frontier*. New York: Cooper Square, 1964.

——. *The Story of Religion in America*. Grand Rapids, MI: Baker, 1973.

Symbolic Union Test

The "symbolic union" test, a refinement of the Supreme Court's landmark ruling in ***Lemon v. Kurtzman* (1971)**, has been used in several cases to detect violations of the **Establishment Clause**. As the test is phrased in *Grand Rapids v. Ball* (1985), a governmental action fails the test if it "is sufficiently likely to be perceived by adherents of the controlling denominations as an endorsement, and by the nonadherents as a disapproval, of their individual religious choices." The Court has expressed special concern that children may be influenced by the symbolic endorsement of religion through state aid to sectarian schools. (KRD) **See also** Education; First Amendment; *Lemon* Test; Wall of Separation.

Bibliography

Hirt, Theodore C. "'Symbolic Union' of Church and State and the 'Endorsement' of Sectarian Activity." *Wake Forest Law Review* 24, no. 4 (Winter 1989): 823-49.

T

Roger Brooke Taney (1777–1864)

Roger B. Taney mirrored the complex political and social world in which he lived. He was a Roman Catholic, but his wife, Anne Key (sister of Francis Scott Key), was an Episcopalian. The couple resolved their religious dilemma by raising the male children as Catholics and the daughters as Episcopalians. Although a Southerner and a slaveholder, Taney defended the Union and freed his slaves. His legacy as a jurist—he was chief justice of the U.S. Supreme Court from 1836 to 1864—is usually defined by his ill-fated decision in the 1857 Dred Scott case, although such an interpretation neglects his important contribution to American jurisprudence. (HLC) **See also** Episcopal Church; Roman Catholicism; Slavery.

Roger B. Taney, chief justice of the U.S. Supreme Court, is best remembered for his role in the controversial Dred Scott decision on slavery in 1857. National Archives.

Bibliography

Newmyer, R. Kent. *The Supreme Court Under Marshall and Taney*. Wheeling, IL: Harlan Davidson, Inc., 1968.

Arthur Tappan (1786–1865)

Arthur Tappan was a New York City businessman who devoted a large share of his earnings to Christian philanthropic causes, including the American Bible Society, the American Sunday School Union, and the American Tract Society. Along with his brother and business partner, **Lewis Tappan**, Arthur Tappan became active in the movement to abolish **slavery**, serving as president of the **American Anti-Slavery Society** until the radical supporters of **William Lloyd Garrison** split the Society in 1839, In 1840, he became organizer and president of the **American and Foreign Anti-Slavery Society**. He also helped financially in the establishment of Oberlin College in Ohio, an educational endeavor featuring evangelist **Charles Grandison Finney** and strong support for abolitionism. (AS) **See also** Abolition; Education; Evangelicals; Liberty Party; Sunday School Movement.

Bibliography

Tappan, Lewis. *The Life of Arthur Tappan*. Westport, CT: Negro Universities Press, 1970 [reprint of 1871 edition].

Winter, Rebecca J. *The Night Cometh: Two Wealthy Evangelicals Face the Nation*. South Pasadena, CA: William Carey Library, 1977.

Lewis Tappan (1788–1873)

Along with his brother and business partner, **Arthur Tappan**, evangelical activist Lewis Tappan worked energetically for the anti-slavery cause. He helped found the **American Anti-Slavery Society**, as well as the **American and Foreign Anti-Slavery Society**. He procured the services of former President **John Quincy Adams** to speak before the Supreme Court in 1841 on behalf of the captured Africans who revolted on the Spanish slave vessel *Amistad* in 1839. The captives were freed and returned to Africa. In the 1840s, Tappan also became an active member of the Liberty Party, which was built solely upon the demand for immediate **abolition** of **slavery**. Tappan used his wealth to support many Christian endeavors for building a more just society. (AS) **See also** Amistad Case; Evangelicals; Liberty Party; Social Justice.

Bibliography

Winter, Rebecca J. *The Night Cometh: Two Wealthy Evangelicals Face the Nation*. South Pasadena, CA: William Carey Library, 1977.

Wyatt-Brown, Bertram. *Lewis Tappan and the Evangelical War Against Slavery*. New York: Atheneum, 1971.

Tax-Exempt Status

Every state in the union grants property tax exemptions to churches, and the federal income tax has exempted religious organizations since its inception. These exemptions posed possible constitutional problems, particularly relating to the **Establishment Clause** of the **First Amendment**. The Establishment Clause forbids the government from aiding religion, not just from establishing an official state religion, and granting tax exemptions was challenged on the grounds that such practices aided religious practice by providing economic relief to churches.

Prior to 1970, the only expression in the U.S. Supreme Court on this issue came from a concurring opinion by Justice **William J. Brennan** in ***Abington Township v. Schempp*** (1963), where he claimed that tax exemptions were constitutional because the benefit conferred was incidental to the religious character of the institutions concerned: "If religious institutions benefit, it is in spite of rather than because of their religious character. For religious institutions simply share the benefits which government makes generally available to educational, charitable, and eleemosynary groups." The Court first ruled directly on the issue in ***Walz v. Tax Commission of the City of New York*** (1970), where a nearly unanimous Court (only Justice **William O. Douglas** dissented) ruled that tax exemptions did not violate the Constitution, stating that the "purpose of a property tax exemption is neither the advancement nor the inhibition of religion." The Court was particularly concerned that taxation would involve the state in a greater entanglement with religious organizations than the Constitution permitted. The Court also believed that termination of exemptions would deeply involve the government in the internal affairs of religious bodies because evaluation of religious properties for tax purposes would be required, and tax liens and foreclosures and litigation concerning tax matters would lead to the kind of government entanglement with religion that the Court had ruled, in ***Lemon v. Kurtzman*** (1971), was proscribed by the **Establishment Clause**. Chief Justice **Warren Burger**, writing for the Court, stated, "the exemption creates only a minimal and remote involvement between church and state. [It] restricts the fiscal relationship between [them], and tends to complement and reinforce the desired separation insulating each from the other."

Walz, however, dealt only with property tax exemptions for property "used exclusively for religious, **education**, or charitable purposes." Although the precedent set in Walz settled the general issue, the Court has faced and likely will continue to face variations on the question. In *Differderfer v. Central Baptist Church* (1972), the Court addressed a challenge to property tax exemptions for church property used as a commercial parking lot. Before the Court could rule, however, the state law was changed, denying exemption for purely commercial property and requiring a pro rata exemption for mixed use property. The problem of diversification among religious organizations led to other exemption problems. The Internal Revenue Service (IRS) granted tax-exempt status to religious schools, independent of racial admissions policies, until 1970, when the IRS concluded that it could no longer justify such exemptions. Bob Jones University, which allowed the enrollment of unmarried blacks but denied admission to applicants engaged in an interracial marriage or known to advocate interracial marriage or dating, lost its tax-exempt status as a result of this policy change by the IRS. The university brought suit against the IRS for exceeding its powers and for violating the **Free Exercise Clause** of the First Amendment. The Supreme Court ruled that the university did not qualify as a tax-exempt organization, stating the "tax exemption depends on meeting certain common-law standards of charity—namely, that an institution seeking tax-exempt status must serve a public purpose and not be contrary to established public policy." To warrant exemption, "an institution. . . must demonstrably serve and be in harmony with the public interest, and the institution's purpose must not be so at odds with the common community conscience as to undermine any public benefit that might otherwise be conferred."

Although all problems pertaining to the tax-exempt status of religious organizations are unlikely to ever be given a complete, definitive statement by the Supreme Court, *Walz* remains the ruling precedent. The Court is unlikely to reverse that precedent, especially because the issue has remained largely unsettled in the courts and the exemptions retain widespread social and political approval. (JM) **See also** Public Aid to Religious Organizations; Wall of Separation.

Bibliography

Kurland, Philip B. *Church and State*. Chicago: University of Chicago Press, 1975.

Stone, Geoffrey R. et. al. *Constitutional Law*. Boston: Little, Brown and Company, 1991.

Nathaniel W. Taylor (1786–1858)

Yale Divinity Professor Nathaniel W. Taylor promoted a moral government theology with implications for civil government. Taylor pictured God as moral governor of the universe, controlling actions of moral beings through divine law and the influences brought to bear upon individuals to obey that law. Taylor was also an active social reformer who argued that Christians have a duty and the power to improve the morality of the United States and American politics. (AS) **See also** Civil Religion; Social Justice.

Bibliography

Foster, Frank Hugh. *A Genetic History of the New England Theology*. Chicago: University of Chicago Press, 1907.

Televangelism

Televangelism is a term used since the early 1980s to describe religious television programming. While the Federal Communication Commission (FCC) had always encouraged broadcasters to carry some religious programming, such television fare did not become influential or controversial until the advent of widespread cable television. Coupled with changes in broadcasting regulations, religious television has become much more visible during the past two decades.

Although easier access to electronic media has allowed increases in several different types of religious programming, the most visible and largest (in terms of audience) has been the segment of religious television associated with evangelical Protestantism. Programs such as *The Old Time Gospel Hour, The 700 Club, The PTL Club* ("PTL" stands for both "People That Love" and "Praise the Lord"), and *Hour of Power* have combined an explicitly "old-fashioned" evangelical religious message with the technology of modern mass communications.

The content of many of these programs has had an explicitly political message. *The Old Time Gospel Hour* was one important vehicle through which **Jerry Falwell** promoted **Moral Majority**, and **Pat Robertson** used *The 700 Club* to launch his bid for the 1988 Republican presidential nomination. Televangelists have been effective at providing religious and political messages to a relatively self-selected audience, and religious television has been a potent means of fund raising as well. (TGJ) **See also** Evangelicals.

Bibliography

Jelen, Ted G. and Clyde Wilcox. "Preaching to the Converted; The Causes and Consequences of Viewing Religious Television." In David C. Leege and Lyman A. Kellstedt, eds. *Rediscovering the Religious Factor in American Politics*. Armonk, NY: M.E. Sharpe, 1993: 255-69.

Stewart, M. Hoover. *Mass Media Religion: The Social Sources of the Electronic Church*. Newbury Park, CA: Sage, 1988.

Temperance and Prohibition

Temperance—the advocacy of moderation and usually abstinence from the use of intoxicating drink—is a theme that has arisen several times in American history. Presidents **Andrew Jackson** (1829–1837) and **Abraham Lincoln** (1861–1865) called for temperance because they believed that democratic government required a moderate, sober populace. However, the movement gained force only after the **Second Great Awakening** when political activity merged with religious fervor. Preachers like **Lyman Beecher** spoke out against the evils of drink. Other **Evangelicals** pushed the movement to the national level in the late nineteenth century. **Frances Willard**'s **Women's Christian Temperance Union (WCTU)** and Alpha J. Kynett's **Anti-Saloon League** were important organizations in the fight against alcohol. **Carrie Amelia Moore Nation**'s hatchet-wielding legions added a fierce militant group to the mix.

In addition to providing the organizations necessary to engage in a successful temperance campaign, religion provided the movement with other elements. Often portrayed as un-American and drunkards, Roman Catholics, especially those of German descent, were often targets of temperance movements. Even the bishop of St. Paul, **John Ireland**, believed that temperance would help "Americanize" Catholics.

By the early twentieth century, the temperance movement had clearly been converted into a prohibition movement that sought the complete end to the manufacture, sale, distribution, and consumption of alcoholic beverages. Even though consumption was at a 40-year low and 27 states and numerous localities had become dry, the movement sought the enactment of a national prohibition law. The shift from teaching moderation to legislating abstinence at a national level received the final push it needed from **World War I**. A successful propaganda campaign linked the Kaiser's policies to his consumption of alcohol. Thus, to be anti-alcohol was to be anti-Kaiser and, therefore, patriotic. With the passage and ratification of the **Eighteenth Amendment** in 1919, the temperance movement was successful at winning the issue at the grassroots levels within the states and at the federal level in Congress. Prohibition was the law of the land for the next 13 years.

However, it quickly became clear that prohibition was not going to work. A thriving business of bootlegging grew into organized crime that sought to control the manufacture and distribution of alcohol. Neither the Volstead Act, passed to enforce the Eighteenth Amendment, nor the increased number of federal agents could curb the rise of organized crime and the flow of liquor. More than 500,000 arrests and 300,000 convictions did not stem the tide. In the end, adoption of the Twenty-first Amendment in 1933 repealed prohibition. The national experiment of noble goals had proven a failure.

Temperance leader Neil Dow spearheaded the first state prohibition law in Maine. National Archives.

With the failure of prohibition, political organizations that had fought for the adoption of prohibition took one of two paths. Either they ceased to exist, or they adopted more limited, and, they hoped, more lasting, goals of educating Americans about the dangers of alcohol and its negative impact on American society. **See also** Roman Catholicism.

Bibliography

Cohen, Daniel. *Prohibition*. Brookfield, CT: Millbrook Press, 1995.

Hamm, Richard F. *Shaping the Eighteenth Amendment*. Chapel Hill: University of North Carolina Press, 1995.

Terrett v. Taylor (1815)

In *Terrett v. Taylor*, 13 U.S. 43 (1815), the U.S. Supreme Court voided, as contrary to the principles of natural justice, two Virginia acts that divested the **Episcopal Church** of title to property. The property had been acquired under the faith of previous laws, and though a church was involved, the primary importance of this case pertained not to church-state issues but to contract law and the constitutionality of state actions that changed the nature of contractual obligations. (JM)

Bibliography

Choper, Jesse H. *Securing Religious Liberty*. Chicago: University of Chicago Press, 1995.

Cord, Robert I. *Separation of Church and State*. New York: Lambeth Press, 1982.

Terrorism

Terrorism has long vexed society. Although broadly viewed as the use of violence to achieve political aims, terrorism has no standard definition. The Federal Bureau of Investigation (FBI) defines terrorism as "the unlawful use of force or violence against persons or property to intimidate or coerce a government, the civilian population, or any segment thereof, in furtherance of political or social objectives." Terrorists, unlike criminals, seek notoriety for their group or cause and hope to implement some larger agenda beyond the immediate attack. Terrorists also try to compensate for lack of numbers and materiel by creating a climate of fear that will leverage some group into accommodating their aims.

For most of its existence, the United States has been largely free of terrorism. Because the nation has sought to build an open, pluralistic **democracy**, the U.S. has not often faced disaffected social groups seeking to achieve, through terrorism, what they could not gain politically. The sense of vulnerability to domestic terrorism has sharpened in recent years, however, and the FBI, which has primary responsibility for investigating domestic terrorist attacks, has carefully monitored that increase.

Where the 1960s saw the rise of leftist, often Marxist, groups, a new trend developed in the 1980s with the rise of militias. Generally characterized by opposition to the federal and state government, strongly racist doctrines, and fears of a conspiracy to establish a new world order, militia groups have stockpiled weapons. The Oklahoma City bombing in April 1995, which claimed 168 lives and was the most destructive terrorist act on U.S. soil, reflects the worst of the militia outlook. Unlike the leftist organizations they have eclipsed, the militias may have a religious dimension, which often takes the form of a virulent **anti-Semitism** and an Aryan millennialism that looks for the ultimate triumph of whites.

Alternatively, some conservative religious groups, such as the Branch Davidians, appear violence-prone, but their destructive energies have turned inward, resorting to mass suicide in prophetic self-fulfillment. While the FBI definition, strictly applied, does not term recent abortion clinic attacks as terrorism, such incidents certainly fit the broader understanding of terrorism as the use of violence (often with religious motivation) to force political change. The most dramatic religiously inspired terrorism in the United States occurred in February 1993, when Islamic radicals bombed New York's World Trade Center, killing six and injuring over 1,000.

While the vast majority of both Muslims and Christians categorically reject terrorism, in a few cases, religious fervor, when coupled with a political agenda, can lead to deadly acts of terrorism. (JML) **See also** Abortion and Birth Control Regulation; Civil Disobedience; Conservatism; Islam; Race Relations.

BIBLIOGRAPHY

McGuckin, Frank, ed. Terrorism in the United States. New York: H.W. Wilson Co., 1997.

Riley, Kevin, and Bruce Hoffman. *Domestic Terrorism: A National Assessment of State and Local Preparedness*. Santa Monica, CA: RAND, 1995.

Terrorism in the United States. Developed by the Terrorist Research and Analysis Center, National Security Division, Federal Bureau of Investigation, Department of Justice. Washington, D.C.: U.S. Government Printing Office. Annual publication.

Tucker, H.H. *Combating the Terrorists: Democratic Responses to Political Violence*. New York: Facts on File, 1988.

Randall A. Terry (1959–)

Randall Terry is the founder of **Operation Rescue**, a pro-life group originally formed to protest abortion through peaceful **civil disobedience**. Terry has spent considerable time in jail since the 1980s for his participation in sit-ins around abortion clinics. He has publically condemned violent protestors. An evangelical Christian, he argues that the United States has lost its moral values, and he indicts church members for their apathy, saying they must be willing to sacrifice to restore God's standards of justice. Congress attempted to curb his activities through the passage of the 1993 Freedom of Access to Clinic Entrances Act that made it unlawful to block the entrances of abortion clinics. (MR) **See also** Abortion and Birth Control Regulation; Evangelicals.

BIBLIOGRAPHY

Wills, Gary. "Evangels of Abortion." *New York Review of Books* (June 15, 1989): 18-19.

Terry, Randall. *Operation Rescue*. Springdale, PA: Whitaker House, 1988.

Thanksgiving and Fast Days

Thanksgiving and fast days are publically appointed days for citizens to appeal to God on behalf of their political community. Thanksgiving days focus primarily on giving thanks for the Almighty's past or present blessings on the political community (e.g., victory in a war). Fast days, usually declared in times of distress, focus more on obtaining God's assistance to deal with (or avert) an impending crisis. Both cultural institutions can be traced back to ancient times, and in America they date back to the first colonial governments. New England **Puritans** were particularly noted for seeking God's blessing and for imploring God's forgiveness for societal sins through public days of devotion. During the **American Revolution**, the **Continental Congress** regularly proclaimed days of both fasting and thanksgiving. After the Revolution, state governments continued their colonial practices. In the earliest years of the nation, thanksgiving and fast days caused little controversy. Even religious dissenters such as **Baptists** and Methodists, who generally opposed government financial support for religion, supported these days of communal worship.

Thanksgiving and fast days continued at the national level after the writing of the Constitution in 1787. **George Washington**, the nation's first president, declared days of thanksgiving in 1789 and 1795. His successor, **John Adams**, proclaimed days of prayer and fasting in 1798.The nation's third president, **Thomas Jefferson**, refused to follow their example, stating that no constitutional power existed for him to declare days of religious obligation. **Andrew Jackson** embraced the same position during an outbreak of Asiatic cholera in 1832, provoking a heated debate in Congress. Later presidents proclaimed days of thanksgiving and prayer on an irregular basis until the administration of **Abraham Lincoln**, who turned a day of thanksgiving into an annual event by reserving the last Thursday in November for this purpose in 1863. The festival has been observed annually ever since. Following his predecessors, Lincoln also appointed periodic days of fasting and prayer during the **Civil War**, a practice that some later presidents also adopted during times of crisis. In 1952, Congress regularized such days by establishing a yearly day of national prayer. (The first Thanksgiving proclamation and President Washington's 1789 Thanksgiving proclamation are reprinted in Appendix 1.) (JGW) **See also** Colonial America; Methodism.

Bibliography

Richardson, James D., ed. *A Compilation of the Messages and Papers of the Presidents*. Washington, DC: Bureau of National Literature, 1911.

Stokes, Anson Phelps. "Government Religious Observance of Special Days and Occasions." In *Church and State in the United States*. New York: Harper and Brothers, 1950.

Theocracy

Theocracy—literally, "rule by God"—involves a cluster of meanings, including a government or society ruled by immediate divine guidance, rule by divinely guided officials, or the domination of political structures by religious structures. Josephus, a Jewish historian of the first century, originated the term to describe Jewish society (i.e., God ruling directly through the Law, or through the king as vicegerent). Theocracy may be contrasted with **democracy**, which is, literally, "rule by the people," and with the constitutional separation of church and state in the United States. Commentators have described the seventeenth-century Puritan societies of Great Britain and America as theocratic. The **Puritans** sought to create divine commonwealths, societies ordered by divine principles. Yet, Puritan communities originated through social compact and functioned with democratic or representative processes (e.g., town meetings, elected officials, written statutes, and civil courts). Clergy and churches had considerable influence, but ecclesiastical and civil structures were intentionally distinct.

Today, those who seek a more explicit integration of religious aims in politics are sometimes accused of seeking to establish a theocracy. This situation points to a fundamental tension in the American political experiment. In contrast to earlier Christendom, the United States has from its inception questioned and finally eschewed direct divine or ecclesiastical rule in favor of representative democracy. Yet, until recently, Americans did not seek a thoroughly secular culture (e.g., the **French Revolution** was far more radical than the American). Hence, Americans have consistently questioned how far religious aims should relate to political systems. (GSS) **See also** Establishment Clause; First Amendment; Judaism; Wall of Separation.

Bibliography

Handy, Robert T. *A Christian America: Protestant Hopes and Historical Realities*. New York: Oxford University Press, 1974.

Neuhaus, Richard John. *The Naked Public Square: Religion and Democracy in America*. Grand Rapids, MI: William B. Eerdmans, 1984.

Theonomy

Theonomists are evangelical Christians who believe in theonomy (literally, the law of God), which stresses the continued application of the social and judicial laws given to biblical **Israel**. Thus, the penal sanctions given to Old Testament Israel would be applied to modern nations like the United States, including, for example, injunctions to execute blasphemers, adulterers, homosexuals, and rebellious children. While theonomy is often equated with Christian Reconstruction, theonomy is a broader category encompassing Reconstructionism. Unlike reconstructionists, theonomists are not necessarily explicit Calvinists. Theonomy is sometimes known as "dominion theology" because it assumes Christians will eventually take dominion over the earth in fulfillment of biblical promises. (ARB) **See also** Calvinism; Christian Reconstructionist Movement; Homosexual Rights.

Bibliography

Bahnsen, Greg L. *Theonomy in Christian Ethics*. Nutley, NJ: Craig Press, 1977.

Barker, William S. and W. Robert Godfrey, eds. *Theonomy: A Reformed Critique*. Grand Rapids, MI: Zondervan Publishing, 1990.

Ronald Frank Thiemann (1946–)

Ronald Thiemann, a Lutheran theologian and proponent of **public theology**, has been dean of the Harvard Divinity School since 1986. While his earlier work is exemplified in such titles as *Revelation and Authority* (1985) and *The Legacy of H. Richard Niebuhr* (1991), his recent theological work focuses on relating religion to the public sphere, as described in his *Constructing a Public Theology: The Church in a Pluralistic Culture* (1991) and *Religion in Public Life: A Dilemma for Democracy* (1996). His work challenges the liberal and, in particular, the Rawlsian exclusion of religion from the public sphere. Thiemann's alternative approach, which recognizes the validity of religiously grounded values as integral to public discourse, is part of a wider movement calling for a public theology. In 1990, Thiemann founded the Harvard Divinity School's Center for the Study of Values and Public Policy to further such a public theology. (ISM) **See also** Liberalsim; Lutheran Church; H. Richard Niebuhr; John Rawls.

Bibliography

Thiemann, Ronald. *Religion in Public Life. A Dilemma for Democracy*. Washington, DC: Georgetown University Press, 1996.

Clarence Thomas (1948–)

Clarence Thomas was born in Georgia in 1948. He graduated from The College of Holy Cross in 1971 and from Yale Law School in 1974. Thomas was appointed assistant secretary for **civil rights** at the United States Department of Education in 1981. In 1982, he was named chairman of the United States Equal Employment Opportunity Commission and served there until 1990. In 1991 he was nominated to the Supreme Court of the United States by President George Bush. The Senate confirmed the appointment, after a series of controversial televised hearings, on October 15, 1991. Thomas has proven to be a conservative voter on the Court, upholding most restrictions on abortions as well as rejecting the "high **wall of separation**" doctrine in regards to religious liberty. (JCW) **See also** Abortion and Birth Control Regulation; Conservatism; Education; Establishment Clause; First Amendment.

BIBLIOGRAPHY

Danforth, John C. *Resurrection: The Confirmation of Clarence Thomas.* New York: Viking, 1994

Mayer, Jane and Jill Abramson. *Strange Justice: The Selling of Clarence Thomas.* New York: Houghton Mifflin, 1994.

Norman Thomas (1884–1968)

Between 1928 and 1948, Norman Thomas, a tireless representative of liberal Christian socialism, ran six times as the Socialist Party candidate for president. After graduating from Union Theological Seminary about 1911, he pastored a church in poverty-stricken East Harlem, a position that led Thomas to adopt such radical solutions to poverty that even Franklin Roosevelt's **New Deal** did not go far enough for him. In 1935, Thomas severed many of his ties to Marxists. His pacifist opposition to **World War II** caused his influence to decline. His last political activities were in opposition to the **Vietnam War**. (MWP) **See also** Liberalism; Pacifism; Peace Movements; Socialism and Communism.

BIBLIOGRAPHY

Fleischman, Harry. *Norman Thomas: A Biography.* New York: Norton, 1964.

Johnpoll, Bernard K. *Pacifist's Progress: Norman Thomas and the Decline of American Socialism.* Chicago: Quadrangle Books, 1970.

Henry David Thoreau (1817–1862)

Henry Thoreau, an essayist and poet, lived and wrote about a simple style of life that combined idealism and practicality into a uniquely American ethic. A friend and disciple of **Ralph Waldo Emerson**, Thoreau held a similar reverence for nature and self-reliance. After graduating from Harvard in 1837, he taught school, helped his father make pencils, and joined Emerson's Transcendentalist discussion group. Although political issues rarely stole his attention from these literary pursuits, Thoreau was strongly opposed to **slavery** and the **Mexican-American War**, and to show his opposition he refused to pay his poll tax. He defended his resistance in *Civil Disobedience* (1849), an essay that deeply influenced India's Mahatma Ghandi in the twentieth century. In the summer of 1845, Thoreau moved into a hut he built on the northwest shore of Walden Pond near Concord, Massachusetts, and lived there until September 6, 1847, writing parts of what would become his most famous work, *Walden, or Life in the Woods* (1854). (BDG) **See also** Abolition; Civil Disobedience; Feethought; Pacifism; Transcendentalism.

BIBLIOGRAPHY

Richardson, Robert D. Jr. *Henry Thoreau: A Life of the Mind.* Berkeley: University of California Press, 1986.

Thoreau, Henry David. *Walden: An Annotated Edition.* Walter Harding, ed. Boston: Houghton Mifflin, 1995.

Thornton v. Caldor, Inc. (1985)

Donald E. Thornton held a managerial position with Caldor that required work on Sunday. Thornton informed his employer that Sunday was his Sabbath and that his religious conviction forbade him to work on that day. Thornton refused a transfer to a Massachusetts store without Sunday hours, resigned, and filed a grievance under a Connecticut statute stating that "An employee's refusal to work on his Sabbath shall not constitute grounds for his dismissal." A Connecticut court ordered Caldor to reinstate Thornton, but in *Estate of Thornton v. Caldor, Inc.*, 472 U.S. 703 (1985), the Supreme Court overruled the lower court on the grounds that the statute violated the **Establishment Clause**. (JM) **See also** First Amendment; Sabbatarianism; Sunday Law Cases.

BIBLIOGRAPHY

Redman, Barbara J. "Sabbatarian Accommodation in the Supreme Court." *Journal of Church and State* 33, no. 3 (Autumn 1991): 495-523.

James Henley Thornwell (1812–1862)

A Southern theologian, James Thornwell served as a professor of logic and belles lettres as well as president of South Carolina College. As **slavery** became a growing theological and political issue, he defended Southern society and slavery, arguing that slavery was condoned by the Bible and was not necessarily an evil institution. Thornwell argued that "the Scriptures not only fail to condem slavery, they also sanction it." Although he claimed that the church was limited to spiritual matters and should not be involved in politics, Thornwell helped the **Presbyterian Church** in the South break its ties to the North when the **Civil War** erupted in 1861. (MWP)

BIBLIOGRAPHY

Farmer, James Oscar, Jr. *The Metaphysical Confederate.* Macon, GA: Mercer University Press, 1986.

Palmer, Benjamin M. *The Life and Letters of James Thornwell.* New York: Arno Press, 1969.

Thornwell, James. *The Rights and Duties of Masters.* 1850.

——. *Our Danger and Our Duty.* 1862.

Paul Tillich (1886–1905)

Theologian Paul Tillich immigrated from Germany in 1933 to become one of the leading religious thinkers in the United States. Influenced by religious socialism and existentialism, Tillich held a theory of religion and culture that was based on a definition of God as "ultimate concern" and that stressed the inevitable religious dimension of all public life, including politics. Tillich's penetrating analysis of such social phenomena as love, power, and justice, and his conceptualization of "**theonomy**" as a criterion for social critique have influenced many politically engaged theologies from the 1960s to the present. (PV) **See also** Socialism and Communism.

BIBLIOGRAPHY

Stone, Ronald H. *Paul Tillich's Radical Social Thought*. Atlanta: John Know Press, 1980.

Tilton v. Richardson (1971)

Tilton v. Richardson, 403 U.S. 672 (1971), involved a challenge to federal grants given to four Catholic colleges in Connecticut to assist in the construction of academic facilities used for the teaching of secular subjects. Chief Justice **Warren E. Burger** argued that even though religious organizations benefited, the legislation's primary purpose was not to advance religion. The Chief Justice also pointed out that whereas the dominant purpose of pre-college church schools was religious indoctrination, college students were less impressionable and more skeptical. The court also recognized that academic freedom further limited the religious nature of sectarian colleges. Consequently, there would be less need for government surveillance and therefore minimal entanglement. In the end, the court ruled that the grants did not violate the separation of church and state. (JP) **See also** Education; Establishment Clause; First Amendment; Public Aid to Religious Organizations; Wall of Separation.

BIBLIOGRAPHY

Eastland, Terry. *Religious Liberty in the Supreme Court*. Washington, DC: Ethics and Public Policy Center, 1993.

Gianell, Donald A. "Lemon and Tilton: The Bitter and the Sweet of the Church-State Entanglement." *The Supreme Court Review* (1971): 147–200.

Glenn Tinder (1923–)

Glenn Tinder taught and wrote about political philosophy and religion, retiring from the University of Massachusetts, Boston, in 1994. His popular book, *Political Thinking: The Perennial Questions* (1989) weighs Christian and secular perspectives, while his *The Political Meaning of Christianity* (1991) seeks to reinterpret the idea of religion positively in the face of secularization and the concomitant loss of community and shared values. (JRV) **See also** Political Participation and Voting Behavior; Secularization Thesis.

BIBLIOGRAPHY

Hewitt, J. Newton. "Glenn Tinder's Niebuhrian Legacy: A Review of 'The Political Meaning of Christianity.'" *Pacificia* 8 (June 1995): 213–17.

Alexis de Tocqueville (1805–1859)

Alexis de Tocqueville was an important observer of nineteenth-century American politics, and of the tendencies of democratic governments generally. Tocqueville is best known for his classic work, *Democracy in America*, in which he describes for a European audience the character of **democracy** in its "natural" setting (i.e., a setting in which democratic values do not need to compete with entrenched aristocracies). *Democracy in America* was based on the observations Tocqueville made of American social and political life during a trip to the United States in 1831.

In *Democracy in America*, Tocqueville argues that the principal problem with democratic regimes is the "tyranny of the majority." In highly egalitarian settings, such as the United States, citizens are naturally skeptical of claims of authority or superiority. The widespread belief that any person (or, inevitably, any idea) is no better or worse than any other means that democratic citizens are likely to defer to any single authority that might exist in any sphere of social life.

Tocqueville suggests that the lack of particular authorities lends public opinion an almost irresistible power. Since democratic citizens typically cannot invoke "superior" judgments in matters of politics, morals, or aesthetics, it follows that any individual citizen probably lacks the intellectual or psychological resources to resist opinions that are widely held. Tocqueville argued that the pervasive power of public opinion led to little independence of thought in the United States, despite a high level of legal freedom of thought and expression. Social pressure, rather than political power, lent American cultural life an unusual quality of conformism.

Tocqueville regarded religion as one of the most important factors in limiting or mitigating the tyranny of the majority. Tocqueville believed that adherence to Christianity was virtually universal in the United States, and that Christians tended to agree on matters of morality. Thus, a consensus on "Christian morality" placed certain topics out of the reach of popular majorities, and provided individual citizens with an authoritative basis from which to criticize prevailing opinions and practices. Adherence to a general Christian tradition created moral and intellectual boundaries, within which American political and social life could be conducted. (TGJ)

BIBLIOGRAPHY

Tocqueville, Alexis de. *Democracy in America*. 2 vols. Phillips Bradley, ed. New York: Vintage Books, 1945.

Torcaso v. Watkins (1961)

The appellant in *Torcaso v. Watkins*, 367 U.S. 488 (1961), was appointed by the governor of Maryland as a notary public. To be seated, he had to agree to take an oath that affirmed his belief in God. He refused to do so and was denied the position. The Supreme Court ruled that the government cannot require a citizen "to profess a belief or a disbelief in any religion." To do so would violate the **First Amendment**'s guarantee of freedom of religion. The Court noted that this principle is deeply seated in the history of the First Amendment and has been consistently upheld. (FHJ) **See also** Establishment Clause; Free Exercise Clause; Religious Tests and Oaths.

Bibliography

Abraham, Henry J. *Freedom and the Court: Civil Rights and Liberties in the United States*. New York: Oxford University Press, 1977.

Pfeffer, Leo. "How Religion Is Secular Humanism?" *The Humanist* 48, no. 5 (September-October 1988): 13-20.

Transcendentalism

Transcendentalism was a literary and philosophical movement that developed in the early nineteenth century. The movement was largely influenced by three seemingly incompatible ideologies. First, from American Puritanism, a strongly Calvinist belief often derided as narrow and morally rigid, the movement adopted a use of introspection. Second, from Unitarianism, a highly rationalized deism that believed in the progress of human nature, transcendentalism took on a strong belief in the development of human reason as a means for progress for both the individual and society. Finally, from Romanticism, the eighteenth-century movement that relied on the imagination and the idealization of nature, transcendentalism drew its belief in the mind as ultimate reality. The movement merged these forces into an ideology that sought a correspondence between mind/spirit and nature.

Trancendentalism had a number of famous adherents, including **Ralph Waldo Emerson.** In his 1836 work *Nature,* Emerson described the philosophic basis of transcendentalism, including the idealism that blended opposition to the material world with Calvinist theology and rejection of artificial restraints on human activity. Another leading writer of the movement was **Henry David Thoreau**, who lived at Emerson's home for some time and later wrote *Walden, or Life in the Woods* (1854). The Transcendental Club of Boston also included educator **Amos Bronson Alcott**, who founded a community known as Fruitlands, and feminist and social activist Margaret Fuller and philosopher **William Ellery Channing**.

Transcendentalism and utopian movements have often been one and the same in the United States. In addition to Alcott's Fruitlands, other communities were founded, including Brook Farm, where the residents sought to achieve the highest in human nature through the socialistic structuring of life. The movement was also active in the **abolition** movement and its members advocated women's rights. The environmental movement of the late twentieth century also has its roots in transcendentalism. **See also** Calvinism; Feminism; Puritans; Utopianism.

Bibliography

Albarese, Catherine. *Corresponding Motion: Transcendental Religion in the New America*. Philadelphia: Temple University Press, 1977.

Boller, Paul F., Jr. *American Transcendentalism, 1830-1860*. New York: Putnam, 1974.

Trusteeship Controversy

Under United States law, lay trustees have the legal ownership of church property. From the last decades of the eighteenth century until the close of the nineteenth century that principle created problems for Catholicism because its bishop-centered organizational structure was unaccustomed to such procedures and sought to vest control of church property in the church hierarchy, i.e., the bishops. Often, when a case involving the owership or control of church property reached court, the Catholic Church found itself facing a judge who was hostile to Catholicism. One of the first such cases arose in 1785, when the laymen who established St. Peter's in New York City attempted to dictate to their bishop who their pastor should be. Over the years, similar problems developed in other cities. In 1822 and 1828, Popes Pius VII and Leo XII issued briefs criticizing trusteeism. During the 1850s, the anti-Catholic **Know-Nothing Party** managed to pass legislation upholding trusteeship in some states. However, beginning with the New York Act of 1863, Catholics managed to alter state laws to bring them more into accord with a church structure ruled by bishops. The Third Plenary Council of Baltimore in 1884 formally acknowledged the state by state approach as an acceptable solution to the problem of trusteeship. (MWP) **See also** Anti-Catholicism; Roman Catholicism.

Bibliography

Carey, Patrick W. *People, Priests and Prelates: Ecclesiastical Democracy and the Tensions of Trusteeism*. Notre Dame, IN: Notre Dame University Press, 1987.

Dignan, P. *History of the Legal Incorporation of Catholic Church Property in the United States, 1784-1932*. New York: P.J. Kenedy & Sons, 1935.

Sojourner Truth (1797–1883)

Sojourner Truth was born as a slave named Isabella Baumfree in Ulster County, New York. Freed by the New York anti-**slavery** law of 1827, she moved to New York City where she had a religious transformation and changed her name to Sojourner Truth. She began to travel throughout New England preaching the word of God. In 1843, Sojourner Truth joined the Northampton Association, a Massachusetts community founded on the ideas of freedom and equality. through the Association, Truth met social reformers and abolitionists, including **Frederick Douglass**. Truth became an active abolitionist, traveling the country to speak about the anti-slavery movement. She earned money for her work by selling copies of her biography as well as picture postcards of herself that were inscribed: "We Sell the Shadow to Support the Substance." A powerful and effective speaker, Truth also was the first prominent black woman to get directly involved with the white women's suffrage movement. She delivered her most famous speech, "Ain't I A Woman?," during the 1851 Convention on Women's Rights in Akron, Ohio. (JCW) **See also** Abolition; Women in Religion and Politics.

BIBLIOGRAPHY

Mabee, Carleton. *Sojourner Truth—Slave, Prophet, Legend.* New York: New York University Press, 1993.

Tuition Tax Credits

Proposals for tuition tax credits—the reduction in taxes paid by parents who send their children to private schools—have been fixtures in the debate over public money for private **education**. Since some private schools are church-affiliated, any proposal for tuition tax credits invariably raises the question of the appropriate relationship between church and state.

Both state and federal governments have proposed (and in some cases passed) legislation providing parents tax relief for private school tuition and other educational expenses. In 1978, both Houses of Congress passed a tuition tax credit, which gave partial federal tax credit for private school tuition. The legislation ultimately failed because the House of Representatives and the Senate could not decide how benefits should be allotted among college and elementary/secondary schools. Several years later, the **Ronald Reagan** administration supported other proposals, although none were enacted, and the idea lay dormant at the national level for many years. Tax credits for primary school tuition have recently been revived as a political issue by a coalition of conservative religious groups and urban school officials.

The constitutional implications of the credits are unsettled. The Supreme Court used to be wary of state aid to religious schools in any form, and, in *Committee for Public Education v. Pearl* (1973), the Court struck down state tuition reimbursements. But, in ***Mueller v. Allen*** (1983), the Court held that tax benefits may be provided to parents sending their children to religious school if those benefits are also available to public school students. Three years later, the Court ruled in ***Witters v. Department of Services for the Blind*** (1986) that it would be constitutional for government money to pay for a blind student to attend Bible college in preparation for a ministerial career. Subsequent cases, such as ***Zobrest v. Catalina Foothills School District*** (1993) and ***Agostini v. Felton*** (1997), have upheld other forms of aid to religious schools.

Advocates of tax credits argue that they not only force public schools to compete in an educational "market," thereby increasing the quality of teaching, but they also maximize the freedom of parents to choose how their children are educated. Opponents claim that the credits violate the **Establishment Clause**, take precious resources from public education, and tend to benefit only the wealthy and middle class. Some religious groups have also voiced concerns that federal tax credits would lead to a nationalization of school finance, opening schools to unwanted centralized monitoring of curriculum and instruction. (KRD) **See also** Conservatism; First Amendment; Public Aid to Religious Organizations; Wall of Separation.

BIBLIOGRAPHY

James, Thomas and Henry Levin, eds. *Public Dollars for Private Schools: The Case of Tuition Tax Credits.* Philadelphia: Temple University Press, 1983.

Young, David and Steven Tigges. "Federal Tuition Credits and the Establishment Clause." *The Catholic Lawyer* 28, no. 1 (Winter 1983): 35-71.

Nat Turner (1800–1831)

Nat Turner was born a slave in 1800 in Southampton County, Virginia. A precocious youth who illegally learned how to read and write, Turner had a series of ecstatic visions that convinced him to lead a struggle against the enslavement of black people. He was instrumental in starting the Southampton Virginia slave revolt in 1831—one of the largest U.S. slave uprisings— which took the lives of more than 60 whites and 200 blacks. After being imprisoned, Turner was interviewed by attorney Thomas Gray, who used his notes as the basis for *Turner's Confessions*. Turner was hanged on November 11, 1831. (JCW) **See also** Abolition; Civil Disobedience; Slavery.

BIBLIOGRAPHY

Oates, Steven B. *The Fires of Jubilee: Nat Turner's Fierce Rebellion.* New York: New American Library, 1975.

U

Uncle Tom's Cabin (1852)

Harriet Beecher Stowe's *Uncle Tom's Cabin* is arguably the most politically influential novel in our nation's history. Originally published serially in 1851, the work seeks to demonstrate the incompatibility of Christianity and **slavery**. The book's namesake is a kind yet courageous slave who functions as the story's Christ figure. For the sake of others, and in the name of his faith, Uncle Tom allows himself to suffer countless indignities, while never losing his dignity. Moralistic in tone, the book had an enormous influence, selling more than 300,000 copies in its first year and rallying anti-slavery sentiment in the northern states, so much so that it is reported that upon meeting Stowe during the **Civil War**, **Abraham Lincoln** called her "the little woman who wrote the book that made this great war." When southerners condemned the book as naive and full of fictitious situations and characters, Stowe responded with *A Key to Uncle Tom's Cabin*, a 262-page book documenting all the evils about which she wrote. Whatever its literary merits, the book has the undeniable virtue of forcing us to confront the problem of the possible disproportion between our religious duties and our duties as citizens. (SJL) **See also** Abolition.

Harriet Beecher Stowe's *Uncle Tom's Cabin* was perhaps the most influential novel in American history. Library of Congress.

BIBLIOGRAPHY

Gossett, Thomas F. *Uncle Tom's Cabin and American Culture*. Dallas: Southern Methodist University Press, 1985.

Stowe, Harriet Beecher. *Uncle Tom's Cabin*. New York: Bantam, 1981.

Unification Church

The Unification Church, officially called the Holy Spirit Association for the Unification of World Christianity, was founded by Korean Minister **Sun Myung Moon** in 1954. Moon claims that Jesus appeared to him in 1936 on Easter Sunday and told him that he had been chosen by God to complete the mission that Jesus had been unable to finish because of the crucifixion. Jesus also revealed that Moon would unify the world into one kingdom of God. While Moon does not directly claim to be a new messiah, he does preach that the second coming of Christ occurred in Korea during the year of his birth.

In 1959, Moon began to recruit followers in the United States, and in 1973 he moved his headquarters to New York. According to Moon, both Satan and God work through countries and the United States is God's nation, the country chosen for salvation. For years, Moon preached that atheistic communism was the major enemy of the God-centered world. Since the fall of communism, the Unification Church has initiated a Federation for World Peace to promote its view on international issues.

In the 1960s and 1970s, the Unification Church recruited extensively on college campuses. Many of these recruits, known as Moonies, sold flowers to raise money for the Church. At that time, the Church was criticized by many who felt that its followers had been brainwashed into joining and working for it.

In 1982, Reverend Moon was convicted of income tax evasion and served a 13-month prison sentence. More recently, the Unification Church has become involved in American politics through its vast network of businesses and organizations. In 1982, it founded the *Washington Times*, a daily newspaper in Washington, D.C., and in 1987 it created the American Freedom Coalition to extend its influence within conservative Christian political circles. Overall, the Unification Church has an estimated membership of 10,000 in the United States and 2 million worldwide. (WVM) **See also** Atheism; Conservatism; Cults; Socialism and Communism.

BIBLIOGRAPHY

Sontag, Frederick. *Sun Myung Moon and the Unification Church*. Nashville, TN: Abington, 1977.

Unitarianism

Unitarianism began as a theological debate during the first three decades of the nineteenth century. As Christians in New England pondered the significance of their new nation, some of them stressed God's benevolence in creating a country where humans could reach their full potential. This confidence in human perfectibility led them to question the necessity of a divine being like Jesus, who, in traditional Trinitarianism (i.e., belief in the trinity of God the Father, God the Son, and God the Holy Spirit), had to be both God and human to save the world.

Early Unitarians contended that Jesus was a man with a special divine mission—a prophet and teacher—but not God. Their God was the creator and benevolent ruler of the universe, who created human beings in the divine image and then set forth guidelines for living a full and perfect life. Unitarian theology encourages philanthropy, humanitarianism, **education**, and a strong sense of civic concern. In the antebellum period, Unitarians were heavily involved in the anti-**slavery** movement, and they also formed numerous humanitarian aid societies to address the needs of the poor in Boston and nearby towns. Contemporary Unitarians are activists for **social justice**, particularly around issues of race and sexual orientation.

Most of the early Unitarians were members of the upper social classes of New England. King's Chapel in Boston was the first church to embrace the new theology, doing so during the **American Revolution**. The appointment of Henry Ware, a Unitarian, as Hollis Professor of Divinity at Harvard, heightened the debate between traditional Trinitarians and Unitarians, and **William Ellery Channing**'s 1819 sermon, *Unitarian Christianity*, set off battles in several churches. In 1820, the decision of the Massachusetts Supreme Court in the **Dedham Case** gave the Unitarian faction financial and administrative control of many of the disputing churches in the Boston area, and a formal schism developed between the Unitarians and the trinitarian Congregationalists.

Unitarians have emphasized religious freedom and complete congregational independence since their inception, and have therefore been progressive leaders in the American debate about religious tolerance. Although the earliest Unitarians remained strongly biblical in orientation, later generations have embraced a more natural theology emphasizing universal salvation and self-actualization. (KMY) **See also** Congregationalism; Homosexual Rights; Race Relations; Secular Humanism.

Bibliography

Ahlstrom, Sydney E. and Carey, Jonathan S. *An American Reformation of Unitarian Christianity*. Middletown, CT: Wesleyan University Press, 1985.

Howe, Daniel Walker. *The Unitarian Conscience: Harvard Moral Philosophy, 1805-1861*. Middletown, CT: Wesleyan University Press, 1988.

Schulz, William F., ed. *The Unitarian Universalist Pocket Guide*. Boston: Skinner House Books, 1993.

Scovel, Carl and Forman, Charles C. *Journey Toward Independence: King's Chapel's Transition to Unitarianism*. Boston: Skinner House Books, 1993.

United Church of Christ

The United Church of Christ was formed in 1957 by the merger of the Evangelical and Reformed Church with the Congregational Christian Churches. The move to unite was explicitly ecumenical, and the theology of the resulting denomination emphasizes both individual and congregational freedom of conscience even as it affirms the traditional Christian faith claims.

From its inception, the United Church of Christ has been involved in **social justice** ministries. The denomination has engaged in political and educational measures to promote equal opportunities for women and minorities, to humanize the criminal justice system, and to facilitate access for people with handicaps. It has been adamantly anti-**war** throughout its history, and, since 1985, has encouraged its member congregations to embrace the "Just Peace Church" pronouncement affirmed by its national body. It has also supported humanitarian aid and missionary social service work in the United States and abroad. Most recently, it has emerged as the leading religious voice in the movement for gay rights.

Often the United Church of Christ's work has been cooperative in nature, planned and carried out in conjunction with other denominations and the National Council of Churches. A member of the Consultation on Church Union since that group was initiated in 1960, the denomination actively participates in the discussion about how various Christian groups might celebrate and act on their connection as one universal church. The Church views its ecumenism as a model for social and political dialogue as well as religious conversation.

Like most mainstream Protestant churches, the United Church of Christ is suffering from a decline in membership, and it is unsure of its ability to speak persuasively to social issues in an increasingly secular national culture. Its enthusiasm for social activism, however, remains undampened. The denomination continues to pass resolutions on **social justice** issues at both its regional and national gatherings, even as the impact of these statements comes into question. (KMY) **See also** Ecumenical Movement; Evangelicals; Homosexual Rights; Pacifism; Race Relations.

Bibliography

History and Program: United Church of Christ. New York: United Church Press, 1986.

Paul, Robert S. *Freedom with Order: The Doctrine of the Church in the United Church of Christ*. New York: United Church Press, 1987.

Thistlethwaite, Susan, ed. *A Just Peace Church*. New York: United Church Press, 1986.

United States v. Ballard (1944)

In the 1940s, a number of persons were convicted for using the mail to defraud, based on the distribution of literature to solicit funds that contained a number of allegedly false representations, one of which read, "The words of the alleged divine entity. . . would be transmitted to mankind through the medium of. . . Guy W. Ballard." In the criminal trial, the jury was instructed to consider only whether the defendants believed the statements in good faith, not whether the statements were actually true. In *United States v. Ballard*, 322 U.S. 78 (1944), the U.S. Supreme Court in a highly divided and complicated decision overturned the decision of the court of appeals, which had vacated the convictions ordering a new trial. The justices were at a loss as to how to separate the issue of belief from the issue of truth. While the judges seem to have agreed that Ballard was guilty of fraud ("The religious views espoused by respondents might seem incredible, if not preposterous, to most people"), they ruled that the truth or falsity of the religious claims could not be subject to trial before a jury. (JM)

Bibliography

Heins, Margorie. "Other People's Faiths." *Hastings Constitutional Law Quarterly* 9, no. 1 (Fall 1981): 153-97.

Noonan, John T., Jr. "How Sincere Do You Have to Be to Be Religious?" *University of Illinois Law Review* (Summer 1989): 713-24.

United States v. Macintosh (1931)

A Canadian was denied U.S. citizenship on the grounds that he did not accept the principles of the U.S. Constitution because he would not promise in advance to bear arms in defense of the United States unless he personally believed the **war** to be morally justified. In *United States v. Macintosh*, 238 U.S. 605 (1931), the U.S. Supreme Court accepted this judgment, stating that "Naturalization is a privilege, to be given, qualified, or withheld as Congress may determine, and which the alien may claim as of right only upon compliance with the terms which Congress imposes." (JM) **See also** Pacifism.

Bibliography

Regan, Richard J. *Private Conscience and Public Law*. New York: Fordham University Press, 1972.

Weber, Paul J., ed. *Equal Protection*. New York: Greenwood, 1990.

Utopianism

Utopianism, the planning of communal living experiments, commenced in America with the first Puritan settlements in the seventeenth century. The impetus for immigrating to the New World was the desire to create carefully crafted civil communities in which the **Puritans** could practice their separatist religious beliefs. However, the rate of migration and the variety among religious dissenters meant that the utopian quality of the experiment was soon diluted.

Some utopian groups, like the Shakers, migrated to the United States after severe persecution in other countries. During the revolutionary period, Shaker leader Mother Ann Lee organized a socialistic Christian community dedicated to sexual abstinence and simple, functional living. The community practiced spiritualism by communicating with the dead, and sought the Pentecostal gifts of speaking in tongues and ecstatic trance. They supported themselves through farming and furniture-making, and their elegantly simple chairs and tables are still prized by contemporary home decorators.

The groups most closely associated with utopianism developed out of the religious perfectionism movement of the 1830s. **John Humphrey Noyes**'s Oneida Community in New York, and the Massachusetts utopias of Hopedale Community, Brook Farm, and Fruitlands were all attempts to organize civil society in ways that would encourage spiritual perfection. Most of the experiments lasted less than a decade. The Oneida Community, which attempted to establish the Kingdom of God on earth through an understanding of Christian love that included a system of "complex marriage" and communal childrearing, endured for over 40 years. It combined the socialized production of flatware with religious idealism and succeeded in creating a flourishing business that supported the community.

Not all utopian movements in the nineteenth century were religious in nature. **Robert Dale Owen**'s New Harmony was dedicated to **education**, freethinking, and human idealism. Most secular utopias were short-lived—New Harmony lasted only a year—suggesting that socialist ideals were insufficient to bind individuals into utopian communities in a nation that encouraged intense religious commitment as the primary basis for social life. Nonetheless, both religious and secular utopianism laid the groundwork for the early twentieth-century **social gospel** movement.

The next wave of utopianism occurred in the 1960s and 1970s. Free love communities and **social justice** experiments abounded in the turbulent years of the **Vietnam War**, **civil rights** movement, and feminist revolution. The 1970 founding of Oyotunji Village, an African-American communitarian experiment in South Carolina, was typical of this era. The Village's charter called for it to combine black nationalist ideals with the African Yoruba religion to promote African religion and culture. In its heyday, Oyotunji Village was home to 200 African Americans. Now the village consists of 12 families. Such decline, if not demise, has been the fate of most American utopian communities. (KMY) **See also** African-American Churches; Communitarianism; Feminism; Freethought; Pentecostals; Polygamy; Socialism and Communism.

Bibliography

Berry, Brian J.L. *America's Utopian Experiments: Communal Havens from Long-Wave Crises*. Hanover: University Press of New England, 1992.

Pitzer, Donald, ed. *America's Communal Utopias*. Chapel Hill: The University of North Carolina Press, 1997.

Vatican I

Vatican I (also known as the first Vatican Council) was convened by Pope Pius IX in 1869–70. The Council was a meeting of the world's bishops, and was intended to formulate a Catholic response to the problems posed to the faith by modernity. Specifically, the Council was intended to counteract the effects of **liberalism** and rationalism, which had been ascendant in the West in the middle and late nineteenth century. Vatican I conceded the existence of a secular sphere of activity, to which the Church could, in principle, be indifferent. However, the main thrust of the Council was a radical reaffirmation of the Church's authority. Perhaps the most important consequence of Vatican I was the formulation of an explicit doctrine of papal infallibility. (TGJ) **See also** Roman Catholicism; Vatican II.

Bibliography

Burns, Gene. *The Frontiers of Catholicism: The Politics of Ideology in a Liberal World.* Berkeley: University of California Press, 1992.

Vatican II

The Second Vatican Council (also known as the Ecumenical Council) was called by Pope John XXIII and deliberated from 1962 through 1965. Vatican II was intended to initiate a search for reunion among the world's Christians, and to increase the importance of the role of the laity in Church affairs. While reaffirming the infallibility of Church doctrine, John XXIII argued that the language used to convey truths must be relevant to contemporary culture. Vatican II produced 16 documents that were intended to modernize the Church's relationship with the world, other religions, and the laity. The Council relaxed a number of Church regulations, and replaced the Tridentine (Latin) Mass with masses conducted in the vernacular of the particular area in which services were held. The Council is considered by some to have rescued the Church from irrelevance by making openings for new movements, such as **liberation theology**, and by others to have undermined the teaching authority that provides Catholicism with its distinctive character. (TGJ) **See also** Ecumenical Movement; Roman Catholicism; Vatican I.

Bibliography

Cuneo, Michael W. *The Smoke of Satan: Conservative and Traditionalist Dissent in Contemporary American Catholicism.* New York: Oxford University Press, 1997.

Davidson, James D., Andrea S. Williams, Richard A. Lamanna, Jan Stenftenagel, Kathleen Maas Weigert, William J. Whalen, and Patricia Wittberg. *The Search for Common Ground: What Unites and Divides Catholic Americans.* Huntington, IN: Our Sunday Visitor, 1997.

Vatican, Diplomatic Relations with

In 1797, the United States appointed John Sartori as its first consul in papal dominions, and from 1847 to 1867 the United States had a chargé d´affaires who represented its interests to the Vatican. After that the United States had no diplomatic relations with the Holy See until 1939 when President Franklin D. Roosevelt sent an informal representative to Pius XII. Roosevelt had met Pius XII in 1936 when the pope was still Cardinal Eugenio Pacelli. At the time, Pacelli was the Vatican's secretary of state and one of his aides was the future archbishop of New York, **Francis Joseph Spellman**.

On December 23, 1939, Roosevelt informed the pope that he was sending Myron C. Taylor, chairman of U.S. Steel and an Episcopalian, to Rome as his personal representative. Franklin Delano Roosevelt was criticized by both liberal and conservative Protestants who feared that any relations with the pope violated the separation of church and state. Roosevelt, however, justified his actions as a way to gather reliable information on fascism and the growing hostilities in Europe.

Roosevelt's decision was a dramatic one considering the strongly anti-Catholic tradition in the United States, which has been largely aimed at the papacy. Many Protestants believed that Catholics could not be trusted in government because their allegiance was to the pope instead of to the country. Additionally, Pope Leo XIII's 1899 encyclical *Testem Benevolemtiae* had specifically condemned certain political and cultural practices that he described as "**Americanism**." However, a personal envoy was a long way from full diplomatic relations.

Another step towards full diplomatic relations was made during the administration of **Richard Nixon**. After visiting Pope Paul VI in 1969 and again in 1970 and praising the pope's world leadership, Nixon officially endorsed the idea of normalized relations with the Vatican. Despite his verbal commitment to the goal, Nixon did little to achieve it. The final step towards full diplomatic relations occurred in 1984 when President **Ronald Reagan** sent an ambassador to the Vatican and, in turn, received the Vatican's representative. Ever since, the United States has maintained full relations with the Vatican. **See also** Anti-Catholicism; Establishment Clause; First Amendment; Roman Catholicism; Wall of Separation.

BIBLIOGRAPHY

Melady, Thomas Patrick. *The Ambassador's Story*. Huntington IN: Our Sunday Visitor, 1994.

Roosevelt, Franklin D. *Wartime Correspondence between President Roosevelt and Pope Pius XII*. New York: Macmillan, 1947.

Denmark Vesey (c.1767–1822)

As a freed slave living in Charleston, South Carolina, Denmark Vesey planned the largest slave revolt in U.S. history. Born in the West Indies and sold to a slave boat captain, Vesey became a resident of Charleston in 1783 and bought his freedom with money won in a lottery in 1800. Aware of the successful Haitian slave revolt, Vesey began to plan one that would involve thousands of blacks in the United States. Warned by a house servant that Vesey's group was using their limited freedom of movement to engage in religious practices as a vehicle for the revolt, authorities suppressed the outbreak. Along with 36 others, Vesey was hanged. As a result, the religious liberty of blacks was severely limited. Vesey's example later inspired the white abolitionist **John Brown** and the black anti-**slavery** activist **Frederick Douglass**, who urged African Americans to enlist in the Union army with the slogan "Remember Denmark Vesey." (MWP) **See also** Abolition.

BIBLIOGRAPHY

Lofton, John. *Denmark Vesey's Revolt: The Slave Plot that Lit a Fuse to Fort Sumter*. Kent, OH: Kent State University Press, 1984.

Vietnam War

The Geneva Accords of 1954 ended the First Indochina War in Vietnam, led to a three-year truce, divided the country at the 17th parallel, and promised elections in 1956. The United States then began providing financial and military support to South Vietnam's president, Ngo Dinh Diem. American involvement in the Second Indochina War began in 1957 when the U.S. helped the south Vietnamese regime confront uprisings that arose after the promised elections were called off because it was obvious that Ho Chi Minh, a Soviet-trained communist, would win. The United States gradually increased military advisors after the Viet Minh, indigenous southerner communists who reignited the conflict in 1957, laid claim to the entire country.

American forces grew from 650 advisors in 1961 to over 16,700 by President **John Fitzgerald Kennedy**'s assassination in November 1963. In early August 1964, President Lyndon Johnson used an inaccurate report of attack by the North Vietnamese on the U.S.S. *Maddox* in the Gulf of Tonkin to get congressional support for retaliation by all necessary measures. Within the context of the Cold War and after the presidential elections of 1964, Johnson approved a two-phase bombing campaign, Operation Barrel Roll against supply trails in Laos, and Operation Rolling Thunder against North Vietnam. From the beginning, the United States attempted to use its massive firepower, great mobility in ships and helicopters, and overwhelming resources to defeat the Viet Minh and the People's Army of Vietnam.

Religious denominations and leaders were divided over the war. Initially many Roman Catholic leaders like Cardinal **Francis Joseph Spellman** supported the war. Much of the support was drawn from the strongly anti-communist stance of the Catholic Church. Also, any of the war's early supporters were Protestant **Evangelicals** like the Reverend **Billy Graham**. However, as the war deepened, support from religious leaders was largely replaced with religious groups opposing the war. **Daniel Berrigan** and **Phillip Berrigan** led the **Catholic Worker Movement** in its opposition. Many **civil rights** leaders and groups opposed the war because of the growing imbalance of blocks as frontline combat troops.

North Vietnam's President Ho Chi Minh and General Vo Nguyen Giap combined fervent nationalism and communism to garner support. Using various military and political strategies, the North was able to prolong a war until it was no longer politically or socially feasible for the Americans to continue fighting. Using a combination of guerrilla, mobile, and offensive warfare, the North Vietnamese forces also attacked political support for the war in the countryside, in the military forces of the South, and in the United States. In 1973, President **Richard Nixon** withdrew American forces under the banner, "Peace with Honor." The North defeated the South and unified the country under communist rule in 1975, leading to a massive exodus of refugees who faced persecution under the new regime. (GT) **See also** Conscientious Objection; Peace Movement; Roman Catholicism; Socialism and Communism.

The Vietnam War divided the nation and religious leaders alike. National Archives.

BIBLIOGRAPHY

Clodfelter, Mark. *The Limits of Air Power: The American Bombing of North Vietnam*. New York: The Free Press, 1989.

Karnow, Stanley. *Vietnam: A History*. New York: Penguin Group, 1991.

Krepinevich, Andrew, Jr. *The Army and Vietnam*. Baltimore: Johns Hopkins University Press, 1990.

Palmer, Bruce, Jr. *The 25-Year War: America's Military Role in Vietnam*. New York: Da Capo Press, 1990.

Virginia Colony

One of the first English colonies in Virginia was founded on Roanoke Island in 1587; it disappeared mysteriously. No other attempt was made until 1607 when a settlement was established at Jamestown. Unlike later colonies to the north that were established for religious reasons, the Jamestown colony was set up as a joint-stock company, and was to be a profit-making business. But so many of the colonists were disinterested in work, that it lost money.

In 1611, Sir Thomas Dale arrived and forced the colonists to work, and in 1612, the first crops of high-quality tobacco were produced; only then did the colony begin to prosper. Offers of 50 acres of free land to new settlers help to attract people to the colony but, as in the other colonies, periodic epidemics limited population growth.

As the colony grew, religion became a growing concern. King James I revoked the colony's charter in 1624 because he feared Puritanism. In response, the colony established the Church of England. By 1643, all nonconformists were required to leave the colony, and in 1661 the colony passed laws against **Baptists** and **Quakers**.

After 1688, the colony became more tolerant of dissenters. In 1776, the new state of Virginia repealed most of the laws that secured the Anglican Church's favored legal status. In 1786, it passed **Thomas Jefferson**'s bill for establishing religious freedom, which completed the task. (MWP) **See also** Colonial America; Puritans; Virginia Declaration of Rights; Virginia Statute for Establishing Religious Freedom.

BIBLIOGRAPHY

Morgan, Edmund S. *American Slavery, American Freedom: The Ordeal of Colonial Virginia*. New York: Norton, 1995.

Morton, Richard L. *Colonial Virginia*. Chapel Hill, NC: Virginia Historical Society, 1960.

Perry, James R. *The Formation of a Society on Virginia's Eastern Shore, 1615-1655*. Chapel Hill, NC: Institute of Early American History and Culture, 1990.

Virginia Declaration of Rights, Article XVI (1776)

Article XVI of the Virginia Declaration of Rights was a seminal, post-colonial statement on the rights of conscience. Authored by **George Mason**, with important substantive amendments from **James Madison**, Article XVI succinctly stated the themes of subsequent debate on religious liberty in Virginia and throughout the new nation. Madison drew on Article XVI to initiate debate in the First Congress on the free exercise of religion, the language of which was eventually adopted in the **First Amendment**. Madison is usually credited with replacing Mason's promise of religious toleration in the initial draft of Article XVI with a **natural rights** declaration that all men are equally entitled to the full and free exercise of religion. In its final form, adopted by the Virginia Convention on June 12, 1776, Article XVI declared "That Religion, or the duty which we owe to our CREATOR, and the manner of discharging it, can be directed only by reason and conviction, not by force or violence; and, therefore, all men are equally entitled to the free exercise of religion, according to the dictates of conscience; and that it is the mutual duty of all to practise Christian forbearance, love, and charity, towards each other." (Article XVI of the Virginia Declaration of Rights is reprinted in Appendix 1.) (DLD) **See also** Free Exercise Clause; Virginia Colony; Virginia Statute for Establishing Religious Freedom.

BIBLIOGRAPHY

Dreisbach, Daniel L. "George Mason's Pursuit of Religious Liberty in Revolutionary Virginia." *Gunston Gazette* II, no. 2 (1997): I-VII.

Rutland, Robert A., ed. *The Papers of George Mason, 1725-1792*. vol. 1. Chapel Hill: University of North Carolina Press, 1970.

Virginia Statute for Establishing Religious Freedom (1786)

The Virginia "Statute for Establishing Religious Freedom," drafted by **Thomas Jefferson** in 1777, is one of the most venerated documents in American history. It was one proposal in an ambitious revision of the laws of Virginia commenced after the political separation from Great Britain. The bill was enacted in January 1786, following the legislative demise of a general assessment proposal that would have required all citizens to pay an annual tax for the support of teachers of the Christian religion. Jefferson's bill failed to gain passage in 1779 when it was first introduced in the Virginia legislature.

In an eloquent preamble (four times the length of the act itself), Jefferson set forth the reasons for the measure: "Almighty God hath created the mind free" and willed "that free it shall remain." Jefferson maintained that the mind of man was, by the intrinsic free-ranging nature and individual variety deliberately created in it by God, not intended to be coerced into intellectual conformity. "[T]he holy author of our religion, who being lord both of body and mind," he argued, chose that religion should be propagated by reason and not by coercion. "[L]egislators and rulers, civil as well as ecclesiastical," have impiously "assumed dominion over the faith of others," and because of their own fallibility and use of coercion have "established and maintained false religions over the greatest part of the world." Jefferson further argued that it is "sinful and tyrannical" to compel a man to support a religion that "he disbelieves and abhors." It is also an infringement on his freedom of choice to force him to support a "teacher of his own religious persuasion," because this inhibits the free encouragement of the minister whose moral pattern and righteousness the citizen finds most persuasive and worthy of support. "[O]ur **civil rights**," Jefferson continued, "have no dependance on our religious opinions, any more than our opinions in physics or geometry"; and, therefore, imposing religious qualifications for civil office deprives the citizen of his "natural right" and tends to corrupt religion by bribery to obtain purely external conformity. It is undesirable to use civil magistrates to suppress the propagation of opinions and principles, even of allegedly false tenets, because "truth is great and . . . has nothing to fear from the conflict" with error "unless by human interposition disarmed of her natural weapons, free argument and debate." Jefferson concluded that "it is time enough" for officers of civil government "to interfere when principles break out into overt acts against peace and good order."

The statute provided in its brief enabling clauses "that no man shall be compelled to frequent or support any religious worship, place, or ministry whatsoever, nor shall be enforced, restrained, molested, or burthened in his body or goods, nor shall otherwise suffer on account of his religious opinions or belief; but that all men shall be free to profess, and by argument to maintain, their opinions in matters of religion, and that the same shall in no wise diminish, enlarge, or affect their civil capacities."

Jefferson selected his authorship of the statute as one of three achievements he wanted memorialized on his gravestone. For more than two centuries, the measure has been a manifesto for religious freedom, not only in Virginia, but also across the nation and around the world. James Madison proclaimed in 1786 that the bill's passage "extinguished for ever the ambitious hope of making laws for the human mind." (Jefferson's draft of a bill establishing religious freedom is reprinted in Appendix 1.) (DLD) **See also** First Amendment; Free Exercise Clause; Natural Rights; Virginia Colony; Virginia Declaration of Rights.

BIBLIOGRAPHY

Dreisbach, Daniel L. "A Perspective on Jefferson's Views on Church-State Relations: The Virginia Statute for Establishing Religious Freedom in Its Legislative Context." *American Journal of Legal History* 35 (1991): 172-204.

Peterson, Merrill D. and Robert C. Vaughan, eds. *The Virginia Statute for Religious Freedom: Its Evolution and Consequences in American History*. New York: Cambridge University Press, 1988.

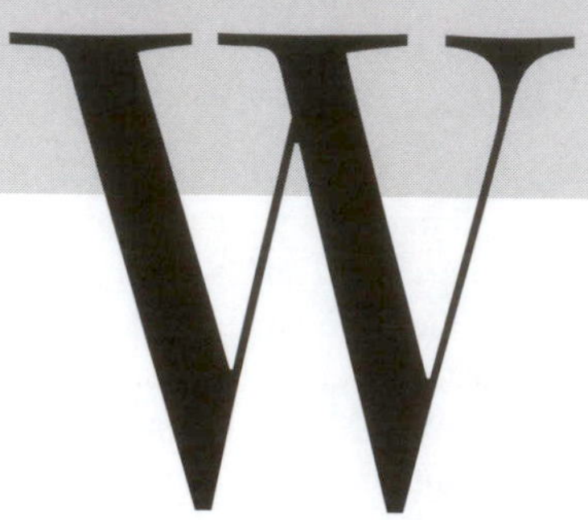

Wall of Separation

The "wall of separation between church and state" is a figure of speech that since the mid-twentieth century has profoundly influenced discourse and policy on church-state relations. It is accepted by many Americans as a pithy description of the constitutionally prescribed church-state arrangement. More important, courts have embraced the metaphor not only as an organizing theme of church-state jurisprudence, but also as a virtual rule of constitutional law in decisions significantly impacting the role of religion in American public life.

The celebrated "wall of separation" metaphor was used by President **Thomas Jefferson** in an 1802 letter to the Danbury Baptist Association of Connecticut to describe the **First Amendment** principles governing church-state relations. Jefferson wrote: "Believing with you that religion is a matter which lies solely between Man & his God, that he owes account to none other for his faith or his worship, that the legitimate powers of government reach actions only, & not opinions, I contemplate with sovereign reverence that act of the whole American people which declared that their legislature should 'make no law respecting an establishment of religion, or prohibiting the free exercise thereof,' thus building a wall of separation between Church & State." Although Jefferson is usually credited with coining the metaphor, at least two other people used it before him in discourse on church and state. The metaphor was mentioned by **Roger Williams**, the colonial champion of religious liberty, and by James Burgh, an eighteenth-century British political writer widely read in revolutionary America.

The "wall" metaphor entered the lexicon of American constitutional law in 1878. In ***Reynolds v. United States*** (1878), the U.S. Supreme Court opined that the Danbury letter "may be accepted almost as an authoritative declaration of the scope and effect of the [first] amendment thus secured." Nearly seven decades later, the metaphor was "rediscovered" by the Supreme Court in the landmark decision of ***Everson v. Board of Education of the Township of Ewing*** (1947). "In the words of Jefferson," wrote Justice **Hugo L. Black** for the Court, "the [First Amendment] clause against establishment of religion by law was intended to erect 'a wall of separation between church and State' . . . . That wall must be high and impregnable. We could not approve the slightest breach." Judicial uses of the metaphor have provoked considerable criticism and controversy.

Jefferson used the "wall" metaphor to illuminate the First Amendment, which he understood was adopted solely as a limitation upon the national government. While Jefferson supported church-state separation in Virginia, it is not clear that he thought his metaphor encapsulated a universal principle of the constitutional and prudential relationship between religion and all civil government. (DLD) **See also** Establishment Clause; Free Exercise Clause; Virginia Declaration of Rights.

Bibliography

Dreisbach, Daniel L. "'Sowing Useful Truths and Principles': The Danbury Baptists, Thomas Jefferson, and the 'Wall of Separation.'" *Journal of Church and State* 39 (1997): 455-501.

Wallace v. Jaffree (1985)

In *Wallace v. Jaffree*, 472 U.S. 38 (1985), the U.S. Supreme Court invalidated an Alabama law providing for a moment of silence for the purpose of "meditation or silent prayer." The Court decided by a 6-3 vote that the law violated the **Establishment Clause** of the **First Amendment**. The opinion of the Court by Justice John Paul Stevens said that the clause requires governmental neutrality and that applying the **Lemon Test** precedent, this law failed to have a secular purpose. Rather, the law was passed to convey to Alabamans that the legislature endorsed prayer activities. Two justices, Lewis Powell and Sandra Day O'Connor, supported the decision while suggesting that some state moment of silence laws might be constitutional. Three dissenting justices indicated dissatisfaction with the Lemon Test precedent followed in the opinion of the Court. The Court also warned against government-sponsored religious activities directed at impressionable children. (JRV)

Bibliography

Sikorski, Robert, ed. *Prayer in Public Schools and the Constitution, 1961-1992*. Controversies in Constitutional Law. New York: Garland Publishing, 1993.

Walz v. Tax Commission of the City of New York (1970)

The Supreme Court's decision in ***Everson v. Board of Education of the Township of Ewing*** (1947) insisted that an impenetrable "**wall of separation**" existed between church and state, and that government had to adopt a position of "strict neutrality" with regard to religion. This idea of government neutrality led to a challenge to the traditional **tax-exempt status** of religious organizations. The resulting case, *Walz v. Tax Commission of the City of New York*, 397 U.S. 664 (1970), marked a departure from the insistence on "strict neutrality" after Justice **Warren E. Burger** announced that government should adopt a position of "benevolent neutrality" toward religion. The Court ruled that any institutions that foster mental or moral improvement and generally help the community should not be inhibited in their activity by the burden of taxation. The true significance of *Walz*, besides eliminating the neutrality standard, was to prohibit the excessive entanglement of church and state. Policies that exempted church properties from taxation tended to minimize the kinds of entanglement between church and state that the Constitution forbade. At the same time, various members of the Court pointed out the difference between tax exemptions and direct subsidies. (JP) **See also** Establishment Clause; First Amendment; Public Aid to Religious Organizations.

BIBLIOGRAPHY

Eastland, Terry. *Religious Liberty in the Supreme Court*. Washington, DC: Ethics and Public Policy Center, 1993.

Michael Walzer (1935–)

As a teacher of social and political thought at Princeton and Harvard Universities, Michael Walzer has concentrated upon the intersection between religion and the role of civil authority, while emphasizing themes of oppression, revolution, and liberation. Walzer's scholarship evidences both the influence of his Jewish faith and modern **liberalism**. (HLC) **See also** Judaism.

BIBLIOGRAPHY

Walzer, Michael. *Exodus and Revolution*. New York: Basic Books, 1985.

——. *The Revolution of the Saints*. Cambridge, MA: Harvard University Press, 1965.

War

War has been part of human existence for as long as can be determined. The three major religions of Mideastern and Western culture have had various perspectives on war. The concept of the "holy war" has been part of **Judaism**, Christianity, and **Islam**. The holy war idea is war directly authorized and sanctified by God, with little ambiguity or qualification. The enemy is the enemy of the people and also the enemy of God. We see the concept in the ancient Jewish invasion of Canaan, in the Christian Crusades, and in Islamic responses to Western influences and incursions.

The "just war" tradition has roots in classical Greek and Roman thinking. It has also been a part of the Christian tradition, particularly after the Emperor Constantine gave official support to Christianity in the early 300s. In broad but fundamental terms, theories of just war seek to answer two questions: What reasons and conditions justify going to war ("jus ad bellum")? and What constitutes just conduct of war ("jus in bello")?

Pacifism involves rejection of the moral legitimacy of war and the refusal to participate in war. It has been a part of the Christian tradition from the early Church. Pacifism normally means principled rejection of all war. It is possible to reject only certain wars as unjust; however, the selective rejection of particular wars is not based on pacifism but on some sense of just war criteria.

The United States was born from war. Churches were among the strongest supporters of the **American Revolution**. The **Civil War**, **World War I**, and **World War II** stand out as times that particularly affected the churches. The Civil War found many triumphantly claiming God for their side. Alternatively, Horace Bushnell and **Abraham Lincoln** sought more sober and complex meanings in the war. World War I so devastated religious optimism that it spurred considerable Christian pacifism in the 1920s and 1930s. Alternatively, World War II led many who had espoused pacifism to repudiate it.

Certain religious groups have established themselves as historic peace churches, especially the **Mennonites** and the **Amish**. They have suffered imprisonment and other punishments for their pacifism (or nonresistance). Still, in periods of conscription, the United States has provided for **conscientious objection** to war on the basis of religious principle. In this regard, because of increasing diversity and secularization in American life, the Supreme Court has construed religious principle in a broad, vaguely theistic sense.

Two matters have spurred considerable thinking about war in recent decades—the **Vietnam War** and nuclear weapons. In the 1960s, Vietnam led many in the churches to question or condemn the morality of that war. In 1983, in the face of nuclear war and growing militarism, the **Conference of Catholic Bishops** issued ***The Challenge of Peace***, condemning the use of nuclear weapons and arguing for **nuclear disarmament**. In 1990-91, the brief war in the Persian Gulf found religious thinkers debating just war issues in the public forum. (GSS) **See also** Just War Theory; Peace Movements; Persian Gulf Conflict.

BIBLIOGRAPHY

Barclay, Oliver R., ed. *Pacifism and War: When Christians Disagree*. Leicester, England: Inter-Varsity Press, 1984.

Holmes, Arthur F., ed. *War and Christian Ethics: Classic Readings on the Morality of War*. Grand Rapids, MI: Baker Book House, 1975.

Kelsay, John and James Turner Johnson, eds. *Just War and Jihad: Historical and Theoretical Perspectives on War and Peace in Western and Islamic Traditions*. New York: Greenwood Press, 1991.

Long, Edward LeRoy, Jr. *War and Conscience in America*. Philadelphia: Westminster Press, 1968.

Booker Taliaferro Washington (1856–1915)

An educator and powerful advocate for Southern black educational and economic self-help programs, Booker T. Washington was the most influential black man in the United States in the post-**Civil War** period. He believed that blacks would be more accepted in Southern communities if they provided the services and products whites needed. Thus, the Tuskegee Institute, of which he was the first president, stressed practical as well as professional training. In Boston in 1900, Washington established the National Negro Business League to provide an economic base for further black advancement. In 1906, he turned down the offer of a cabinet post.

Washington was conciliatory and gradualist in his approach to **civil rights**, believing that blacks had to gradually earn the respect of whites and political rights through their own efforts at economic and social advancement. This approach, summed up in his speech at the opening of the 1895 Atlanta Cotton States Exposition, turned black intellectuals against him, especially **W.E.B. DuBois**, who accused Washington of downplaying civil rights, of "practically accepting the alleged inferiority of the Negro races." Civil rights leaders of the 1960s viewed Washington's approach as reactionary. However, by the late 1980s, many ex-militants disillusioned with government-sponsored **welfare** programs began to endorse economic strategies for black advancement that were similar to those advocated by Washington.

Born into **slavery** at Hale's Ford, Virginia, Washington graduated in 1876 from the Hampton Normal and Agricultural Institute in Virginia. He died November 14, 1915, at Tuskegee, Alabama. (Washington's "The Religious Life of the Negro" speech is reprinted in Appendix 1.) (ISM) **See also** Race Relations.

BIBLIOGRAPHY

Harlan, Louis R. *Booker T. Washington: The Making of a Black Leader, 1856-1901*. New York: Oxford University Press, 1972.

Washington, Booker T. *Up from Slavery*. Garden City, NY: Doubleday & Co., 1901.

George Washington (1732–1799)

Rightly called the "father of his country" for his service as leader of the Continental Army, president of the Constitutional Convention, and first president of the United States, George Washington was a strong proponent of religious liberty in the U.S. In **Washington's letter to the Hebrew Congregation** (1790) in Newport, Rhode Island, he spoke of his desire that every religious group should continue to "sit in safety under his own vine and fig tree and there shall be none to make him afraid." He was particularly distressed by recent clashes between various Christian denominations, especially between Catholics and Protestants.

Washington's tolerant attitude toward religious differences may have stemmed from his own non-sectarian, perhaps even deistical, personal views. A lifelong member of the **Episcopal Church** and vestryman in Truro Parish in Virginia,

This picture shows George Washington in prayer at Valley Forge during the darkest days of the Revolutionary War. Library of Congress.

Washington had deep and earnest religious sensibilities and trusted his own well-being and that of the new nation to the workings of a just and benign Providence.

Although he was the strongest possible advocate of liberty of conscience, Washington insisted in his Farewell Address (1796) that religion and the morality it produces were "indispensable supports" of political prosperity. Thus, he initially backed a general assessment bill for the support of the Virginia churches because, as he wrote to **George Mason** (1785), "I am not amongst the number of those who are so much alarmed at the thought of making people pay towards the support of that which they profess." Still, as Washington explained to a group of New England Presbyterians concerned over the omission of God and Jesus Christ from the new Constitution, it was the job of ministers and not the government to lead people to faith. As president, however, Washington did not hesitate to issue Thanksgiving Proclamations in keeping with "the duty of all nations to acknowledge the providence of Almighty God." In 1787, Washington supported the new Constitution because he was convinced that the new general government it created could never be "so administered as to render the liberty of conscience insecure." (JHM) **See also** Deism; Presbyterian Church; Roman Catholicism; Washington's Farewell Address.

BIBLIOGRAPHY

Boller, Paul F. Jr. "George Washington and Religious Liberty." *William and Mary Quarterly* (1960): 486-506.

Washington's Farewell Address (1796)

Although it is best remembered for its recommendations concerning foreign policy, the Farewell Address was a summary of the first president's mature thoughts about the new nation. After announcing his intention to retire and not seek a third presidential term, **George Washington** gave his considered advice on subjects he thought necessary for the long-term safety and happiness of the American people.

Washington warned the nation to distrust the passions of political parties, be wary of foreign influence in domestic politics, and avoid an entangling foreign policy, but his two main themes were the Union as the core of American nationhood and national independence in world affairs. Central to both are a well-formed constitution, the habits of good citizenship, and the proper dispositions among the people—meaning especially the twin pillars of religion and morality, which are "a necessary spring of popular government." (Washington's Farewell Address is reprinted in Appendix 1.) (MS)

BIBLIOGRAPHY

Burton Ira Kaufman, ed. *Washington's Farewell Address: The View from the 20th Century.* Chicago: Quadrangle Books, 1969.

Spalding, Matthew and Patrick J. Garrity. *A Sacred Union of Citizens: George Washington's Farewell Address and the American Character.* Lanham, MD: Rowman & Littlefield, 1996.

Washington's Letter to the Hebrew Congregation (1790)

Soon after he became president, **George Washington** wrote an important series of letters to each religious denomination in America, the general theme of which is the relationship between religious freedom and civic responsibility. Washington's best and most significant elaboration of this idea is his letter to the Hebrew Congregation of Newport, Rhode Island, in August 1790. "It is now no more that toleration is spoken of as if it were the indulgence of one class of people that another enjoyed the exercise of their inherent **natural rights**, for, happily, the Government of the United States, which gives to bigotry no sanction, to persecution no assistance, requires only that they who live under its protection should demean themselves as good citizens in giving it on all occasions their effectual support." By protecting the right of freedom of religion, the new government deserved the support and affection of all religious Americans. To preserve their freedoms, a religious people had to become vigilant and active citizens–thereby infusing the general citizenry with their virtues and characteristics. (Washington's letter is reprinted in Appendix 1.) (MS)

BIBLIOGRAPHY

Allen, William B. *George Washington: A Collection.* Indianapolis: Liberty Classics, 1988.

Francis Wayland (1796–1865)

Francis Wayland, a Baptist minister, had a major impact on American **education** during his long presidency of Brown University (1827–1855). He changed the emphasis of education from the gentlemanly study of literary classics to practical training for professional life. He also opposed **slavery**, and in his sermon, "The Moral Dignity of the Missionary Enterprise," championed Christian missions. Wayland is recognized as one of the leading Baptist thinkers in the period before the **Civil War**. (MWP) **See also** Baptists; Missionaries.

BIBLIOGRAPHY

Wayland, Francis. *A Memoir of the Life and Labors of Francis Wayland.* New York: Sheldon & Co., 1967.

Max Weber (1864–1920)

One of the leading social scientists of the twentieth century, Max Weber is best known in the United States as the author of *The Protestant Ethic and the Spirit of Capitalism.* In this work, Weber argues that capitalism is a secularized form of **Calvinism** wherein the Calvinistic duty to work ceaselessly to show that one is predestined for salvation in the other world is transformed into the duty to accumulate as much wealth as possible in this world. (SJL)

BIBLIOGRAPHY

Weber, Max. *The Protestant Ethic and the Spirit of Capitalism.* Talcott Parsons, translator. New York: Scribner's, 1958.

George Weigel (1951–)

Pope John Paul II has called George Weigel, along with **Michael Novak** and the Reverend **Richard John Neuhaus**, one of the the three most important Catholics in American politics. A prolific author, Weigel particularly has attacked the errors of political realism in which power (and the pursuit of power) animates the thoughts and actions of individuals and states, and argues that politics and ethics are connected in domestic and foreign policy. Currently, he is writing the authorized biography of the Holy Father. (EES) **See also** Roman Catholicism.

BIBLIOGRAPHY

Weigel, George. *Catholicism and the Renewal of American Democracy.* New York: Paulist Press, 1989.

——. *Freedom and Its Discontents.* Washington, DC: Ethics & Public Policy Center, 1991.

——. *Idealism Without Illusions: U.S. Foreign Policy in the 1990s.* Grand Rapids, MI: Eerdmans, 1994.

Theodore Dwight Weld (1803–1895)

Theodore Weld was one of the greatest American revivalists and a leading figure in the early nineteenth-century **abolition** and temperance movements. **Charles Grandison Finney** was a powerful force in shaping the young Weld, whom Finney first met in 1825 at a revival in upstate New York. After Weld led revivals for several years, he decided to attend Lane Theological Seminary in Cincinnati, Ohio, beginning in 1832. However, in the spring of 1834, Weld was expelled for his abolitionist activities. Weld then went to the newly formed Oberlin College, which was under the direction of Finney and had the financial backing of **Arthur Tappan** and **Lewis Tappan**.

Weld became active in the **American Anti-Slavery Society** and wrote two works against **slavery**—*The Bible Against Slavery* (1839) and *American Slavery As It Is* (1839). His writings influenced others, including **Harriet Beecher Stowe**, author of ***Uncle Tom's Cabin***. The divisive split of the **American Anti-Slavery Society** in 1839 over the issue of woman suffrage and **William Lloyd Garrison**'s position of non-political moral persuasion, led Weld to retire from political activities. He spent the remainder of his life as a farmer and teacher, refraining from further involvement in reform movements. **See also** Temperance and Prohibition.

BIBLIOGRAPHY

Abzug, Robert H. *Passionate Liberator: Theodore Dwight Weld and the Dilemma of Reform.* New York: Oxford University Press, 1980.

Welfare

Welfare is a complicated issue for Americans, and has been throughout the history of the United States. Whether and how to provide for the poor, who are alternately viewed as individual victims in need of charity or slothful, lazy people who deserve their poverty, have been questions since the **Puritans** first settled the **Massachusetts Bay Colony** in the seventeenth century. Sometimes the issue of **social justice** has merged with welfare concerns. At other times, moral reform has been the orienting focus of welfare. But whatever the secondary issues, Americans have shown a profound ambivalence about poverty that has manifested itself in both anger toward and indifference to the welfare of the poor, as well as in benevolence and social reform movements.

Two religious understandings of the seventeenth century have shaped the American mindset toward the poor and welfare. The first is "**pietism**," which focused on the inner workings of the spiritual life and on humility expressed through service. In essence, pietism demanded that individuals serve other less fortunate people to remind themselves of the provisions God makes in their own lives, and to express God's care for the world. Seventeenth-century piety was concerned with charity, but not with social change. Pietism assumed that the poor would always exist, and that service to the poor was essential to Christian faith development.

Coupled with pietism was the Puritanism of that era. Puritans focused on the covenantal nature of relationships. They were suspicious of individualism and disorder, and promoted a strong work ethic. Because their civil and religious lives were intertwined, their degree of economic productivity was interpreted religiously as reward for righteousness or punishment for sinfulness. Effort, obedience, and sober attention to work had high social value; creativity and entrepreneurial endeavors caused social scandal and elicited communal pressure to conform. Welfare was a function of the communal covenant to care for one another as long as the poor remained in good standing within the community.

The eighteenth century reinforced the concept of a religious obligation to provide welfare for the poor. Jonathan Edwards, a prominent preacher of the **First Great Awakening** revival, argued that the provision of welfare was the consistent Christian response to God's gift of grace, and that God's demand that Christians love their enemies meant that even persons who were poor because of their own shortcomings deserved assistance. During this century, the role of government shifted from that of Puritan disciplinarian to that of social services agent.

The late eighteenth and early nineteenth centuries introduced the idea of populism into the American perspective on poverty and welfare. Populism denoted a fascination with the wisdom and practices of the "common" people: poor farmers, miners, factory workers. The anti-intellectualism of this era, coupled with Scottish Common Sense philosophy, led to a romanticization of the working poor as God's blessed people. At the same time, concern for the welfare of the poor raised the issue of social justice and permitted American Christians to argue for **abolition** and **labor** unions.

With the idea of populism, however, came a second nineteenth-century concept: Social Darwinism. This concept worked against the populist impulse to valorize the working class because it assumed that failure to succeed in the marketplace resulted from social deficiencies that rendered one less fit to survive in an evolutionary world. Americans in this era valued progress highly. Even if they theologically rejected Darwinian theories, as did most evangelicals, they still held that society was progressively moving toward an ideal state termed the "Kingdom of God."

Also moderating the nineteenth-century populist impulse was the era's embrace of laissez-faire economics, which emphasized the freedom of Americans to buy and sell whatever they wanted with minimum government interference. Economic reformers, therefore, often defined their agendas with narrow legislative goals, which they pursued only if they could not win voluntary compliance from rising industrialists. The philanthropic activities of men like Andrew Carnegie created a moral dilemma for nineteenth-century reformers because the practice of charitable giving by the wealthy superficially addressed the issue of welfare without really altering the circumstances of the urban poor. Yet reformers were reluctant to criticize these wealthy industrialists because reform societies depended on their donations and because reformers genuinely believed that the American system of **capitalism** was the most progressive economic form available.

The dominant themes of nineteenth-century welfare practices, then, were the moral reform of the poor and the modest regulation of industrial working conditions. Charitable societies viewed the city, with its high levels of poverty and social disorder, as a dangerous threat to American progress. Poor families were stereotyped as ignorant, immoral, lazy, and prone to promiscuity. **Henry Ward Beecher**, a widely admired preacher, attributed poverty to the poor's lack of industriousness, frugality, and wise planning. Middle-class reformers sought to "convert" slum families from social failure and moral crisis to stable middle-class values and lifestyles. Children and young adults, because of their potential for redirection, received particular attention from such groups as the Children's Aid Society and the Young Men's and Women's Christian Associations (YMCA and YWCA).

The **Social Gospel** movement of the late nineteenth and early twentieth centuries attempted to expand the focus of welfare from charity alone to charity coupled with strenuous advocacy for social change. While even evangelical groups like the **Salvation Army** called for a social revival of the "wicked" cities, Social Gospelers like **Walter Rauschenbusch** received little mainstream support because of Americans' basic acceptance of the Puritan linkage of poverty to sinfulness. What little response had been generated within liberal Christianity disappeared when the Great Depression of the 1930s stripped churches of their benevolence funds.

Part of the legacy of the 1960s **civil rights** movement is that it pushed the federal government and religious groups to "rediscover" poverty as a pressing social concern. President Lyndon Johnson declared war on poverty in 1964, using as his weapons Affirmative Action, Project Head Start, the Community Action Program, and the Model Cities Program. Welfare advocates lobbied for urban renewal rather than the demolition of inner city neighborhoods. Black and Hispanic churches, despite their limited resources, set out to combat the persistent anti-urbanism of suburban white churches and to push for social responsibility.

Today, the Christian and civil response to poverty and welfare continues to vacillate between condemnation of the poor and calls for social reform. **Evangelicals**, who cling to the "evil city" perspective and prioritize evangelism over social action, have actively opposed government-sponsored welfare programs. Instead, they advocate "workfare," in which recipients of government aid perform services in exchange for support. They have also lobbied for strict sanctions against mothers who have additional children while receiving public assistance, and condemn the Aid to Families with Dependent Children program, with its focus on families headed by single mothers, as an affront to fathers and extended families. They reject the eighteenth-century governmental shift from disciplinarian to social services agent, arguing that it is not the government's responsibility to care for the poor. Instead, they believe the poor are the church's responsibility, and that the church should help the poor become self-sufficient. They characterize welfare as a system that pays people not to work and creates a charity mentality.

More liberal Christians have responded to evangelical arguments with the observation that improvements in the poverty level in this country depend on expanding the economy, and thus welfare is an appropriate response while economic opportunities are being developed or redistributed. Preacher and activist **William Sloane Coffin** argues that poor people exist because rich people exist, and that sharing the surpluses of wealth is an issue of required justice, not a voluntary issue of benevolence. Liberals, like their Social Gospel forebears, contend that the poor need not always be with us, and that it is cheaper to eradicate poverty than to maintain it. Thus, they see welfare as a matter of charity connected to a larger process of justice. Calling on the idea of the Kingdom of God, they reject any attempt to spiritualize poverty and its relief as a heavenly issue. Nonetheless, liberals also worry about creating a charity mentality, in which the poor identify themselves as helpless victims and the middle-class and rich support welfare programs to assuage their own guilt at having more than they need.

The American Catholic Bishops articulated their views on welfare in their 1986 pastoral letter, *Economic Justice for All: Catholic Social Teaching and the U.S. Economy*. They argued that God chooses to side with the poor out of mercy and love, and that Christians should do the same. While carefully supporting free enterprise, the letter focuses on the communal nature of human life, and the religious obligation of respect and care for all persons. **Richard John Neuhaus**, a prominent Catholic scholar of religion and politics, has written extensively on the "preferential option for the poor" that should inform American political life. He rejects the stereotype of the poor as immoral, arguing instead that many poverty-stricken individuals hold family loyalty and religious devotion as central values.

According to national polls, church members, regardless of their religious beliefs, are more inclined to charity and social outreach than non-church members. This inclination is critical to addressing the problem of over 30 million poor in the United States. Whether welfare consists of governmental programs like Aid to Families with Dependent Children, or citizen initiatives like Millard Fuller's Habitat for Humanity, or religious soup kitchens and food pantries, the need for welfare is obvious. The debate about the root causes of poverty, and thus the deservedness of welfare, coexists with the reality of undernourished children, homelessness, and the working poor. Americans continue to struggle with the legacy of their pietist, Puritan, populist, and progressive past as they seek an appropriate response to the suffering of the poor. They can choose to deny the real existence of poverty, as Americans did in the gilded ages of the 1890s, 1920s, and 1980s. They can choose to denigrate the poor as ignorant, immoral, and in need of strict instruction, as the welfare reform movements of the mid-nineteenth century and the 1990s have done. Or they can choose to advocate major social change, as the Social Gospelers did. The twenty-first century offers all these possibilities for the issue of welfare in the United States. (KMY) **See also** Liberalism; National Catholic Welfare Conference; Reformation; Religion and Urban Issues; Secular Humanism; Socialism and Communism.

Bibliography

Coffin, William Sloan. *Passion for the Possible: A Message to U.S. Churches*. Louisville: Westminster/John Knox Press, 1993.

Conn, Harvie M. *The American City and the Evangelical Church*. Grand Rapids, MI: Baker Books, 1994.

Kelly, George A. *The Catholic Church and the American Poor*. New York: Alba House, 1976.

Neuhaus, Richard John, ed. *The Preferential Option for the Poor*. Grand Rapids, MI: Eerdmans Publishing Company, 1988.

Olasky, Marvin. *The Tragedy of American Compassion*. Washington: Regency, 1992.

Perkins, John M. *Beyond Charity: The Call to Christian Community Development*. Grand Rapids, MI: Baker Books, 1993.
Walters, Ronald G. *American Reformers, 1815-1860*. New York: Hill and Wang, 1978.

West Virginia State Board of Education v. Barnette (1943)

In *West Virginia State Board of Education v. Barnette*, 329 U.S. 624 (1943), the United States Supreme Court overruled a three-year-old precedent established in ***Minersville School District v. Gobitis***. In that decision, the Court had upheld a Pennsylvania statue that required children in public schools to recite the **Pledge of Allegiance**. Subsequently in *Barnette*, the Court held that such a requirement violated the Free Speech and Press provisions of the **First Amendment**, as applied to the states by the Due Process Clause of the **Fourteenth Amendment**.

In *Barnette*, the plaintiff argued that the requirement of reciting the Pledge violated the **Free Exercise Clause** of the First Amendment, since, as a Christian Scientist, his children could not say the Pledge of Allegiance without violating the religious prohibition against worshipping a graven image. However, the Court's majority opinion, written by Justice Robert Jackson, stated that the most fundamental question at stake was free expression, and that religious freedom was a secondary issue. The Free Exercise issue was given more weight in concurrences by Justices **William Douglas**, **Hugo Black**, and Frank Murphy, who argued that the state could only interfere with religious freedom for reasons that were "imperative" or "necessary."

In dissent, Justice **Felix Frankfurter** argued (in a manner that may have anticipated the 1990 decision in ***Employment Division of Oregon v. Smith***) that the West Virginia statute did not mandate accepting particular religious dogma, but simply intended to pursue the secular goal of good citizenship, which, according to Frankfurter, falls well within the police powers of the state. (TGJ) **See also** Christian Science.

BIBLIOGRAPHY

Eastland, Terry. Religious Liberty in the Supreme Court. Washington, DC: Ethics and Public Policy Center, 1993.
Employment Division, Department of Human Resources of Oregon v. Smith, 494 U.S. 872 (1990).
Minersville School District v. Gobitis, 310 U.S. 586 (1940).

George Whitefield (1714–1770)

George Whitefield, a Calvinist clergyman, was the most renowned preacher of the **First Great Awakening** (1740-1743), effectively shaping the American religious consciousness and also establishing the paradigm of modern mass evangelism. From 1738 to 1770, Whitefield came to America on seven separate occasions to preach, drawing crowds of thousands. Controversial with established religious leaders, Whitefield encouraged the questioning of hierarchy in the established church. His message of "new birth" and his anti-Anglican stance made him a symbol of American patriotism during the pre-revolutionary years. (PV) **See also** Calvinism; Colonial America.

George Whitefield was the most effective preacher of the First Great Awakening. Library of Congress.

BIBLIOGRAPHY

Stout, Harry. *The Divine Dramatist: George Whitefield and the Rise of Modern Evangelism*. Grand Rapids, MI: Eerdmans, 1991.

Walt Whitman (1819–1892)

Walt Whitman is an American poet best known for the many editions of his collection of poems entitled *Leaves of Grass*. Until his mid-30s, Walt Whitman was a little known newspaper editor, but in 1855, he published the first edition of *Leaves of Grass,* which offered poetry with an optimistic vision of the country's future. Leading transcendentalists like **Ralph Waldo Emerson** and **Henry David Thoreau** were encouraged by the young poet's art and message. By the third (1860) edition, *Leaves of Grass* had taken on a sensuality that brought accusations of obscenity. Ralph Waldo Emerson, initially excited about the new poet, later complained that he wanted Whitman to make songs about the nation and discovered that he "seemed content to make the inventories." Whitman's defenders claim that he spoke about generalities by focusing on particulars. Much of his work took a post-Christian flavor that reflected his general skepticism of authority. Whitman hoped that the country would prosper because of its faith in **democracy** and in the common man. (MWP) **See also** Transcendentalism.

BIBLIOGRAPHY

Kuebrich, David. *Minor Prophecy: Walt Whitman's New American Religion*. Bloomington: Indiana University Press, 1989.

Widmar v. Vincent (1981)

The University of Missouri at Kansas City generally made its facilities available for use to student organizations, but a student religious organization was informed by university officials that it could not use campus facilities for its meetings because such gatherings would violate a policy that prohibited use of university buildings and grounds "for purposes of religious worship or religious teaching." The university said it believed such a policy was required by the **Establishment Clause** of the **First Amendment** of the Constitution to avoid state entanglement with and support of religion.

In *Widmar v. Vincent*, 454 U.S. 263 (1981), the Supreme Court took another view of the Establishment Clause. It held that the university's exclusionary policy violated the constitutional requirement that state policies be content-neutral. Once the state created a public forum—providing meeting space for over 100 student organizations—it must demonstrate a "compelling state interest" in the regulation of free speech for forbidding a group to take part in that forum. Such restriction must pass a three-prong test: (1) it must have a secular purpose, (2) must not advance or inhibit religion, and (3) must not foster "excessive entanglement" with religion. (FHJ) **See also** Equal Access Act; Free Speech Approach to Religious Liberty.

BIBLIOGRAPHY

Breneman, Scott C. "*Widmar v. Vincent* and the Public Forum Doctrine: Time to Reconsider the Public School Prayer. (Case Note)." *Wisconsin Law Review* no. 1 (January-February 1984): 147-94.

Aaron Wildavsky (1930–1994)

Born in New York City, Aaron Wildavsky was an eminent political scientist who returned to spiritual concerns with great intensity towards the end of his life. Best known as a student of public policy, Wildavsky authored a classic study of the budget process and served as president of the American Political Science Association. Turning to the study of the "macropolitics of regimes," he composed books on Moses and Joseph that saw these Old Testament figures as models of political leadership. (HLC)

BIBLIOGRAPHY

Wildavsky, Aaron. *Assimilation Versus Separation: Joseph the Administrator and the Politics of Religion in Biblical Israel*. New Brunswick, NJ: Transaction Press, 1992.

——. *The Nursing Father: Moses as a Political Leader*. Tuscaloosa: University of Alabama Press, 1984.

Emma Willard (1787–1870)

An important advocate of female **education** in the nineteenth century, Emma Willard founded the Troy Female Seminary in 1821. A Congregationalist and later Episcopalian, Willard was firmly convinced that women had a unique role to play in the creation of good, moral citizens. Unlike many of her contemporaries, she believed that women needed to receive a rigorous academic education. Willard's chief influences came through the more than 12,000 women who graduated from Troy Seminary between 1821 and 1872. She also wrote several textbooks and was an early lobbyist for state support of female educational institutions. (MDH) **See also** Congregationalism; Episcopal Church; Women in Religion and Politics.

BIBLIOGRAPHY

Goodsell, Willystine, ed. *Pioneers of Women's Education in the United States: Emma Willard, Catherine Beecher, Mary Lyons*. New York: AMS Press, 1970.

Lutz, Alma. *Emma Willard: Pioneer Educator of American Women*. Westport, CT: Greenwood Press, 1983.

Frances Elizabeth Caroline Willard (1839–1898)

A skilled organizer and political advocate, Frances Willard played a major role in making the prohibition movement a powerful political force. Trained as a teacher, Willard became the president of Northwestern Female College (1871) and dean of women at Northwestern University when the college merged with the university (1873). The following year she resigned to work with the **Women's Christian Temperance Union (WCTU)**. Willard quickly rose to become its national president (1879), an office she held until her death. Like many in the **temperance** movement, she also fought for women's suffrage and protective laws for working women. (MWP) **See also** Women in Religion and Politics.

BIBLIOGRAPHY

Dillon, Mary E. *Francis Willard: From Politics to Prayer*. Chicago: University of Illinois Press, 1944.

William Penn Essays

These 24 essays written in 1829 by evangelical reformer **Jeremiah Evarts** criticized efforts by the federal government to compel the Cherokee to leave their ancestral lands in Georgia. Printed in newspapers around the nation, the essays were a tour de force of law, logic, and morality. Evarts made his case by appealing to **natural rights**, national honor, the obligation of contracts, Biblical justice, and the law of nations. U.S. Supreme Court Chief Justice John Marshall called Evarts' essays the "most conclusive argument that he ever read on any subject whatever." The essays are one of the finest examples of political rhetoric by an American religious reformer. (JGW) **See also** Cherokee Removal.

BIBLIOGRAPHY

Evarts, Jeremiah. *The "William Penn Essays" and Other Writing by Jeremiah Evarts*. Francis Paul Prucha, ed. Knoxville: University of Tennessee Press, 1981.

West, John G., Jr. *The Politics of Revelation and Reason: Religion and Civic Life in the New Nation*. Lawrence: University Press of Kansas, 1996.

Roger Williams (1603–1683)

Roger Williams, the founder of **Rhode Island Colony**, emigrated to the **Massachusetts Bay Colony** in 1631. A separatist who rejected the establishment of the Church of England, Williams soon left Massachusetts Bay and settled in the separatist colony of Plymouth, where disapproval of his radical views forced his return to Massachusetts Bay in 1634. Williams was banished from the Bay Colony in 1635 because of his rejection of the legitimacy of the colony's leaders and laws. With few options remaining, he settled among the Narragansett Indians in present-day Rhode Island.

In 1643, he went to England to obtain a charter for a new colony. The following year, his thoughts on religion and politics were published in his book, *The Bloody Tenets of Persecution*. In the work, he rejected the common belief that religious uniformity was necessary for social peace. Instead, he argued that religious freedom could only be secure if religious tolerance were extended to all. Although Williams's Rhode Island did not welcome **Quakers** or Catholics, it became a politically secure and religiously tolerant colony for other groups, including **Baptists** and Jews. **See also** Colonial America; Judaism; Pilgrims; Roman Catholicism.

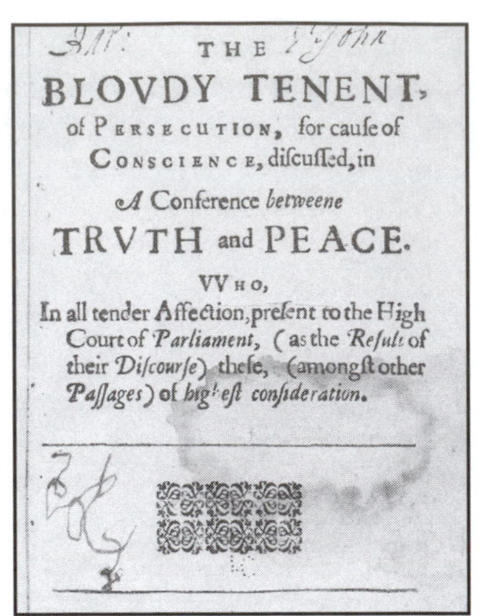
THE BLOVDY TENENT, of PERSECUTION, for cause of CONSCIENCE, discussed, in A Conference betweene TRVTH and PEACE. VVHO, In all tender Affection, present to the High Court of Parliament, (as the Result of their Discourse) these, (amongst other Passages) of highest consideration.

Roger Williams, founder of Rhode Island Colony, collected his thoughts on religion and politics in "The Bloody Tenet of Persecution." Library of Congress.

BIBLIOGRAPHY

Garrett, John. *Roger Williams*. New York: Macmillan, 1970.

Miller, Perry. *Roger Williams: His Contributions to the American Tradition*. Indianapolis: Bobbs-Merrill, 1953.

Morgan, Edmund S. *Roger Williams: The Church and State*. New York: Harcourt Brace & World, 1967.

Francis Graham Wilson (1901–1976)

As a teacher and author, Francis G. Wilson contributed substantially to the mid-twentieth-century revival of the study of Christian political thought, especially its importance to American political theory. A convert to **Roman Catholicism**, Wilson published many books and articles on public opinion, American political theory, and Catholicism's response to the modern world. (HLC)

BIBLIOGRAPHY

Wilson, Francis Graham. *The American Political Mind*. New York: McGraw Hill, 1949.

James Wilson (1742–1798)

James Wilson was a signer of the **Declaration of Independence** and the Constitution, one of America's first law professors, and a Supreme Court justice. His Christian beliefs had an important influence on his contributions to the creation of the American Republic. Born in Scotland, Wilson graduated from St. Andrews and attended one year of divinity school before emigrating to America in 1765. Firmly believing that the primary purpose of government was to protect God-given **natural rights**, he became an important leader in the **American Revolution**. In 1774, Wilson provided the first argument that Parliament had absolutely no sovereignty over the American colonies, and in 1776 he cast the deciding vote in favor of the Declaration of Independence.

Convinced that democratic institutions were the best way to create moral laws, Wilson was the foremost advocate of a strong, democratic government at the Federal Constitutional Convention. Second only to **James Madison** in his influence on the Constitution, Wilson went on to play a central role in the ratifying debates and was the moving force behind the Pennsylvania Constitution of 1790. Finally, as a law professor and Supreme Court justice, he produced some of the period's most profound commentary on the Constitution and American law. He died fleeing creditors in 1798. (MDH) **See also** Colonial America; Democracy.

BIBLIOGRAPHY

Hall, Mark David. *The Political and Legal Philosophy of James Wilson, 1742-1798*. Columbia:University of Missouri Press, 1997.

McCloskey, Robert, ed. *The Works of James Wilson*. 2 vols. Cambridge: Harvard University Press, 1967.

Woodrow Wilson (1856–1924)

Woodrow Wilson was both a man of intellect and a man of action, having served as president of Princeton University (1902-1910), governor of New Jersey (1911-1913), and president of the United States (1913-1921). Wilson was a unique American statesman, one whose actions can only be properly appreciated in the light of their religious and spiritual underpinnings. The son of a **Presbyterian** minister, Wilson never strayed far from his **Puritan** roots, having been at the center of the late nineteenth-century Progressive movement. Wilson is widely recognized as the architect of the modern American state, in both its domestic and international policy dimensions. He employed his idealistic (some say utopian) vision of American greatness to expand the scope of federal power and to transform the **Democratic Party** into an engine for moral and social progress. In his famous War Message to Congress in April 1917, Wilson set the tone for the next seven decades of American foreign policy by calling on the United States to "make the world safe for democracy." At home or abroad, Wilson's leadership was characterized by a passionate, moralistic reformism, especially his advocacy of national self-determination at the Versailles peace conference (1919), that left an indelible mark on American politics. (GSB) **See also** Democracy; World War I.

BIBLIOGRAPHY

Butler, Gregory S. "Visions of a Nation Transformed: Modernity and Ideology in Wilson's Political Thought." *Journal of Church and State* 39 (Winter 1997): 37-51.

Schulte-Nordholt, Jan Willen. *Woodrow Wilson: A Life for World Peace*. Herbert H. Rowen, trans. Berkeley: University of California Press, 1991.

John Winthrop (1588–1649)

John Winthrop was one of the leaders of the great English **Puritan** migration to New England that began in 1630. A lawyer by training, Winthrop was elected first governor of the **Massachusetts Bay Colony** in 1631, an office he held almost annually until his death in 1649. While aboard ship in the Atlantic, Winthrop delivered a lay sermon in which he expressed his belief that New England would be like "a city upon a hill." Winthrop also helped to organize the New England Confederacy (1643) and became its first president.

Winthrop has sometimes been associated with the more fanatical elements among the New England Puritans, probably because the banishment of **Anne Hutchinson** occurred while he was governor. Although he rejected direct **democracy** because "there was no such government in Israel," Winthrop nevertheless opened the franchise, which had originally been restricted to members of the Massachusetts Bay Company, to include all church members. Winthrop was arguably a moderating influence in Massachusetts Bay and was by no means an autocratic ruler; he was accused of leniency and compromise by his critics, especially among the clergy. (JHM) **See also** Colonial America.

BIBLIOGRAPHY

Morgan, Edmund S. *The Puritan Dilemma: The Story of John Winthrop*. Boston: Little, Brown and Co., 1958.

William Wirt (1772–1834)

Initially a Deist, William Wirt became an Evangelical Christian in 1804. Some of Wirt's essays provide good examples of evangelical life in his day. He served as U.S. attorney general from 1817 through 1829 under Presidents James Monroe and **John Quincy Adams**. During his tenure as attorney general, he participated in some of the nation's most important cases, including *McCulloch v. Maryland* (1819) and *Gibbons v. Ogden* (1824). In 1832, he served as the presidential standard-bearer for the Anti-Masonic Party. (MWP) **See also** Deism; Evangelicals; Anti-Masonic Movement.

BIBLIOGRAPHY

Kennedy, John P. *Memoirs of the Life of William Wirt*. Philadelphia: Lea and Blanchard, 1849.

Oberg, Michael L. "William Wirt and the Trials of Republicanism." *Virginia Magazine of History and Biography* 99 (July 1991): 305-26.

Wisconsin v. Yoder (1972)

The ruling of the Supreme Court in *Wisconsin v. Yoder*, 406 U.S. 205 (1972), allowed members of a religious order to claim exemption from a state law that was dangerous to their way of life. Members of the Old Order **Amish** and Conservative Amish **Mennonite** Church had been convicted of violating a Wisconsin law requiring all children to attend school until they were 16 years old. The Amish parents had removed their children from the public schools after the eighth grade, preferring to train their children in an informal, vocational manner for the Amish lifestyle. They claimed that public **education** was dangerous to their way of life and a threat to their children's salvation and their own. The Supreme Court's decision, written by Chief Justice **Warren E. Burger**, allowed the Amish the exemption and put forth three criteria against which their claims, and similar claims in the future, should be weighed: the sincerity of the religious beliefs, the fundamentality of the outlawed practices to the religion, and the adequacy of the substitute measures that the religion proposed to achieve the goals of the law. (BDG)

BIBLIOGRAPHY

Pfeffer, Leo. *Religion, State, and the Burger Court*. Buffalo: Prometheus Books, 1984.

John Witherspoon (1723–1794)

During the period of his American career (1768–1794), John Witherspoon was one of the foremost figures in New Jersey, if not all of America. A native Scot, Witherspoon emigrated to the colonies to assume the presidency of the College of New Jersey at Princeton. He combined careers as **Presbyterian** divine, educator, author, and statesman. Witherspoon served in the New Jersey legislature and the **Continental Congress**, signed the **Declaration of Independence** and the Articles of Confederation, and was a member of the New Jersey convention that ratified the Constitution.

An orthodox Calvinist in theology and a Federalist in political matters, Witherspoon led in the nationalization of the Presbyterian Church in the United States and was a staunch proponent of independence and American political unity. He preached one of the more influential political sermons of the revolutionary era, "The Dominion of Providence Over the Passions of Men" (1776), and encouraged his colleagues in the Continental Congress to declare independence, arguing that America was not only ripe for independence but in danger of rotting from the want of it. Witherspoon was also a member of the American Philosophical Society, introduced the word "campus" into the American vocabulary, and coined the term "**Americanism**." (JHM) **See also** American Revolution; Calvinism; Colonial America; Samuel Stanhope Smith.

BIBLIOGRAPHY

Collins, Varnum Lansing. *President Witherspoon*. New York: Arno Press, 1969.

Witters v. Department of Services for the Blind (1986)

In *Witters v. Department of Services for the Blind*, 474 U.S. 481 (1986), a unanimous Supreme Court held that it would not violate the **Establishment Clause** of the **First Amendment** for a blind student to use Washington State funds to pay educational expenses at a Bible college where he was studying for the ministry. Justice Thurgood Marshall, writing for the Court, argued that because the vocational aid was paid directly to the student, any state funds that went to the Bible college did so, not as a result of state action, but by the independent choice of the aid recipient. (SM)

BIBLIOGRAPHY

Monsma, Stephen. "Religion and Schooling in Contemporary America: Confronting our Cultural Pluralism." Garland Reference Library of Social Science. vol. 1127. New York: Garland, 1997.

Wolman v. Walter (1977)

Ohio adopted a statute that laid out a scheme for providing aid to nonpublic schools. The statute included the provision of secular textbooks, standardized tests and scoring services that were used in the public schools, psychological services, instructional materials and equipment of the kind used in public schools, and field trip transportation. The scheme was challenged on the grounds that such aid violated the **Establishment Clause** of the **First Amendment**. In *Wolman v. Walter*, 433 U.S. 229 (1977), the U.S. Supreme Court held that the scheme was constitutional with the exception of those portions providing instructional materials and equipment and field trip services, because the latter could be used for inculcating religious doctrines. (JM) **See also** Education.

Bibliography

Bryson, Joseph E. *The Supreme Court and Public Funds for Religious Schools*. Jefferson, NC: McFarland, 1990.

Women in Religion and Politics

The engagement of women in American politics has of necessity been related to religious understandings of women's roles in American culture. In a nation settled as a collection of religious commonwealths and comfortable with the **Reformation** ideal of the family as a unit represented by the male head of household, political action by women has seemed at times irreligious and unnecessary. Nevertheless, women have engaged in political activity and have effected political change throughout American history, sometimes aided by religious ideals, and sometimes in spite of religious opposition.

In the seventeenth century, women's political action took the form of religious dissent. Since religious and civil authority coincided in the New England commonwealths, unconventional theological beliefs or religious practices had social consequences. **Anne Hutchinson**'s claim to have received special divine revelations, and her consequent dismissal of much of Boston's religious leadership as unrepentant sinners, resulted in her expulsion from the **Massachusetts Bay Colony**. Her campaign to reform Boston society failed, but she used her notoriety to create a new settlement, Portsmouth, in **Rhode Island Colony**, an act that can certainly be characterized as political.

Women were also active in nineteenth-century politics. The **temperance** movement served to politicize feminine culture through its demand that the public recognize women's values and formalize their ideals as law. Women banded together to pray and sing outside saloons. Some extraordinarily bold women, such as Carrie Nation, would lead groups of women from saloon to saloon, preaching the evils of drink and smashing whiskey barrels. Most women saw their role as less centered in the public arena. They focused their attention on discouraging drinking among their husbands, brothers, and sons. However public the action, the temperance movement marked a new role for women in public affairs, and various temperance groups soon linked themselves with other social action issues like women's suffrage, prison reform, and **labor** unions. The largest temperance group, the **Women's Christian Temperance Union (WCTU)**, maintained close ties with the largest labor union, the Knights of Labor, throughout the 1880s and 1890s.

In general, women found it easier to organize in small communities, where neighborly ties facilitated acceptance of social causes. The multiplicity of church groups and social circles stymied organizational efforts in larger towns because women were less interested in banding together with strangers. Women's organizations also tended to understand themselves as temporary associations focused on the propagation of a particular moral view and the amelioration of some form of immorality. Uncomfortable with conventional political power—even the women's suffrage movement positioned the vote as more important for moral suasion than for equality—nineteenth-century women eschewed power as a morally corrupting force.

In the twentieth century, women have been vastly underrepresented in American politics, but gains have been made as more women run for and win public office. But the percentage of offices held by women remains in the single digits, whereas half the population is female. And real barriers to political office exist. When Geraldine Ferraro ran for vice president in 1984, her candidacy was forcefully opposed by several prominent American Catholic leaders, such as Archbishop (now Cardinal) Bernard Law, because she refused to translate her own Catholic opposition to **abortion** into law. Joined by fundamentalist and conservative **Evangelicals** who condemned Ferraro's "unfeminine" behavior as well as her pro-choice politics, the Catholic hierarchy succeeded in tying religion and gender together as the central issues of the election.

The late twentieth-century concern with family values plays on the nineteenth-century theme of female moral power, once again asserting that women's greater moral strength demands that they influence politics through an ethics of care and a politics of moral persuasion. Although this moral superiority can exert itself in direct leadership and legislative power, and there is no longer a temporal limit on women's participation in politics, the religious ideology of female virtue still opens women's political actions to moral questions not commonly applied to men's politics. (KMY) **See also** Fundamentalists; Roman Catholicism.

Bibliography

Andolsen, Barbara Hilkert, Gudorf, Christine E., and Pellauer, Mary D., eds. *Women's Consciousness, Women's Conscience*. San Francisco: Harper & Row, 1985.

Epstein, Barbara Leslie. *The Politics of Domesticity: Women, Evangelism, and Temperance in Nineteenth Century America*. Middletown, CT: Wesleyan University Press, 1981.

Ginzberg, Lori D. *Women and the Work of Benevolence: Morality, Politics, and Class in the 19th-Century United States*. New Haven, CT: Yale University Press, 1990.

Ruether, Rosemary Radford and Keller, Rosemary Skinner, eds. *Women & Religion in America, Volume 1: The Nineteenth Century*. San Francisco: Harper & Row, 1981.

Women's Christian Temperance Union (WCTU)

The idea of a society dedicated to **temperance** began at a Chautauqua meeting in Cleveland, Ohio, in 1874. The purpose of the Women's Christian Temperance Union was to encourage people to totally abstain from alcoholic beverages and to end the commercial sale of liquor. **Frances E. Willard**, a Methodist woman, became the WCTU's first corresponding secretary and later became its president during the years 1879 to 1898. The organization worked for the passage of local and state prohibition laws. It also played a major role in the passage of the **Eighteenth Amendment**, banning the sale of liquor in the U.S. The amendment was ratified on January 29, 1919, but repealed in 1933 by the Twenty-first Amendment. Today, the organization remains committed to its original purpose. (MWP) **See also** Methodism.

BIBLIOGRAPHY

Parker, Alison. *Purifying America*. Urbana: University of Illinois Press, 1997.

Willard, Frances E. *Glimpse of Fifty Years*. New York: Source Book Press, 1970.

James E. Wood, Jr. (1922–)

An ardent civil libertarian and church-state separationist, Dr. James Wood directed the J.M. Dawson Institute of Church-State Studies at Baylor University from 1959 to 1973 and again from 1980 to 1994. He also edited the Institute's respected *Journal of Church and State*. From 1972 through 1980, he headed the **Baptist** Joint Committee on Public Affairs in Washington, D.C. (ARB)

BIBLIOGRAPHY

Davis, Derek, ed. *The Separation of Church and State Defended: Selected Writings of James E. Wood, Jr.* Waco, TX: J.M. Dawson Institute of Church-State Studies, 1995.

Samuel Worcester (1798–1859)

Samuel Worcester was a missionary to the Cherokee for the **American Board of Commissioners for Foreign Missions**. He served initially at the Cherokee capital city of Echota, Georgia, (1825-1835), and then, after the Cherokees' forced removal from Georgia, in Arkansas and finally at the Park Hill Mission in Indian Territory (now Oklahoma). In 1831, Worcester and Elizur Butler were imprisoned by the state of Georgia for refusing to swear allegiance to Georgia and for protesting the 1830 Indian Removal Act. The appeal against a four-year sentence led to a U.S. Supreme Court decision (*Worcester v. Georgia*, 1832) which found for the defendants and which established that an Indian tribe's weakness or inability to use resources did not permit the forfeiture of the tribe's land. Worcester established the largest mission in Indian Territory, translated and printed many religious and secular works into Cherokee, and remained with the Cherokee until his death. (AOT) **See also** Cherokee Removal; Jeremiah Evarts; Missionaries; William Penn Essays.

BIBLIOGRAPHY

Bass, Althea. "Cherokee Messenger." *Civilization of the American Indian Series*. vol. 12, University of Oklahoma Press, 1996.

McLoughlin, W.G. "Civil Disobedience and Evangelism among the Missionaries to the Cherokees, 1829-1839." *Journal of Prebyterian History* 51 (1973): 116-39.

World War I (1914–1918)

World War I pitted the triple alliance of Germany, Austria-Hungary, and Italy (later to be replaced by Ottoman Turkey) against the triple entente of France, Great Britain, and Russia (they were later joined by the United States, China, Italy, and many other smaller nations). It ended the relatively peaceful century Europe had enjoyed following Napoleon's defeat in 1815. The war was triggered by the assassination of Austrian Archduke Francis Ferdinand and his wife Sophie in Sarajevo, Serbia, by the Serbian nationalist Gavrila Princip. Upon Serbia's failure to meet the Austro-Hungarian ultimatum, war broke out on July 28, 1914. It ended on November 11, 1918, and the Treaty of Versailles in 1919 established the peace conditions.

The results of the war were far-reaching. The imperial dynasties of Austria-Hungary, Germany, Russia, and the Ottoman Empire collapsed, and nationalism and the principle of self-determination took central stage. The Bolsheviks took power in Russia under Vladmir Lenin and imposed communism as state policy. World War I led to the destabilization of European society, both politically and culturally, and this laid the foundation for **World War II**. Germany deeply resented the Versailles settlement, which had placed blame for the war on Germany and required full reparations from Germany. This also destroyed the cultural liberalism that was manifest in the European belief in progress.

The religious consequences of the war were profound. The war caused a deep disillusionment that was articulated by Karl Barth in his epochal work, *The Commentary on Romans* (1919 and 1921), which led to the rise of the theological movement known as Protestant realism or Neo-Orthodoxy. American theologians and social ethicists such as **H. Richard Niebuhr**, **Reinhold Niebuhr**, Paul Lehmann, and many others were influenced by Barth's commentary, as well as by the social writings of the theologian **Paul Tillich**. They began the Protestant Realism school in America. The churches in the United States and their leaders generally supported the war effort, encouraging American participation in 1917. (DH) **See also** Socialism and Communism; Woodrow Wilson.

BIBLIOGRAPHY

Barth, Karl. *The Epistle to the Romans.* Trans. from 6th ed. by Edwyn C. Hoskyns. New York: Oxford, 1933.

Busch, Eberhard. *Karl Barth: His Life from Letters and Autobiographical Texts.* Trans. by John Bowden. Philadelphia: Fortress, 1976.

Moellering, Ralph L. *Modern War and the American Churches: A Factual Study of the Christian Conscience on Trial from 1939 to the Cold War Crisis of Today.* New York: American Press, 1956.

Piper, John F., Jr. *The American Churches in World War I.* Athens: Ohio Universtiy Press, 1985.

Repington, Charles A. *The First World War.* 2 vols. Brookfield, VT: Ashgate Publishers, 1992.

World War II (1939–1945)

World War II was the largest and bloodiest war in human history, with an estimated 40 to 50 million deaths incurred in over six years of combat. The war spanned most of the globe, with war theaters in Africa, Europe, the Pacific Islands, and much of Asia. It began on September 3, 1939, when Great Britain and France declared war on Germany after its invasion of Poland. The principal combatants were the Allied powers (United States, Soviet Union, Great Britain, France, China, and many other nations) and the Axis powers (Germany, Italy, and Japan). The war with Germany ended on May 8, 1945, and the war with Japan on September 2, 1945.

World War II was a pivotal event in shaping world politics to the present day. It resulted in a shift in world power from the continent of Europe to the United States and the Soviet Union. The subsequent Cold War between the Soviet Union and the Warsaw Pact countries on one side and the United States and the NATO countries on the other began with the struggle to include European countries in each side's "sphere of influence." World War II included the use of nuclear weapons, and the threat of further use of such weapons defined the history of the entire Cold War period from 1945 up to the collapse of the Berlin Wall in 1989 and the dissolution of the USSR in 1991. The United Nations, an international organization devoted to prospects of world peace, arbitration, and conflict resolution, was formed as a result of the conflict.

President Franklin D. Roosevelt signs the declaration of war against Japan. Library of Congress.

World War II led to significant ecclesiastical and theological developments. The World Council of Churches, which included Protestants and Orthodox communions and Roman Catholic observers, was founded in 1948 with the purpose of uniting the churches. The religious conflict within Germany over the state **Lutheran Church**'s support of Nazism led to sharp theological protest. Karl Barth, whose opposition to German dictator Adolf Hitler led to the loss of his theological position in Germany and exile in Switzerland, was the principal author of the "Barmen Declaration" against the German Christian movement, that insisted that a Christian's ultimate loyalty was to God and not to the state. **Paul Tillich**, another prominent German theologian, was one of the first intellectuals forced to leave Germany for opposing national socialism. He emigrated to the United States and became one of the country's most influential theologians. One of the most well-known German theologians was Dietrich Bonhoeffer, who was executed for complicity in the conspiracy to kill Hitler in 1944. His works, especially *The Cost of Discipleship* have had a deep influence on American and ecumenical Christianity.

The American churches and their leaders overwhelmingly supported American involvement in the war. The agenda of Nazism had, even before the war, forced theologian **Reinhold Niebuhr** to abandon his **pacifism** and membership in the Fellowship of Reconciliation and to advocate the removal of tyrants by force. He argued for a "Christian Realism" that recognized that in a sinful world, justice could only be achieved through armed resistance. The **Holocaust** of the European Jews forced attention upon ethnic and religious genocide and compelled Western Christian Churches to re-examine their contributions to the rise and support of **anti-Semitism.** (DH) **See also** Ecumenical Movement; Judaism; Nuclear Disarmament; Roman Catholicism; World War I.

Bibliography

Busch, Eberhard. *Karl Barth: His Life From Letters and Autobiographical Texts.* Translated by John Bowden. Philadelphia: Fortress, 1976.

Meyer, Donald B. *The Protestant Search for Political Realism, 1919–1941.* Berkeley: University of California Press, 1961.

Polenberg, Richard. *War and Society: The United States, 1941–1945.* Westport: Greenwood Press, 1980.

Soper, David W. *Major Voices in American Theology: Six Contemporary Leaders.* Philadelphia: Westminster, 1953.

Wells, Ronald A., ed. *The Wars of America: Christian Views.* Grand Rapids: Eerdmans, 1981.

Frances Wright (1795–1852)

Born into a wealthy family in Scotland, Frances Wright invested some of her wealth into Nashoba, a community for freed slaves in Tennessee, in 1825. (A blend of **socialism** and free love soon led to the community's failure.) Wright also delivered lectures in which she attacked religion and church involvement in politics. Together with **Robert Dale Owen**, Wright published the *Free Enquirer*, advocating the ideas of free-thinkers. Her opposition to **slavery** included support for the colonization of slaves outside the United States. (MWP) **See also** Abolition; Freethought; Women in Religion and Politics.

Bibliography

Lane, Margaret. *Frances Wright and the Great Experiment.* Lantham, MD: Rowman, 1972.

Waterman, William R. *Frances Wright.* New York: AMS Press, 1981.

Andrew Young (1932–)

As a black civil rights leader and politician, Andrew Young has had a varied political career. Trained as a **United Church of Christ** clergyman, he worked in the 1960s for the **Southern Christian Leadership Conference (SCLC)**, serving as its executive director from 1964 through 1967. From 1970 until 1972, he was chair of the Atlanta Community Relations Committee. Entering politics, he was one of Georgia's representatives in the U.S. House of Representatives from 1973 through 1977. In 1977, President **Jimmy Carter** appointed Young American ambassador to the United Nations, a post he held until 1979. He was elected mayor of Atlanta in 1980 and re-elected in 1984, serving until 1989. (MWP)

Bibliography

Young, Andrew. *A Way Out of No Way*. Nashville: T. Nelson, 1994.

Brigham Young (1801–1877)

Brigham Young, second president of the **Church of Jesus Christ of Latter-day Saints** (LDS or "Mormon" church), led thousands of Mormons from Illinois to Utah, where his strong leadership established a religious, economic, and political community unlike any other. He left an indelible mark on the American West.

After joining the church in 1832, Young became known for his enthusiastic service. His involvement in the Mormon migrations to Missouri and Illinois prepared him to lead the difficult mass migration to Utah in 1844 when the the Church was expelled from Illinois after the murder of founder **Joseph Smith**. Mormon settlers arrived in Utah in 1847. Under Young's leadership, the church expanded remarkably. The nearly 400 communities established by Young ranged from Canada to Mexico and were populated by the Church's many converts. Young's political vision was for an autonomous State of Deseret, and he was the first political leader of the territory, but tensions between the church and the federal government prompted the appointment of non-Mormons as territorial governors beginning in 1857. Young's pragmatic decision-making

After the murder of Joseph Smith, Brigham Young, pictured here with his wives and family, led the Mormons to Utah. Library of Congress.

led to a variety of economic experiments that included mercantile cooperatives, farming, and industry. Having 20 wives, he also was known for promoting polygyny, a practice that contributed to delays in the passing of Utah's statehood until 1896, after the official Mormon rejection of **polygamy**. (MEN)

Bibliography

Arrington, Leonard J. *Bringham Young: American Moses*. New York: Alfred A. Knopf, 1985.

Bringhurst, Newell G. *Brigham Young and the Expanding American Frontier*. Boston, 1986.

Z

Zion City, Illinois

Founded by the Christian healing evangelist John Alexander Dowie at the turn of the century, Zion City, Illinois, was intended to be a community organized and governed according to the theocratic principles of the Bible. Located north of Chicago near the Illinois-Wisconsin state line, the life of the city has long been closely associated with Dowie's Christian Catholic Church, which even today is located in the geographic heart of the city. In 1992, the city was forced to abandon the traditional city seal, which, until that time, had been the logo of the Christian Catholic Church. (ARB) **See also** Utopianism.

Dowieites, the followers of John Alexander Dowie, gather for services in Zion City, Illinois, in 1912. Photo by M.M. Webb. National Archives.

Bibliography

Cook, Philip L. *Zion City, Illinois: Twentieth Century Utopia*. Syracuse, NY: Syracuse University Press, 1996.

Wacker, Grant. "Marching to Zion: Religion in a Modern Utopian Community." *Church History* 54 (December 1985): 496-511.

Zionism

The roots of Zionism are ancient, going back to the love of displaced Jews for their homeland as expressed in Psalm 137:1: "By the rivers of Babylon we sat and wept when we remembered Zion." The roots of modern Zionism are more secular. During the nineteenth century, Europeans began basing their identity on nationality. Sensing resistance to their assimilation into any existing country, some Jews began to call for their own nation. In 1897, Theodore Herzl, an Austrian, organized the first Zionist Congress in Basel, Switzerland. It called for a homeland for Jews in Palestine, then ruled by Ottoman Turkey. Over the years, small groups of Jews settled in Palestine. During **World War I**, Great Britain issued the Balfour Declaration, promising to support a Jewish homeland in Palestine. British rule of Palestine after the war awakened Zionist hopes, but the growing hostility of the region's Arab population kept the British from acting. After **World War II**, the United Nations attempted to divide the land between Jews and Arabs. The effort failed; when the British left in 1948, a bloody war established temporary borders that continue to be contested by both sides. Over the years, American Jews have strongly supported the modern Jewish state of **Israel**. (MWP) **See also** Anti-Semitism; Holocaust; Judaism.

Bibliography

Glazer, Nathan. *American Judaism*. Chicago:University of Chicago Press, 1972.

Silverberg, Robert. *If I Forget Thee O Jerusalem: American Jews and the State of Israel*. New York: Morrow, 1970.

Zobrest v. Catalina Foothills School District (1993)

When a school district refused to provide a deaf child with a sign-language interpreter for classes at a Catholic high school, the parents brought suit, alleging that the Individuals with Disabilities Education Act and the **Free Exercise Clause** of the **First Amendment** required the school district to provide the interpreter, and that such provision did not violate the **Establishment Clause**. In *Zobrest v. Catalina Foothills School District,* 509 U.S. 1 (1993), the U.S. Supreme Court ruled that the Establishment Clause was not violated by the Individuals with Disabilities Education Act, stating, "Government programs that neutrally provide benefits to a broad class of citizens defined without reference to religion are not readily subject to an Establishment Clause challenge just because sectarian institutions may also receive an attenuated financial benefit." As a result, the school district was required to provide an interpreter to the student. (JM) **See also** Education; Roman Catholicism.

BIBLIOGRAPHY

Dietrich, James J. "Equal Protection, Neutrality, and the Establishment Clause." *Catholic University Law Review* 43, no. 4 (Summer 1994): 1209-45.

Johnson, Julie. "Striking a Balance Between the Establishment Clause and Rights of Handicapped Students." *The Journal of Law and Education* 23, no. 1 (Winter 1994): 107-14.

Zoning

Zoning refers to the setting aside of certain sections of land within city limits for specific uses. Through zoning, the state's interest in promoting the orderly development of land is fulfilled. The zoning regulations pertain to the land and the buildings and structures on the land. This function falls within the police power of the state to promote order, safety, health, morals, and the general welfare. The U.S. Supreme Court has allowed local governments to use zoning to protect public interests, even reaching to regulating land use that might be harmful to "family values."

The matter of zoning restrictions has become a major issue in recent years for religious properties and activities, as municipalities have increasingly sought to limit or regulate church property as a legitimate exercise of police power via the authority vested in them by state zoning enabling acts.

The power of a municipality to limit the use of property for religious use is not necessarily a violation of the **free exercise** of religion, since this clause of the **First Amendment** guarantees unrestrained freedom to believe, but not unlimited freedom to act. Because every use of church property, whether worship facility, a house as a meeting place, or a recreation facility, is a form of religious conduct, rather than belief, the conduct is not free from regulation.

Though a city has the right of police power to determine zoning restrictions, it may not do so arbitrarily. To regulate religious interests, the municipality must overcome the presumption of a religious organization's First Amendment right of free exercise. The ordinance must be reasonable and achieve a legitimate end relating to health, safety, morals, or public welfare.

Not only the First Amendment protects religious groups from arbitrary zoning restrictions; the due process clause of the **Fourteenth Amendment** requires moderation in state action. The municipality may not exert unfair application of zoning ordinances against a religious organization.

Generally, the majority view has been that churches, by their very nature, are in conformity with the ends of zoning since they promote public morals and general welfare. Attempts to exclude churches from residential areas have been looked on with distrust. Churches have, thus, been included within residential districts, though required to conform to building codes and other reasonable zoning requirements. The zoning authority might attempt to dress up the exclusion under the need to protect against hazards of traffic congestion and noise that might threaten the reasonable welfare of a residential neighborhood, but the traditional disposition of the courts has been to strike down such ordinances.

Increasingly, however, zoning determinations that allow exclusion of churches from residential districts have been upheld by some courts. In *Lakewood, Ohio Congregation of Jehovah's Witnesses, Inc. v. City of Lakewood*, the Sixth Circuit Court of Appeals upheld a zoning ordinance that restricted the construction of structures to areas which comprised only 10 percent of the total land area of the city. This ruling signals a trend, in some jurisdictions at least, from the traditional deference accorded to church property. Due to this, churches, synagogues, mosques, and temples may now be faced with challenges from homeowners that the construction of a religious building in a residentially zoned district would increase the traffic and noise, change the character of the neighborhood, or even decrease the property value of the district. Thus, courts may be willing to uphold a blanket exclusionary zoning ordinance if it is able to determine that such buildings are in such number that public safety, expressed through noise and traffic and the like, may be adversely affected, or if the inclusion of such a facility would decrease the property value of the neighborhood, in derogation of public welfare.

Often these cases deal with the attempt to determine that the buildings in question are not of a religious nature from the city's perspective, such as a homeless shelter, athletic facility, or non-traditional structure for worship. The attempt to exclude a religious organization, however, runs into two major challenges. The municipality would be basing its decision on the religious nature of the property use and the ordinance might be failing to adopt the least restrictive means to accomplishing the legitimate ends of providing for public safety and general welfare. The first of these challenges concerns the attempt to define what is a "church." Such a matter was presented in *Synod of Chesapeake, Inc. v. Newark*, where the church was disallowed from continuing occupancy of a former single-family residence that had been converted by the congregation into a combination worship facility, office, and coffeehouse for students. The court overturned the city's order, ruling that the activities constituted a church. In the landmark case of *Sherbert v. Verner*, the Supreme Court determined that even a compelling state action must be tempered by using the least drastic means to accomplishing its ends. Unfortunately, the logic of that case has been undercut in recent years in such decisions as ***Employment Division of Oregon v. Smith*** (1990). Thus, whether courts will continue to insist that zoning boards use the "least restrictive means" when regulating land use by churches is somewhat in doubt.

Religious and non-profit organizations must give careful consideration in approaching a zoning board and should anticipate issues before a dispute arises. Documents and information are easily procured from zoning agencies relating to the property district of the group and can then be used to develop plans that conform to the policies. This is much preferable to expending considerable expense and planning to discover whether the new structure is non-conforming or excluded based on zoning restrictions. (HWH)

BIBLIOGRAPHY

House, H. Wayne. *Christian Ministries and the Law.* Grand Rapids, MI: Baker, 1992.

Rohan, P. "Zoning and Land Use Controls, §1.02[4] (1978). Note, Land Use Regulation and the Free Exercise Clause" *Columbia Law Review* 84 (1984): 1562, 1568.

Reynolds, Laurie. "Zoning the Church: The Police Power Versus the First Amendment," *Boston University Law Review* 64 (1984): 767, 772.

Zorach v. Clauson (1952)

In *Zorach v. Clauson*, 343 U.S. 306 (1952), the U.S. Supreme Court upheld a New York "**release-time**" program that permitted public school students, on the written request of their parents, to leave school premises during regular school hours to receive religious instruction from teachers paid from private funds in facilities maintained by participating religious societies. Nonparticipating students remained at the public school for secular instruction. In upholding the program, the Court noted that no expenditures of public funds maintained the program, and that the school neither promoted the program nor made comment on attendance or nonattendance. The New York program differed from the Illinois release-time program invalidated in ***McCollum v. Board of Education* (1948)**, which offered religious instruction in public school classrooms during school hours. Writing for the Court in *Zorach*, Justice **William O. Douglas** affirmed that "[g]overnment may not finance religious groups nor undertake religious instruction nor blend secular and sectarian education nor use secular institutions to force one or some religion on any person. But we find no constitutional requirement which makes it necessary for government to be hostile to religion and to throw its weight against efforts to widen the effective scope of religious influence." Lacking evidence of coerced participation in the program, the Court held that public schools may accommodate their schedules to a program of religious instruction conducted off school premises by private teachers for students who desire it. (DLD) **See also** Education.

BIBLIOGRAPHY

Eastland, Terry. *Religious Liberty in the Supreme Court.* Washington, DC: Ethics and Public Policy Center, 1993.

Appendices

1

Speeches and Documents

1. Mayflower Compact (1620)

In The Name of God, Amen.We whose names are underwritten, the loyal subjects of our dread sovereign Lord, King James, by the grace of God, of Great Britain, France and Ireland, King, defender of the faith, etc., having undertaken for the glory of God and advancement of the Christian faith, and honor of our King and country, a voyage to plant the first colony in the Northern parts of Virginia, do by these presents solemnly and mutually in the presence of God, and of one another, covenant and combine ourselves together into a civil body politic for our better ordering and preservation and furtherance of the ends aforesaid, and by virtue hear of to enact, constitute and frame such just and equal laws, ordinances, acts, constitutions and offices, from time to time, as shall be thought most convenient for the general good of the Colony, unto which we promise all due submission and obedience. In Witness whereof we have hereunder subscribed our names at Cape Cod the 11th of November, in the year of the reign of our Lord, King James of England, France and Ireland, the eighteenth, and of Scotland the fifty fourth, Ano Dom. 1620.

2. The Fundamental Orders of Connecticut (1639)

For as much as it hath pleased Almighty God by the wise disposition of his divine providence so to order and dispose of things that we the Inhabitants and Residents of Windsor, Hartford and Wethersfield are now cohabiting and dwelling in and upon the river of Connectecotte and the lands thereunto adjoining; and well knowing where a people are gathered together, the word of God requires that to maintain the peace and union of such a people there should be an orderly and decent Government established according to God, to order and dispose of the affairs of the people at all seasons as occasion shall require; do therefore associate and conjoin ourselves to be as one Public State or Commonwealth; and do for ourselves and our successors and such as shall be adjoined to us at any time hereafter, enter into Combination and Confederation together, to maintain and preserve the liberty and purity of the Gospel of our Lord Jesus which we now profess, as also, the discipline of the Churches, which according to the truth of the said Gospel is now practiced amongst us; as also in our civil affairs to be guided and governed according to such Laws, Rules, Orders and Decrees as shall be made, ordered, and decreed as followeth:

1. It is Ordered, sentenced, and decreed, that there shall be yearly two General Assemblies or Courts, the one the second Thursday in April, the other the second Thursday in September following; the first shall be called the Court of Election, wherein shall be yearly chosen from time to time, so many Magistrates and other public Officers as shall be found requisite: Whereof one to be chosen Governor for the year ensuing and until another be chosen, and no other Magistrate to be chosen for more than one year: provided always there be six chosen besides the Governor, which being chosen and sworn according to an Oath recorded for that purpose, shall have the power to administer justice according to the Laws here established, and for want thereof, according to the Rule of the Word of God; which choice shall be made by all that are admitted freemen and have taken the Oath of Fidelity, and do cohabit within this Jurisdiction having been admitted Inhabitants by the major part of the Town wherein they live or the major part of such as shall be then present.

2. It is Ordered, sentenced, and decreed, that the election of the aforesaid Magistrates shall be in this manner: every person present and qualified for choice shall bring in (to the person deputed to receive them) one single paper with the name of him written in it whom he desires to have Governor, and that he that hath the greatest number of papers shall be Governor for that year. And the rest of the Magistrates or public officers to be chosen in this manner: the Secretary for the time being shall first read the names of all that are to be put to choice and then shall severally nominate them distinctly, and every one that would have the person nominated to be chosen

shall bring in one single paper written upon, and he that would not have him chosen shall bring in a blank; and every one that hath more written papers than blanks shall be a Magistrate for that year; which papers shall be received and told by one or more that shall be then chosen by the court and sworn to be faithful therein; but in case there should not be six chosen as aforesaid, besides the Governor, out of those which are nominated, then he or they which have the most written papers shall be a Magistrate or Magistrates for the ensuing year, to make up the aforesaid number.

3. It is Ordered, sentenced, and decreed, that the Secretary shall not nominate any person, nor shall any person be chosen newly into the Magistracy which was not propounded in some General Court before, to be nominated the next election; and to that end it shall be lawful for each of the Towns aforesaid by their deputies to nominate any two whom they conceive fit to be put to election; and the Court may add so many more as they judge requisite.

4. It is Ordered, sentenced, and decreed, that no person be chosen Governor above once in two years, and that the Governor be always a member of some approved Congregation, and formerly of the Magistracy within this Jurisdiction; and that all the Magistrates, Freemen of this Commonwealth; and that no Magistrate or other public officer shall execute any part of his or their office before they are severally sworn, which shall be done in the face of the court if they be present, and in case of absence by some deputed for that purpose.

5. It is Ordered, sentenced, and decreed, that to the aforesaid Court of Election the several Towns shall send their deputies, and when the Elections are ended they may proceed in any public service as at other Courts. Also the other General Court in September shall be for making of laws, and any other public occasion, which concerns the good of the Commonwealth.

6. It is Ordered, sentenced, and decreed, that the Governor shall, either by himself or by the Secretary, send out summons to the Constables of every Town for the calling of these two standing Courts one month at least before their several times: And also if the Governor and the greatest part of the Magistrates see cause upon any special occasion to call a General Court, they may give order to the Secretary so to do within fourteen days' warning: And if urgent necessity so required, upon a shorter notice, giving sufficient grounds for it to the deputies when they meet, or else be questioned for the same; And if the Governor and major part of Magistrates shall either neglect or refuse to call the two General standing Courts or either of them, as also at other times when the occasions of the Commonwealth require, the Freemen thereof, or the major part of them, shall petition to them so to do; if then it be either denied or neglected, the said Freemen, or the major part of them, shall have the power to give order to the Constables of the several Towns to do the same, and so may meet together, and choose to themselves a Moderator, and may proceed to do any act of power which any other General Courts may.

7. It is Ordered, sentenced, and decreed, that after there are warrants given out for any of the said General Courts, the Constable or Constables of each Town, shall forthwith give notice distinctly to the inhabitants of the same, in some public assembly or by going or sending from house to house, that at a place and time by him or them limited and set, they meet and assemble themselves together to elect and choose certain deputies to be at the General Court then following to agitate the affairs of the Commonwealth; which said deputies shall be chosen by all that are admitted Inhabitants in the several Towns and have taken the oath of fidelity; provided that none be chosen a Deputy for any General Court which is not a Freeman of this Commonwealth.

The aforesaid deputies shall be chosen in manner following: every person that is present and qualified as before expressed, shall bring the names of such, written in several papers, as they desire to have chosen for that employment, and these three or four, more or less, being the number agreed on to be chosen for that time, that have the greatest number of papers written for them shall be deputies for that Court; whose names shall be endorsed on the back side of the warrant and returned into the Court, with the Constable or Constables' hand unto the same.

8. It is Ordered, sentenced, and decreed, that Windsor, Hartford, and Wethersfield shall have power, each Town, to send four of their Freemen as their deputies to every General Court; and Whatsoever other Town shall be hereafter added to this Jurisdiction, they shall send so many deputies as the Court shall judge meet, a reasonable proportion to the number of Freemen that are in the said Towns being to be attended therein; which deputies shall have the power of the whole Town to give their votes and allowance to all such laws and orders as may be for the public good, and unto which the said Towns are to be bound.

9. It is Ordered, sentenced, and decreed, that the deputies thus chosen shall have power and liberty to appoint a time and a place of meeting together before any General Court, to advise and consult of all such things as may concern the good of the public, as also to examine their own Elections, whether according to the order, and if they or the greatest part of them find any election to be illegal they may seclude such for present from their meeting, and return the same and their reasons to the Court; and if it be proved true, the Court may fine the party or parties so intruding, and the Town, if they see cause, and give out a warrant to go to a new election in a legal way, either in part or in whole. Also the said deputies shall have power to fine any that shall be disorderly at their meetings, or for not coming in due time or place according to appointment; and they may return the said fines into the Court if it be refused to be paid, and the Treasurer to take notice of it, and to escheat or levy the same as he does other fines.

10. It is Ordered, sentenced, and decreed, that every General Court, except such as through neglect of the Governor and the greatest part of the Magistrates the Freemen themselves do call, shall consist of the Governor, or some one

chosen to moderate the Court, and four other Magistrates at least, with the major part of the deputies of the several Towns legally chosen; and in case the Freemen, or major part of them, through neglect or refusal of the Governor and major part of the Magistrates, shall call a Court, it shall consist of the major part of Freemen that are present or their deputies, with a Moderator chosen by them: In which said General Courts shall consist the supreme power of the Commonwealth, and they only shall have power to make laws or repeal them, to grant levies, to admit of Freemen, dispose of lands undisposed of, to several Towns or persons, and also shall have power to call either Court or Magistrate or any other person whatsoever into question for any misdemeanor, and may for just causes displace or deal otherwise according to the nature of the offense; and also may deal in any other matter that concerns the good of this Commonwealth, except election of Magistrates, which shall be done by the whole body of Freemen.

In which Court the Governor or Moderator shall have power to order the Court, to give liberty of speech, and silence unseasonable and disorderly speakings, to put all things to vote, and in case the vote be equal to have the casting voice. But none of these Courts shall be adjourned or dissolved without the consent of the major part of the Court.

11. It is Ordered, sentenced, and decreed, that when any General Court upon the occasions of the Commonwealth have agreed upon any sum, or sums of money to be levied upon the several Towns within this Jurisdiction, that a committee be chosen to set out and appoint what shall be the proportion of every Town to pay of the said levy, provided the committee be made up of an equal number out of each Town.

14th January 1639 the 11 Orders above said are voted.

3. The Act of Toleration of Maryland Colony (1649)

An Act Concerning Religion.

Forasmuch as in a well governed and Christian Common Wealth matters concerning Religion and the honor of God ought in the first place to bee taken, into serious consideration and endeavored to bee settled, Be it therefore ordered and enacted by the Right Honorable Cecilius Lord Baron of Baltimore absolute Lord and Proprietary of this Province with the advise and consent of this General Assembly:

That whatsoever person or persons within this Province and the Islands thereunto belonging shall from henceforth blaspheme God, that is Curse him, or deny our Savior Jesus Christ to bee the son of God, or shall deny the holy Trinity the father son and holy Ghost, or the Godhead of any of the said Three persons of the Trinity or the Unity of the Godhead, or shall use or utter any reproachful Speeches, words or language concerning the said Holy Trinity, or any of the said three persons thereof, shall be punished with death and confiscation or forfeiture of all his or her lands and goods to the Lord Proprietary and his heirs.

And bee it also Enacted by the Authority and with the advise and assent aforesaid, That whatsoever person or persons shall from henceforth use or utter any reproachful words or Speeches concerning the blessed Virgin Mary the Mother of our Savior or the holy Apostles or Evangelists or any of them shall in such case for the first offense forfeit to the said Lord Proprietary and his heirs Lords and Proprietors of this Province the sum of five pound Sterling or the value thereof to be Levied on the goods and chattels of every such person so offending, but in case such Offender or Offenders, shall not then have goods and chattels sufficient for the satisfying of such forfeiture, or that the same bee not otherwise speedily satisfied that then such Offender or Offenders shall be publically whipped and bee imprisoned during the pleasure of the Lord Proprietary or the Lieutenant or chief Governor of this Province for the time being. And that every such Offender or Offenders for every second offense shall forfeit ten pound sterling or the value thereof to bee levied as aforesaid, or in case such offender or Offenders shall not then have goods and chattels within this Province sufficient for that purpose then to bee publically and severely whipped and imprisoned as before is expressed. And that every person or persons before mentioned offending herein the third time, shall for such third Offense forfeit all his lands and Goods and bee for ever banished and expelled out of this Province.

And be it also further Enacted by the same authority advise and assent that whatsoever person or persons shall from henceforth upon any occasion of Offense or otherwise in a reproachful manner or Way declare call or denominate any person or persons whatsoever inhabiting, residing, trafficing, trading or commercing within this Province or within any the Ports, Harbors, Creeks or Havens to the same belonging an heretic, Schismatic, Idolater, puritan, Independent, Presbyterian popish priest, Jesuit, Jesuit papist, Lutheran, Calvinist, Anabaptist, Brownist, Antinomian, Barrowist, Roundhead, Separatist, or any other name or term in a reproachful manner relating to matter of Religion shall for every such Offense forfeit and loose the sum of ten shillings sterling or the value thereof to bee levied on the goods and chattels of every such Offender and Offenders, the one half thereof to be forfeited and paid unto the person and persons of whom such reproachful words are or shall be spoken or uttered, and the other half thereof to the Lord Proprietary and his heirs Lords and Proprietors of this Province. But if such person or persons who shall at any time utter or speak any such reproachful words or Language shall not have Goods or Chattels sufficient and overt within this Province to bee taken to satisfy the penalty aforesaid or that the same bee not otherwise speedily satisfied, that then the person or persons so offending shall be publicly whipped, and shall suffer imprisonment without bail or maineprise [bail] until he, she or they respectively shall satisfy the party so offended or grieved by such reproachful Language by asking him or her respectively forgiveness publically for such his Offense before the Magistrate of chief Officer or Officers of the Town or place where such Offense shall be given.

And be it further likewise Enacted by the Authority and consent aforesaid That every person and persons within this Province that shall at any time hereafter profane the Sabbath or Lords day called Sunday by frequent swearing, drunkenness or by any uncivil or disorderly recreation, or by working on that day when absolute necessity do not require it shall for every such first offense forfeit 2s 6d sterling or the value thereof, and for the second offense 5s sterling or the value thereof, and for the third offense and so for every time he shall offend in like manner afterwards 10s sterling or the value thereof. And in case such offender and offenders shall not have sufficient goods or chattels within this Province to satisfy any of the said Penalties respectively hereby imposed for profaning the Sabbath or Lords day called Sunday as aforesaid, That in Every such case the party so offending shall for the first and second offense in that kind be imprisoned till he or she shall publicly in open Court before the chief Commander Judge or Magistrate, of that County Town or precinct where such offense shall be committed acknowledge the Scandal and offense he hath in that respect given against God and the good and civill Government of this Province, And for the third offense and for every time after shall also bee publicly whipped.

And whereas the enforcing of the conscience in matters of Religion hath frequently fallen out to be of dangerous Consequence in those commonwealths where it hath been practiced, And for the more quiet and peaceable government of this Province, and the better to preserve mutual Love and amity amongst the Inhabitants thereof, Be it Therefore also by the Lord Proprietary with the advise and consent of this Assembly Ordained and enacted (except as in this present Act is before Declared and set forth) that no person or persons whatsoever within this Province, or the Islands, Ports, Harbors, Creeks, or havens thereunto belonging professing to believe in Jesus Christ, shall from henceforth bee any ways troubled, Molested or discountenanced for or in respect of his or her religion nor in the free exercise thereof within this Province or the Islands thereunto belonging nor any way compelled to the belief or exercise of any other Religion against his or her consent, so as they be not unfaithful to the Lord Proprietary, or molest or conspire against the civill Government established or to bee established in this Province under him or his heirs. And that all and every person and persons that shall presume Contrary to this Act and the true intent and meaning thereof directly or indirectly either in person or estate willfully to wrong disturb trouble or molest any person whatsoever within this Province professing to believe in Jesus Christ for or in respect of his or her religion or the free exercise thereof within this Province other than is provided for in this Act that such person or persons so offending, shall be compelled to pay treble damages to the party so wronged or molested, and for every such offense shall also forfeit 20s sterling in money or the value thereof, half thereof for the use of the Lord Proprietary, and his heirs Lords and Proprietors of this Province, and the other half for the use of the party so wronged or molested as aforesaid, Or if the party so offending as aforesaid shall refuse or bee unable to recompense the party so wronged, or to satisfy such fine or forfeiture, then such Offender shall be severely punished by public whipping and imprisonment during the pleasure of the Lord Proprietary, or his Lieutenant or chief Governor of this Province for the time being without bail or maineprise.

And bee it further also Enacted by the authority and consent aforesaid That the Sheriff or other Officer or Officers from time to time to bee appointed and authorized for that purpose, of the County Town or precinct where every particular offense in this present Act contained shall happen at any time to bee committed and whereupon there is hereby a forfeiture fine or penalty imposed shall from time to time distain and seize the goods and estate of every such person so offending as aforesaid against this present Act or any part thereof, and sell the same or any part thereof for the full satisfaction of such forfeiture, fine, or penalty as aforesaid, Restoring unto the party so offending the Remainder or overplus of the said goods or estate after such satisfaction so made as aforesaid.

The freemen have assented.

4. The First Thanksgiving Proclamation (1676)

The Holy God having by a long and Continual Series of his Afflictive dispensations in and by the present War with the Heathen Natives of this land, written and brought to pass bitter things against his own Covenant people in this wilderness, yet so that we evidently discern that in the midst of his judgments he has remembered mercy, having remembered his Footstool in the day of his sore displeasure against us for our sins, with many singular Intimations of his Fatherly Compassion, and regard; reserving many of our Towns from Desolation Threatened, and attempted by the Enemy, and giving us especially of late with many of our Confederates many signal Advantages against them, without such Disadvantage to ourselves as formerly we have been sensible of, if it be the Lord's mercy that we are not consumed, It certainly bespeaks our positive Thankfulness, when our Enemies are in any measure disappointed or destroyed; and fearing the Lord should take notice under so many Intimations of his returning mercy, we should be found an Insensible people, as not standing before Him with Thanksgiving, as well as lading him with our Complaints in the time of pressing Afflictions:

The Council has thought meet to appoint and set apart the 29th day of this instant June, as a day of Solemn Thanksgiving and praise to God for such his Goodness and Favor, many Particulars of which mercy might be Instanced, but we doubt not those who are sensible of God's Afflictions, have been as diligent to espy him returning to us; and that the Lord may behold us as a People offering Praise and thereby glorifying Him; the Council does commend it to the Respective Ministers, Elders and people of this Jurisdiction; Solemnly and seriously to keep the same Beseeching that being persuaded by the mercies of God we may all, even this whole people offer up our bodies and souls as a living and acceptable Service unto God by Jesus Christ.

5. Clause XVI of the Virginia Declaration of Rights (1776)

XVI That religion, or the duty which we owe to our Creator and the manner of discharging it, can be directed by reason and conviction, not by force or violence; and therefore, all men are equally entitled to the free exercise of religion, according to the dictates of conscience; and that it is the mutual duty of all to practice Christian forbearance, love, and charity towards each other.

6. Thomas Jefferson's Draft for a Bill Establishing Religious Freedom (1779)

Section I.

Well aware that the opinions and beliefs of men depend not on their own will, but follow involuntarily the evidence proposed to their minds; that Almighty God hath created the mind free, and manifested his supreme will that free it shall remain by making it altogether insusceptible of restraint; that all attempts to influence it by temporal punishments, or burthens, or by civil incapacitations, tend only to beget habits of hypocrisy and meanness, and are a departure from the plan of the holy author of our religion, who being lord both of body and mind, yet chose not to propagate it by coercions on either, as was in his Almighty power to do, but to extend it by its influence on reason alone; that the impious presumption of legislators and rulers, civil as well as ecclesiastical, who, being themselves but fallible and uninspired men, have assumed dominion over the faith of others, setting up their own opinions and modes of thinking as the only true and infallible, and as such endeavoring to impose them on others, hath established and maintained false religions over the greatest part of the world and through all time: That to compel a man to furnish contributions of money for the propagation of opinions which he disbelieves and abhors, is sinful and tyrannical; that even the forcing him to support this or that teacher of his own religious persuasion, is depriving him of the comfortable liberty of giving his contributions to the particular pastor whose morals he would make his pattern, and whose powers he feels most persuasive to righteousness; and is withdrawing from the ministry those temporary rewards, which proceeding from an approbation of their personal conduct, are an additional incitement to earnest and unremitting labors for the instruction of mankind; that our civil rights have no dependence on our religious opinions, any more than our opinions in physics or geometry; that therefore the proscribing any citizen as unworthy of the public confidence by laying upon him an incapacity of being called to offices of trust and emolument, unless he profess or renounce this or that religious opinion, is depriving him injuriously of those privileges and advantages to which, in common with his fellow citizens, he has a natural right; that it tends also to corrupt the principles of that very religion it is meant to encourage, by bribing, with a monopoly of worldly honors and emoluments, those who will externally profess and conform to it; that though indeed these are criminal who do not withstand such temptation, yet neither are those innocent who lay the bait in their way; that the opinions of men are not the object of civil government, nor under its jurisdiction; that to suffer the civil magistrate to intrude his powers into the field of opinion and to restrain the profession or propagation of principles on supposition of their ill tendency is a dangerous fallacy, which at once destroys all religious liberty, because he being of course judge of that tendency will make his opinions the rule of judgment, and approve or condemn the sentiments of others only as they shall square with or differ from his own; that it is time enough for the rightful purposes of civil government for its officers to interfere when principles break out into overt acts against peace and good order; and finally, that truth is great and will prevail if left to herself; that she is the proper and sufficient antagonist to error, and has nothing to fear from the conflict unless by human interposition disarmed of her natural weapons, free argument and debate; errors ceasing to be dangerous when it is permitted freely to contradict them.

Section II.

WE the General Assembly of Virginia do enact that no man shall be compelled to frequent or support any religious worship, place, or ministry whatsoever, nor shall be enforced, restrained, molested, or burthened in his body or goods, nor shall otherwise suffer, on account of his religious opinions or beliefs; but that all men shall be free to profess, and by argument to maintain, their opinions in matters of religion, and that the same shall in no wise diminish, enlarge, or affect their civil capacities.

Section III.

AND though we well know that this Assembly, elected by the people for the ordinary purposes of legislation only, have no power to restrain the acts of succeeding Assemblies, constituted with powers equal to our own, and that therefore to declare this act irrevocable would be of no effect in law; yet we are free to declare, and do declare, that the rights hereby asserted are of the natural rights of mankind, and that if any act shall be hereafter passed to repeal the present or to narrow its operation, such act will be an infringement of natural right.

7. James Madison's "Memorial and Remonstrance" (1785)

To the Honorable the General Assembly of the Commonwealth of Virginia

A Memorial and Remonstrance

We the subscribers, citizens of the said Commonwealth, having taken into serious consideration, a Bill printed by order of the last Session of General Assembly, entitled "A Bill establishing a provision for Teachers of the Christian Religion," and conceiving that the same if finally armed with the sanctions of a law, will be a dangerous abuse of power, are bound as faithful members of a free State to remonstrate against it, and to declare the reasons by which we are determined. We remonstrate against the said Bill,

1. Because we hold it for a fundamental and undeniable truth, "that religion or the duty which we owe to our Creator and the manner of discharging it, can be directed only by reason and conviction, not by force or violence." The Religion then of every man must be left to the conviction and conscience of every man; and it is the right of every man to exercise it as these may dictate. This right is in its nature an unalienable right. It is unalienable, because the opinions of men, depending only on the evidence contemplated by their own minds cannot follow the dictates of other men: It is unalienable also, because what is here a right towards men, is a duty towards the Creator. It is the duty of every man to render to the Creator such homage and such only as he believes to be acceptable to him. This duty is precedent, both in order of time and in degree of obligation, to the claims of Civil Society. Before any man can be considerd as a member of Civil Society, he must be considered as a subject of the Governour of the Universe: And if a member of Civil Society, do it with a saving of his allegiance to the Universal Sovereign. We maintain therefore that in matters of Religion, no man's right is abridged by the institution of Civil Society and that Religion is wholly exempt from its cognizance. True it is, that no other rule exists, by which any question which may divide a Society, can be ultimately determined, but the will of the majority; but it is also true that the majority may trespass on the rights of the minority.

2. Because Religion be exempt from the authority of the Society at large, still less can it be subject to that of the Legislative Body. The latter are but the creatures and vicegerents of the former. Their jurisdiction is both derivative and limited: it is limited with regard to the co-ordinate departments, more necessarily is it limited with regard to the constituents. The preservation of a free Government requires not merely, that the metes and bounds which separate each department of power be invariably maintained; but more especially that neither of them be suffered to overleap the great Barrier which defends the rights of the people. The Rulers who are guilty of such an encroachment, exceed the commission from which they derive their authority, and are Tyrants. The People who submit to it are governed by laws made neither by themselves nor by an authority derived from them, and are slaves.

3. Because it is proper to take alarm at the first experiment on our liberties. We hold this prudent jealousy to be the first duty of Citizens, and one of the noblest characteristics of the late Revolution. The free men of America did not wait till usurped power had strengthened itself by exercise, and entangled the question in precedents. They saw all the consequences in the principle, and they avoided the consequences by denying the principle. We revere this lesson too much soon to forget it. Who does not see that the same authority which can establish Christianity, in exclusion of all other Religions, may establish with the same ease any particular sect of Christians, in exclusion of all other Sects? That the same authority which can force a citizen to contribute three pence only of his property for the support of any one establishment, may force him to conform to any other establishment in all cases whatsoever?

4. Because the Bill violates the equality which ought to be the basis of every law, and which is more indispensible, in proportion as the validity or expediency of any law is more liable to be impeached. If "all men are by nature equally free and independent," all men are to be considered as entering into Society on equal conditions; as relinquishing no more, and therefore retaining no less, one than another, of their natural rights. Above all are they to be considered as retaining an "equal title to the free exercise of Religion according to the dictates of Conscience." Whilst we assert for ourselves a freedom to embrace, to profess and to observe the Religion which we believe to be of divine origin, we cannot deny an equal freedom to those whose minds have not yet yielded to the evidence which has convinced us. If this freedom be abused, it is an offence against God, not against man: To God, therefore, not to man, must an account of it be rendered. As the Bill violates equality by subjecting some to peculiar burdens, so it violates the same principle, by granting to others peculiar exemptions. Are the Quakers and Menonists the only sects who think a compulsive support of their Religions unnecessary and unwarrantable? Can their piety alone be entrusted with the care of public worship? Ought their Religions to be endowed above all others with extraordinary privileges by which proselytes may be enticed from all others? We think too favorably of the justice and good sense of these denominations to believe that they either covet pre-eminences over their fellow citizens or that they will be seduced by them from the common opposition to the measure.

5. Because the Bill implies either that the Civil Magistrate is a competent Judge of Religious Truth; or that he may employ Religion as an engine of Civil policy. The first is an arrogant pretension falsified by the contradictory opinions of Rulers in all ages, and throughout the world: the second an unhallowed perversion of the means of salvation.

6. Because the establishment proposed by the Bill is not requisite for the support of the Christian Religion. To say that it is, is a contradiction to the Christian Religion itself, for every page of it disavows a dependence on the powers of this world: it is a contradiction to fact; for it is known that this Religion both existed and flourished, not only without the support of human laws, but in spite of every opposition from them, and not only during the period of miraculous aid, but long after it had been left to its own evidence and the ordinary care of Providence. Nay, it is a contradiction in terms; for a Religion not invented by human policy, must have pre-existed and been supported, before it was established by human policy. It is moreover to weaken in those who profess this Religion a pious confidence in its innate excellence and the patronage of its Author; and to foster in those who still reject it, a suspicion that its friends are too conscious of its fallacies to trust it to its own merits.

7. Because experience witnesseth that eccelsiastical establishments, instead of maintaining the purity and efficacy of Religion, have had a contrary operation. During almost fifteen centuries has the legal establishment of Christianity been on trial. What have been its fruits? More or less in all places, pride and indolence in the Clergy, ignorance and servility in the laity, in both, superstition, bigotry and persecution. Enquire of the Teachers of Christianity for the ages in which it appeared in its greatest lustre; those of every sect, point to the ages prior to its incorporation with Civil policy. Propose a restoration of this primitive State in which its Teachers depended on the voluntary rewards of their flocks, many of them predict its downfall. On which Side ought their testimony to have greatest weight, when for or when against their interest?

8. Because the establishment in question is not necessary for the support of Civil Government. If it be urged as necessary for the support of Civil Government only as it is a means of supporting Religion, and it be not necessary for the latter purpose, it cannot be necessary for the former. If Religion be not within the cognizance of Civil Government how can its legal establishment be necessary to Civil Government? What influence in fact have ecclesiastical establishments had on Civil Society? In some instances they have been seen to erect a spiritual tyranny on the ruins of the Civil authority; in many instances they have been seen upholding the thrones of political tyranny: in no instance have they been seen the guardians of the liberties of the people. Rulers who wished to subvert the public liberty, may have found an established Clergy convenient auxiliaries. A just Government instituted to secure & perpetuate it needs them not. Such a Government will be best supported by protecting every Citizen in the enjoyment of his Religion with the same equal hand which protects his person and his property; by neither invading the equal rights of any Sect, nor suffering any Sect to invade those of another.

9. Because the proposed establishment is a departure from the generous policy, which, offering an Asylum to the persecuted and oppressed of every Nation and Religion, promised a lustre to our country, and an accession to the number of its citizens. What a melancholy mark is the Bill of sudden degeneracy? Instead of holding forth an Asylum to the persecuted, it is itself a signal of persecution. It degrades from the equal rank of Citizens all those whose opinions in Religion do not bend to those of the Legislative authority. Distant as it may be in its present form from the Inquisition, it differs from it only in degree. The one is the first step, the other the last in the career of intolerance. The maganimous sufferer under this cruel scourge in foreign Regions, must view the Bill as a Beacon on our Coast, warning him to seek some other haven, where liberty and philanthropy in their due extent, may offer a more certain repose from his Troubles.

10. Because it will have a like tendency to banish our Citizens. The allurements presented by other situations are every day thinning their number. To superadd a fresh motive to emigration by revoking the liberty which they now enjoy, would be the same species of folly which has dishonoured and depopulated flourishing kingdoms.

11. Because it will destroy that moderation and harmony which the forbearance of our laws to intermeddle with Religion has produced among its several sects. Torrents of blood

have been split in the old world, by vain attempts of the secular arm, to extinguish Religious discord, by proscribing all difference in Religious opinion. Time has at length revealed the true remedy. Every relaxation of narrow and rigorous policy, wherever it has been tried, has been found to assuage the disease. The American Theatre has exhibited proofs that equal and compleat liberty, if it does not wholly eradicate it, sufficiently destroys its malignant influence on the health and prosperity of the State. If with the salutary effects of this system under our own eyes, we begin to contract the bounds of Religious freedom, we know no name that will too severely reproach our folly. At least let warning be taken at the first fruits of the threatened innovation. The very appearance of the Bill has transformed "that Christian forbearance, love and charity," which of late mutually prevailed, into animosities and jealousies, which may not soon be appeased. What mischiefs may not be dreaded, should this enemy to the public quiet be armed with the force of a law?

12. Because the policy of the Bill is adverse to the diffusion of the light of Christianity. The first wish of those who enjoy this precious gift ought to be that it may be imparted to the whole race of mankind. Compare the number of those who have as yet received it with the number still remaining under the dominion of false Religions; and how small is the former! Does the policy of the Bill tend to lessen the disproportion? No; it at once discourages those who are strangers to the light of revelation from coming into the Region of it; and countenances by example the nations who continue in darkness, in shutting out those who might convey it to them. Instead of Levelling as far as possible, every obstacle to the victorious progress of Truth, the Bill with an ignoble and unchristian timidity would circumscribe it with a wall of defence against the encroachments of error.

13. Because attempts to enforce by legal sanctions, acts obnoxious to so great a proportion of Citizens, tend to enervate the laws in general, and to slacken the bands of Society. If it be difficult to execute any law which is not generally deemed necessary or salutary, what must be the case, where it is deemed invalid and dangerous? And what may be the effect of so striking an example of impotency in the Government, on its general authority?

14. Because a measure of such singular magnitude and delicacy ought not to be imposed, without the clearest evidence that it is called for by a majority of citizens, and no satisfactory method is yet proposed by which the voice of the majority in this case may be determined, or its influence secured. The people of the respective counties are indeed requested to signify their opinion respecting the adoption of the Bill to the next Session of Assembly." But the representatives of the Counties will be that of the people. Our hope is that neither of the former will, after due consideration, espouse the dangerous principle of the Bill. Should the event disappoint us, it will still leave us in full confidence, that a fair appeal to the latter will reverse the sentence against our liberties.

15. Because finally, "the equal right of every citizen to the free exercise of his Religion according to the dictates of conscience" is held by the same tenure with all our other rights. If we recur to its origin, it is equally the gift of nature; if we weigh its importance, it cannot be less dear to us; if we consult the "Declaration of those rights which pertain to the good people of Virginia, as the basis and foundation of Government," it is enumerated with equal solemnity, or rather studied emphasis. Either then, we must say, that the Will of the Legislature is the only measure of their authority; and that in the plenitude of this authority, they may sweep away all our fundamental rights; or, that they are bound to leave this particular right untouched and sacred: Either we must say, that they may control the freedom of the press, may abolish the Trial by Jury, may swallow up the Executive and Judiciary Powers of the State; nay that they may despoil us of our very right of suffrage, and erect themselves into an independent and hereditary Assembly or, we must say, that they have no authority to enact into the law the Bill under consideration. We the Subscribers say, that the General Assembly of this Commonwealth have no such authority: And that no effort may be omitted on our part against so dangerous an usurpation, we oppose to it, this remonstrance; earnestly praying, as we are in duty bound, that the Supreme Lawgiver of the Universe, by illuminating those to whom it is addressed, may on the one hand, turn their Councils from every act which would affront his holy prerogative, or violate the trust committed to them: and on the other, guide them into every measure which may be worthy of his [blessing, may re]dound to their own praise, and may establish more firmly the liberties, the prosperity and the happiness of the Commonweath.

8. The Northwest Ordinance (1787)

An Ordinance for the government of the Territory of the United States northwest of the River Ohio.

Be it ordained by the United States in Congress assembled, That the said territory, for the purposes of temporary government, be one district, subject, however, to be divided into two districts, as future circumstances may, in the opinion of Congress, make it expedient.

Be it ordained by the authority aforesaid, That the estates, both of resident and nonresident proprietors in the said territory, dying intestate, shall descend to, and be distributed among their children, and the descendants of a deceased child, in equal parts; the descendants of a deceased child or grandchild to take the share of their deceased parent in equal parts among them: And where there shall be no children or descendants, then in equal parts to the next of kin in equal degree; and among collaterals, the children of a deceased brother or sister of the intestate shall have, in equal parts among them, their deceased parents' share; and there shall in no case be a distinction between kindred of the whole and half blood; saving, in all cases, to the widow of the intestate her third part of the real estate for life, and one third part of the personal estate; and this law relative to descents and dower, shall remain in full force until altered by the legislature of the district. And until the governor and judges shall adopt laws as hereinafter mentioned, estates in the said territory may be devised or bequeathed by wills in writing, signed and sealed by him or her in whom the estate may be (being of full age), and attested by three witnesses; and real estates may be conveyed by lease and release, or bargain and sale, signed, sealed and delivered by the person being of full age, in whom the estate may be, and attested by two witnesses, provided such wills be duly proved, and such conveyances be acknowledged, or the execution thereof duly proved, and be recorded within one year after proper magistrates, courts, and registers shall be appointed for that purpose; and personal property may be transferred by delivery; saving, however to the French and Canadian inhabitants, and other settlers of the Kaskaskies, St. Vincents and the neighboring villages who have heretofore professed themselves citizens of Virginia, their laws and customs now in force among them, relative to the descent and conveyance, of property.

Be it ordained by the authority aforesaid, That there shall be appointed from time to time by Congress, a governor, whose commission shall continue in force for the term of three years, unless sooner revoked by Congress; he shall reside in the district, and have a freehold estate therein in 1,000 acres of land, while in the exercise of his office.

There shall be appointed from time to time by Congress, a secretary, whose commission shall continue in force for four years unless sooner revoked; he shall reside in the district, and have a freehold estate therein in 500 acres of land, while in the exercise of his office. It shall be his duty to keep and preserve the acts and laws passed by the legislature, and the public records of the district, and the proceedings of the governor in his executive department, and transmit authentic copies of such acts and proceedings, every six months, to the Secretary of Congress: There shall also be appointed a court to consist of three judges, any two of whom to form a court, who shall have a common law jurisdiction, and reside in the district, and have each therein a freehold estate in 500 acres of land while in the exercise of their offices; and their commissions shall continue in force during good behavior.

The governor and judges, or a majority of them, shall adopt and publish in the district such laws of the original States, criminal and civil, as may be necessary and best suited to the circumstances of the district, and report them to Congress from time to time: which laws shall be in force in the district until the organization of the General Assembly therein, unless disapproved of by Congress; but afterwards the Legislature shall have authority to alter them as they shall think fit.

The governor, for the time being, shall be commander in chief of the militia, appoint and commission all officers in the same below the rank of general officers; all general officers shall be appointed and commissioned by Congress.

Previous to the organization of the general assembly, the governor shall appoint such magistrates and other civil officers in each county or township, as he shall find necessary for the preservation of the peace and good order in the same: After the general assembly shall be organized, the powers and duties of the magistrates and other civil officers shall be regulated and defined by the said assembly; but all magistrates and other civil officers not herein otherwise directed, shall during the continuance of this temporary government, be appointed by the governor.

For the prevention of crimes and injuries, the laws to be adopted or made shall have force in all parts of the district, and for the execution of process, criminal and civil, the governor shall make proper divisions thereof; and he shall proceed from time to time as circumstances may require, to lay out the parts of the district in which the Indian titles shall have been extinguished, into counties and townships, subject, however, to such alterations as may thereafter be made by the legislature.

So soon as there shall be five thousand free male inhabitants of full age in the district, upon giving proof thereof to the governor, they shall receive authority, with time and place, to elect a representative from their counties or townships to represent them in the general assembly: Provided, That, for every five hundred free male inhabitants, there shall be one representative, and so on progressively with the number of free male inhabitants shall the right of representation increase, until the number of representatives shall amount to twenty five; after which, the number and proportion of representatives shall be regulated by the legislature: Provided, That no person be eligible or qualified to act as a representative unless he shall have been a citizen of one of the United States three years, and be a resident in the district, or unless he shall have resided in the district three years; and, in either case, shall likewise hold in his own right, in fee simple, 200 acres of land within the same; Provided, also, That a freehold in fifty acres of land in the district, having been a citizen of one of the states, and being resident in the district, or the like freehold and two years residence in the district, shall be necessary to qualify a man as an elector of a representative.

The representatives thus elected, shall serve for the term of two years; and, in case of the death of a representative, or removal from office, the governor shall issue a writ to the county or township for which he was a member, to elect another in his stead, to serve for the residue of the term.

The general assembly or legislature shall consist of the governor, legislative council, and a house of representatives. The Legislative Council shall consist of five members, to continue in office five years, unless sooner removed by Congress; any three of whom to be a quorum: and the members of the Council shall be nominated and appointed in the following manner, to wit: As soon as representatives shall be elected, the Governor shall appoint a time and place for them to meet together; and, when met, they shall nominate ten persons, residents in the district, and each possessed of a freehold in 500 acres of land, and return their names to Congress; five of whom Congress shall appoint and commission to serve as aforesaid; and, whenever a vacancy shall happen in the council, by death or removal from office, the house of representatives shall nominate two persons, qualified as aforesaid, for each vacancy, and return their names to Congress; one of whom Congress shall appoint and commission for the residue of the term. And every five years, four months at least before the expiration of the time of service of the members of council, the said house shall nominate ten persons, qualified as aforesaid, and return their names to Congress; five of whom Congress shall appoint and commission to serve as members of the council five years, unless sooner removed. And the governor, legislative council, and house of representatives, shall have authority to make laws in all cases, for the good government of the district, not repugnant to the principles and articles in this ordinance established and declared. And all bills, having passed by a majority in the house, and by a majority in the council, shall be referred to the governor for his assent; but no bill, or legislative act whatever, shall be of any force without his assent. The governor shall have power to convene, prorogue, and dissolve the general assembly, when, in his opinion, it shall be expedient.

The governor, judges, legislative council, secretary, and such other officers as Congress shall appoint in the district, shall take an oath or affirmation of fidelity and of office; the governor before the president of Congress, and all other officers before the governor. As soon as a legislature shall be formed in the district, the council and house assembled in one room, shall have authority, by joint ballot, to elect a delegate to Congress, who shall have a seat in Congress, with a right of debating but not voting during this temporary government.

And, for extending the fundamental principles of civil and religious liberty, which form the basis whereon these republics, their laws and constitutions are erected; to fix and establish those principles as the basis of all laws, constitutions, and governments, which forever hereafter shall be formed in the said territory: to provide also for the establishment of States, and permanent government therein, and for their admission to a share in the federal councils on an equal footing with the original States, at as early periods as may be consistent with the general interest:

It is hereby ordained and declared by the authority aforesaid, That the following articles shall be considered as articles of compact between the original States and the people and States in the said territory and forever remain unalterable, unless by common consent, to wit:

Article 1: No person, demeaning himself in a peaceable and orderly manner, shall ever be molested on account of his mode of worship or religious sentiments, in the said territory.

Article 2: The inhabitants of the said territory shall always be entitled to the benefits of the writ of habeas corpus, and of the trial by jury; of a proportionate representation of the people in the legislature; and of judicial proceedings according to the course of the common law. All persons shall be bailable, unless for capital offenses, where the proof shall be evident or the presumption great. All fines shall be moderate; and no cruel or unusual punishments shall be inflicted. No man shall be deprived of his liberty or property, but by the judgment of his peers or the law of the land; and, should the public exigencies make it necessary, for the common preservation, to take any person's property, or to demand his particular services, full compensation shall be made for the same. And, in the just preservation of rights and property, it is understood and declared, that no law ought ever to be made, or have force in the said territory, that shall, in any manner whatever, interfere with or affect private contracts or engagements, bona fide, and without fraud, previously formed.

Article 3: Religion, morality, and knowledge, being necessary to good government and the happiness of mankind, schools and the means of education shall forever be encouraged. The utmost good faith shall always be observed towards the Indians; their lands and property shall never be taken from them without their consent; and, in their property, rights, and liberty, they shall never be invaded or disturbed, unless in just and lawful wars authorized by Congress; but laws founded in justice and humanity, shall from time to time be made for preventing wrongs being done to them, and for preserving peace and friendship with them.

Article 4: The said territory, and the States which may be formed therein, shall forever remain a part of this Confederacy of the United States of America, subject to the Articles of Confederation, and to such alterations therein as shall be constitutionally made; and to all the acts and ordinances of the United States in Congress assembled, conformable thereto. The inhabitants and settlers in the said territory shall be subject to pay a part of the federal debts contracted or to be contracted, and a proportional part of the expenses of government, to be apportioned on them by Congress according to the same common rule and measure by which apportionments thereof shall be made on the other States; and the taxes for paying their proportion shall be laid and levied by the authority and direction of the legislatures of the district or districts, or new States, as in the original States, within the time agreed upon by the United States in Congress assembled. The legislatures of those districts or new States, shall never interfere with the primary disposal of the soil by the United States in Congress assembled, nor with any regulations Congress may find necessary for securing the title in such soil to the bona fide purchasers. No tax shall be imposed on lands the property of the United States; and, in no case, shall nonresident proprietors be taxed higher than residents. The navigable waters leading into the Mississippi and St. Lawrence, and the carrying places between the same, shall be common highways and forever free, as well to the inhabitants of the said territory as to the citizens of the United States, and those of any other States that may be admitted into the confederacy, without any tax, impost, or duty therefor.

Article 5: There shall be formed in the said territory, not less than three nor more than five States; and the boundaries of the States, as soon as Virginia shall alter her act of cession, and consent to the same, shall become fixed and established as follows, to wit: The western State in the said territory, shall be bounded by the Mississippi, the Ohio, and Wabash Rivers; a direct line drawn from the Wabash and Post Vincents, due North, to the territorial line between the United States and Canada; and, by the said territorial line, to the Lake of the Woods and Mississippi. The middle State shall be bounded by the said direct line, the Wabash from Post Vincents to the Ohio, by the Ohio, by a direct line, drawn due north from the mouth of the Great Miami, to the said territorial line, and by the said territorial line. The eastern State shall be bounded by the last mentioned direct line, the Ohio, Pennsylvania, and the said territorial line: Provided, however, and it is further understood and declared, that the boundaries of these three States shall be subject so far to be altered, that, if Congress shall hereafter find it expedient, they shall have authority to form one or two States in that part of the said territory which lies north of an east and west line drawn through the southerly bend or extreme of Lake Michigan. And, whenever any of the said States shall have sixty thousand free inhabitants therein, such State shall be admitted, by its delegates, into the Congress of the United States, on an equal footing with the original States in all respects whatever, and shall be at liberty to form a permanent constitution and State government: Provided, the constitution and government so to be formed, shall be republican, and in conformity to the principles contained in these articles; and, so far as it can be consistent with the general interest of the confederacy, such admission shall be allowed at an earlier period, and when there may be a less number of free inhabitants in the State than sixty thousand.

Article 6: There shall be neither slavery nor involuntary servitude in the said territory, otherwise than in the punishment of crimes whereof the party shall have been duly convicted: Provided, always, That any person escaping into the same, from whom labor or service is lawfully claimed in any one of the original States, such fugitive may be lawfully reclaimed and conveyed to the person claiming his or her labor or service as aforesaid.

Be it ordained by the authority aforesaid, That the resolutions of the 23rd of April, 1784, relative to the subject of this ordinance, be, and the same are hereby repealed and declared null and void.

9. George Washington's Thanksgiving Proclamation (October 3, 1789)

By the President of the United States of America. A Proclamation.

Whereas it is the duty of all Nations to acknowledge the providence of Almighty God, to obey his will, to be grateful for his benefits, and humbly to implore his protection and favor—and whereas both Houses of Congress have by their joint Committee requested me 'to recommend to the People of the United States a day of public thanksgiving and prayer to be observed by acknowledging with grateful hearts the many signal favors of Almighty God especially by affording them an opportunity peaceably to establish a form of government for their safety and happiness.'

Now therefore I do recommend and assign Thursday the 26th day of November next to be devoted by the People of these States to the service of that great and glorious Being, who is the beneficent Author of all the good that was, that is, or that will be—That we may then all unite in rendering unto him our sincere and humble thanks—for his kind care and protection of the People of this Country previous to their becoming a Nation—for the signal and manifold mercies, and the favorable interpositions of his Providence which we experienced in the tranquillity, union, and plenty, which we have since enjoyed—for the peaceable and rational manner, in which we have been enabled to establish constitutions of government for our safety and happiness, and particularly the national One now lately instituted—for the civil and religious liberty with which we are blessed; and the means we have of acquiring and diffusing useful knowledge; and in general for all the great and various favors which he hath been pleased to confer upon us.

And also that we may then unite in most humbly offering our prayers and supplications to the great Lord and Ruler of Nations and beseech him to pardon our national and other transgressions—to enable us all, whether in public or private stations, to perform our several and relative duties properly and punctually—to render our national government a blessing to all the people, by constantly being a Government of wise, just, and constitutional laws, discreetly and faithfully executed and obeyed—to protect and guide all Sovereigns and Nations (especially such as have shewn kindness onto us) and to bless them with good government, peace, and concord—To promote the knowledge and practice of true religion and virtue, and the encrease of science among them and us—and generally to grant unto all Mankind such a degree of temporal prosperity as he alone knows to be best.

Given under my hand at the City of New-York the third day of October in the year of our Lord 1789.

10. Constitutional Clauses Addressing Religion (1789-91)

Article VI, Clause 3

The Senators and Representatives before mentioned, and the Members of the several State Legislatures, and all executive and judicial Officers, both of the United States and of the several States, shall be bound by Oath or Affirmation, to support this Constitution; but no religious Test shall ever be required as a Qualification to any Office or public Trust under the United States.

First Amendment

Congress shall make no law respecting an establishment of religion, or prohibiting the free exercise thereof; or abridging the freedom of speech, or of the press; or the right of the people peaceably to assemble, and to petition the Government for a redress of grievances.

11. George Washington's Letter to the Hebrew Congregation in Newport, Rhode Island (August 18, 1790)

Gentlemen.

While I receive, with much satisfaction, your Address replete with expressions of affection and esteem; I rejoice in the opportunity of assuring you, that I shall always retain a grateful remembrance of the cordial welcome I experienced in my visit to Newport, from all classes of Citizens.

The reflection on the days of difficulty and danger which are past is rendered the more sweet, from a consciousness that they are succeeded by days of uncommon prosperity and security. If we have wisdom to make the best use of the advantages with which we are now favored, we cannot fail, under the just administration of a good Government, to become a great and a happy people.

The Citizens of the United States of America have a right to applaud themselves for having given to mankind examples of an enlarged and liberal policy: a policy worthy of imitation. All possess alike liberty of conscience and immunities of citizenship. It is now no more that toleration is spoken of, as if it was by the indulgence of one class of people, that another enjoyed the exercise of their inherent natural rights. For happily the Government of the United States, which gives to bigotry no sanction, to persecution no assistance requires only that they who live under its protection should demean themselves as good citizens, in giving it on all occasions their effectual support.

It would be inconsistent with the frankness of my character not to avow that I am pleased with your favorable opinion of my Administration, and fervent wishes for my felicity. May the Children of the Stock of Abraham, who dwell in this land, continue to merit and enjoy the good will of the other Inhabitants; while every one shall sit in safety under his own vine and fig tree, and there shall be none to make him afraid. May the father of all mercies scatter light and not darkness in our paths, and make us all in our several vocations useful here, and in his own due time and way everlastingly happy.

12. President George Washington's Farewell Address (1796)

Friends and Fellow-Citizens:

The period for a new election of a citizen, to administer the executive government of the United States, being not far distant, and the time actually arrived, when your thoughts must be employed designating the person, who is to be clothed with that important trust, it appears to me proper, especially as it may conduce to a more distinct expression of the public voice, that I should now apprise you of the resolution I have formed, to decline being considered among the number of those out of whom a choice is to be made.

I beg you at the same time to do me the justice to be assured that this resolution has not been taken without a strict regard to all the considerations appertaining to the relation which binds a dutiful citizen to his country; and that in withdrawing the tender of service, which silence in my situation might imply, I am influenced by no diminution of zeal for your future interest, no deficiency of grateful respect for your past kindness, but am supported by a full conviction that the step is compatible with both.

The acceptance of, and continuance hitherto in, the office to which your suffrages have twice called me, have been a uniform sacrifice of inclination to the opinion of duty, and to a deference for what appeared to be your desire. I constantly hoped, that it would have been much earlier in my power, consistently with motives, which I was not at liberty to disregard, to return to that retirement, from which I had been reluctantly drawn. The strength of my inclination to do this, previous to the last election, had even led to the preparation of an address to declare it to you; but mature reflection on the then perplexed and critical posture of our affairs with foreign nations, and the unanimous advice of persons entitled to my confidence impelled me to abandon the idea.

I rejoice, that the state of your concerns, external as well as internal, no longer renders the pursuit of inclination incompatible with the sentiment of duty, or propriety; and am persuaded, whatever partiality may be retained for my services, that, in the present circumstances of our country, you will not disapprove my determination to retire.

The impressions, with which I first undertook the arduous trust, were explained on the proper occasion. In the discharge of this trust, I will only say, that I have, with good intentions, contributed towards the organization and administration of the government the best exertions of which a very fallible judgment was capable. Not unconscious, in the outset, of the inferiority of my qualifications, experience in my own eyes, perhaps still more in the eyes of others, has strengthened the motives to diffidence of myself; and every day the increasing weight of years admonishes me more and more, that the shade of retirement is as necessary to me as it will be welcome. Satisfied, that, if any circumstances have given peculiar value to my services, they were temporary, I have the consolation to believe, that, while choice and prudence invite me to quit the political scene, patriotism does not forbid it.

In looking forward to the moment, which is intended to terminate the career of my public life, my feelings do not permit me to suspend the deep acknowledgment of that debt of gratitude, which I owe to my beloved country for the many honors it has conferred upon me; still more for the steadfast confidence with which it has supported me; and for the opportunities I have thence enjoyed of manifesting my inviolable attachment, by services faithful and persevering, though in usefulness unequal to my zeal. If benefits have resulted to our country from these services, let it always be remembered to your praise, and as an instructive example in our annals, that under circumstances in which the passions, agitated in every direction, were liable to mislead, amidst appearances sometimes dubious, vicissitudes of fortune often discouraging, in situations in which not unfrequently want of success has countenanced the spirit of criticism, the constancy of your support was the essential prop of the efforts, and a guarantee of the plans by which they were effected. Profoundly penetrated with this idea, I shall carry it with me to my grave, as a strong incitement to unceasing vows that Heaven may continue to you the choicest tokens of its beneficence; that your union and brotherly affection may be perpetual; that the free constitution, which is the work of your hands, may be sacredly maintained; that its administration in every department may be stamped with wisdom and virtue; that, in fine, the happiness of the people of these States, under the auspices of liberty, may be made complete, by so careful a preservation and so prudent a use of this blessing, as will acquire to them the glory of recommending it to the applause, the affection, and adoption of every nation, which is yet a stranger to it.

Here, perhaps I ought to stop. But a solicitude for your welfare which cannot end but with my life, and the apprehension of danger, natural to that solicitude, urge me, on an occasion like the present, to offer to your solemn contemplation, and to recommend to your frequent review, some sentiments which are the result of much reflection, of no inconsiderable observation, and which appear to me all-important to the permanency of your felicity as a people. These will be offered to you with the more freedom, as you can only see in them the disinterested warnings of a parting friend, who can possibly have no personal motive to bias his counsel. Nor can I forget, as an encouragement to it, your indulgent reception of my sentiments on a former and not dissimilar occasion.

Interwoven as is the love of liberty with every ligament of your hearts, no recommendation of mine is necessary to fortify or confirm the attachment. . . .

Of all the dispositions and habits, which lead to political prosperity, Religion and Morality are indispensable supports. In vain would that man claim the tribute of Patriotism, who should labor to subvert these great pillars of human happiness, these firmest props of the duties of Men and Citizens. The mere Politician, equally with the pious man, ought to respect and to cherish them. A volume could not trace all their connections with private and public felicity. Let it simply be asked, Where is the security for property, for reputation, for life, if the sense of religious obligation desert the oaths, which are the instruments of investigation in Courts of Justice? And let us with caution indulge the supposition, that morality can be maintained without religion. Whatever may be conceded to the influence of refined education on minds of peculiar structure, reason and experience both forbid us to expect, that national morality can prevail in exclusion of religious principle.

It is substantially true, that virtue or morality is a necessary spring of popular government. The rule, indeed, extends with more or less force to every species of free government. Who, that is a sincere friend to it, can look with indifference upon attempts to shake the foundation of the fabric?

Promote, then, as an object of primary importance, institutions for the general diffusion of knowledge. In proportion as the structure of a government gives force to public opinion, it is essential that public opinion should be enlightened. . . .

Though, in reviewing the incidents of my administration, I am unconscious of intentional error, I am nevertheless too sensible of my defects not to think it probable that I may have committed many errors. Whatever they may be, I fervently beseech the Almighty to avert or mitigate the evils to which they may tend. I shall also carry with me the hope, that my Country will never cease to view them with indulgence; and that, after forty-five years of my life dedicated to its service with an upright zeal, the faults of incompetent abilities will be consigned to oblivion, as myself must soon be to the mansions of rest.

Relying on its kindness in this as in other things, and actuated by that fervent love towards it, which is so natural to a man, who views it in the native soil of himself and his progenitors for several generations; I anticipate with pleasing expectation that retreat, in which I promise myself to realize, without alloy, the sweet enjoyment of partaking, in the midst of my fellow-citizens, the benign influence of good laws under a free government, the ever favorite object of my heart, and the happy reward, as I trust, of our mutual cares, labors, and dangers.

George Washington
United States, September 17th, 1796

13. Thomas Jefferson's Letter to the Danbury Baptist Association of Connecticut (1802)

To Messrs. Nehemiah Dodge, Ephraim Robbins, & Stephen S. Nelson, a committee of the Danbury association in the state of Connecticut.

Gentlemen

The affectionate sentiments of esteem and approbation which you are so good as to express towards me, on behalf of the Danbury Baptist association, give me the highest satisfaction. My duties dictate a faithful & zealous pursuit of the interests of my constituents, & in proportion as they are persuaded of my fidelity to those duties, the discharge of them becomes more and more pleasing.

Believing with you that religion is a matter which lies solely between Man & his God, that he owes account to none other for his faith or his worship, that the legitimate powers of government reach actions only, & not opinions, I contemplate with sovereign reverence that act of the whole American people which declared that their legislature should "make no law respecting an establishment of religion, or prohibiting the free exercise thereof," thus building a wall of separation between Church & State, adhering to this expression of the supreme will of the nation in behalf of the rights of conscience, I shall see with sincere satisfaction the progress of those sentiments which tend to restore to man all his natural rights, convinced he has no natural right in opposition to his social duties.

I reciprocate your kind prayers for the protection & blessing of the common father and creator of man, and tender you for yourselves & your religious association, assurances of my high respect & esteem.

14. Excerpts from Joseph Story's *Commentaries* on the Constitution (1833)

Sections 1837- 1843: Oaths of Office and Religious Tests

§1837. The next clause is, "The senators and representatives before mentioned, and the members of the several state legislatures and all executive and judicial officers, both of the United States and of the several states, shall be bound by oath or affirmation to support the constitution. But no religious test shall ever be required as a qualification to any office or public trust under the United States."

§1838. That all those, who are entrusted with the execution of the powers of the national government, should be bound by some solemn obligation to the due execution of the trusts reposed in them, and to support the constitution, would seem to be a proposition too clear to render any reasoning necessary in support of it. It results from the plain right of society to require some guaranty from every officer, that he will be conscientious in the discharge of his duty. Oaths have a solemn obligation upon the minds of all reflecting men, and especially upon those, who feel a deep sense of accountability to a Supreme being. If, in the ordinary administration of justice in cases of private rights, or personal claims, oaths are required of those, who try, as well as of those, who give testimony, to guard against malice, falsehood, and evasion, surely like guards ought to be interposed in the administration of high public trusts, and especially in such, as may concern the welfare and safety of the whole community. But there are known denominations of men, who are conscientiously scrupulous of taking oaths (among which is that pure and distinguished sect of Christians, commonly called Friends, or Quakers,) and therefore, to prevent any unjustifiable exclusion from office, the constitution has permitted a solemn affirmation to be made instead of an oath, and as its equivalent.

§1839. But it may not appear to all persons quite so clear, why the officers of the state governments should be equally bound to take a like oath, or affirmation; and it has been even suggested, that there is no more reason to require that, than to require, that all of the United States officers should take an oath or affirmation to support the state constitutions. A moment's reflection will show sufficient reasons for the requisition of it in the one case, and the omission of it in the other. The members and officers of the national government have no agency in carrying into effect the state constitutions. The members and officers of the state governments have an essential agency in giving effect to the national constitution. The election of the president and the senate will depend, in all cases, upon the legislatures of the several states; and, in many cases, the election of the house of representatives may be affected by their agency. The judges of the state courts will frequently be called upon to decide upon the constitution, and laws, and treaties of the United States; and upon rights and claims growing out of them. Decisions ought to be, as far as possible, uniform; and uniformity of obligation will greatly tend to such a result. The executive authority of the several states may be often called upon to exert powers, or allow rights, given by the constitution, as in filling vacancies in the senate; during the recess of the legislature; in issuing writs of election to fill vacancies in the house of representatives; in officering the militia: and giving effect to laws for calling them; and in the surrender of fugitives from justice. These, and many other functions, devolving on the state authorities, render it highly important, that they should be under a solemn obligation to obey the constitution. In common sense, there can be no well-founded objection to it. There may be serious evils growing out of an opposite course. One of the objections, taken to the articles of confederation, by an enlightened state, (New-Jersey,) was, that no oath was required of members of congress, previous to their admission to their seats in congress. The laws and usages of all civilized nations, (said that state,) evince the propriety of an oath on such occasions; and the more solemn and important the deposit, the more strong and explicit ought the obligation to be.

§1840. As soon as the constitution went into operation, congress passed an act, prescribing the time and manner of taking the oath, or affirmation, thus required, as well by officers of the several states, as of the United States. On that occasion, some scruple seems to have been entertained, by a few members, of the constitutional authority of congress to pass such an act. But it was approved without much opposition. At this day, the point would be generally deemed beyond the reach of any reasonable doubt.

§1841. The remaining part of the clause declares, that "no religious test shall ever be required, as a qualification to any office or public trust, under the United States." This clause is not introduced merely for the purpose of satisfying the scruples of many respectable persons, who feel an invincible repugnance to any religious test, or affirmation. It had a higher object; to cut off for ever every pretense of any alliance between church and state in the national government. The framers of the constitution were fully sensible of the dangers from this source, marked out in the history of other ages and countries; and not wholly unknown to our own. They knew, that bigotry was unceasingly vigilant in its stratagems, to secure to itself an exclusive ascendancy over the human mind; and that intolerance was ever ready to arm itself with all the terrors of the civil power to exterminate those, who doubted its dogmas, or resisted its infallibility. The Catholic and the Protestant had alternately waged the most ferocious and unrelenting warfare on each other; and Protestantism itself, at the very moment, that it was proclaiming the right of private judgment, prescribed boundaries to that right, beyond which if any one dared to pass, he must seal his rashness with the blood of martyrdom. The history of the parent country, too, could not fail to instruct them in the uses, and the abuses of religious tests. They there found the pains and penalties of non-conformity written in no equivocal language, and enforced with a stern and vindictive jealousy. One hardly knows, how to repress the sentiments of strong indignation, in reading the cool vindication of the laws of England on this subject, (now, happily, for the most part abolished by recent enactments,) by Mr. Justice Blackstone, a man, in many respects distinguished for habitual moderation, and a deep sense of justice. "The second species," says he "of non-conformists, are those, who offend through a mistaken or perverse zeal. Such were esteemed by our laws, enacted since the time of the reformation, to be papists, and protestant dissenters; both of which were supposed to be equally schismatics in not communicating with the national church; with this difference, that the papists divided from it upon material, though erroneous, reasons; but many of the dissenters, upon matters of indifference, or, in other words, upon no reason at all. Yet certainly our ancestors were mistaken in their plans of compulsion and intolerance. The sin of schism, as such, is by no means the object of temporal coercion and punishment. If, through weakness of intellect, through misdirected piety, through perverseness and acerbity of temper, or, (which is often the case,) through a prospect of secular advantage in herding with a party, men quarrel with the ecclesiastical establishment, the civil magistrate has nothing to do with it; unless their tenets and practice are such, as threaten ruin or disturbance to the state. He is bound, indeed, to protect the established church; and, if this can be better effected, by admitting none but its genuine members to offices of trust and emolument, he is certainly at liberty so to do; the disposal of offices being matter of favor and discretion. But, this point being once secured, all persecution for diversity of opinions, however ridiculous or absurd they may be, is contrary to every principle of sound policy and civil freedom. The names and subordination of the clergy, the posture of devotion, the materials and color of the minister's garment, the joining in a known, or an unknown form of prayer, and other matters of the same kind, must be left to the option of every man's private judgment."

§1842. And again: "As to papists, what has been said of the protestant dissenters would hold equally strong for a general toleration of them; provided their separation was founded only upon difference of opinion in religion, and their principles did not also extend to subversion of the civil government. If once they could be brought to renounce the supremacy of the pope, they might quietly enjoy their seven sacraments, their purgatory, and auricular confession; their worship of reliques and images; nay even their transubstantiation. But while they acknowledge a foreign power, superior to the sovereignty of the kingdom, they cannot complain, if the laws of that kingdom will not treat them upon the footing of good subjects."

§1843. Of the English laws respecting papists, Montesquieu observes, that they are so rigorous, though not professedly of the sanguinary kind, that they do all the hurt, that can possibly be done in cold blood. To this just rebuke, (after citing it, and admitting its truth,) Mr. Justice Blackstone has no better reply to make, than that these laws are seldom exerted to their utmost rigor; and, indeed, if they were, it would be very difficult to excuse them. The meanest apologist of the worst enormities of a Roman emperor could not have shadowed out a defense more servile, or more unworthy of the dignity and spirit of a freeman. With one quotation more from the same authority, exemplifying the nature and objects of the English test laws, this subject may be dismissed. "In order the better to secure the established church against perils from nonconformists of all denominations, infidels, Turks, Jews, heretics, papists, and sectors, there are, however, two bulwarks erected, called the corporation and test acts. By the former of which, no person can be legally elected to any office relating to the government of any city or corporation, unless, within a twelvemonth before, he has received the sacrament of the Lord's supper according to the rights of the church of England; and he is also enjoined to take the oaths of allegiance and supremacy, at the same time, that he takes the oath of office; or, in default of either of these requisites, such election shall be void. The other, called the test-act, directs all officers, civil and military, to take the oaths, and make the declaration against transubstantiation, in any of the king's courts at Westminster, or at the quarter sessions, within six calendar months.

Sections 1865-1873: Religious Clauses of First Amendment

§1864. The first is, "Congress shall make no law respecting an establishment of religion, or prohibiting the free exercise thereof; or abridging the freedom of speech, or of the press; or the right of the people peaceably to assemble, and to petition government for a redress of grievances."

§1865. And first, the prohibition of any establishment of religion, and the freedom of religious opinion and worship. How far any government has a right to interfere in matters touching religion, has been a subject much discussed by writers upon public and political law. The right and the duty of the interference of government, in matters of religion, have been maintained by many distinguished authors, as well those, who were the warmest advocates of free governments, as those, who were attached to governments of a more arbitrary character. Indeed, the right of a society or government to interfere in matters of religion will hardly be contested by any persons, who believe that piety, religion, and morality are intimately connected with the well being of the state, and indispensable to the administration of civil justice. The promulgation of the great doctrines of religion, the being, and attributes, and providence of one Almighty God; the responsibility to him for all our actions, founded upon moral freedom and accountability; a future state of rewards and punishments; the cultivation of all the personal, social, and benevolent virtues;—these never can be a matter of indifference in any well ordered community. It is, indeed, difficult to conceive, how any civilized society can well exist without them. And at all events, it is impossible for those, who believe in the truth of Christianity, as a divine revelation, to doubt, that it is the especial duty of government to foster, and encourage it among all the citizens and subjects. This is a point wholly distinct from that of the right of private judgment in matters of religion, and of the freedom of public worship according to the dictates of one's conscience.

§1866. The real difficulty lies in ascertaining the limits, to which government may rightfully go in fostering and encouraging religion. Three cases may easily be supposed. One, where a government affords aid to a particular religion, leaving all persons free to adopt any other; another, where it creates an ecclesiastical establishment for the propagation of the doctrines of a particular sect of that religion, leaving a like freedom to all others; and a third, where it creates such an establishment, and excludes all persons, not belonging to it, either wholly, or in part, from any participation in the public honors, trusts, emoluments, privileges, and immunities of the state. For instance, a government may simply declare, that the Christian religion shall be the religion of the state, and shall be aided, and encouraged in all the varieties of sects belonging to it; or it may declare, that the Catholic or Protestant religion shall be the religion of the state, leaving every man to the free enjoyment of his own religious opinions; or it may establish the doctrines of a particular sect, as of Episcopalians, as the religion of the state, with a like freedom; or it may establish the doctrines of a particular sect, as exclusively the religion of the state, tolerating others to a limited extent, or excluding all, not belonging to it, from all public honors, trusts, emoluments, privileges, and immunities.

§1867. Now, there will probably be found few persons in this, or any other Christian country, who would deliberately contend, that it was unreasonable, or unjust to foster and encourage the Christian religion generally, as a matter of sound policy, as well as of revealed truth. In fact, every American colony, from its foundation down to the revolution, with the exception of Rhode Island, (if, indeed, that state be an exception,) did openly, by the whole course of its laws and institutions, support and sustain, in some form, the Christian religion; and almost invariably gave a peculiar sanction to some of its fundamental doctrines. And this has continued to be the case in some of the states down to the present period, without the slightest suspicion, that it was against the principles of public law, or republican liberty. Indeed, in a republic, there would seem to be a peculiar propriety in viewing the Christian religion, as the great basis, on which it must rest for its support and permanence, if it be, what it has ever been deemed by its truest friends to be, the religion of liberty. Montesquieu has remarked, that the Christian religion is a stranger to mere despotic power. The mildness so frequently recommended in the gospel is incompatible with the despotic rage, with which a prince punishes his subjects, and exercises himself in cruelty. He has gone even further, and affirmed, that the Protestant religion is far more congenial with the spirit of political freedom, than the Catholic. "When," says he, "the Christian religion, two centuries ago, became unhappily divided into

Catholic and Protestant, the people of the north embraced the Protestant, and those of the south still adhered to the Catholic. The reason is plain. The people of the north have, and will ever have, a spirit of liberty and independence, which the people of the south have not. And, therefore, a religion, which has no visible head, is more agreeable to the independence of climate, than that, which has one." Without stopping to inquire, whether this remark be well founded, it is certainly true, that the parent country has acted upon it with a severe and vigilant zeal; and in most of the colonies the same rigid jealousy has been maintained almost down to our own times. Massachusetts, while she has promulgated in her BILL OF RIGHTS the importance and necessity of the public support of religion, and the worship of God, has authorized the legislature to require it only for Protestantism. The language of that bill of rights is remarkable for its pointed affirmation of the duty of government to support Christianity, and the reasons for it. "As," says the third article, "the happiness of a people, and the good order and preservation of civil government, essentially depend upon piety, religion, and morality; and as these cannot be generally diffused through the community, but by the institution of the public worship of God, and of public instructions in piety, religion, and morality; therefore, to promote their happiness and to secure the good order and preservation of their government the people of this Commonwealth have a right to invest their legislature with power to authorize, and require, and the legislature shall from time to time authorize and require, the several towns, parishes, &c. &c. to make suitable provision at their own expense for the institution of the public worship of God, and for the support and maintenance of public protestant teachers of piety, religion, and morality, in all cases where such provision shall not be made voluntarily." Afterwards there follow provisions, prohibiting any superiority of one sect over another, and securing to all citizens the free exercise of religion.

§1868. Probably at the time of the adoption of the constitution, and of the amendment to it, now under consideration, the general, if not the universal, sentiment in America was, that Christianity ought to receive encouragement from the state, so far as was not incompatible with the private rights of conscience, and the freedom of religious worship. An attempt to level all religions, and to make it a matter of state policy to hold all in utter indifference, would have created universal disapprobation, if not universal indignation.

§1869. It yet remains a problem to be solved in human affairs, whether any free government can be permanent, where the public worship of God, and the support of religion, constitute no part of the policy or duty of the state in any assignable shape. The future experience of Christendom, and chiefly of the American states, must settle this problem, as yet new in the history of the world, abundant, as it has been, in experiments in the theory of government.

§1870. But the duty of supporting religion, and especially the Christian religion, is very different from the right to force the consciences of other men, or to punish them for worshipping God in the manner, which, they believe, their accountability to him requires. It has been truly said, that "religion or the duty we owe to our Creator, and the manner of discharging it, can be dictated only by reason and conviction, not by force or violence," Mr. Locke himself, who did not doubt the right of government to interfere in matters of religion, and especially to encourage Christianity, at the same time has expressed his opinion of the right of private judgment, and liberty of conscience, in a manner becoming his character, as a sincere friend of civil and religious liberty. "No man, or society of men," says he, "have any authority to impose their opinions or interpretations on any other, the meanest Christian; since, in matters of religion, every man must know, and believe, and give an account for himself." The rights of conscience are, indeed, beyond the just reach of any human power. They are given by God, and cannot be encroached upon by human authority, without a criminal disobedience or, the precepts or natural, as well as revealed religion.

§1871. The real object of the amendment was, not to countenance, much less to advance Mahometanism, or Judaism, or infidelity, by prostrating Christianity; but to exclude all rivalry among Christian sects, and to prevent any national ecclesiastical establishment, which should give to an hierarchy the exclusive patronage of the national government. It thus cut off the means of religious persecution, (the vice and pest of former ages,) and of the subversion of the rights of conscience in matters of religion, which had been trampled upon almost from the days of the Apostles to the present age. The history of the parent country had afforded the most solemn warnings and melancholy instructions on this head; and even New England, the land of the persecuted puritans, as well as other colonies, where the Church of England had maintained its superiority, would furnish out a chapter, as full of the darkest bigotry and intolerance, as any, which could be found to disgrace the pages of foreign annals. Apostasy, heresy, and nonconformity had been standard crimes for public appeals, to kindle the flames of persecution, and apologize for the most atrocious triumphs over innocence and virtue.

§1872. Mr. Justice Blackstone, after having spoken with a manly freedom of the abuses in the Romish church respecting heresy; and, that Christianity had been deformed by the demon of persecution upon the continent, and that the island of Great Britain had not been entirely free from the scourge, defends the final enactments against nonconformity in England, in the following set phrases, to which, without any material change, might be justly applied his own sarcastic remarks upon the conduct of the Roman ecclesiastics in punishing heresy. "For nonconformity to the worship of the church," (says he,) "there is much more to be pleaded than for the former, (that is, reviling the ordinances of the church,) being a matter of private conscience, to the scruples of which our present laws have shown a very just, and Christian indulgence. For undoubtedly all persecution and oppression of weak consciences, on the score of religious persuasions, are highly unjustifiable upon every principle of natural reason, civil liberty, or sound religion. But care must be taken not to carry this indulgence into such extremes, as may endanger the national church. There is always a difference to be made between toleration and establishment." Let it be remembered, that at the very moment, when the learned commentator was penning these cold remarks, the laws of England merely tolerated protestant dissenters in their public worship upon certain conditions, at once irritating and degrading; that the test and corporation acts excluded them from public and corporate offices, both of trust and profit; that the learned commentator avows, that the object of the test and corporation acts was to exclude them from office, in common with Turks, Jews, heretics, papists, and other sectors; that to deny the Trinity, however conscientiously disbelieved, was a public offense, punishable by fine and imprisonment; and that, in the rear of all these disabilities and grievances, came the long list of acts against papists, by which they were reduced to a state of political and religious slavery, and cut off from some of the dearest privileges of mankind.

§1873. It was under a solemn consciousness of the dangers from ecclesiastical ambition, the bigotry of spiritual pride, and the intolerance of sects, thus exemplified in our domestic, as well as in foreign annals, that it was deemed advisable to exclude from the national government all power to act upon the subject. The situation, too, of the different states equally proclaimed the policy, as well as the necessity of such an exclusion. In some of the states, Episcopalians constituted the predominant sect; in others, Presbyterians; in others, Congregationalists; in others, Quakers; and in others again, there was a close numerical rivalry among contending sects. It was impossible, that there should not arise perpetual strife, and perpetual jealousy on the subject of ecclesiastical ascendancy, if the national government were left free to create a religious establishment. The only security was in extirpating the power. But this alone would have been an imperfect security, if it had not been followed up by a declaration of the right of the free exercise of religion, and a prohibition (as we have seen) of all religious tests. Thus, the whole power over the subject of religion is left exclusively to the state governments, to be acted upon according to their own sense of justice, and the state constitutions; and the Catholic and the Protestant, the Calvinist and the Armenian, the Jew and the Infidel, may sit down at the common table of the national councils, without any inquisition into their faith, or mode of worship.

15. Angelina Grimke's *Appeal to Christian Women* (1836)

But perhaps you will be ready to query, why appeal to women on this subject? We do not make the laws which perpetuate slavery. No legislative power is vested in us; we can do nothing to overthrow the system, even if we wished to do so. To this I reply, I know you do not make the laws, but I also know that you are the wives and mothers, the sisters and daughters of those who do; and if you really suppose you can do nothing to overthrow slavery, you are greatly mistaken. You can do much in every way: four things I will name. 1st. You can read on this subject. 2d. You can pray over this subject. 3d. You can speak on this subject. 4th. You can act on this subject. I have not placed reading before praying because I regard it more important, but because, in order to pray aright, we must understand what we are praying for; it is only then we can "pray with the understanding and the spirit also."

1. Read then on the subject of slavery. Search the Scriptures daily, whether the things I have told you are true. Other books and papers might be a great help to you in this investigation, but they are not necessary, and it is hardly probable that your Committees of Vigilance will allow you to have any other. The Bible then is the book I want you to read in the spirit of inquiry, and the spirit of prayer. Even the enemies of Abolitionists acknowledge that their doctrines are drawn from it. In the great mob in Boston, last autumn, when the books and papers of the Anti-Slavery Society were thrown out of the windows of their office, one individual laid hold of the Bible and was about to toss it out to the ground, when another reminded him that is was the Bible he had in his hand. "O! 'tis all one," he replied, and out went the sacred volume, along with the rest. We thank him for the acknowledgment. Yes, "it is all one," for our books and papers are mostly commentaries on the Bible, and the Declaration. Read the Bible then, it contains the words of Jesus, and they are spirit and life. Judge for yourselves whether he sanctioned such a system of oppression and crime.

2. Pray over this subject. When you have entered into your closets, and shut the doors, then pray to your father, who seeth in secret, that he would open your eyes to see whether slavery is sinful, and if it is, that he would enable you to bear a faithful, open and unshrinking testimony against it, and to do whatsoever your hands find to do, leaving the consequences entirely to him, who still says to us whenever we try to reason away duty from the fear of consequences, "What is that to thee, follow thou me." Pray also for that poor slave, that he may be kept patient and submissive under his hard lot, until God is pleased to open the door of freedom to him without violence or bloodshed. Pray too for the master that his heart may be softened, and he made willing to acknowledge, as Joseph's brethren did, "Verily we are guilty concerning our brother," before he will be compelled to add in consequence of Divine judgment, "therefore is all this evil come upon us." Pray also for all your brethren and sisters who are laboring in the righteous cause of Emancipation in the Northern States, England and the world. There is great encouragement for

prayer in these words of our Lord. "Whatsoever ye shall ask the Father in my name, he will give it to you"—Pray then without ceasing, in the closet and the social circle.

3. Speak on this subject. It is through the tongue, the pen, and the press, that truth is principally propagated. Speak then to your relatives, your friends, your acquaintances on the subject of slavery; be not afraid if you are conscientiously convinced it is sinful, to say so openly, but calmly, and to let your sentiments be known. If you are served by the slaves of others, try to ameliorate their conditions as much as possible; never aggravate their faults, and thus add fuel to the fire of anger already kindled, in a master and mistress's bosom; remember their extreme ignorance, and consider them as your Heavenly Father does the less culpable on this account, even when they do wrong things. Discountenance all cruelty to them, all starvation, all corporal chastisement; these may brutalize and break their spirits, but will never bend them to willing, cheerful obedience. If possible, see that they are comfortably and seasonably fed, whether in the house or the field; it is unreasonable and cruel to expect slaves to wait for their breakfast until eleven o'clock, when they rise at five or six. Do all you can, to induce their owners to clothe them well, and then allow them many little indulgences which would contribute to their comfort. Above all, try to persuade your husband, father, brothers, and sons, that slavery is a crime against God and man, and that it is a great sin to keep human beings in such abject ignorance; to deny them the privilege of learning to read and write. The Catholics are universally condemned, for denying the Bible to the common people, but, slaveholders must not blame them, for they are doing the very same thing, and for the very same reason, neither of these systems can bear the light which bursts from the pages of that Holy Book. And lastly, endeavour to inculcate submission on the part of the slaves, but whilst doing this be faithful in pleading the cause of the oppressed.

Will you behold unheeding,
Life's holiest feelings crushed,
Where woman's heart is bleeding,
Shall woman's voice be hushed?

4. Act on this subject. Some of you own slaves yourselves. If you believe slavery is sinful, set them at liberty, "undo the heavy burdens and let the oppressed go free." If they wish to remain with you, pay them wages, if not let them leave you. Should they remain teach them, and have them taught the common branches of an English education; they have minds and those minds ought to be improved. So precious a talent as intellect, never was given to be wrapt in a napkin and buried in the earth. It is the duty of all, as far as they can, to improve their own mental faculties, because we are commanded to love God with all our minds, as well as with all our hearts, and we commit a great sin, if we forbid or prevent that cultivation of the mind in others, which would enable them to perform this duty. Teach your servants then to read &c, and encourage them to believe it is their duty to learn, if it were only that they might read the Bible.

But some of you may say, if we do free our slaves, they will be taken up and sold, therefore there will be no use in doing it. Peter and John might just as well have said, we will not preach the gospel, for if we do, we shall be taken up and put in prison, therefore there will be no use in our preaching. Consequences, my friends, belong no more to you, than they did to these apostles. Duty is ours and events are God's. If you think slavery is sinful, all you have to do is to set your slaves at liberty, do all you can to protect them, and in humble faith and fervent prayer, commend them to your common Father. He can take care of them; but if for wise purposes he sees fit to allow them to be sold, this will afford you an opportunity of testifying openly, wherever you go, against the crime of manstealing. Such an act will be clear robbery, and if exposed, might, under the Divine direction, do the cause of Emancipation more good, than any thing that could happen, for, "He makes even the wrath of man to praise him, and the remainder of wrath he will restrain."

But you may say we are women, how can our hearts endure persecution? And why not? Have not women stood up in all the dignity and strength of moral courage to be the leaders of the people, and to bear a faithful testimony for the truth whenever the prevalence of God has called them to do so? Are there no women in that noble army of martyrs who are now singing the song of Moses and the Lamb? Who led out the women of Israel from the house of bondage, striking the timbrel, and singing the song of deliverance on the banks of that sea whose waters stood up like walls of crystal to open a passage for their escape? It was a woman; Miriam, the prophetess, the sister of Moses and Aaron. Who went up with Barak to Kadesh to fight against Jabin, King of Canaan, into whose hand Israel had been sold because of their iniquities? It was a woman!

What human voice first proclaimed to Mary that she should be the mother of our Lord? It was a woman! Elizabeth, the wife of Zacharias; Luke I: 42 & 43. Who united with the good old Simeon in giving thanks publicly in the temple, when the child, Jesus, was presented there by his parents, "and spake of him to all them that looked for redemption in Jerusalem?" It was a woman! Anna the prophetess. Who first proclaimed Christ as the true Messiah in the streets of Samaria, once the capital of the ten tribes? It was a woman! Who ministered to the Son of God whilst on earth, a despised and persecuted Reformer, in the humble garb of a carpenter? They were women!

But why, my dear friends, have I thus been endeavouring to lead you through the history of more than three thousand years, and to point you to that great cloud of witnesses who have gone before, "from works to rewards?" Have I been seeking to magnify the sufferings, and exalt the character of woman, that she "might have praise of man?" No! no! my object has been to arouse you, as the wives and mothers, the daughters and sisters, of the South, to a sense of your duty as woman, and as Christian women, on that great subject, which has already shaken our country, from the St. Lawrence and the lakes, to the Gulf of Mexico, and from the Mississippi to the shores of the Atlantic; and will continue mightily to shake it, until the polluted temple of slavery falls and crumbles into ruin.

The women of the South can overthrow this horrible system of oppression and cruelty, licentiousness and wrong. Such appeals to your legislatures would be irresistible, for there is something in the heart of man which will bend under moral persuasion. There is a swift witness for truth in his bosom, which will respond to truth when it is uttered with calmness and dignity. If you could obtain but six signatures to such a petition in only one state, I would say, end up that petition, and be not in the least discouraged by the scoffs and jeers of the heartless, or the resolution of the house to lay it on the table. It will be a great thing if the subject can be introduced into your legislatures in any way, even by women, and they will be the most likely to introduce it there in the best possible manner, as a matter of morals and religion, not of expediency or politics. You may petition, too, the different ecclesiastical bodies of the slave states. Slavery must be attacked with the whole power of truth and the sword of the spirit. You must take it up on Christian ground; and fight against it with Christian weapons, whilst your feet are shod with the preparation of the gospel of peace.

Sisters in Christ, I have done. As a Southern, I have felt it was my duty to address you. I have endeavoured to set before you the exceeding sinfulness of slavery, and to point you to the example of those noble women who have been raised up in the church to effect great revolutions, and to suffer for the truth's sake. I have appealed to your sympathies as women, to your sense of duty as Christian woman. I have attempted to vindicate the Abolitionists, to prove the entire safety of immediate Emancipation, and to plead the cause of the poor and oppressed. I have done—I have sowed the seeds of truth, but I well know, that even if an Apollos were to follow in my steps to water them, "God only can give the increase." To Him then who is able to prosper the work of his servant's hand, I commend this Appeal in fervent prayer, that as he "hath chosen the weak things of the world, to confound the things which are mighty," so He may cause His blessing, to descend and carry conviction to the hearts of many Lydias through these speaking pages. Farewell—Count me not your "enemy because I have told you the truth," but believe me in unfeigned affection,

Your sympathizing Friend,

16. South Carolina Governor John H. Hammond's "Slavery Is Not a Sin" Speech (1853)

On Slavery in the abstract, then, it would not be amiss to have as little as possible to say. Let us contemplate it as it is. And thus contemplating it, the first question we have to ask ourselves is, whether it is contrary to the will of God, as revealed to us in his Holy Scriptures—the only certain means given us to ascertain his will. If it is, then Slavery is a sin. And I admit at once that every man is bound to set his face against it, and to emancipate his slaves, should he hold any.

Let us open these Holy Scriptures. In the twentieth chapter of Exodus, seventeenth verse, I find the following words: "Thou shalt not covet thy neighbour's house, thou shalt not covet thy neighbor's wife, nor his man-servant, nor his maid-servant, nor his ox, nor his ass, nor anything that is thy neighbor's"—which is the tenth of those commandments that declare the essential principles of the great moral law delivered to Moses by God himself. Now, discarding all technical and verbal quibbling as wholly unworthy to be used in interpreting the Word of God, what is the plain meaning, undoubted intent, and true spirit of this commandment? Does it not emphatically and explicitly forbid you to disturb your neighbor in the enjoyment of his property; and more especially of that which is here specifically mentioned as being lawfully, and by this commandment made sacredly his? Prominent in the catalogue stands his "man-servant and his maid-servant," who are thus distinctly consecrated as his property, and guaranteed to him for his exclusive benefit, in the most solemn manner. You attempt to avert the otherwise irresistible conclusion, that Slavery was thus ordained by God, by asserting that the word "slave" is not used here, and is not to be found in the Bible. And I have seen many learned dissertations on this point from abolition pens. It is well known that both the Hebrew and Greek words translated "servant" in the Scriptures, mean also, and most usually, "slave." The use of the one word, instead of the other, was a mere matter of taste with the translators of the Bible, as it has been with all the commentators and religious writers, the latter of whom have, I believe, for the most part, adopted the term "slave," or used both terms indiscriminately. If, then, these Hebrew and Greek words include the idea of both systems of servitude, the conditional and unconditional, they should, as the major includes the minor proposition, be always translated "slaves," unless the sense of the whole text forbids it. The real question, then is, what idea is intended to be conveyed by the words used in the commandment quoted? And it is clear to my mind, that as no limitation is affixed to them, and the express intention was to secure to mankind the peaceful enjoyment of every species of property, that the terms "men-servants and maid-servants" include all classes of servants, and establish a lawful, exclusive, and indefeasible interest equally in the "Hebrew brother who shall go out in the seventh year," and "the yearly hired servant," and "those purchased from the heathen round about," who were to be "bondmen forever," as the property of their fellow-man.

You cannot deny that there were among the Hebrews "bondmen forever." You cannot deny that God especially authorized his chosen people to purchase "bondmen forever" from the heathen, as recorded in the twenty-fifth chapter of Leviticus, and that they are there designated by the very Hebrew word used in the tenth commandment. Nor can you deny that a "BONDMAN FOREVER" is a "SLAVE;" yet you endeavor to hand an argument of immortal consequence upon the wretched subterfuge, that the precise word "slave" is not to be found in the translation of the Bible. As if the translators were canonical expounders of the Holy Scriptures, and their words, not God's meaning, must be regarded as his revelation.

It is vain to look to Christ or any of his Apostles to justify such blasphemous perversions of the word of God. Although Slavery in its most revolting form was everywhere visible around them, no visionary notions of piety or philanthropy ever tempted them to gainsay the LAW, even to mitigate the cruel severity of the existing system. On the contrary, regarding Slavery as an established, as well inevitable condition of human society, they never hinted at such a thing as its termination on earth, any more than that "the poor may cease out of the land," which God affirms to Moses shall never be: and they exhort "all servants under the yoke" to "count their masters as worthy of all honor:" "to obey them in all things according to the flesh; not with eye-service as men-pleasers, but in singleness of heart, fearing God;" "not only the good and gentle, but also the forward:" "for what glory is it if when ye are buffetted for your faults ye shall take it patiently? but if when ye do well and suffer for it ye take it patiently, this is acceptable of God." St. Paul actually apprehended a runaway slave, and sent him to his master! Instead of deriving from the Gospel any sanction for the work you have undertaken, it would be difficult to imagine sentiments and conduct more strikingly in contrast, than those of the Apostles and the abolitionists.

It is impossible, therefore, to suppose that Slavery is contrary to the will of God. It is equally absurd to say that American Slavery differs in form or principle from that of the chosen people. We accept the Bible terms as the definition of our Slavery, and its precepts as the guide of our conduct. We desire nothing more. Even the right to "buffet," which is esteemed so shocking, finds its express license in the gospel. 1 Peter ii. 20. Nay, what is more, God directs the Hebrews to "bore holes in the ears of their brothers" to mark them, when under certain circumstances they become perpetual slaves. Exodus xxi. 6.

I think, then, I may safely conclude, and I firmly believe, that American Slavery is not only not a sin, but especially commanded by God through Moses, and approved by Christ through his apostles. And here I might close its defense; for what God ordains, and Christ sanctifies, should surely command the respect and toleration of man. But I fear there has grown up in our time a transcendental religion, which is throwing even transcendental philosophy into the shade—a religion too pure and elevated for the Bible; which seeks to erect among men a higher standard of morals than the Almighty has revealed, or our Savior preached; and which is probably destined to do more to impede the extension of God's kingdom on earth than all the infidels who have ever lived. Error is error. It is as dangerous to deviate to the right hand as the left. And when men, professing to be holy men, and who are by numbers so regarded, declare those things to be sinful which our Creator has expressly authorized and instituted, they do more to destroy his authority among mankind than the most wicked can effect, by proclaiming that to be innocent which he has forbidden. To this self-righteous and self-exalted class belong all the abolitionists whose writings I have read. With them it is no end of the argument to prove your propositions by the text of the Bible, interpreted according to its plain and palpable meaning, and as understood by all mankind for three thousand years before their time. They are more ingenious at construing and interpolating to accommodate it to their new fangled and ethereal code of morals than ever were Voltaire and Hume in picking it to pieces, to free the world from what they considered a delusion. When the abolitionists proclaim "man-stealing" to be a sin, and show me that it is so written down by God, I admit them to be right, and shudder at the idea of such a crime. But when I show them that to hold "bondmen forever" is ordained by God, they deny the Bible, and set up in its place a law of their own making. I must then cease to reason with them on the branch of the question. Our religion differs as widely as our manners. The great judge in our day of final account must decide between us.

17. Lyrics to "The Battle Hymn of the Republic" by Julia Ward Howe (1862)

Mine eyes have seen the glory of the coming of the Lord; He is trampling out the vintage where the grapes of wrath are stored; He has loosed the fateful lightning of His terrible swift sword: His truth is marching on.
Glory! Glory! Hallelujah!
Glory! Glory! Hallelujah!
Glory! Glory! Hallelujah!
His truth is marching on.
I have seen Him in the watch-fires of a hundred circling camps; They have builded Him an altar in the evening dews and damps; I can read His righteous

sentence by the dim and flaring lamps; His day is marching on.
[Chorus]
I have read a fiery gospel writ in burnish'd rows of steel; "As ye deal with my condemners, So with you my grace shall deal'; Let the Hero, born of woman, crush the serpent with his heel; Since God is marching on.
[Chorus]
He has sounded forth the trumpet that shall never call retreat; He is sifting out the hearts of men before His judgment-seat; Oh, be swift, my soul, to answer Him! be jubilant, my feet!; Our God is marching on.
[Chorus]
In the beauty of the lilies Christ was born across the sea; With a glory in His bosom that transfigures you and me; As He died to make men holy, let us die to make men free; While God is marching on.
[Chorus]

18. The Second Inaugural Address of President Abraham Lincoln (1865)

At this second appearing to take the oath of the Presidential office there is less occasion for an extended address than there was at the first. Then a statement somewhat in detail of a course to be pursued seemed fitting and proper. Now, at the expiration of four years, during which public declarations have been constantly called forth on every point and phase of the great contest which still absorbs the attention and engrosses the energies of the nation, little that is new could be presented. The progress of our arms, upon which all else chiefly depends, is as well known to the public as to myself, and it is, I trust, reasonably satisfactory and encouraging to all. With high hope for the future, no prediction in regard to it is ventured.

On the occasion corresponding to this four years ago all thoughts were anxiously directed to an impending civil war. All dreaded it, all sought to avert it. While the inaugural address was being delivered from this place, devoted altogether to saving the Union without war, urgent agents were in the city seeking to destroy it without war; seeking to dissolve the Union and divide effects by negotiation. Both parties deprecated war, but one of them would make war rather than let the nation survive, and the other would accept war rather than let it perish, and the war came.

One-eighth of the whole population were colored slaves, not distributed generally over the Union, but localized in the southern part of it. These slaves constituted a peculiar and powerful interest. All knew that this interest was somehow the cause of the war. To strengthen, perpetuate, and extend this interest was the object for which the insurgents would rend the Union even by war, while the Government claimed no right to do more than to restrict the territorial enlargement of it. Neither party expected for the war the magnitude or the duration which it has already attained. Neither anticipated that the cause of the conflict might cease with or even before the conflict itself should cease. Each looked for an easier triumph, and a result less fundamental and astounding. Both read the same Bible and pray to the same God, and each invokes His aid against the other. It may seem strange that any men should dare to ask a just God's assistance in wringing their bread from the sweat of other men's faces, but let us judge not, that we be not judged. The prayers of both could not be answered. That of neither has been answered fully. The Almighty has His own purposes. "Woe unto the world because of offenses; for it must needs be that offenses come, but woe to that man by whom the offense cometh." If we shall suppose that American slavery is one of those offenses which, in the providence of God, must needs come, but which, having continued through His appointed time, He now wills to remove, and that He gives to both North and South this terrible war as the woe due to those by whom the offense came, shall we discern therein any departure from those divine attributes which the believers in a living God always ascribe to Him? Fondly do we hope, fervently do we pray, that this mighty scourge of war may speedily pass away. Yet, if God wills that it continue until all the wealth piled by the bondsman's two hundred and fifty years of unrequited toil shall be sunk, and until every drop of blood drawn with the lash shall be paid by another drawn with the sword, as was said three thousand years ago, so still it must be said "the judgments of the Lord are true and righteous altogether."

With malice toward none, with charity for all, with firmness in the right as God gives us to see the right, let us strive on to finish the work we are in, to bind up the nation's wounds, to care for him who shall have borne the battle and for his widow and his orphan, to do all which may achieve and cherish a just and lasting peace among ourselves and with all nations.

19. Philip Schaff's Speech on "The Idea of Religious Freedom" (1888)

What is the distinctive character of American Christianity in its organized social aspect and its relation to the national life, as compared with the Christianity of Europe?

It is a free church in a free state, or a self-supporting and self-governing Christianity in independent but friendly relation to the civil government.

This relationship of church and state marks an epoch. It is a new chapter in the history of Christianity, and the most important one which America has so far contributed. It lies at the base of our religious institutions and operations, and they cannot be understood without it. . . .

The relationship of church and state in the United States secures full liberty of religious thought, speech, and action, within the limits of the public peace and order. It makes persecution impossible.

Religion and liberty are inseparable. Religion is voluntary, and cannot and ought not to be forced.

This is a fundamental article of the American creed, without distinction of sect or party. Liberty, both civil and religious, is an American instinct. All natives suck it in with the mother's milk; all immigrants accept it as a happy boon, especially those who flee from oppression and persecution abroad. Even those who reject the modern theory of liberty enjoy the practice, and would defend it in their own interest against any attempt to overthrow it.

Such liberty is impossible on the basis of a union of church and state, where the one of necessity restricts or controls the other. It requires a friendly separation, where each power is entirely independent in its own sphere. The church, as such, has nothing to do with the state except to obey its laws and to strengthen its moral foundations; the state has nothing to do with the church except to protect her in her property and liberty; and the state must be equally just to all forms of belief and unbelief which do not endanger the public safety.

The family, the church, and the state are divine institutions demanding alike our obedience, in their proper sphere of jurisdiction. The family is the oldest institution, and the source of church and state. The patriarchs were priests and kings of their households. Church and state are equally necessary, and as inseparable as soul and body, and yet as distinct as soul and body. The church is instituted for the religious interests and eternal welfare of man; the state for his secular interests and temporal welfare. The one looks to heaven as the final home of immortal spirits, the other upon our mother earth. The church is the reign of love; the state is the reign of justice. The former is governed by the gospel, the latter by the law. The church exhorts, and uses moral suasion; the state commands, and enforces obedience. The church punishes by rebuke, suspension, and excommunication; the state by fines, imprisonment, and death. Both meet on questions of public morals, and both together constitute civilized human Society and ensure its prosperity.

The root of this theory we find in the New Testament.

In the ancient world religion and politics were blended. Among the Jews religion ruled the state, which was a theocracy. Among the heathen the state ruled religion; the Roman emperor was the supreme pontiff (pontifex maximus), the gods were national, and the priests were servants of the state.

Christianity had at first no official connection with the state. . . .

For three hundred years the Christian church kept aloof from politics, and, while obeying the civil laws and paying tribute, maintained at the same time the higher law of conscience in refusing to comply with idolatrous customs and in professing the faith in the face of death. The early Apologists—Justin Martyr, Tertullian, Lactantius—boldly claimed the freedom of religion as a natural right.

The American System Compared with Other Systems

The American relationship of church and state differs from all previous relationships in Europe and in the colonial period of our history; and yet it rests upon them and reaps the benefit of them all. For history is an organic unit, and American history has its roots in Europe.

1. The American system differs from the ante-Nicene or pre-Constantinian separation of church and state, when the church was indeed, as with us, self-supporting and self-governing, and so far free within, but under persecution from without, being treated as a forbidden religion by the then heathen state. In America the government protects the church in her property and rights without interfering with her internal affairs. By the power of truth and the moral heroism of martyrdom the church converted the Roman Empire and became the mother of Christian states.

2. The American system differs from the hierarchical control of the church over the state, or from priest government, which prevailed in the Middle Ages down to the Reformation, and reached its culmination in the Papacy. It confines the church to her proper spiritual vocation, and leaves the state independent in all the temporal affairs of the nation. The hierarchical theory was suited to the times after the fall of the Roman Empire and the ancient civilization, when the state was a rude military despotism, when the church was the refuge of the people, when the Christian priesthood was in sole possession of learning and had to civilize as well as to evangelize the barbarians of northern and western Europe. By her influence over legislation the church abolished bad laws and customs, introduced benevolent institutions, and created a Christian state controlled by the spirit of justice and humanity and fit for self-government.

3. The American system differs from the Erastian or Caesaro-Papal control of the state over the church, which was obtained in the old Byzantine Empire, and prevails in modern Russia, and in the Protestant states of Europe, where the civil

government protects and supports the church, but at the expense of her dignity and independence, and deprives her of the power of self-government. The Erastian system was based on the assumption that all citizens are also Christians of one creed, but is abnormal in the mixed character of government and people in the modern state. In America, the state has no right whatever to interfere with the affairs of the church, her doctrine, discipline, and worship, and the appointment of ministers. It would be a great calamity if religion were to become subject to our ever-changing politics.

4. The American system differs from the system of toleration, which began in Germany with the Westphalia Treaty, 1648; in England with the Act of Toleration, 1689, and which now prevails over nearly all Europe; of late years, nominally at least, even in Roman Catholic countries, to the very gates of the Vatican, in spite of the protest of the Pope. Toleration exists where the government supports one or more churches, and permits other religious communities under the name of sects (as on the continent), or dissenters and nonconformists (as in England), under certain conditions. In America there are no such distinctions, but only churches or denominations on a footing of perfect equality before the law. To talk about any particular denomination as the church, or the American church, has no meaning, and betrays ignorance or conceit. Such exclusiveness is natural and logical in Romanism, but unnatural, illogical, and contemptible in any other church. The American laws know no such institution as "the church," but only separate and independent organizations.

Toleration is an important step from state-churchism to free-churchism. But it is only a step. There is a very great difference between toleration and liberty. Toleration is a concession, which may be withdrawn; it implies a preference for the ruling form of faith and worship, and a practical disapproval of all other forms. It may be coupled with many restrictions and disabilities. We tolerate what we dislike but cannot alter; we tolerate even a nuisance, if we must. Acts of toleration are wrung from a government by the force of circumstances and the power of a minority too influential to be disregarded.

In our country we ask no toleration for religion and its free exercise, but we claim it as an inalienable right. "It is not toleration," says Judge Cooley, "which is established in our system, but religious equality." Freedom of religion is one of the greatest gifts of God to man, without distinction of race and color. He is the author and lord of conscience, and no power on earth has a right to stand between God and the conscience. A violation of this divine law written in the heart is an assault upon the majesty of God and the image of God in man. Granting the freedom of conscience, we must, by logical necessity, also grant the freedom of its manifestation and exercise in public worship. To concede the first and to deny the second, after the manner of despotic governments, is to imprison the conscience. To be just, the state must either support all or none of the religions of its citizens. Our government supports none, but protects all.

5. Finally—and this we would emphasize as especially important in our time—the American system differs radically and fundamentally from the infidel and red-republican theory of religious freedom. The word freedom is one of the most abused words in the vocabulary. True liberty is a positive force, regulated by law; false liberty is a negative force, a release from restraint. True liberty is the moral power of self-government; the liberty of infidels and anarchists is carnal licentiousness. The American separation of church and state rests on respect for the church; the infidel separation, on indifference and hatred of the church, and of religion itself.

The infidel theory was tried and failed in the first Revolution of France. It began with toleration, and ended with the abolition of Christianity, and with the reign of terror, which in turn prepared the way for military despotism as the only means of saving society from anarchy and ruin. Our infidels and anarchists would reinact this tragedy if they should ever get the power. They openly profess their hatred and contempt of our Sunday-laws, our Sabbaths, our churches, and all our religious institutions and societies. Let us beware of them! The American system grants freedom also to irreligion and infidelity, but only within the limits of the order and safety of society. The destruction of religion would be the destruction of morality and the ruin of the state. Civil liberty requires for its support religious liberty, and cannot prosper without it. Religious liberty is not an empty Sound, but an orderly exercise of religious duties and enjoyment of all its privileges. It is freedom in religion, not freedom from religion; as true civil liberty is freedom in law, and not freedom from law. . . .

Republican institutions in the hands of a virtuous and God-fearing nation are the very best in the world, but in the hands of a corrupt and irreligious people they are the very worst, and the most effective weapons of destruction. An indignant people may rise in rebellion against a cruel tyrant; but who will rise against the tyranny of the people in possession of the ballot-box and the whole machinery of government? Here lies our great danger, and it is increasing every year.

Destroy our churches, close our Sunday-schools, abolish the Lord's Day, and our republic would become an empty shell, and our people would tend to heathenism and barbarism. Christianity is the most powerful factor in our society and the pillar of our institutions. It regulates the family; it enjoins private and public virtue; it builds up moral character; it teaches us to love God supremely, and our neighbor as ourselves; it makes good men and useful citizens; it denounces every vice; it encourages every virtue; it promotes and serves the public welfare; it upholds peace and order. Christianity is the only possible religion for the American people, and with Christianity are bound up all our hopes for the future.

This was strongly felt by Washington, "the father of his country, first in war, first in peace, and first in the hearts of his countrymen"; and no passage in his immortal Farewell Address is more truthful, wise, and worthy of constant remembrance by every American statesman and citizen than that in which he affirms the inseparable connection of religion with morality and national prosperity.

20. Andrew Carnegie's "Gospel of Wealth" (1889)

The problem of our age is the administration of wealth, so that the ties of brotherhood may still bind together the rich and poor in harmonious relationship. The conditions of human life have not only been changed, but revolutionized, within the past few hundred years. In former days there was little difference between the dwelling, dress, food, and environment of the chief and those of his retainers. . . . The contrast between the palace of the millionaire and the cottage of the laborer with us to-day measures the change which has come with civilization.

This change, however, is not to be deplored, but welcomed as highly beneficial. It is well, nay, essential for the progress of the race, that the houses of some should be homes for all that is highest and best in literature and the arts, and for all the refinements of civilization, rather than that none should be so. Much better this great irregularity than universal squalor. Without wealth there can be no Maecenas [Note: a rich Roman patron of the arts]. The "good old times" were not good old times . Neither master nor servant was as well situated then as to day. A relapse to old conditions would be disastrous to both—not the least so to him who serves—and would sweep away civilization with it. . . .

We start, then, with a condition of affairs under which the best interests of the race are promoted, but which inevitably gives wealth to the few. Thus far, accepting conditions as they exist, the situation can be surveyed and pronounced good. The question then arises—and, if the foregoing be correct, it is the only question with which we have to deal—What is the proper mode of administering wealth after the laws upon which civilization is founded have thrown it into the hands of the few? And it is of this great question that I believe I offer the true solution. It will be understood that fortunes are here spoken of, not moderate sums saved by many years of effort, the returns from which are required for the comfortable maintenance and education of families. This is not wealth, but only competence, which it should be the aim of all to acquire.

There are but three modes in which surplus wealth can be disposed of. It can be left to the families of the decedents; or it can be bequeathed for public purposes; or, finally, it can be administered during their lives by its possessors. Under the first and second modes most of the wealth of the world that has reached the few has hitherto been applied. Let us in turn consider each of these modes. The first is the most injudicious. In monarchial countries, the estates and the greatest portion of the wealth are left to the first son, that the vanity of the parent may be gratified by the thought that his name and title are to descend to succeeding generations unimpaired. The condition of this class in Europe to-day teaches the futility of such hopes or ambitions. The successors have become impoverished through their follies or from the fall in the value of land. . . . Why should men leave great fortunes to their children? If this is done from affection, is it not misguided affection? Observation teaches that, generally speaking, it is not well for the children that they should be so burdened. Neither is it well for the state. Beyond providing for the wife and daughters moderate sources of income, and very moderate allowances indeed, if any, for the sons, men may well hesitate, for it is no longer questionable that great sums bequeathed oftener work more for the injury than for the good of the recipients. Wise men will soon conclude that, for the best interests of the members of their families and of the state, such bequests are an improper use of their means. . . .

As to the second mode, that of leaving wealth at death for public uses, it may be said that this is only a means for the disposal of wealth, provided a man is content to wait until he is dead before it becomes of much good in the world. . . . The cases are not few in which the real object sought by the testator is not attained, nor are they few in which his real wishes are thwarted. . . .

The growing disposition to tax more and more heavily large estates left at death is a cheering indication of the growth of a salutary change in public opinion. . . . Of all forms of taxation, this seems the wisest. Men who continue hoarding great sums all their lives, the proper use of which for public ends would work good to the community, should be made to feel that the community, in the form of the state, cannot thus be deprived of its proper share. By taxing estates heavily at death, the state marks its condemnation of the selfish millionaire's unworthy life.

. . . This policy would work powerfully to induce the rich man to attend to the administration of wealth during his life, which is the end that society should always have in view, as being that by far most fruitful for the people....

There remains, then, only one mode of using great fortunes: but in this way we have the true antidote for the temporary unequal distribution of wealth, the reconciliation of the rich and the poor—a reign of harmony—another ideal, differing, indeed from that of the Communist in requiring only the further evolution of existing conditions, not the total overthrow of our civilization. It is founded upon the present most intense individualism, and the race is prepared to put it in practice by degrees whenever it pleases. Under its sway we shall have an ideal state, in which the surplus wealth of the few will become, in the best sense, the property of the many, because administered for the common good, and this wealth, passing through the hands of the few, can be made a much more potent force for the elevation of our race than if it had been distributed in small sums to the people themselves. Even the poorest can be made to see this, and to agree that great sums gathered by some of their fellow-citizens and spent for public purposes, from which the masses reap the principal benefit, are more valuable to them than if scattered among them through the course of many years in trifling amounts. . . .

This, then, is held to be the duty of the man of Wealth: First, to set an example of modest, unostentatious living, shunning display or extravagance; to provide moderately for the legitimate wants of those dependent upon him; and after doing so to consider all surplus revenues which come to him simply as trust funds, which he is called upon to administer, and strictly bound as a matter of duty to administer in the manner which, in his judgment, is best calculated to produce the most beneficial result for the community—the man of wealth thus becoming the sole agent and trustee for his poorer brethren, bringing to their service his superior wisdom, experience, and ability to administer—doing for them better than they would or could do for themselves.

21. Pope Leo XIII's Encyclical *Testem Benevolentiae Nostrae* (1899)

To Our Beloved Son, James Cardinal Gibbons, Cardinal Priest of the Title Sancta Maria, Beyond the Tiber, Archbishop of Baltimore:

LEO XIII, Pope-Beloved Son, Health and Apostolic Blessing: We send to you by this letter a renewed expression of that good will which we have not failed during the course of our pontificate to manifest frequently to you and to your colleagues in the episcopate and to the whole American people, availing ourselves of every opportunity offered us by the progress of your church or whatever you have done for safeguarding and promoting Catholic interests. Moreover, we have often considered and admired the noble gifts of your nation which enable the American people to be alive to every good work which promotes the good of humanity and the splendor of civilization. Although this letter is not intended, as preceding ones, to repeat the words of praise so often spoken, but rather to call attention to some things to be avoided and corrected; still because it is conceived in that same spirit of apostolic charity which has inspired all our letters, we shall expect that you will take it as another proof of our love; the more so because it is intended to suppress certain contentions which have arisen lately among you to the detriment of the peace of many souls.

It is known to you, beloved son, that the biography of Isaac Thomas Hecker, especially through the action of those who under took to translate or interpret it in a foreign language, has excited not a little controversy, on account of certain opinions brought forward concerning the way of leading Christian life.

We, therefore, on account of our apostolic office, having to guard the integrity of the faith and the security of the faithful, are desirous of writing to you more at length concerning this whole matter.

The underlying principle of these new opinions is that, in order to more easily attract those who differ from her, the Church should shape her teachings more in accord with the spirit of the age and relax some of her ancient severity and make some concessions to new opinions. Many think that these concessions should be made not only in regard to ways of living, but even in regard to doctrines which belong to the deposit of the faith. They contend that it would be opportune, in order to gain those who differ from us, to omit certain points of her teaching which are of lesser importance, and to tone down the meaning which the Church has always attached to them. It does not need many words, beloved son, to prove the falsity of these ideas if the nature and origin of the doctrine which the Church proposes are recalled to mind. The Vatican Council says concerning this point: "For the doctrine of faith which God has revealed has not been proposed, like a philosophical invention to be perfected by human ingenuity, but has been delivered as a divine deposit to the Spouse of Christ to be faithfully kept and infallibly declared. Hence that meaning of the sacred dogmas is perpetually to be retained which our Holy Mother, the Church, has once declared, nor is that meaning ever to be departed from under the pretense or pretext of a deeper comprehension of them." -*Constitutio de Fide Catholica*, Chapter iv.

We cannot consider as altogether blameless the silence which purposely leads to the omission or neglect of some of the principles of Christian doctrine, for all the principles come from the same Author and Master, "the Only Begotten Son, Who is in the bosom of the Father."-John i, 18. They are adapted to all times and all nations, as is clearly seen from the words of our Lord to His apostles: "Going, therefore, teach all nations; teaching them to observe all things whatsoever I have commanded you, and behold, I am with you all days, even to the end of the world."-Matt. xxviii, 19. Concerning this point the Vatican Council says: "All those things are to be believed with divine and catholic faith which are contained in the Word of God, written or handed down, and which the Church, either by a solemn judgment or by her ordinary and universal magisterium, proposes for belief as having been divinely revealed."-*Const. de Fide*, Chapter iii.

Let it be far from anyone's mind to suppress for any reason any doctrine that has been handed down. Such a policy would tend rather to separate Catholics from the Church than to bring in those who differ. There is nothing closer to our heart than to have those who are separated from the fold of Christ return to it, but in no other way than the way pointed out by Christ.

The rule of life laid down for Catholics is not of such a nature that it cannot accommodate itself to the exigencies of various times and places. (VOL. XXIV-13.) The Church has, guided by her Divine Master, a kind and merciful spirit, for which reason from the very beginning she has been what St. Paul said of himself: "I became all things to all men that I might save all."

History proves clearly that the Apostolic See, to which has been entrusted the mission not only of teaching but of governing the whole Church, has continued "in one and the same doctrine, one and the same sense, and one and the same judgment,"-*Const. de Fide*, Chapter iv.

But in regard to ways of living she has been accustomed to so yield that, the divine principle of morals being kept intact, she has never neglected to accommodate herself to the character and genius of the nations which she embraces.

Who can doubt that she will act in this same spirit again if the salvation of souls requires it? In this matter the Church must be the judge, not private men who are often deceived by the appearance of right. In this, all who wish to escape the blame of our predecessor, Pius the Sixth, must concur. He condemned as injurious to the Church and the spirit of God who guides her the doctrine contained in proposition lxxviii of the Synod of Pistoia, "that the discipline made and approved by the Church should be submitted to examination, as if the Church could frame a code of laws useless or heavier than human liberty can bear."

But, beloved son, in this present matter of which we are speaking, there is even a greater danger and a more manifest opposition to Catholic doctrine and discipline in that opinion of the lovers of novelty, according to which they hold such liberty should be allowed in the Church, that her supervision and watchfulness being in some sense lessened, allowance be granted the faithful, each one to follow out more freely the leading of his own mind and the trend of his own proper activity. They are of opinion that such liberty has its counterpart in the newly given civil freedom which is now the right and the foundation of almost every secular state.

In the apostolic letters concerning the constitution of states, addressed by us to the bishops of the whole Church, we discussed this point at length; and there set forth the difference existing between the Church, which is a divine society, and all other social human organizations which depend simply on free will and choice of men.

It is well, then, to particularly direct attention to the opinion which serves as the argument in behalf of this greater liberty sought for and recommended to Catholics.

It is alleged that now the Vatican decree concerning the infallible teaching authority of the Roman Pontiff having been proclaimed that nothing further on that score can give any solicitude, and accordingly, since that has been safeguarded and put beyond question a wider and freer field both for thought and action lies open to each one. But such reasoning is evidently faulty, since, if we are to come to any conclusion from the infallible teaching authority of the Church, it should rather be that no one should wish to depart from it, and moreover that the minds of all being leavened and directed thereby, greater security from private error would be enjoyed by all. And further, those who avail themselves of such a way of reasoning seem to depart seriously from the over-ruling wisdom of the Most High—which wisdom, since it was pleased to set forth by most solemn decision the authority and supreme teaching rights of this Apostolic See—willed that decision precisely in order to safeguard the minds of the Church's children from the dangers of these present times.

These dangers, viz., the confounding of license with liberty, the passion for discussing and pouring contempt upon any possible subject, the assumed right to hold whatever opinions one pleases upon any subject and to set them forth in print to the world, have so wrapped minds in darkness that there is now a greater need of the Church's teaching office than ever before, lest people become unmindful both of conscience and of duty.

We, indeed, have no thought of rejecting everything that modern industry and study has produced; so far from it that we welcome to the patrimony of truth and to an ever-widening scope of public well-being whatsoever helps toward the progress of learning and virtue. Yet all this, to be of any solid benefit, nay, to have a real existence and growth, can only be on the condition of recognizing the wisdom and authority of the Church.

Coming now to speak of the conclusions which have been deduced from the above opinions, and for them, we readily believe there was no thought of wrong or guile, yet the things themselves certainly merit some degree of suspicion. First, all external guidance is set aside for those souls who are striving after Christian perfection as being superfluous or indeed, not useful in any sense —the contention being that the Holy Spirit pours richer and more abundant graces than formerly upon the souls of the faithful, so that without human intervention He teaches and guides them by some hidden instinct of His own. Yet it is the sign of no small over-confidence to desire to measure and determine the mode of the Divine communication to mankind, since it wholly depends upon His own good pleasure, and He is a most generous dispenser of his own gifts. "The Spirit breatheth whereso He listeth."-John iii, 8.

"And to each one of us grace is given according to the measure of the giving of Christ."-Eph. iv, 7.

And shall any one who recalls the history of the apostles, the faith of the nascent church, the trials and deaths of the martyrs—and, above all, those olden times, so fruitful in saints—dare to measure our age with these, or affirm that they received less of the divine outpouring from the Spirit of Holiness? Not to dwell upon this point, there is no one who calls in question the truth that the Holy Spirit does work by a secret descent into the souls of the just and that He stirs them alike by warnings and impulses, since unless this were the case all outward defense and authority would be unavailing. "For if any persuades himself that he can give assent to saving, that is, to gospel truth when proclaimed, without any illumination of the Holy Spirit, who give's unto all sweetness both to assent and to hold, such an one is deceived by a heretical spirit."-From the Second Council of Orange, Canon 7.

Moreover, as experience shows, these monitions and impulses of the Holy Spirit are for the most part felt through the medium of the aid and light of an external teaching authority.

To quote St. Augustine. "He (the Holy Spirit) co-operates to the fruit gathered from the good trees, since He externally waters and cultivates them by the outward ministry of men, and yet of Himself bestows the inward increase."-*De Gratia Christi*, Chapter xix. This, indeed, belongs to the ordinary law of God's loving providence that as He has decreed that men for the most part shall be saved by the ministry also of men, so has He wished that those whom He calls to the higher planes of holiness should be led thereto by men; hence St. Chrysostom declares we are taught of God through the instrumentality of men.-Homily I in Inscrib. Altar. Of this a striking example is given us in the very first days of the Church.

For though Saul, intent upon blood and slaughter, had heard the voice of our Lord Himself and had asked, "What dost Thou wish me to do?" yet he was bidden to enter Damascus and search for Ananias. Acts ix: "Enter the city and it shall be there told to thee what thou must do."

Nor can we leave out of consideration the truth that those who are striving after perfection, since by that fact they walk in no beaten or well-known path, are the most liable to stray, and hence have greater need than others of a teacher and guide. Such guidance has ever obtained in the Church; it has been the universal teaching of those who throughout the ages have been eminent for wisdom and sanctity—and hence to reject it would be to commit one's self to a belief at once rash and dangerous.

A thorough consideration of this point, in the supposition that no exterior guide is granted such souls, will make us see the difficulty of locating or determining the direction and application of that more abundant influx of the Holy Spirit so greatly extolled by innovators. To practice virtue there is absolute need of the assistance of the Holy Spirit, yet we find those who are fond of novelty giving an unwarranted importance to the natural virtues, as though they better responded to the customs and necessities of the times and that having these as his outfit man becomes more ready to act and more strenuous in action. It is not easy to understand how persons possessed of Christian wisdom can either prefer natural to supernatural virtues or attribute to them a greater efficacy and fruifulness. Can it be that nature conjoined with grace is weaker than when left to herself?

Can it be that those men illustrious for sanctity, whom the Church distinguishes and openly pays homage to, were deficient, came short in the order of nature and its endowments, because they excelled in Christian strength? And although it be allowed at times to wonder at acts worthy of admiration which are the outcome of natural virtue—is there anyone at all endowed simply with an outfit of natural virtue? Is there any one not tried by mental anxiety, and this in no light degree? Yet ever to master such, as also to preserve in its entirety the law of the natural order, requires an assistance from on high. These single notable acts to which we have alluded will frequently upon a closer investigation be found to exhibit the appearance rather than the reality of virtue. Grant that it is virtue, unless we would "run in vain" and be unmindful of that eternal bliss which a good God in his mercy has destined for us, of what avail are natural virtues unless seconded by the gift of divine grace? Hence St. Augustine well says: "Wonderful is the strength, and swift the course, but outside the true path." For as the nature of man, owing to the primal fault, is inclined to evil and dishonor, yet by the help of grace is raised up, is borne along with a new greatness and strength, so, too, virtue, which is not the product of nature alone, but of grace also, is made fruitful unto everlasting life and takes on a more strong and abiding character.

This overesteem of natural virtue finds a method of expression in assuming to divide all virtues in active and passive, and it is alleged that whereas passive virtues found better place in past times, our age is to be characterized by the active. That such a division and distinction cannot be maintained is patent—for there is not, nor can there be, merely passive virtue. "Virtue," says St. Thomas Aquinas, "designates the perfection of some faculty, but end of such faculty is an act, and an act of virtue is naught else than the good use of free will," acting, that is to say, under the grace of God if the act be one of supernatural virtue.

He alone could wish that some Christian virtues be adapted to certain times and different ones for other times who is unmindful of the apostle's words: "That those whom He foreknew, He predestined to be made conformable to the image of His Son."- Romans viii, 29. Christ is the teacher and the exemplar of all sanctity, and to His standard must all those conform who wish for eternal life. Nor does Christ know any change as the ages pass, "for He is yesterday and to-day and the same forever."-Hebrews xiii, 8. To the men of all ages was the precept given: "Learn of Me, because I am meek and humble of heart."-Matt. xi, 29.

To every age has He been made manifest to us as obedient even unto death; in every age the apostle's dictum has its force: "Those who are Christ's have crucified their flesh with its vices and concupiscences." Would to God that more nowadays practiced these virtues in the degree of the saints of past times, who in humility, obedience and self-restraint were powerful "in word and in deed" —to the great advantage not only of religion, but of the state and the public welfare.

From this disregard of the angelical virtues, erroneously styled passive, the step was a short one to a contempt of the religious life which has in some degree taken hold of minds. That such a value is generally held by the upholders of new views, we infer from certain statements concerning the vows which religious orders take. They say vows are alien to the spirit of our times, in that they limit the bounds of human liberty; that they are more suitable to weak than to strong minds; that so far from making for human perfection and the good of human organization, they are hurtful to both; but that this is as false as possible from the practice and the doctrine of the Church is clear, since she has always given the very highest approval to the religious method of life; nor without good cause, for those who under the divine call have freely embraced that state of life did not content themselves with the observance of precepts, but, going forward to the evangelical counsels, showed themselves ready and valiant soldiers of Christ. Shall we judge this to be a characteristic of weak minds, or shall we say that it is useless or hurtful to a more perfect state of life?

Those who so bind themselves by the vows of religion, far from having suffered a loss of liberty, enjoy that fuller and freer kind, that liberty, namely, by which Christ hath made us free. And this further view of theirs, namely, that the religious life is either entirely useless or of little service to the Church, besides being injurious to the religious orders cannot be the opinion of anyone who has read the annals of the Church. Did not your country, the United States, derive the beginnings both of faith and of culture from the children of these religious families? to one of whom but very lately, a thing greatly to your praise, you have decreed that a statue be publicly erected. And even at the present time wherever the religious families are found, how speedy and yet how fruitful a harvest of good works do they not bring forth! How very many leave home and seek strange lands to impart the truth of the gospel and to widen the bounds of civilization; and this they do with the greatest cheerfulness amid manifold dangers! Out of their number not less, indeed, than from the rest of the clergy, the Christian world finds the preachers of God's word, the directors of conscience, the teachers of youth and the Church itself the examples of all sanctity.

Nor should any difference of praise be made between those who follow the active state of life and those others who, charmed with solitude, give themselves to prayer and bodily mortification. And how much, indeed, of good report these have merited, and do merit, is known surely to all who do not forget that the "continual prayer of the just man" avails to placate and to bring down the blessings of heaven when to such prayers bodily mortification is added.

But if there be those who prefer to form one body without the obligation of the vows let them pursue such a course. It is not new in the Church, nor in any wise censurable. Let them be careful, however, not to set forth such a state above that of religious orders. But rather, since mankind are more disposed at the present time to indulge themselves in pleasures, let those be held in greater esteem "who having left all things have followed Christ."

Finally, not to delay too long, it is stated that the way and method hitherto in use among Catholics for bringing back those who have fallen away from the Church should be left aside and another one chosen, in which matter it will suffice to note that it is not the part of prudence to neglect that which antiquity in its long experience has approved and which is also taught by apostolic authority. The scriptures teach us that it is the duty of all to be solicitous for the salvation of one's neighbor, according to the power and position of each. The faithful do this by religiously discharging the duties of their state of life, by the uprightness of their conduct, by their works of Christian charity and by earnest and continuous prayer to God. On the other hand, those who belong to the clergy should do this by an enlightened fulfillment of their preaching ministry, by the pomp and splendor of ceremonies especially by setting forth that sound form of doctrine which Saint Paul inculcated upon Titus and Timothy. But if, among the different ways of preaching the word of God that one sometimes seems to be preferable, which directed to non-Catholics, not in churches, but in some suitable place, in such wise that controversy is not sought, but friendly conference, such a method is certainly without fault. But let those who undertake such ministry be set apart by the authority of the bishops and let them be men whose science and virtue has been previously ascertained. For we think that there are many in your country who are separated from Catholic truth more by ignorance than by ill-will, who might perchance more easily be drawn to the one fold of Christ if this truth be set forth to them in a friendly and familiar way.

From the foregoing it is manifest, beloved son, that we are not able to give approval to those views which, in their collective sense, are called by some "Americanism." But if by this name are to be understood certain endowments of mind which belong to the American people, just as other characteristics belong to various other nations, and if, moreover, by it is designated your political condition and the laws and customs by which you are governed, there is no reason to take exception to the name. But if this is to be so understood that the doctrines which have been adverted to above are not only indicated, but exalted, there can be no manner of doubt that our venerable brethren, the bishops of America, would be the first to repudiate and condemn it as being most injurious to themselves and to their country. For it would give rise to the suspicion that there are among you some who conceive and would have the Church in America to be different from what it is in the rest of the world.

But the true church is one, as by unity of doctrine, so by unity of government, and she is catholic also. Since God has placed the center and foundation of unity in the chair of Blessed Peter, she is rightly called the Roman Church, for "where Peter is, there is the church." Wherefore, if anybody wishes to be considered a real Catholic, he ought to be able to say from his heart the selfsame words which Jerome addressed to Pope Damasus: "I, acknowledging no other leader than Christ, am bound in fellowship with Your Holiness; that is, with the chair of Peter. I know that the church was built upon him as its rock, and that whosoever gathereth not with you, scattereth."

We having thought it fitting, beloved son, in view of your high office, that this letter should be addressed specially to you. It will also be our care to see that copies are sent to the bishops of the United States, testifying again that love by which we embrace your whole country, a country which in past times has done so much for the cause of religion, and which will by the Divine assistance continue to do still greater things. To you, and to all the faithful of America, we grant most lovingly, as a pledge of Divine assistance, our apostolic benediction.

Given at Rome, from St. Peter's, the 22nd day of January, 1899, and the thirty-first of our pontificate.

22. Booker T. Washington's "The Religious Life of the Negro" Speech (1905)

In everything that I have been able to read about the religious life of the Negro, it has seemed to me that writers have been too much disposed to treat of it as something fixed and unchanging. They have not sufficiently emphasized the fact that the Negro people, in respect to their religious life, have been, almost since they landed in America, in a process of change and growth.

The Negro came to America with the pagan ideas of his African ancestors; he acquired under slavery a number of Christian ideas, and at the present time he is slowly learning what those ideas mean in practical life. He is learning, not merely what Christians believe, but what they must do to be Christians.

The religious ideas which the Negroes brought with them to America from Africa were the fragments of a system of thought and custom, which, in its general features, is common to most barbarous people. What we call "fetishism" is, I suppose, merely the childish way of looking at and explaining the world, which did not, in the case of the people of West Africa, preclude a belief in the one true God, although He was regarded by them as far away and not interested in the little affairs of men.

But the peculiarity of their primitive religion, as I have learned from a very interesting book written by one who has been many years a missionary in Africa, consists in this, that it sought for its adherents a purely "physical salvation."

In the religion of the native African there was, generally speaking, no place of future reward or punishment, no heaven and no hell, as we are accustomed to conceive them. For this reason, the Negro had little sense of sin. He was not tortured by doubts and fears, which are so common and, we sometimes feel, so necessary a part of the religious experiences of Christians. The evils he knew were present and physical.

During the period of servitude in the New World, the Negro race did not wholly forget the traditions and habits of thought that it brought from Africa. But it added to its ancestral stock certain new ideas.

Slavery, with all its disadvantages, gave the Negro race, by way of recompense, one great consolation, namely, the Christian religion and the hope and belief in a future life. The slave, to whom on this side of the grave the door of hope seemed closed, learned from Christianity to lift his face from earth to heaven, and that made his burden lighter. In the end, the hope and aspiration of the race in slavery fixed themselves on the vision of the resurrection, with its "long white robes and golden slippers."

This hope and this aspiration, which are the theme of so many of the old Negro hymns, found expression in the one institution that slavery permitted to the Negro people—the Negro Church. It was natural and inevitable that the Negro Church, coming into existence as it did under slavery, should permit the religious life of the Negro to express itself in ways almost wholly detached from morality. There was little in slavery to encourage the sense of personal responsibility.

The attitude of some Negro communities in this respect is very clearly illustrated in the story of the slave who was a "professor" of religion, in the current phrase of the time, but made his master so much trouble by his persistence in certain immoral practices that it was finally necessary to call in a clergyman to try to reform him. The clergyman made the attempt, and sought to bring the terrors of the law to bear upon the slave's conscience.

"Look yeah, Massa," said the culprit, "don't de Scripture say, Dem who b'lieves an' is baptize' shall be saved?"

"Certainly," was the reply, and the clergyman went on to explain the passage to him, but the slave interrupted him again.

"Jus' you tell me now, Massa, don't de good book say dese words: 'Dem as b'lieve and is baptize' shall be saved?'"

"Yes, but—"

"Dat's all I want to know, sar. Now, wat's de use of talkin' to me. You ain't ago'n to make me believe wat de blessed Lord say ain't so, not if you tries forever."

This illustrates one of the difficulties that we have to contend with to-day. In our Tuskegee Negro Conference, we have constantly to insist that the people draw moral distinctions within the limits of their own communities, that they get rid of immoral ministers and school-teachers, and refuse to associate with people whom they know to be guilty of immoral practices.

It has been said that the trouble with the Negro Church is that it is too emotional. It seems to me that what the Negro Church needs is a more definite connection with the social and moral life of the Negro people. Could this connection be effected in a large degree, it would give to the movement for the upbuilding of the race the force and inspiration of a religious motive. It would give to the Negro religion more of that missionary spirit, the spirit of service, that it needs to purge it of some of the worst elements that still cling to it.

The struggle to attain a higher level of living, to get land, to build a home, to give their children an education, just because it demands more earnestness and steadfastness of purpose, gives a steadiness and a moral significance to the religious life, which is the thing the Negro people need at present.

A large element of the Negro Church must be recalled from its apocalyptic vision back to the earth; the members of the Negro race must be taught that mere religious emotion that is guided by no definite idea and is devoted to no purpose is vain.

It is encouraging to notice that the leaders of the different denominations of the Negro Church are beginning to recognize the force of the criticism made against it, and that, under their leadership, conditions are changing. In one of these denominations, the A. M. E. Zion Church alone, $2,000,000 was raised, from 1900 to 1904, for the general educational, moral and material improvement of the race. Of this sum, $1,000,000 was contributed for educational purposes alone. The A. M. E. Church and the Baptists did proportionally as well.

The mere fact that this amount of money has been raised for general educational purposes, in addition to the sum expended in each local community for teachers, for building schoolhouses and supplementing the State appropriations for schools, shows that the colored people have spent less money in saloons and dispensaries; that less has been squandered on toys and gimcracks that are of no use. It shows that there has been more saving, more thought for the future, more appreciation of the real value of life.

In this connection, it is well to have in mind that the industrial schools have performed a great and useful service, in so far as they have impressed upon the young men who go out from these schools as preachers the importance of learning a trade, something of agriculture, so that they can give the members of their congregations an example of industrial thrift.

At Tuskegee Institute, we insist upon the importance of service. Every student in this department is expected to do, in connection with his other work either as a teacher or preacher, some part of the social and religious work that is carried on under the direction of the Bible Training School in the surrounding country. We are seeking to imbue these young men who are going forth as leaders of their people with the feeling that the great task of uplifting the race, though it may be for others merely a work of humanity, for them, and every other member of the Negro race, is a work of religion.

In this great modern world, where every individual has so many interests and life is so complicated there is a tendency to let religion and life drift apart. I meet men every day who, honest and upright though they be, have lost in their daily lives this connection with religion, and are striving vainly to regain it. There is no one great dominating motive in their lives which enters into every task and gives it significance and zest.

It is one of the compensations which hardships bring, that the race problem is a thing so real and so present to the Negro people that it enters, as a motive, into everything they do. It is this that makes it possible for them to realize that the acts of every individual have an importance far beyond the measure in which they make or mar his or her personal fortunes.

So soon as a man, white or black, really learns to comprehend that fact, he will cease to whine and complain, and he will be content to do his best, humble though it be, to improve his own condition, and to help his less fortunate fellows.

Slowly but surely, and in ever larger numbers, the members of my race are learning that lesson; they are realizing that God has assigned to their race a man's part in the task of civilization; they are learning to understand their duty, and to face uncomplainingly and with confidence the destiny that awaits them.

23. Humanist Manifesto (1933)

The time has come for widespread recognition of the radical changes in religious beliefs throughout the modern world. The time is past for mere revision of traditional attitudes. Science and economic change have disrupted the old beliefs. Religions the world over are under the necessity of coming to terms with new conditions created by a vastly increased knowledge and experience. In every field of human activity, the vital movement is now in the direction of a candid and explicit humanism. In order that religious humanism may be better understood we, the undersigned, desire to make certain affirmations which we believe the facts of our contemporary life demonstrate.

There is great danger of a final, and we believe fatal, identification of the word religion with doctrines and methods which have lost their significance and which are powerless to solve the problem of human living in the Twentieth Century. Religions have always been means for realizing the highest values of life. Their end has been accomplished through the interpretation of the total environing situation (theology or world view), the sense of values resulting therefrom (goal or ideal), and the technique (cult), established for realizing the satisfactory life. A change in any of these factors results in alteration of the outward forms of religion. This fact explains the changefulness of religions through the centuries. But through all changes religion itself remains constant in its quest for abiding values, an inseparable feature of human life.

Today man's larger understanding of the universe, his scientific achievements, and deeper appreciation of brotherhood, have created a situation which requires a new statement of the means and purposes of religion. Such a vital, fearless, and frank religion capable of furnishing adequate social goals and personal satisfactions may appear to many people as a complete break with the past. While this age does owe a vast debt to the traditional religions, it is none the less obvious that any religion that can hope to be a synthesizing and dynamic force for today must be shaped for the needs of this age. To establish such a religion is a major necessity of the present. It is a responsibility which rests upon this generation. We therefore affirm the following:

FIRST: Religious humanists regard the universe as self-existing and not created.

SECOND: Humanism believes that man is a part of nature and that he has emerged as a result of a continuous process.

THIRD: Holding an organic view of life, humanists find that the traditional dualism of mind and body must be rejected.

FOURTH: Humanism recognizes that man's religious culture and civilization, as clearly depicted by anthropology and history, are the product of a gradual development due to his interaction with his natural environment and with his social heritage. The individual born into a particular culture is largely molded by that culture.

FIFTH: Humanism asserts that the nature of the universe depicted by modern science makes unacceptable any supernatural or cosmic guarantees of human values. Obviously humanism does not deny the possibility of realities as yet undiscovered, but it does insist that the way to determine the existence and value of any and all realities is by means of intelligent inquiry and by the assessment of their relations to human needs. Religion must formulate its hopes and plans in the light of the scientific spirit and method.

SIXTH: We are convinced that the time has passed for theism, deism, modernism, and the several varieties of "new thought".

SEVENTH: Religion consists of those actions, purposes, and experiences which are humanly significant. Nothing human is alien to the religious. It includes labor, art, science, philosophy, love, friendship, recreation—all that is in its degree expressive of intelligently satisfying human living. The distinction between the sacred and the secular can no longer be maintained.

EIGHTH: Religious Humanism considers the complete realization of human personality to be the end of man's life and seeks its development and fulfillment in the here and now. This is the explanation of the humanist's social passion.

NINTH: In the place of the old attitudes involved in worship and prayer the humanist finds his religious emotions expressed in a heightened sense of personal life and in a cooperative effort to promote social well-being.

TENTH: It follows that there will be no uniquely religious emotions and attitudes of the kind hitherto associated with belief in the supernatural.

ELEVENTH: Man will learn to face the crises of life in terms of his knowledge of their naturalness and probability. Reasonable and manly attitudes will be fostered by education and supported by custom. We assume that humanism will take the path of social and mental hygiene and discourage sentimental and unreal hopes and wishful thinking.

TWELFTH: Believing that religion must work increasingly for joy in living, religious humanists aim to foster the creative in man and to encourage achievements that add to the satisfactions of life.

THIRTEENTH: Religious humanism maintains that all associations and institutions exist for the fulfillment of human life. The intelligent evaluation, transformation, control, and direction of such associations and institutions with a view to the enhancement of human life is the purpose and program of humanism. Certainly religious institutions, their ritualistic forms, ecclesiastical methods, and communal activities must be reconstituted as rapidly as experience allows, in order to function effectively in the modern world.

FOURTEENTH: The humanists are firmly convinced that existing acquisitive and profit-motivated society has shown itself to be inadequate and that a radical change in methods, controls, and motives must be instituted. A socialized and cooperative economic order must be established to the end that the equitable distribution of the means of life be possible. The goal of humanism is a free and universal society in which people voluntarily and intelligently cooperate for the common good. Humanists demand a shared life in a shared world.

FIFTEENTH AND LAST: We assert that humanism will: (a) affirm life rather than deny it; (b) seek to elicit the possibilities of life, not flee from them; and (c) endeavor to establish the conditions of a satisfactory life for all, not merely for the few. By this positive morale and intention humanism will be guided, and from this perspective and alignment the techniques and efforts of humanism will flow.

So stand the theses of religious humanism. Though we consider the religious forms and ideas of our fathers no longer adequate, the quest for the good life is still the central task for mankind. Man is at last becoming aware that he alone is responsible for the realization of the world of his dreams, that he has within himself the power for its achievement. He must set intelligence and will to the task.

24. Economic Justice for All: A Pastoral Letter on Catholic Social Teaching and the U.S. Economy (1986)

Introduction

Brothers and Sisters in Christ:

1. We are believers called to follow Our Lord Jesus Christ and proclaim his Gospel in the midst of a complex and powerful economy. This reality poses both opportunities and responsibilities for Catholics in the United States. Our faith calls us to measure this economy, not by what it produces but also by how it touches human life and whether it protects or undermines the dignity of the human person. Economic decisions have human consequences and moral content; they help or hurt people, strengthen or weaken family life, advance or diminish the quality of justice in our land.

2. This is why we have written *Economic Justice for All: A Pastoral Letter on Catholic Social Teaching and the U.S. Economy*. This letter is a personal invitation to Catholics to use the resources of our faith, the strength of our economy, and the opportunities of our democracy to shape a society that better protects the dignity and basic rights of our sisters and brothers, both in this land and around the world.

3. This pastoral letter has been a work of careful inquiry, wide consultation, and prayerful discernment. The letter has been greatly enriched by this process of listening and refinement. We offer this introductory pastoral message to Catholics in the United States seeking to live their faith in the marketplace—in homes, offices, factories, and schools; on farms and ranches; in boardrooms and union halls; in service agencies and legislative chambers. We seek to explain why we wrote the pastoral letter, to introduce its major themes, and to share our hopes for the dialogue and action it might generate.

Why We Write

4. We write to share our teaching, to raise questions, to challenge one another to live our faith in the world. We write as heirs of the biblical prophets who summon us "to do right, and to love goodness, and to walk humbly with your God" (Mi. 6:8). We write as followers of Jesus who told us in the Sermon on the Mount: "Blessed are the poor in spirit .... Blessed are the meek .... Blessed are they who hunger and thirst for righteousness .... You are the salt of the earth .... You are the light of the world" (Mt. 5:1-6, 13-14). These words challenge us not only as believers but also as consumers, citizens, workers, and owners. In the parable of the Last Judgment, Jesus said, "For I was hungry and you gave me food, I was thirsty and you gave me drink .... As often as you did it for one of my least brothers, you did it for me" (Mt. 25:35-40). The challenge for us is to discover in our own place and time what it means to be "poor in spirit" and "the salt of the earth" and what it means to serve "the least among us" and to "hunger and thirst for righteousness."

5. Followers of Christ must avoid a tragic separation between faith and everyday life. They can neither shirk their earthly duties nor, as the Second Vatican Council declared, "immerse [them]selves in earthly activities as if these latter were utterly foreign to religion, and religion were nothing more than the fulfillment of acts of worship and the observance of a few moral obligations" (*Pastoral Constitution on the Church in the Modern World,* no. 43).

6. Economic life raises important social and moral questions for each of us and for the society as a whole. Like family life, economic life is one of the chief areas where we live out our faith, love our neighbor, confront temptation, fulfill God's creative design, and achieve holiness. Our economic activity in factory, field, office, or shop feeds our families—or feeds our anxieties. It exercises our talents—or wastes them. It raises our hopes—or crushes them. It brings us into cooperation with others—or sets us at odds. The Second Vatican Council instructs us "to preach the message of Christ in such a way that the light of the Gospel will shine on all activities of the faithful" (*Pastoral Constitution*, no. 43). In this case, we are trying to look at economic life through the eyes of faith, applying traditional church teaching to the U.S. economy.

7. In our letter, we write as pastors, not public officials. We speak as moral teachers, not economic technicians. We seek not to make some political or ideological point but to lift up the human and ethical dimensions of economic life, aspects too often neglected in public discussion. We bring to this task a dual heritage of Catholic social teaching and traditional American values.

8. As Catholics, we are heirs of a long tradition of thought and action on the moral dimensions of economic activity. The life and words of Jesus and the teachings of his Church call us to serve those in need and to work actively for social and economic justice. As a community of believers, we know that our faith is tested by the quality of justice among us, that we can best measure our life together by how the poor and the vulnerable are treated. This is not a new concern for us. It is as old as the Hebrew prophets, as compelling as the Sermon on the Mount, and as current as the powerful voice of Pope John Paul II defending the dignity of the human person.

9. As Americans, we are grateful for the gift of freedom and committed to the dream of "liberty and justice for all." This nation, blessed with extraordinary resources, has provided an unprecedented standard of living for millions of people. We are proud of the strength, productivity, and creativity of our economy, but we also remember those who have been left behind in our progress. We believe that we honor our history best by working for the day when all our sisters and brothers share adequately in the American dream.

10. As bishops, in proclaiming the Gospel for these times we also manage institutions, balance budgets, meet payrolls. In this we see the human face of our economy. We feel the hurts and hopes of our people. We feel the pain of our sisters and brothers who are poor, unemployed, homeless, living on the edge. The poor and vulnerable are on our doorsteps, in our parishes, in our service agencies, and in our shelters. We see too much hunger and injustice, too much suffering and despair, both in our country and around the world.

11. As pastors, we also see the decency, generosity, and vulnerability of our people. We see the struggles of ordinary families to make ends meet and to provide a better future for their children. We know the desire of managers, professionals, and business people to shape what they do by what they believe. It is the faith, goodwill, and generosity of our people that gives us hope as we write this letter.

Principal Themes of the Pastoral Letter

12. The pastoral letter is not a blueprint for the American economy. It does not embrace any particular theory of how the economy works, nor does it attempt to resolve disputes between different schools of economic thought. Instead, our letter turns to Scripture and to the social teaching of the

Church. There, we discover what our economic life must serve, what standards it must meet. Let us examine some of these basic moral principles.

13. Every economic decision and institution must be judged in light of whether it protects or undermines the dignity of the human person. The pastoral letter begins with the human person. We believe the person is sacred—the clearest reflection of God among us. Human dignity comes from God, not from nationality, race, sex, economic status, or any human accomplishment. We judge any economic system by what it does "for" and to people and by how it permits all to "participate" in it. The economy should serve people, not the other way around.

14. Human dignity can be realized and protected only in community. In our teaching, the human person is not only sacred but social. How we organize our society—in economics and politics, in law and policy—directly affects human dignity and the capacity of individuals to grow in community. The obligation to "love our neighbor" has an individual dimension, but it also requires a broader social commitment to the common good. We have many partial ways to measure and debate the health of our economy: Gross National Product, per capita income, stock market prices, and so forth. The Christian vision of economic life looks beyond them all and asks, Does economic life enhance or threaten our life together as a community?

15. All people have a right to participate in the economic life of society. Basic justice demands that people be assured a minimum level of participation in the economy. It is wrong for a person or a group to be excluded unfairly or to be unable to participate or contribute to the economy. For example, people who are both able and willing, but cannot get a job are deprived of the participation that is so vital to human development. For, it is through employment that most individuals and families meet their material needs, exercise their talents, and have an opportunity to contribute to the larger community. Such participation has a special significance in our tradition because we believe that it is a means by which we join in carrying forward God's creative activity.

16. All members of society have a special obligation to the poor and vulnerable. From the Scriptures and church teaching, we learn that the justice of a society is tested by the treatment of the poor. The justice that was the sign of God's covenant with Israel was measured by how the poor and unprotected—the widow, the orphan, and the stranger—were treated. The kingdom that Jesus proclaimed in his word and ministry excludes no one. Throughout Israel's history and in early Christianity, the poor are agents of God's transforming power. "The Spirit of the Lord is upon me, therefore he has anointed me. He has sent me to bring glad tidings to the poor" (Lk. 4:18). This was Jesus's first public utterance. Jesus takes the side of those most in need. In the Last Judgment, so dramatically described in St. Matthew's Gospel, we are told that we will be judged according to how we respond to the hungry, the thirsty, the naked, the stranger. As followers of Christ, we are challenged to make a fundamental "option for the poor"—to speak for the voiceless, to defend the defenseless, to assess life styles, policies, and social institutions in terms of their impact on the poor. This "option for the poor" does not mean pitting one group against another, but rather, strengthening the whole community by assisting those who are the most vulnerable. As Christians, we are called to respond to the needs of all our brothers and sisters, but those with the greatest needs require the greatest response.

17. Human rights are the minimum conditions for life in community. In Catholic teaching, human rights include not only civil and political rights but also economic rights. As Pope John XXIII declared, "all people have a right to life, food, clothing, shelter, rest, medical care, education, and employment." This means that when people are without a chance to earn a living, and must go hungry and homeless, they are being denied basic rights. Society must ensure that these rights are protected. In this way, we will ensure that the minimum conditions of economic justice are met for all our sisters and brothers.

18. Society as a whole, acting through public and private institutions, has the moral responsibility to enhance human dignity and protect human rights. In addition to the clear responsibility of private institutions, government has an essential responsibility in this area. This does not mean that government has the primary or exclusive role, but it does have a positive moral responsibility in safeguarding human rights and ensuring that the minimum conditions of human dignity are met for all. In a democracy, government is a means by which we can act together to protect what is important to us and to promote our common values.

19. These six moral principles are not the only ones presented in the pastoral letter, but they give an overview of the moral vision that we are trying to share. This vision of economic life cannot exist in a vacuum; it must be translated into concrete measures. Our pastoral letter spells out some specific applications of Catholic moral principles. We call for a new national commitment to full employment. We say it is a social and moral scandal that one of every seven Americans is poor, and we call for concerted efforts to eradicate poverty. The fulfillment of the basic needs of the poor is of the highest priority. We urge that all economic policies be evaluated in light of their impact on the life and stability of the family. We support measures to halt the loss of family farms and to resist the growing concentration in the ownership of agricultural resources. We specify ways in which the United States can do far more to relieve the plight of poor nations and assist in their development. We also reaffirm church teaching on the rights of workers, collective bargaining, private property, subsidiarity, and equal opportunity.

20. We believe that the recommendations in our letter are reasonable and balanced. In analyzing the economy, we reject ideological extremes and start from the fact that ours is a "mixed" economy, the product of a long history of reform and adjustment. We know that some of our specific history as

recommendations are controversial. As bishops, we do not claim to make these prudential judgments with the same kind of authority that marks our declarations of principle. But we feel obliged to teach by example how Christians can undertake concrete analysis and make specific judgments on economic issues. The Church's teachings cannot be left at the level of appealing generalities.

21. In the pastoral letter, we suggest that the time has come for a "New American Experiment"—to implement economic rights, to broaden the sharing of economic power, and to make economic decisions more accountable to the common good. This experiment can create new structures of economic partnership and participation within firms at the regional level, for the whole nation, and across borders.

22. Of course, there are many aspects of the economy the letter does not touch, and there are basic questions it leaves to further exploration. There are also many specific points on which men and women of goodwill may disagree. We look for a fruitful exchange among differing viewpoints. We pray only that all will take to heart the urgency of our concerns; that together we will test our views by the Gospel and the Church's teaching; and that we will listen to other voices in a spirit of mutual respect and open dialogue.

A Call to Conversion and Action

23. We should not be surprised if we find Catholic social teaching to be demanding. The Gospel is demanding. We are always in need of conversion, of a change of heart. We are richly blessed, and as St. Paul assures us, we are destined for glory. Yet, it is also true that we are sinners; that we are not always wise or loving or just; that, for all our amazing possibilities, we are incompletely born, wary of life, and hemmed in by fears and empty routines. We are unable to entrust ourselves fully to the living God, and so we seek substituted forms of security in material things, in power, in indifference, in popularity, in pleasure. The Scriptures warn us that these things can become forms of idolatry. We know that, at times, in order to remain truly a community of Jesus's disciples, we will have to say "no" to certain aspects of our culture, to certain trends and ways of acting that are opposed to a life of faith, love and justice. Changes in our hearts lead naturally to a desire to change how we act. With what care, human kindness, and justice do I conduct myself at work? How will my economic decisions to buy, sell, invest, divest, hire, or fire serve human dignity and the common good? In what career can I best exercise my talents so as to fill the world with the Spirit of Christ? How do my economic choices contribute to the strength of my family and community, to the values of my children, to a sensitivity to those in need? In this consumer society, how can I develop a healthy detachment from things and avoid the temptation to assess who I am by what I have? How do I strike a balance between labor and leisure that enlarges my capacity for friendships, for family life, for community? What government policies should I support to attain the well-being of all, especially the poor and vulnerable?

24. The answers to such questions are not always clear—or easy to live out. But conversion is a lifelong process. And it is not undertaken alone. It occurs with the support of the whole believing community, through baptism, common prayer, and our daily efforts, large and small, on behalf of justice. As a Church, we must be people after God's own heart, bonded by the Spirit, sustaining one another in love, setting our hearts on God's kingdom, committing ourselves to solidarity with those who suffer, working for peace and justice, acting as a sign of Christ's love and justice in the world. The Church cannot redeem the world from the deadening effects of sin and injustice unless it is working to remove sin and injustice in its own life and institutions. All of us must help the Church to practice in its own life what it preaches to others about economic justice and cooperation.

25. The challenge of this pastoral letter is not merely to think differently, but also to act differently. A renewal of economic life depends on the conscious choices and commitments of individual believers who practice their faith in the world. The road to holiness for most of us lies in our secular vocations. We need a spirituality that calls forth and supports lay initiative and witness not just in our churches but also in business, in the labor movement, in the professions, in education, and in public life. Our faith is not just a weekend obligation, a mystery to be celebrated around the altar on Sunday. It is a pervasive reality to be practiced every day in homes, offices, factories, schools, and businesses across our land. We cannot separate what we believe from how we act in the marketplace and the broader community, for this is where we make our primary contribution to the pursuit of economic justice.

26. We ask each of you to read the pastoral letter, to study it, to pray about it, and match it with your own experience. We ask you to join with us in service to those in need. Let us reach out personally to the hungry and the homeless, to the poor and the powerless, and to the troubled and the vulnerable. In serving them, we serve Christ. Our service efforts cannot substitute for just and compassionate public policies, but they can help us practice what we preach about human life and human dignity.

27. The pursuit of economic justice takes believers into the public arena, testing the policies of government by the principles of our teaching. We ask you to become more informed and active citizens, using your voices and votes to speak for the voiceless, to defend the poor and the vulnerable, and to advance the common good. We are called to shape a constituency of conscience, measuring every policy by how it touches the least, the lost, and the left-out among us. This letter calls us to conversion and common action, to new forms of stewardship, service, and citizenship.

28. The completion of a letter such as this is but the beginning of a long process of education, discussion and action. By faith and baptism, we are fashioned into new creatures, filled with the Holy Spirit and with a love that compels us to seek out a new profound relationship with God, with the human family, and with all created things. Jesus has entered our

history as God's anointed son who announces the coming of God's kingdom, a kingdom of justice and peace and freedom. And, what Jesus proclaims, he embodies in his actions. His ministry reveals that the reign of God is something more powerful than evil, injustice, and the hardness of hearts. Through his crucifixion and resurrection, he reveals that God's love is ultimately victorious over all suffering, all horror, all meaninglessness, and even over the mystery of death. Thus, we proclaim words of hope and assurance to all who suffer and are in need.

29. We believe that the Christian view of life, including economic life, can transform the lives of individuals, families, schools, and our whole culture. We believe that with your prayers, reflection, service and action, our economy can be shaped so that human dignity prospers and the human person is served. This is the unfinished work of our nation. This is the challenge of our faith.

25. Christian Coalition's "Contract with the American Family" (1995)

Introduction

In the 1994 midterm elections, the American people elected the first Republican Congress in 40 years in what was the largest transfer of power from a minority party to a majority party in the twentieth century. The message of the election was clear: the American people want lower taxes, less government, strong families, protection of innocent human life, and traditional values.

The 104th Congress devoted its first hundred days to the Contract with America, including a Balanced Budget Amendment, tax relief for families, welfare reform, and term limits. The Christian Coalition enthusiastically supported the Contract and launched one of the most extensive grassroots campaigns in its history to support the Contract's passage. The Coalition will continue this effort as the Contract moves through the Senate.

The problems our nation faces are not all fiscal in nature. The American people are increasingly concerned about the coarsening of the culture, the breakup of the family, and a decline in civility. A recent *Los Angeles Times poll* reported that 53 percent of Americans believe the moral problems facing our country are more important than the economic problems. Other survey data indicates that 80 percent of Americans believe there is a problem of declining morality within our nation.

The Contract with the American Family is a bold agenda for Congress intended to strengthen families and restore common-sense values. The Contract represents a valuable contribution to a congressional agenda beyond the first hundred days. These provisions are the ten suggestions, not the Ten Commandments. There is no deadline or specified time period during which they are to be enacted. But Congress would be well advised to act with all due and deliberate speed. The provisions in the Contract enjoy support from 60 to 90 percent of the American people.

These items do not represent the pro-family movement's entire agenda. There are many other prominent pro-family organizations that will work on many other issues—women in combat, welfare reform, budget policy—in the months ahead. This contract is designed to be the first word, not the last word, in developing a bold and incremental start to strengthening the family and restoring values.

Restoring Religious Equality

A constitutional amendment to protect the religious liberties of Americans in public places.

With each passing year, people of faith grow increasingly distressed by the hostility of public institutions toward religious expression. Public interest law firms dedicated to preserving religious liberties receive thousands of calls every year on issues pertaining to the rights of students in public schools. . . .

Returning Education Control to the Local Level

Transfer funding of the federal Department of Education to families and local school boards. . . .

Promoting School Choice

Enactment of legislation that will enhance parents' choice of schools for their children.

Protecting Parental Rights

Enactment of a Parental Rights Act and defeat of the UN Convention on the Rights of the Child. . . .

Family-Friendly Tax Relief

Reduce the tax burden on the American family, eliminate the marriage penalty, and pass the Mothers and Homemakers' Rights Act to remedy the unequal treatment that homemakers receive under the Internal Revenue Service Code with respect to saving for retirement. . . .

Restoring Respect for Human Life

Protecting the rights of states that do not fund abortion, protecting innocent human life by placing real limits on late-term abortions, and ending funds to organizations that promote and perform abortions. . . .

Encouraging Support of Private Charities

Enactment of legislation to enhance contributions to private charities as a first step toward transforming the bureaucratic welfare state into a system of private and faith-based compassion.

Restricting Pornography

Protecting children from exposure to pornography on the Internet and cable television, and from the sexual exploitation of child pornographers.

1. Enactment of legislation to protect children from being exposed to pornography on the Internet. . . .

2. Enactment of legislation to require cable television companies to completely block the video and audio on pornography channels to non-subscribers. . . .

3. Amending the federal child pornography law to make illegal the possession of any child pornography. . . .

Privatizing the Arts

The National Endowment for the Arts, National Endowment for the Humanities, Corporation for Public Broadcasting, and Legal Services Corporation should become voluntary organizations funded through private contributions. . . .

Crime Victim Restitution

Funds given to states to build prisons should encourage work, study, and drug testing requirements for prisoners in state correctional facilities, as well as requiring restitution to victims subsequent to release. . . .

Conclusion

The Contract with the American Family is the first word, not the last word, on a cultural agenda for the 104th Congress during the post-100-day period. The ideas included in this document are suggestions, not demands, and are designed to be a help, not a hindrance, to Members of Congress as they seek to fulfill their mandate for dramatic change.

Christian Coalition welcomes the support of Republicans and Democrats alike as it seeks passage of the items in this bold legislative agenda. There is no specified deadline on acting on the Contract. The Coalition and its grassroots members will work on behalf of these mainstream proposals in this Congress and in as many subsequent sessions of Congress as necessary to secure passage.

The Contract with the American Family emerged from a survey of Christian Coalition members and supporters conducted in March and April, 1995. It has been improved during the drafting process by extensive polling and focus groups and consultations with members of Congress and their staffs. Each item in the Contract enjoys support from between 60 and 90 percent of the American people. More than half of the items in the Contract already have legislative sponsors, and several have already been passed by committee.

The American people now have a Congress that is receptive to their desire for religious liberty, stronger families, lower taxes, local control of education, and tougher laws against crime. With the Contract with the American Family, the nation now has an agenda with broad support that addresses time-honored values and cultural issues for the 104th Congress and beyond.

2
List of Organizations

Acton Institute for the Study of Religion and Liberty
161 Ottawa Street NW, Suite 301
Grand Rapids, MI 49503
(616) 454-3080
sirico@acton.org
President: Robert A. Sirico
website: http://www.acton.org

Founded in 1990, the Acton Institute seeks to provide a forum to discuss classical liberalism's principles including limited government and religious pluralism. The organization holds a number of programs to foster intelligent conversation of topics that involve religion and liberty. It conducts several student programs, including an essay contest, and issues awards for students.

American Atheists
PO Box 140195
Austin, TX 78714
(512) 458-1244
(512) 467-9525 Fax
President: Ellen Johnson
website: http://www.atheists.org

Founded in 1969 by Madalyn Murray O'Hair, who had successfully challenged a school prayer law in *Murray v. Curlett* (1963), the American Atheists seeks the complete separation of church and state as well as defending the civil rights of atheists. The groups offers speakers, conducts seminars and has published over 100 books. It is publisher of the monthly magazine *American Atheist*.

American Baptist Churches (American Baptist Historical Society)
PO Box 851
Valley Forge, PA 19482-0851
(610) 768-2378
(610) 768-2374
Administrator: Beverly Carlson
website: http://www.abc-coe.org

Founded in 1853, the group promotes the study of Baptist history and theology, as well as maintaining libraries housing related documents. The group publishes *American Baptist Quarterly*, a journal that covers such issues as Baptist identity, ethnic diversity, and church-state issues. It also publishes two semi-annual newsletters.

American Center for Law and Justice
PO Box 64429
Virginia Beach, VA 23464
(804) 579-2489
(804) 579-2836 Fax
Executive Director: Keith A. Fournier
website: http://www.acli.org

Founded in 1990 to promote the legal rights of Christians in the United States, the organization offers legal services and advice, as well as support for attorneys working in defense of religious liberties. The group opposes non-traditional families, legalized abortion, and restrictions against public preaching. The Center has published *In Defense of Liberty, Religion and the Public School Student*, and *Taking the Gospel to the Streets*, as well as the quarterly *Law & Justice Journal*.

American Civil Liberties Union
125 Broad Street, 18th Floor
New York, NY 10004
President: Nadine Strossem
website: http://www.aclu.org

Founded in 1920, the ACLU is one of the nation's largest civil rights organizations with more than 275,000 members. It is active in a broad array of issues including the strict separation of church and state. It engages in ligitation, education and lobbying to achieve its goals. It has played an active part in several important Supreme Court decisions affecting religion. It maintains an extensive library, and it produces a number of pamphlets, books and studies.

American Friends Service Committee
1501 Cherry Street
Philadelphia, PA 19102
(215) 241-7000
(800) 226-9816
(215) 864-0101 Fax
E-mail: afscinfo@afsc.org
website: http://www.afsc.org

Founded in 1917, this organization offers peace education, refugee relief work, and community organizing to people in 22 countries, and it works with other groups to alleviate minority problems in areas such as equal rights, housing, and employment. The organization opposes militarism, human suffering, and violence, and it functions as a multinational, nondenominational peace group.

American Health and Temperance Association
c/o DeWitt Williams
12501 Old Columbia Pike
Silver Spring, MD 20904-6600
(301) 680-6733
(301) 680-6464 Fax
Executive Director: DeWitt Williams

Founded in 1826, the American Health and Temperance Association was formerly known as the American Health and Temperance Society, and later as the American Temperance Society. The group promotes a drug-free and alcohol-free life through public information, research programs, children's services, and a speakers' bureau. Its goal is to inform others about the effects of alcohol, tobacco, and narcotics. Publications include *Health Connection Catalog*, *Listen*, *Vibrant Life*, and *Winner*.

American Humanist Association
7 Harvard Drive
PO Box 1188
Amherst, NY 14226-7188
(716) 839-5080
(800) 743-6646
(716) 839-5079 Fax
Executive officer: Frederick Edwards
website: http://www.infidels.org/

Founded in 1941 as a humanist organization dedicated to spreading the concept of mutual responsibility through discussion groups, educational programs, and the media, the group offers counseling services, library holdings, and a number of publications, including films, magazines, and brochures.

American Israel Public Affairs Committee
440 1st Street NW, Suite 600
Washington, DC 20001
(202) 639-5200
(202) 347-4889 Fax
Executive Director: Neil Sher
website: http://www.aipac.org

The American Israel Public Affairs Committee was founded in 1954 as the Zionist Committee for Public Affairs. The group actively lobbies the United States government on issues affecting US-Israel relations and it also offers informative and educational resources about American foreign policy in the Middle East.

American Jewish Alternatives to Zionism
347 5th Avenue, Suite 900
New York, NY 10016
(212) 213-9125
(212) 213-9142 Fax

Founded in 1969 as a group of anti-Zionist Americans primarily of Jewish descent, the organization is concerned with the influence of Zionism on the U.S. and the Middle East. It supports justice issues and offers specialized education, pamphlets, and quarterly reports.

American Jewish Committee
c/o Institute of Human Relations
165 East 56th Street
New York, NY 10022
(212) 751-4000
(212) 838-2120 Fax
Executive Director: David Harris
website: http://www.ajc.org

The American Jewish Committee was founded in 1906. Currently the organization offers programs in education, research, and human relations. It also seeks to end bigotry and to instill religious and civil rights. Publications include the monthly journal *American Jewish Committee—Commentary*, and *American Jewish Yearbook: A Record of Events and Trends in American and Worldwide Jewish Life*, a compendium of related articles.

American Jewish Congress
Stephen Wise Congress House
15 East 84th Street
New York, NY 10028
(212) 879-4500
(212) 249-3672 Fax
Executive Director: Phil Baum
Office of Governmental and Public Affairs
2027 Massachusetts Avenue NW
Washington, DC 20036
(202) 332-4001
(202) 387-3434 Fax
E-mail: washrep@ajcongress.org
Director: David A. Harris
website: http://www.ajcongress.org

Founded in 1918 by Rabbi Stephen S. Wise, Justice Louis D. Brandeis, and other distinguished Jewish individuals, the American Jewish Congress is the legal voice of the American Jewish Community. It works to safeguard and protect basic freedoms enshrined in the Bill of Rights. A liberal advocacy group based in New York City, it maintains a Government Affairs office in Washington, DC. The group seeks to ensure the creative survival of the Jewish people, and it is dedicated to activism inspired by Jewish teachings and values. Its stated political goals include the maintenance of the complete separation of church and state, advocacy on behalf of Israel, advancement of social and economic justice, fighting anti-Semitism in the United States, and the promotion of Jewish religious, institutional, communal, and cultural life. The organization is active in lobbying the federal government and it maintains a legislative alert system to distribute information regarding issues before Congress. It has taken leadership roles in the fight against school vouchers, the protection of abortion, including late-term abortions, promotion of civil rights, and maintenence of the separation of church and state. It has an active publishing program that includes *Congress Monthly*, *JUDAISM*, *Radical Islamic Fundamentalism Update*, *Proudly Jewish*, *Actively Feminist*, and other publications.

American Jewish League for Israel
130 East 59th Street
New York, NY 10022
(212) 371-1583
(212) 371-3265 Fax
President: Dr. Martin L. Kalmanson

The American Jewish League for Israel was founded in 1957. Its goals are to strengthen Jewish life, the state of Israel, and ties with American Jewry. The League sponsors the University Scholarship fund, which provides tuition to U.S. students in Israel, and it publishes both the monthly *AJLI Newsletter* and the monthly *News Bulletin of the American Jewish League for Israel*.

American Life League
PO Box 1350
Stafford, VA 22555
(703) 659-2586
(703) 659-2586 Fax
President: Judie Brown
E-mail: jbrown@all.org
website: http://www.all.org

Founded in 1982 as a pro-life, pro-family organization, the League focuses on issues concerning abortion, euthanasia, organ transplanting, population management, and world hunger. The League provides educational materials; books, such as *Choice in Matters of Life and Death*; magazines, such as the bimonthly *All About Issues*; flyers; programs; and other informational resources. It also produces *Celebrate Life*, a weekly national TV program.

American Peace Society
1319 18th Street NW
Washington, DC 20036-1802
(202) 96-6267
(202) 296-5149 Fax
President: Dr. Evron M. Kirkpatrick

Founded in 1828, the American Peace Society focuses on advancing judicial practices and other peaceful avenues to assist in adjusting differences among nations. The Society publishes the quarterly journal *World Affairs*.

American Zionist Movement
110 East 59th Street
New York, NY 10022
(2112) 318-6100
(212) 935-3578 Fax
Telex; 4948197 AMZION
Executive Director: Karen Rubinstein
website: http://www.azm.org

Founded in 1939, the organization was formerly known as the American Zionist Emergency Council, the American Zionist Council, and the American Zionist Federation. The Movement unifies 22 separate organizations to provide a combined front in favor of Zionist education, economic development, political action, and similar issues, and it publishes the *Zionist Advocate*.

American Zionist Youth Council
110 East 59th Street
New York, NY 10022
(212) 339-6914
(212) 755-4781 Fax
Contact: Gideon Elad
website: http://www.azm.org

The American Zionist Youth Council was founded in 1951 in conjunction with efforts made by the American Zionist Movement; it combines the efforts of 10 separate groups. The group coordinates Zionist youth activities, helps interpret Israel to children and teens, and initiates related practices.

American Zionist Youth Foundation
110 East 59th Street, 3rd floor
New York, NY 10022
(212) 318-6123
(800) 27-ISRAE (Fax)
website: http://www.azm.org

Founded in 1963, the organization sponsors educational services, programs, and activities for young American Jews to inform them about Judaism and Israel. The Foundation conducts cultural exchange programs, supports Jewish student activism, sponsors the annual Salute to Israel Parade, and provides various publications. It also offers tour and study programs in Israel.

Americans for God
PO Box 342
Damascus, MD 20872
(301) 253-3496
President: John C. Webb Jr.

Americans for God was formed in 1968. The organization denounces federal bans on prayer and Bible teaching in public schools, and it also provides public information on sex education, ozone depletion, chemical pollution, and the national debt. The organization promotes the preservation of natural resources and the spiritual ideals of prayer, the Bible, God, and such Americans as George Washington and Thomas Jefferson. It publishes *the American Standard*.

Americans for Religious Liberty
PO Box 6656
Silver Spring, MD 20916
(301) 598-2447
(301) 438-8424 Fax

Founded in 1980, the group's beliefs include preservation of religious, intellectual, and personal freedom, separation of church and state, and reproductive rights. The group achieves its goals by conducting research, maintaining a speakers' bureau, and engaging in government litigation. Publications include *The Case Against School Vouchers*, *Catholic Schools: The Facts*, *The December Wars*, and *Religious Liberty in Crisis*.

Americans United for Separation of Church and State
1816 Jefferson Place NW
Washington, DC 20036
(202) 466-3234
(202) 466-2587 Fax
Executive Director: Barry Lynn
website: http://www.au.org

Founded in 1947, the organization is committed to the constitutional principle of the separation of church and state. It engages in litigation and lobbying to achieve its goals, and acts as a media contact to get its viewpoints into the mainstream press. With more than 50,000 members in a network of volunteers, Americans United also conducts educational programs and runs a speakers' bureau. It publishes the monthly magazine *Church and State*.

Anti-Defamation League of the B'nai B'rith
823 UN Plaza
New York, NY 10017-3560
website: http://www.adl.org

Founded in 1913, the ADL is an international organization that fights anti-Semitism. It seeks justice and fair treatment of all citizens and engages in a variety of activities to pursue that goal, including litigation, education programs, and community service. The ADL office in Washington, DC, is charged with lobbying the federal government, foreign embassies, and non-governmental organizations.

Archonist Club
c/o William L. Knaus
682 Callahan Place
Mendota Heights, MN 55118
(612) 454-6961
Regent: Cheryl Andrea Bruhn

The Archonist Club was formed in 1967, and it supports an end to questionable foreign alignments. It also backs equal rights, a return to voluntary prayer in public schools, alternate power source research, tax reform, and a de-emphasis on sports in American culture. The group believes that decisions in government and society should be based on logic and morality as they apply to the Scriptures, management principles, and similar topics. It also conducts research and surveys.

Baptist Joint Committee on Public Affairs
200 Maryland Avenue NE
Washington, DC 20002

(202) 544-4226
(202) 544-2094
E-mail: BJCPA@erols.com
website: http://www.bjcpa.org

Formed in 1936, the Committee represents several separate groups as a constituency to the government, media, and general public, while also providing information to each of these divisions. It supports human rights, religious liberty, and successful church-state relations. Its publications include *Baptist News Service*, *Report from the Capitol*, and other materials.

Baptist Peace Fellowship of North America
499 Paterson Street
Memphis, TN 38111
(901) 324-7675
(901) 324-5921 Fax
Executive Director: Ken Sehested
website: http://www.primetime.com/~bpnfa/

Founded in 1984, the Baptist Peace Fellowship of North America consists of Baptists from several different groups that are interested in bringing attention to peace and justice issues. The Fellowship offers educational, charitable, and children's programs, as well as a speakers' bureau. Publications include *Dreaming God's Dream: Curriculum Guide for Church, School, and Home, Recipe for Peacemaking*, the quarterly *Baptist Peacemakers*, and the bimonthly newsletter *Peacework*.

Baptist World Alliance
6733 Curran Street
McLean, VA 22101-6005
(703) 790-8980
(703) 893-5160 Fax
website: http://www.bwanet.org

Founded in 1905, the Baptist World Alliance is an international Baptist organization currently representing over 38,000,000 members. Goals include assisting issues concerning world aid, relief programs, evangelism, communication, and refugee aid. The Alliance encourages the observation of the annual Baptist World Alliance Day, and publications include *The Baptist World* and *Baptist World Alliance News*.

Bread for the World
c/o Dorota Munoz
1100 Wayne Avenue, Suite 1000
Silver Spring, MD 20910
(301) 608-2400
(800) 822-7323
(301) 608-2401 Fax
E-mail: bread@igc.org
website: http://www.bread.org

Founded in 1973 as a multinational organization of Christians united against poverty and hunger, the group conducts research and offers educational resources through the Bread of the World Institute and focuses on such issues as military spending, agriculture, Third World nations, trade, unemployment, poverty, and hunger. It works with local congressional representatives and provides a speakers' bureau and reference library holdings. Publications include *Christian Faith and Public Policy: No Grounds for Divorce* and *Harvesting Peace: The Arms Race and Human Need*.

Buddhist Peace Fellowship
PO Box 4650
Berkeley, CA 94704
(510) 525-8596
(510) 525-7973 Fax
E-mail: bpf@bpf.com
Coordinator: Alan Senauke
website: http://www.bpf.com

Founded in 1978, the Buddhist Peace Fellowship is dedicated to world peace, social justice, nonviolence, and environmental activism. The Fellowship also provides support for the homeless and Buddhist prisoners, as well as working toward disarmament and environmental campaigns. It publishes *Turning Wheel* and other texts.

Care Net
109 Carpenter Drive, Suite 100
Sterling, VA 20164
(703) 478-5661
(703) 478-5668 Fax
E-mail: Etlanna@ix.net.com.com
President: Guy M. Condon

Care Net was founded in 1975 as the Christian Action Council. The group offers help to women, men, and unborn children threatened by abortion. Care Net publishes a quarterly newsletter, *Faces of Care Net*.

Catholic Council on Working Life
c/o Martin Burns
300 W. Washington, Suite 1200
Chicago, IL 60606
(312) 372-1646

Founded in 1943, the Catholic Council on Working Life works toward the study and promotion of moral, ethical, and Christian social principles in American life. The Council focuses on urban problems, as well as economic and political policies and practices.

Catholic Interracial Council of New York
899 10th Avenue
New York, NY 10019
(212) 237-8255
(212) 237-8607 Fax

The Catholic Interracial Council of New York was formed in 1934 to promote interracial justice. The Council works with parishes, governmental offices, and volunteer groups to support equality and social justice for all races, religions, and ethnic groups, and it sponsors a speakers' bureau, research programs, community action activities, and education forums, as well as publishing the quarterly *Interracial Review*.

Catholic Peace Fellowship
339 Lafayette Street
New York, NY 10012
(212) 369-1590
Secretary: Thomas C. Correll

Founded in 1964, the Catholic Peace Fellowship is dedicated to peace and justice advocacy. The Fellowship also provides educational programs for social change and it informs the public of the benefits of the Roman Catholic principle of nonviolence. The group counsels conscientious objectors, promotes disarmament and civil disobedience, and publishes the newsletter, *Catholic Peace Fellowship Bulletin*.

Catholic Women for the ERA
1006 Hatch Street
Cincinnati, OH 45202
Co-coordinator: Maggie Quinn

Founded in 1974, the group is composed of Catholic women in favor of the Equal Rights Amendment. Members write and lobby in favor of the amendment, as well as contact other Catholic groups to gain their support for the ERA.

Catholics for a Free Choice
1436 U Street NW, No. 301
Washington, DC 20009
(202) 986-6093
(202) 332-7995 Fax
President: Frances Kissling
website: http://www.igc.apc.org/catholicvote/pageone.html/

Catholics for a Free Choice was formed in 1972. It comprises Roman Catholics in support of legal reproductive health care. The group supports social and economic programs for women, families, and children, especially in the areas of family planning, abortion, and freedom in childbearing and childrearing. Publications include *The History of Abortion in the Catholic Church*, *Powerful Conceptions: A Series on Bishops and Birth Control*, and *Conscience: A Newsjournal of Prochoice Catholic Opinion*.

Center for Law and Religious Freedom
4208 Evergreen Lane, Suite 222
Annandale, VA 22003
(703) 642-1070
(703) 642-1075 Fax
E-mail: cls@interramp.com
Director: Steven T. McFarland

Founded in 1975, The Center trains lawyers in handling religious freedom cases, monitoring relevant judicial developments, and educating the general public on legal principles involving freedom of speech and religion. Publications include *Center for Law and Religious Freedom—Focus: On Justice, Reconciliation*, and *Religious Freedom*; *Defender*; and *Juris: For Jurisprudence and Legal History*.

Center for Public Justice
PO Box 48368
Washington, DC 20002
(410) 571-6300
(410) 571-6365
E-mail: inquires@cpjustice.org
website: http://cpjustice.org
Executive Director: James W. Skillen

The Center for Public Justice supports justice issues related to welfare, school choice, and other issues. Its publications include *Public Justice Report* and *Civic Connection*.

Chalcedon Foundation
PO Box 158-WP
Vallecito, CA 95251
(209) 736-4365
President: R. J. Rushdoony
website: http://www.chalcedon.edu

Founded in 1964, the Chalcedon Foundation is a religious education organization that conducts research and publishes reports. Its extensive publications include the *Chalcedon Report* and the *Journal of Church Reconstruction*. Additionally, the organization maintains a speaker's bureau and holds educational programs.

Christian Anti-Communism Crusade
PO Box 890
227 East 6th Street
Long Beach, CA 90801
(310) 437-0941
(310) 432-2074 Fax
E-mail: njmc@gte.net
President: Fred C. Schwarz

Formed in 1953 to inform Christians and other people of faith about the negative points of communism, the Crusade analyzes the philosophy, morality, strategy, tactics, and organizational structure of communism to educate others on these topics. The organization sponsors various seminars and projects in pursuit of its goals, and it publishes *News Letter*, *The Three Faces of Revolution*, *What is Communism?*, *Why Communism Kills*, *Why I Am Against Communism*, and *Can You Trust the Communists (to Be Communists)?*.

Christian Century Foundation
407 South Dearborn Street, Suite 1405
Chicago, IL 60605-1150
(312) 427-5380
(312) 427-1302
President and Editor: James M. Wall

Founded in 1884, the Christian Century Foundation interprets contemporary issues from a Christian perspective through magazines and other periodicals. Publications include the *Christian Century* and the *Christian Ministry*.

Christian Coalition
1801-L Sara Drive
Chesapeake, VA 23320
(757) 424-2630
Executive Director: Randy Tate
website: http://www.cc.org

Founded in 1989 out of the organization developed by Reverend Pat Robertson for his 1988 Republican Party presidential campaign, the Christian Coalition is a conservative political organization comprising evangelical Christians, Roman Catholics, and other pro-family groups. The organization is one of the nation's most effective grassroots organizations and contributed greatly to the Repbulican takeover of Congress in 1994. The group performs many functions, including lobbying, information distribution, and get-out-the-vote activities. Its legislative agenda is best outlined in its 1995 Contract with the American Family. It also produces a voter's guide that outlines candidates' positions on key issues of interest to its constituency.

Christian Crusade
PO Box 977
Tulsa, OK 74102
(918) 438-4234
(918) 438-4235 Fax
E-mail: christcrew@aol.com
President: Dr. Billy James Hargis

The Christian Crusade was founded in 1949. The group opposes socialist and communist philosophies, American participation in the United Nations, and federal government administration of schools, housing, and private business. The Crusade supports the gospel of Jesus Christ and Christian ideals, and it sponsors the Good Samaritan Children's Foundation, which in turn supports orphanages, schools, hospitals, leprosy clinics, and surgery programs for handicapped children. The group publishes *Christian Crusade Newspaper*.

Christian Family Renewal
Box 73
Clovis, CA 93613
(209) 297-7818

Founded in 1970 by Christians concerned with problems plaguing the modern family, the organization sponsors Christian business solutions, educational counseling, home study programs, and nutrition services. It publishes books, pamphlets, and the quarterly *Jesus and Mary Are Calling You*.

Christian Law Association
PO Box 4010
Seminole, FL 34645
(813) 399-8300
President: Dr. David Gibbs

Formed in 1977, the Association provides legal defense to Christians, churches, and ministries in cases involving their First Amendment Rights and it offers educational and informational material on First Amendment Rights, the effects of the law on the conservative Christian community, and general legal procedures. The Association publishes the monthly *Teacher's Forum*.

Christian Legal Society
4208 Evergreen Lane, Suite 222
Annandale, VA 22003-3251
(703) 642-1070
(703) 642-1075 Fax
Executive Director: Samuel B. Casey
website: http://www.clsnet.com

Founded in 1961 as a collection of lawyers, judges, law teachers, and law students dedicated to professionally serving Christ through high standards of justice and ethical morality, the Society provides a speakers' bureau, lawyer referral, information on legal issues of concern to the religious community, mediation services, and student ministry retreats. It publishes *Christian Legal Society Quarterly* and various books relevant to its mission.

Christian Renewal Effort for Emerging Democracies (CREED)
787 Princeton Kingston Road
Princeton, NJ 08540-4165
(609) 497-0224
(609) 497-0622 Fax
President: Dr. Ernest Gordon

Founded in 1980 as the Christian Rescue Effort for the Emancipation of Dissidents, the group's goals include combating religious persecution, teaching moral responsibility, and assisting refugees. Activities include providing Bibles and other resources to all Christians, conducting research, and supporting charitable and educational programs.

Christians in Crisis
1111 Fairgrounds Rd.
Grand Rapids, MN 55744
(218) 326-2688
(800) 286-5115
President; Sidney Reiners
website: http://www.crisis.net

Founded in 1981 as the Christian Forum Research Foundation, Christians in Crisis believes in the protection of religious freedom for people of all faiths. The organization assists victims of war, persecution, and poverty, as well as those discriminated against for their religious beliefs. It distributes Christian literature, maintains a speakers' bureau, and publishes the bimonthly *Christians in Crisis*.

Christic Institute
PO Box 845
Malibu, CA 90265-0845
(310) 287-1556
(310) 287-1559 Fax
National Director: Sara M. Nelson

Founded in 1978, the organization conducts research, supports litigation, and provides legal support in favor of public issues connected to religious principles. The Institute also publishes audiotapes, videos, and other books and resources, including *Cover Up*, *In Contempt of Congress*, and *The Killing of Karen Silkwood*.

Church State Council
1228 N Street, Suite 8
Sacramento, CA 95814
(916) 446-2552
(916) 446-6543
Director: Alan Reinach
E-mail: 74617.631@compuserve.com

The Church State Council is an educational group associated with the Seventh-Day Adventist Church. The group pursues the dual purpose of working to ensure freedom of religion at the greatest extent possible while maintaining a distinct separation of church and state through educational programs that it offers to churches and other interested groups.

Church Women United
475 Riverside Drive, Room 812
New York, NY 10115-0832
(212) 870-2347
(212) 870-2338 Fax
General Director: Marguerite Belisle

Founded in 1941, Church Women United has existed under a variety of names, including the United Council of Church Women, the Department of United Church Women of the National Council of Churches, and Church Women United in the USA. The organization advocates peace, justice, human rights, and the empowerment of women. It publishes *Churchwoman*, a quarterly magazine.

Churches Center for Theology and Public Policy
4500 Massachusetts Avenue NW
Washington, DC 20016-5690
Executive Director: Dr. James A. Nash

Founded in 1976, the organization's goals include examining the role of Christian faith on politics and examining current policies in relation to disarmament, foreign relations, health care, world economy, and minority rights. The Center also tries to affirm the lay ministry among politicians, activists, bureaucrats, and other parties. It publishes *Center Circles*, *Shalom Papers*, and various articles for scholarly journals.

Commission for Racial Justice
c/o United Church of Christ
700 Prospect Avenue
Cleveland, OH 44115-1110
(216) 736-2161
(216) 736-2171 Fax
Executive Director: Bernice Powell Jackson
website: http://www.ucc.org

Known formerly as the United Church of Christ Ministers for Racial and Social Justice, the Commission for Racial Justice was founded in 1967. The group works to increase the role and impact of

African Americans and other persons of color within the United Church of Christ. The Commission publishes *Civil Rights Journal*, a weekly newsletter.

Commission on Social Action of Reform Judaism
838 5th Avenue
New York, NY 10021
(212) 650-4160
(212) 650-4169 Fax
Contact: Rabbi David Saperstein

Founded in 1953 to encourage and support the importance of Judaism in everyday life, as well as to provide education on domestic and international social justice issues, the commission provides information, reports, and other publications to various reform synagogues in the United States and Canada.

Concerned Women for America
370 L'Enfant Promenade SW, Suite 800
Washington, DC 20024
(202) 488-7000
(202) 488-0806 Fax
President: Beverly LaHaye
website: http://www.cwfa.org

Concerned Women for America was founded in 1979, and it acts as an educational and legal defense foundation dedicated to protecting family rights, preserving American values, and meeting the cultural, political, and social needs of others. The organization broadcasts a live daily radio program and publishes *Family Voice* magazine.

Culture Watch
464 19th Street
Oakland, CA 94612
(510) 835-4692
(512) 835-3017 Fax
Editor: Bill Berkowitz
website: http://www.igc.apc.org/culturewatch/

Culture Watch is a monthly magazine containing an annotated bibliography of publications by the Religious Right; the publication also monitors the political agendas of conservative religious groups.

J.M. Dawson Institute for Church State Studies
Baylor University
PO Box 97308
Waco, TX 76798
(254) 710-1510
(254) 710-1571
Director: Derek Davis
website: http://www.baylor.edu/~church_state/

Founded in 1968, the Dawson Institute offers research facilities on issues of church and state. The group has a special collection library that focuses on such issues and offers a degree granting program that also focuses on church and state issues. It publishes the highly acclaimed *Journal of Church and State*.

Discovery Institute
1402 Third Ave., Suite 400
Seattle, WA 98101
(206) 292-0401
(206) 682-5320 Fax
E-mail: discovery@discovery.org
President: Bruce Chapman
website: http://www.discovery.org

Started in 1992, Discovery Institute is a non-partisan, non-sectarian research center for public policy. Its programs dealing with religion and politics include The George Washington Fellows Program, a summer seminar for college students, the C. S. Lewis and Public Life Project, which explores the connections between faith and public life through the writings of C. S. Lewis, and the Center for the Renewal of Science and Culture, which promotes the study of the social and political consequences of scientific materialism and underwrites research by scholars formulating the paradigm of "intelligent design."

Eagle Forum
Box 618
Alton, IL 62002
(618) 462-5415
(618) 462-8909 Fax
President: Phyllis Schlafly
website: http://www.eagleforum.org

The Eagle Forum was formed in 1975; the group promotes pro-family attitudes, traditional morality, national defense, and private business. Goals of the organization include ending tax discrimination, developing more secure education rights, opposing the ERA, and promoting a stronger approach to national defense. The Forum publishes *The Phyllis Schlafly Report*.

Episcopal Peace Fellowship
PO Box 28156
Washington, DC 20038-8156
(202) 783-3380
(202) 393-3695 Fax
Executive Secretary: Mary H. Miller
website: http://www.nonviolence.org/epf/

Founded in 1939, the Episcopal Peace Fellowship works for social peace by increasing awareness of the peacemaking messages in the gospel. The Fellowship opposes racism, capital punishment, militarism, nuclear weapons, and the draft, and it provides support to prisoners, conscientious objectors, war resisters, and tax resisters. Publications include *Cross Before Flag* and the quarterly *Episcopal Peace Fellowship Newsletter*.

Ethics and Public Policy Center
1015 15th Street, NW
Washington, DC 20005
(202) 682-1200
(202) 408-0632 Fax
E-mail: ethics@eppc.org
President: Elliot Abrams

Started in 1976, the Ethics and Public Policy Center promotes the study of the connections between religion, morality, and public life. Scholars affiliated with the group include Catholic thinker George Weigel and Protestant public policy analyst Michael Cromartie, director of the group's Evangelical Studies Project. The group also has a regular book publishing program.

Evangelicals for Social Action (ESA)
10 Lancaster Avenue
Wynnewood, PA 19096
(215) 645-9390
(800) 650-6600
(215) 649-8090 Fax
E-mail: esa@esa.mhs.compuserve.com
website: http://www.libertynet.org/esa/

The ESA was formed in 1978, and it supports policy changes in issues concerning peace, justice, poverty, abortion, disarmament, penal reform, and the environment. The group hopes to incorporate a wholistic biblical outlook in these areas, and it manages library holdings and offers informative programs. The group publishes *Christian Monographs on Public Policy* and the quarterly *Green Cross Magazine*.

Family Research Council
700 13th Street, Suite 500
Washington, DC 20005
(202) 393-2100
(202) 393-2134 Fax
President: Gary Bauer
website: http://www.townhall.com/frc/

Founded in 1980, the Family Research Council was originally called the Family Research Group and later the Family Research Council of America. The group distributes information and shares expertise with members of Congress, government officials and agencies, policy makers, the media, and the public. The Council also focuses on a number of other issues, including teen suicide, family values, housing, adolescent pregnancy, single parent support, taxation, and the potential effects of parental absence.

Federation of Islamic Associations in the U.S. and Canada
25351 Five Mile & Aubery Road
Redford, MI 48239
(313) 534-3295
(313) 534-1474 Fax
E-mail: mounira@concentric.net
website: http://www.islamerica.com

Founded in 1951 to unite Muslim groups in the U.S. and Canada under the focus of religious, political, social, and educational issues, the Federation's goals include the promotion of Muslim life and heritage, defense of human rights, and improvement of relations between Muslim and non-Muslim groups. The Federation offers charitable functions, youth programs, reference library holdings, book publications, and a weekly radio show called "Muslim Star: Voice of American-Canadian Muslims."

Fellowship of Reconciliation
PO Box 271
Nyack, NY 10960
(914) 358-4601
(914) 358-4924
E-mail: fornatl@ igc.org
website: http:\\www.nonviolence.org/~nvweb/for

The Fellowship of Reconciliation was founded in 1915, and it promotes peace and justice through education, training, and nonviolent action. The Fellowship offers library holdings, booklets, brochures, books, pamphlets, and greeting cards, and it publishes *Fellowship*.

Focus on the Family
Colorado Springs, CO 80995
(719) 531-5181
(800) A-FAMILY
President: James Dobson
website: http://www.fotf.org

Founded in 1977, Focus on the Family has developed into one of the nation's largest Christian groups. The organization airs seven radio broadcasts, some of which are distributed nationally, and it publishes 10 magazines. Its goal is to strengthen the American family through the inclusion of God in daily life.

Foundation for a Christian Civilization
PO Box 1868
York PA 17405
(717) 225-7197
(717) 225- 7479 Fax
President: Raymond E. Drake

Formed in 1973 to educate people about the values of the Christian religious and cultural heritage, the Foundation supports family and youth programs, research in cultural and intellectual development, and cultural exchange programs. Publications include *America Needs Fatima* and *Tradition, Family, and Property Magazine*.

Freedom from Religion Foundation
PO Box 750
Madison, WI 53701
(608) 256-8900
(608) 256-5800
(608) 256-1116 Fax
E-mail: ffrf@mailbag.com
website: http://www.infidels.org/org/ffrf/

Founded in 1978, the Freedom from Religion Foundation promotes separation of church and state, as well as the First Amendment. The group opposes government favoritism toward religious groups, religious stands against women and homosexual rights, and similar issues. The Foundation offers a number of publications, including *The Book of Ruth*, *The Born Again Skeptic's Guide to the Bible*, *Woe to the Women—the Bible Tells Me So*, and *Losing Faith in Faith—From Preacher to Atheist.*

Friends Committee on National Legislation
245 2nd Street NE
Washington, DC 20002
(202) 547-6000
(202) 547-6019 Fax
Executive Secretary: Joe Volk
website: http://www.fcnl.org

Founded in 1943 as an organization of Quakers concerned about the connection between politics and religion, the Committee focuses on human rights, health care, disarmament, refugees, U.S. foreign policy, militarism, UN affairs, and Native Americans issues. It provides legal testimony, statistics, and various publications, including *Action Bulletin* and *Visions of a Warless World*.

Friends Peace Committee
1515 Cherry Street
Philadelphia, PA 19102
(215) 241-7232
(215) 241-7233
(215) 567-2096 Fax

The Friends Peace Committee was founded in 1892, and it supports international peace through Quaker views on nonviolent social change. The Committee focuses on issues dealing with disarmament, the draft, foreign policy, and other related issues, and it provides speakers, literature, and other information, as well as counseling services.

Friends World Committee for Consultation
Sect. of the Americas
1506 Race Street
Philadelphia, PA 19102
(215) 241-7250
(215) 241-7285 Fax
Executive Secretary: Asia Bennett
website: http://www.quaker.org/fwcc/

Founded in 1937 to maintain understanding and unity among multinational Quakers, the group also focuses on peace and justice issues, as well as publishing books, reports, the *FWCC Friends Directory*, a semi-annual newsletter called *Friends World News*, and *Newsletter of the Americas*.

General Board of Church and Society of the United Methodist Church
100 Maryland Avenue NE
Washington, DC 20002
(202) 488-5600
(202) 488-5619 Fax
General Secretary: Thom White Wolf Fassett

Founded in 1917 to conduct research, education, and action programs, the organizations areas of focus include substance abuse, delinquency and crime, arms control, world peace, health care, race relations, hunger, environmental issues, and civil liberties. It publishes a monthly magazine, *Christian Social Action*, as well as providing pamphlets and audiovisuals.

Gloria Dei Press
919 Vogan Toll Road
Jackson, CA 95642
Editor: Margaret Scott

Formed in 1989 as a merger of Gloria Dei Enterprises and United Parents Under God, the Press is dedicated to pro-life and pro-family issues. It provides researched information, fund raising, workshops, and a speakers' bureau, and it supports a lifestyle founded on traditional Judeo-Christian laws and the U.S. Constitution.

Institute for the Study of Religion in Politics
PO Box 69
Rancho Cordova, CA 95741
(916) 635-8739
E-mail: etnet@calweb.com
President: Laurence Dene McGriff
website: http://www.isrp.org

The Institute collects, studies and disseminates information relating to the intrusion of religion into politics in the United States and in the world. The group believes that attempting to re-establish a Christian civil religion is more dangerous than the secular humanism that it also opposes.

Institute on Religion and Democracy
1521 16th Street NW, Suite 300
Washington, DC 20036
(202) 986-1440
(202) 986-3159 Fax
President: Diane Kippers

The Institute on Religion and Democracy was founded in 1981, and it examines the connection between religion and government in an effort to restore democratic values to churches. The Institute disagrees with some church movements that appear to be leftist and neglectful of democratic values. Publications include *Episcopal Action Briefing*, *Faith and Freedom*, and *United Methodist Action Briefing*.

Institute on Religion and Public Life
156 Fifth Avenue, Suite 400
New York, NY 10010
(212) 627-2288
(212) 627-2184 Fax
President: Richard John Neuhaus
website: http://www.firstthings.com/

Started in the 1980s, the Institute sponsors conferences and publishes the interfaith journal *First Things*, edited by Richard John Neuhaus.

Interfaith Center on Corporate Responsibility
475 Riverside Drive, Room 566
New York, NY 10115
(212) 870-2293
(212) 870-2023 Fax
Executive Director: Timothy H. Smith

Founded in 1974, the organization conducts research in a number of areas, including equal employment opportunity, nuclear weapons production, drug exports, economic conversion, and alternative investments. The Center helps coordinate corporate responsibilities with social ethics and it works with government officials, universities, corporations, and other business responsibility groups. The Center publishes *Corporate Examiner*.

Interfaith Center to Reverse the Arms Race
132 North Euclid
Pasadena, CA 91101
(818) 449-9430
Executive Director: Judith Glass

Founded in 1980 as an educational resources center dedicated to reversing the arms race, the Center organizes conferences and workshops, offers a speakers' bureau and film rentals, maintains a library, and provides pamphlets, books, and brochures. It also publishes a quarterly newsletter, *ICRAR Challenge*.

International Association for Religious Freedom
777 United Nations Plaza, 7th Floor
New York, NY 10017-3521
(212) 867-9255
(212) 867-9245 Fax
President: Duncan Whitespipe

Founded in 1969, the International Association for Religious Freedom promotes the work and ideals of religious freedom. It also publishes *Terra Una*.

International League for the Repatriation of Russian Jews
2 Fountain Lane, Suite 2J
Scarsdale, NY 10583
(800) 775-3225
(914) 683-3221 Fax
Chairman: James Rapp

Founded in 1968 to help Jews in the former USSR emigrate to Israel, the League also offers counseling, job training, and educational programs for Jews coming to the U.S. from the former Soviet Union, and it provides a speakers' bureau, books, and other resources.

International Religious Liberty Association
c/o Dr. Bert B. Beach
12 501 Old Columbia Pike
Silver Spring, MD 20904-6600
(301) 680-6680
(301) 680-6695 Fax

Founded in 1888 as a multinational group dedicated to promoting religious liberty as the right and freedom of all people, the Association denounces discrimination against any individual. Formerly known as the National Religious Liberty Association, the group currently publishes *Conscience et Liberté* and the bimonthly *Liberty*.

Jewish Labor Bund
25 East 21st Street
New York, NY 10010
(212) 475-0055
(212) 473-5102 Fax
Secretary: Benjamin Nadel

Founded in 1897 as a Jewish political and cultural organization, the group coordinates international activities with other Bund groups, and promotes the ideals and beliefs of socialism among Jews. It also conducts cultural and educational programs in Yiddish.

Jewish Women International
1828 L Street NW, Suite 250
Washington, DC 20036
(202) 857-1300
(202) 857-1380 Fax

Founded in 1897 as the Women's Supreme Council, the group later changed its name to B'nai B'rith and finally to Jewish Women International. Projects by the group include domestic violence awareness, leadership training, self-esteem programs, Holocaust awareness, philanthropic functions, hospital visits, and other activities. The Council maintains a treatment center for emotionally disturbed children in Jerusalem, Israel. Publications include *Mingled Roots: A Guide for Jewish Grandparents of Interfaith Grandchildren* and a quarterly newsletter, *Women's World*.

Knights of Columbus
1 Columbus Plaza
New Haven, CT 06510-3326
(203) 772-2130
(203) 772-3000 Fax
Director: Virgil C. Dechant
website: http://www.kofc-supreme-council.org

The Knights of Columbus was formed in 1882, and it currently includes around 1,540,000 members. This multinational group, which is comprised of Catholic men 18 years of age or older, coordinates annual conventions and manages lending libraries that provide reference materials on the Church and U.S. history to the general public. It also publishes a monthly magazine, *Columbia*, and a monthly newsletter called *Squires*.

Lutheran Peace Fellowship
1710 11th Avenue
Seattle, WA 98122-2420
Coordinator: Bonnie Block

The Lutheran Peace Fellowship was founded in 1941. Its goals include working for world peace, providing counseling and materials to people in legal problems due to their beliefs in disarmament, and the spreading of the Lutheran pacifist position. The Fellowship also provides training in nonviolent confrontation, maintains a speakers' bureau, supports a government-free military chaplaincy, and backs other practices used in preaching God's vision of peace. It publishes a quarterly newsletter, *Peace Notes*, as well as other materials.

Maryknoll Mission Center of New England
80 Emerson Road
East Walpole, MA 02032-1349
(508) 668-6830
Executive Officer: Gerald E. Kelly
website: http://www.maryknoll.org

Founded in 1911 as the Maryknoll Center for Justice Concerns to increase awareness of the Third World and its problems, specifically situations involving world hunger, multinational corporations, and tensions in Latin America, the Center pursues its goals by designing college and public education courses on the Third World. It also maintains public libraries containing information on U.S. foreign policy, Third World and developing countries, spirituality, and other related topics. The Center publishes *Maryknoll*, a monthly magazine covering the Catholic foreign mission.

Mennonite Central Committee
21 South 12th Street
PO Box 500
Akron, PA 17501-0500
(717) 859-1151
(717) 859-2171 Fax
902210 Telex
website: http://www.mennonitecc.ca/mcc/

Founded in 1920, the Mennonite Central Committee participates in programs relating to agricultural and economic development, education, health, and employment development. The Committee also works toward providing relief, peace, and disaster services to needy areas, and it currently has over 900 workers in over 50 countries across the globe. Publications include the quarterly *A Common Place*, *Conciliation*, and a variety of newsletters.

Methodist Federation for Social Action
76 Clinton Avenue
Staten Island, NY 10301
(718) 273-6372
Executive Director: Rev. George D. McClain
website: http://www.umc.org

Founded in 1907 as the Methodist Federation for Social Service, Methodist Federation for Social Action is an independent group of clergy members from the United Methodist Church dedicated to spreading the gospel of Jesus Christ to strive for world peace. The group's goals include the abolition of war and nuclear arms, promotion of social and economic planning against discrimination, and the defense of civil liberties and rights as set forth by biblical tradition and the United Nation's Declaration of Human Rights. It publishes the bimonthly newsletter *Social Questions Bulletin*.

Mordechai Anielewitz Circle of Americans for Progressive Israel
27 West 20th Street, Suite 902
New York, NY 10011
(212) 255-8760
(212) 627-1287 Fax

The Mordechai Anielewitz Circle of Americans for Progressive Israel was founded in 1980 as a section of Americans for Progressive Israel; this new group comprises people between the ages of 25 and 40 who are interested in progressive Zionist thought, history, and practice. The group seeks to educate its members through periodic meetings held in New York City, Philadelphia, and San Francisco. It also maintains a library and a speakers' bureau, and provides informational and educational mailings.

National Association of Evangelicals
PO Box 28
Wheaton, IL 60189
(630) 665-0500
(630) 665-8575 Fax
E-mail: nae@nae.net
Chairman: R. Lamar Vest
Office for Governmental Affairs
1023 15th Street NW, Suite 500
Washington, DC 20005
(202) 789-1011
(202) 842-0392 Fax
E-mail: oga@nae.net
website: http://www.nae.net

The National Association of Evangelicals (NAE) is a voluntary association of individuals, denominations, churches, schools, and organizations comprising approximately 43,000 congregations nationwide from 49-member denominations and individual congregations from an additional 27 denominations, as well as several hundred independent churches. The group's Office of Governmental Affairs in Washington, DC, is active in lobbying the federal government on behalf of the group's nearly 30 million members. The organization is active in securing housing for the poor, strengthening obscenity and pornography laws, supporting better education, and ensuring religious freedom for all.

National Catholic Coalition for Responsible Investment
1000 6th Street
Charleston, WV 25302
(304) 342-2716
(304) 344-1678 Fax
Chairman: Richard Zelik

The National Catholic Coalition for Responsible Investment is a joint project of six national Catholic organizations, as well as regional coalitions of dioceses, religious orders, health care facilities, and educational institutes. The group was founded in 1973 to encourage Catholic groups owning stock in corporations to consider their ethical and religious role as investors. It achieves these goals by sponsoring educational and informative workshops on theology, corporate responsibility, and the corporate world in general.

National Catholic Conference for International Justice
3033 4th Street NE
Washington, DC 20017-1102
(202) 529-6480
(202) 526-1262
Contact: Joseph M. Conrad Jr.

Founded in 1959, the National Catholic Conference for International Justice currently has a membership of over 6,000. Established as a Catholic organization working for interracial justice and social concerns in the United States, the Conference works separately and with other groups to halt discrimination in community development, education, and employment. Publications include *Commitment*, a quarterly newsletter, and such other materials as educational pamphlets.

National Catholic Council on Alcoholism and Related Drug Programs
1550 Hendrickson Street
Brooklyn, NY 11234-3514
(718) 951-7177
(718) 951-7233 Fax
Contact: Msgr. K. Martin

Founded in 1949 as a multinational organization dedicated to providing consultation and supportive services for all religious people suffering from drug and alcohol dependency, this group focuses on healing addicts with spiritual, physical, and mental rehabilitation. It also educates priests and other Catholics on substance abuse issues, as well as sponsoring other related workshops and programs. The Council publishes an annual magazine called the *Black Book* and the quarterly *Newsletter & Addiction Report*, along with the book *Wine as Sacramental Matter and the Use of Mustum*. The National Catholic Council on Alcoholism and Related Drug Programs was formerly known as the National Clergy Conference on Alcoholism and the National Clergy Council on Alcoholism and Related Drug Problems.

National Christian Leadership Conference for Israel
134 East 39th Street
New York, NY 10016
(212) 213-8636
(212) 683-3475
Executive Director: David Blewett

Founded in 1978 to help unite, coordinate, and support the activities of various U.S. Christian groups working on behalf of Israel, this group conducts research, maintains reference libraries, and holds a speakers' bureau. It publishes a semiannual newsletter, *Honor the Promise*, and the *National Christian Leadership Conference for Israel* brochure.

National Christian Life Community of the United States of America
3601 Lindell Boulevard No. 421
Street Louis, MO 63108-3393
(314) 977-7370
(314) 822-3919 Fax

Founded in 1963, the National Christian Life Community of the United States of America was formerly known as the Sodality Movement and Queens Work and later as the United States National Federation of Christian Life Communities. Goals of the group include social work, reform work and training, elimination of issues caused by economic gaps between the rich and the poor, and the development of spiritual freedom. The group forms Christian Life Communities to help meet these goals. The organization publishes a quarterly newsletter titled *Christian Life Communities HARVEStreet.*

National Coalition for the Protection of Children and Families
800 Compton Road, Suite 9224
Cincinnati, OH 45231
(513) 521-6227
(513) 521-6337 Fax
President: Jerry R. Kirk

Formerly known as the National Consultation on Pornography and Obscenity and later as the National Coalition Against Pornography, the organization was founded in 1983 to petition government and corporate officials into strictly upholding existing child protection and obscenity laws. The group also seeks to ban child pornography and to distance minors from harmful material. It provides materials explaining ways to combat illegal pornography, sexual violence, and child victimization, and it publishes a newsletter called *Standing Together*.

National Coalition of American Nuns
7315 South Yale
Chicago, IL 60621
(312) 651-8372
Director: Sr. Margaret Ellen Traxler

Founded in 1969, the National Coalition of American Nuns currently has around 1,800 members. The group is dedicated to researching and speaking on issues related to human rights and social justice. It publishes the quarterly *NCAN Newsletter*, and it also holds an annual conference.

National Conference of Catholic Bishops
3211 4th Street NE
Washington, DC 20017
(202) 541-3000
website: http://www.nccbuscc.org

Originally founded in 1919, the Conference adopted its current name in 1966. Its new agenda is to fulfill Vatican II's mandate that bishops jointly exercise the pastoral office. Through a number of committees made up exclusively of bishops, the NCCB prepares proposals for the bishops to consider at general meetings. It has published several pastoral letters on issues of social justice and nuclear war.

National Conference of Christians and Jews
71 5th Avenue, Suite 1100
New York, NY 16003-3095
(212) 206-0006
(212) 255-6177
President: Sanford Cloud Jr.
website: http://www.nccj.org

Founded in 1928, this organization promotes tolerance for all religious groups and races through education and cooperation. It works to eliminate prejudices that strain religious, business, social, and political relations. The Conference also organizes programs on a variety of topics, including equal opportunity employment and community relations, as well as conducting workshops and sponsoring Brotherhood/Sisterhood Week. It promotes a number of newsletters and other publications.

National Conference on Soviet Jewry
1640 Rhode Island Avenue, 5th Floor
Washington, DC 20036
(202) 898-2500
(202) 898-0822
Executive Director: Mark B. Levin

Founded in 1964 as a coalition of 45 Jewish organizations, the group seeks to help Jews legally leave the former Soviet Union, while providing assistance and defending the rights of those who wish to remain. The Conference also helps coordinate public, religious, educational, and charitable activities, along with other public events and seminars. It provides information to the government, universities, and the media and publishes a number of pamphlets and reports.

National Council of Catholic Women
1275 K Street NW, Suite 975
Washington, DC 20005
(202) 682-0334
(202) 682-0338 Fax
Executive Director: Annette Kane

Founded in 1920 as a coalition of 7,000 separate Catholic women's organizations, the Council allows Catholic women to share resources, speak on current issues, and develop leadership and management skills. It also monitors social justice issues, helps raise funds for foreign relief, and assists in developing religious, educational, and social programs. The Council publishes *Catholic Woman*, a bimonthly newsletter.

National Council of Churches (National Council of the Churches of Christ in the U.S.A.)
475 Riverside Drive
New York, NY 10115
(212) 870-2227
(212) 870-2030 Fax
E-mail: carol_fouke.parti@ecunet.org
General Secretary: Joan B. Campbell
website: http://www.wfn.org

Founded in 1950 to unite Protestant, Anglican, and Orthodox denominations, the Council publishes religious education materials and public policy statements, provides disaster relief and refugee assistance, and supports family life. It also provides assistance to underdeveloped nations, promoting justice, equality, and environmental issues in the process, and publishes the quarterly *Ecu-Link* newsletter and the annual *Yearbook of American and Canadian Churches*.

National Council of Jewish Women
53 West 23rd Street
New York, NY 10010
(212) 645-4048
(212) 645-7466 Fax
National President: Susan Katz

Founded in 1893, the National Council of Jewish Women currently has approximately 90,000 members. The group sponsors educational causes, social action, and community service programs. It also supports social welfare, equality, constitutional rights, and civil liberties issues. The Council publishes a number of brochures and informative handbooks along with its quarterly magazine, the *NCJW Journal*, and it maintains the Institute for Innovation in Education at Hebrew University in Jerusalem, Israel, and the Center for the Child in New York City.

National Interreligious Service Board for Conscientious Objectors
1830 Connecticut Avenue NW
Washington, DC 20009-5732
(202) 483-2220
(202) 483-1246 Fax
E-mail: nisbco@ige.apc.org
Executive Director: Philip L. Borkholden
website: http://www.nonviolence.org/~nvweb/nisbco/

Founded in 1940 as an international service organization for conscientious objectors, the Board provides information, professional counseling, speakers, and an extensive referral service. It also works with military objectors, as well as keeping abreast on pertinent governmental legislation. It provides library holdings, database and computer services, and a number of independent publications, such as *National Service and Religious Values*, the monthly *Reporter for the Conscience Sake*, and the annual *Draft Counselors Manual*.

National League for the Separation of Church and State
16935 West Bernardo Drive, Suite 103
San Diego, CA 92127
(619) 676-0430

Founded in 1876 as the Liberal League by Robert G. Ingersoll and Dan M. Bennett, the group changed its name in 1965. The present name more accurately reflects the organization's opposition to any religious influence on public policies. It publishes the magazine, *Truth Seeker*, and promotes its ideas through education rather than litigation.

National Office for Black Catholics
3025 4th Street NE
Washington, DC 20017
(202) 635-1778
Director: Walter Hubbard

Founded in 1970, the National Office for Black Catholics currently has a membership of around 1,000,000 black priests, sisters, brothers, and laypersons of the Catholic Church. The organization coordinates community development activities, provides youth leadership training, and combats poverty and deprivation. It initiates programs to sensitize the black community to its historical, cultural, and religious history, and sponsors and supports the Pastoral Ministry Institute, the Afro-American Culture and Worship Workshop, and other councils and committees. The Office publishes the bimonthly *Impact* newsletter.

National Office of Jesuit Social Ministries
1424 16th Street NW, Suite 300
Washington, DC 20036
(202) 462-7008
(202) 462-7009 Fax

Founded in 1972, the National Office of Jesuit Social Ministries represents the Jesuit concern for social justice and coordinates efforts with similar organizations in the U.S. The Office also supports legislation that shares its goals.

National Reform Association
PO Box 97086
Pittsburgh, PA 15229
(412) 331-4081
(412) 331-4081 Fax
Director: Jerry Bowyer
website: http://www.natreformassn.org

Founded in 1864 to promote the Christian principles of civil government in American life, the Association promotes government officials who support the ideals of the Christian family and the pursuit of peace. It teaches respect for human life, urges public recognition of the "Lord's Day" as one of worship and rest, and offers microfilm material to the Andover-Harvard Theological Library in Cambridge, Massachusetts, and University Microfilms International in Ann Arbor, Michigan. The Association publishes *Christian Statesman*, a bimonthly journal.

National Religious Broadcasters
7839 Ashton Avenue
Manassas, VA 22110
(703) 330-7000
(703) 330-7100 Fax
President: Dr. Brandt Gustavson
website: http://www.nrb.org

National Religious Broadcasters was founded in 1944 as a multinational organization of religious radio and television program producers, station owners and operators, and foreign broadcasters to support their joint efforts. The organiztion sponsors conventions, international tours, and professional training courses, as well as acting as the central information source for religious broadcast media. It publishes the annual *Directory of Religious Media*, the monthly *Religious Broadcasting Magazine*, and a number of brochures.

National Right to Life Committee (NRLC)
419 7th Street NW, Suite 500
Washington, DC 20004
(202) 626-8800
President: Wanda Franz
website: http://www.nrlc.org

Founded in 1973, NRLC is a grass-roots pro-life organization that seeks to protect all human life. The group sponsors educational programs, seeks legislation to protect the unborn, and conducts research on social, political, and medical issues related to abortion. NRLC is active in lobbying Congress, maintains a speakers' bureau, and issues statements for the press. It also publishes a number of books and pamphlets in addition to its newspaper, *National Right to Life News*.

Natural Law Party
51 West Washington Avenue
Fairfield, Iowa 52556
(515) 472-2040
info@natural-law.org
Party Chair: Kingsley Brooks
website: http://www.natural-law.org

Founded in 1992, the Natural Law Party (NLP) is one of the fastest growing political parties in the U.S. In the 1996 elections, the party sponsored over 400 candidates, and its presidential candidate, John Hagelin, received over 100,000 votes and was on the ballot in 48 states. The party's goal is to "bring the light of science into politics." It advocates prevention-oriented government, conflict-free politics, and proven solutions designed to bring national life into harmony with natural law. The party's organizers are followers of Maharishi Mahesh Yogi and they blend holistic approaches, transcendental meditation, "yogic flying," and other peaceful New Age remedies. The party's platform calls for cutting taxes deeply and responsibly while simultaneously balancing the budget, and advocating natural health care programs, educational initiatives and curriculum innovations, crime prevention and rehabilitation, and reductions in government waste and special interest control of politics. The party has national party status from the Federal Elections Committee and received over $500,000 in federal matching funds in 1996.

NETWORK
801 Pennsylvania Avenue SE, Suite 460
Washington, DC 20003-2167
(202) 547-5556
(202) 547-5510 Fax
E-mail: network@igc.apc.org

Founded in 1971, this organization works for legislative rights that will enable individuals to participate in the decision-making process of issues relevant to them, such as employment, housing, healthcare, and human rights. The organization conducts informative workshops, monitors congressional activity, and communicates with appropriate government officials. Publications include a bimonthly magazine titled *NETWORK Connection*, the bimonthly *NETWORKer*, and other resources.

New Call to Peacemaking
21 South 12th Street
PO Box 500
Akron, PA 17501-0500
(717) 859-1958
(717) 859-1958 Fax
Coordinator: John Stoner

The organization works with and combines resources with other church organizations to create peace initiative programs, uphold conscientious objection, peacefully denounce nuclear armament, and support other peace efforts. The organization provides pamphlets, magazines, books, and a quarterly newsletter, *Call to Peacemaker*.

Operation Rescue (OR)
PO Box 740066
Dallas, TX 75374
(214) 348-8866
(214) 348-7172 Fax
National Director: Flip Benham
website: http://www.orn.org

Founded in 1987 by Randall Terry, Operation Rescue organizes sit-ins and other forms of protest to persuade women to forego abortion. Since it began its activities, the group has had more than 50,000 members arrested and has prevented over 1,000 abortions from occurring.

Order of the Cross Society
PO Box 7638
Fort Lauderdale, FL 33338
(305) 564-5588
Steward: Rev. K. Chandler

The Order of the Cross Society was formed in 1975, and it supports civil government, the value of family, and just-business practices. Topics the group opposes include government subsidization, legalized abortion, and unjust social security practices. It encourages individuals and businesses to review their actions in light of Christian practices.

Pax Christi
348 East 10th Street
Erie, PA 16503
(814) 453-4955
(814) 452-4784 Fax
website: http://www.nonviolence.org/pcusa/

Founded in 1972, Pax Christi consists of 11,500 Roman Catholics committed to the Christian ideal of nonviolence. Goals of the group include military disarmament, economic justice, interracial equality, human rights, global restoration, and peace education. The organization coordinates a speakers' bureau, charitable events, and educational programs, and publishes its own quarterly newspaper, *The Catholic Peace Voice*.

Peace Mission Movement
Woodmont
1622 Spring Mill Road
Gladwyne, PA 19035
(610) 525-5598
(610) 525-0634 Fax
E-mail: fdipmm@libertynet.org
website: http://www.libertynet.org/nfd.pmm

Founded in 1933, the group is a spiritual movement dedicated to living by Father Divine's International Modest Code, which calls for a lifestyle devoid of drinking, smoking, obscenity, vulgarity, profanity, undue mixing of the sexes, and the taking of gifts or bribes. The goal of the Movement is to recognize God's presence by conforming to the Sermon on the Mount, the U.S. Constitution, and the Declaration of Independence. It publishes *Enlightenment*, a quarterly newsletter.

Plymouth Rock Foundation
Fisk Mill
PO Box 577
Marlborough, NH 03455
(603) 876-4685
(603) 876-4128 Fax
Executive Director: Rus Walton

Formed in 1970 to advance the principles of civil government and an American reformation based on Christian principles, the Foundation conducts seminars, workshops, and a student art/essay contest. The Foundation works with Christian Freedom Institutes and Christian Committees of Correspondence. Its publications include *A Worthy Company*, *American Christian Heritage Series*, *American Christian Statesmen Series*, *Dating and Courtship*, *Fundamentalists for American Christians*, and various newsletters, manuals, and other materials.

Presbyterian Peace Fellowship
Box 271
Nyack, NY 10960
(914) 358-4601
(914) 358-4924 Fax

Founded in 1983 as a voluntary group of ministers and laypersons dedicated to the principles of reconciliation, universal peace, and justice, the Fellowship's activities include testifying against military conscription, assisting conscientious objectors, and working with various peace groups. The Fellowship publishes *Briefly*, a quarterly newsletter.

Priests for Equality
PO Box 5243
West Hyattsville, MD 20782
(301) 699-0042
(301) 864-2182 Fax
National Secretary: Rev. Joseph A. Dearborn
website: http://www.igc.apc.org/quixote/pfe/

Priests for Equality was founded in 1975 by Catholic priests seeking equality for women within the Catholic Church and society. Work includes research, studies, and activities dedicated to gaining women the right to be ordained, to be recognized as equals, and to participate fully in both the church and general society. The organization publishes a quarterly newsletter, pamphlets, and papers.

Prison Fellowship Ministries
PO Box 17500
Washington, DC 20041-0500
(703) 478-0100
E-mail: bgil@pfm.org
website: http://www.pfm.org

Founded in 1976 by Charles W. Colson, former special counsel to President Richard Nixon, after serving time in prison for a Watergate-related offense, Prison Fellowship Ministries is a not-for-profit, volunteer-based organization that ministers to prisoners, ex-prisoners, victims, and their families, and promotes biblical standards of justice in the criminal justice system.

Promise Keepers
PO Box 103001
Denver, CO 80250
(800) 888-7595
President: Bill McCartney
website: http://www.promisekeepers.com

Founded in 1990 by former University of Colorado head football coach Bill McCartney, the organization seeks to strengthen men as husbands, fathers, and members of their communities. The group is nonpartisan and pursues spiritual renewal and community service. More than 2 million men have attended Promise Keeper rallies, including its 1997 Stand in the Gap meeting in Washington, DC.

Religious Action Center for Reform Judaism
2027 Massachusetts Avenue NW
Washington, DC 20036
(202) 387-2800
(202) 667-9070 Fax
Director: Rabbi David Saperstein
website: http://www.cdinet.com/rac/

The Religious Action Center for Reform Judaism was founded in 1961. The group serves as government liaison for the Union of American Hebrew Congress and the Central Conference of American Rabbis. It also monitors federal legislation and reports back to interested parties, and it conducts seminars, conferences, and workshops on social injustice issues. Publications include *Chai/Impact Newsletter*, *The Challenge of the Religious Right: A Jewish Response*, and *Preventing the Nuclear Holocaust: A Jewish Response*.

Religious Coalition for Reproductive Choice
1025 Vermont Avenue NW, Suite 1130
Washington, DC 20005
(202) 628-7700
(202) 628-7716 Fax
Executive Director: Ann Thompson Cook
website: http://www.rcrc.org

The Coalition was founded in 1973 to educate the media and the general public about the support such mainstream churches as United Methodist, Jewish, United Church of Christ, Presbyterian, and Episcopalian, give reproductive options and rights. The Coalition promotes pro-choice policy making, an end to anti-abortion violence, and reproductive health clinics. It also provides counseling services and various publications, including *Abortion and the Holocaust: Twisting the Language*, *Judaism and Abortion*, and their own newsletter. The organization was formerly known as the Religious Coalition for Abortion Rights.

Religious Heritage of America
1750 South Brentwood Boulevard, Suite 502
St. Louis, MO 63144-1341
(314) 962-0001

Founded in 1951, the organization led the campaign that successfully added the phrase "under God" to the Pledge of Allegiance in 1954. It is presently an interfaith group that seeks to recall, define and perpetuate traditional American values. It organizes tours to religious, historical, and cultural sites for both youths and adults.

Religious Network for Equality for Women
475 Riverside Drive, Room 812-A
New York, NY 10115
(212) 870-2995
(212) 870-2338 Fax
Coordinator: Dr. Zelle W. Andrews

Founded in 1976, Religious Network for Equality for Women promotes legal and economic justice for women, as well as other women's rights issues. The Network conducts an economic literacy program and other educational actions while also lobbying for national civil rights and economic reform legislation. It participates in the campaign to ratify the United Nations Convention on Elimination of Discrimination Against Women and publishes *Learning Economics*.

Religious Roundtable
PO Box 11467
Memphis, TN 38111
(901) 458-3795
(910) 324-0265 Fax

The organization was founded in 1978 to achieve an American society formed around Judeo-Christian ethics. It works to form public and government policy concerning the American family, freedom of religion, and Israel. The organization opposes abortion, child abuse, homosexuality, and pornography, and conducts prayer meetings and sponsors Christians for a Strong America.

Religious Task Force on Central America and Mexico
3053 4th Street NE
Washington, DC 20017-1102
(202) 529-0441
E-mail: rtfca@igc.org

Religious Task Force on Central America and Mexico was formed in 1980, and its interests include social justice and church involvement with disadvantaged people in South America. It provides coordination of religious-based campaigns and education to individuals about the treatment of Central Americans, as well as an end to U.S. intervention and military aid in these locations. The organization has produced a number of publications, including *Action Alerts for Organizations and Communities*, *Central America/Mexico Report*, and *Like Grains of Wheat*.

Rockford Institute Center on Religion and Society
2275 Half Day Rd., Suite 350
Deerfield, IL 60015
(708) 317-8062
(708) 383-1108
(800) 383-0680
(708) 317-8141 Fax

Founded in 1984 as a division of the Rockford Institute, the Center is an interreligious, multinational organization dedicated to research, education, and change in prevalent social issues. The main goal of the organization is to address the role of religion in society. It maintains a speakers' bureau and public libraries, and it publishes the *Religion and Society Report*, a monthly newsletter.

Rutherford Institute
PO Box 7482
Charlottesville, VA 22900
(804) 978-3888
E-mail: tristaff@rutherford.org
President: John W. Whitehead
website: http://www.rutherford.org

Founded in 1982, the organization is an international civil liberties legal and educational organization. It pursues its support of the religious heritage of American and civil rights through litigation, and it also conducts an extensive publishing program that includes books, papers, and periodicals.

Simon Wiesenthal Center
9760 W. Pico Boulevard
Los Angeles, CA 90035-4792
(310) 553-9036
(310) 553-8007 Fax
website: http://www.wisenthal.com

Formed in 1978 as an international center for Holocaust remembrance, as well as in defense of human rights and the Jewish people, the Center offers a number of educational programs, including International Social Action and Media, Holocaust Studies and Research, and Educational Outreach. The Center operates the Museum of Tolerance, which focuses on American prejudice and the Nazi Holocaust. It also provides a number of publications, including *Genocide: Critical Issues of the Holocaust*, the quarterly newsletter *Response*, and the quarterly *Commitment*.

Sojourners
2401 15th St. NW
Washington, DC 20009
(202) 328-8842
(202) 328-8757 Fax
President: James E. Wallis

Founded in 1971 as the People's Christian Coalition, Sojourners adopted its present name in 1980. Largely composed of Evangelical Christians, the group seeks to present an alternative perspective from the left on such issues as race, poverty, politics, and culture. It also publishes the magazine *Sojourners*.

Southern Baptist Convention
127 Ninth Ave. North
Nashville, TN 37234
(615) 251-2000
website: http://www.sbcnet.com

Founded in 1845, the Southern Baptist Convention has more than 40,000 churches associated with more than 15 million members. Its purpose is to provide a general organization for Baptists in the United States. It is active in missions throughout the world and it maintains several auxiliary organizations, including a Sunday School board to carry out its missions. The SBC has become active in cultural and political issues, including supporting boycotts of companies that transgress its beliefs and teachings.

Southern Christian Leadership Conference
334 Auburn Avenue NE
Atlanta, GA 30312
(404) 522-1420
(404) 524-7957 Fax
President: Martin Luther King III
website: http://www.sclcnational.com

Founded in 1957, the SCLC participated in the Montgomery Bus Boycott and wanted to continue its nonviolent fight for civil rights in the United States. The group's mission has expanded beyond its initial anti-discrimination objectives to include job creation, voter registration, drug sentencing guidelines, and capital punishment.

Unitarian Universalist Association Black Concerns Working Group
25 Beacon Street
Boston, MA 02108
(617) 742-2100
(617) 367-3237 Fax

Founded in 1985, the Unitarian Universalist Association Black Concerns Working Group is dedicated to racial justice issues. The group offers regional workshops, coordinates special events, and maintains a speakers' bureau to raise public awareness of racism. It publishes *No Problem—Again*.

Unitarian Universalist Service Committee
130 Prospect Street
Cambridge, MA 02139-1845
(617) 868-6600
(617) 868-7102 Fax
website: http://www.uusc.org

Formed in 1963 as a nondenominational, international human rights organization, the Committee provides human rights education and citizen action programs on such issues as assisting at-risk children in the U.S. and taking social action on international issues. It also supports women and reproductive rights, and publishes various reports and books, such as *Journey to Understanding*, *Promise the Children*, and *Roots and Visions: The First Fifty Years of the Unitarian Universalist Service Committee*.

Unitarian Universalist Women's Federation
25 Beacon Street
Boston, MA 02108
(617) 742-2100
(617) 742-2402 Fax
Executive Director: Mairi Maeks

Founded in 1963, the group works for women's rights and human rights issues. The Federation supports abortion and reproductive rights, quality standards for childcare centers, and family issues. It also works with the aging and with programs dealing with women's spirituality and multi-cultural issues. The Federation publishes a number of books and pamphlets.

United Black Christians
1380 Hyde Park Boulevard, No. 815
Chicago, Il 60615
President: Patricia Eggleston

Founded in 1970, United Black Christians currently has over 70,000 members. Formerly known as the United Black Churchmen, this group seeks to increase the relevance of the United Church of Christ in the struggle for liberation and justice.

United Church of Christ Coordinating Center for Women in Church and Society
700 Prospect Avenue
Cleveland, OH 44115
(216) 736-2150
(216) 736-2156 Fax
E-mail: langa@ucc.org
Executive Director: Mary Susan Gast
website: http://www.ucc.org

Founded in 1980 to eliminate sexism in the church and society, the Center works toward legislation and advocacy of women's issues. It provides speakers and workshops on relevant material, as well as maintaining library resources. The Center works with a number of other organizations with similar goals and it publishes *Mom's Morning Out*, *Women Pray*, and the quarterly journal *Common Lot*.

United Church of Christ Office for Church in Society
700 Prospect Avenue
Cleveland, OH 44115
(216) 736-2174
(216) 7336-2176 Fax
Executive Director: Valerie E. Russell
website: http://www.uss.org

Founded in 1976, the United Church of Christ Office for Church in Society organizes religious resources and texts for various social action and education programs concerning the Church. It acts as liaison with the United Church of Christ's legislation ministry office and it catalogs, identifies, and analyzes world wide issues to recommend solutions to these problems. The Office publishes *Courage in the Struggle for Justice and Peace*, a newsletter.

United States Catholic Conference
3211 4th Street NE
Washington, DC 20017
(202) 541-3000
website: http://www.nccbuscc.org

Founded in 1966 as the lobbying arm of the Catholic Church in America, the group lobbies on issues that are of concern to the Church, including abortion, social and economic justice, and human rights. It maintains administrative offices that conduct research and educational activities in addition to its lobbying.

Voice of Liberty Association
692 Sunnybrook Drive
Decatur, GA 30033
(404) 633-3634
Executive Secretary: Martha O. Andrews

The Voice of Liberty Association was formed in 1961 from a membership consisting of conservatives and patriotic groups. The Association opposes secular humanism through specialized education programs and other methods, and it publishes *Basics of National Identity* and *Voice of Liberty*.

William Penn House
515 East Capitol Street
Washington, DC 20003
(202) 543-5560
Director: Gregory L. Howell
website: http://www.quaker.org/penn-house/

The William Penn House was founded in 1966. It holds seminars to assist Quakers and students in understanding American government policy, and current events, and it explores ways to bring about changes worldwide. The organization publishes a quarterly newsletter, *Penn Notes*.

Woman's Christian Temperance Union (WCTU)
1730 Chicago Avenue
Evanston, IL 60201-4585
(708) 864-1396
(708) 864-1397
(708) 864-9497 Fax
President: Sarah F. Ward
website: http://www.uctu.org

Founded in 1874, WCTU is a nonpartisan, interdenominational Christian women's group dedicated to educating people about the dangers of alcohol, narcotic drugs, and tobacco on the human body and American society. It conducts a number of educational activities, including essay, picture, and speech contests. It also publishes and disseminates information on temperance. The WTCU maintains an extensive library and museum at the Frances E. Willard Home. In addition to its numerous pamphlets and reports, it also publishes two quarterlies, *Promoter* and *The Union Signal*.

World Conference on Religion and Peace
777 United Nations Plaza
New York, NY 10017
(212) 687-2163
Secretary General: Dr. William F. Vendley

Founded in 1966 as a multinational organization of clergy and laypeople from all major religions, the Conference works to provide a united front in favor of arms limitation, economic order, human rights, natural resource conservation, and peace education. The organization has offered world conferences and publishes relevant material.

World Council of Churches
Case Postale 2100
Ch-1211 Geneva 2, Switzerland
22 7916111
22 7910 361 Fax
Telex: 415730 01K CH
website: http://www.wcc-coe.org

The World Council of Churches was founded in 1948. It focuses on issues concerning service, unity, faith, mission and evangelism, church and society, racism, youth work, medical assistance for developing countries, and other related topics. The Council provides special programs on these topics and publishes 25 to 30 books annually, as well as weekly, monthly, and quarterly works.

Young Women's Christian Association of the United States of America
726 Broadway
New York, NY 10003
(212) 614-2700
(212) 677-9716 Fax
Executive Director: Dr. Prema Matillai
website: http://www.ywca.org

Founded in 1858, the YWCA offers service programs in the areas of health education, recreation, and self-betterment. It also offers counseling and assistance on issues pertaining to education, employment, human sexuality, emotional and physical health, juvenile justice, and volunteerism and citizenship. The YWCA advocates economic and social justice, equality, human rights, an end to racism, and peace issues.

3

Timeline

Date	Religion	United States	World
1787	Article VI, clause 3 of the U.S. Constitution bans religious tests for federal office.	U.S. Constitution adopted.	Louis XVI of France calls the Estates-General, the French representative assembly, into session.
1788		New Hampshire is the ninth state to ratify the Constitution, bringing it into effect.	In Great Britain, Warren Hastings goes on trial for mismanagement in India.
1789	John Carroll becomes the first Roman Catholic bishop in the United States; Lutheran Rev. Frederick Muhlenburg is elected first Speaker of the House.	George Washington is sworn in as the first president of the U.S.	French Revolution begins.
1790	President Washington sends a letter concerning religious freedom to the Newport Congregation.	The first U.S. census is completed in August.	Sweden defeats Russia in a decisive naval battle and secures its independence.
1791	The First Amendment to the Constitution is ratified as part of the Bill of Rights.	Bill of Rights is adopted as first 10 amendments to the Constitution.	The British Parliament's Canada Constitutional Act divides Canada into two provinces—Upper Canada (Ontario) and Lower Canada (Quebec).
1792		First political parties in the United States are formed with Alexander Hamilton leading the Federalists and Thomas Jefferson the Republicans.	Denmark becomes the first European nation to abolish the slave trade.
1793	Congress enacts the first Fugitive Slave Law, which is widely ignored and largely ineffective.	U.S. declares its neutrality in the European conflicts between Revolutionary France and her neighbors.	Louis XVI of France is executed.
1794	The first Methodist Church for African Americans is founded in Philadelphia by Richard Allen.	Whiskey Rebellion erupts in western Pennsylvania.	Polish nationals fail to overthrow Russian rule.

Date	Religion	United States	World
1795		Treaty of San Lorenzo settles border between U.S. and Spanish Florida.	French troops occupy the Netherlands.
1796	In his Farewell Address, George Washington reminds Americans of the beneficial effects of religion.	A game protection act is passed to protect Native American hunting lands from white settlers.	Napoleon continues to wage war in Europe, extending France's territorial domain.
1797	Second Great Awakening begins to spread in New England.	First Special Session of Congress is called to discuss strained U.S. relations with France.	Austria and France sign Treaty of Campo Formio in which France takes control of Belgium and Austria takes Venice.
1798	Quaker George Logan leads a "peace mission" to France.	Congress passes the Alien and Sedition Acts.	Pope flees Rome as French troops take the city.
1799		George Washington dies at Mt. Vernon.	British put down Irish independence movement.
1800	Rev. John Mason publishes a pamphlet accusing presidential candidate Thomas Jefferson of being anti-Christian.	Thomas Jefferson is elected president.	Spain cedes Louisiana to France.
1801		Tripolitan War (undeclared) begins when the U.S. refuses to pay more tribute to the pasha for protection from North African pirates.	Czar Paul I of Russia is assassinated and succeeded by his son, Alexander I.
1802	Jefferson's letter to the Danbury Baptist Association speaks of a "wall of separation" between church and state.	The U.S. Military Academy at West Point is founded.	Napoleon becomes First Consul of France for life.
1803	Lyman Beecher urges Christians to start voluntary associations in his address "The Practicality of Suppressing Vice by Means of Societies Instituted for That Purpose."	The U.S. Supreme Court establishes judicial review in its landmark decision, *Marbury v. Madison.*	Swiss cantons regain their independence with the passage of the Act of Mediation.
1804	Anti-dueling campaign commences after Aaron Burr kills Alexander Hamilton in a duel.	The Twelfth Amendment, which changes electoral procedures, is adopted.	Haiti declares independence after defeating French forces.

Date	Religion	United States	World
1805		U. S. and Great Britain edge closer to war with conflict over trade in West Indies.	Lord Nelson defeats Spanish and French fleets at Trafalgar.
1806	First American Foreign Missions Board is founded.	Aaron Burr is arrested and charged with treason, although acquitted in 1807.	Prussia enters the war against France.
1807		To prevent the loss of American shipping to the warring European navies, the Embargo Act bans imports and exports with any foreign country.	Prussian Prime Minister Baron von Stein emancipates the serfs.
1808	The first Bible society is formed in Philadelphia by William White.	U.S. prohibits the importation of slaves.	Congress of Erfurt renews Franco-Russian Alliance.
1809	Elizabeth Ann Seton founds her first Catholic elementary school.	The Non-Intercourse Act repeals the Embargo Act and allows trade with all countries except France and Great Britain.	Ecuador gains independence from Spain.
1810	American Board of Commissioners for Foreign Missions is formed by Congregationalists.	The term "gerrymandering" is coined in response to politically motivated congressional redistricting in Massachusetts.	Venezuela declares independence from Spain.
1811		William Henry Harrison defeats a band of Native American warriors at Tippecanoe in the Indiana Territory.	George III of England is declared insane and George, Prince of Wales, becomes Prince Regent.
1812	William Ellery Channing argues for pacifism and criticizes the government's attempts to stifle anti-war speech.	First foreign aid act is passed, sending $50,000 to Venezuela for earthquake relief; War of 1812 begins with Great Britain.	Napoleon launches his ill-fated Russian campaign.
1813	President James Madison issues his second proclamation for a national day of prayer; later in life he will argue privately against the practice.	Oliver Perry defeats the British in the Battle of Lake Erie.	Persia cedes territory to Russia in the Treaty of Gulistan.
1814		British forces burn Washington, D.C.	Napoleon is banished to the island of Elba.

Date	Religion	United States	World
1815	Boston Society for the Moral and Religious Instruction of the Poor is founded to extend Sunday school education to all.	After the Treaty of Ghent ends the War of 1812; Andrew Jackson defeats the British at the Battle of New Orleans.	Napoleon is defeated by Wellington at Waterloo.
1816	The American Bible Society is founded in New York.	Second Bank of the U.S. is chartered.	
1817	Thomas Hopkins Gallaudet founds the first free school for the deaf in Connecticut.	First Seminole War begins when settlers attack Native Americans in Florida and the Seminoles retaliate by attacking towns in Georgia.	Simon Boliver establishes an independent government in Venezuela.
1818		U.S. and Canada agree to the 49th parallel as border.	Chile declares its independence from Spain.
1819		U.S. purchases Florida from Spain.	British East India Company establishes a colony at Singapore.
1820	Elihu Embree begins publication of *The Emancipator*, an early abolitionist paper that identifies slavery as an evil.	Missouri Compromise is adopted—Maine enters Union as a free state and Missouri enters as a slave state.	Leaders of the Cato Street murder conspiracy against British Cabinet members are executed.
1821	Emma Willard founds the Troy Theological Seminary for women.		Peru, Guatemala, Panama, and Santo Domingo all gain independence from Spain.
1822	Jedidiah Morse submits his report on the religious conditions of Native Americans to the secretary of war.	President James Monroe vetoes the Cumberland Road Bill stating that the federal government has no business controlling public roads.	Greeks draft a constitution and declare independence from Turkish rule.
1823	Gabriel Richard becomes the first Roman Catholic priest to serve in the House of Representatives when he is elected from the Michigan Territory.	President James Monroe issues the Monroe Doctrine, which makes the Americas off-limits to European imperialism.	The Confederation of United Provinces of Central America is formed.
1824	The American Sunday School Union is formed.	John Quincy Adams is the first president elected without a national majority.	Civil War erupts in the Turkish Ottoman Empire.
1825	Robert Owen founds his utopian community at New Harmony, Indiana.		Decembrist Revolt in Russia is crushed by the czar's forces.
1826	Free Mason William Morgan is killed in New York giving rise to a more solidified anti-Masonic movement.	John Adams and Thomas Jefferson both die on the 50th Fourth of July.	Burmese War ends with Treaty of Yandabu.

Date	Religion	United States	World
1827	Ezra Stiles Ely delivers a Fourth of July oration entitled "The Duty of Church Freemen to Elect Christian Rulers," wherein he calls for the formation of a Christian party.		Peru secedes from Colombia.
1828	The American Peace Society is founded.	Tariff of Abominations is adopted.	Russia declares war on the Turkish Ottoman Empire.
1829	After Congress is flooded with petitions protesting Sunday mails, Senator Richard Johnson issues a report defending the practice.	The "spoils system" becomes part of American politics when President Andrew Jackson replaces government employees with political supporters.	Swiss cantons revise their constitution guaranteeing universal suffrage, freedom of press, and equality before the law.
1830	Evangelicals such as Jeremiah Evarts petition Congress to guarantee the treaty rights of the Cherokee.	Congress passes the Indian Removal Act, which requires the relocation of all Native Americans east of the Mississippi to the Oklahoma Territory.	After a revolution in Paris, Louis Philippe is made king of France.
1831	Christian missionaries are blamed for the slave revolt in Virginia led by Nat Turner.	The U.S. Supreme Court denies a petition from the Cherokee protesting their removal from Georgia, citing a lack of original jurisdiction.	Belgium declares independence from the Netherlands.
1832	William Wirt runs for the presidency on the Anti-Masonic Party ticket.	South Carolina Convention issues the ordinances of nullification calling the tariffs of 1828 and 1832 null and void.	Reform Bill in Great Britain redistributes seats in the House of Commons.
1833	The Congregational Church is disestablished as the state church of Massachusetts, the last state to have an established religion.	President Andrew Jackson withdraws government funds from the Bank of the U.S.	Slavery is abolished in the British Empire.
1834	Methodist minister Jason Lee founds a mission and permanent settlement in the Willamette Valley in Oregon.	U.S. Senate censures President Andrew Jackson for removing government funds from the Bank of the U.S.	Quadruple Alliance among Great Britain, France, Portugal, and Spain supports the constitutional government of Spain's Isabella II.
1835	Rev. Lyman Beecher issues "A Plea for the West" in which he decries a growing American Catholicism.	Texas declares independence from Mexico.	The Municipal Corporation Act creates the borough system of government in England.

Date	Religion	United States	World
1836	The first McGuffey Reader appears; it blends education and the teaching of morality.	Mexican army attacks the Alamo, killing the fort's 200 defenders.	France banishes Charles Louis Napoleon Bonaparte to America when his revolt plans fail.
1837		A severe financial panic occurs, due in large part to President Andrew Jackson's easy credit policies.	Victoria becomes Queen of Great Britain and Ireland.
1838		The Trail of Tears occurs as the last remaining Native Americans east of the Mississippi are forcibly moved to the Oklahoma Territory.	In southern Africa, Boers defeat Zulus in the Battle of Blood River.
1839	American Anti-Slavery Society splits, with William Lloyd Garrison leading the more radical abolition faction.	War between U.S. and Canada over logging rights in Maine is averted when both sides agree to establish a commission to settle the issue.	First Opium War between China and Great Britain.
1840	*The Beacon*, an anti-religion paper, advocates labor reform and social justice while condemning religion as the root cause of most social inequity.	Congress establishes the independent treasury system.	Muhammad Ali rejects the terms of the Treaty of London.
1841	Former President John Quincy Adams defends the *Amistad* mutineers.	President William H. Harrison dies one month after taking office; John Tyler becomes the first vice president to succeed to the presidency.	The five Great Powers—Great Britain, France, Prussia, Austria, and Russia—guarantee Ottoman Turkey's sovereignty.
1842		Webster-Ashburton Treaty settles Canadian border dispute between U.S. and Great Britain.	Treaty of Nanking ends Opium War; Great Britain founds a colony at Hong Kong.
1843	Amos Bronson Alcott founds the transcendentalist commune, Fruitlands, in Concord, Massachusetts.	The Oregon Trail is opened for settlers moving west.	A military revolt in Spain deposes General Espartero; Isabella II is declared queen.
1844	James A. Birney runs for president on the Liberty Party ticket.	The gag rule barring discussion of slavery in the U.S. House of Representatives is finally lifted.	Dominican Republic declares independence from Haiti.
1845	Southern Baptist Convention is formed as Baptists splinter over the issue of slavery.	Texas and Florida become states.	The Swiss Sonderbund is formed to protect Catholic cantons.

Date	Religion	United States	World
1846	Maine adopts statewide prohibition.	War with Mexico begins.	British repeal the Corn Laws which bar the import and export of grain.
1847	Mormons settle in Utah under the leadership of Brigham Young.	U.S. forces capture Mexico City.	Liberia, in West Africa, becomes an independent republic.
1848	The doctrine of Manifest Destiny is used to justify the war with Mexico.	Treaty of Guadalupe Hidalgo ends Mexican-American War; the U.S. acquires huge tracts of land in the Southwest from Mexico.	Karl Marx and Friedrich Engels publish the *Communist Manifesto.*
1849	Henry David Thoreau publishes *Resistance to Civil Government,* wherein he asserts the right to disobey an unjust law.	Its population swollen by the Gold Rush, California calls for a convention to adopt a constitution.	Under Guiseppe Mazzini, Rome is declared a republic.
1850	The Fugitive Slave Act requires the return of runaway slaves and imposes penalties on people who help a slave escape.	Compromise of 1850 attempts to settle the slave question in the territories.	Taiping Rebellion begins in China; Hung Hiu-tsuen proclaims himself emperor.
1851	The Young Men's Christian Association (YMCA) is founded in the U.S. to promote good moral character as well as physical well-being.	*New York Times* begins publication.	Cuba declares its independence from Spain.
1852	Harriet Beecher Stowe's novel, *Uncle Tom's Cabin*, is published.	A reluctant Franklin Pierce of New Hampshire is elected president as a compromise candidate in the growing slavey controversy.	Louis Napoleon, president of France, proclaims himself Emperor Napoleon III and begins the Second French Empire.
1853	The Know Nothing Party (American Party), a nativist and anti-Catholic party, is founded.	By Gadsden Purchase, U.S. buys southern Arizona and New Mexico from Mexico for $10 million.	The Crimean War between Russia and an alliance that includes France and Great Britain begins.
1854	The Massachusetts Emigrant Aid Society, which becomes the New England Emigrant Aid Society, is founded by Eli Thayer to help anti-slavery settlers in Kansas.	"Bleeding Kansas" begins, as slave and free forces clash over the state's admission to the Union.	Pope Pius IX issues the article of faith of the Immaculate Conception of the Blessed Virgin Mary.
1855		Conflict continues in Kansas as the state forms both free and slave governments.	Taiping Rebellion comes to an end in China.

Date	Religion	United States	World
1856	John Brown leads a raid on pro-slavery settlers in Missouri.	The anti-slavery Republican Party holds its first convention and nominates John C. Fremont for president.	South African Republic is organized under the leadership of Mathinius Pretorius.
1857		Speculation in U.S. railroad equities causes a financial and economic crisis in Europe; Supreme Court's Dred Scott decision aggravates the slavery debate.	Czar Alexander II begins emancipation of serfs in Russia.
1858	A religious revival is sparked by the financial panic of 1857; revivals are held in major cities, including New York and Philadelphia.	The Lecompton Constitution is again rejected by Kansas voters and Kansas statehood must wait until 1861; Lincoln-Douglas debates take place in Illinois Senate race.	The government of British India is transferred from the East India Company to the British Crown.
1859	John Brown is arrested and hung for his raid on a federal arsenal at Harper's Ferry, Virginia.	Abolitionist John Brown leads a raid on the federal arsenal at Harper's Ferry, Virginia.	German National Association is formed to unite Germany under Prussian rule.
1860		South Carolina secedes from Union in protest over Abraham Lincoln's election to the presidency.	Giuseppe Garibaldi proclaims Victor Emmanuel II king of Italy.
1861	James H. Thornwell defends slavery and helps Southern Presbyterians to break away from Northern Presbyterians.	Confederates take Fort Sumter in South Carolina and the Civil War begins.	Warsaw Massacre occurs as the Russian military opens fire on demonstrators against Russian rule.
1862	Julia Ward Howe writes the words to the "Battle Hymn of the Republic."	Union forces are defeated at the Second Battle of Bull Run.	Otto I of Greece is forced to resign after a military coup.
1863	Confederate churches behind federal lines are guaranteed non-interference by President Abraham Lincoln.	President Lincoln issues the Emancipation Proclamation; three-day Battle of Gettysburg is fought in July.	French capture Mexico City and proclaim Archduke Maximilian of Austria emperor of Mexico.
1864	The phrase "In God We Trust" is placed on two-cent piece at the direction of Salmon P. Chase, secretary of the Treasury.	Union General William T. Sherman marches to Atlanta and occupies Savannah.	First International Workingmen's Association is founded by Karl Marx.
1865	Lincoln's second inaugural address calls upon God and His mercy to aid in the war and in the healing of the nation.	Abraham Lincoln is assassinated and Vice President Andrew Johnson becomes president.	In southern Africa, Boers of Orange Free State and Basutos declare war on each other.

Date	Religion	United States	World
1866	The quasi-religious Lost Cause Myth begins to take shape in the South.	Fourteenth Amendment to the Constitution, which prohibits voting discrimination against African-American males, is ratified.	The sultan of Turkey grants the right of primogeniture to Ismail, Khedive of Egypt.
1867		Russia sells Alaska to U.S. for $7.2 million.	Giuseppe Garibaldi's March on Rome ends with his defeat by French and papal forces at Mentana.
1868		President Andrew Johnson is impeached for violating the Tenure of Office Act; he is acquitted by the Senate.	The last shogun of Japan, Kekei, abdicates and the Meiji Dynasty is restored.
1869	The Prohibition Party is formed.	U.S. Grant takes office as president.	Red River Rebellion begins in Canada.
1870	A labor dispute brings Solomon Washington Gladden—father of the Social Gospel movement—into more active politics.	Standard Oil is founded by John D. Rockefeller.	After a revolt in Paris, the Third French Republic is proclaimed.
1871		Treaty of Washington settles disputes between U.S. and Great Britain.	France cedes Alsace-Lorraine and pays 5-billion-franc indemnity to end Franco-Prussian War.
1872	Charles Taze Russell forms the Jehovah's Witnesses.	U.S. General Amnesty Act pardons most ex-Confederates.	Three Emperors League of Germany, Russia, and Austria-Hungary is formed in Berlin.
1873	The Comstock Act prohibits the use of the mails to transmit obscenity.	Financial panic hits New York.	Republic proclaimed in Spain.
1874	The Women's Christian Temperance Union (WCTU) is formed at a temperance meeting in Cleveland, Ohio.	First zoo in the United States opens in Philadelphia.	In the South Pacific, the Fiji Islands become part of Great Britain.
1875	James G. Blaine proposes the Blaine Amendment forbidding public monies for religious purposes.	William Marcy "Boss" Tweed escapes from jail and flees to Cuba.	Political unrest begins against Turkish rule in Bosnia and Herzegovina.
1876	Liberal League, which seeks the complete separation of church and state, is founded by Robert G. Ingersoll.	General George Custer is massacred with his troops by Native Americans at the Battle of Little Big Horn.	Korea becomes independent nation.

Date	Religion	United States	World
1877		Electoral Commission decides 1876 presidential election in favor of Republican Rutherford B. Hayes, even though Democrat Samuel Tilden won a majority of the popular vote.	Queen Victoria is proclaimed empress of India.
1878	The wall of separation metaphor from Jefferson's Danbury Letter is cited in the Supreme Court case, *Reynolds v. U.S.*	District of Columbia's government is reorganized to a presidential commission in which the residents have no vote.	Treaty of Berlin settles the "Eastern Question," that is, what to do with the failing Turkish Ottoman Empire.
1879		Specie payments re-instituted after 18-year suspension.	In southern Africa, the British Zulu War comes to an end.
1880	The Salvation Army is formed in the United States.	U.S. Supreme Court rules that African Americans cannot be excluded from juries.	Chile declares war on Bolivia and Peru.
1881		President James Garfield is assassinated; Chester Arthur becomes president.	In southern Africa, British recognize independent Transvaal Republic in the Treaty of Pretoria.
1882	The Knights of Columbus, a fraternal order for Catholic men, is formed.	U.S. bans Chinese immigrants for 10 years.	Hague Convention sets a three-mile limit for territorial waters.
1883		The Northern Pacific Railroad line is completed.	The last male member of the French royal House of Bourbon, Comte de Chambord, dies.
1884	During the 1884 presidential election, the anti-Catholicism of the Republican Party is expressed by a Blaine supporter who calls the Democratic Party the party of "rum, Romanism and rebellion."	Mugwumps walk out of the Republican National Convention when James Blaine is nominated for president.	Berlin Conference on African Affairs opens with representatives from 14 nations in attendance.
1885		Fencing of public lands in the West is prohibited.	Belgium, Germany, and Great Britain extend their territorial control of Africa.
1886	Dr. Stanton Coit establishes the first settlement house in New York.	The American Federation of Labor (AFL) is founded.	Bonaparte and Orleans families are banished from France.

Date	Religion	United States	World
1887	The Edmunds-Tucker Act dissolves the Mormon Church as a corporation.	Dawes Severalty Act replaces reservation system with parcels given to individual Native Americans.	Queen Victoria celebrates her Golden Jubilee.
1888	Philip Schaff's *Church and State in the United States* celebrates the amicable relations between the two.	The first secret ballot is used in Louisville, Kentucky.	Jack the Ripper murders six women in London.
1889	Andrew Carnegie writes his article "Wealth," in which he states that it is God's providence that some are wealthy.	Oklahoma is opened to non-Indian settlers.	Cecil Rhodes's British South Africa Company is granted a royal charter.
1890	The U.S. Supreme Court states in *Davis v. Beason* that the U.S. is a Christian nation.	Samoan Treaty gives joint control of Samoa to Germany, Great Britain, and the U.S.	Swiss government adopts social insurance for citizens.
1891		A mob in Valparaiso, Chile, attacks American sailors from the USS *Baltimore*; war is narrowly adverted.	The Triple Alliance of Germany, Austria, and Italy is renewed for 12 years.
1892	Charles H. Parkhurst's sermon denouncing Tammany Hall corruption leads to the 1894 Lexow Investigation of political corruption.	Iron and steel workers strike over wages and working conditions.	Belgian forces defeat Arab slave traders in the upper Congo.
1893		Hawaii is annexed and then released by the U.S.	Second Irish Home Rule Bill passed by the British House of Commons but rejected by the Lords.
1894		Coxey's Army of the unemployed marches from Massillon, Ohio, to Washington, D.C.	Chinese defeated at Port Arthur by Korean and Japanese troops.
1895	The Anti-Saloon League, an interdenominational temperance organization, is founded by Howard Russell, A. J. Kynett, Methodist Bishop Luther Wilson, and Catholic Archbishop John Ireland.	U.S. is almost drawn into war with Great Britain over a border dispute between British Guiana and Venezuela.	Rhodesia is formed from British South Africa Company territory south of the Zambezi River.
1896	Utah is admitted as a state after the Mormon Church rejects polygamy.	U.S. Supreme Court upholds the separate-but-equal doctrine in *Plessy v. Ferguson.*	Armenians are massacred in Constantinople.

Date	Religion	United States	World
1897	Congregational minister Charles M. Sheldon publishes *In His Steps*; the book becomes a bestseller.	The first shipment of Klondike gold reaches San Francisco.	Peace of Constantinople settles war between Turkey and Greece over Crete.
1898		Treaty of Paris ends Spanish-American War; Spain cedes Cuba, Puerto Rico, Guam, and Philippines for $20 million.	Emile Zola is imprisoned for his open letter (*J'Accuse*) to the French president on the Dreyfus Affair.
1899	Pope Leo XIII issues *Testem Benevolentiae Nostrae,* which criticizes Americanism.	Philippines demand independence from U.S.	Dreyfus Affair, in which a French officer is accused of spying for the Germans, comes to an end with a pardon by the French president.
1900	William Jennings Bryan runs unsuccessfully for president on an anti-imperialism and free silver platform.	U.S. population is 76 million at the start of the new century.	Boxer rebellions against Europeans begin in China.
1901		President William McKinley is assassinated; Vice President Theodore Roosevelt becomes president.	The First Nobel Peace Prize is awarded to Henri Dunant and Frederic Passy.
1902		U.S. gains control over Panama Canal.	National bankruptcy declared by Portugal.
1903		U.S. Marines land in Panama to support its independence from Colombia.	The Russian Social Democratic Party splits between the Mensheviks and the Bolsheviks at the London Congress.
1904		American troops end occupation of Cuba.	Russo-Japanese War begins.
1905	Anti-Saloon League support is critical in defeating Ohio's incumbent Republican governor Myron Herrick and replacing him with dry Democrat John Patterson.	Despite efforts to limit immigration, over 1 million enter the U.S.	Norwegian Parliament decides to separate from Sweden and elects Prince Charles of Denmark to be King Haakon VII of Norway.
1906	The American Jewish Committee is formed.	U.S. troops occupy Cuba after failed Liberal revolt.	All India Moslem League founded by Aga Kahn.
1907	Walter Rauschenbusch, Social Gospel advocate, publishes *Christianity and the Social Crisis.*	J.P. Morgan stops bank panic by importing $100 million in gold from Europe.	Open Door Policy on access to China adopted by France and Japan.

Date	Religion	United States	World
1908	Thirty Protestant denominations form the Federal Council of Churches of Christ in America.	First Model T (Tin Lizzie) rolls off an assembly line in Detroit.	Bulgaria declares its independence under Czar Ferdinand I.
1909		Violence erupts at the Pressed Steel Car Company during a strike; five strikers are killed.	Civil War erupts in Honduras.
1910	*The Fundamentals*, a publication that demarcates the five basic truths of Christianity, is published.	Powerful speaker of the House "Uncle" Joe Cannon is stripped of the power to appoint committee members.	China abolishes slavery.
1911	The Maryknoll Center for Justice Concerns, which focuses on Latin America, is founded.	U.S. signs commercial treaties with Japan.	Winston Churchill is appointed First Lord of the British Admiralty.
1912		Arizona and New Mexico enter the Union.	Turkey closes Dardanelles to shipping.
1913	The Anti-Defamation League of B'nai B'rith is founded to fight anti-Semitism.	Ratification of the Sixteenth Amendment to the U.S. Constitution establishes a federal income tax.	First and Second Balkan Wars show instability of the region and foreshadow the outbreak of World War I.
1914	Gary, Indiana, adopts the first release-time program in the country.	U.S. Marines are detained in Mexico when they stop for supplies; the incident leads to the resignation of Mexican President Victoriano Huerta.	World War I begins with the assassination of Austrian Archduke Francis Ferdinand in Sarajevo.
1915	The Ku Klux Klan is revived on anti-immigration, anti-Catholic, anti-Semitic as well as racist grounds.	Cornell University German Instructor Erich Muenter blows up the reception room of the U.S. Senate, shoots J. Pierpont Morgan, Jr., and then commits suicide.	Germany sinks the ocean liner *Lusitania*.
1916	Louis Brandeis is confirmed as an associate justice of the U.S. Supreme Court despite anti-Semitic attacks on his nomination.	Pancho Villa, Mexican revolutionary general, crosses U.S. border and raids Columbus, New Mexico.	Rebellion in Ireland on Easter led by Sinn Fein.
1917	Jehovah's Witnesses and other pacifist church members are criticized as unpatriotic because of their opposition to World War I.	Literacy Test for U.S. citizenship is passed over President Woodrow Wilson's veto.	Mata Hari is executed as a spy by the French.

Date	Religion	United States	World
1918	Evangelists like Billy Sunday hold "Hang the Kaiser" rallies to increase support for the war effort.	Eugene V. Debs, leader of the Socialist Party, is sentenced to a 10-year prison term for violating the espionage and sedition law.	Armistice signed between Allies and Germany ends the fighting in World War I.
1919	Ratification of the Eighteenth Amendment to the U.S. Constitution begins prohibition.	The Treaty of Versailles concludes World War I.	Red Army takes Ufa, marking the beginning of White defeat in the Russian Civil War.
1920	The American Civil Liberties Union is founded in response to the Red Scare, but also pursues policies and litigation to maintain a high wall of separation between church and state.	U.S. Senate votes against joining the League of Nations.	The International Court of Justice is established in The Hague, Netherlands.
1921		President Warren G. Harding commutes Eugene Debs's 10-year prison sentence.	Reza Khan leads coup d'etat in Teheran, Iran.
1922	Moral Re-Armament is founded at Princeton by Frank Buchman.	A revitalized Ku Klux Klan gains political strength in the South and Midwest.	USSR is officially formed.
1923	J. Gresham Machen's *Christianity & Liberalism* argues that one cannot be a good Christian and espouse liberal theology.	Teapot Dome Oil scandal breaks in Washington.	Beer Hall Putsch by Adolf Hitler fails to overthrow the German government.
1924	The National Origins Act, supported by groups including the KKK, limits immigrants from Southern and Eastern Europe, effectively restricts Catholic and Jewish immigration.	J. Edgar Hoover is appointed Director of the Bureau of Investigation, renamed the Federal Bureau of Investigation in 1935.	Benito Mussolini wins Italian elections.
1925	John Scopes goes on trial in Tennessee for teaching evolution in violation of state law.		Japan grants universal suffrage to men.
1926	American Eugenics Society sponsors a sermon contest.	President Calvin Coolidge pledges non-intervention in conflict between Mexican government and the Mexican Catholic Church.	Turkey enacts reforms that end polygamy and modernize female attire.
1927		Nicola Sacco and Bartolomeo Vanzetti are executed for murder.	Economic collapse in Germany.

Date	Religion	United States	World
1928	New York Governor Alfred Smith becomes the first Catholic to be nominated by a major political party (Democratic Party) for president; his religion is a factor in his defeat.	More Marines are sent to Nicaragua to fight guerrillas.	Kellogg-Briand Pact outlawing war is signed by 65 nations.
1929	H. Richard Niebuhr publishes *The Social Sources of Denominationalism* wherein he explores the social causes of the proliferation of denominations in the U.S.	The stock market crashes, helping to plunge the nation into the Great Depression.	Unrest between Arabs and Jews in Palestine over Jewish use of the Wailing Wall.
1930	Nation of Islam is founded by W. D. Fard in Detroit.	Protectionist Smoot-Hawley tariff is enacted with President Herbert Hoover's support.	Revolutions in Brazil and Argentina bring new governments.
1931	Jane Addams shares the Nobel Peace Prize with Nicholas Butler for efforts in world peace.	President Herbert Hoover calls for a one-year moratorium on payment of European reparations and war debts to the U.S.	Austrian Credit-Anstalt collapses and causes a financial crisis in Central Europe.
1932		Troops under General Douglas MacArthur are summoned to disperse ex-serviceman who are rallying in Washington for payment of their military bonuses.	Mohandas Gandhi is arrested as Indian Congress is declared illegal by British.
1933	The Humanist Manifesto is issued by 11 prominent university professors; it argues that humans control their destiny and discounts God in human affairs.	U.S. Congress passes independence bill for Philippines.	Hitler is granted dictatorial powers in Germany by passage of the Enabling Law.
1934	Father Charles Coughlin founds the National Union for Social Justice, a group critical of the New Deal.	Congress grants President Franklin Roosevelt the power to reduce tariffs.	Soviet Union is admitted to the League of Nations.
1935	Alcoholics Anonymous, an alcohol recovery program that recognizes the need for God in one's life, is formed.	Political demagogue Huey Long is assassinated by Dr. Carl Weiss in the Louisiana Capitol Building.	Italy invades Abyssinia (Ethiopia) despite League of Nation's condemnation and sanctions.
1936		Bruno Richard Hauptman is convicted of kidnapping and killing Lindbergh baby.	German troops occupy the Rhineland; Spanish Civil War begins.

Date	Religion	United States	World
1937		Violence erupts at Republic Steel strike in Chicago; 4 are killed and 84 injured.	British Royal Commission on Palestine recommends the establishment of separate Arab and Jewish states.
1938		The House Un-American Activities Committee is formed and chaired by Marin Dies (D-TX).	Japan continues its aggression in China.
1939	J. Frank Norris advocates U.S. intervention against Hitler.	Sit-down strikes are ruled illegal by the U.S. Supreme Court.	Great Britain, France, and U.S. recognize Franco's government as Spanish Civil War ends.
1940	The U.S. Supreme Court in *Cantwell v. Connecticut* strikes down local ordinances requiring proselytizers to obtain permits.	Franklin D. Roosevelt is re-elected to an unprecedented third term as president.	The German bombings of London ("the Blitz") begin; France falls to the Germans.
1941	Military chaplain Howell M. Forgy utters his famous phrase "Praise the Lord and pass the ammunition" as Pearl Harbor is attacked.	U.S. naval base at Pearl Harbor is attacked by Japan; U.S. declares war the next day (December 8).	Germany invades Soviet Union.
1942	The government uses the Espionage Act to prevent influential anti-Communist and New Deal critic Father Coughlin from distributing his magazine *Social Justice* through the mail.	Office of Price Administration freezes rents and begins rationing of staples like sugar, coffee, and gasoline.	American and Philippine prisoners of war are led on a forced march in which many die (Bataan Death March).
1943	In *West Virginia Board of Education v. Barnette*, the U.S. Supreme Court reverses *Minersville v. Gobitis* (1940), its decision on compulsory flag salutes in public schools.	War Relations Board orders a government takeover of coal mines when 500,000 miners strike.	Italy surrenders unconditionally to Allies.
1944	National Religious Broadcasters is formed.	Sky-rocketing inflation raises cost of living (30%).	D-Day landings in Normandy, France (June 6).
1945	Labor schools are held by the Catholic Church to warn members of the dangers of Communist infiltration of labor unions.	U.S. drops atomic bomb on Hiroshima and Nagasaki; Japan surrenders five days later.	Hitler commits suicide (April 30) and one week later the war ends in Europe (V.E. Day).
1946		New York is made the permanent home for the United Nations.	Nuremberg trials come to an end with 12 sentenced to death, 2 to life in prison, and 2 acquitted.

Date	Religion	United States	World
1947	The U.S. Supreme Court upholds the use of taxpayer money to bus children to parochial schools in *Everson v. Board of Education*.	Taft-Hartley Act restricting the power of labor unions is passed over President Harry Truman's veto.	India wins its independence from Great Britain and is divided into India and Pakistan.
1948	President Harry Truman recognizes Israel.	Marshall Plan, giving $17 billion in aid to Europe, is passed.	Mohandas Gandhi is assassinated.
1949	Christian Crusade, a strident anti-Communist organization, is founded by Billy James Hargis.	North Atlantic Treaty Organization (NATO) is founded under U.S. leadership.	Mao Tse-tung leads a successful communist revolution in China.
1950		Alger Hiss is sentenced for perjury.	North Korea invades South Korea.
1951	William F. Buckley, Jr., publishes *God and Man at Yale*, wherein he criticizes liberalism's destruction of the humanities.	Julius and Ethel Rosenberg are sentenced to death for espionage.	Conservatives regain control of the British Parliament and Winston Churchill becomes prime minister again.
1952	The U.S. Supreme Court upholds a release-time program in *Zorach v. Clauson*, seemingly undercutting its decision in *McCollum v. Board of Education* (1948).	Dwight D. Eisenhower resigns as Supreme Commander in Europe and is elected president.	Great Britain produces an atomic bomb.
1953	President Dwight D. Eisenhower's inauguration is opened with a prayer.	Department of Health, Education and Welfare is created.	Marshal Josip Tito is elected president of Yugoslavia under the country's new constitution.
1954	"Under God" is added to the Pledge of Allegiance.	U.S. Supreme Court rules that segregated public schools are unconstitutional in *Brown v. Board of Education, Topeka, Kansas*.	Gamal Abdel Nasser seizes power in Egypt.
1955	"In God We Trust" is added to all currency.	AFL and CIO merge under the leadership of George Meany.	The Vienna Treaty restores Austria's independence.
1956	Racial Segregation of the Methodist Church comes to an end.	Victor Riesel, labor columnist, is blinded by acid thrown by a gangster.	Soviet troops crush unrest in Hungary.
1957	Nearly 2 million attend the rallies of Billy Graham's crusade in New York City.	President Eisenhower issues "Eisenhower Doctrine" pledging protection of the Middle East from Communist aggression and expansion.	The Rome Treaty is signed by "the Six"—France, West Germany, Italy, Netherlands, Belgium, and Luxembourg—marking the beginning of the Common Market.

Date	Religion	United States	World
1958		Alaska becomes the 49th state.	United Arab Republic is formed from Egypt and Syria under the leadership of Gamal Abdel Nasser.
1959	Pat Robertson buys a bankrupt UHF TV station in Portsmouth, Virginia, and begins CBN.	Hawaii becomes the 50th state.	Fidel Castro successfully overthrows Cuban President Fulgenico Batista.
1960	The election of Roman Catholics to public office is condemned by the Southern Baptist Convention.	U-2 pilot Gary Powers is shot down and captured over USSR.	Adolf Eichmann, former chief of the Gestapo, is arrested and sent to Israel to stand trial.
1961	John F. Kennedy is inaugurated as the first Roman Catholic president.	Bay of Pigs invasion of Cuba is a failure.	Berlin Wall is constructed by the Soviets.
1962	The U.S. Supreme Court bars state-composed prayer in public schools in *Engel v. Vitale*.	Cuban Missile crisis heats up the Cold War.	Pope John XXIII opens the 21st Ecumenical Council (Vatican II).
1963	Martin Luther King, Jr., issues the Letter from a Birmingham Jail.	President John F. Kennedy is assassinated by Lee Harvey Oswald; Vice President Lyndon B. Johnson becomes president.	Buddhist priests and nuns in South Vietnam immolate themselves in protest of American-backed Diem regime.
1964	The Becker Amendment attempts to overturn recent Supreme Court decisions on school prayer and Bible reading.	Ratification of the Twenty-fourth Amendment bars poll taxes.	China announces it has the atomic bomb.
1965	Conscientious objection is upheld by the U.S. Supreme Court in *U.S. v. Seeger*.	25,000 march in civil rights demonstration in Selma, Alabama.	In southern Africa, Rhodesia declares itself an independent nation.
1966	The National Catholic Welfare Conference is reorganized into the National Conference of Catholic Bishops and the United States Catholic Conference.	U.S. Supreme Court limits police interrogation powers in *Miranda v. Arizona*.	Mao Tse-tung launches the cultural revolution in China.
1967		Massive anti-Vietnam War demonstrations in Washington, D.C.	Six-Day War between Israel and Arab nations.
1968	Billy Graham publicly announces his support for Richard Nixon.	Martin Luther King, Jr., civil rights leader, is assassinated by James Earl Ray.	Soviet Union invades Czechoslovakia.

Date	Religion	United States	World
1969	Madalyn Murray O'Hair founds American Atheists, Inc.	The Chicago Eight are indicted for violation of the anti-riot clause of the Civil Rights Act.	Yasser Arafat is elected chairman of the Palestine Liberation Organization (PLO).
1970	In *Walz v. Tax Commission,* the U.S. Supreme Court rules that tax exemption does not violate the First Amendment.	Four student protesters of the Vietnam War are killed by National Guardsmen at Kent State University (Ohio).	Civil war ends in Nigeria.
1971	The U.S. Supreme Court establishes the Lemon Test for analyzing Establishment Clause questions in *Lemon v. Kurtzman*.	Ratification of the Twenty-sixth Amendment to the U.S. Constitution lowers the voting age to 18.	Women are granted the right to vote in Switzerland.
1972	Dean M. Kelley shocks many with his book, *Why Conservative Churches Are Growing*.	Vice presidential candidate Senator Thomas Eagleton of Missouri resigns from the Democratic Party's presidential ticket when it is learned he has a history of mental depression.	Arab terrorists take nine hostages and kill two Israeli athletes during Munich Olympics; the hostages are killed in shoot-outs with West German police and soldiers.
1973	The U.S. Supreme Court announces a constitutional right to an abortion in *Roe v. Wade*.	Watergate scandal deepens and begins to threaten Richard Nixon's presidency.	Ireland, Great Britain, and Denmark become full members of the European Economic Community.
1974		Richard Nixon is forced to resign the presidency under threat of impeachment; Gerald Ford becomes president.	Constantine Caramanlis returns from exile to resume premiership of Greece after military government resigns.
1975	Elizabeth Ann Seton becomes the first American-born saint.	Vietnam War comes to an end.	Suez Canal reopens after 8 years of being closed.
1976	*Time* Magazine declares 1976 as the year of the Evangelical.	Patty Hearst, former hostage of the Symbionese Liberation Army, is found guilty of armed robbery.	Israeli commandos successfully raid the Entebbe Airport in Uganda to free 105 hostages being held by pro-Palestinian hijackers.
1977	James Dobson founds Focus on the Family.	Trans-Alaskan oil pipeline opens.	Adolpho Suarez is victorious in Spain's first democratic elections in 41 years.

Date	Religion	United States	World
1978	Congress passes the American Indian Religious Freedom Act making it U.S. policy to protect the natural right of Native Americans to practice their religions.	Proposition 13 is adopted by California voters and begins the taxpayers' revolt.	John Paul II—the first non-Italian in 455 years—is elevated to the papacy.
1979	Rev. Jerry Falwell founds the Moral Majority.	U.S. embassy in Iran is seized by supporters of the Ayatollah Khomeini.	Conservative Party leader Margaret Thatcher becomes the first woman prime minister of Great Britain.
1980	The Hyde Amendment, which limits federal funding of abortions, is unsuccessfully challenged on First Amendment grounds in *Harris v. McRae.*	Eight members of Congress are indicted in an FBI investigation dubbed Abscam.	Polish government recognizes Solidarity labor union under the leadership of Lech Walesa.
1981	The Sanctuary Movement attempts to protect illegal aliens from being deported by U.S.	First space shuttle flight.	Egyptian President Anwar Sadat is murdered by military officers.
1982		Nearly 1 million anti-nuke demonstrators rally in New York City.	Argentina and Great Britain go to war over the Falkland Islands.
1983	The Nation's Catholic Bishops issue "The Challenge of Peace" in which they condemn the growing arms race and the proliferation of nuclear weapons.	216 marines are killed in a Beirut bombing.	Benigno Aquino, Philippine President Ferdinand Marcos's chief rival, is assassinated at the Manilla airport.
1984	President Ronald Reagan restores full diplomatic relations with the Vatican after a 117-year lapse.	U.S. Commission on Civil Rights votes to discontinue use of quotas.	Indian Army crushes Sikh uprising in Punjab region of India.
1985	U.S. Supreme Court strikes down the practice of "a moment of silence" in *Wallace v. Jafree.*	John Walker and Jonathan Jay Pollard are arrested for spying—Walker for the Russians and Pollard for the Israelis.	Racial violence in South Africa threatens the government's control.
1986	U.S. Catholic bishops call for greater economic equity in their pastoral letter, "Economic Justice for All."	U.S. military bombs Libyan targets.	Jean-Claude Duvalier, self-proclaimed president for life, flees Haiti.
1987	Randall Terry founds the militant pro-life group, Operation Rescue.	The Dow falls 508 points to 1738.74 on "Black Friday."	Mikhail Gorbechev implements glasnost and perestroika reforms in Soviet Union.

Date	Religion	United States	World
1988	Rev. Pat Robertson is unsuccessful in his bid for the Republican Party's presidential nomination.	Four indicted in the Iran-Contra scandal.	Benazir Bhutto becomes the first woman to head a Muslim nation, Pakistan.
1989	The Christian Coalition is formed out of Pat Robertson's 1988 presidential campaign.	U.S. invades Panama and arrests Panamanian dictator Manuel Noriega.	Berlin Wall comes down.
1990	The U.S. Supreme Court is seen as undercutting Native American religious freedom in its decision in *Employment Division v. Smith.*	Savings and Loan crisis deepens with the Keating Five allegations.	Iraqi army invades Kuwait.
1991	James Hunter's *Culture Wars* describes the changes in American religious denominations.	U.S. leads Gulf War coalition under the command of Chief of Staff General Colin Powell and General Norman Schwarzkopf.	The USSR officially comes to an end when Boris Yeltsin assumes the presidency of Russia.
1992	Pat Buchanan gives fierce competition to incumbent Republican George Bush in the presidential primaries.	The decision in the police brutality case against Los Angeles police for the beating of Rodney King leads to rioting in Los Angeles.	War rages in Bosnia-Herzegovina.
1993	In response to several U.S. Supreme Court decisions (but especially *Employment Division v. Smith* [1990]), Congress passes the Religious Freedom Restoration Act.	A terrorist bomb explodes at the World Trade Center in New York City killing six; Muslim fundamentalists are suspected.	Israel and the PLO sign a treaty that would establish Palestinian self-rule.
1994		For the first time in 40 years, Congress is controlled by the Republican Party.	Nelson Mandela, former political prisoner, is elected the first black president of South Africa.
1995	Nation of Islam leader Louis Farrakhan holds the Million Man March in Washington, D.C.	A budget dispute between Democratic President Bill Clinton and the Republican-controlled Congress shuts down the government for 21 days.	India continues economic reforms by privatizing previously government-owned companies.
1996	Congress enacts the Communication Decency Act as an attempt to control pornography on the Internet.	The Unabomber, Theodore Kaczynski, is arrested after 16 bombs and 17 years.	An IRA bomb explodes near South Quays Station in London ending a 17-month cease-fire.

Date	Religion	United States	World
1997	The Religious Freedom Restoration Act (1993) is struck down as unconstitutional by the U.S. Supreme Court in *City of Boerne v. Flores*.	Oklahoma City bombing trials of Timothy McVeigh and Terry Nichols end in convictions.	Hong Kong is returned to China.
1998	James C. Dobson and Gary Bauer consider founding a distinctly Christian third party.	First balanced budget in over 30 years is submitted to Congress.	Economic crisis rocks Asian economies.

Index

by Kay Banning

Bold-face page references are to full entries.

Index

Index

Index